TRENDS AND ISSUES IN INSTRUCTIONAL DESIGN AND TECHNOLOGY

TRENDS AND ISSUES IN INSTRUCTIONAL DESIGN AND TECHNOLOGY

Fourth Edition

Edited by

Robert A. Reiser
Florida State University

John V. Dempsey
University of South Alabama

330 Hudson Street, New York, NY 10013

Vice President and Editor in Chief: Kevin M. Davis
Portfolio Manager: Drew Bennett
Content Producer: Miryam Chandler
Portfolio Management Assistant: Maria Feliberty
Executive Product Marketing Manager: Christopher Barry
Executive Field Marketing Manager: Krista Clark
Procurement Specialist: Deidra Smith
Cover Designer: Cenveo, Carie Keller
Cover Art: Fotolia/mimacz
Media Producer: Allison Longley
Editorial Production and Composition Services: SPi Global
Full-Service Project Manager: Jason Hammond, SPi Global
Printer/Binder: LSC Communications-Menasha
Cover Printer: Lehigh Phoenix
Text Font: Times LT Pro 10/12

Library of Congress Cataloging-in-Publication Data: [CIP data is available at the Library of Congress.]

1   16

ISBN 10:   0-13-423546-0
ISBN 13: 978-0-13-423546-2

Contents

Preface

This book provides readers with a clear picture of the field of instructional design and technology (IDT). Many textbooks in the IDT field focus on the skills needed by instructional designers and technologists. However, we believe that professionals in the field should be able to do more than just perform the skills associated with it. They should also be able to clearly describe the nature of the field, be familiar with the field's history and its current status, and be able to describe the trends and issues that have affected it and those that are likely to do so in the future. This book will help readers attain these goals.

Organization of the Book

This book is organized into ten sections. The first section of the book focuses on definitions and the history of the field. Key terms in the field are defined, and a history of the field is presented.

The second section reviews **instructional design models**, including traditional models and several examples of models that are emerging in the field.

The **theories and models of learning and instruction** that serve as the basis for the field are the subjects of Section III. Wide arrays of viewpoints are discussed, ranging from cognitive and behavioral perspectives to some of the views of teaching and learning associated with constructivism, motivation, and the learning sciences.

Section IV focuses on two of the often overlooked phases of the instructional design process, namely **evaluating and managing instructional programs and projects**. Particular emphasis is placed on current methods of evaluation, including return on investment, as well as the use of learning analytics.

The fifth section of the book focuses on **performance improvement**. The key ideas and practices associated with performance improvement are discussed, and a variety of noninstructional solutions to performance problems, such as performance support and informal learning, are described.

Section VI describes **what IDT professionals do in a variety of work settings**. These settings include business and industry, the military, health care, K–12 schools, and higher education in the United States. The work that IDT professionals do in Europe and Asia is also discussed. This section should be particularly useful to new designers considering career options and others not familiar with the wide variety of professional areas supported by instructional design and technology professionals.

Section VII focuses on **how to get an IDT position and succeed at it**. In addition to offering suggestions to job seekers and providing advice to those seeking to serve as consultants in the field, the section describes some of the organizations and publications that will foster the growth of IDT professionals.

The eighth section of the text is concerned with **technology and learning**. Emerging technologies and recent trends are covered from the perspective of their effects on learning and instructional systems.

Increasingly, the importance of **instructional strategies** in our educational processes and institutions is being acknowledged by all stakeholders. Section IX reviews some of the models, strategies, and tactics that are driving improved teaching and learning environments.

The final section of the book addresses some of the **current issues in the field of instructional design and technology**. Topics such as diversity, accessibility, professional ethics, open educational resources, and the changing conceptions of high-quality design are among the important issues that are addressed.

What's New in This Edition?

This edition of this book includes **seventeen new chapters**. These chapters provide an in-depth look at many topics that were either not covered in the previous edition or were addressed by different authors. The subjects of these chapters include:

- Alternatives to the ADDIE model (Chapter 4)
- The Successive Approximation Model (Chapter 5)
- Measuring the return on investment in technology-based learning (Chapter 11)
- Learning analytics (Chapter 12)
- Performance support (Chapter 15)
- Informal learning (Chapter 16)
- Integrating technology into K–12 education (Chapter 20)
- Instructional design in higher education (Chapter 21)
- Instructional design trends in Europe (Chapter 22)
- Performance consulting (Chapter 25)
- Social media (Chapter 28)
- Mobile learning (Chapter 29)
- MOOCs (Chapter 30)
- Social interdependence and small group learning (Chapter 32)
- Problem-based learning (Chapter 34)
- Authentic learning (Chapter 35)
- Open educational resources (Chapter 38)

In addition to these new chapters, **many of the other chapters have been extensively revised** so as to describe how recent developments inside and outside of the field have affected the trend or issue that is the focus of that chapter. Oftentimes these developments center around technological advances or new ideas regarding learning theories or instructional strategies.

As was the case with the previous edition of this book, **each chapter includes an end-of-chapter summary of the key principles and practices discussed in that chapter**. These summaries are designed to help students recall the key ideas expressed throughout each chapter.

The **case-based application questions** that appear at the end of each chapter should also be mentioned. While a few questions of this type appeared in the first three editions of this book, in this edition the majority of application questions present students with authentic ("real world") problems and require them to solve those problems. We have used these sorts of application questions in our classes for quite a few years, and our students have indicated that trying to solve them has really helped them to learn how to apply the key principles and practices associated with the various trends they are studying.

Acknowledgments

This book would not have been possible if it were not for all the hard work done by the many individuals who have written chapters for it. As a group, they voluntarily spent many hundreds of hours putting together a series of chapters that provides readers with what we consider to be a thoughtful overview of the field of instructional design and technology, and the trends and issues that are affecting it. We would like to express our deepest thanks and sincere appreciation to all of these authors for their outstanding efforts. We really believe they did an excellent job, and we are confident that after you read the chapters they wrote, you will feel the same way.

We would also like to express our sincere appreciation to Meredith Fossel, our former editor at Pearson Teacher Education, and Miryam Chandler, our content producer at Pearson. Their help in putting together this manuscript proved to be invaluable. And we would like to give special recognition to Jason Hammond, the vendor project manager at SPi Gobal. Jason's work in coordinating and managing the entire production process, as well as his very careful proofreading, was simply outstanding.

Thank you, Jason!

Introduction

Robert A. Reiser
Florida State University

and

John V. Dempsey
University of South Alabama

Many of us who have been in this field for a while have had the experience of facing our parents and trying to explain our profession to them. Long explanations, short explanations—the end result is always the same. Our parents go cross-eyed and mumble something like, "That's nice, dear."

How about your parents? How much do they know about the field you are now studying, the field this book is about? They probably can't describe it very well; perhaps they can't even name it. But that puts them in some pretty good company. Many professionals in this field have trouble describing it. Indeed, many of them aren't sure exactly what to call it—instructional technology, educational technology, instructional design, instructional development, instructional systems, or *instructional design and technology* (IDT), the name we, the editors of this book, have decided to use. Just what is the nature of the field that practitioners call by so many names? This is the basic question that the authors of the chapters in this book have attempted to answer.

This volume grew from each of our experiences in teaching a "Trends and Issues" course at our respective universities (together, we have a total of more than fifty years of experience teaching a course of this nature!). For many years, we used an ever-changing collection of readings from a variety of sources. For all the differences between our two courses, there were greater similarities. (Dempsey was, after all, a student in Reiser's Trends and Issues course shortly after movable type was invented.) So, it was natural that we spoke together on several occasions about the kind of text we would like to have, if we had our druthers.

When the folks at Pearson Education encouraged us in our delusions, our first idea was to produce a book of reprints from germane periodicals. As our discussions continued, however, we decided to invite a number of the most talented individuals we know in the field to contribute original manuscripts. The result is this book, *Trends and Issues in Instructional Design and Technology*.

The many talented authors and leaders in the field who have contributed to this book join with us in the hope that by the time you finish reading it, you will have a clearer picture of the nature of the field of instructional design and technology, and the trends and issues that have affected it in the past, today, and in the future. If we succeed in our efforts, then you may be able to clearly describe our field to your parents, or anyone who will take the time to listen.

Chapter 1

What Field Did You Say You Were In?

Defining and Naming Our Field[1]

Robert A. Reiser

Florida State University

What are the boundaries of the field we are in? How shall we define it? Indeed, what shall we call it? These are important questions that professionals in our field should be able to answer or, because there is no generally accepted "correct" answer, at least be able to discuss intelligently. This chapter is intended to provide you with information that should help you formulate some tentative answers to these questions. In this chapter, we will examine how the definition of the field has changed over the years, present two new definitions, and discuss the term that we will use in this book as the label for our field.

Before beginning to examine the definitions of our field, it is important to point out that not only have the definitions changed, but the actual name of the field itself has often varied. Over the years, a variety of different labels have been used, including, among others, such terms as audiovisual instruction, audiovisual communications, and educational technology. However, in the United States the term that has been used most frequently has been *instructional technology*. This is the term that will be used in the next few sections of this chapter. However, the issue of the proper name for the field will be revisited near the end of the chapter.

What is the field of instructional technology? This is a difficult question to answer because the field is constantly changing. New ideas and innovations affect the practices of individuals in the field, changing, often broadening, the scope of their work. More-over, as is the case with many professions, different individuals in the field focus their attention on different aspects of it, oftentimes thinking that the work they do is at the heart of the field, that their work is what instructional technology is "really all about."

Over the years, there have been many attempts to define the field. Several such efforts have resulted in definitions accepted by a large number of professionals in the field, or at least by the professional organizations to which they belonged. However, even when a leading organization in the field has endorsed a particular definition, professionals in the field have operated from a wide variety of different personal, as well as institutional, perspectives. This has held true among intellectual leaders as well as practitioners. Thus, throughout the history of the field, the thinking and actions of a substantial number of professionals in the field have not been, and likely never will be, captured by a single definition.

Early Definitions: Instructional Technology Viewed As Media

Early definitions of the field of instructional technology focused on instructional media—the physical means via which instruction is presented to learners. The roots of the field have been traced back at least as far as the first decade of the twentieth century, when one of these media—educational film—was first being produced (Saettler, 1990). Beginning with this period, and extending through the 1920s, there was a marked

---

[1]I would like to thank Walter Dick, Kent Gustafson, and the late Don Ely for providing me with invaluable feedback on earlier versions of this manuscript, portions of which previously appeared in *Educational Technology Research and Development* (Reiser & Ely, 1997).

increase in the use of visual materials (such as films, pictures, and lantern slides) in the public schools. These activities were all part of what has become known as the visual instruction movement. Formal definitions of visual instruction focused on the media that were used to present that instruction. For example, one of the first textbooks on visual instruction defined it as "the enrichment of education through the 'seeing experience' [involving] the use of all types of visual aids such as the excursion, flat pictures, models, exhibits, charts, maps, graphs, stereographs, stereopticon slides, and motion pictures" (Dorris, 1928, p. 6).

From the late 1920s through the 1940s, as a result of advances in such media as sound recordings, radio broadcasting, and motion pictures with sound, the focus of the field shifted from visual instruction to audiovisual instruction. This interest in media continued through the 1950s with the growth of television. Thus, during the first half of the twentieth century, most of those individuals involved in the field that we now call instructional technology were focusing their attention on instructional media.

Today, many individuals who view themselves as members of the instructional technology profession still focus much, if not all, of their attention on the design, production, and use of instructional media. Moreover, many individuals both within and outside of the field of instructional technology equate the field with instructional media. Yet, although the view of instructional technology as media has persisted over the years, during the past fifty years other views of instructional technology have emerged and have been subscribed to by many professionals in the field.

The 1960s and 1970s: Instructional Technology Viewed As a Process

Beginning in the 1950s and particularly during the 1960s and 1970s, a number of leaders in the field of education began discussing instructional technology in a different way—that is, rather than equating it with media, they discussed it as being a process. For example, Finn (1960) indicated that instructional technology should be viewed as a way of looking at instructional problems and examining feasible solutions to those problems; and Lumsdaine (1964) indicated that educational technology could be thought of as the application of science to instructional practices. As you will see, most of the definitions of the 1960s and 1970s reflect this view of instructional technology as a process.

The 1963 Definition

In 1963, the first definition to be approved by the major professional organization within the field of educational technology was published, and it, too, indicated that the field was not simply about media. This definition (Ely, 1963), produced by a commission established by the Department of Audiovisual Instruction (now known as the Association for Educational Communications and Technology), was a departure from the "traditional" view of the field in several important respects.

First, rather than focusing on media, the definition focused on "the design and use of messages which control the learning process" (p. 38). Moreover, the definition statement identified a series of steps that individuals should undertake in designing and using such messages. These steps, which included planning, production, selection, utilization, and management, are similar to several of the major steps often associated with what has become known as systematic instructional design (more often simply referred to as instructional design). In addition, the definition statement placed an emphasis on learning, rather than instruction. The differences identified here reflect how, at that time, some of the leaders in the field saw the nature of the field changing.

The 1970 Definitions

The changing nature of the field of instructional technology is even more apparent when you examine the next major definition statement, produced in 1970 by the Commission on Instructional Technology. The commission was established and funded by the United States government in order to examine the potential benefits and problems associated with increased use of instructional technology in schools. The commission's report, entitled *To Improve Learning* (Commission on Instructional Technology, 1970), provided *two* definitions of instructional technology. The first definition reflected the older view of instructional technology, stating:

> In its more familiar sense, it [instructional technology] means the media born of the communications revolution which can be used for instructional purposes alongside the teacher, textbook, and blackboard . . . The pieces that make up instructional technology [include]: television, films, overhead projectors, computers, and other items of "hardware" and "software" . . . (p. 21)

In contrast to this definition, the Commission on Instructional Technology offered a second definition that described instructional technology as a process, stating:

> The second and less familiar definition of instructional technology goes beyond any particular medium or device. In this sense, instructional technology is more than the sum of its parts. It is a systematic way of designing, carrying out, and evaluating the whole process of learning and teaching in terms of specific objectives, based on research on human learning and communication, and employing a combination of human and nonhuman resources to bring about more effective instruction. (p. 21)

Whereas the commission's first definition seems to reinforce old notions about the field of instructional technology, its second definition clearly defines the field differently, introducing a variety of concepts that had not appeared in previous "official" definitions of the field. It is particularly important to note that this definition mentions a "systematic" process that includes the specification of objectives, and the design, implementation, and evaluation of instruction, each term representing one of the steps in the systematic instructional design procedures that were beginning to be discussed in the professional literature of the field (e.g., Finn, 1960; Gagné, 1965; Hoban, 1977; Lumsdaine, 1964; Scriven, 1967). The definition also indicates that the field is based on research and that the goal of the field is to bring about more effective learning (echoing the 1963 emphasis on this concept). Finally, the definition discusses the use of both nonhuman and human resources for instructional purposes, seemingly downplaying the role of media.

The 1977 Definition

In 1977, the Association for Educational Communication and Technology (AECT) adopted a new definition of the field. This definition differed from the previous definitions in several ways. Perhaps most noteworthy was its length—it consisted of sixteen statements spread over seven pages of text, followed by nine pages of tables elaborating on some of the concepts mentioned in the statements, as well as nine more chapters (more than 120 pages) that provided further elaboration. Although the authors clearly indicated that no one portion of the definition was adequate by itself, and that the sixteen parts were to be taken as a whole, the first sentence of the definition statement provides a sense of its breadth:

> Educational technology is a complex, integrated process involving people, procedures, ideas, devices, and organization, for analyzing problems and devising, implementing, evaluating, and managing solutions to those problems, involved in all aspects of human learning. (p. 1)

Much like the second 1970 definition put forth by the commission, the 1977 definition placed a good deal of emphasis on a systematic ("complex, integrated") design process; the various parts of the definition mentioned many of the steps in most current-day systematic design processes (e.g., design, production, implementation, and evaluation). It is particularly interesting to note that the 1977 definition statement was the first such statement to mention the analysis phase of the planning process, which at that time was beginning to receive increasing attention among professionals in the field.

The 1977 definition also broke new ground by incorporating other terminology that, within a period of a few years, was to become commonplace in the profession. For example, the definition included the terms *human learning problems* and *solutions,* foreshadowing the frequent current-day use of these terms, especially in the context of performance improvement.

The 1977 definition also included detailed tables describing the various learning resources associated with the field. This list gave equal emphasis to people, materials, and devices, thus reinforcing the notion that the work of instructional technologists was not limited to the development and use of media.

The 1994 Definition: Beyond Viewing Instructional Technology As a Process

During the period from 1977 to the mid-1990s, many developments affected the field of instructional technology.[2] Whereas behavioral learning theory had previously served as the basis for many of the instructional design practices employed by those in the field, cognitive and constructivist learning theories began to have a major influence on design practices. The profession was also greatly influenced by technological advances such as the microcomputer, interactive video, CD-ROM, and the Internet. The vast expansion of communications technologies led to burgeoning interest in distance learning, and "new" instructional strategies such as collaborative learning gained in popularity. As a result of these and many other influences, by the mid-1990s the field of instructional technology was immensely different from what it was in 1977, when the previous definition of the field had been published. Thus, it was time to redefine the field.

Work on a new definition of the field officially commenced in 1990 and continued until 1994, when AECT published *Instructional Technology: The Definitions and Domains of the Field* (Seels & Richey, 1994). This book contains a detailed description of the field, as well as the following concise definition statement:

> Instructional Technology is the theory and practice of design, development, utilization, management, and evaluation of processes and resources for learning. (p. 1)

As is evident in the definition, the field is described in terms of five domains—design, development, utilization, management, and evaluation—or five areas of study and practice within the field. The interrelationship between these domains is visually represented by a wheel-like visual, with each domain on the perimeter and connected to a "theory and practice" hub. This representation scheme was designed, in part, to prevent readers from coming to the erroneous conclusion that these domains are linearly related (Richey & Seels, 1994).

Unlike the second 1970 definition and the 1977 AECT definition, the 1994 definition does not describe the field as process oriented. In fact, the authors of the 1994 definition state they purposely excluded the word *systematic* in their definition so as to reflect current interests in alternative design methodologies such as constructivist approaches (Richey & Seels, 1994). Nonetheless, the five domains that are identified in the definition are similar to the steps that comprise the "systematic" processes described in the previous two definitions. Indeed, each of the five terms (design, development, utilization, management, and evaluation) or a synonym is used directly or indirectly in one or both of the previous two definitions.

The 1994 definition statement moves in some other new directions and revisits some old ones. For example, much like the 1963 definition statement, the 1994 statement describes the field in terms of theory and practice, emphasizing the notion that the field of instructional technology is not only an area of practice, but also an area of research and study. The documents in which the 1970 and 1977 definition statements appear also discuss theory and practice, but the definition statements themselves do not mention these terms.

In at least two respects the 1994 definition is similar to its two most recent predecessors. First, it does not separate teachers from media, incorporating both into the phrase "resources for learning." Second, it focuses on the improvement of learning as the goal of the field, with instruction being viewed as a means to that end.

---

[2]Many of these developments are discussed in detail in Chapter 2 of this book.

Although the 1994 definition discusses instruction as a means to an end, a good deal of attention is devoted to instructional processes. The authors indicate that the "processes . . . for learning" (Seels & Richey, 1994, p. 1) mentioned in their definition refer to both design and delivery processes. Their discussion of the latter revolves around a variety of instructional strategies and reflects the profession's current interest in a wide variety of instructional techniques, ranging from traditional lecture/discussion approaches to open-ended learning environments.

Two More Recent Definitions

In the past few years, there have been several definitions published. In this section of the chapter, we will focus on two of these: one that an AECT committee has recently produced and one that we, the authors of this textbook, have developed.

The Latest AECT Definition

In 2008, an AECT committee produced a book that presented a new definition of the field of educational technology (AECT Definition and Terminology Committee, 2008). The definition statement that appears in the book is as follows:

> Educational technology is the study and ethical practice of facilitating learning and improving performance by creating, using, and managing appropriate technological processes and resources. (p. 1)

One of the many useful features of the book is a series of chapters devoted to explaining each of the key terms in the definition statement and discussing how the new definition differs from previous ones. Some of the key terms that the authors discuss in the chapter are described next.

One key term in the new definition is the word *ethical*. This term focuses attention on the fact that those in the profession must maintain a high level of professional conduct. Many of the ethical standards professionals in the field are expected to adhere to are described in the AECT Code of Ethics (Association for Educational Communications and Technology, 2007).

The new definition also focuses on the notion that the instructional interventions created by professionals in the field are intended to *facilitate* learning. The authors contrast this viewpoint with those expressed in earlier definitions, in which it was stated or implied that the instructional solutions that were produced would cause or control learning. The new perspective recognizes the important role that learners play in determining what they will learn, regardless of the instructional intervention they are exposed to.

The new definition also indicates that one of the goals of professionals in the field is to *improve performance*. The authors indicate this term emphasizes that it is not sufficient to simply help learners acquire inert knowledge. Instead, the goal should be to help learners *apply* the new skills and knowledge they have acquired.

Unlike previous definitions, in which terms such as *design, development,* and *evaluation* were often used to denote major processes or domains within the field, the new definition uses the words *creating, using,* and *managing* to describe the major

functions performed by educational technology professionals. The *creation* function includes all of the steps involved in the generation of instructional interventions and learning environments, including analysis, design, development, implementation, and evaluation. The *utilization* function includes the selection, diffusion, and institutionalization of instructional methods and materials; and the *management* function incorporates project, delivery system, personnel, and information management. The authors point out that these three less technical terms are used to describe the major functions so as to convey a broader view of the processes used within the field.

The definition also uses the adjective *technological* to describe the types of processes professionals in the field engage in, and the type of resources they often produce. The authors, drawing on the work of Galbraith (1967), indicate that technological processes are those that involve "the systematic application of scientific or other organized knowledge to accomplish practical tasks" (AECT Definition and Terminology Committee, 2008, p. 12). The authors also indicate that technological resources refer to the hardware and software that is typically associated with the field, including such items as still pictures, videos, computer programs, DVD players, among others.

The Definition Used Here

One of the many strengths of the new AECT definition of educational technology is that the definition clearly indicates that *a focus on systematic design processes* and *the use of technological resources* are both integral parts of the field. The definition that we will use in this textbook emphasizes these two aspects of the field as well as the recent influence the human performance technology movement has had on the profession.

As will be pointed out in later chapters in this textbook, in recent years, many professionals in the field of instructional design and technology (ID&T), particularly those who have been primarily trained to design instruction, have been focusing their efforts on improving human performance in the workplace. Although such improvements may be brought about by employing *instructional interventions,* which are often delivered either via training courses and/or training materials, careful analysis of the nature of performance problems often leads to the development and use of *noninstructional solutions* (i.e., solutions other than training courses and/or training materials). Numerous examples of noninstructional solutions to performance problems are described in other chapters in this book, including, but not limited to, the chapters on human performance improvement (Chapter 14), performance support (Chapter 15), informal learning (Chapter 16), social media (Chapter 28), and mobile learning (Chapter 29). This new emphasis on improving human performance in the workplace via noninstructional, as well as instructional, methods has been dubbed the performance improvement movement. We believe that any definition of the field of instructional design and technology should reflect this new emphasis. The definition that we have developed, and that we will use in this book, clearly does so. The definition is as follows:

> The field of instructional design and technology (also known as instructional technology) encompasses the analysis of learning

and performance problems, and the design, development, implementation, evaluation and management of instructional and non-instructional processes and resources intended to improve learning and performance in a variety of settings, particularly educational institutions and the workplace. Professionals in the field instructional design and technology often use systematic instructional design procedures and employ instructional media to accomplish their goals. Moreover, in recent years, they have paid increasing attention to non-instructional solutions to some performance problems. Research and theory related to each of the aforementioned areas is also an important part of the field.

As noted earlier, this definition highlights two sets of practices that have, over the years, formed the core of the field. We believe that these two practices—the use of media for instructional purposes and the use of systematic instructional design procedures (often simply called *instructional design*)—are the key defining elements of the field of instructional design and technology. Individuals involved in the field are those who spend a significant portion of their time working with media and/or with tasks associated with systematic instructional design procedures. We believe that one strength of this definition is the prominent recognition it gives to both aspects of the field. More importantly, we feel the proposed definition, unlike those that have preceded it, clearly points to the efforts that many professionals in the field are placing on improving human performance in the workplace through a variety of instructional and non-instructional means. There is no doubt that many of the concepts and practices associated with performance improvement have been integrated into the training that future ID&T professionals receive (Fox & Klein, 2003), and the activities those individuals undertake once they enter the profession (Van Tiem, 2004). The definition we have put forward clearly reflects this reality.

Naming the Field: Why Should We Call It Instructional Design and Technology?

The definition proposed in this chapter also differs from most of the previous definitions in that it refers to the field as *instructional design and technology,* rather than *instructional technology.* Why? Most individuals outside of our profession, as well as many inside of it, when asked to define the term *instructional technology,* will mention computers, DVDs, mobile devices, and the other types of hardware and software typically associated with the term *instructional media.* In other words, most individuals will equate the term *instructional technology* with *instructional media.* This is the case in spite of the all the broadened definitions of instructional technology that have appeared over the past thirty to forty years. In light of this fact, perhaps it is time to reconsider the label we use for the broad field that encompasses the areas of instructional media, instructional design, and more recently, performance improvement. Any of a number of terms come to mind, but one that seems particularly appropriate is *instructional design and technology.* This term, which has also been employed by one of the professional organizations in our field (Professors of Instructional Design and Technology), mentions both of the areas focused upon in earlier definitions. Performance improvement, the most recent area to have a major impact on the field, is not directly mentioned because adding it to the term *instructional design and technology* would make that term unwieldy, and because in recent years instructional design practices have broadened so that many of the concepts associated with the performance improvement movement are now regularly employed by those individuals who call themselves instructional designers.

Here, our field will be referred to as *instructional design and technology,* and we will define this term as indicated in the previous section; however, regardless of the term that is used as the label for our field and the specific definition you prefer, it is important to understand the ideas and practices that are associated with the field, and the trends and issues that are likely to affect it. The purpose of this book is to introduce you to many of those ideas, practices, trends, and issues. As you proceed through this book, we anticipate that your view of the field will evolve, and we are confident that your understanding of the field will increase. Moreover, we expect that you will be able to add your reasoned opinion to the ongoing debate concerning the "proper" definition and label for the field we have called instructional design and technology.

Summary of Key Principles

1. **Over the years, a variety of different labels have been used as the name for the field that in this book we refer to as *instructional design and technology.*** In recent years, other frequently used names for the field have included *instructional technology* and *educational technology.*

2. **Definitions of the field have also changed over the years.** Changes in definitions are appropriate because as new ideas and innovations affect the practices of individuals in the field, definitions of the field should be revised so as to make mention of those new practices.

3. **Whereas early definitions of the field focused on the instructional media that were being produced by professionals in the field, starting in the 1960s and 1970s a number of leaders in the field, working both as individuals and as members of professional committees, developed definitions that indicated instructional (or educational) technology was a process.** In particular, a process for systematically designing instruction.

4. **The goals specified in the various definition statements have also shifted over the years.** Whereas the earlier definitions indicated that goal of the field was to bring about more effective instruction, later definitions indicated that the primary goal was to improve learning. The most recent definition statements expanded this aim, indicating that the goal of the field is to improve (or facilitate) learning *and* performance.

5. **The definition of the field that we are using in this book focuses on the systematic design of instruction and the use of media for instructional purposes —the two sets of practices that continue to form the foundation of our field.** The definition also focuses on the efforts by many professionals in our field to use a variety of instructional *and* noninstructional means to improve human performance in the workplace.

Application Questions

1. **Define the field:** Reexamine the various definitions of the field that have been mentioned in this chapter, as well as several other definitions that you find online and/or in other sources. Then, prepare your own definition of the field. This definition may either be one you create, one that was taken verbatim from this chapter or another source, or one that is a modified version of an existing definition. In any case, be sure to reference the sources you used in preparing your definition. After you prepare your definition, describe why you feel it is a good one.

2. **Name the field:** As mentioned in this chapter, there are many labels for the field you are now studying. These labels include *educational technology, instructional technology, instructional design and technology, instructional design, and performance improvement,* among others. Examine some outside resources in which several of these labels are defined and discussed. Then, identify which label you feel is the best one for the field, and describe why you feel that way.

References

AECT Definition and Terminology Committee. (2008). In A. Januszewski & M. Molenda (Eds.), *Educational technology: A Definition with Commentary*. New York: Lawrence Erlbaum.

Association for Educational Communications and Technology. (1977). *Educational technology: Definition and glossary of terms*. Washington, DC: Association for Educational Communications and Technology.

Association for Educational Communications and Technology. (2007). *AECT: Code of professional ethics*. Retrieved from http://www.aect.org/About/Ethics.asp

Commission on Instructional Technology. (1970). *To improve learning: An evaluation of instructional technology*. Washington, DC: United States Government Printing Office.

Dorris, A. V. (1928). *Visual instruction in the public schools*. Boston: Ginn.

Ely, D. P. (Ed.). (1963). The changing role of the audiovisual process in education: A definition and a glossary of related terms. *AV Communication Review, 11.*

Finn, J. D. (1960). Technology and the instructional process. *AV Communication Review, 8,* 5–26.

Fox, E. J., & Klein, J. D. (2003). What should instructional designers and technologists know about human performance technology? *Performance Improvement Quarterly, 16,* 87–98.

Gagné, R. M. (1965). The analysis of instructional objectives for the design of instruction. In R. Glaser (Ed.), *Teaching machines and programmed learning, II: Data and directions*. Washington, DC: National Education Association.

Galbraith, J. K. (1967). *The new industrial state*. Boston: Houghton Mifflin.

Hoban, C. F., Jr. (1977). A systems approach to audio-visual communications: The Okoboji 1956 keynote address. In L. W. Cochran (Ed.), *Okoboji: A 20 year review of leadership 1955-1974*. Dubuque, IA: Kendall/Hunt.

Lumsdaine, A. A. (1964). Educational technology, programmed learning, and instructional science. In E. R. Hilgard (Ed.), *Theories of learning and instruction: The sixty-third yearbook of the National Society for the Study of Education, Part I*. Chicago: University of Chicago Press.

Reiser, R. A., & Ely, D. P. (1997). The field of educational technology as reflected in its definitions. *Educational Technology Research and Development, 45,* 63–72.

Richey, R. C., & Seels, B. (1994). Defining a field: A case study of the development of the 1994 definition of instructional technology. In D. P. Ely (Ed.), *Educational media and technology yearbook: 1994*. Englewood, CO: Libraries Unlimited.

Saettler, P. (1990). *The evolution of American educational technology*. Englewood, CO: Libraries Unlimited.

Scriven, M. (1967). The methodology of evaluation. In *Perspectives of curriculum evaluation* (American Educational Research Association Monograph Series on Curriculum Evaluation, No. 1). Chicago: Rand McNally.

Seels, B. B., & Richey, R. C. (1994). *Instructional technology: The definition and domains of the field*. Washington, DC: Association for Educational Communications and Technology.

Van Tiem, D. M. (2004). Interventions (solutions) usage and expertise in performance technology practice: An empirical investigation. *Performance Improvement Quarterly*., *17*, 23–44.

Chapter 2

A History of Instructional Design and Technology[1]

Robert A. Reiser

Florida State University

As was indicated in the first chapter of this book, over the years, two practices—the use of systematic instructional design procedures (often simply called *instructional design*) and the use of media for instructional purposes—have formed the core of the field of instructional design and technology. This chapter will review the history of the field by examining the history of both instructional media and instructional design. From a historical perspective, most of the practices related to instructional media have occurred independent of developments associated with instructional design. Therefore, the history of each of these two sets of practices will be described separately. It should also be noted that although many important events in the history of the field of instructional design and technology have taken place in other countries, the emphasis in this chapter will be on events that have taken place in the United States.

History of Instructional Media

The term *instructional media* has been defined as the physical means via which instruction is presented to learners (Reiser & Gagné, 1983). Under this definition, every physical means of instructional delivery, from the live instructor to the textbook to the computer and so on, would be classified as an instructional medium. It may be wise for practitioners in the field to adopt this viewpoint; however, in most discussions of the history of instructional media, the three primary means of instruction

prior to the twentieth century (and still the most common means today)—the teacher, the chalkboard, and the textbook—have been categorized separately from other media (cf. Commission on Instructional Technology, 1970). In order to clearly describe the history of media, this viewpoint will be employed in this chapter. Thus, instructional media will be defined as the physical means, other than the teacher, chalkboard, and textbook, via which instruction is presented to learners.

School Museums

In the United States, the use of media for instructional purposes has been traced back to at least as early as the first decade of the twentieth century (Saettler, 1990). It was at that time that school museums came into existence. As Saettler (1968) has indicated, these museums "served as the central administrative unit[s] for visual instruction by [their] distribution of portable museum exhibits, stereographs [three-dimensional photographs], slides, films, study prints, charts, and other instructional materials" (p. 89). The first school museum was opened in St. Louis in 1905, and shortly thereafter school museums were opened in Reading, Pennsylvania and Cleveland, Ohio. Although few such museums have been established since the early 1900s, the district-wide media center may be considered a modern-day equivalent.

Saettler (1990) has also stated that the materials housed in school museums were viewed as supplementary curriculum materials. They were not intended to supplant the teacher or the textbook. Throughout the past one hundred years, this early view of the role of instructional media has remained prevalent in the educational community at large. That is, during this time

[1] I would like to thank Fabrizio Fornara and Weinan Zhao for their assistance in identifying and analyzing reports regarding current-day use of instructional media.

period most educators have viewed instructional media as supplementary means of presenting instruction. In contrast, teachers and textbooks are generally viewed as the primary means of presenting instruction, and teachers are usually given the authority to decide what other instructional media they will employ. Over the years, a number of professionals in the field of instructional design and technology (e.g., Heinich, 1970) have argued against this notion, indicating that (a) teachers should be viewed on an equal footing with instructional media—as just one of many possible means of presenting instruction; and (b) teachers should not be given sole authority for deciding what instructional media will be employed in classrooms. In the broad educational community, however, these viewpoints have not prevailed.

The Visual Instruction Movement and Instructional Films

As Saettler (1990) has indicated, in the early part of the twentieth century, most of the media housed in school museums were visual media, such as films, slides, and photographs. Thus, at the time, the increasing interest in using media in the school was referred to as the "visual instruction" or "visual education" movement. The latter term was used at least as far back as 1908, when the Keystone View Company published *Visual Education,* a teacher's guide to lantern slides and stereographs.

Besides magic lanterns (lantern slide projectors) and stereopticons (stereograph viewers), which were used in some schools during the second half of the nineteenth century (Anderson, 1962), the motion picture projector was one of the first media devices used in schools. In the United States, the first catalog of instructional films was published in 1910. Later that year, the public school system of Rochester, New York, became the first to adopt films for regular instructional use. In 1913, Thomas Edison proclaimed: "Books will soon be obsolete in the schools. . . . It is possible to teach every branch of human knowledge with the motion picture. Our school system will be completely changed in the next ten years" (cited in Saettler, 1968, p. 98).

During the ten-year period Edison was referring to (i.e., 1914–1923), the visual instruction movement did grow. Five national professional organizations for visual instruction were established, five journals focusing on visual instruction began publication, more than twenty teacher-training institutions began offering courses in visual instruction, and at least a dozen large-city school systems developed bureaus of visual education (Saettler, 1990). By the end of that ten-year period, however, the revolutionary changes in education envisioned by Edison had not come about. Cuban (1986) indicates that the impact of the visual instruction was limited because of a wide variety of factors, including teacher resistance to change, the difficulty teachers had in operating film equipment, the paucity and poor instructional quality of relevant films in many subject areas, and the costs associated with purchasing and maintaining films and equipment.

The Audiovisual Instruction Movement and Instructional Radio

During the remainder of the 1920s and through much of the 1930s, technological advances in such areas as radio broadcasting, sound recordings, and sound motion pictures led to increased interest in instructional media. With the advent of media incorporating sound, the visual instruction movement became known as the audiovisual instruction movement (Finn, 1972; McCluskey, 1981). However, McCluskey (1981), a leader in the field during this period, indicates that while the field continued to grow, the educational community at large was not greatly affected by that growth. He states that by 1930, commercial interests in the visual instruction movement had invested and lost more than $50 million, only part of which was due to the Great Depression, which began in 1929.

In spite of the adverse economic effects of the Great Depression, the audiovisual instruction movement continued to evolve. According to Saettler (1990), one of the most significant events in this evolution was the merging, in 1932, of the three existing national professional organizations for visual instruction. As a result of this merger, leadership in the movement was consolidated within one organization, the Department of Visual Instruction (DVI), which at that time was part of the National Education Association. Over the years, this organization, which was created in 1923 and is now called the Association for Educational Communications and Technology (AECT), has maintained a leadership role in the field of instructional design and technology.

During the 1920s and 1930s, a number of textbooks on the topic of visual instruction were written. Perhaps the most important of these textbooks was *Visualizing the Curriculum,* written by Charles F. Hoban, Sr., Charles F. Hoban, Jr., and Stanley B. Zissman (1937). In this book, the authors stated that the value of audiovisual material was a function of their degree of realism. The authors also presented a hierarchy of media, ranging from those that could only present concepts in an abstract fashion to those that allowed for very concrete representations (Heinich, Molenda, Russell, & Smaldino, 1999). Some of these ideas had previously been discussed by others, but had not been dealt with as thoroughly. In 1946, Edgar Dale further elaborated upon these ideas when he developed his famous "Cone of Experience." Throughout the history of the audiovisual instruction movement, many have indicated that part of the value of audiovisual materials is their ability to present concepts in a concrete manner (Saettler, 1990).

A medium that gained a great deal of attention during this period was radio. By the early 1930s, many audiovisual enthusiasts were hailing radio as the medium that would revolutionize education. For example, in referring to the instructional potential of radio, films, and television, the editor of publications for the National Education Association stated that "tomorrow they will be as common as the book and powerful in their effect on learning and teaching" (Morgan, 1932, p. ix). However, contrary to these sorts of predictions, over the next twenty years, radio had very little impact on instructional practices. Cuban (1986) indicates that poor equipment, poor reception of radio signals, scheduling problems, and teacher resistance to change were among the many factors that resulted in this lack of impact.

World War II

With the onset of World War II, the growth of the audiovisual instruction movement in the schools slowed; however, audiovisual devices were used extensively in the military services and in industry. For example, during the war the U.S. Army Air Force produced more than 400 training films and 600 filmstrips, and during a two-year period (from mid-1943 to mid-1945) it was estimated that there were over 4 million showings of training films and filmstrips to U.S. military personnel. Although there was little time and opportunity to collect hard data regarding the effect of these films on the performance of military personnel, several surveys of military instructors revealed that they felt that the training films and filmstrips used during the war were effective training tools (Saettler, 1990). Apparently, at least some of the enemy agreed; in 1945, after the war ended, the German Chief of General Staff said: "We had everything calculated perfectly except the speed with which America was able to train its people. Our major miscalculation was in underestimating their quick and complete mastery of film education" (cited in Olsen & Bass, 1982, p. 33).

During the war, training films also played an important role in preparing U.S. civilians to work in industry. In 1941, the federal government established the Division of Visual Aids for War Training. From 1941 to 1945, this organization oversaw the production of 457 training films. Most training directors reported that the films reduced training time without having a negative impact on training effectiveness, and that the films were more interesting and resulted in less absenteeism than traditional training programs (Saettler, 1990).

In addition to training films and film projectors, a wide variety of other audiovisual materials and equipment were employed in the military forces and in industry during World War II. Those devices that were used extensively included overhead projectors, which were first produced during the war; slide projectors, which were used in teaching aircraft and ship recognition; audio equipment, which was used in teaching foreign languages; and simulators and training devices, which were employed in flight training (Olsen & Bass, 1982; Saettler, 1990).

Theories of Communication

During the decade after World War II, many leaders in the audiovisual instruction movement became interested in various theories or models of communication, such as the model put forth by Shannon and Weaver (1949). These models focused on the communication process, a process involving a sender and a receiver of a message, and a channel, or medium, through which that message is sent. The authors of these models indicated that during planning for communication it was necessary to consider all the elements of the communication process, and not just focus on the medium (e.g., Berlo, 1963). Several leaders in the audiovisual movement, such as Dale (1953) and Finn (1954), also emphasized the importance of the communication process. Although at first, audiovisual practitioners were not greatly influenced by this notion (Lumsdaine, 1964; Meierhenry, 1980), the expression of this point of view eventually helped expand the focus of the audiovisual movement (Ely, 1963; Ely, 1970; Silber, 1981).

Instructional Television

Perhaps the most important factor to affect the audiovisual movement in the 1950s was the increased interest in television as a medium for delivering instruction. Prior to the 1950s, there had been a number of instances in which television had been used for instructional purposes (Gumpert, 1967; Taylor, 1967). During the 1950s, however, there was a tremendous growth in the use of instructional television. This growth was stimulated by at least two major factors.

One factor that spurred the growth of instructional television was the 1952 decision by the Federal Communications Commission to set aside 242 television channels for educational purposes. This decision led to the rapid development of a large number of public (then called "educational") television stations. By 1955, there were seventeen such stations in the United States, and by 1960 that number had increased to more than fifty (Blakely, 1979). One of the primary missions of these stations was the presentation of instructional programs. As Hezel (1980) indicates: "The teaching role has been ascribed to public broadcasting since its origins. Especially prior to the 1960s, educational broadcasting was seen as a quick, efficient, inexpensive means of satisfying the nation's instructional needs" (p. 173).

The growth of instructional television during the 1950s was also stimulated by funding provided by the Ford Foundation. It has been estimated that during the 1950s and 1960s the foundation and its agencies spent more than $170 million on educational television (Gordon, 1970). Those projects sponsored by the foundation included a closed-circuit television system that was used to deliver instruction in all major subject areas at all grade levels throughout the school system in Washington County (Hagerstown), Maryland; a junior-college curriculum which was presented via public television in Chicago; a large-scale experimental research program designed to assess the effectiveness of a series of college courses taught via closed circuit television at Pennsylvania State University; and the Midwest Program on Airborne Television Instruction, a program designed to simultaneously transmit televised lessons from an airplane to schools in six states.

By the mid-1960s, much of the interest in using television for instructional purposes had abated. Many of the instructional television projects developed during this period had short lives. For example, by 1963 the Ford Foundation decided to focus its support on public television in general, rather than on in-school applications of instructional television (Blakely, 1979). In addition, many school districts discontinued instructional television demonstration projects when the external funding for those projects was halted (Tyler, 1975b). Moreover, instructional programming was still an important part of the mission of public television, but that mission was now wider, encompassing other types of programming, such as cultural and informational presentations (Hezel, 1980). In light of these and other developments, in 1967 the Carnegie Commission on Educational Television concluded:

> The role played in formal education by instructional television has been on the whole a small one . . . nothing which approached the true potential of instructional television has been realized

in practice. . . . With minor exceptions, the total disappearance of instructional television would leave the educational system fundamentally unchanged. (pp. 80–81)

Many reasons have been given as to why instructional television was not adopted to a greater extent. These include teacher resistance to change, especially *top-down change* (change mandated by school administrators with little or no input from teachers), the mediocre instructional quality of many of the television programs (many of them did little more than present a teacher delivering a lecture), the expense of installing and maintaining television systems in schools, and the failure to provide teachers with adequate guidance as to how to integrate the use of instructional television into their instructional practices (Chu & Schramm, 1975; Cuban, 1986; Gordon, 1970; Tyler, 1975b).

Using Computers for Instructional Purposes

After the interest in instructional television faded, the next technological innovation to catch the attention of a large number of educators was the computer. Although widespread interest in the computer as an instructional tool did not occur until the 1980s, computers were first used in education and training at a much earlier date. Much of the early work in computer-assisted instruction (CAI) was done in the 1950s by researchers at IBM, who developed the first CAI author language and designed one of the first CAI programs to be used in the public schools. Other pioneers in this area included Gordon Pask, whose adaptive teaching machines made use of computer technology (Lewis & Pask, 1965; Pask, 1960; Stolorow & Davis, 1965), and Richard Atkinson and Patrick Suppes, whose work during the 1960s led to some of the earliest applications of CAI at both the public school and university levels (Atkinson & Hansen, 1966; Suppes & Macken, 1978). Other major efforts during the 1960s and early 1970s included the development of CAI systems such as PLATO and TICCIT. However, in spite of the work that had been done, by the end of the 1970s, CAI had had very little impact on education (Pagliaro, 1983).

By the early 1980s, a few years after personal computers became available to the general public, the enthusiasm surrounding this tool led to increasing interest in using computers for instructional purposes. By January 1983, computers were being used for instructional purposes in more than 40 percent of all elementary schools and more than 75 percent of all secondary schools in the United States (Center for Social Organization of Schools, 1983).

Many educators became attracted to personal computers as an instructional tool because they were relatively inexpensive, were compact enough for desktop use, and could perform many of the functions performed by the large computers that had preceded them. As was the case when other new media were first introduced into the instructional arena, many expected that this medium would have a major impact on instructional practices. For example, Papert (1984) indicated that the computer was going to be "a catalyst of very deep and radical change in the educational system" (p. 422) and that by 1990 one computer per child would be a common state of affairs in schools in the United States.

At first, optimistic predictions about the extent to which computers would transform instructional practices appeared to be wrong. By the mid-1990s that impact had been rather small. Surveys revealed that by 1995, although schools in the United States possessed, on average, one computer for every nine students, the impact of computers on instructional practices was minimal, with a substantial number of teachers reporting little or no use of computers for instructional purposes. Moreover, in most cases, the use of computers was far from innovative. In elementary schools, teachers reported that computers were being primarily used for drill and practice, and at the secondary level, reports indicated that computers were mainly used for teaching computer-related skills such as word processing (Anderson & Ronnkvist, 1999; Becker, 1998; Office of Technology Assessment, 1995). However, as we'll discuss next, events during the first fifteen years of the current century indicate that computers and other new technologies are having more of an impact on education and training than many of the media that preceded these innovations.

Recent Developments

During the past fifteen years, rapid advances in computers and other digital technology, including the Internet, have led to a rapidly increasing interest in, and use of, these media for instructional purposes. This conclusion appears to be true across a wide variety of training and educational settings, including business and industry, higher education, and K-12 education. One of the largest areas of growth has involved the use of online instruction in all of the aforementioned settings. For example, in higher education the percentage of students taking online courses has dramatically increased. In 2002, whereas approximately 10 percent of the students enrolled in institutions of higher learning were taking at least one online course, by 2011 approximately 32 percent of such students were doing so (Allen & Seaman, 2013). The same general trend can also be noted at the middle school and high school levels. In 2008, 9 percent of middle school students took at least one online course, whereas 19 percent did so in 2010; and at the high school level, the percentage of students grew from 10 percent in 2008 to 30 percent in 2010 (Blackboard, 2011). Moreover, the use of online instruction has also greatly increased in business and industry. In 2003, 13 percent of the training in business and industry was delivered online, whereas by 2014 that percentage had more than doubled, with 28 percent of the training being online (ASTD Research, 2010; ATD Research, 2015a).

In business and industry, the increasing role that technology is playing in the delivery of training goes beyond online instruction. In recent years, in addition to online instruction, a wide variety of technologies, such as video, satellite, CD-ROM, and mobile devices, have served on a steadily increasing basis as the means via which training is presented. Whereas in 2004, 26 percent of all training in business and industry was delivered via technology, by 2014 the percentage of training that was delivered via technology had risen to 41 percent (ASTD Research, 2008; ATD Research, 2015a).

Mobile devices, such as smartphones and tablets, are another form of media that are playing an increasingly large role in the delivery of instruction. For example, a recent survey reveals that more than one-third of business organizations now provide their employees with learning programs that are delivered via mobile devices (ATD Research, 2015b). Mobile devices are also being used for learning on a frequent basis in higher education. In a 2015 survey, 64 percent of college students reported that they used smartphones for their schoolwork at least two or three times per week, and 40 percent indicated that they used tablets for schoolwork at least that frequently (Pearson, 2015a). In addition, many students in grades 4 through 12 are using mobile devices. In 2015, of the students surveyed at those grade levels, 41 percent reported that they used smartphones, and 37 percent reported that they used tablets, at least two or three times per week (Pearson, 2015b).

In sum, most of the evidence presented in this section of this chapter clearly indicates that in recent years there has been a significant increase in the use of instructional media in a variety of settings. What are some of the reasons for this increased usage? In business and industry, the Internet has been viewed as a means of providing instruction and information to widely dispersed learners at a relatively low cost. Moreover, in many cases, the easy accessibility of computers makes it possible for learners to receive instruction and/or performance support when and where they need it, oftentimes as they are performing particular job tasks.

In higher education, distance education via the Internet has been seen as a low-cost method of providing instruction to students who, due to a variety of factors (e.g., job and family responsibilities, geographic locations), might not otherwise have been able to receive it. Moreover, institutions of higher education often view online courses as a significant source of additional revenue.

Another reason that the newer media are being used to a greater extent may be due to their increased interactive capabilities. Moore (1989) describes three types of interactions among the agents usually involved in an instructional activity. These interactions are between learners and instructional content, between learners and the instructor, and among learners themselves. Due to their attributes, the instructional media that were prevalent during some portion of the first two-thirds of the past century (e.g., films and instructional television) were primarily employed as a means of having learners interact with instructional content. In contrast, through the use of such features as e-mail, chat rooms, and bulletin boards, the Internet is often used as a means of having learners interact with their instructor and with other learners, as well as with instructional content. This is one example of how some of the newer media make it easier to promote the various types of interactions described by Moore.

In addition, advances in computer technology, particularly with regard to the increasing multimedia capabilities of this medium, have made it easier for educators to design learning experiences that involve more complex interactions between learners and instructional content than has previously been the case. For example, as the amount and type of information (e.g., print, video, audio) that can be presented by computers has increased, the type of feedback, as well as the type of problems, that can be presented to learners has greatly expanded. These increased instructional capabilities have attracted the attention of many educators. Moreover, the ability of computers to present information in a wide variety of forms, as well as to allow learners to easily link to various content, has attracted the interest of instructional designers having a constructivist perspective. They and others who are particularly concerned with presenting authentic (i.e., "real world") problems in learning environments in which learners have a great deal of control of the activities they engage in and the tools and resources they use, find the new digital technology more accommodating than its predecessors.

Finally, in recent years technologies such as personal computers, mobile devices, and the Internet have become pervasive, and the use of the tools and technologies associated with social networking (e.g., Facebook, LinkedIn) and social media (e.g., blogs, wikis, YouTube, Twitter) has become widespread. These tools and technologies have become commonplace devices for individuals to share information and acquire new skills and knowledge. In light of this fact, it is not surprising that educators are frequently turning to these devices as a means of supporting instruction, learning, and on-the-job performance.

Conclusions Regarding the History of Instructional Media

Of the many lessons we can learn by reviewing the history of instructional media, perhaps one of the most important involves a comparison between the anticipated and actual effects of media on instructional practices. As Cuban (1986) has pointed out, as you look back over the history of instructional media during the twentieth century, you are likely to note a recurrent pattern of expectations and outcomes. As a new medium enters the educational scene, there is a great deal of initial interest and much enthusiasm about the effects it is likely to have on instructional practices. However, enthusiasm and interest eventually fade, and an examination reveals that the medium has had a minimal impact on such practices. For example, Edison's optimistic prediction that films would revolutionize education proved to be incorrect, and the enthusiasm for instructional television that existed during the 1950s greatly abated by the mid-1960s, with little impact on instruction in the schools. However, since the start of the twenty-first century, that pattern seems to have changed. Computers and other digital technologies seem to be having a more profound impact on the way in which instruction is presented, whether it is at the K-12 level, in higher education, or in business and industry. While a full-scale revolution—one in which the classroom teacher is removed as one of the primary means of delivering instruction—has not taken place and is unlikely to come about at any time in the foreseeable future (which, in my opinion, is a good thing), it seems clear to me that computers and the other digital media that have been discussed in this chapter have brought about far greater changes in the way instruction is delivered than the media that preceded them.

History of Instructional Design

As mentioned, in addition to being closely associated with instructional media, the field of instructional design and technology has also been closely associated with the use of systematic instructional design procedures. As is indicated in Chapter 3, a variety of sets of systematic instructional design procedures (or models) have been developed, and have been referred to by such terms as *the systems approach*, *instructional systems design (ISD)*, *instructional development*, and *instructional design* (which is the term I will use in the remainder of the chapter). Although the specific combination of procedures often varies from one instructional design model to the next, most of the models include the analysis of instructional problems and the design, development, implementation, and evaluation of instruction procedures and materials intended to solve those problems. How did this instructional design process come into being? This portion of this chapter will focus on answering that question.

The Origins of Instructional Design: World War II

The origins of instructional design procedures have been traced to World War II (Dick, 1987). During the war, a large number of psychologists and educators who had training and experience in conducting experimental research were called upon to conduct research and develop training materials for the military services. These individuals, including Robert Gagné, Leslie Briggs, John Flanagan, and many others, exerted considerable influence on the characteristics of the training materials that were developed, basing much of their work upon instructional principles derived from research and theory on instruction, learning, and human behavior (Baker, 1973; Saettler, 1990).

Moreover, psychologists used their knowledge of evaluation and testing to help assess the skills of trainees and select the individuals who were most likely to benefit from particular training programs. For example, at one point in the war, the failure rate in a particular flight training program was unacceptably high. In order to overcome this problem, psychologists examined the general intellectual, psychomotor, and perceptual skills of individuals who were able to successfully perform the skills taught in the program, and then developed tests that measured these traits. These tests were used to screen candidates for the program, with those individuals who scored poorly being directed into other programs. As a result of using this examination of entry skills as a screening device, the military was able to significantly increase the percentage of personnel who successfully completed the program (Gagné, personal communication, 1985).

Immediately after the war, many of the psychologists responsible for the success of World War II military training programs continued to work on solving instructional problems. Organizations such as the American Institutes for Research were established for this purpose. During the late 1940s and throughout the 1950s, psychologists working for such organizations started viewing training as a system, and developed a number of innovative analysis, design, and evaluation procedures (Dick, 1987). For example, during this period, a detailed task analysis methodology was developed by Robert B. Miller while he worked on projects for the military (Miller, 1953, 1962). His work and those of other early pioneers in the instructional design field are summarized in *Psychological Principles in System Development*, edited by Gagné (1962b).

More Early Developments: The Programmed Instruction Movement

The programmed instruction movement, which ran from the mid-1950s through the mid-1960s, proved to be another major factor in the development of the systems approach. In 1954, B. F. Skinner's article, "The Science of Learning and the Art of Teaching," began what might be called a minor revolution in the field of education. In this article and later ones (e.g., Skinner, 1958), Skinner described his ideas regarding the requirements for increasing human learning and the desired characteristics of effective instructional materials. Skinner stated that such materials, called programmed instructional materials, should present instruction in small steps, require active responses to frequent questions, provide immediate feedback, and allow for learner self-pacing. Moreover, because each step was small, it was thought that learners would answer all questions correctly and thus be positively reinforced by the feedback they received.

The process Skinner and others (cf. Lumsdaine & Glaser, 1960) described for developing programmed instruction exemplified an empirical approach to solving educational problems: Data regarding the effectiveness of the materials were collected, instructional weaknesses were identified, and the materials were revised accordingly. In addition to this trial and revision procedure, which today would be called formative evaluation, the process for developing programmed materials involved many of the steps found in current instructional design models. As Heinich (1970) indicates:

> Programmed instruction has been credited by some with introducing the systems approach to education. By analyzing and breaking down content into specific behavioral objectives, devising the necessary steps to achieve the objectives, setting up procedures to try out and revise the steps, and validating the program against attainment of the objectives, programmed instruction succeeded in creating a small but effective self-instructional system – a technology of instruction. (p. 123)

The Popularization of Behavioral Objectives

As indicated, those involved in designing programmed instructional materials often began by identifying the specific objectives learners who used the materials would be expected to attain. In the early 1960s, Robert Mager, recognizing the need to teach educators how to write objectives, wrote *Preparing Objectives for Programmed Instruction* (Mager, 1962). This small, humorously written programmed book, now in its second edition (Mager, 1984), has proved to be quite popular, with sales over 1.5 million copies. The book describes how to write objectives that include a description of desired learner behaviors, the conditions under which the behaviors are to be performed, and the standards (criteria) by which the behaviors are to be judged. Many current-day adherents of the instructional design process advocate the preparation of objectives that contain these three elements.

Although Mager popularized the use of objectives, the concept was discussed and used by educators at least as far back at the early 1900s. Among those early advocates of the use of clearly stated objectives were Bobbitt, Charters, and Burk (Gagné, 1965a). However, Ralph Tyler has often been considered the father of the behavioral objectives movement. In 1934, he wrote: "Each objective must be defined in terms which clarify the kind of behavior which the course should help to develop" (cited in Walbesser & Eisenberg, 1972). During the famous Eight-Year Study that Tyler directed, it was found that in those instances in which schools did specify objectives, those objectives were usually quite vague. By the end of the project, however, it was demonstrated that objectives could be clarified by stating them in behavioral terms, and those objectives could serve as the basis for evaluating the effectiveness of instruction (Borich, 1980; Tyler, 1975a).

In the 1950s, behavioral objectives were given another boost when Benjamin Bloom and his colleagues published *Taxonomy of Educational Objectives* (Bloom, Engelhart, Furst, Hill, & Krathwohl, 1956). The authors of this work indicated that within the cognitive domain there were various types of learning outcomes, that objectives could be classified according to the type of learner behavior described therein, and that there was a hierarchical relationship among the various types of outcomes. Moreover, they indicated that tests should be designed to measure each of these types of outcomes. As we shall see in the next two sections of this chapter, similar notions described by other educators had significant implications for the systematic design of instruction.

The Criterion-Referenced Testing Movement

In the early 1960s, another important factor in the development of the instructional design process was the emergence of criterion-referenced testing. Until that time, most tests, called norm-referenced tests, were designed to spread out the performance of learners, resulting in some students doing well on a test and others doing poorly. In contrast, a criterion-referenced test is intended to measure how well an individual can perform a particular behavior or set of behaviors, irrespective of how well others perform. As early as 1932, Tyler had indicated that tests could be used for such purposes (Dale, 1967). And later, Flanagan (1951) and Ebel (1962) discussed the differences between such tests and the more familiar norm-referenced measures. However, Robert Glaser (1963; Glaser & Klaus, 1962) was the first to use the term *criterion-referenced measures.* In discussing such measures, Glaser (1963) indicated that they could be used to assess student entry-level behavior and to determine the extent to which students had acquired the behaviors an instructional program was designed to teach. The use of criterion-referenced tests for these two purposes is a central feature of instructional design procedures.

Robert M. Gagné: Domains of Learning, Events of Instruction, and Hierarchical Analysis

Another important event in the history of instructional design occurred in 1965, with the publication of the first edition of *The Conditions of Learning,* written by Robert Gagné (1965b). In this book, Gagné described five domains, or types, of learning outcomes—verbal information, intellectual skills, psychomotor skills, attitudes, and cognitive strategies—each of which required a different set of conditions to promote learning. Gagné also provided detailed descriptions of these conditions for each type of learning outcome.

In the same volume, Gagné also described nine *events of instruction,* or teaching activities, that he considered essential for promoting the attainment of any type of learning outcome. Gagné also described which instructional events were particularly crucial for which type of outcome, and discussed the circumstances under which particular events could be excluded. Now in its fourth edition (Gagné, 1985), Gagné's description of the various types of learning outcomes and the events of instruction remain cornerstones of instructional design practices.

Gagné's work in the area of learning hierarchies and hierarchical analysis also has had a significant impact on the instructional design field. In the early 1960s and later in his career (e.g., Gagné, 1962a, 1985; Gagné, Briggs, and Wager, 1992; Gagné & Medsker, 1996), Gagné indicated that skills within the intellectual skills domain have a hierarchical relationship to each other, so that in order to readily learn to perform a superordinate skill, one would first have to master the skills subordinate to it. This concept leads to the important notion that instruction should be designed so as to ensure that learners acquire subordinate skills before they attempt to acquire superordinate ones. Gagné went on to describe a hierarchical analysis process (also called learning task analysis or instructional task analysis) for identifying subordinate skills. This process remains a key feature in many instructional design models.

Sputnik: The Indirect Launching of Formative Evaluation

In 1957, when the Soviet Union launched *Sputnik,* the first orbiting space satellite, there began a series of events that would eventually have a major impact on the instructional design process. In response to the launching of *Sputnik,* the United States government, shocked by the success of the Soviet effort, poured millions of dollars into improving math and science education in the United States. The instructional materials developed with these funds were usually written by subject-matter experts and produced without tryouts with learners. Years later, in the mid-1960s, when it was discovered that many of these materials were not particularly effective, Michael Scriven (1967) pointed to the need to try out drafts of instructional materials with learners prior to the time the materials were in their final form. This process would enable educators to examine the materials and, if necessary, revise them while the materials were still in their formative stages. Scriven coined this tryout and revision process *formative evaluation,* and contrasted it with what he labeled *summative evaluation,* the testing of instructional materials after they are in their final form.

Although the terms formative and summative evaluation were coined by Scriven, the distinction between these two approaches was previously made by Lee Cronbach (1963). Moreover, during the 1940s and the 1950s, a number of educators, such as

Arthur Lumsdaine, Mark May, and C. R. Carpenter, described procedures for evaluating instructional materials that were still in their formative stages (Cambre, 1981). However, in spite of the writings of such educators, very few of the instructional products developed in the 1940s and 1950s went through any sort of formative evaluation process. This situation changed somewhat in the late 1950s and through the1960s, as many of the programmed instructional materials developed during that period were tested while they were being developed. However, authors such as Susan Markle (1967) decried a lack of rigor in testing processes. In light of this problem, Markle prescribed detailed procedures for evaluating materials both during and after the design process. These procedures are much like the formative and summative evaluation techniques generally prescribed today.

Early Instructional Design Models

In the early and mid-1960s, the concepts that were being developed in such areas as task analysis, objective specification, and criterion-referenced testing were linked together to form a process, or model, for systematically designing instructional materials. Among the first individuals to describe such models were Gagné (1962b), Glaser (1962, 1965), and Silvern (1964). These individuals used terms such as "instructional design," "system development," "systematic instruction," and "instructional system" to describe their models. Other instructional design models created and employed during this decade included those described by Banathy (1968), Barson (1967), and Hamerus (1968).

The 1970s: Burgeoning of Interest in the Systems Approach

During the 1970s, the number of instructional design models greatly increased. Building upon the works of those who preceded them, many individuals created new models for systematically designing instruction (e.g., Dick & Carey, 1978; Gagné & Briggs, 1974; Gerlach & Ely, 1971; Kemp, 1971), several of which became "standards" in the field. Indeed, updated versions of at least two of these models (Dick, Carey, & Carey, 2009; Morrison, Ross, Kemp, & Kalman, 2010) are still frequently taught to graduate students studying instructional design (Johnson, Xin, Mackal, & Reiser, 2012.).

During the 1970s, interest in the instructional design process flourished in a variety of different sectors. In 1975, several branches of the U.S. military adopted an instructional design model (Branson et al., 1975) intended to guide the development of training materials within those branches. In academia, during the first half of the decade, many instructional improvement centers were created with the intent of helping faculty use media and instructional design procedures to improve the quality of their instruction (Gaff, 1975; Gustafson & Bratton, 1984). Moreover, many graduate programs in instructional design were created (Partridge & Tennyson, 1979; Redfield & Dick, 1984; Silber, 1982). In business and industry, many organizations, seeing the value of using instructional design to improve the quality of training, began adopting the approach (cf. Mager, 1977; Miles, 1983). Internationally, many nations,

such as South Korea, Liberia, and Indonesia, saw the benefits of using instructional design to solve instructional problems in those countries (Chadwick, 1986; Morgan, 1989). These nations supported the design of new instructional programs, created organizations to support the use of instructional design, and provided support to individuals desiring training in this field. Many of these developments were chronicled in the *Journal of Instructional Development*, a journal that was first published during the 1970s.

The 1980s: Growth and Redirection

In many sectors, the interest in instructional design that burgeoned during the previous decade continued to grow during the 1980s. Interest in the instructional design process remained strong in business and industry (Bowsher, 1989; Galagan, 1989), the military (Chevalier, 1990; Finch, 1987; McCombs, 1986), and in the international arena (Ely & Plomp, 1986; Morgan, 1989).

In contrast to its influence in the aforementioned sectors, during the 1980s, instructional design had minimal impact in other areas. In the public school arena, some curriculum development efforts involved the use of basic instructional design processes (e.g., Spady, 1988), and some instructional design textbooks for teachers were produced (e.g., Dick & Reiser, 1989; Gerlach & Ely, 1980; Sullivan & Higgins, 1983). However, in spite of these efforts, evidence indicated that instructional design was having little impact on instruction in the public schools (Branson & Grow, 1987; Burkman, 1987b; Rossett & Garbosky, 1987). In a similar vein, with a few exceptions (e.g., Diamond, 1989), instructional design practices had a minimal impact in higher education. Whereas instructional improvement centers in higher education were growing in number through the mid-1970s, by 1983 more than one-fourth of these organizations were disbanded and there was a general downward trend in the budgets of the remaining centers (Gustafson & Bratton, 1984). Burkman (1987a, 1987b) provides an enlightening analysis of the reasons why instructional design efforts in schools and universities have not been successful, and contrasts these conditions with the more favorable conditions that exist in business and the military.

During the 1980s, there was a growing interest in how the principles of cognitive psychology could be applied in the instructional design process, and a number of publications outlining potential applications were described (e.g., Bonner, 1986; Divesta & Rieber, 1987; "Interview with Robert M. Gagné," 1982; Low, 1980). However, several leading figures in the field have indicated that the actual effects of cognitive psychology on instructional design practices during this decade were rather small (Dick, 1987; Gustafson, 1993).

A factor that did have a major effect on instructional design practices in the 1980s was the increasing interest in the use of personal computers for instructional purposes. With the advent of these devices, many professionals in the instructional design field turned their attention to producing computer-based instruction (Dick, 1987; Shrock, 1995). Others discussed the need to develop new models of instructional design to accommodate the interactive capabilities of this technology (Merrill, Li, & Jones). Moreover, computers began to be used as tools to automate some instructional design tasks (Merrill & Li, 1989).

The 1990s: Recognizing the Importance of Performance

Beginning in the 1990s and continuing on into the current century, one of the trends that has had a major impact on the field has been the human performance improvement movement (see Section 4 of this book). This movement—with its emphasis on on-the-job performance (rather than learning), business results, and noninstructional solutions to performance problems—has broadened the scope of the instructional design field.

During the 1990s another factor that began to have a major influence on the field was the growing interest in constructivist views of teaching and learning. For example, the constructivist emphasis on designing "authentic" learning tasks—tasks that reflect the complexity of the real-world environment in which learners will be using the skills they are learning—has had an effect on how instructional design is being practiced and taught.

During this decade, instructional designers also began to have an interest in using computers not only as an instructional tool to enhance learning, but also as an aid to improve on-the-job performance. In particular, it was during this decade that an interest in using electronic performance support tools and systems to support on-the-job performance began to flourish. In addition, during this decade instructional designers began to discuss the use of computer-based knowledge management systems to support learning and performance (viz., Schwen, Kalman, Hara, & Kisling, 1998).

Instructional Design in the Twenty-First Century

During the first fifteen years of the twenty-first century, several developments have had a major influence on the field of instructional design. One such development involves the increasing use of the Internet as a means of presenting instruction to learners. As noted in an earlier section of this chapter, during this period there has been significant growth in online learning in higher education, business and industry, and K-12 schools. Along with this growth has come the realization that instructional designers play a vital part in the creation of online courses. This realization has opened new job opportunities for those in the instructional design field and has also presented new challenges as instructional design

professionals attempt to identify interesting and effective means of delivering instruction online.

Another recent development that has had a major impact on the instructional design field has been the increasing reliance on informal learning, as opposed to formal training, as a means of improving learning and performance in the workplace. In recent years, as people in the workplace have increasingly turned to innovations such as social media (Chapter 28), mobile devices (Chapter 29), and performance support tools (Chapter 15) to help them perform their jobs, the need for formal training has deceased. As a result, many instructional designers have had to expand their professional toolkits; they have needed to learn how to design and promote the use of these alternate means of facilitating skill acquisition.

A third factor that has affected the instructional design field in recent years involves the concerns that some individuals in the field expressed about "traditional" instructional design models, such as the ADDIE model. These concerns include the view that oftentimes traditional models often take too long to implement, that effective instruction can be designed in a more efficient manner using simpler design models. This concern and a number of others are discussed in several chapters in this book (e.g., see Chapter 4 and Chapter 39). In spite of these concerns, and/or perhaps because a substantial number of professionals in the field have adapted the design processes they employ in light of them, the demand for instructional designers in business and industry and higher education remains strong today, and is likely to remain strong in the foreseeable future.

Conclusion

Although this chapter has provided separate accounts of the history of instructional media and the history of instructional design, there is an obvious overlapping between these two areas. Many instructional solutions arrived at through the use of instructional design processes require the employment of the instructional media discussed in the first half of this chapter. Moreover, many individuals (e.g., Clark, 1994, 2001; Kozma, 1994; Morrison, 1994; Reiser, 1994; Shrock, 1994) have argued that the effective use of media for instructional purposes requires careful instructional planning, such as that prescribed by models of instructional design. In the field of instructional design and technology, those whose work is influenced by the lessons learned from the history of media *and* the history of instructional design will be well positioned to have a positive influence on future developments within the field.

Summary of Key Principles

1. **Throughout most of the 1900s, as each new medium (i.e., films, radio, and television) entered the world of education, there was a great deal of optimism regarding the extent to which that medium would change instructional practices.** Contrary to expectations, however, none of the aforementioned media had nearly the effect that the optimists envisioned.

2. **The likely reasons as to why each medium had minimal effects on practice are many.** Those that are frequently cited include teacher resistance to change, especially top-down change, the costs associated with purchasing and maintaining the necessary media hardware, the poor instructional quality of media software, and failure to provide teachers with adequate

guidance as to how to integrate the new media into their instructional practices.

3. **In recent years, computers and related technologies have had a greater effect on instructional practices and learning than did the various media that preceded them.** The interactive capabilities of these media, their ability to present information and instruction in a wide variety of forms, and the ease with which learners can create and share their own knowledge and skills via these media appear to be some of the primary reasons why these media have had a greater influence on instruction and learning.

4. **Portions of most of the instructional design models that were created in the 1960s and 1970s, and which still remain popular today, can be traced back to developments in education and training during the 1940s through the 1960s.** Advances in military training during World War II, new directions in instruction emanating from the programmed instruction movement, and new ideas involving behavioral objectives, criterion-referenced testing, learning hierarchies, and formative evaluation are often reflected in the various steps in these models.

5. **In the 1980s and 1990s, many instructional design models and practices were influenced by the principles derived from cognitive psychology and the new views of teaching and learning associated with constructivism.** Moreover, during that period the performance improvement movement led many instructional designers to begin thinking about the importance of positively influencing on-the-job performance and identifying noninstructional, as well as instructional, means of doing so.

6. **During the first fifteen years of the twenty-first century, several factors have had a major influence on the field of instructional design.** The increasing interest in e-learning has opened new opportunities for instructional designers, the increasing reliance on informal learning as a means of improving learning and performance has resulted in many instructional designers having to expand their professional toolkits, and concerns that have been expressed about "traditional" instructional design models has led some in the profession to propose and use alternate models of design.

Application Questions

1. During the previous school year, all the students assigned to four subject area teachers (math, language arts, social studies, and science) in the seventh grade at a local middle school were given laptop computers and provided with wireless Internet access at home and in school for an entire year. The students took the laptops home every evening and brought them into classes every day. Teachers were also provided with laptops and wireless Internet access twenty-four hours a day, every day of the week (24/7), for the entire year. Moreover, all of the curriculum materials (textbooks, workbooks, student study guides, teacher curriculum guides, etc.) that the teachers normally used during the school year were installed on the laptops.

   Assume that you were assigned as one of the evaluators for the project described, and that throughout the year you examined how this innovation (providing teachers and students with 24/7 access to laptops, curriculum materials, and wireless Internet service) changed the way instruction was presented in the classrooms of the four teachers who were involved in the project. Further assume that your findings clearly indicated that the innovation had very little effect on the manner in which instruction was presented in the teachers' classrooms. Now do the following:

   a. Describe at least three possible reasons (factors) why the project described had very little effect on the instructional practices employed by the teachers. Each of the factors you identify should be related to the factors mentioned in this chapter as to why earlier forms of instructional media (i.e., films, radio, and television) had very limited effects on instructional practices.

   b. Describe at least two strategies that could have been employed to help mitigate the factors that you think contributed to the minimal effect this project had on instructional practices. Indicate why you think each of these strategies might have been helpful.

2. Congratulations! Your instructional design consulting company has just been selected as one of the finalists to receive a contract to design a print-based instructional unit that will teach sixth-grade students throughout the United States how to multiply fractions. Now, in order to receive the contract, the contracting agency has asked you to prepare a memo in which you describe why your company is well suited to take on this task. As noted in the next paragraph, however, this memo isn't your normal memo!

   The agency's chief contract officer feels that the contract should be awarded to someone who understands the history of instructional design and can apply the ideas from that history to today's instructional design tasks. Therefore, he has asked that each of the finalists send him a 250- to 300-word memo in which they select four of the six historical periods provided here, and briefly describe how an instructional design principle derived from the period might be used in the design and/or presentation of the instructional unit on fractions. Write the memo!

Historical periods:

- World War II
- Programmed instruction movement
- Behavioral objectives movement

- Criterion-referenced testing movement
- Early work of Robert M. Gagné
- Formative evaluation movement

References

Allen, I. E., & Seaman, J. (2013). *Changing Course: Ten years of tracking online education in the United States.* Wellesley, MA: Babson Survey Research Group.

Anderson, C. (1962). *Technology in American education: 1650–1900* (Report No. OE-34018). Washington, DC: Office of Education, U.S. Department of Health, Education, and Welfare.

Anderson, R. E., & Ronnkvist, A. (1999). *The presence of computers in American schools: Teaching, learning and computing: 1998 national survey* (Report #2). Irvine, CA: Center for Research on Information Technology and Organizations (ERIC Document Reproduction Service No. ED 430 548).

Andrews, D. H., & Goodson, L. A. (1980). A comparative analysis of models instructional design. *Journal of Instructional Development, 3*(4), 2–16.

ASTD Research. (2008). *2008 state of the industry report.* Alexandria, VA: American Society for Training & Development.

ASTD Research. (2010). *2010 state of the industry report.* Alexandria, VA: American Society for Training & Development.

ATD Research. (2015a). *2015 state of the industry report.* Alexandria, VA: Association for Talent Development.

ATD Research. (2015b). *The mobile landscape 2015: Building toward anytime, anywhere learning.* Alexandria, VA: Association for Talent Development.

Atkinson, R. C., & Hansen, D. N. (1966). Computer-assisted instruction in initial reading: The Stanford project. *Reading Research Quarterly, 2*, 5–25.

Baker, E. L. (1973). The technology of instructional development. In R. M. W. Travers (Ed.), *Second handbook of research on teaching.* Chicago: Rand McNally.

Banathy, B. H. (1968). *Instructional systems.* Belmont, CA: Fearon.

Barson, J. (1967). *Instructional systems development. A demonstration and evaluation project: Final report.* East Lansing, MI: Michigan State University (ERIC Document Reproduction Service No. ED 020 673).

Becker, H. J. (1998). Running to catch a moving train: Schools and information technologies. *Theory into Practice, 37*(1), 20–30.

Berlo, D. K. (1963). You are in the people business. *Audiovisual Instruction, 8*, 372–381.

Blackboard. (2011). *Learning in the 21st century: 2011 trends update.* Washington, DC: Blackboard K-12.

Blakely, R. J. (1979). *To serve the public interest: Educational broadcasting in the United States.* Syracuse, NY: Syracuse University Press.

Bloom, B. S., Engelhart, M. D., Furst, E. J., Hill, W. H., & Krathwohl, D. R. (1956). *Taxonomy of educational objectives: The classification of educational goals. Handbook 1: Cognitive Domain.* New York: David McKay.

Bonner, J. (1986). Implications of cognitive theory for instructional design. *Educational Communication and Technology Journal, 36*, 3–14.

Borich, G. D. (1980). *A state of the art assessment of educational evaluation.* Austin, TX: University of Texas (ERIC Document Reproduction Service No. ED 187 717).

Bowsher, J. E. (1989). *Educating America: Lessons learned in the nation's corporations.* New York: Wiley.

Branson, R. K., & Grow G. (1987). Instructional systems development. In R. M. Gagné (Ed.), *Instructional technology: Foundations* (pp. 397–428). Hillsdale, NJ: Lawrence Erlbaum.

Branson, R. K., Rayner, G. I., Cox, J. L., Furman, J. P., King, F. J., & Hannum, W. H. (1975). *Inter-service procedures for instructional systems development.* Fort Monroe, VA: U.S. Army Training and Doctrine Command.

Burkman, E. (1987a). Factors affecting utilization. In R. M. Gagné (Ed.), *Instructional technology: Foundations* (pp. 429–456). Hillsdale, NJ: Lawrence Erlbaum.

Burkman, E. (1987b). Prospects for instructional systems design in the public schools. *Journal of Instructional Development, 10*(4), 27–32.

Cambre, M. A. (1981). Historical overview of formative evaluation of instructional media products. *Educational Communication and Technology Journal, 29*, 3–25.

Carnegie Commission on Educational Television. (1967). *Public television: A program for action.* New York: Harper & Row.

Center for Social Organization of Schools. (1983). *School uses of microcomputers: Reports from a national survey* (Issue no. 1). Baltimore, MD: Johns Hopkins University, Center for Social Organization of Schools.

Chadwick, C. B. (1986). Instructional technology research in Latin America. *Educational Communication and Technology Journal, 34*, 247–254.

Chevalier, R. D. (1990). Improving efficiency and effectiveness of training: A six year case study of systematic change. *Performance and Instruction, 29*(5), 21–23.

Chu, G. C., & Schramm, W. (1975). *Learning from television: What the research says* (rev. ed.). Washington, DC: National Association of Educational Broadcasters.

Clark, R. E. (1994). Media will never influence learning. *Educational Technology Research and Development, 42*(2), 21–29.

Clark, R. E. (2001). What is next in the media and methods debate? In R. E. Clark (Ed.), *Learning from media.* Greenwich, CT: Information Age.

Commission on Instructional Technology. (1970). *To improve learning: An evaluation of instructional technology* (vol. 1). New York: Rowker.

Cronbach, L. J. (1963). Course improvement through evaluation. *Teachers' College Record, 64,* 672–683.

Cuban, L. (1986). *Teachers and machines: The classroom use of technology since 1920.* New York: Teachers College Press.

Dale, E. (1946). *Audio-visual methods in teaching* (1st ed.). New York: Holt, Rinehart and Winston.

Dale, E. (1953). What does it mean to communicate? *AV Communication Review, 1,* 3–5.

Dale, E. (1967). Historical setting of programmed instruction. In P. C. Lange (Ed.), *Programmed instruction: The sixty-sixth yearbook of the National Society for the Study of Education, Part 11.* Chicago: University of Chicago Press.

Diamond, R. M. (1989). *Designing and improving courses and curricula in higher education: A systematic approach.* San Francisco: Jossey-Bass.

Dick, W. (1987). A history of instructional design and its impact on educational psychology. In J. Glover & R. Roning (Eds.), *Historical foundations of educational psychology.* New York: Plenum.

Dick, W., & Carey, L. (1978). *The systematic design of instruction* (1st ed.). Glenview, IL: Scott, Foresman.

Dick, W., Carey, L., & Carey, J. O. (2009). *The systematic design of instruction* (7th ed.). Upper Saddle River, NJ: Pearson Education.

Dick W., & Reiser, R. A. (1989). *Planning effective instruction.* Englewood Cliffs, NJ: Prentice-Hall.

Divesta, F. J., & Rieber, L. P. (1987). Characteristics of cognitive engineering: The next generation of instructional systems. *Educational Communication and Technology Journal, 35,* 213–230.

Ebel, R. L. (1962). Content standard test scores. *Educational and Psychological Measurement, 22,* 15–25.

Ely, D. P. (Ed.). (1963). The changing role of the audiovisual process in education: A definition and glossary of related terms. *AV Communication Review, 11*(1).

Ely, D. P. (1970). Toward a philosophy of instructional technology. *British Journal of Educational Technology, 1*(2), 81–94.

Ely, D. P., & Plomp, T. (1986). The promises of educational technology: A reassessment. *International Review of Education. 32,* 231–249.

Finch, C. R. (1987). Instructional systems development in the military. *Journal of Industrial Teacher Education, 24*(4), 18–26.

Finn, J. D. (1954). Direction in AV communication research. *AV Communication Review, 2,* 83–102.

Finn, J. D. (1972). The emerging technology of education. In R. J. McBeath (Ed.), *Extending education through technology: Selected writings by James D. Finn.* Washington, DC: Association for Educational Communications and Technology.

Flanagan, J. C. (1951). Units, scores, and norms. In E. T. Lindquist (Ed.), *Educational measurement.* Washington, DC: American Council on Education.

Gaff, J. G. (1975). *Toward faculty renewal: Advances in faculty, instructional, and organizational development.* San Francisco: Jossey-Bass.

Gagné, R. M. (1962a). The acquisition of knowledge. *Psychological Review, 69,* 355–365.

Gagné, R. M. (1962b). Introduction. In R. M. Gagné (Ed.), *Psychological principles in system development.* New York: Holt, Rinehart and Winston.

Gagné, R. M. (1965a). The analysis of instructional objectives for the design of instruction. In R. Glaser (Ed.), *Teaching machines and programmed learning, II: Data and directions.* Washington, DC: National Education Association.

Gagné, R. M. (1965b). *The conditions of learning* (1st ed.). New York: Holt, Rinehart and Winston.

Gagné, R. M. (1985). *The conditions of learning* (4th ed.). New York: Holt, Rinehart and Winston.

Gagné, R. M., & Briggs, L. J. (1974). *Principles of instructional design* (1st ed.). New York: Holt, Rinehart, and Winston.

Gagné, R. M., Briggs, L. J., & Wager, W. W. (1992). *Principles of instructional design* (4th ed.). New York: Holt, Rinehart, and Winston.

Gagné, R. M., & Medsker, K. L. (1996). *The conditions of learning: Training applications.* Fort Worth, TX: Harcourt Brace.

Galagan, P. A. (1989). IBM gets its arms around education. *Training and Development Journal, 43*(1), 34–41.

Gerlach, V. S., & Ely, D. P. (1971). *Teaching and media: A systematic approach* (1st ed.). Englewood Cliffs, NJ: Prentice-Hall.

Gerlach, V. S., & Ely, D. P. (1980). *Teaching and media: A systematic approach* (2nd ed.). Englewood Cliffs, NJ: Prentice-Hall.

Glaser, R. (1962). Psychology and instructional technology. In R. Glaser (Ed.), *Training research and education.* Pittsburgh: University of Pittsburgh Press.

Glaser, R. (1963). Instructional technology and the measurement of learning outcomes: Some questions. *American Psychologist, 18,* 519–521.

Glaser, R. (1965). Toward a behavioral science base for instructional design. In R. Glaser (Ed.), *Teaching machines and programmed learning, II: Data and directions.* Washington, DC: National Education Association.

Glaser, R., & Klaus, D. J. (1962). Proficiency measurement: Assessing human performance. In R. M. Gagné (Ed.), *Psychological principles in system development.* New York: Holt, Rinehart and Winston.

Gordon. G. N. (1970). *Classroom television: New frontiers in ITV.* New York: Hastings House.

Gumpert, G. (1967). Closed-circuit television in training and education. In A. E. Koenig & R. B. Hill (Eds.), *The farther vision: Educational television today.* Madison, WI: University of Wisconsin Press.

Gustafson, K. L. (1993). Instructional design fundamentals: Clouds on the horizon. *Educational Technology, 33*(2), 27–32.

Gustafson, K., & Bratton, B. (1984). Instructional improvement centers in higher education: A status report. *Journal of Instructional Development, 7*(2), 2–7.

Hamerus, D. (1968). *The systems approach to instructional development: The contribution of behavioral science to instructional technology.* Monmouth: OR: Oregon State System of Higher Education, Teaching Research Division.

Heinich, R. (1970). Technology and the management of instruction (Association for Educational Communications and Technology Monograph No. 4). Washington, DC: Association for Educational Communications and Technology.

Heinich, R., Molenda, M., Russell, J. D., & Smaldino, S. E. (1999). *Instructional media and technologies for learning* (6th ed.). Upper Saddle River, NJ: Prentice Hall.

Hezel, R. T. (1980). Public broadcasting: Can it teach? *Journal of Communication, 30,* 173–178.

Hoban, C. F., Sr., Hoban, C. F., Jr., & Zissman, S. B. (1937). *Visualizing the curriculum.* New York: Dryden.

Interview with Robert M. Gagné: Developments in learning psychology: Implications for instructional design; and effects of computer technology on instructional design and development. (1982). *Educational Technology, 22*(6), 11–15.

Johnson, T. E., Xin, X., Mackal, M. & Reiser, R. A. (2012). Textbooks used in graduate programs in instructional design and technology: Comparisons across time and countries. *Educational Technology, 52*(4), 25–32.

Kemp, J. E. (1971). *Instructional design: A plan for unit and course development.* Belmont, CA: Fearon.

Kozma, R. B. (1994). Will media influence learning: Reframing the debate. *Educational Technology Research and Development, 42*(2), 7–19.

Lewis, B. N., & Pask, G. (1965). The theory and practice of adaptive teaching systems. In R. Glaser (Ed.), *Teaching machines and programmed learning II: Data and directions.* Washington, DC: National Education Association.

Low, W. C. (1980). Changes in instructional development: The aftermath of an information processing takeover in psychology. *Journal of Instructional Development, 4*(2), 10–18.

Lumsdaine, A. A. (1964). Educational technology, programmed learning, and instructional science. In E. R. Hilgard (Ed.), *Theories of learning and instruction: The sixty-third yearbook of the National Society for the Study of Education, Part 1.* Chicago: University of Chicago Press.

Lumsdaine, A. A., & Glaser, R. (Eds.). (1960). *Teaching machines and programmed learning: A source book.* Washington, DC: National Education Association.

Mager, R. F. (1962). *Preparing objectives for programmed instruction.* Belmont, CA: Fearon.

Mager, R. F. (1977). The "winds of change." *Training and Development Journal, 31*(10), 12–20.

Mager, R. F. (1984). *Preparing instructional objectives* (2nd ed.). Belmont, CA: Lake.

Markle, S. M. (1967). Empirical testing of programs. In P. C. Lange (Ed.), *Programmed instruction: The sixty-sixth yearbook of the National Society for the Study of Education, Part II.* Chicago: University of Chicago Press.

McCluskey, F. D. (1981). DVI, DAVI, AECT: A long view. In J. W. Brown & S. N. Brown (Eds.), *Educational media yearbook: 1981.* Littleton, CO: Libraries Unlimited.

McCombs, B. L. (1986). The instructional systems development (ISD) model: A review of those factors critical to its successful implementation. *Educational Communications and Technology Journal, 34,* 67–81.

Meierhenry, W. C. (1980). Instructional theory: From behaviorism to humanism to synergism. *Instructional Innovator, 25*(1), 16–18.

Merrill, M. D., & Li, Z. (1989). An instructional design expert system. *Journal of Computer-Based Instruction, 16*(3), 95–101.

Merrill, M. D., Li, Z., & Jones, M. K. (1990a). Limitations of first generation instructional design. *Educational Technology, 30*(1), 7–11.

Merrill, M. D., Li, Z., & Jones, M. K. (1990b). Second generation instructional design (ID2). *Educational Technology, 30*(2), 7–14.

Miles, G. D. (1983). Evaluating four years of ID experience. *Journal of Instructional Development, 6*(2), 9–14.

Miller, R. B. (1953). *A method for man-machine task analysis* (Tech. Rep. No. 53–137). Wright-Patterson Air Force Base, Ohio: Wright Air Development Center.

Miller, R. B. (1962). Analysis and specification of behavior for training. In R. Glaser (Ed.), *Training research and education*. Pittsburgh: University of Pittsburgh Press.

Moore, M. G. (1989, April). Three modes of interaction. In *Issues in Instructional Interactivity*. Forum conducted at the meeting of the National University Continuing Education Association, Salt Lake City, UT.

Morgan, J. E. (1932). Introduction. In B. H. Darrow, *Radio: The assistant teacher*. Columbus, OH: R.H. Adams.

Morgan, R. M. (1989). Instructional systems development in third world countries. *Educational Technology Research and Development*, *37*(1), 47–56.

Morrison, G. R. (1994). The media effects question: "Unsolvable" or asking the right question. *Educational Technology Research and Development*, *42*(2), 41–44.

Morrison, G. R., Ross, S. M., Kemp, J. E., & Kalman, H. (2010). *Designing effective instruction* (6th ed.) Hoboken, NJ: Wiley.

Office of Technology Assessment. (1995). *Teachers & technology: Making the connection*. Washington, DC: Office of Technology Assessment.

Olsen, J. R., & Bass, V. B. (1982). The application of performance technology in the military: 1960–1980. *Performance and Instruction*, *21*(6), 32–36.

Pagliaro, L. A. (1983). The history and development of CAI: 1926–1981, an overview. *Alberta Journal of Educational Research*, *29*(1), 75–84.

Papert, S. (1984). New theories for new learnings. *School Psychology Review*, *13*(4), 422–428.

Partridge, M. I., & Tennyson, R.D. (1979). Graduate programs in instructional systems: A review of selected programs. *Journal of Instructional Development*, *2*(2), 18–26.

Pask, G. (1960). Electronic keyboard teaching machines. In A. A. Lumsdaine & R. Glaser (Eds.), *Teaching machines and programmed learning: A source book*. Washington, DC: National Education Association.

Pearson. (2015a). *Pearson student mobile device survey 2015: National report: College students*. Upper Saddle River, NJ: Pearson Education.

Pearson. (2015b). *Pearson student mobile device survey 2015: National report: Students in grades 4–12*. Upper Saddle River, NJ: Pearson Education.

Redfield, D. D., & Dick, W. (1984). An alumni-practitioner review of doctoral competencies in instructional systems. *Journal of Instructional Development*, *7*(1), 10–13.

Reiser, R. A. (1994). Clark's invitation to the dance: An instructional designer's response. *Educational Technology Research and Development*, *42*(2), 45–48.

Reiser, R. A., & Gagné, R. M. (1983). *Selecting media for instruction*. Englewood Cliffs, NJ: Educational Technology.

Rossett, A., & Garbosky, J. (1987). The use, misuse, and non-use of educational technologists in public education. *Educational Technology*, *27*(9), 37–42.

Saettler, P. (1968). *A history of instructional technology*. New York: McGraw-Hill.

Saettler, P. (1990). *The evolution of American educational technology*. Englewood, CO: Libraries Unlimited.

Schwen, T. M., Kalman, H. K., Hara, N., & Kisling, E. L. (1998). Potential knowledge management contributions to human performance technology research and practice. *Educational Technology Research and Development*, *46*(4), 73–89.

Scriven, M. (1967). The methodology of evaluation. In *Perspectives of Curriculum Evaluation* (American Educational Research Association Monograph Series on Curriculum Evaluation, No. 1). Chicago: Rand McNally.

Shannon, C. E., & Weaver, W. (1949). *The mathematical theory of communication*. Urbana, IL: University of Illinois Press.

Shrock, S. A. (1994). The media influence debate: Read the fine print, but don't lose sight of the big picture. *Educational Technology Research and Development*, *42*(2), 49–53.

Shrock, S. A. (1995). A brief history of instructional development. In G. J. Anglin (Ed.), *Instructional technology: Past, present, and future*. Englewood, CO: Libraries Unlimited.

Silber, K. H. (1981). Some implications of the history of educational technology: We're all in this together. In J. W. Brown & S. N. Brown (Eds.), *Educational media yearbook: 1981*. Littleton, CO: Libraries Unlimited.

Silber, K. H. (1982). An analysis of university training programs for instructional developers. *Journal of Instructional Development*, *6*(1), 15–28.

Silvern, L. C. (1964). *Designing instructional systems*. Los Angeles: Education and Training Consultants.

Skinner, B. F. (1954). The science of learning and the art of teaching. *Harvard Educational Review*, *24*, 86–97.

Skinner, B. F. (1958). Teaching machines. *Science,* 128, 969–977.

Spady, W. G. (1988). Organizing for results: The basis for authentic restructuring and reform. *Educational Leadership*, *46*(2), 4–8.

Stolorow, L. M., & Davis, D. (1965). Teaching machines and computer-assisted systems. In R. Glaser (Ed.), *Teaching machines and programmed learning, II: Data and directions*. Washington, DC: National Education Association.

Sullivan, H. J., & Higgins, N (1983). *Teaching for competence*. New York: Teachers College Press.

Suppes, P., & Macken, E. (1978). The historical path from research and development to operational use of CAI. *Educational Technology*, *18*(4), 9–12.

Taylor, B. J. (1967). The development of instructional television. In A. E. Koenig & R. B. Hill (Eds.), *The farther vision: Educational television today.* Madison, WI: University of Wisconsin Press.

Tyler, R. W. (1975a). Educational benchmarks in retrospect: Educational change since 1915. *Viewpoints, 51*(2), 11–31.

Tyler, R. W. (1975b). Have educational reforms since 1950 created quality education? *Viewpoints, 51*(2), 35–57.

Walbesser, H. H., & Eisenberg, T. A. (1972). A *review of the research on behavioral objectives and learning hierarchies.* Columbus, OH: Ohio State University, Center for Science and Mathematics Education (ERIC Document Reproduction Service No. ED 059 900).

Chapter 3

Characteristics of Foundational Instructional Design Models

Robert Maribe Branch

University of Georgia

Instructional design is a system of procedures for developing education and training materials in a consistent and reliable fashion. Although the exact origins of the instructional design process can be debated, Silvern, (1965) presented an early attempt to apply General Systems Theory (GST) as an approach to accomplishing learning tasks and solving instructional problems. Silvern's model, and practically all other early instructional design models, was based in behaviorism. Although behaviorism is commonly associated with B. F. Skinner and Stimulus-Response theory, many early behaviorists held far more encompassing theoretical and philosophical perspectives. Burton, Moore, and Magliaro (1996) broadly defined behaviorism as the philosophy and values associated with the measurement and study of human behavior. Cognitive psychologists, particularly from the perspective of information processing, such as Gagné (1985), have also made major contributions to the underlying theories of instructional design.

Soon after behaviorism was acknowledged as a tenet of instructional design, general systems theory (Bertalanffy, 1968) emerged as another fundamental tenet of instructional design. The general systems concept is characterized as being systematic, systemic, responsive, interdependent, redundant, dynamic, cybernetic, synergistic, and creative. *Systematic* means agreeing to adopt rules and procedures as a way to move through a process. However, being systematic does not mean blindly following a sequence without reflection on the process. *Systemic* stresses the application of creative problem-solving methods.

The evidence that something is systemic is when you can observe that all components of a system respond when a single component within that system is stimulated. *Responsive*, within the context of instructional design, means accepting whatever goals are established as its orientation. *Interdependence* means that all elements within a system are connected to every other element within that same system, and therefore, all elements depend on each other to accomplish the system's goals. *Redundancy* refers to duplicate processes and duplicate procedures that are intended to prevent failure of the entire system. *Dynamic* means the system can adjust to changing conditions and constantly monitors its environment. *Cybernetic* means the elements efficiently communicate among themselves for the purpose to steer, govern, and guide. Cybernetics is most often associated with theories related to automated control systems. *Synergistic* means that together, all the elements can achieve more than the individual elements can achieve alone. Thus, the whole is greater than the sum of its parts. *Creativity* in instructional design refers to the use of special human talents and imagination in generating original ideas that permit instructional designers to expand the limitations of any system.

The nine features of the general systems theory described above allow a systems approach to facilitate the complexities of an educational situation by responding to multiple components that form the system, the interactions within a system, and the interactions that occur between different systems. Different learning outcomes often require various applications to a general systems concept.

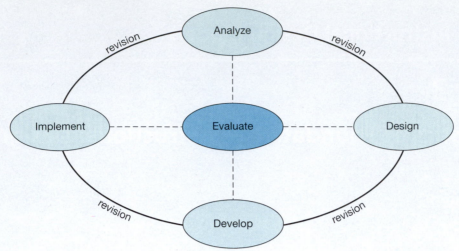

FIGURE 3.1   The core elements of the ADDIE model.

The ADDIE Process

A wide variety of instructional design models (sets of recommended procedures) have been generated since the 1970s (Branch & Dousay, 2015; Gustafson & Branch, 2002), and the majority of those models consist of five phases. These five phases are often referred to as the ADDIE process, or ADDIE model (Figure 3.1). ADDIE is an acronym for Analyze, Design, Develop, Implement, and Evaluate. ADDIE is based on a systematic product development concept. The concept of systematic product development has existed since the formation of social communities. Creating products using an ADDIE process remains one of today's most effective tools; however, ADDIE is not a specific, fully elaborated model in its own right, but rather a paradigm that refers to a family of models that share a common underlying structure (Branch, 2009). According to Molenda (Molenda, 2008), the ADDIE label seems to have evolved informally through oral tradition, rather than having been formalized as a term by a single author. Molenda further asserts that ADDIE has become a colloquial term used to describe a systematic approach to instructional design.

Analyze often includes conducting a needs assessment (Rossett, 1993), identifying a performance problem in a business setting or some other environment (Gilbert, 1978; Harless, 1975), and stating a goal (Mager, 1984a). Design includes writing objectives in measurable terms (Mager, 1984b; Dick, Carey, & Carey, 2015; Smith & Ragan, 1999), classifying learning as to type (Gagné, Wager, Golas, & Keller, 2005; Merrill, 1983), specifying learning activities (Briggs, Gustafson, & Tillman, 1991), and specifying media (Reiser & Gagné, 1983; Smaldino, Lowther, Russell, & Mims, 2015). Development includes preparing student and instructor materials (both print and electronic) as specified during design (Morrison, Ross, & Kemp, 2004). Implementation includes delivering the instruction in the settings for which it was designed (Greer, 1996). Evaluation includes both formative and summative evaluation, as well as revision (Dick et al., 2015). Formative evaluation involves collecting data to identify needed revisions to the instruction while summative evaluation involves collecting data to assess

the overall effectiveness and worth of the instruction. Revision involves making needed changes based on the formative evaluation data.

Instructional design activities typically are not completed in a linear step-by-step manner, although they may be portrayed that way for initial understanding and convenience. For example, during the life of a project, as data are collected and the design team gains insights, it is often necessary to move back and forth among the activities of analysis, design, and formative evaluation and revision. This iterative and self-correcting nature of the instructional design process is one of its greatest strengths.

Linear vs. Curvilinear Depictions of the Instructional Design Process

One of the most popular and influential instructional design models is the model created by Dick, Carey, and Carey (Dick, Carey, & Carey, 2015), which is depicted in Figure 3.2.

While instructional design has traditionally been portrayed as a linear process, consisting of rectilinear rows of boxes connected by straight lines with one-way arrows and a return line that is parallel to other straight lines, similar to the model as depicted in Figure 3.2, it is worth noting here that the actual practice of instructional design might be better communicated as a curvilinear flow diagram. Curvilinear compositions of ovals connected by curved lines with two-way arrows effectively acknowledge the complex reality upon which instructional design is practiced. Curvilinear portrayals of instructional design models tend to communicate more iterations, which characterize the actual way instructional design is typically practiced (Branch, 1996). Figure 3.3 illustrates another example of an instructional design model based on the systems approach to instructional design that employs some curvilinear elements. Instructional design is also often portrayed as a conceptual waterfall (Figure 3.4), fostering the notion that instructional design is practiced as an overlapping, recurring, and iterative process.

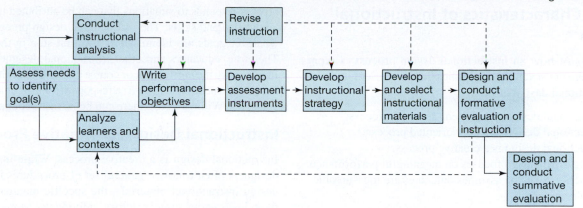

FIGURE 3.2   Reprinted by permission. A linear depiction of an instructional design model (Dick, Carey, & Carey, 2015).

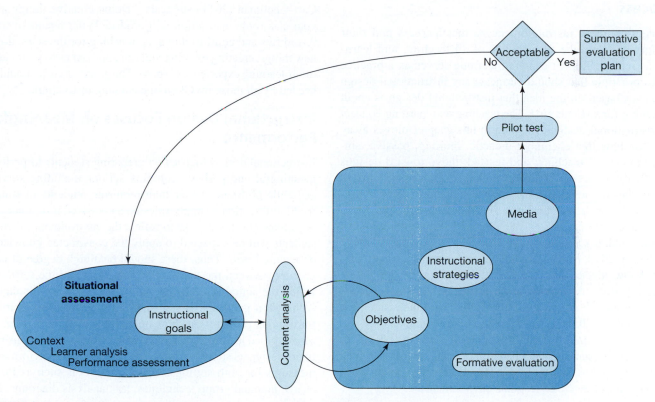

FIGURE 3.3   A curvilinear depiction of an instructional design model (Branch, 1996).

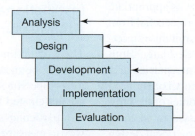

FIGURE 3.4   A depiction of the instructional design process based on the waterfall concept.

Seven Characteristics of Instructional Design

Regardless of how an instructional design process is represented, there are seven characteristics that are present in almost all instructional design efforts:

1. Instructional design is a student-centered process.
2. Instructional design is a goal-oriented process.
3. Instructional design is a creative process.
4. Instructional design focuses on meaningful performance.
5. Instructional design assumes outcomes are measureable, reliable, and valid.
6. Instructional design is an empirical, iterative, and self-correcting process.
7. Instructional design typically is a team effort.

Instructional Design Is a Student-Centered Process

Student-centered instruction means that learners and their performance are the focal points of all teaching and learning activities. Student-centered learning serves as a practice and a principle that should permeate any instructional design endeavor based on the idea that instructional design is about designing for students first. The teaching and learning concept of instructional design promoted in this chapter moves away from designs that encumber didactic, limiting, passive, singular modes of teaching, and instead, move toward designs that facilitate active, multifunctional, inspirational, situated approaches to intentional learning. "Facilitation begins by trying to care for each student as a person and through practicing observable actions such as attending and valuing through eye contact, nodding your head, and listening" (Cornelius-White & Harbaugh, 2010, p. 49). Teaching, then, becomes a way to promote knowledge construction and skill development. Self-study and group study, technology-based instruction, and teacher-based strategies are all options to be considered, with the result often being a mix of all these and other strategies. Students may also be given opportunities to confirm or modify learning objectives in some circumstances. This change in perspective from teaching to learning represents a paradigm shift of immense power when planning for effective educational environments.

Instructional Design Is a Goal-Oriented Process

Establishing well-defined project goals is central to the instructional design process. Goals should reflect client expectations for an instructional design project and, if met, ensure its appropriate implementation. However, many well-intended projects fail from lack of agreement on the goals or the decision to omit this important step in the false belief that this can be settled later. Both identifying and managing client expectations are particularly important to the project manager, but team members also need to share a common vision of the anticipated outcomes of the project. The ultimate question for an instructional system is: *Have the goals of the project been attained?* The instructional design process responds to situations that can be attributed to a lack of knowledge and skills. The instructional design process accepts whatever goals are identified as the first step in the process. Therefore, educators and other instructional designers need to first identify the curriculum or course goals before initiating any kind of instructional design as a response to a lack of knowledge and skills. Without goals, there can be no instructional design.

Instructional Design Is a Creative Process

Instructional design is a creative process. While instructional designers often follow a general set of procedures in order to design instructional materials, the specific manner in which they do so varies greatly across individuals. Moreover, individual instructional designers usually vary the procedures they employ from one situation to another; and in most cases, instructional designers, rather than relying on templates, use their creativity in designing and developing instructional activities. In an instructional design text geared toward teachers, Carr-Chellman (2011) suggests: "Doing creative things with your classroom instruction will produce better results overall. Avoid ruts and comfort and keep reaching for the stars, doing new things, creating exciting and fun approaches to your classroom-learning experiences" (p. 4). This point of view should be heeded by all those involved in designing instruction.

Instructional Design Focuses on Meaningful Performance

Instructional design focuses on preparing students to perform meaningful and perhaps complex actions including solving authentic problems rather than requiring students to simply recall information or apply rules on a contrived task. Learning objectives are stated so as to reflect the environment in which students will be expected to apply the constructed knowledge or acquired skill. Thus, there should be a high degree of congruence between the learning environment and the setting in which the actual knowledge and skills should be displayed. Although it is usually easier to identify performance settings for training programs such as operating a drill press, than for school-based learning such as a college biology course, instructional designers should strive to identify authentic performance measures for both settings. Operational tools such as PERT charts, nominal group techniques, task analysis diagrams, lesson plan templates, worksheets for generating objectives, and production schedule templates contextualize the instructional design process, and as such, make instructional design a practical approach to addressing educational problems that are due to a lack of knowledge and skill.

Instructional Design Outcomes Are Measureable, Reliable, and Valid

The instructional design process centers around outcomes that can be measured. In other words, it focuses on a behavior—a specific skill, knowledge, and/or attitude—that learners are anticipated to acquire as a result of their having engaged in a particular set of instructional activities. If there is not a way to measure whether a learner is able to perform a specific behavior, then the instructional designer cannot judge whether the instruction as designed was effective.

When it comes to measuring whether learners have acquired specific behavior, reliability and validity are issues of major concern. Reliability refers to the consistency of the assessment across time and individuals. If the assessment technique cannot consistently measure whether someone has acquired a desired outcome, then its reliability is compromised and the designer cannot adequately determine if the instruction as designed was effective. Validity refers to the degree to which an assessment technique or tool actually measures what it is supposed to measure. For example, if the objective is to safely and efficiently operate a drill press, then a valid (authentic) assessment technique would likely involve having an observer with a checklist observe the learner performing selected drilling operations and also examining the quality of the products created. Conversely, a multiple-choice, paper-and-pencil test would not be a valid measure.

Instructional Design Is an Empirical, Iterative, and Self-Correcting Process

Data are the heart of the instructional design process. Data collection begins during the initial analysis phase and continues through implementation. For example, during the analysis phase, data may be collected so as to compare a student's actual knowledge and skill to the desired knowledge and skill for the student. Guidance and feedback from subject-matter experts ensures the accuracy and relevance of the knowledge and skills to be taught. Results of research and prior experience guide the selection of instructional strategies and media. Data collected during formative tryout identifies needed revisions, and data from the field after implementation indicates whether the instruction is effective. Although the data may not always bring good news, they are always *friendly* in that they provide a rational basis for decision making and a basis for successfully completing the project. Thus, the instructional design process usually is empirical, iterative, and self-correcting.

Instructional Design Typically Is a Team Effort

Although it is possible for a single individual to complete an instructional design project, instructional design typically is a team effort. The process of instructional design is a collaboration among a design team, clients, sponsors, primary stakeholders, and secondary stakeholders. Collaboration can be understood on a multitude of levels for instructional design processes and practices. There are considerations to be made for collaboration in terms of the roles, the content, and the philosophical perspectives in instructional design. Due to their size, scope, and technical complexity, most instructional design projects require the specialized skills of a variety of individuals. An instructional design team typically will consist of a subject-matter expert, an instructional designer, one or more production personnel, clerical support, and a project manager. Sometimes a single individual may play more than one role on a team, but larger projects invariably require greater specialization. For example, high-tech projects may require computer programmers, videographers, editors, graphic artists, and interface designers. Demands for logistic support in the form of clerical staff, librarians, business managers, and system support expand as the size and duration of projects increase.

The Purpose of Instructional Design Models

While ADDIE illustrates the conceptual components of instructional design, there remains a need to indicate how instructional design is practiced relative to different realities and various educational problems. Reiser (2001) noted: "although the specific combination of procedures often varies from one instructional design model to the next, most of the models include design, development, implementation and evaluation of instructional procedures and materials intended to solve those problems" (p. 58). Models are conceptual representations of reality. Models simplify reality because the reality often it is too complex to portray and because much of that complexity is unique to specific situations. Thus, models generally seek to identify what is generic and applicable across multiple contexts. Instructional design models serve this purpose by describing how to conduct the various steps that comprise the instructional design process. Instructional design models also allow people to visualize the overall process, establish guidelines for its management, and communicate among team members and with clients. A wide variety of ID models have been created to describe how the ID process might be carried out in different settings (Branch & Dousay, 2015; Gustafson & Branch, 1997; Gustafson & Branch, 2002). Ertmer and Quinn (2003, 2007) and Ertmer, Quinn, and Glazewski (2014) have published useful sets of case studies in instructional design from a variety of settings.

An effective instructional design model will have a high correlation between the amount of complexity contained within the model and the amount of complexity of the instructional situation, or otherwise referred to as the space dedicated to intentional learning. Spaces dedicated to intentional learning are complex and, therefore, the instructional design process should be equally complex. The notion of the need for equitable complexity is consistent with the law of requisite variety (Ashby, 1957), which suggests that in order to properly facilitate the quantity and diversity of a situation, you must have an equal quantity and diversity of responses. Requisite variety offers a rationale for matching the complexity of an instructional situation and the complexity required by an instructional design model to accomplish the desired learning goals within the same instructional situation.

One of the most influential instructional design model builders was Silvern (1965) in the 1950s and 1960s. Silvern's work with the military and aerospace industry resulted in an extremely complex and detailed instructional design model with multiple variations that drew heavily on general systems theory. Silvern's instructional design model is rarely used today, but it remains an excellent original resource for those willing to wade through Silvern's sometime obscure writing.

Students of the instructional design process easily observe Silvern's influence on the content of contemporary instructional design models. An example of the evolution of the instructional design process is observed through the advent of whole task models of instructional design. Whole task models facilitate the implementation of *First Principles of Instructional Design* (Merrill, 2002, 2007, 2009) by specifying the content to be learned at the beginning of the instructional design process and then constructing a progression of increasingly complex tasks.

Effective instructional design models, first and foremost, should account for several independent complicated entities, including but not limited to students and their peers, content, delivery systems, time, goals, and the instructor. Second, instructional design models should provide opportunities for relevant entities to enter and exit the instructional design process at various points depending on a particular learning tasks. Third, instructional design models display resilience by satisfying the many stakeholder expectations by employing multiple paths to success. Fourth, instructional design models are characterized by cybernetic attributes that permit instructional designers who use them to treat the diversity associated with uncertainty and unpredictability as assets in the instructional design process.

Conclusion

Instructional design is a complex process that requires more than writing objectives, publishing training manuals, and placing lesson plans online. Because instructional design is an applied product development process, the expertise required to practice instructional design includes minimum competencies such as those promoted by the International Board of Standards for Training, Performance and Instruction (Kozalka, Russ-Eft, & Reiser, 2013). An instructional design process works best when it is matched to a corresponding context. However, educational contexts are often complex and feature complex issues related to teaching and learning. Therefore, effective instructional design models need to be sensitive to different educational contexts and be responsive to complex teaching and learning situations. Instructional design should accommodate emerging theories about intentional learning and the broad array of contexts in which instructional design is being applied, such as open online courses, the flipped classroom, online learning environments, and the exponential growth of open educational resources (OERs). Finally, instructional design is a student-centered, goals-oriented, empirical process, directed toward reliable and valid measurement of meaningful knowledge and skills.

Summary of Key Principles

1. **Instructional design is student centered. Students and their performance are the focal point of instructional design activities.** Teaching is a means to facilitate knowledge construction and student performance. Students actively participate in confirming learning objectives and instructional strategies.

2. **Instructional design focuses on measurable outcomes. There should be a high correlation between student work during a course and the work that will be expected by a student upon completion of a course.** Thus, evaluation tools used during the instructional design, development, and implementation process should be situated within reality and administered within authentic contexts.

3. **Instructional design is best practiced as a partnering process.** The success of an instructional development project often depends on the ability of the instructional

designer to effectively collaborate with the primary stakeholders. The collaborative effort typically requires the lead designer to serve as a project manager where the client, subject-matter experts, and core team members are all considered partners in the process.

4. **Instructional design is a systematic process that is employed to develop education and training programs in a consistent and reliable fashion.**

5. **Instructional design is empirical, iterative, and self-correcting.** Collecting data from multiple sources initiates the instructional design process, typically in the form of analyses, and continues through the entire instructional design process, commonly through formative and summative evaluation. These data provide evidence as to the effectiveness of the actions taken during the design process and increase the probability of a high-quality learning product.

Application Questions

1. Study the rectilinear, curvilinear, and waterfall portrayals of the instructional design process mentioned in this chapter. Then, either adapt one of these models for your own context or create an entirely new instructional design model that best accommodates your situation. What components did you consider essential for your instructional design model?

2. You have recently been hired by a large plumbing company to design a course to train recent high school graduates how to perform some basic plumbing skills. Describe how you might use each of the seven characteristics of instructional design that were described in this chapter to help you design an effective course.

References

Ashby, W. R. (1957). Requisite variety. In W. R. Ashby, *An introduction to cybernetics*. London, England: Chapman and Hall, Limited. http://pespmc1.vub.ac.be/books/IntroCyb.pdf

Banathy, B. H. (1987). Instructional systems design. In R. M. Gagné (Ed.), *Instructional technology: Foundations*. Hillsdale, NJ: Lawrence Erlbaum Associates, Incorporated.

Bertalanffy, L. (1968). *General systems theory*. New York: Braziller.

Branch, R. (1996). Instructional design as a response to the complexities of instruction. In N. Venkataiah (Ed.), *Educational technology* (pp. 21–49). New Delhi: S. B. Nangia for APH Publishing Corporation.

Branch, R. (2009). *Instructional design: The ADDIE approach*. New York: Springer.

Branch, R., & Dousay, T. (2015). *Survey of instructional design models* (5th ed.). Bloomington, IN: Association for Educational Communications and Technology.

Briggs, L. J., Gustafson, K. L., & Tillman, M. H. (Eds.). (1991). *Instructional design: Principles and applications* (2nd ed.). Englewood Cliffs, NJ: Educational Technology Publications.

Burton, J., Moore, D., & Magliaro, S. (1996). Behaviorism and instructional technology. In D. Jonassen (Ed.), *Handbook of research for educational communications and technology*. New York: Macmillan.

Carr-Chellman, A. A. (2011). *Instructional design for teachers: Improving classroom practice*. New York: Routledge.

Cornelius-White, J. H. D., & Harbaugh, A. P. (2010). *Learner-centered instruction: Building relationships for student success*. Los Angeles: Sage Publications, Incorporated.

Dick, W., Carey, L., & Carey, L. (2015). *The systematic design of instruction* (8th ed.). Upper Saddle River, NJ: Pearson Education..

Ertmer, P. A., & Quinn, J. (2003). *The ID casebook: Case studies in instructional design* (2nd ed.). Upper Saddle River, NJ: Prentice Hall.

Ertmer, P. A., & Quinn, J. (2007). *The ID casebook: Case studies in instructional design* (3rd ed.). Upper Saddle River, NJ: Prentice Hall.

Ertmer, P. A., Quinn, J., & Glazewski, K. D. (2014). *The ID casebook: Case studies in instructional design* (4th ed.). Upper Saddle River, NJ: Prentice Hall.

Gagné, R. M. (1985). *The conditions of learning*. New York: Holt, Rinehart and Winston.

Gagné, R. M., Wager, W. W., Golas, K. C., & Keller, J. M. (2005). *Principles of Instructional Design* (5th ed.). Belmont, CA: Thomson Wadsworth.

Gilbert, T. (1978). *Human competence: Engineering worthy performance*. New York: McGraw-Hill.

Greer, M. (1996). *The project manager's partner: A step-by-step guide to project management*. Amherst, MA: HRD Press.

Gustafson, K. L., & Branch, R. (1997). Revisioning models of instructional development. *Educational Technology Research and Development, 45*(3), 73–89.

Gustafson, K. L., & Branch, R. (2002). Survey of instructional development models (4th ed.). Syracuse, NY: Syracuse University (ERIC Clearinghouse on Information Resources).

Harless, J. (1975). *An ounce of analysis is worth a pound of cure*. Newnan, GA: Harless Performance Guild.

Mager, R. (1984a). *Goal analysis*. Belmont, CA: Pitman Management and Training.

Mager, R. (1984b). *Preparing instructional objectives* (2nd ed.). Belmont, CA: Pitman Management and Training.

Merrill, M. D. (1983). Component display theory. In C. M. Reigeluth (Ed.), *Instructional design: Theories and models: An overview of their current status* (pp. 279–334). Hillsdale, NJ: Lawrence Erlbaum Associates, Incorporated.

Merrill, M. D. (2002). First principles of instruction. *Educational Technology Research and Development, 50*(3), 43–59.

Merrill, M. D. (2007). First principles of instruction: A synthesis. In R. A. Reiser & J. V. Dempsey (Eds.), *Trends and issues in instructional design and technology* (2nd ed.) (Vol. 2, pp. 62–71). Upper Saddle River, NJ: Merrill/Prentice Hall.

Merrill, M. D. (2009). First principles of instruction. In C. M. Reigeluth & A. Carr (Eds.), *Instructional design theories and models: Building a common knowledge base* (Vol. III). New York: Routledge Publishers.

Molenda, M. (2008). Historical foundations. In J. M. Spector, M. David Merrill, J. van Merrienboer, & M. P. Driscoll (Eds.), *Handbook of research on educational communications and technology* (3rd ed.). New York: Lawrence Erlbaum Associates.

Morrison, G., Ross, S., & Kemp, J. (2004). *Designing effective instruction* (5th ed.). Hoboken, NJ: Wiley and Sons, Incorporated.

Reiser, R. A. (2001). A history of instructional design and technology, part II: A history of instructional design. *Educational Technology Research and Development, 49*(2), 57–67 (ERIC Document Reproduction Service No. EJ 629 874).

Reiser, R., & Gagné, R. (1983). *Selecting media for instruction*. Englewood Cliffs, NJ: Educational Technology Publications.

Rossett, A. (1993). Needs assessment. In G. J. Anglin (Ed.), *Instructional technology: Past, present, and future* (2nd ed.) (pp. 156–169). Englewood, CO: Libraries Unlimited.

Silvern, L. C. (1965). *Basic analysis*. Los Angeles: Education and Training Consultants Company.

Smaldino, S. E., Lowther, D. L., Russell, J. D., & Mims, C. (2015). *Instructional technology and media for learning* (11th ed.). Upper Saddle River, NJ: Pearson.

Smith, P. L., & Ragan, T. J. (1999). *Instructional design* (3rd ed.). Hoboken, NJ: Wiley & Sons, Incorporated.

Chapter 4

SAM and Pebble-in-the-Pond: Two Alternatives to the ADDIE Model

Michael W. Allen

Allen Interactions Inc.

M. David Merrill

Utah State University

ADDIE has been the most popular instructional design and development model of the past several decades. In this paper the authors argue that we need to move beyond ADDIE to more appropriate models for instructional design and development. Allen has proposed a successive approximation model (SAM) for instructional design and development (Allen, 2012) and Merrill has proposed a Pebble-in-the-Pond model for instructional design (Merrill, 2013). This chapter identifies some of the limitations of the ADDIE model, briefly describes the key characteristics of the SAM and Pebble models and how they help overcome some of the limitations of ADDIE, and identifies the differences and similarities of these two models and how they are complementary with one another.

ADDIE

ADDIE is a process model developed for and adopted by the military to hasten and standardize production of training materials, often by persons having less than a thorough background in instructional design. As originally conceived, the model was a sequential or "waterfall" model, indicating that each phase was to be completed before the next began (Figure 4.1).

ADDIE was enthusiastically adopted by the military for its clear delineation of steps, grouped into five ordered project phases: Analysis, Design, Development, Implementation, and Evaluation. Dependency on prior steps required thorough completion of each step before moving on. So once consideration had been given, decisions made, and designs documented, the task was completed and final. This made for a clear, regimented, and highly manageable process. If, however, previously determined requirements shifted as work on subsequent tasks was in progress or even completed, it created inefficiencies at best and potentially chaos with budget and schedule overruns.

Frustrations

ADDIE is a logical and well thought-out process. Those new to the design and production of instructional products can appreciate and find comfort in the structure, although the model doesn't explain how to perform tasks—just *which* tasks need to be performed and when. It is an easily defended process that covers all the bases, at least from the point of view of a content-based model.

Both authors have witnessed considerable strife over many years of experience with teams using ADDIE. A common cause was when downstream work was disrupted by significant changes made to approved specifications. As people saw courseware come to life based on specification documents, there was almost always surprise—some good, but often more bad. Unexpected interpretations of the specifications caused rework, budgetary problems, and faultfinding. *"That's not what we meant by . . . Why did you think you should have . . . ?"*

Exhausted and annoyed team members would begrudgingly compromise when most of the allocated time had already been spent, but at some point workers or management would resolutely refuse to make further adjustments. In the end, few people were proud of the resulting courseware. No one found the final product to closely approximate the original, enthusiastic expectations.

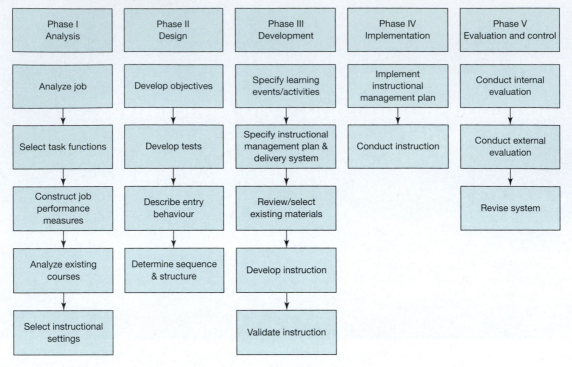

FIGURE 4.1 The ADDIE ISD model for instructional systems development.

Weaknesses

Although various forms of ADDIE differ in their strengths and weaknesses, let's list and review some of the common problems.

1. **ADDIE works through documentation.**
    Specification documents, even storyboards, are surprisingly easy to misinterpret. Experience has caused many teams to insist on rigorous documentation to prevent misinterpretation, but while such steps can reduce misinterpretation, not being able to see a learning event in action means the design cannot be evaluated on some of its most important attributes. Further, rigorous documentation adds considerably to project costs and slows the process. With much of the design still open for a wide range of expectations, communication by documentation, and looking at parts and pieces of the design for some considerable span of time before the whole becomes visible, are far from optimal.

    The solution is not to push for endless detail in specifications. Indeed, it is with best intentions and expertise that we can follow directions and yet end up with a product that all view as falling short. The problem lies in the very process of attempting to design via documents rather than working in the medium of delivery. To arrive at optimal designs, designers need to see and explore alternative designs with as much functionality operative as possible for assessment.

2. **ADDIE ranges from linear to amorphous.**
    Stepwise dependency is regularly debunked and appropriately so. Nevertheless, changing this characteristic of ADDIE introduces a new model. Changing the model but retaining the original name is confusing. One doesn't know which version of today's ADDIE models provides the official definition of the name. Perhaps the bigger issue is that various adaptations of ADDIE suggest nearly all tasks flow into many, if not all others. While conceptually, all components have relationships with others, instructional designers and developers need more guidance than this. It seems with ADDIE, we have either too much rigidity or too much flexibility.

3. **ADDIE loses sight of the learner experience.**
    Studying the steps within the phases (see Figure 4.1), the majority of the steps focus on content, sequencing, delivery, and assessment. This is a more suitable view when the instructional approach is primarily one of presentation and testing than when trying to provide meaningful, memorable, and motivational experiences—hallmarks of the successive approximations model (SAM) or effective, efficient, and engaging experiences—hallmarks of the Pebble-in-the-Pond model.

4. **ADDIE is a meticulously slow process.**
    Although rapid prototyping is incorporated in some versions of ADDIE, a process *based* on rapid prototyping places emphasis on the learner experience. Content is developed as demanded by the experience as it unfolds through iterations. Time and resources are spent experimenting with various ways to engage learners, support alternative decisions and actions they might make, and show consequences of these actions (both good and bad). Examples and counterexamples emerge; needed demonstrations are identified.

5. **ADDIE fails to involve stakeholders.**
    An important aspect of many projects is achieving the continuing support of stakeholders, including prospective learners. With ADDIE, conducting analyses, writing design

specifications, and performing considerable amounts of work before a clear, testable version of a prospective design becomes available, it's easy for stakeholders to be surprised at their first view of the emerging instruction—even if they've approved documents leading to the product finally at hand; and much of the project time and budget is spent before any learner can be observed and before any learner can give feedback. ADDIE projects are at considerable risk if stakeholders are displeased or if learners respond quite differently from expectations.

6. **We need a simpler model.**

   We need a simpler and yet more effective model. We need a faster and more collaborative model. We need a model that fosters creativity; that's practical. We need a model that focuses on the learning experience and assures achievement of identified performance outcomes. For these and many other reasons, Pebble-in-the-Pond and SAM are attractive alternatives. Although one was developed primarily in academia and the other in the commercial arena, they are strikingly complimentary.

SAM

We introduce the successive approximation model (SAM) briefly here and mention only a few of its more auspicious characteristics. Please refer to Chapter 5 for a more complete description of SAM.

The primary defining characteristics of SAM are:

1. SAM is a design and development process providing maximum opportunities for review, evaluation, and correction of decisions throughout the process.
2. SAM is optimized to produce the best possible instruction with given constraints of time and budget.
3. Sketching and "disposable" prototypes are used to share ideas visually and assess functionally.
4. Devising an initial treatment for all content before polishing the treatment for any content is a key feature of the process.

SAM is a process model for design and development, but not a design model per se. While SAM provides support and benefits to many if not all models of instruction, very much (including Merrill's First Principles) is not entirely impartial. It was devised to emphasize learning experiences over presentations of content. Learning events are scaffolded or wire-framed first to assess the learning opportunity they could yield. Before accepting the design, content is fitted into only the most promising structures and tested with live learners as soon as possible for refinement of text, media, and complete functionality. If the design fails at this point, minimal time and effort has been invested in it, allowing it to be comfortably discarded. Other design ideas can be considered without stretching the schedule or budget. Content is then articulated and the learner-centric product is fleshed out once the design direction is verified. Let's see how this is actually accomplished.

There are two versions of SAM—a basic, two-phase version (the generally preferred version) and an extended, three-phase version (needed for larger projects). Figure 4.2 illustrates the primary phases and components of the basic version of SAM.

Easily noted from Figure 4.2 are circles of activity sitting atop a left-to-right backbone of project flow, moving from information gathering to rollout. This overall design reflects the intent of the model to address the simultaneous needs for effective, creative design and for getting projects delivered within time and budgetary constraints. Indeed, SAM is as concerned with practicality and project manageability as it is with achieving maximum instructional impact.

1. **Preparation Phase**

   It only makes sense to collect background information that can provide useful direction. This is done expeditiously rather than exhaustively in SAM for two reasons: (1) It's possible to sink large amounts of time and effort into analysis and yet, as the project progresses, still find key questions unanswered. (2) During subsequent exploratory work in search of an optimal instructional strategy, everything can change, including who is to be taught, what the goals are, how instruction will be delivered, and what the scope of content will be. It's smart and efficient to minimize effort until you have a prospective direction in mind and specific questions in hand. But you need to start somewhere. Fundamental questions, therefore, focus information gathering on identified performance needs, past instructional successes and failures, assumptions held by key individuals, schedule and budgetary constraints, and so on.

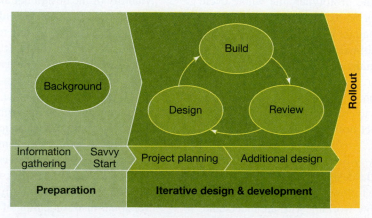

FIGURE 4.2 Successive Approximation (two-phase) Model (SAM) for instructional design and development.

With background information in hand, a meeting/work session, usually of two days in length, is held for key stakeholders with the project manager and design team. Called the Savvy Start, this meeting quickly reviews gathered background information, states the desired outcome behaviors together with thoughts about how they'll be measured, and, under the leadership of an instructional designer, sketches what the last learning activity in the course might look like. This will be an activity in which learners are performing targeted skills and demonstrating the mastery needed to have completed the course of instruction successfully.

The Savvy Start is a carefully structured event in which multiple instructional designs are always considered. Even if everyone enthusiastically accepts the first idea, it is set aside for two additional attempts to do better. Three design efforts, each one first sketched then prototyped during the two days, are usually enough to produce a superior design. As each design candidate is put on the table for discussion, the question becomes, *Why shouldn't we do this?*

Answers to this fundamental question will sometimes be:

Because this would be boring.
Because learners won't see the relevance.
Because I see now that we're really training the wrong people.
Because it will take too long and cost too much.
Because it's pretty rare that anyone really needs to do this.

The answer will often be:

Because I think I have a better idea.

The Savvy Start follows the same process as is diagramed for iterative design and development. It begins with a proposed design that is sketched out sufficiently for the group's understanding. Several ideas are usually advanced to this stage initially and one or more are taken further into rapid prototyping. Since most of the prototypes will be used only for evaluation of ideas and then discarded, they are developed/built and shown very quickly. Text and graphics are rough placeholders, but the sequence of events including student activities and the types of feedback to be given for specific student actions must be clearly shown.

Following review of the prototypes, the whole cycle is repeated before moving on to content that enables the performance skills being taught by this first design. Working backwards from the ultimate skills to be taught toward enabling skills, the team must not spend too much time in attempts to perfect any treatment. As additional content is considered, new insights will suggest ways to improve previous designs or needs to create broad consistency. Premature attempts to perfect designs prove inefficient and time consuming.

In most cases, the Savvy Start doesn't provide nearly enough time to complete the design of a project. Additional design work will continue following the same process usually by a smaller team now working with an understanding of the expectations of those people no longer directly involved. Having confirmed answers to all key questions and having some representative designs in hand, the team is also now prepared to accurately estimate the work remaining and generate a concrete project plan.

2. **Iterative Design and Development Phase**
There is great benefit from continually interleaving design and development. Prototypes can be refined incrementally until they become the final product; and as development advances, opportunities for design improvement can be reviewed and improvements made, often with minimal disruption. It's important to realize that ideas for improvement never stop germinating, and the best ones often occur in the midst of development, or worse, toward product completion. When design and development are interleaved throughout the process, efficiencies often allow incorporating at least some aspects of late-arriving ideas.

There's a risk of falling into perpetual redesign, because designs can always be improved. But there is an important process rule that minimizes this concern: Because we are careful to cover all the content in iterative design passes, something like frosting layers of a cake, and because we insist on usable, functional prototypes evolving toward the final product, we always have the best product available and usable at any time delivery is required—an invaluable advantage of this "agile" process.

In the two-phase model, iterative design and development continue until either time runs out or the product is judged ready for trial rollout. It's wise to reserve time for future iterations after some field experience with the product.

3. **Separated Design and Development Phases**
The three-phase model of SAM depicted in Figure 4.3 separates iterative design and iterative development. The iterative design phase produces prototypes for each type of content included in the project, a project plan, and if given the green light for the plan, the design for the remaining content.

As work moves into development, a Design Proof is generated to confirm suitability of all decisions, from visual style to method of delivery. It integrates samples of all components to test and prove viability. It has greater functionality or usability than the design prototypes and is built with the same tools that will produce the final deliverable. In this way, the design proof tests not only the viability of the design but also the production system.

The design proof provides a critical opportunity for the team and stakeholders to feel confident that the parts create a desirable whole. It's also a chance to be sure no technical problems lie ahead to prevent delivery of the proposed design.

Content development then proceeds following the same iterative pattern of taking small steps and evaluating them so that corrections can be made before too much work is done to make corrections impractical. An alpha version is produced with all expected components present and usable, with notes describing any known problems and omissions. Final proofing is not usually completed at this point. This version is also something of a test to help complete the list of items that need to be added, completed, or modified.

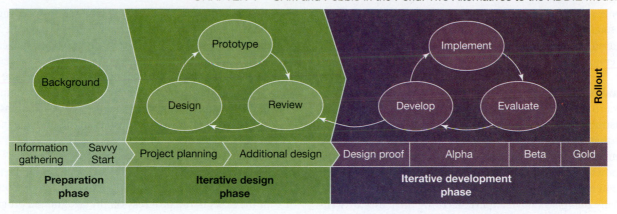

FIGURE 4.3   Successive Approximation (three-phase) Model (SAM) for instructional design and development.

A Beta version is then produced. With this version, developers believe the product is ready for release. Experience suggests there is almost always a need to address some problems that have been overlooked, so the Beta version is likely to need some final refinement. If not, however, the release becomes Gold and rolls out.

Pebble-in-the-Pond[1]

Figure 4.4 illustrates the primary products in the Pebble-in-the-Pond model for instructional design. The metaphor is an environmental pond in which instruction is to occur. The pebble is an instance of a problem that learners need to be able to solve in the context of the pond. The problem pebble thrown into the instructional pond is the trigger for the instructional design process. The instructional product comprising the first ripple is a prototype demonstration of an instance of this problem and how it might be solved. The second ripple is a progression of problem instances. The instructional products comprising this second ripple are further demonstrations or applications (practice exercises) for each problem in the progression. The third ripple is the component skills required to solve this class of problems. The instructional products comprising this third ripple are demonstrations or applications for each of the component skills as they are taught in the context of the problems in the progression. The fourth ripple involves enhancing instructional strategies, oftentimes by providing a structural framework that provides learner guidance and by providing opportunities for peer interaction. The fifth ripple is a finalization of the functional prototype including the final design for the interface, navigation, and supplemental instructional materials. The sixth ripple contains data collection, formative evaluation, and prototype revision.

The Pebble-in-the-Pond model is more constrained than the ISD procedure illustrated in Figure 4.1. The Pebble

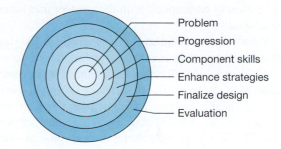

FIGURE 4.4   A Pebble-in-the-Pond model for instructional design.

model focuses primarily on the instructional design phase of the whole instructional development process. Instructional development, as illustrated in Figure 4.1, includes some steps that are not included in the Pebble model as it is presented here, but this does not imply that these steps are unimportant. The Pebble model assumes that some front-end analysis has already determined that there is a problem that can be solved by instruction rather than by some other means. It assumes that the content area and some form of instructional goal have been previously identified through front-end analysis or some other appropriate methodology. The Pebble model is a design rather than development model. This means that the important steps of production, implementation, and summative evaluation are not considered in this model. The model does involve the development of a functional prototype, but does not include the final production of multimedia objects, packaging, and other production concerns. The Pebble model results in a functional prototype that can be used as the model on which the final production is based. Finally, implementation of a course in an organization is a complex process in its own right. The involvement of stakeholders and organizations in the implementation of a course is also beyond the scope of the Pebble model. Summative evaluation of the course after it has been implemented involves concerns that have also been treated in other sources and are therefore not considered here. In short, the Pebble model starts with the existence of an instructional pond consisting of a problem that learners in this context need to learn to solve. The model starts with a previous identification of the context, the subject matter, the learning population,

---

[1]The material on the Pebble-in-the-Pond model of instructional design was adapted from Chapter 11, "A Pebble-in-the-Pond Model for Instructional Design." In Merrill (2013), *First principles of instruction: Identifying and designing effective, efficient, and engaging instruction.*

and some idea of the instructional goal. The model concludes with a functional prototype that serves as a specification for the production, implementation, and summative evaluation of the final version of the course.

1. **Design a Problem Demonstration**
   Traditional ISD advocates the early specification of instructional objectives. The problem with this approach is that instructional objectives are abstract representations of the knowledge to be taught, rather than the knowledge itself. Often the specification of the actual content is delayed until the development phase of ISD. Many designers have experienced the difficulty of writing meaningful objectives early in the design process. Often, after the development starts, the objectives written early in the process are abandoned or revised to more closely correspond with the content that is finally developed.

   Pebble-in-the-Pond avoids this problem by starting with the content to be taught (i.e., an instance of the whole problem to be solved) rather than some abstract representation of this content (i.e., objectives). Pebble-in-the-Pond assumes that the designer has already identified an instructional goal (not detailed objectives) and a learner population. The first step, the pebble, is to specify an instance that demonstrates the whole problem that learners will be able to solve following the instruction. The word, *specify*, indicates that a complete instance of the problem should be demonstrated, not just some information about the problem. A complete instance of a problem includes the information that the learner is given and the transformation of this information that will result when the problem is solved. The best way to specify this instance of the problem is to design a demonstration showing in detail every step required to solve the problem. It is also desirable at this point to design an application that requires learners to solve the problem.

2. **Design a Progression of Problems**
   Having specified an instance of a typical problem for the goals of the instruction, the next ripple in the pond is to specify a progression of problem instances that gradually increase in complexity, difficulty, or the number of component skills required to complete each task. Each instance in the progression should be completely specified including the givens, the solution, and the steps necessary to solve the problem. The component skills for each problem should then be identified. These component skills should be reviewed to be sure that by solving each instance of the problem in the progression, learners will acquire all the intended knowledge and skill required by the instructional goals. If the problem progression does not include all the required knowledge and skill, additional problem instances should be added to the progression, or the instances in the progression should be modified to require the necessary knowledge and skill.

   In a problem-centered approach, the early problem instance in the progression should be demonstrated to learners. As the learner progresses from one problem instance to

the next, the learner should be required to solve more and more of each instance in the sequence. The specification of the instances in the sequence is accomplished by designing a demonstration or application for each of the instances in the sequence. Design a demonstration for the first one or two problem instances; design a combination demonstration application for the next one or two problem instances; and design application for the remaining problem instances in the sequence.

3. **Design Instruction for Component Skills**
   The third ripple in the pond is to design prototype instruction for the component skills required to complete each of the tasks in the progression. In designing a progression of problems, it is necessary to consider the component skills that are required by each of the problem instances in the progression to be certain that all of these component skills are taught. One advantage of a progression of problem instances is that the component skills required for one problem in the progression are also required for subsequent problems. In this situation, it is possible to demonstrate the skill the first time it is taught and then to provide application for this skill on subsequent occasions. In this phase of the Pebble model, each of the component skills are carefully identified for each of the problems in the progression. This chart of skills is then examined to determine when a given skill is first taught. This occasion is then tagged for a demonstration of the skill. When the skill is required for a second instance of the problem, then the skill is tagged for application. The next activity in this ripple is to prepare a prototype demonstrations and applications for each of the component skills as determined by this analysis of their occurrence during the progression of problems.

4. **Design Instructional Strategy Enhancements**
   The result of the first three ripples in the Pebble model is a functional prototype of your course that includes a demonstration or application strategy for each of the problems in the progression and a demonstration or application strategy for each of the component skills required to solve these problems. The remaining ripples in the instructional design pond fine-tune these instructional strategies by enhancing their potential e3 (effective, efficient, engaging) quality.

   One form of enhancement is to provide a structural framework that can provide guidance during the problem demonstrations and coaching during the problem applications.

   Perhaps the instruction could also be enhanced by providing an opportunity for learners to work together. A peer collaboration situation might provide a better opportunity for learners to demonstrate their acquisition of the desired skills. There are several possibilities for this collaboration. One alternative is to have a group of three students work together to come up with a single solution. A second form of collaboration would be for each student in a collaboration group to come up with his or her own solution and then present the solution to members of their collaboration group for critique. In this situation, there could be more than one correct solution to the problem. A further enhancement might be to have another one or two students evaluate the solutions for accuracy.

5. **Finalize Instructional Design**

The next ripple in the Pebble model is to bring your prototype to a final form ready for evaluation, production, and implementation. Perhaps the first consideration at this point is to troubleshoot and bulletproof your navigation. Navigation includes the devices that enable a learner to move from one place in the instruction to another. Even with a great instructional strategy, nothing can kill motivation and interfere with learning more than ineffective navigation. Learners should be able to easily determine where they are in a course. They should be able to quickly return to an overall menu of the course. The navigation should be as clear as possible with clear identification of what happens.

Depending on your artistic inclinations, you may have been working on an interface while developing strategies for problem and component skill demonstration and application. If your artistic inclinations are as limited, you may have developed a utilitarian prototype that shows the strategy but leaves something to be desired for its aesthetic appeal. You have a functional prototype at this point; now is the time to consult with a graphic designer to develop an appealing interface for the product. You may want to encourage the graphic designer to add a mockup of the graphic design to the prototype. Like the cover of a book, the interface of your product is what makes the first impression. If the interface is unappealing, then learners may undertake learning with less than a positive attitude about what's next.

If you have developed a technology-based instructional product, it may be desirable to accompany it with supplemental material. This might include a user's guide; it might include offline materials to supplement what is in the online course.

6. **Design Assessment and Evaluation**

The final ripple in the Pebble model is to design appropriate data collection procedures, conduct a formative evaluation, and revise the prototype. Examine the application strategies to identify where learner responses actually demonstrate competency in a component skill or in problem solution. Adapt the prototype to enable you to collect this data. Conduct a tryout of your prototype. Use the data to revise your prototype and make it ready for production.

This is also the ripple where questionnaires, interview forms, and other instruments should be designed to gather information to help you revise the prototype of the course. For course revision, these items may include questions about format, navigation, and interface. You may also want learners to identify areas were they felt confused either by the content or by the operation of the learning system. If you plan a one-on-one formative evaluation of your prototype, this is the time to begin to consider the questions you will ask as learners participate in your instruction. You may want to consider embedding some of these questions into the course itself.

Once you have adapted your prototype to enable you to collect performance data and have developed appropriate questionnaires soliciting learner attitudes about the course, you are ready to conduct a tryout of the prototype. The data from these individual and small group tryouts give you information about where there are problems in the course. The final step is to revise your prototype to overcome the problems you discover from this formative evaluation.

Unique Properties of Pebble-in-the-Pond

1. **Principle Oriented**

The ISD/ADDIE approach illustrated in Figure 4.1, and most of the modifications of this approach, emphasize a series of steps that are supposed to result in an instructional product that is effective and efficient in accomplishing the goal of the instruction. The problem is not that the steps are the wrong steps, but rather that the emphasis is on the procedure rather than on the instructional design product that results from carrying out a step in the procedure. Designers must be taught not only to carry out the prescribed steps, but to observe the consequence of each step to be sure that it is characterized by the properties that define an effective instructional product. If a designer specifies a performance goal for a given step in the instructional analysis and this goal fails to adequately specify performance that is appropriate for that kind of learning or the conditions under which this performance should occur, then when using this objective to specify presentation or practice instructional events, it is likely that these events will also fail to implement all of the required properties for an effective or efficient demonstration, practice, or assessment. The steps in the instructional design procedure are not what lead to an e3 learning consequence; rather, it is the products that these steps produce that are the conditions for the desired learning outcomes.

The Pebble-in-the-Pond model attempts to implement First Principles of Instruction. Merrill (2013) suggests recommended or prescribed steps that are thought to implement First Principles of Instruction that have been found to lead to instructional products that result in an e3 learning consequence. In the Pebble model these instructional products are a mockup of the actual instruction, using multimedia or placeholders to create a functional prototype of the instruction rather than an abstract description. The Pebble approach is based on the properties for e3 demonstrations and applications prescribed in First Principles of Instruction. If a demonstration instructional event fails to implement the prescribed properties for the type of learning involved, then the designer is encouraged to revise the prototype demonstration until it does implement the prescribed properties.

2. **Problem-Portrayal First**

The ISD model illustrated in Figure 4.1 commences with a number of steps that provide *information about* the content to be presented. The early steps in the traditional ISD model are information oriented rather than portrayal oriented; that is, they describe what is to be done rather than showing it. For example, a goal statement is information; it describes the problem that learners will be able to solve as a result of the instruction. A goal analysis is information; it describes the steps learners will have to execute and the subordinate skills learners must have in order to accomplish the goal. The performance objectives are information; they describe the performance associated with each step or subordinate skill. Even the instructional strategies are often represented as information; they are often merely descriptions of how learners will interact with the content.

In contrast, the Pebble-in-the Pond approach begins the design process with *a portrayal of* an instance of the problem learners will learn to solve. This problem is a portrayal of the goal to be accomplished rather than an abstract description of the problem and its solution. An actual portrayal of the problem to be solved and a demonstration of its solution are far less ambiguous than an abstract description of the problem. The Pebble approach compresses steps in the ISD process by moving directly to the development of a functional prototype of the actual instructional strategy, subsuming goal analysis, performance objectives, and media selection into a combined instructional design activity. This rapid prototyping approach leads to an interim instructional product that can be formatively evaluated and revised as the design proceeds thus resulting in a more efficient design process. This is one implementation of a successive approximation model of instructional design.

3. **Problem Centered**

The ISD model illustrated in Figure 4.1 prescribes a *cumulative content sequence*. A cumulative content sequence first teaches the subordinate skills for the first step in the goal analysis and then teaches the step that depends on these subordinate skills. The sequence then proceeds to the next step in the goal analysis sequence until all of the subordinate skills and steps in the process have been presented. Finally after all the steps required to accomplish the instructional goal have been taught, learners are required to use the skills in an integrated way to solve a problem or accomplish a complex task. This cumulative content sequence often suffers from several limitations. First, if the content is complex and there are a large number of subordinate skills or steps in the sequence, then it is possible that by the time learners are required to apply the skills, they may have already forgotten some of the skills acquired early in the sequence. Second, without a context for where a given skill will be used, its relevance may not be apparent to learners. Without an assurance of relevance, the motivation for learning the skill is reduced and effective learning hindered. Acquiring skills in a cumulative fashion brings to mind the teacher phrase we all learned to dread, "You won't understand this now, but later it will be really important to you!" This often is processed by the student to mean, "This is not important to me now because later I'll have to learn it again anyway."

The Pebble-in-the-Pond approach overcomes this problem by demonstrating an instance of the problem to be solved as one of the first learning activities in the sequence. Seeing a portrayal of an actual problem and a demonstration of its solution is far more easily understood by learners than an abstract statement describing the problem. The Pebble approach then demonstrates the component skills

specifically required for this problem and demonstrates how each of these specific instances of each skill was used to solve the problem. Rather than an abstract objective stating what the learner will be able to do, learners are shown what they will be able to do with a concrete demonstration of an actual instance of the problem.

The content sequence in the Pebble model is not cumulative; it is problem centered. The component skills are taught in the context of a progression of problem instances. After the first instance of the problem and its component skills are demonstrated, a second instance of the problem is shown to the learners. Learners are then required to apply the skills they learned for the first problem instance to this second problem instance. If there are new component skills required for this problem instance, they are demonstrated to the learner in the context of this problem. This sequence of demonstrating and applying component skills is repeated until all of the component skills have been demonstrated multiple times and learners have had multiple opportunities to apply these skills to new instances of the problem.

In the Pebble design process, therefore, rather than describing both the goal and the problem, an actual instance of the problem to be solved is identified; a demonstration of an instance of this problem is designed and prototyped; and an application for an instance of this problem is designed and prototyped. In other words, in the Pebble approach the actual content to be learned is identified, demonstrated, and designed for application early in the instructional design process. The Pebble design approach is thus problem centered.

4. **Rapid Prototyping**

The ISD model illustrated in Figure 4.1 produces a number of instructional design products as a result of carrying out the steps in the instructional design procedure described. As indicated, most of these instructional design products are abstract descriptions of the content and instructional strategy to be developed. The actual use of the content materials themselves or multimedia representations of this content do not take place until after the objectives, assessment, and instructional strategy have been described. Typically this process produces an instructional design document. A significant problem with this approach is the number of translation errors that can occur when developing the actual instruction from the abstract design document. This is not so much a problem when a single designer carries out all of the steps of the process, but when a team of people is involved it is frequently the case that the instructional strategies, as implemented, are often significantly different from the design envisioned by the designer who wrote the strategy specification. This translation problem results in misunderstandings and almost always delays the efficient development of the instruction. Critics have been quick to identify the long delays that result as a significant weakness of the ISD process.

The Pebble model attempts to overcome this problem by using actual materials or placeholders to develop a functional prototype of the strategies, interactions, and assessments. A *functional prototype* is a mockup of the instructional strategy that includes actual content material or placeholders for this material, that allows learner interaction with the instructional strategies, and that approximates the learner interaction available in the final product. A functional prototype uses a development tool that allows rapid development, is easily modified, and can be used for formative evaluation with actual learners. Developing a functional prototype is incorporated as part of the Pebble-in-the-Pond model for instructional design (Allen, 2003, 2012).

Model Comparison

SAM and Pebble share viewpoints on the drawbacks of ADDIE as well as on nearly all critical aspects of a better process for the design of learning experiences. Terms vary slightly, and some points are given greater emphasis than others. Yet one has to search for significant points of difference in concepts, values, and procedures. Such concurrence, especially given that the models were independently developed, applied, and verified over many years and with many projects, lends considerable confidence that these models are not only viable but also advantageous to the designer.

While the authors have their preferences and have become confident in their recommended procedures, both continue to look for enhancements and refinements. Both also recognize projects are performed within constraints. There is sometimes little choice but to sacrifice some preferred methods to accommodate constraints. Here's where experience is invaluable, as knowing the consequences of alternatives informs designers with respect to which sacrifice to make and to what extent.

We can point out some differences between Pebble and SAM, the purpose of which is to help you better understand the models and perhaps craft your own adaptations. Below are some specific comparisons, although as noted, the differences are minor in contrast to similarities and agreements.

Scope

Pebble is a design model squarely focused on methods of instructional product design. Based on a decomposition of effective learning products, Pebble charts the process of designing the components essential for teaching specific types of skills.

SAM is a design and development process, covering tasks from stakeholder identification to release of the final instructional product. It speaks to such issues as verifying that initially identified goals, learners, and content are, in fact, the best goals, people to be trained, and content to be learned.

Both models are optimized for construction of the kinds of learning experiences the authors agree we should all be building. The authors are very much in agreement about the attributes of instruction that are important. At the highest level, Merrill strives for effective, efficient, and engaging instruction (e3) with Pebble; Allen uses SAM to create meaningful, memorable, and motivational learning experiences. Both models value active learning experiences that cause learners to encounter authentic problems (Merrill) or challenges (Allen), with sufficient practice to reach applicable skill levels.

Sequence

Pebble asks designers to begin with an identified problem the learner needs to learn to solve or a task the learner needs to learn to perform. The process assumes that some analysis of the need has been accomplished in order to identify the problem or task to be learned. Prototypes of problems or tasks are prepared to be sure they are fully defined, appropriate as instructional targets, and workable for instruction. It's important to begin with problems or tasks that are to be encountered in the world—not just components of those tasks. By then identifying essential attributes in the problems, a class of problems can be defined that, when learned, learners will have reached the instructional goal with transferability to useful application.

Design work then proceeds in a prescribed order through "ripples" of components that emanate from the problem set and will compose instruction on solving the problems or performing the tasks. The components to be designed are (in order): problem or task progression, component skills with demonstrations and application strategies, instructional strategy enhancements, final design (including navigation, user interface, and supplemental materials), and assessment and evaluation.

SAM similarly assumes some background analysis has been done—enough to propose who may need to learn what. The process looks first at the final skills learners need to demonstrate as evidence they have reached acceptable mastery. SAM prescribes that a team of stakeholders, led by an instructional designer, should initiate product design in a work session called the Savvy Start. The team typically includes the project funder/owner, project manager, instructional designer, a manager of the people to be trained, a typical learner, a subject-matter expert, and a prototyper. The team works backward, addressing the final learning and performance activities first, then moving through prerequisites until learning events are designed for entry-level skills. Because stakeholders often have preconceptions of appropriate learning events, it helps to get these notions on the table early on. So the team begins by quickly proposing a design for the last learning events for the project, based on whatever thoughts they may have, then asks the question, *Why shouldn't we do this?*

There will be many reasons why initial proposals are probably not the best ideas, but even more than instructional approaches should be examined. Questioning whether the right people are being trained, whether the right goals have been identified, and whether the content is appropriate, among many other foundational concerns, is perfectly appropriate. Sometimes it becomes clear a major shift in direction should be taken.

As ideas congeal, it is helpful to quickly prototype some of them, fully intending to throw the prototypes away after they've helped the team examine their thoughts. With appropriate tools and a skilled prototyper, prototypes can be produced quickly, sometimes even as the team is discussing options or while they take a break. Again, thinking about why a prototyped approach shouldn't be built is easier and more productive than answering the question, *What should we do?* Examining a prototype comfortably involves all stakeholders and gives the instructional designer an understanding of perspectives, misconceptions, and whose criteria must be met for project acceptance.

Prototypes

Both models find functional prototypes essential. They are a primary means of expressing, sharing, and evaluating a candidate design. With content, logic, and media in play, team members can see precisely what is being proposed. At first, disposable prototypes can be produced by carefully *avoiding* polish and sophistication. Designers focus on demonstrating key instructional constructs for evaluation. Because time and effort are kept to a minimum in early prototype production, there's little tendency to defend them in light of new ideas that may arise in reaction. In fact, a primary purpose of early prototypes is to confirm that no better ideas are to be found.

Both models also favor iterative design over painstaking attempts to produce the final design in a single pass, but SAM specifically urges designers to discard, at least temporarily, their first and second prototypes in search of what might be a better approach. The third prototype may be an entirely new approach or an amalgamation of new ideas and ideas explored in previous prototypes.

Documentation

Both models minimize documentation. Design specification documents are not only time consuming to prepare, but also easily misinterpreted. As noted, readers may read their own preferences and expectations into such design documents, approve them, and then be quite surprised when the product contrasts significantly with their expectations. Prototypes cover many of the needs often addressed in documentation, but does so faster and better.

Objectives

Both models, in contrast to other approaches, delay preparation of instructional objectives. Instead, the initial focus is on developing content and instructional approaches in prototype application. This approach not only moves projects along faster, but also avoids preparing instructional objectives out of the context of real content and needing to modify them later as a better understanding of appropriate objectives emerges.

Components

Both models prescribe that the final demonstration should be as authentic as possible, meaning that the context is as similar as possible to the situation in which the performance will occur, the challenge or problem is typical of challenges or problems to be encountered, and the activity or learning activities, such as the range of choices, level of prompting, performance aids, and the manner in which the learner meets the challenge or solves the problem, are all similar to how the learner will perform. Feedback for the final learning experiences is intrinsic, meaning it is primarily shown as a realistic consequence of the learners' actions.

Project Planning

As a design only model, Pebble doesn't specifically address project planning, whereas SAM addresses development as well as the design process. People who commission the development of learning products want to know upfront how much projects would cost and how long development would take. The request is an understandable one, but many factors are involved to answer just the one question of the *optimal* amount to spend. Even determining the *minimal* amount requires determining what the instructional strategy will be, what type and how much media will be needed, how much usable content exists and how much more will need to be created, and so on. It's an easy and common error to spend too little and waste the entire budget along with a great deal of learner time in use of ineffective instruction, but it's also quite possible to spend more than is beneficial. Some work needs to be done to answer the question accurately and responsibly.

The Savvy Start exercise prescribed in SAM provides much of the basis for generating a project plan, budget, and schedule. During this event, which typically lasts two days, the team finds or generates information needed, including the scope of skills to be developed, the instructional approach to be taken, the content and media components required by the approach, the complexity of instructional interactions, availability of key resource people, and the delivery platforms to be used. While other questions may remain and not all of these data may be forthcoming immediately, the Savvy Start provides in a very short amount of time much of the basis for generating a project plan.

Development

As an iterative, small-step process, SAM shares many of the concepts and values of Agile software development (www.agilealliance.org). It keeps project clients in the loop and able to see the project developing so that design corrections remain affordable as long as possible.

Multiple operating versions of the project are produced, beginning with the initial functional prototypes and evolving into a *design proof,* which demonstrates all unique components without much replication so as to remain open to modification. User interface is functional in e-learning applications. Final media for some content appear in operational interactions, so quality and timing can be reviewed. Connection with an LMS is tested along with transfer of collected data, scoring, and reporting. In essence, a deep slice of the final instructional product is available to review as the standard for all subsequent content development.

Conclusion

As an instructional design and development model ADDIE often leads to frustration among team members, inefficiencies in both time and cost, and disappointing learning outcomes from the resulting instruction. A simpler model is needed that relies more on the actual content to be taught rather than specification documents, that utilizes rapid prototyping, and that relies on an iterative design and development process. SAM and Pebble are instructional development models that attempt to overcome many of the weaknesses of ADDIE. This chapter describes some of the principal properties of each of these models and compares these models to each other and to ADDIE. The authors believe that although these models were developed independently, that both SAM and Pebble are complimentary and that their use will result in a more efficient design and development experience and will result in learning experiences that are more meaningful, memorable, and motivational and learning outcomes that are more effective, efficient, and engaging.

Summary of Key Principles

1. **The legacy ADDIE (Analysis, Design, Development, Implementation, and Evaluation) process has become a family of processes due to the many adaptations made to overcome its weaknesses.** The original ADDIE was described as a linear, phase-based process in which the work of one phase was completed before the next began. As such, errors and omissions made in one phase cause problems down line. Further, as a document-based process, misinterpretation of documents inevitably led to problems. While it identified important tasks to be done, it was also slow, cumbersome, and complicated—all qualities that stifled much needed creativity and focus on the learner experience.

2. **SAM and Pebble models were created to overcome problems identified from many years of experience with ADDIE.** These processes recognize the importance of creating learner experiences that are effective, efficient, and engaging. Consistent with today's Agile concepts for software development, they emphasis the importance of operational prototypes and minimize the use of documentation that is too easily misinterpreted.

3. **SAM and Pebble, in their use of iterative design, are efficient models optimized through elimination of unneeded tasks and performance of tasks at optimal times and levels.**

4. **Both process models focus on targeted outcome performance and problems learners will need to be able to solve.** The goal is to produce highly beneficial learning experiences, not to check off a long list of design and development tasks.

5. **While SAM and Pebble were developed independently, the great similarity and use over many years lends considerable credibility.** No model is perfect, but ADDIE has many drawbacks overcome by these contemporary models.

Application Questions

1. **Applying SAM:** An organization that certifies cafeteria food workers wants cooks to understand the interaction that can occur between foods kept in refrigeration and to place foods in refrigerators to minimize spoilage.
   a. Identify the tasks learners need to perform and the prerequisite knowledge and skills for each.
   b. Sketch a learning experience that would lead to satisfactory performance and discuss with one or more other people to get their reactions.
   c. Sketch a second learning experience responding to comments and suggestions you received, but also trying out a very different approach than you used the first time. Discuss with others.

2. **Applying Pebble-in-the-Pond:** Select a course or module you are preparing to teach.

   Identify a real-world problem or complex skill that this module is intended to teach the learner to solve or complete. Create a demonstration of an instance of the problem or task and an application requiring the learner to solve or complete another instance of this problem or task.

References

Allen, M. W. (2003). *Michael Allen's guide to e-learning.* Hoboken, NJ: John Wiley & Sons.

Allen, M. W. (2012). *Leaving ADDIE for SAM: An Agile model for developing the best learning experiences.* Alexandria, VA: ASTD Press.

Merrill, M. D. (2013). *First principles of instruction: Identifying and designing effective, efficient and engaging instruction.* Hoboken, NJ: Pfeiffer.

Chapter 5

The Successive Approximation Model (SAM): A Closer Look

Michael W. Allen

Allen Interactions Inc.

Introduction

Every day, learning professionals face the challenges of designing and developing engaging learning experiences within typical constraints of tight budgets and even tighter timelines. The demands of the modern workplace challenge the capability of instructional design methods to deliver on time and within budget without compromising instructional impact. Traditional processes too often produce unsatisfactory results, even without such constraints, and have increasingly dimmer prospects as constraints continue tightening.

Successful instruction is much more than the transmission of information, yet that's what many resort to in response to pressure for faster, less expensive production. No matter how well organized and complete instructional materials may be, content-centered instruction cannot deliver optimally effective learning experiences because of its focus on content presentation rather than on meaningful and lasting learning experiences. To achieve the impact that justifies design and development time and also the nonrefundable aggregate of learner time, it is essential for learning experiences to be *meaningful* to the individual learner, *memorable* to provide sustained performance guidance, and *motivational* to activate new behaviors.

Meaningful, memorable, and motivational are not easy criteria to meet, but all are essential. With care, skill, and an appropriate process, they are indeed achievable. Nevertheless, we continue to see diminishing project budgets and less patience for thoughtful design and development. Organizations want training developed more quickly and often by people with minimal knowledge of instructional design and human learning. Yet, presumably, they also want training that leads to desired performance.

A greater understanding of what constitutes a smart level of investment would certainly help, but regardless of the constraints, all would benefit greatly from a simpler and faster approach to design and development that produces effective learner-adaptive experiences. Support for more effective collaboration would help as well, to shorten development time while taking advantage of more perspectives and talents. We need a model that fosters creativity and yet is practical and efficient. We're looking for a lot of help.

Although ADDIE (a legacy model specifying phases of analysis, design, development, implementation, and evaluation) has appealing logic and draws out important tasks, all successful models must include or address, as pointed out in Chapter 4 of this book, an arduous and risky model known more for obsession with detailing, scoping, and sequencing content than for creating compelling learning experiences that adapt to individual needs as learners progress. It is a risky model because in using it critical aspects of designs are not typically revealed in functional or testable form until late in the process, when suggestions for modification are difficult to afford. The ability to try out a design, whether in the classroom or on a computer, is essential to understanding and evaluating its strengths and weaknesses. The earlier a design can be fully evaluated, the better, as good ideas for modification will almost certainly arise. Design revelations that arise late during that design process can lead to better approaches, but are often, and regrettably, unmanageable.

The successive approximation model (SAM) (Allen, 2012) focuses more directly on the construction of learning experiences, giving attention to learner emotions, energy, activity, needs, and accomplishments. It is fundamentally iterative and exploratory, which allows alternative designs to be considered very early in the process. It even looks for learner input at the start and throughout the process. ADDIE tasks are integrated throughout SAM, but are limited to addressing identified project needs, rather than attempting broad, time-consuming thoroughness without clear justification and usefulness.

SAM is much less daunting than ADDIE, sharing many concepts with Agile—a software development methodology in which requirements and solutions evolve through collaboration of, and repeated considerations from, cross-functional teams. Scope is kept small and focused so an initial implementation can be made functional quickly. Functionality is then maintained throughout the remainder of the process as additional capabilities are identified, added, and evaluated. Consistent with Agile principles and experience, SAM is fast, practical, and responsible for producing many outstanding, award-winning courses of instruction within given constraints.

So how does SAM achieve all these benefits? Let's review the process and discuss key principles and activities.

Successive Approximation Model (SAM)

The model's name reveals two essential concepts. First, "successive" tells us that tasks are done in a prescribed order and repeated. Indeed, a foundation of SAM is that several attempts to design and build an effective learning experience are more likely to yield a successful one than is a single attempt. We can have much greater confidence in our design when we consider several designs, even if we ultimately go with our first one.

The second essential concept, "approximation," recognizes that no design is perfect and never will be; improvement is always possible. And since improvement is always possible, any given design is only one approximation of the theoretical ultimate design.

Successive approximations are, therefore, *repeated attempts to achieve closer proximity to perfection* (without expecting to achieve it). Not expecting to achieve perfection provides great relief and suggests comforting pragmatism. Since perfection is an unrealistic goal, the number of iterations one should undertake becomes a simple, practical consideration. Experience

suggests that three iterations usually return substantial benefit, while further revisions, especially before field testing, return declining benefits.

Two- and Three-Phase Versions

The iterative nature of SAM allows it to adjust readily to project variables, such as the size of the project, and even to major changes to initial assumptions, such as who should be trained first, what form of delivery will be used, the instructional approach to be selected, and type of amount and media to be used. Indeed, because the process questions everything to attain the most impact, the ability to accommodate changes efficiently is essential. The small steps and frequent iterations permit SAM to respond efficiently when problems and opportunities arise.

The original and basic version of SAM prescribed only two phases: a preparatory or backgrounding phase and an interleaved design, build, and review phase (later called a design and development phase). This two-phase model is depicted in Figure 5.1.

In projects undertaken by smaller teams (one up to about five individuals, most of whom have both design and development skills), there is great benefit from using this simple two-phase process; however, more structure is required when projects are larger, more people are involved, and more money is at risk. Planning for larger projects is typically more extensive; special-purpose prototypes are often required to keep all design attributes consistent, and development is usually less integrated with design.

For larger projects and especially for those engaging a separate development team, foundational designs (plans for how the content will be presented) are often validated and then used repeatedly during the development phase. In these cases, SAM employs a three-phase approach (Figure 5.2).

As can be seen by examining Figures 5.1 and 5.2, there is a great deal of similarity between the two-phase and three-phase models. So as to provide you with a clear picture of the entire process, let's discuss the three-phase model, but keep in mind that most of that description applies to the two-phase model as well.

In the lower portion of Figure 5.1 is a visual representation of the workflow for the two-phase SAM. The two phases are (1) *preparation*, which includes information gathering and

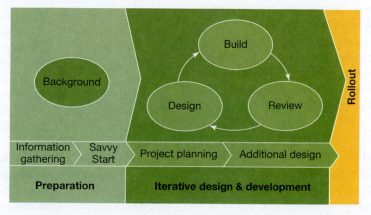

FIGURE 5.1 Two-phase successive approximation model (SAM).

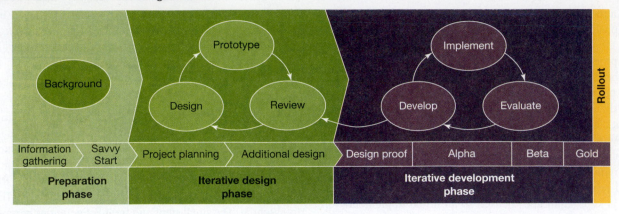

FIGURE 5.2   Three-phase successive approximation model (SAM).

an important project initiation event called Savvy Start; and (2) *iterative design and development,* in which alternative designs are built out just enough for evaluative review, then redesigned to explore how the design might be improved.

Preparation Phase

For speed and efficiency, the preparation phase is completed quickly. It is the time for gathering background information about a project, clarifying conflicting information, noting initial goals, and so forth. This information will, in turn, support discussion that centers on the perceived performance problem that appears to be preventing attainment of a goal. During this phase, the project team determines key aspects that help to set the target, identify special issues, and rule out options.

SAM then moves into a structured meeting called a Savvy Start, in which collected information and assumptions are reviewed with stakeholders. In quick attempts to imagine what the eventual training might look like, questions will arise that require additional information gathering. Such directed information gathering is far more efficient than broadly collecting information that might be valuable.

Information Gathering

At the start of any instructional design project, it can be tempting to begin by collecting content to be organized and sequenced for use in the course. Typically, a learning design/development team initiates an instructional project by collecting data: policy documents, procedural guides, training content from past courses, etc. Doing this at the start of the process, however, easily shifts focus away from *performance* and toward *information*—as if the project were about information. When implementing SAM, however, it is especially important to avoid articulating content this soon. While existing materials may prove valuable and useful, in this phase, SAM suggests simply noting what materials exist and moving on to quickly propose what the goals and *key performance issue(s)* may be.

The information gathering process includes:

- *Identifying key players and their commitment to participate.* Key players include:
  - Decision and budget maker
  - Opportunity owner
  - Subject-matter expert (SME)
  - Performance supervisor
  - Recent learners
  - Target learners
  - The organization's deployment manager
- *Identifying the organization's primary opportunity* and its dependency on specific behavioral changes. For example, an aircraft manufacturer has the opportunity to further improve performance among its employees in handling safety issues with reduced risk of injury or death, but this opportunity is dependent upon the learners being willing and able to engage in learning so as to change their behavior when it comes to practicing sound safety measures.

Background information to be gathered for these tasks includes:

- Previous performance improvement efforts (if any) and their outcomes
- Programs currently in use (if any)
- Available content materials
- Organizational responsibilities for training
- Constraints, such as schedule, budget, and legal requirements
- Name of the ultimate decision maker
- Aspect that will define project success
- Budget constraints
- Deadline

During information gathering, the team does preparation work quickly, taking paths of least resistance. This approach differs from the start of a traditional ADDIE process, in which much time is often spent collecting potentially relevant information that may or may not turn out to be helpful. Because so many dynamic forces interplay in determining what people do and when they do it, the deeper one probes the more one can see opportunities to investigate further. This can cause "analysis paralysis," which can overwhelm and delay a project.

In contrast to ADDIE, SAM tries to avoid delays and unnecessary efforts by undertaking performance analysis in the context of considering alternative instructional treatments intended to identify and address performance issue(s). As we'll see, SAM prioritizes analysis by considering designs quickly proposed, based on the information at hand. Asking, "Why shouldn't we do this?" can quickly propagate questions. If answers aren't known, then researching them will be time well spent. When more information is needed, the team goes after it with a clear purpose and justification.

Once the preliminary data are gathered, the preparation phase moves from information gathering to the Savvy Start.

The Savvy Start

The *Savvy Start* is a brainstorming event in which the design team and key stakeholders (e.g., the budget maker, the individual who owns the performance problem, the individual who supervises performers, the subject-matter expert [SME], and potential and recent learners) review the collected background information and generate initial design ideas. (Table 5.1 lists the participants and responsibilities needed in the Savvy Start.) Brainstorming begins with jumping into solutions stakeholders may already have in mind. From these initial ideas, instructional events are brainstormed, sketched, and prototyped quickly.

The Savvy Start meeting is an iterative process of review, design, prototype, and review. As shown in Figure 5.3, the Savvy Start uses the same cycle of iterations to be used in the following iterative design and iterative development phases, but the iterations are performed very quickly—over just hours rather than days. The cycle is repeated as many times as possible during the meeting.

First, background information provided prior to the meeting is reviewed so that there can be at least a temporary assumption of the goals and problems to be addressed. These may change as the team begins to understand the situation and options better. People often come to projects with ideas of what should be done. It's important to make sure these ideas, which may actually be expectations and even strong preferences, are shared

and evaluated, lest they disrupt work by coming to the fore later on after other approaches are pursued. So, the team is asked to contribute an initial round of ideas. The instructional designer helps and guides the group toward approaches known to be effective for specific types of learning outcomes and sketch alternatives for discussion, perhaps following David Merrill's *First Principles of Instruction* (Merrill, 2013), which integrate beautifully with SAM. One or more sketches are then given to a prototyper (a designer/developer who can quickly build functional prototypes of the sketches) to quickly develop, perhaps as the group continues its discussions or during a break. As soon as possible, the prototype is presented to the group for review. With proper tools and experience, prototypes are produced repeatedly and reviewed within the Savvy Start.

During a Savvy Start, a variety of ideas and preferences surface, the need for research and more information may become apparent, and attractive instructional approaches emerge. Different approaches will need to be thoughtfully considered and refined, and possibly modified extensively—even replaced. Attendees should expect this to happen, and recognize it as a sign of progress.

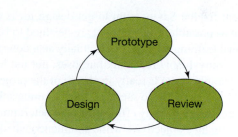

FIGURE 5.3   Savvy Start iterations.

TABLE 5.1   Savvy Start Roles and Responsibilities

Role	Responsibilities
Budget maker	This person can explain budgetary constraints, knows if the budget will be (or was) set, and knows what assumptions have been made.
Person who owns the performance problem	This person will help to determine the organization's expectations for successful performance.
Person who supervises performers	Supervisors are closest to the actual performance issues and will provide the most concrete examples of performance problems that need to be solved.
Subject-matter expert (SME)	This person can provide insight into the content and direction for the instruction.
Potential learners	These people can share a novice's perspective that is invaluable for effective design.
Recent learners	Recent learners can help the team understand the strengths and weaknesses of current instruction, what is easy and hard to learn, and what may be best to learn on the job.
Project manager	The manager directs resources and schedules project work, making sure effective communication occurs.
Instructional designer	The designer(s) will advise the team on effective timing of instructional approaches, select or create instructional treatments to be considered, and oversee content creation.
Prototyper	This person will sketch and/or build prototypes to give the team the opportunity to visualize their ideas as they evaluate alternatives.

Duration

The Savvy Start session may take only a half day, but may take as much three full days, or sometimes even longer. The optimal length depends on many factors, such as the diversity of opinion among stakeholders, the complexity of the skills and behaviors being taught, variance in learner readiness, and so on. The length possible often depends on incidental factors, such as availability of people or meeting space, but even with all these relevant factors, two days are often just right and should be scheduled if at all possible. It's important to achieve as much as possible while the group is convened, as it may not be possible to reassemble again, or as responsively as the project might need if insufficient consensus is not achieved at the start.

While the involvement of key stakeholders is essential to truly understanding the project's boundaries and expectations, these people usually can't afford the time necessary to reach needed depth or cover all of the content. Having the right people in the room is critical to achieve the most impactful outcomes from the Savvy Start.

Design, Prototype, and Review

It is important for the Savvy team to get design ideas on the table as soon as possible, whether they are destined to become part of the final learning package or eventually abandoned. This activity proves invaluable for many purposes, not the least of which is determining who is really in charge of the project and what outcomes are essential to success. Brainstorming solutions in this manner is an amazingly efficient way of determining the primary performance objectives, while simultaneously dealing with the organization's hierarchy that can so easily obscure important success goals.

Prototyping is the essential activity of Savvy Starts because visual representations make it possible to discuss and agree to a design with much less ambiguity and individual interpretation than results from verbal descriptions. The Savvy team reveals and shares critical information during the process of designing and reviewing rapidly constructed, disposable prototypes. The prototypes promote brainstorming and creative problem solving, help the team determine what really is and isn't important in the project, and help align the team's values.

It's hard to overstate how effective and efficient the Savvy Start is. The basic process is discuss, brainstorm, sketch, prototype, and review. The fundamental review question as the team looks at their first prototypes is, *Why shouldn't we do this?* In the first cycle, answers may erupt quickly and easily; but even if they aren't, important progress occurs by quickly throwing out a possibility and thinking about its shortfalls. These answers become important guides for the next cycle: repeat.

The whole process takes place rapidly in an effort to create viable instructional treatments that the team can commit to. Working quickly and minimizing personal investment by not prematurely polishing a design reduces the temptation to commit to any design that has significant flaws. Quickly created designs that fail to adequately address the performance issue(s) are easily discarded and new ones created.

Design, prototyping, and review continue to be done iteratively in small steps. Only exemplary samples of the instructional content are worked to completion. Additional content is created later, but even then, iteratively.

Savvy Start Products

The essential products of the Savvy Start are:

- Rough, exemplary prototypes
- Savvy Start Summary Report, a document that details the discussions and decisions made in the meeting
- Objectives X Treatments Matrix, a document that lists primary instructional objectives and aligns them with defined treatments

Each of these essential products will support the continued design to take place during the next phase of SAM: the iterative design phase.

Highlights of the Savvy Start include the following:

- *Design cycles:* evaluate the direction suggested by gathered information, assumptions, and early ideas
- *Prototypes:* provide just enough to communicate and test ideas
- *Performance outcome objectives:* clarify success for the overall project and for individual learners
- *Evaluation:* done merely by discussion at this point, may result in redefining and changing the entire project—even the business problem to be addressed and the intended learners
- *Speed* is the key!

A Note on Instructional Objectives

Instructional objectives are an essential component of effective instructional design. The instructional treatments SAM seeks to create and test are based on defined performance needs. The team may work from initial instructional objectives provided to the design team from stakeholders or identified in early preparation-phase discussions, at the start of the project, or determine them during the Savvy Start. Regardless of where they originate, instructional objectives are vital to keeping the design on track throughout the SAM process.

The Savvy Start concludes with the confirmation of performance outcome goals, instructional objectives, and prototypes for at least a portion of the content. The team then moves into the second phase of SAM: iterative design.

Iterative Design Phase

The iterative design phase (Figure 5.4) picks up after the Savvy Start has concluded. Most SAM leaders prefer to work backward through the content, addressing the final learning activities first. When this recommended procedure is followed, the Savvy Start will have focused on the culminating learning activities that should have learners integrating their skills in the performance of authentic activities. Design attention then moves progressively backward toward more basic skills, each design preparing learners for the previously designed learning events.

Unless the project is very small, there is considerably more work to do, including more design work, during this

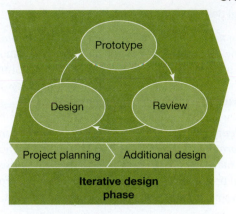

FIGURE 5.4 Iterative design phase.

phase. At first glance, the diagram may suggest a perpetually iterating process that could be difficult to contain and manage, but as we'll discuss, cycles have specific purposes and criteria to meet. The simple and nearly always appropriate guideline for SAM, however, is to cycle three times and move on.

The Savvy Start should produce enough information to produce a project plan. Although it's unfortunate that organizations often attempt to create a plan before an exercise such as the Savvy Start produces vital information, it can lead to undesirable results. The Savvy Start informs planning in critical ways, making it possible to identify tasks, who will hold responsibilities for them, reasonable timelines, and probable costs.

Additional design takes place through more iteration, but by a smaller team focused on covering additional content, resolving inconsistencies among designs, and solving problems that have arisen along the way.

Note that with larger projects or teams, documentation and coordination are prerequisites to success, but SAM pushes for minimal documentation. This holds true during the iterative design phase as well as other phases in SAM. The project team should produce only the most essential documents, all of which should be questioned as to whether face-to-face communication, or even the visual transfer of ideas through prototypes, wouldn't be more effective.

Project Planning

Project planning involves a quantitative assessment of remaining project development details affecting timeline and budget. Three-phase SAM, especially, involves careful consideration not only of cost and quality management, but also of related communication, risk, schedule, scope, and staffing implications.

Project planning should reflect the essential SAM concept that no project is ever perfect, but through repeated work can evolve and become closer to perfection. This notion lends a great deal of practicality; it urges project managers to put projects into use and think of making future iterations based on feedback from the field. The point relevant to planning is that by quickly producing a first-round project and then planning for successive improvements as time allows, there can be more certainty of project availability on a preset date than with other approaches.

From the time functional prototypes are available, SAM projects always have usable courseware. Its quality will continually increase, but at any point that it's necessary to begin instruction, the best product possible within the project's constraints will be available.

For ultimate practicality, as the team plans for project tasks, each task is given a level of priority for the each iteration:

Threshold	Must be completed in the current iteration
Target	Is expected to be completed in the current iteration
Future	Will be held back for a future iteration
Epic	To be considered after the current project has been put in use

Based on the designs created or selected in the Savvy Start, the team can create a project plan that has integrity. With Savvy Start input, the team can estimate content writing, media development, and programming for the overall project plan.

Guidelines for project planning tasks include the following:

- Capture discussions and decisions by preparing and circulating a *Savvy Start Summary Report*.
- Prepare initial *Media and Content Style Guides*. These guides are likely to be incomplete until additional design cycles have been completed. It's easy and efficient to capture additional style preferences as the team becomes aware of them.
- Prepare an initial draft of a *Content Development Plan* that indicates responsibilities and estimates of which material(s) will be needed. Prioritize items by threshold, target, and future.

The biggest risk in project planning lies with learning and performance objectives for which no solutions have yet been prototyped.

Additional Design

Additional design activities are identical to the design–prototype–review events of the Savvy Start and often occur concurrently with project planning, to maintain momentum of the Savvy Start. For example, in the Savvy Start, the design team for an aircraft manufacturing company was only able to prototype five of the nine design treatments identified. During the additional design phase, the team will prototype the remaining treatments after reviewing existing prototyped treatments for completeness and consistency.

Breadth Before Depth

During this phase, the team will likely be leaner, and keeping in mind decisions made in the Savvy Start and expectations set there, the team will be able to progress more quickly. It remains important, however, to follow the rule of *breadth before depth*. That is, the team must consider all of the content to understand whether a broad variety of instructional treatments will be necessary, or just a few will suffice.

The breadth before depth rule is harder to follow than it appears and can actually be the biggest liability of using

SAM. With each iteration, design becomes more articulated and reaches greater depth. The team will be tempted to immediately follow up on ideas as they surface, feeling that it's efficient to continue iterations, build on ideas while they are fresh and in mind, and "complete" the design. The problem is that new, "better" ideas are likely to emerge from every iteration, and it takes discipline not to pursue them—launching into perpetual iterations, spending too much time on a single content segment, and leaving too little time for adequate design for remaining content.

Generally, no content area should receive more than three iterations until all types of content have received similar attention. One very important benefit of considering all content before polishing any one treatment to its final level is that it's very typical to find similar content recurring throughout a course of instruction, whether it's applying a procedure, making decisions, predicting outcomes, or other types of content. It may be possible to provide a powerful treatment that covers large amounts of content, rather than building many treatments that cannot receive much attention.

The initial task is to scan through all the content and to design basic instruction for each new type of content encountered. Then the project manager can decide if there is time to iterate further on some or all of the designs. Very often, there's less time remaining than expected; but covering all the content initially ensures a deliverable course.

Prototypes

Prototypes continue in additional design activities to be important to communicate and test ideas. A usable prototype is better than any description, specification, or storyboard. It substitutes for many pages of documentation that can be time consuming both to write and read. A prototype communicates by example, making it easy for people to understand, ask constructive questions, and make detailed comments.

Following the Savvy Start, where prototypes are focused on achieving consensus on design principles, the team may develop additional prototypes, including some special-purpose prototypes.

Depending on the selected means of delivery, one or more of the following types of prototypes may prove helpful:

- *Media prototypes* integrate media elements to demonstrate the desired "look-and-feel." Layout, colors, fonts, images, and samples of other elements are brought together to form a clear design example and set criteria for full product development.
- *Functional prototypes* are derived by enhancing prototypes created during the Savvy Start to make them usable by and testable with learners. Functional prototypes provide navigational and interactive elements so learners can move through and complete the activities successfully.
- *Integrated prototypes* combine functional and media prototypes with sample content to provide a complete, representative sample of the product design.
- *Technical prototypes* are created to test delivery platform compatibility, communication with a learning management system (LMS), or any technical or design components that instructional delivery will depend upon.

Additional design tasks include:

- *Using the same iterative process of design, prototype, and review.* Key decision makers should review and approve final prototypes before development begins. Simply trusting that these key people will be happy with how things are evolving, unseen, is not a good practice.
- *Reviewing all content and organizing it by similarities to identify the smallest number of necessary treatments and prototypes.* Except for small projects and those with a very narrow focus, there isn't enough time to create functional prototypes for each segment of content. Focus is on developing a prototype for each *type* of content.

The Iterative Development Phase

The iterative development phase is depicted in Figure 5.5. The iterations that are so advantageous to the design phase process are equally powerful for development phase activities. Iterations allow stakeholders to have a continuing means of evaluating decisions and making corrections within project constraints. The importance of this advantage cannot be overstated. Because a functional product becomes available quickly, stakeholders can get an invaluable glimpse of the design becoming reality before the team engages in time-consuming refinements.

Design Proof

Given a set of prototypes from phase two to address treatments for each type of content, user interface, media integration, and other components, the first product of phase three is a *design proof* to assure that all the components will work together as expected. The design proof is a visual, functional demonstration of the proposed solution. The design proof also integrates samples of all components to test and prove viability. It has greater functionality or usability than the design prototypes and is built with the same tools that will produce the final deliverable. In this way, the design proof not only tests the viability of the design, but also the production system.

The design proof provides a critical opportunity for the team and stakeholders to feel confident that the parts create a desirable whole. It's also a chance to be sure no technical problems lie ahead to prevent delivery of the proposed design.

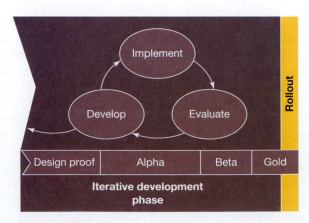

FIGURE 5.5 Iterative development phase.

Approval or disapproval will determine whether:

- Additional design work needs to take place. If so, the process returns to iterative design to produce needed designs.
- Another development iteration should take place to make corrections.
- Iterative development can proceed to producing an alpha version of the final product.

If technology is involved, the design proof needs to run on the equipment and network to be used by learners and demonstrate functional communication with the LMS, if one is to be used. If the design proof includes role playing, field demonstrations, or other activities, then the team needs to conduct trial runs of these activities to be sure all details have been incorporated to make these activities run smoothly.

Design proof evaluation is a critical event in the process. Design proofs scout out potential problems so they don't become last-minute crises. Evaluating the design proof is the best opportunity for the design team and the stakeholders to check how the course will function as a whole. At this point, it is possible to get the clearest sense of what the overall solution is becoming while still having time to note corrections that are clearly needed.

Design Proof Highlights

- The first production cycle results in the design proof, which provides an opportunity to confirm all design decisions by presenting and testing a functional application on the intended delivery platform.
- Design proofs test:
  - Design viability
  - Whether the design communicates requirements effectively
  - Suitability of development tools
  - Ability to deliver required learning experiences reliably and repeatedly
- Design proofs combine sample content, including examples of all components, with design treatments. Text and media are polished and representative of the final quality to be expected for all similar elements.

Alpha Release

The *alpha release* is a complete version of the instructional application to be validated against the approved design. By this point, the team should have implemented all content and media into the alpha. The team should document any outstanding problems that may exist, particularly if evaluation needs to begin before all issues can be rectified. No major, undocumented issues are expected to be found, but it's nevertheless common for them to surface despite everyone's best efforts.

Evaluation of the alpha release identifies deviations from style guides, graphical errors, text changes, sequencing problems, missing content, lack of clarity, and functional problems.

Alpha Highlights

- The second production cycle (or set of cycles for large projects) produces the alpha from approved designs.
- Full content development integration occurs in this cycle. Samples no longer suffice.

- The alpha is nearly the final version of the complete instructional program that will be validated against the approved design.
- Completion and approval of the alpha signals the beginning of the validation cycles.
- Alpha reviewers should ideally find only minor to moderate deviations from style guides, writing issues, graphical errors, and functional problems.

Beta Release

Because reviewers nearly always find errors in alpha releases, the team schedules a second cycle, called the *validation* cycle. Validation is part of the process that leads to a second final product candidate, the *beta release*. The beta is a modified version of the alpha that incorporates the needed changes that reviewers have identified during alpha evaluation.

If the team makes the corrections carefully and as expected, reviewers should discover few errors in the beta release. At this point, these errors should include only minor typographical errors or corrections in graphics.

Beta Highlights

- The SAM process considers the beta release to be the first gold release candidate. The beta should have no functional errors, but if it does, an additional iteration may be needed to produce a second beta release and additional prospective releases if significant errors continue to surface.
- User acceptance testing enabled by the beta version is a time for learners to experience the course and provide feedback and insight prior to the final deliverable. Not only SMEs, but also actual learners representative of the target population, should evaluate the beta release during user acceptance testing sessions.

Gold Release

Construction of the *gold release* is the final stage in the iterative development phase. At this point, while no project ever reaches perfection, the courseware becomes fully usable within the parameters of previously approved project guidelines.

Gold Highlights

- If reviewers identify any problems in the courseware, the team must fix these issues before the beta release can be given the gold crown. At this point, the team would produce a modified version of a beta, "beta 2" (sometimes called "gold candidate 2"), and, if necessary, a succession of numbered candidates, until all problems are resolved.
- When the beta performs as expected and reviewers encounter no additional problems, it becomes the gold release without further development and is ready for *rollout* implementation.
- Hopefully, but all too rarely, rollout signals the beginning of an evaluation study to determine whether learners actually achieve the targeted behaviors and whether these new behaviors secure the expected performance success.

Relative Advantages of Two-Phase and Three-Phase Models

When examining the relative merits of the two-phase and three-phase successive approximation models, the two-phase model is the process this author most prefers. This model has many advantages, especially in its rapid response to problems and opportunities and in its fostering of creativity. Another primary advantage of this model is that design and/or implementation can be adjusted as soon as opportunities or needs can be seen in the developing courseware. Immediate, in-stream opportunity or problem identification prevents going too far down an undesirable path and minimizes the amount of work discarded when corrections are made. It fosters quick experimentation, evaluation, and correction. It avoids being locked into a design that needs no further development to evaluate. The closeness of a small team facilitates efficient communication and minimizes time-consuming documentation and formalities. Of course, it also requires careful time management, as with iterations there is the liability of getting caught in a whirlpool and never escaping.

The three-phase model, however, works better when design and development is being done by a larger group and especially with teams of specialists, where concurrent work is usually necessary to get the work done as quickly as possible. More coordination is needed when more people are involved, of course, and this can be an additional investment. Documenting styles and various standards, although it does take time, can result in increased efficiencies that participants in the two-phase model would likely reject as too constraining. In short, while both models prove very effective, the three-phase model will need to be chosen when the group of workers exceeds about a half dozen. When the group is smaller, choose the two-phase model.

Conclusion

SAM is a fun, energetic, and agile approach to the otherwise daunting task of designing highly effective instructional programs. It is practical in its recognition that no program will achieve perfection and that compromises are always necessary to meet ever-present constraints. After a minimal effort to collect background information, a specially structured, two-day meeting is held with stakeholders, learners, an instructional designer, project manager, and a rapid prototyper. In this meeting, called a Savvy Start, alternative instructional approaches are advanced starting with the last learning activity to be provided and working backward toward the beginning of the course.

Looking at ideas advanced by the team, the process repeatedly asks, *Why shouldn't we do this?* If there's no obvious objection, a prototype is built to further probe into the strengths and weaknesses of the idea. The first idea is set aside and in two more iterations, two other approaches are considered. The best of the three is selected and the team moves on to other content.

As discussed in this chapter, there are two versions of SAM, one for smaller projects, which integrates design and development from beginning to delivery, and an extended process, which separates development into its own iterative phase. Through experiences of many teams producing countless courses of instruction, SAM has helped many organizations produce more effective, spirited courseware faster and easier.

Summary of Key Principles

1. **Instructional designers are under pressure to produce instructional products faster than ever before.** While the legacy ADDIE process is an exhaustive process, it can have trouble meeting today's requirements for expeditious development of instruction.

2. **An effective process recognizes that success often includes meeting the expectations of multiple people holding varying perspectives.** While the challenges of creating effective learning experiences are difficult in and of themselves, most instructional products are developed in an environment where satisfying multiple individuals is essential. Since conflicting views are sometimes strongly held, better processes recognize the importance of achieving a working consensus as soon as possible.

3. **No project is perfect.** To successfully deal with the constraints teams must work within, it's helpful to realize that all projects can be improved. Stopping short of perfection will happen no matter how much time is taken. The objective is therefore to produce the best product possible within given constraints.

4. **The successive approximation model (SAM)** is an iterative model designed to produce products rapidly, create effective instructional experiences, bring stakeholders to consensus so their criteria can be met, and produce the best product possible within given constraints.

5. **SAM's advantages stem from taking small steps of interleaved design, development, and evaluation.** Instead of attempting an overarching analysis, producing extensive documentation, and seeking sign-off approvals to develop a complete course of instruction, SAM reorganizes the steps and simplifies the work not only for efficiency, but to foster design correction as better ideas emerge (as they always will).

6. **Analysis is undertaken primarily within the process.** As an initial step, background information that's readily available is collected, such as identification of the trainee population, outcome goals, options for delivery, rollout date, and so on. But since it's not unusual for any (and even all) of these factors to be changed as alternatives are considered, initial analysis is done quickly. Just enough information is gathered to serve as a springboard for the project.

7. **The Savvy Start brings primary stakeholders together with instructional design experts.** This critical meeting, typically of two days in length, works to ferret

out various preferences, expectations, and constraints. Previously collected background information is presented and usually modified by the groups before they are asked what they think would be a good approach. The designer participates to be sure proven approaches are considered. One idea is selected for a discussion, stimulated by the question, *Why shouldn't we do this?*

8. **Prototyping is essential.** It isn't until stakeholders can actually see and partially experience an instructional event that they can effectively evaluate a design. Prototyping, whether it's for roleplaying setup, a game,

or an e-learning activity, provides a basis for effective evaluation and for consideration of new ideas.

9. **In its simplest form, SAM interleaves design, development, and evaluation until it's necessary to roll the product out.** This version of SAM is best for beginners to undertake and guarantees the best product possible is produced within the amount of time allowed. An extended version of SAM is optimized for larger projects and larger teams (more than five or six), in which content development is performed in separate iterations.

Application Questions

1. The vice-president of sales at a custom furniture company feels that while their training of new sales people is about the best it can be, having refined it over decades, it remains a slow and costly process. After five weeks of classroom training, they find trainees still falter on the job, sometimes damaging permanently any future prospects with clients. She has set aside an undisclosed budget to develop new training to be rolled out in ten weeks and wants you to lead the development using the SAM process she's heard good things about. After collecting some background information, you've learned that the director of training has been urging the company to develop e-learning so that the more experienced salespeople can get into the field faster while those needing more skill development get the training they need. The sales VP, however, has been arguing that they simply need to record some of their best sales people in action and give everyone access to the videos.

   a. Who do you invite to the Savvy Start and why?

   b. Someone suggests you start with ideas to develop entry-level skills. Do you agree or disagree? Why?

   c. What do you do if the vice-president of sales attends but doesn't express any preference for video presentation? Or if the training director attends but doesn't describe the advantages of e-learning presented?

   d. Describe what might happen if you let unexpressed differences go unexplored at the Savvy Start.

   e. You see some very good ideas accepted by the group, but realize they would be expensive. Do you raise this concern in this meeting? Why or why not?

2. Imagine you have completed most of the two days allowed for a Savvy Start and the group has reviewed several prototypes, noting likes and dislikes in each. How would you handle the following situations?

   a. A completely new idea arises, which everyone seems to like.

   b. You've only been able to cover about 20 percent of the skills learners need to develop. What do you tell the group about how the 80 percent might be covered?

   c. You see some very promising elements in the designs people like, but also some pitfalls that need to be addressed. How do you handle them?

References

Allen, M. W. (2012). *Leaving ADDIE for SAM: An Agile model for developing the best learning experiences.* Alexandria, VA: ASTD Press.

Merrill, M. D. (2013). *First principles of instruction: Identifying and designing effective, efficient and engaging instruction.* Hoboken, NJ: Pfeiffer.

Chapter 6

Psychological Foundations of Instructional Design

Marcy P. Driscoll

Florida State University

This chapter provides an overview of the major psychological concepts and principles of learning that are foundational to the field of instructional design (ID). The behavioral learning theory of B. F. Skinner, for example, contributed concepts such as reinforcement, feedback, behavioral objectives, and practice to the design of instruction. Cognitive theories such as information processing and schema theory shifted the focus of the ID field to attributes of learners and the role of prior knowledge in learning new knowledge and skills. Situated learning theory shifted the ID field toward consideration of sociocultural factors in learning and the importance of the community in which knowledge and skills are acquired and practiced. Instructional theories such as Gagné's and constructivist approaches provide guidance for designing learning environments that facilitate the acquisition of desired skills, knowledge, and attitudes. Finally, connectivism is raising interesting questions about the role digital tools and technology could play in transforming the learning process.

Regardless of the differences among psychological perspectives on learning, an underlying assumption of most is that instruction will bring about learning. This assumption is what is important to those in the ID field. As Gagné (1995/1996) put it, "There are, after all, some useful human activities that are acquired without instruction, and others that result from self-instruction. But most practical and purposeful activities, such as the pursuits involved in vocational and technical training, are learned in settings that employ instruction" (p. 17).

Learning Defined

Most people have an intuitive notion of what it means to learn—they can do something that they could not do before or they know something that they did not know before. But learning must be distinguished from human development, or maturation, which also leads to abilities that were not present before. For example, young children are soon able to grasp objects in both hands simultaneously as they develop muscular control and coordination. Human development occurs as a natural process whereby "everyone, barring those with serious disorders, succeeds and succeeds well" (Gee, 2004, p. 11). Familiar examples of human development include learning to walk and learning one's native language.

Changes in ability that are only temporary must also be distinguished from learning, because learning implies a kind of permanence. Thus, the increased abilities of an athlete taking a performance-enhancing drug would not be thought of as learning.

Finally, some scholars make a further distinction between learning as an instructed process and learning as a cultural process (Gee, 2004). People learn many things by virtue of the cultural group to which they belong, such as social norms, rituals, and games. These are not typically the goals of instruction, whereas school subjects such as learning calculus or physics, are. As indicated earlier, overt instruction is what instructional designers care most about.

In most psychological theories, learning is defined as "a persisting change in human performance or performance potential"

(Driscoll, 2005, p. 9), with performance potential referring to the fact that what is learned may not always be exhibited immediately. Indeed, you may remember many instances in which you were never asked to demonstrate what you had learned until a unit or final test was administered. It is important to note, however, that such demonstrations of learning are important for instructional designers to establish the effectiveness of instruction. How else can they determine the impact of instruction if they do not, in some way, ask the learners to perform what was to be learned in the first place?

Learning is defined further by how it is thought to occur. In most psychological theories, learning comes about as a consequence of "the learner's experience and interaction with the world" (Driscoll, 2005, p. 9), and this interaction is understood as an individual process. That is, individuals interact with the world surrounding them, and this experience leads to an increased ability to perform in a particular way. A focus on the individual learner is why there has been such historical interest in differences among individuals and why the performance of individual learners is assessed after instruction. What differs among particular learning theories is how they describe the observed outcomes of learning and how they explain the learning process. Some of these differences are described in later sections of the chapter.

In recent years, however, perspectives have emerged that call into question the individuality of learning. Adherents of a sociocultural view believe that "[psychological] individuality can only be properly identified and analyzed after the levels of community have been factored out" (Lemke, 1997, p. 49). In other words, learning is to be understood in terms of the activities of people living within a particular sociocultural setting. In this view, learning is more than a change in performance of a single individual; it can encompass the performance of a group of individuals sharing a common purpose or intent or engaged in a common practice. Furthermore, learning is characterized not just by the processes within an individual learner but also by the processes shared by and affecting the members of a defined group. It is in this perspective that learning as an instructed process begins to merge with learning as a cultural process.

Connectivism takes social learning a step further, reflecting a rapidly changing society that is "more complex, connected socially, global, and mediated by increasing advancements in technology" (Duke, Harper, & Johnston, 2013, p. 6). Similar to the sociocultural view, connectivism as a theory attempts to address organizational knowledge that can reside outside the individual. Learning becomes a process of connecting ideas, evaluating diverse information sources, and deciding what is relevant or important to make knowledge actionable (Siemens, 2005). In the connectivist view, learning may begin with the individual, but knowledge can grow exponentially as individuals collaborate within a network and constantly update information. In this view, an individual's existing state of knowledge is less important than the ability to connect within a network, and it is advancing technology that makes these connections possible.

In the sections that follow, major psychological concepts and principles of learning are explored and their implications for ID

discussed. In some cases, such implications have already been observed as influences on the field. In others, implications are being imagined and proposed as potential and future influences on the field.

Behavioral Learning Theory

B. F. Skinner, throughout his life and career, advocated an approach to the study of psychology and learning that is focused on behavior (see, for example, Skinner, 1938, 1969, 1987). At the core of his radical behaviorism is Skinner's belief that learning can be understood, explained, and predicted entirely on the basis of observable events—namely, the behavior of the learner along with its environmental antecedents and consequences. Antecedents refer to the cues occurring in the environment that signal the appropriateness of a given behavior. A stop sign, for example, signals to the driver that the appropriate behavior is to apply the brakes. Likewise, a teacher's admonition to "listen up!" signals to learners that they should stop talking and pay attention. According to Skinner, the consequences of a behavior then determine whether it is repeated and thus considered to be learned. For instance, a learner who is rewarded with a teacher's smile for paying attention in class will be more likely to follow the teacher's direction at a later time than one whose behavior goes unnoticed. Similarly, a learner who tries a new strategy for finding information on the World Wide Web is more likely to keep using it if it proves to be successful (and is thus reinforced) than if the strategy does not yield the sought-for information.

The principles of behavior modification that Skinner and his disciples investigated in their research and tried out in instructional applications have had significant impact on the ID field. To begin with, behavioral learning theory is empirically based, which means that behavior is observed both before and after an intervention such as instruction has been implemented, and the observed changes in performance are related to what occurred during the intervention. If there is no change in behavior, then the intervention cannot be considered effective. In the ID field, these observations are part of formative evaluation, which is conducted to collect information about whether instruction resulted in learning and how it might be improved to result in even better learner performance.

The emphasis in this theory on the behavior of the learner also contributed to concepts such as behavioral objectives and the importance of practice in instruction. For example, prior to instruction, teachers and instructional designers can determine whether learners have already acquired a desired behavior by observing them. Desired behaviors that are not exhibited can be specified as objectives, or learning outcomes, to be addressed in the instruction that is being designed and developed. In a similar way, specifying desired behaviors as objectives points out the need to ensure that learners have sufficient opportunities to practice these behaviors as they learn.

Finally, behavioral theory influenced early conceptions of instructional feedback. That is, feedback was assumed to be essentially equivalent to reinforcement. When learners responded correctly during instruction, immediate feedback that the answer was correct was expected to reinforce the response. Likewise, feedback that an answer was wrong was expected to reduce the incidence of incorrect responding. Because of the anticipated reinforcing benefits of feedback, instructional designs (such as programmed instruction) resulted that broke instruction into small steps and required learners to respond frequently (see, for example, Holland & Skinner, 1961), thus virtually assuring errorless performance. Unfortunately, these designs were boring to learners, who could also "peek" ahead at answers before they responded, which meant that the presumed benefits of feedback were rarely realized (Kulhavy, 1977).

Cognitive Information Processing Theory

The informational value of feedback became apparent when researchers and practitioners began to adopt the perspective of information processing theory. This view rose to prominence among psychologists in the 1970s, and variations of it continue to be investigated and articulated today. Like behavioral theory, information processing theory regards the environment as playing an important role in learning. Where information processing theory differs from behavioral theory, however, is in its assumption of internal processes within the learner that explain learning. "The birth of computers after World War II provided a concrete way of thinking about learning and a consistent framework for interpreting early work on memory, perception, and learning. Stimuli became inputs; behavior became outputs. And what happened in between was conceived of as information processing" (Driscoll, 2005, p. 74).

Atkinson and Shriffin (1968) proposed a multistage, multistore theory of memory that is generally regarded as the basis for information processing theory. Three memory systems in the learner (sensory, short-term, and long-term memory) are assumed to receive information from the environment and transform it for storage and use in memory and performance. With sensory memory, learners perceive organized patterns in the environment and begin the process of recognizing and coding these patterns. Short-term, or working, memory permits the learner to hold information briefly in mind to make further sense of it and to connect it with other information that is already in long-term memory. Finally, long-term memory enables the learner to remember and apply information long after it was originally learned.

In addition to stages through which information passes, processes such as attention, encoding, and retrieval are hypothesized to act upon information as it is received, transformed, and stored for later recall and use. For instance, learners who fail to pay attention will never receive the information to be learned in the first place. To be most influential on learning, attention must often be directed so that learners heed specific aspects of the information they are being asked to learn. Similarly, the process of encoding provides a means for learners to make personally meaningful connections between new information and their prior knowledge. Finally, retrieval enables learners to recall information from memory so that it can be applied in an appropriate context.

Feedback from an information processing perspective, then, serves two functions during learning. First, it provides the learner with knowledge about the correctness of his or her response or the adequacy of his or her performance. While this knowledge is certainly important during learning, it is not sufficient for correcting misconceptions or other errors in performance. The second function of feedback, therefore, is to provide corrective information to the learner that can be used to modify performance. In essence, feedback completes a learning cycle where the feedback can be used to continually modify what is stored in memory and used to guide performance.

In addition to changing our conception of feedback in instructional design, information processing theory shifted our focus to various attributes of instruction and how they can facilitate or impede information processing and, thereby, learning. It also put increased emphasis on the role of prior knowledge in learning new knowledge and skills. For instance, a learner who already knows a good deal about the topic of instruction can call to mind many cues that will be helpful in processing whatever information is new. A learner with little prior knowledge, however, can make few connections between what is already known and what he or she is being asked to learn.

To assist learners in processing information, practitioners have incorporated strategies into their instructional designs that direct attention, facilitate encoding and retrieval, and provide practice in a variety of contexts. The use of boldface and italic print in text materials, for example, can draw learners' attention to important information just as the use of color in diagrams or slides can help learners distinguish important features of visual information. Graphical diagrams and imagery strategies can help learners make meaningful connections between their prior knowledge and the new information they are learning. Finally, providing many different kinds of examples or problems in different contexts can help learners apply the knowledge they are acquiring to situations where it is relevant.

Schema Theory and Cognitive Load

What distinguishes experts from novices in the way they structure knowledge and in their ability to solve problems? Questions like this have prompted developments in learning theory that, while still cognitive in orientation, diverge from information processing perspectives. According to schema theory, knowledge is represented in long-term memory as packets of information called schemas. Schemas organize information in categories that are related in systematic and predictable ways. For instance, my knowledge or schema of "farm" may encompass categories of information such as kinds of animals raised there, types of crops grown, implements used, and so on. Learners use existing schemas to interpret events and solve problems, and they develop new and more complex schemas through experience and learning.

Automation is important in the construction of schemas, because learners have only so much processing capacity. "Indeed, knowledge about working memory limitations suggest[s] humans are particularly poor at complex reasoning unless most of the elements with which we reason have previously been stored in long-term memory" (Sweller, van Merriënboer, & Paas, 1998, p. 254). More sophisticated and automatic schemas free a learner's working memory capacity, allowing processes such as comprehension and reasoning to occur. However, a high cognitive load is put on learners when they do not have appropriate or automated schemas to access, or when the learning task imposes a heavy demand on working memory processes.

From their investigations of cognitive load theory, Sweller and colleagues suggested instructional strategies designed to reduce extraneous cognitive load in instructional materials. These include providing worked examples and partially completed problems that learners review or finish solving. Worked examples appear to be effective not only in well-structured domains (such as algebra) but also in complex domains that are largely heuristic in nature (such as troubleshooting in engineering; Renkl, Hilbert, & Schworm, 2009). In multimedia instruction, Mayer and Moreno (2003) suggest that narration, rather than on-screen text, be used with animation or diagrams so that learners' attention is not split between two sources of visual input. The split-attention effect can also be reduced in text-based instruction by integrating explanations within diagrams instead of requiring learners to mentally integrate text and pictures (Sweller et al., 1998).

Finally, the evolution of cognitive load theory focused increasing attention in the instructional design field on learning of complex, cognitive skills. Van Merriënboer and his colleagues proposed the 4C/ID model for complex learning, which calls for learning tasks to be sequenced in ways that reduce cognitive load (van Merriënboer, Kirschner, & Kester, 2003; van Merriënboer & Kirschner, 2007). That is, learners are gradually introduced to a series of task classes, each of which represents, on a simple to complex continuum, a version of the whole task. These are supplemented with just-in-time information and part-task practice, depending on the learner's growing expertise and the need for automaticity.

Situated Learning Theory

Whereas the context of learning is recognized as important in information processing theory, it takes on a more central and defining role in situated learning theory. As an emergent trend in the cognitive sciences (Robbins & Aydede, 2009), situated learning or situated cognition theory is regarded by its proponents as "a work in progress" (Kirshner & Whitson, 1997). There is growing consensus, however, about what it means to say that "learning is always situated" (Sawyer & Greeno, 2009) and what this could imply for instructional design.

Unlike behavioral and information processing theory, situated learning theory relies more on social and cultural determinants of learning than it does on individual psychology. Specifically, knowledge is presumed to accrue in "meaningful actions, actions that have relations of meaning to one another in terms of some cultural system" (Lemke, 1997, p. 43). For example, children selling candy on the streets of Brazil developed techniques for manipulating numbers that are related to currency exchanges, whereas their age-mates in school learned standard number orthography (Saxe, 1990). To understand why the candy sellers acquired the particular mathematical knowledge that they did and why it was so different from what their age-mates learned requires reference, at least in part, to the "mathematical and economic problems linked to the practice" of candy selling (p. 99).

Thus, learning from a situated perspective occurs through the learner's participation in the practices of a community, practices that are mutually constituted by the members of the community. Consider, for example, the instructional design profession as a community of practice. As a student, you are a newcomer to the community, engaged in learning its models and practices and becoming ever more competent as you gain experience in these practices. With increasing participation, newcomers become old-timers in the community, individuals who control the resources and affect the practices of the community at large. Faculty members in programs, for example, change the practices of the field through their participation in research and development.

According to Wenger (1998), learning as participation can be defined:

- individually (i.e., as members engage in the practices of a community);
- community-wide (i.e., as members refine the practices of a community and recruit new members); and
- organizationally (i.e., as members sustain the interconnected communities of practice through which "an organization knows what it knows and thus becomes effective and valuable as an organization)" (p. 8).

Organizations that hire instructional designers, for example, constitute their own communities of practice that embody the ways in which design is conducted in the context of their businesses. Yet their practices are influenced by the academic communities from which they recruit their instructional designers. It should also be obvious that the influence of interconnected communities of practice works in both directions; academic programs modify their practices from time to time based on what they learn from the organizations where they place their graduates.

Proponents of situated learning theory point to its strength as integrating knowing with doing. That is, one learns a subject matter by doing what experts in that subject matter do (Lave, 1990/1997). For example, Scardamalia and Bereiter (1994, 1996a) studied a community-of-learners approach to instruction called Computer-Supported Intentional Learning Environment (CSILE). This approach—and its upgraded version, Knowledge Forum (Scardamalia, 2004; Zhang, Scardamalia, Reeve, & Messina, 2009)—is a computer tool that enables students to engage in the discourse of a subject-matter discipline in a scholarly way. They focus on a problem and build a communal database, or "knowledge space," of information about the problem. With current Web technologies, CSILE/ Knowledge Forum has the capability now of linking experts in the field with students in the classroom in mutually constituted knowledge-building efforts (Scardamalia & Bereiter, 1996b). Students continually improve their ideas as they consult others' work, and they collectively determine next steps based on gaps in their knowledge. Evidence suggests that the tools embodied in Knowledge Forum can facilitate high-level collective cognitive responsibility and dynamic knowledge building among members of the learning community (Zhang et al., 2009).

The influence of situated learning theory can also be seen in designs for anchored instruction. The Cognition and Technology Group at Vanderbilt (1990) proposed anchored instruction as a means of providing a situated context for problem solving. Specifically, they developed video adventure programs containing a series of embedded problems that engaged the viewers in attempting to solve the problems. The video adventure story provides a realistic, situated "anchor" for activities such as identifying problems, making hypotheses, proposing multiple solutions, among others. The expectation is that students will engage in authentic practices of the discipline in which a given set of problems is anchored—whether mathematics, science, or history, for example.

Anchored instruction has been criticized for providing a simulation of a community of practice, casting the learners as observers rather than participants (Tripp, 1993). The Vanderbilt group, however, evolved an approach where students begin with a video-based problem but then move through cycles of learning where they consult various knowledge resources, share ideas, and revise their understandings (Schwartz, Lin, Brophy, & Bransford, 1999). Web-based software provides a visual representation of the learning cycle and facilitates students' action and reflection, as well as their interaction with others. As with CSILE/Knowledge Forum, this affords an opportunity for learners to collaborate within a broader community and leave a legacy for others to use and build upon.

Gagné's Theory of Instruction

Although many learning theorists may be interested in what their work means for instruction, the explanation of learning is their primary concern. Robert M. Gagné, on the other hand, was primarily concerned with instruction and how what is known about learning can be systematically related to the design of instruction. He proposed an integrated and comprehensive theory of instruction that is based primarily on two foundations: cognitive information processing theory and Gagné's own observations of effective teachers in the classroom. A long-term collaborator of Gagné, Briggs (1980) wrote also that "I never asked Gagné about this, but I believe his early work in [designing training programs for] the Air Force must have been an important factor in his later derivation of his (a) taxonomy of learning outcomes, (b) concept of learning hierarchies, and (c) related concepts of instructional events and conditions of learning" (pp. 45–46).

As it evolved, then, Gagné's theory of instruction came to comprise three components:

- A taxonomy of learning outcomes that defined the types of capabilities humans can learn
- Internal and external learning conditions associated with the acquisition of each category of learning outcome
- Nine events of instruction that each facilitate a specific cognitive process during learning

Taxonomies of learning existed before and since Gagné's formulation, but none other besides his includes all three domains in which individuals are presumed to learn: cognitive, affective, and psychomotor. According to Gagné (1972, 1985; Gagné &

Medsker, 1996; Gagné, Wager, Golas, & Keller, 2005), there are five major categories of learning:

- Verbal information (i.e., knowing "that" or "what")
- Intellectual skills (i.e., applying knowledge)
- Cognitive strategies (i.e., employing effective ways of thinking and learning)
- Attitudes (i.e., feelings and beliefs that govern choices of personal action)
- Motor skills (i.e., executing precise, smooth, and accurately timed movements)

The reason for defining different categories of learning outcomes stems from the assumption that they must all require different conditions for learning. For example, learning to ride a bicycle (a motor skill) is different in fundamental ways from learning the multiplication table (verbal information), which is different in fundamental ways from learning to solve scientific problems (intellectual skill).

The differences in conditions of learning across categories of learning outcomes provide guidelines for which conditions must be included in instruction for specifically defined instructional goals. For example, instruction on the goal of "perform CPR" (motor skill) is likely to include a demonstration of the procedure, individual practice on the procedure, and perhaps a job aid depicting each step. On the other hand, instruction on an attitudinal goal implicit in job training on an electronic support system (such as, "choose to use the help function before seeking human assistance") is likely to provide a human model and focus on the benefits of making the desired choice.

In addition to conditions of learning that are unique to each learning outcome, there are conditions of learning that facilitate the process of learning in general. Gagné conceived of the nine events of instruction as learning conditions to support internal processes such as attention, encoding, and retrieval. The events of instruction are presented briefly here:

1. Gaining attention—a stimulus change to alert the learner and focus attention on desired features.
2. Informing the learner of the objective—a statement or demonstration to form an expectancy in the learner as to the goals of instruction.
3. Stimulating recall of prior learning—a question or activity to remind the learner of prerequisite knowledge.
4. Presenting the stimulus—an activity or information that presents the content of what is to be learned.
5. Providing learning guidance—a cue or strategy to promote encoding.
6. Eliciting performance—an opportunity to practice or otherwise perform what is being learned.
7. Providing feedback—information of a corrective nature that will help learners improve their performance.
8. Assessing performance—an opportunity to demonstrate what has been learned.
9. Enhancing retention and transfer—examples or activities that prompt the learner to go beyond the immediate context of instruction.

The application of Gagné's theory in instructional design is often a highly analytical affair, and it is therefore possible to lose sight of the overall context for learning while dealing with all the details of instruction. As a means of helping instructional designers integrate multiple goals into instruction, Gagné and Merrill (1990) proposed the notion of an enterprise schema. The enterprise schema defines the context for learning, the reason for learning a particular set of goals in the first place. For example, the enterprise schema of "managing a lemonade stand" provides a meaningful context for learning how to exchange currency, how to calculate needed supplies based on an anticipated volume of business, and so on.

Constructivism

Constructivism is not a single theory, but a collection of views sharing a fundamental assumption about learning that contrasts sharply with the assumptions underlying theories such as information processing. The contrast can be drawn this way. In information processing theory, learning is mostly a matter of going from the outside in. The learner receives information from the environment, transforms it in various ways, and acquires knowledge that is subsequently stored in memory. In constructivist approaches, on the other hand, learning is more a matter of going from the inside out. The learner actively imposes organization and meaning on the surrounding environment and constructs knowledge in the process.

From a radical constructivist point of view, knowledge constructions do not have to correspond with reality to be meaningful, but most constructivist researchers agree that not all knowledge constructions are equally viable. To sort out which ideas are viable and which are not, learners must test their personal understandings against those of others, usually peers and teachers.

Constructivism has been felt keenly in the world, partly because it seems to contrast so starkly with the other foundations, such as information processing and Gagné's theories, that have influenced practices in our field. Some of the philosophical issues related to these views are taken up in Chapter 5 and so will not be repeated here. Rather, I have chosen to describe a few of what I perceive to be the greatest impacts of constructivism on the field.

To begin with, constructivist researchers focused attention on high-level, complex learning goals, such as "the ability to write persuasive essays, engage in informal reasoning, explain how data relate to theory in scientific investigations, and formulate and solve moderately complex problems that require mathematical reasoning" (Cognition and Technology Group at Vanderbilt, 1991, p. 34). While these kinds of goals are certainly definable using taxonomies such as Gagné's, under such approaches they do not necessarily assume the prominence that constructivists would assign to them. Addressing broad and complex learning goals is also consistent with constructivist beliefs that individuals do not all learn the same things from instruction.

Constructivism has also had a substantial impact on views pertaining to the learning conditions and instructional strategies believed to support constructivist learning goals. To engage learners in knowledge construction, facilitate tests of their understanding, and prompt reflection on the knowledge generation process itself, constructivist researchers have recommended the creation and use of complex learning environments. Such learning environments should:

- engage learners in activities authentic to the discipline in which they are learning;
- provide for collaboration and the opportunity to engage multiple perspectives on what is being learned;
- support learners in setting their own goals and regulating their own learning; and
- encourage learners to reflect on what and how they are learning.

The rapid growth in computer technologies has assisted researchers in creating different kinds of technology-mediated learning environments that implement these strategies. It remains somewhat difficult to judge the effectiveness of these systems, however, because advances in assessment have not kept up well with advances in technology. Furthermore, constructivists argue that assessment of individual student learning should involve authentic practices observed during learning and would not necessarily reveal a uniform level of accomplishment across learners.

The popularity of constructivist learning environments and the difficulty in designing effective ones has led to criticism that they simply do not work. Kirschner, Sweller, and Clark (2006) conducted an analysis of "minimally guided" learning environments and concluded that, "Insofar as there is any evidence from controlled studies, it almost uniformly supports direct, strong instructional guidance rather than constructivist-based minimal guidance during the instruction of novice to intermediate learners" (p. 82). While others have taken issue with Kirschner et al.'s analysis (e.g., Hmelo-Silver, Duncan, & Chinn, 2007), an important point to take from it is that constructivist learning environments can and do differ greatly in the amount and kind of instructional support that they provide for learners. In a study of conceptual change in science, for example, Hardy, Jonen, Möller, and Stern (2006) found that all students benefitted through their participation in a constructivist learning environment on the topic of "floating and sinking." But students held fewer misconceptions and adopted better scientific explanations when the teacher structured tasks to highlight relevant aspects and facilitated student reflection on their insights.

Connectivism

The final theory to be considered in this chapter has its roots in the neural networks of cognitive science and artificial intelligence (e.g., Nielson, 2015). Its proponents argue that connectivism as a learning theory is very different from, and indeed incommensurable with, in Thomas Kuhn's conception, all the other theories discussed here. According to Downes (2014), learning is defined in connectivism as "the formation of connections in a network," and "networks 'learn' by automatically adjusting the set of connections between individual neurons or nodes." Learning results, then, not in "the accumulation of more and more facts or memories but the ongoing development of a richer and richer neural tapestry."

Siemens (2005) articulated a set of connectivist principles that serve as a basis for application in both individual and organizational settings:

- Learning and knowledge rests in diversity of opinions.
- Learning is a process of connecting specialized nodes or information sources.
- Learning may reside in non-human appliances.
- Capacity to know more is more critical than what is currently known.
- Nurturing and maintaining connections is needed to facilitate continual learning.
- Ability to see connections between fields, ideas, and concepts is a core skill.
- Currency (accurate, up-to-date knowledge) is the intent of all connectivist learning activities.
- Decision making is itself a learning process. Choosing what to learn and the meaning of incoming information is seen through the lens of a shifting reality. While there is a right answer now, it may be wrong tomorrow due to alterations in the information climate affecting the decision. (pp. 5–6)

These principles suggest that information is ever changing as new contributions are made to the network. The learning process must be cyclical as a result, dependent on learners' abilities to find new information, filter out extraneous information, and share their realizations (Kop & Hill, 2008). Assessment of learning also changes under connectivism and involves recognition of expertise by other participants in the network (Downes, 2014).

Proponents relate connectivism explicitly to the transformative possibilities offered by emerging technologies and argue that other existing theories of learning cannot adequately explain learning in environments such as Web 2.0 (Bell, 2011; Clarà & Barbarà, 2013). Connectivist massive open online courses (cMOOCs), for example, are designed to take advantage of Web 2.0 capabilities and create a dynamic environment where learners determine the content of learning, decide who can participate, and how they will communicate. In fact, cMOOCs are assumed to instantiate the pedagogy associated with connectivism and are being used to explore and refine that pedagogy.

Connectivism as a learning theory is not without its detractors. Critics deem it a phenomenon or a pedagogy and claim it is underdeveloped as a theory of learning. Despite broad dissemination of connectivism through books, articles, and blogposts, there has been little empirical research elaborating or testing its guiding principles (Bell, 2011). Clarà and Barbarà (2013) argued that it "underconceptualizes interaction and dialogue" (p. 131), and Kop & Hill (2008) pointed to the high level of learner autonomy that is required for students to be successful in connectivist learning environments. Perhaps the most important contribution of connectivism to date is driving a useful conversation about the transformative possibilities for learning that are offered by emerging technologies.

Conclusion

This chapter has presented a brief introduction to some of the major psychological principles and avenues of thought that have contributed (and continue to contribute) to professional practices in the field of instructional design. Behavioral and cognitive information processing theory came out of research programs dominating psychology in the 1960s and 1970s. Gagné's theory evolved through two decades of research from the 1960s to 1980s and integrates cognitive with behavioral views. These theories collectively form the bedrock on which the field of instructional design was founded and initially developed. They provided, and continue to provide, useful and reliable guidance for designing effective instruction.

Constructivism, schema theory, and situated learning theory now offer the ID field other ways of thinking about learning. Along with advances in technology, they promise design strategies for producing learning environments more complex, more authentic, and more appealing than ever before. The long-term implications of these theories to the ID field are not yet fully known, but they surely offer an invitation to professionals new to the field to help shape that legacy.

Summary of Key Principles

1. **Observe the behavior of learners to identify what students need to know, where they need practice, and when they have met a desired standard of performance.** This can also help you make judgments about the effectiveness of instruction in facilitating students' learning.

2. **Use instructional strategies that direct learners' attention, help them make relevant information personally meaningful, and provide them practice in a variety of contexts to facilitate transfer.**

3. **To help students learn complex skills, use instructional strategies such as worked examples and partially completed problems to reduce cognitive load.**

4. **Provide opportunities for students to work in communities of learning, where they tackle complex problems, share information, challenge each other's perspectives, and arrive at common understandings.**

5. **Align conditions of learning with the type of learning outcome students are expected to attain.** Be sure to incorporate the nine events of instruction to facilitate the overall process of learning.

6. **Engage learners in authentic activities and collaborative problem solving.** Use instructional strategies that enable students to set their own goals, monitor their own progress, and reflect on their own learning.

Application Questions

1. Assume that you are trying to teach learners how to calculate and compare the unit costs (e.g., price per ounce) of various sizes and/or brands of the same product. Select three of the theories of learning discussed in this chapter. For each of the three, describe the nature of the instructional activities that you would design if you were adhering to that theory as you were planning the instruction.

2. Select two instructional goals that represent simple versus complex learning outcomes. How would the learning theories discussed in this chapter be employed to develop instruction to teach the goals you have selected? How would the instruction differ in each case? Would one or another theory be more applicable to one goal versus the other? Why?

References

Atkinson, R. C., & Shriffin, R. M. (1968). Human memory: A proposed system and its control processes. In K. Spence and J. Spence (Eds.), *The psychology of learning and motivation* (Vol. 2). New York: Academic Press.

Bell, F. (2011). Connectivism: Its place in theory-informed research and innovation in technology-enabled learning. *International Review of Research in Open and Distance Learning, 12*(3), 98–118.

Briggs, L. J. (1980, February). Thirty years of instructional design: One man's experience. *Educational Technology, 20*(2), 45–50.

Clarà, M., & Barberà, E. (2013). Learning online: Massive open online courses (MOOCs), connectivism, and cultural psychology. *Distance Education, 34*(1), 129–136.

Cognition and Technology Group at Vanderbilt. (1990, April). Anchored instruction and its relationship to situated cognition. *Educational Researcher, 30*(3), 2–10.

Cognition and Technology Group at Vanderbilt. (1991, May). Technology and the design of generative learning environments. *Educational Technology, 31*, 34–40.

Downes, S. (April, 2014). *Connectivism as learning theory*. http://halfanhour.blogspot.com/2014/04/connectivism-as-learning-theory.html

Driscoll, M. P. (2005). *Psychology of learning for instruction* (3rd ed.). Needham Heights, MA: Allyn and Bacon.

Duke, B., Harper, G., & Johnston, M. (2013). Connectivism as a digital age learning theory. *The International HETL Review, Special Issue*, 4–13.

Gagné, R. M. (1972). Domains of learning. *Interchange, 3*, 1–8.

Gagné, R. M. (1985). *The conditions of learning* (4th ed.). New York: Holt, Rinehart, and Winston.

Gagné, R. M. (1995/1996). Learning processes and instruction. *Training Research Journal, 1*(1), 17–28.

Gagné, R. M., & Medsker, K. L. (1996). *The conditions of learning: Training applications*. Fort Worth, TX: Harcourt Brace College Publishers.

Gagné, R. M., & Merrill, M. D. (1990). Integrative goals for instructional design. *Educational Technology Research & Development, 38*, 23–30.

Gagné, R. M., Wager, W. W., Golas, K. C., & Keller, J. M. (2005). *Principles of instructional design* (5th ed.). Belmont, CA: Wadsworth/Thomson Learning.

Gee, J. P. (2004). *Situated language and learning: A critique of traditional schooling*. New York: Routledge.

Hardy, I., Jonen, A., Möller, K., & Stern, E. (2006). Effects of instructional support within constructivist learning environments for elementary school students' understanding of "floating and sinking." *Journal of Educational Psychology, 98*(2), 307–326.

Hmelo-Silver, C. E., Duncan, R. G., & Chinn, C. A. (2007). Scaffolding and achievement in problem-based and inquiry learning: A response to Kirschner, Sweller, and Clark (2006). *Educational Psychologist, 42*(2), 99–107.

Holland, J., & Skinner, B. F. (1961). *The analysis of behavior*. New York: McGraw-Hill.

Kirschner, P. A., Sweller, J., & Clark, R. E. (2006). Why minimal guidance during instruction doesn't work: An analysis of the failure of constructivist, discovery, problem-based, experiential, and inquiry-based teaching. *Educational Psychologist, 41*(2), 75–86.

Kirshner, D., & Whitson, J. A. (Eds.). (1997). *Situated cognition: Social, semiotic, and psychological perspectives*. Mahweh, NJ: Lawrence Erlbaum Associates.

Kop, R. & Hill, A. (2008). Connectivism: Learning theory of the future or vestige of the past? *International Review of Research in Open and Distance Learning, 9*(3), 1–13.

Kulhavy, R. (1977). Feedback in written instruction. *Review of Educational Research, 47*(2), 211–232.

Lave, J. (1990/1997). The culture of acquisition and the practice of understanding. Reprinted in D. Kirshner & J. A. Whitson (Eds.), *Situated cognition: Social, semiotic, and psychological perspectives*. Mahweh, NJ: Lawrence Erlbaum Associates.

Lemke, J. L. (1997). Cognition, context, and learning: A social semiotic process. In D. Kirshner & J. A. Whitson (Eds.), *Situated cognition: Social, semiotic, and psychological perspectives*. Mahweh, NJ: Lawrence Erlbaum Associates.

Mayer, R. E., & Moreno, R. (2003). Nine ways to reduce cognitive load in multimedia learning. *Educational Psychologist, 38*(1), 43–52.

Nielson, M. A. (2015). *Neural networks and deep learning.* Determination Press.

Renkl, A., Hilbert, T., & Schworm, S. (2009). Example-based learning in heuristic domains: A cognitive load theory account. *Educational Psychology Review, 21*(1), 67–78.

Robbins, P., & Aydede, M. (2009). A short primer on situated cognition. In P. Robbins & M. Aydede (Eds.), *The Cambridge handbook of situated cognition.* Cambridge: The Cambridge University Press.

Sawyer, R. K., & Greeno, J. G. (2009). Situativity and learning. In P. Robbins & M. Aydede (Eds.), *The Cambridge handbook of situated cognition.* Cambridge: The Cambridge University Press.

Saxe, G. B. (1990). *Culture and cognitive development: Studies in mathematical understanding.* Hillsdale, NJ: Lawrence Erlbaum Associates.

Scardamalia, M. (2004). CSILE/Knowledge Forum®. In A. Kovalchick & K. Dawson (Eds.), *Education and technology: An encyclopedia.* Santa Barbara, CA: ABC-CLIO.

Scardamalia, M., & Bereiter, C. (1994). Computer support for knowledge-building communities. *The Journal of the Learning Sciences, 3*(3), 265–283.

Scardamalia, M., & Bereiter, C. (1996a). Adaptation and understanding: A case for new cultures of schooling. In S. Vosniadou, E. deCorte, R. Glaser, & H. Mandl (Eds.), *International perspectives on the design of technology-supported learning environments.* Mahweh, NJ: Lawrence Erlbaum Associates.

Scardamalia, M., & Bereiter, C. (1996b). Engaging students in a knowledge society. *Educational Leadership,* November, 6–10.

Schwartz, D. L., Lin, X., Brophy, S., & Bransford, J. D. (1999). Toward the development of flexibly adaptive instructional designs. In C. M. Reigeluth (Ed.), *Instructional-design theories and models* (Vol. II). Mahweh, NJ: Lawrence Erlbaum Associates.

Siemens, G. (2005). Connectivism: A learning theory for the digital age. *International Journal of Instructional Technology & Distance Learning,* http://www.itdl.org/jan_05/article01.htm

Skinner, B. F. (1938). *The behavior of organisms: An experimental analysis.* Englewood Cliffs, NJ: Prentice-Hall.

Skinner, B. F. (1969). *Contingencies of reinforcement.* Englewood Cliffs, NJ: Prentice-Hall.

Skinner, B. F. (1987). Whatever happened to psychology as the science of behavior? *American Psychologist, 42,* 780–786.

Sweller, J., van Merriënboer, J. J. G., & Paas, F. G. W. C. (1998). Cognitive architecture and instructional design. *Educational Psychology Review, 10*(3), 251–296.

Tripp, S. D. (1993). Theories, traditions, and situated learning. *Educational Technology, 33*(3), 71–77.

van Merriënboer, J. J. G., & Kirschner, P. A. (2007). *Ten steps to complex learning: A systematic approach to four-component instructional design.* Mahwah, NJ: Erlbaum.

van Merriënboer, J. J. G., Kirshner, P. A., & Kester, L. (2003). Taking the load off a learner's mind: Instructional design for complex learning. *Educational_ Psychologist, 38*(1), 5–13.

Wenger, E. (1998). *Communities of practice.* New York: Cambridge University Press.

Zhang, J., Scardamalia, M., Reeve, R., & Messina, R. (2009). Designs for collective cognitive responsibility in knowledge-building communities. *The Journal of the Learning Sciences, 18,* 7–44.

Chapter 7
Constructivism for Active, Authentic Learning

Brent G. Wilson

University of Colorado, Denver

If you spend time with professional educators—K–12 teachers, education professors, or even corporate trainers—you will run into the term *constructivism*. As its name suggests, constructivism sees learning as a process of constructing or making something. Constructivism says that people learn by *making sense out of the world*; they make meaning out of what they encounter. Exactly how people do so is something that learning theorists debate, some arguing for fairly mechanistic processes of information encoding and retrieval, others seeing the process in qualitative, experiential terms. Whatever the exact process of meaning construction, instructors and instructional designers try to create conditions for meaningful learning in classrooms and courses, and on the job.

This chapter examines the place of constructivism in the field of instructional design and technology (IDT). To do this, we briefly show where constructivism fits into the history and evolution of the field. We present some potential benefits and problems with the approach, then conclude with some thoughts about its continuing role in the profession.

Basic Principles of Constructivism

As an educational philosophy, constructivism came to prominence in the 1990s (e.g., Dunlap & Grabinger, 1996; Savery & Duffy, 1996; Wilson, Teslow, & Osman-Jouchoux 1995). The basic precepts include:

- Learning is an *active process of meaning-making* gained in and through our experience and interactions with the world.

- Learning opportunities arise as people encounter *cognitive conflict or challenge*, and through naturally occurring as well as planned *problem-solving* activities.
- Learning is a *social activity* involving collaboration, negotiation, and participation in authentic practices of communities.

Because this is how learning is, instruction that lines up with those realities is likely to be more successful. A typical example of constructivist instruction presents a complex problem or challenge within a resource-rich environment, with learners working together and assuming responsibility for activities and decisions, and teachers in a support role. Instructional designers look for prescriptive guidelines, so constructivism became a set of principles for creating meaningful, engaging instruction. See Table 7.1 for a set of prescriptions for constructivist design.

The principles in Table 7.1 suggest a renegotiation of teacher and learner roles. Instruction is not so much *done to* learners, rather it *engages* learners in a process of inquiry and meaningful activity. The instructor's role shifts from "sage on the stage" to "guide on the side." And while the principles are framed in terms of a human instructor in the classroom, the instructor function can be done through careful design of learning materials, particularly through online technologies.

Constructivist teaching is often contrasted with the traditional teacher-centered approach, with students passively receiving content presented in lectures and textbooks. This has mistakenly been characterized as *behaviorist*—a mistake because behaviorist learning requires, above all, active responding; and when examined closely, both lectures and textbooks

TABLE 7.1	Constructivism Expressed as a Set of Prescriptions for Designing Instruction

The Problem	• Design instruction around a problem or small set of problems that is:
	  • Authentic—similar to those encountered outside of school
	  • Complex—involving multiple interconnected factors
	  • "Rich" or "wicked"—with many possible framings, solution paths, and solutions
	• Anchor individual skills to a larger valued goal.

The Environment	• Design the learning environment to resemble a real-world situation, with access to tools, information, and natural resources. • Provide opportunities for performance feedback in the form of natural consequences.
The Learner's Role	• Encourage learner ownership by highlighting the relevance of the problem and encouraging pursuit of interests. • Grant learners the main responsibility for knowledge advancement. • Provide opportunities for social interaction, communication, and collaborative teams. • Encourage learner reflection.
The Instructor's Role	• Emphasize guidance and facilitation—"guide on the side" rather than "sage on the stage." • Focus on deep engagement rather than coverage of topics. • Build on prior knowledge and experience.

are highly evolved tools and not as passive as they appear (Friesen, 2011, 2013). It is no mistake, though, that learners, whether in K–12, higher education, or training settings, are too often underengaged, underchallenged, passive, or disengaged mentally and physically. So constructivism remains a compelling idea for learners and instructors at all levels of education and training.

Instructional Models Linked to Constructivism

Here we describe some noteworthy instructional models developed during the early years of the constructivist movement that are still in use today.

Problem-based learning. Working with medical-school faculty, Howard Barrows (1988) developed a model for centering instruction around a key statement of a problem, prompting team-based inquiry and problem-solving processes. The problem-based learning (PBL) model spawned hundreds of projects and research studies in a variety of disciplines, and has been largely successful in terms of student learning (Hmelo-Silver, 2004).

Case- and scenario-based learning. In the 1990s, John Bransford and colleagues produced a series of videodisc lessons presenting a problem in an everyday context, requiring math for its solution. These authentic "macrocontexts" for classroom discussion and problem solving were proven useful as instructional strategies (Cognitive and Technology Group at Vanderbilt, 1990) and influential as instructional designers borrowed elements of these cases for incorporation into their own instructional and training products.

Cognitive apprenticeship. Based on a theory of situated cognition, Alan Collins and John Seely Brown developed an instructional model meant to include key aspects of informal learning (Collins, Brown, & Newman, 1989), similar to how apprentices learn from their masters in work settings. This model became popular among instructional designers seeking a framework for designing authentic but replicable instruction.

Interactive learning environments. Carl Bereiter and Marlene Scardamelia developed an online environment for collaborative problem solving, reasoning, and argumentation (Scardamalia & Bereiter, 1991). The online environment had built-in tools for structuring arguments and making a case based on evidence. The focus on knowledge creation continues in a number of online environments in a wide variety of subjects and grade levels.

We provide a few more examples later in the chapter, as we explore current and future uses of constructivism.

Potential Benefits

Proponents of constructivism point to a number of strengths of the position, summarized here.

Correspondence to how people really learn. Constructivism's depiction of learning through active engagement and meaningful activity is generally corroborated by findings in neuroscience, anthropology, and education. A research community known as the learning sciences has continued a serious research agenda based on constructivist-compatible ideas (Sawyer, 2006).

Higher-order learning outcomes. Constructivist teaching focuses on problem solving and critical thinking, and higher-order cognitive outcomes. These higher forms of learning, while challenging to accomplish, are critical objectives for education and training, and closer to the demands of expertise in the "real world." Focus on higher-order learning helps IDT professionals move beyond narrow technical training to include "softer" training for leaders and professionals.

Better integration of affect and emotion.   Constructivist learning seeks to integrate emotion, affect, and engagement into discussions of learning and cognition. This holistic approach is generally good because instruction becomes more than an "academic" thing—it draws on the whole person and leads to more realistic representations of expertise.

More relevance to job and out-of-the-classroom performance.   Because of its emphasis on authentic performance in realistic settings, constructivist learning can be more relevant to out-of-the-classroom needs. As learners encounter more complex problems and tasks during instruction, they should be able to transfer that knowledge to work settings more easily. For certain kinds of job needs, a very focused tutorial or job aid available at work may be more appropriate than a constructivist learning experience. Generally though, constructivist principles should lead to greater relevance to jobs and the outside world.

Potential Concerns

Like all approaches, constructivism solves some problems while perhaps creating others. There are some situations where a constructivist solution is a perfect fit, and then others where it may be a stretch. In this section, we examine some of the downsides to adopting a constructivist stance.

In most courses, instructors are the hardest workers. They are the most active and engaged; they rarely fall asleep in class. They make the hardest and most interesting decisions and solve the most problems; and they tend to learn the most (their first few times teaching anyway). This is reversed in constructivist instruction: Learners are put in situations where *they* have to do the really interesting work. They take on jobs that the instructor might otherwise do—choosing an area to work on or an approach to solving a problem; determining roles of team members; judging sources and methods; evaluating quality and appropriateness of solutions; giving feedback and consulting with other learners. While, in theory, handing over these responsibilities to learners may sound great, a number of questions quickly emerge:

- Are learners prepared to take on this new work?
- Are they motivated and emotionally mature enough to work independently and look after each other's interests?
- Do they have the prior knowledge they need to handle complex, authentic environments?
- Do they have adequate access to needed information?

In general, learners are most helped by *scaffolding* when first performing challenging, complex tasks. The scaffolding metaphor draws on Vygotsky's idea of a zone of proximal development, where children can perform complex tasks but only with assistance from a guiding adult (Wood, Bruner, & Ross, 1976). In our field, the concept refers to a variety of supports, helps, information resources, and advisement aimed to help learners through initial performance of a complex task The best scaffolding is uniquely tailored to the learner and their learning goals (Sawyer, 2006). Scaffolding supports are intended to be temporary, until learners are able to do the work more independently.

In this light, high-quality constructivist teaching requires more support, more access to resources, more attention to detail, more progress monitoring, and more carefully crafted guidance than traditional instructor-led teaching. Setting up a constructivist learning experience and getting it working right can be a huge pain for instructional designers, nearly always requiring field testing to get it right. If done well, though, the investment can result in significant learning gains—and just as important—more fully engaged learners. After iterations of design and revision, the instructor may end up truly acting as the "guide on the side," enjoying the energy, engagement, and active learning of individuals and teams.

As learning becomes more student centered, questions also arise concerning the role of the instructor. Maintaining control and surviving a transition to student-centered learning are probably the top concerns for many instructors. Teaching a class is like a fine-tuned choreography, and instructional designers who try to upset the dance by changing steps and inserting new routines can easily lose their audience in the process. The shift toward constructivist learning is indeed a major decision and commitment, involving new learning for students and instructors alike. Instructors who are being asked to make this shift should be supported in their efforts, and have access to knowledgeable mentors, information resources, and a supportive incentive/management structure to make this change successfully.

A Cautionary Case

Consider the case of Professor George. George thinks of himself as a constructivist. His courses contain just a few articles as assigned readings but lots of elective readings. Students complete just two major projects, one individually completed and one assigned to groups of three or four students. He rarely lectures but rather turns class time to students to work on their projects. Each project has a rubric with criteria to guide students, also used for grading. Students approach him about their work, and he advises and helps them find resources.

Unfortunately, George's students report a frustrating experience. They come into the class lacking knowledge, and too often exit with the same concern. A feeling of disorientation pervades. They are tired of not knowing where to look, pursuing unpromising leads, waiting for help or guidance. Only gradually do they create a picture of things—but too late to really be of help to them on their assignments.

The moral of the story: It's possible to follow the precepts of constructivist learning and still have less than successful instruction. Potential problems, beyond those already discussed, that instructional designers need to think about include:

- *Low-level outcomes due to inefficient activity.* George's students may be working actively on "authentic" tasks within complex environments, but their efforts are not directed at the right work. Too much time is spent on low-payoff activities: vague information searching, attending to unimportant tasks and details, trying to solve problems using means-end strategies (essentially educated guessing, and trying again). In spite of all their activity (or perhaps because of it), a close look at their learning is disappointing: Not much new information has been acquired, and not enough higher-level problem solving and schema acquisition has occurred.

- *Misalignment with standards and objectives.* Constructivist learning approaches tend to focus on just a few projects and cases. For curricula with broader learning requirements, this can be a disproportionate investment of time and attention, leaving other objectives unaddressed. Making things fit within a strictly defined curriculum can require some larger rethinking of overall goals and objectives.

- *Mistaking activity for targeted learning.* Many students, instructors, and instructional designers are prone to confuse busy activity with learning. While activity does equate to learning at some general level, activity does not assure mastery of a *targeted* learning objective. Thorough assessment of *targeted* learning can verify whether students' active engagement is actually resulting in their picking up the needed knowledge and skills of the lesson. In addition, multiple assessments—ongoing and summative, formal and informal—can provide a redundancy to assure mastery of any critical learning objectives.

- *Seduction of media/production values.* Constructivism and technology go hand in hand because of the scaffolding, support, and affordances for engagement available through various tools and resources on the Web. Many Web resources are of high presentation quality and compete well with entertainment media; but instructional designers should be careful in their selection of these media resources. We often gravitate to cool video clips that look and sound compelling but don't really further understand the content. Media can be effective as a first introduction to a subject, or as illustration or support. But learners need encouragement to go deeper and make connections to subject matter and solution paths. Sometimes the richer media may be less relevant than the mundane text-based page or article.

- *Hard to measure benefits.* The full learning accrued from constructivist teaching methods can be hard to pin down using objective assessments. The easiest way to teach a fixed and narrow learning target would usually be straight ahead, direct instruction; but constructivist methods lead to broader outcomes—a competent, confident problem solver who loves the subject matter. These outcomes may be seen as secondary to bottom-line skills of literacy and math computation, or technical mastery of job competencies. Instructional designers should strive to identify and/or create assessment techniques that adequately address both the bottom-line skills *and* these harder-to-measure outcomes.

- *Ties to privilege and access.* Critical theorists have offered critiques of constructivism that cast it as another privilege enjoyed by the White middle class (Popkevitz, 1998). Lower class, high minority schools are rarely the innovators in this area. In work settings, lower paid workers often receive technical training that is less engaging and authentic when compared to management training. Access to enabling technologies also varies across class, race, and culture. When learners are not well prepared with prior knowledge

and academic study skills, constructivism may be seen as a dispensable luxury. Even when constructivist lessons are employed, do all students really benefit? Critiques of privilege and power tend to examine the winners and losers of any ideology or intervention—and constructivism needs to undergo the same scrutiny.

When Constructivist Strategies May NOT Be a Good Idea

In general, I recommend serious consideration of constructivist strategies as a method for instruction because it generally fits how people learn. No single approach is complete and perfect, however. Here are some times when a constructivist strategy may *not* be a good idea:

- The content consists of technical material with fixed known rules and procedures or models that must be mastered or remembered with precision.
- Curriculum is driven by high-stakes exams that are mandated and external to the instruction.
- The situation requires short time frames with limited time and resources to devote to teaching and the preparation of materials.
- Learners may expect and want to be provided the material and the answers, led by an instructor and driven by the content or an exam.
- The school or business does not support a learner-centered culture—lacking supports for instructors or facilities or technology—or a tradition of learner-centered teaching.

In these cases, an alternative to constructivist teaching may be a better choice, but for practical constraints instead of theoretical reasons. Instructional theories are rarely applied in a strict fashion, however, so any situation could likely benefit from some consideration of constructivist principles in the design process.

Current Projects

The projects and models described in this section, developed and in use more recently, illustrate constructivism's continuing influence today.

Active learning classrooms (ALC). Several universities are redesigning classroom space to accommodate constructivist learning activities (Cotner, Loper, Walker, & Brooks, 2013). The active learning classroom (ALC) model, developed at the University of Minnesota, places a teacher station in the middle of a set of nine-person roundtables, with generous access to technology for instructor and students. Cotner and colleagues found that biology students in ALC classrooms outperformed expectations based on ACT scores, whereas students in traditional classrooms did not. Although universities rely on large-enrollment lecture courses for cost reasons, learner-centered physical spaces are growing in popularity in many universities.

Flipped learning. In 2007, two small-town science teachers in the mountains of Colorado, Jon Bergmann and Aaron Sams, made their recorded lectures available for student viewing at home and then used classroom time for student consultation and problem solving. They called it *flipped learning* or the *flipped classroom*—and interest took off (Noonoo, 2012). Their website (the Flipped Learning Network at http://www.flippedlearning. org) includes a variety of research reports showing growth in adoption and positive effects of flipped-learning activities. Note that the model still makes use of lectures, but students gain a measure of control over them, treating a recorded lecture as a *learning resource* that they can access and use, rather than an *imposed experience* that they must sit through regardless of their learning state.

Mobile learning.   Mobile learning is variously defined as learning via mobile devices, or learning that can only or best be done via mobile devices. As ownership and use of mobile devices continues to grow, the learning potential grows as well, but learners need compatible resources designed for mobile access (Chen, Sailhamer, Bennett, & Bauer, 2015). Accessing learning resources via a mobile device is not in itself constructivist (e.g., a museum tour requiring only listening and moving to the next station). Yet overall, mobile learning presents an opportunity for more site-specific, in-context access to learning exchanges, which are consistent with constructivist principles.

Serious e-learning.   In March 2014, four respected e-learning theorists (Michael Allen, Julie Dirksen, Clark Quinn, and Will Thalheimer) launched a "serious learning manifesto" consisting of design principles and standards that all e-learning products should address. The manifesto was a response to quality concerns about e-learning products typically generated in many settings, where poorly designed products were seen to threaten the legitimacy of the profession. The design principles (Table 7.2) are wide ranging, but most are completely consistent with a constructivist approach.

See the website for more detail and supporting principles (Serious eLearning Manifesto, http://elearningmanifesto.org/). Notably absent from the principles is any mention of accommodating learners with special needs or reaching marginalized groups, concerns common in schools and universities but increasingly the responsibility of corporate training providers as well.

Connectivism.   In 2005, Canadians George Siemens and Stephen Downes developed an approach to learning called connectivism, stressing the active creation of meaning by engaging networks of human and information resources and based on ideas derived from the open Web and online learning. Siemens (2005) offers a set of descriptive principles:

* Learning and knowledge rests in diversity of opinions.
* Learning is a process of connecting specialized nodes or information sources.
* Learning may reside in non-human appliances.
* Capacity to know more is more critical than knowing what is currently known.
* Nurturing and maintaining connections is needed to facilitate continual learning.
* Ability to see connections between fields, ideas, and concepts is a core skill.
* Currency (accurate, up-to-date knowledge) is the intent of all connectivist learning activities.
* Decision making is itself a learning process. Choosing what to learn and identifying the meaning of incoming information is seen through the lens of a shifting reality. While there is a right answer now, it may be wrong tomorrow due to alterations in the information climate affecting the decision.

Connectivism was influential in the design of the first massive open online courses (MOOCs) and among advocates of open education resources (OER). While criticized for its lack of rigorous grounding, connectivism remains a popular concept among practitioners in search of open inquiry environments that fully utilize the power of the Web. I see connectivism as largely compatible with constructivist precepts, with a pro-information, pro-online bias that may work wonderfully for some.

Maker movement.   The maker movement is the technology side of the DIY (do-it-yourself) culture consisting of hobbyists and artisans who build things, whether for learning, interest, or profit. Examples of maker products include 3D printing, robotics, HAM radio, and DIY electronics. Many of these activities have clear potential for learning and are seen in preengineering curricula. Concepts associated with the maker movement include tinkering, visual thinking, and the learn-to-code movement in schools. These are all related to the learning theory of *constructionism* (not constructivism), first promoted by Seymour Paper, focusing on learning through making things.

This sampling of projects and movements shows the long life and continuing impact of constructivism in current thinking and practice. The proliferation of "isms" can be daunting—constructivism, constructionism, connectivism—but in a way, the success of constructivism has led to its taking on new forms and labels over time.

TABLE 7.2	Serious E-learning Principles (from the Serious eLearning Manifesto)
Typical E-learning	**Serious E-learning**
Content focused	Performance focused
Efficient for authors	Meaningful to learners
Attendance driven	Engagement driven
Knowledge delivery	Authentic contexts
Fact testing	Realistic decisions Individualized challenges
One size fits all	Spaced practice
One-time events	Real-world consequences
Didactic feedback	

Conclusion

Instructional design depends on good theories of knowledge, learning, and instruction; but keep in mind, every instructional theory is seriously *underspecified*—that is, it doesn't really tell you everything you need to design a lesson based on that theory. Too much depends on the local situation, the goals and constraints, and expertise of participants. Instructional theories are necessarily abstract and general, leaving so much to real-life teams and individuals. Constructivism in its many faces and forms contributes to that theory base. At the same time, the field depends on skilled professionals who know what to *do with* a good theory—to use it in combination with local knowledge and ideas for making good instruction.

Constructivism has nearly achieved the status of common sense among educators, even while it has evolved into a number of instructional models and approaches. The term "constructivist" remains a good shorthand, suggesting instruction that is more meaningful, authentic, and problem based. These are enduring values among instructional designers and will have a place in our discourse for many years to come.

Summary of Key Principles

1. **Constructivism is both a philosophy or stance toward learning and an approach to designing instruction.** The philosophy emphasizes learners' construction of meaning through collaboration and engagement with the world. Constructivist instruction is typically built around authentic problems and projects, with problem solving and higher-order thinking skills, rather than narrow technical skills, being the target of learning.

2. **Constructivist teaching involves new roles for students and instructor.** Students take on much of the work traditionally assigned to the instructor (e.g., selecting topics, choosing instructional resources), whereas the instructor serves as a "guide on the side" rather than the "sage on the stage." This shift requires preparation and support for both students and instructor.

3. **A principal concern is preparing learners to take more responsibility for their own learning.** Students often lack the prior knowledge or dispositions to succeed with these added responsibilities, which is why they come as learners. Constructivist teaching asks a lot of learners, both cognitively and emotionally. Scaffolding strategies (temporary supports meant to recede over time) give learners that extra boost as they initially perform complex tasks, leading to richer, deeper learning outcomes.

4. **Constructivism typically takes more work, not less.** Compared to traditional approaches, constructivist designs generally require more careful design, performance monitoring, scaffolding, and field testing, in order to provide the needed guidance and support to learners.

5. **Constructivism has had a major impact on the practices of many instructional designers.** Constructivist values are reflected in a number of projects and models, and continue to influence professional standards in the field.

6. **The key to successful constructivist instruction— indeed of all instructional design—lies in the details of the doing,** at least as much as in the particular theory or model being applied.

Application Questions

1. **Nurses training:** The training director at a local hospital has asked you to design a three-hour (maximum) training session for the nurses that will result in their engaging in friendlier behaviors when they interact with the family members of patients. Twenty nurses will attend each training session, which will be offered repeatedly until all of the nurses in the hospital have had the opportunity to attend.

   In addition the training director, who has just taken the *Theories of Learning* course in her online masters degree program, suggests: "And can you design the session using a constructivist approach? I'd like nurses to somehow get engaged in something meaningful, not just see a lecture or be taught a set of rules."

   As a start, she has asked for a one-page (approximately 400-word) memo briefly describing the following:
   • The instructional activities that will take place during the training session

   • How those activities embody most of the instructional principles associated with constructivism (*be sure to clearly indicate what those principles are and how the activities embody those principles*)

   Write the memo!

2. **Online teaching—psych class:** As an instructional designer within the Faculty Teaching Center, you are working with Maya, a tenured psychology professor doing a makeover and redesign of a human motivation class offered to psychology majors. Now entering her fourth year teaching the course online, she feels experienced and qualified to teach online. In an effort to make the course more engaging and meaningful, she revised one unit into a project-based assignment for teams of three or four students working together in private work areas. The response from students was encouraging—they generally like the project as a diversion from weekly readings and online discussion.

The problem is, teams vary considerably in the quality of the submitted work, leading to some less than desirable grades for about a third of the class. Because of the course schedule, students move immediately to the next unit upon submission of work and do not review each other's submissions.

"I like the direction we're heading," affirms Serge. "A couple of teams reported frustration about the unit though; they seemed to be grasping for help about how to do it better. How can I give them better guidance without being too heavy handed? I don't want them just to copy a template or example I provide."

What are the next steps in the consultation process? Drawing on constructivist principles, what questions would you put to Maya, or what advice would you give her? What could you draw from your reading of benefits and concerns about constructivist teaching that might inform the conversation?

References

Barrows, H. (1988). *The tutorial process*. Springfield, IL: SIU School of Medicine.

Chen, B., Sailhamer, R., Bennett, L., & Bauer, S. (2015). Students' mobile learning practices in higher education: A multi-year study. *EDUCAUSE Review*. Retrieved from http://www.educause.edu/ero/article/students-mobile-learning-practices-higher-education-multi-year-study

Cognitive and Technology Group at Vanderbilt. (1990). Anchored instruction and its relationship to situated cognition. *Educational Researcher, 19*(6), 2–10.

Collins, A., Brown, J. S., & Newman, S. E. (1989). Cognitive apprenticeship: Teaching the crafts of reading, writing, and mathematics. In L. B. Resnick (Ed.), *Knowing, learning, and instruction: Essays in honor of Robert Glaser* (pp. 453–494). Hillsdale, NJ: Lawrence Erlbaum Associates.

Cotner, S., Loper, J., Walker, J. D., & Brooks, D. C. (2013). "It's not you, it's the room." Are the high-tech, active learning classrooms worth it? *Journal of College Science Teaching, 42*(6), 82–88.

Dunlap, J., & Grabinger, R. (1996). Rich environments for active learning in the higher education classroom. In B. G. Wilson (Ed.), *Constructivist learning environments: Case studies in instructional design* (pp. 65–82). Englewood Cliffs, NJ: Educational Technology Publications.

Friesen, N. (2011, April). The lecture as a transmedial pedagogical form: A historical analysis. *Educational Researcher*, 95–102.

Friesen, N. (2013). The past and likely future of an educational form: A textbook case. *Educational Researcher, 42*(9), 498–508.

Hmelo-Silver, C. E. (2004). Problem-based learning: What and how do students learn? *Educational Psychology Review, 16*(3), 235–266.

Noonoo, S. (2012). Flipped learning founders set the record straight. *THE Journal, The Flipped Classroom* [Web log comment]. Retrieved from http://thejournal.com/articles/2012/06/20/flipped-learning-founders-q-and-a.aspx

Savery, J. R., & Duffy, T. M. (1996). In B. G. Wilson (Ed.),- *Constructivist learning environments: Case studies in instructional design* (pp. 135–148). Englewood Cliffs, NJ: Educational Technology Publications.

Sawyer, R. K. (Ed.). (2006). *The Cambridge handbook of the learning sciences*. New York: Cambridge University Press.

Scardamalia, M., & Bereiter, C. (1991). Higher levels of agency for children in knowledge building: A challenge for the design of new knowledge media. *The Journal of the Learning Sciences, 1*(1), 37–68.

Serious eLearning Manifesto. (n. d.). Retreived from http://elearningmanifesto.org/

Siemens, G. (2005). Connectivism: A learning theory for the digital age. *Journal of Instructional Technology and Distance Learning International, 2*(1). Retrieved from http://www.itdl.org/Journal/Jan05/article01.htm

Wilson, B., Teslow, J., & Osman-Jouchoux, R. (1995). The impact of constructivism (and postmodernism) on ID fundamentals. In B. B. Seels (Ed.), *Instructional design fundamentals: A reconsideration* (pp. 137–157). Englewood Cliffs, NJ: Educational Technology Publications.

Wood, D., Bruner, J., & Ross, G. (1976). The role of tutoring in problem solving. *Journal of Child Psychology and Psychiatry, 17*(2), 89–100.

Chapter 8

The Learning Sciences: Where They Came from and What It Means for Instructional Designers

Christopher Hoadley
New York University

James P. Van Haneghan
University of South Alabama

The goal of this chapter is to describe the learning sciences perspective. We address questions about how this perspective emerged, what makes it unique, how it goes beyond previous perspectives on learning, and what research findings and practical tools for the instructional designer result from taking this perspective. To start the chapter, we will take a journey back about forty years ago.

At that time, cognitive psychology was moving into the mainstream of psychology and becoming increasingly entwined with educational applications. Overall, there were three major trends that led to the blossoming of a cognitive psychology relevant to education. First, the departure from purely behaviorist models of psychology allowed for alternative theoretical bases for understanding human learning. Second, the emergence of the interdisciplinary field of cognitive science legitimized mixing and matching approaches from disciplines as varied as computer science, anthropology, linguistics, and philosophy with traditional psychological theories and research methods, which helped bring to the forefront context and culture as key factors in learning (apart from learners' individual psychology, or the particulars of an instructional design). Third, the rise of computer technology opened the doors to a design mindedness that matched well with teaching and educational psychology, arguably the first design-oriented domains within psychology.

Multiple Theories of Learning in Psychology

By the 1970s, psychology was in a marked transition. The dominant paradigm in the early twentieth century was behaviorism that focused on linking discrete stimuli to responses through association or reinforcement; however, behaviorism was challenged by a number of alternative paradigms that emerged after World War II. Work in linguistics, information theory, and the emergence of the computer led to ideas that sparked the questioning of behaviorism. For example, Chomsky (1959) suggested that behaviorist concepts could not explain the generativity of language. The growing movement toward taking "thoughts" and "ideas" seriously as psychological phenomenon was termed *cognitivism*. As behaviorism was being challenged by cognitive models of thinking, cognitive scientists were building artificial intelligence models of human cognition, and ideas about cognitive development were being developed and studied. For example, Schank and Abelson's (1977) book that melded together artificial intelligence and human thinking about events led to a great deal of research using the script concept to describe how people understood and behaved in real-world contexts (e.g., how one conceptualized a visit to a restaurant). Developmental psychologists were busy testing out Piaget's theory of cognitive development to test its explanatory limits. The Laboratory for Comparative Human Cognition (LCHC) led by Cole (e.g., Cole & Means, 1981) was busy examining how many of the tasks researchers took for granted as indicative of cognitive skill were viewed differently in other cultures. Meanwhile, cognitive psychologists were investigating the implications of the cognitive architecture of human thinking by studying memory, perception, language acquisition, and how people acquire and automatize skills (Gardner, 1985). At every turn, these psychological concepts were suggesting new ways to think about education and learning.

Computer science had a unique role in this mix of disciplines, both as a tool for empirical science and as a platform for intervention. Researchers saw the promise of cognitive science (both psychology and artificial intelligence work) to perhaps change the practices and approaches we had held onto so long in education. John Anderson and colleagues began studying "intelligent tutoring systems" (Anderson, Boyle, & Reiser, 1985) in which carefully constructed artificial intelligence models of problem solving in a domain such as algebra could direct a computer to provide guidance to learners. These tutoring systems were used to test and refine the induced models of how people think, but they also could be used to try to prompt and support students by solving problems along with them, and then giving feedback when the students' problem solving started to stray. Papert's (1980) book *Mindstorms* showed how children could invent and create using the LOGO computer language. The premise put forth by Papert was that learning could take place in interaction with tools for construction, and computers could be general-purpose tools for letting learners construct artifacts that reflected their understanding of a wide variety of domains. Bransford created the Learning Technology Center at Vanderbilt University in 1984 to develop new ways of using technology (especially video and computers) to help children learn; their interventions drew on what was known about how experts and novices think differently in learning domains, but also drew on ideas about more contextual aspects of learning, such as the use of authentic problems to motivate students. The recognition that technological artifacts and tools could change the way we think and learn was something that went hand in hand with the cognitive revolution; rather than simply deliver fine-tuned messages to students about what they should know, the cognitivists began exploring how learners constructed knowledge as they did the work of making sense of the world around them. Along with new theories of learning, new ways of researching needed to be developed because the process no longer was to simply test a theory, but to see how practices changed when new artifacts and ideas were introduced.

Broadening the Study of Learning to Include Context

Research from several different fronts seemed to point to the central role of context in understanding learning and development. As early as the 1970s, Cronbach (1975) highlighted the weaknesses in psychology's reduction of the study of education to two-way linear interactions between individual differences and educational interventions. What this perspective is blind to is both higher-order (nonlinear) interactions and the effects of learning contexts. Cole's LCHC group found that depending upon the context, what was intelligent behavior could be construed differently. Those studying Piaget's theory found that children's competence on tasks of logical thinking was alterable by changing the context of the task (e.g., McGarrigle & Donaldson, 1974). Those trying to implement tools like LOGO found that success required more than giving children the opportunity to interact with the computer program, and that the effects of a tool like LOGO did not generalize as widely as

people thought they might (Pea, Kurland, & Hawkins, 1985). Other attempts to implement what cognitive scientists thought would be effective in the classroom also ran into problems. Researchers studying memory wondered why students did not access the knowledge they had, and set out to discover what it would take to help them access their available knowledge.

The recognition of the importance of context suggested that the unit of analysis for understanding learning had to be larger than the individual person. People learned things with other people and generally learned with culturally developed tools and artifacts. Hence, studying these interactions, tools, and artifacts meant considering ideas from fields like sociology and anthropology, semiotics and linguistics as part of the research and theory-building process.

Four somewhat related theoretical ideas emerged to help frame this new understanding. First, there was the rediscovery of Vygotsky's theoretical work as presented in the *Mind and Society* compilation (Vygotsky & Cole, 1978). Vygotsky died in 1934, but his ideas were not widely known outside of the Soviet Union (and were suppressed there); hence, the ideas were largely unknown in the United States. They contained within them, however, ideas that resonated with the findings of individuals applying cognitive science in the everyday world. First, instead of being secondary, the importance of culture and the artifacts were primary. Both the learning of the individual and the adaptation of the species were tied to cultural artifacts and tools. People's cognitive processes are created in conjunction with the tools of the culture, and at the same time, the tools of the culture are enhanced by the thinking of people and societies. Additionally, Vygotsky's idea of the zone of proximal development (ZDP) led people to think differently about learning, assessment, and development. The idea of the ZPD is that the cutting edge of learning is not what students can do individually, but what they can accomplish with the help of a more able other.

Out of these ideas, in particular ZPD, Brown and Campione (1994) developed the Fostering Community of Learners model for teaching science. The approach involved developing group projects around thematic science units that featured (a) distributed expertise among students and (b) activities that create a discourse around topics that looked more like what scientists do than typically classroom science that focuses on vocabulary memorization and "canned" labs.

Also coming out of the renaissance of thinking about Vygotsky was the notion of distributed intelligence (Pea, 1993). As Pea notes, the concept of historically changing tools for thinking that arise from human cultures in Vygotsky's theory fit well with the notion that technologies provided tools that changed thinking processes in people. Pea and others suggested that the transformative potential of new forms of technology that were emerging not only made activities easier, but actually changed how they were carried out. In other words, what was intelligence was actually changed by changing the tools for thinking. Thus, Vygotsky's model also provided a way to conceptualize the transformative impacts of new technology.

Second was the idea of situated learning (Greeno & The Middle School Mathematics Through Applications Project Group, 1998; Kirshner & Whitson, 1997; Lave, 1988;

Lave & Wenger, 1991). For example, Lave (1988), who worked cross culturally and in everyday contexts like grocery shopping, found that learning in these informal environments was not something widely generalized, but tended to be highly tied to the activity context and its meaning for the people involved. Such analysis raised serious questions for traditional schooling, where the learning of students in formal classroom settings would purportedly transfer to new contexts in the everyday world. In contrast, a basic tenet of situated cognition is that in order to promote skill transfer from the learning setting to the "real world" setting in which the skills are expected to be employed, the conditions in the learning setting should be as similar as possible to those that the learner will encounter in the real world.

A third idea was that of anchored instruction (Cognition and Technology Group at Vanderbilt, 1990). The anchored instruction model arose out of the notion that in order for people to access knowledge, they need not only to experience it, but to experience it such that they can know when to use it. It is "conditionalized" (National Research Council Committee on Learning Research and Educational Practice, 1999) to particular classes of events. Without anchoring the knowledge to situations where the purpose of the knowledge is clear, then is likely to become inert. Ideas like these, and interest in applying knowledge in real contexts, led researchers to look for new perspectives. Out of work on anchored instruction came the *Adventures of Jasper Woodbury* (Cognition and Technology Group at Vanderbilt, 1992), a series of videodiscs (later CD-ROMs) that was involved in helping middle school students develop skills in solving complex mathematics problems by presenting the problems to them in simulated real-world contexts designed to be of interest to the students.

Fourth, Schank, bolstered by the insights gained from his computer models of how people think in the real world (e.g., Riesbeck & Schank, 1989), started a center for learning sciences that focused on developing similarly innovative approaches to professional development and training. Schank is generally seen as the first to use the term *learning sciences*, but his concept of the learning sciences did not encompass the diversity of perspectives that today make up the field (Hoadley, 2007). In 1991, the *Journal for the Learning Sciences* was started (Kolodner, 1991), followed by the International Society for the Learning Sciences.

As initiatives like these emerged, they contained some common elements that made traditional research methods problematic; yet researchers felt they were learning something fundamental about how students can learn. Traditional research and evaluation methods, such as randomized experiments, require controlling variables and manipulating only a few things at a time. Traditional program evaluation methods focused largely on outcomes without paying enough attention to the learning of researchers during the process of designing these interventions. Researchers felt they were learning something fundamental about learning as they developed new instructional approaches, and consequently felt the need to develop new methodological approaches. Brown (1992) and Collins (1992) created what was initially talked about as design experiments and later more generally described as design-based research (Design-Based Research Collective, 2003). The basic method involved documenting what was going on in an applied setting and examining the impact of complex instructional implementations as they went through different phases of design and development.

An example of design-based research is a project in which the second author has been involved. The project involves the development of engineering design challenges for middle school students. In that initiative, both the process of developing the modules and the examination of their effectiveness are being studied. Initial analyses involve examining frame by frame videotaped observations, seeing the effectiveness of the design model in action. Later on as the revision of the modules takes place, the results of adding new kinds of instructional tools or assessments to the modules will be examined along with more formal instructional outcomes. The focus will be on the innovative instructional processes and tools that are part of the creation of new instruction in school or other contexts. The process goes through periods of design and testing, with the processes and products of instruction being the the focus. Just as an engineer may come up with a design for a product that can be used in a variety of applications and tells us something fundamental about the nature of something, so too can instructional designers engage in a process that yields a process or product that can be applied to a variety of contexts and can tell us something fundamental about learning.

Although the notion of the learning sciences emerged before its publication, Stokes's (1997) book, *Pasteur's Quadrant,* framed nicely what learning scientists were attempting to do. Dismissing the unidimensional "applied vs. pure" distinction in science, he proposed two dimensions: application relevance and theory mindedness. The traditional view of the continuum as applied to basic research limited theoretical advances to tightly controlled experimental research. What Stokes pointed out was that the applied versus basic continuum only dealt with one dimension, practical use. It did not address the other dimension of theoretical relevance. Pasteur used practical problems that were studied without some of the tight controls of the laboratory, yet his research had important implications for basic theories in microbiology. Learning scientists, too, endeavor to do applied research that helps students and provides basic knowledge to the field of learning and instructional design. Stokes's book reminded researchers that applied research could yield generalizable findings that go beyond the specific context to a whole class of situations.

The Emergence of the Learning Sciences as a Design Science

Apart from its reliance on the multiple disciplines of cognitive science, and its willingness to consider context, the learning sciences are also noteworthy for their commitment to making education happen in authentic contexts. This commitment has several implications. First, the implementation requirement moves the learning sciences toward interventionist (and away from purely explanatory or predictive) goals. Second, because of the messiness of doing research in context, learning scientists are forced to consider methods that do not rely on tight experimental control. Hence, learning scientists have worked on developing design-based research methods.

To explore the role of design in the learning sciences, it helps to go back to the history of education as a discipline. Whereas learning is pervasive throughout the history of the human race, formal teaching, especially as practiced in the classroom, is a more recent invention. Our current practice of universal, formal primary education, oriented toward basic literacies (linguistic and mathematical), is only a few centuries old. Lagemann (2000) describes how the twentieth century saw the consolidation of teaching as an academic discipline, and how newly founded colleges of education had to fight for academic legitimacy. Since the enlightenment, the academy has placed increasing importance on scientific forms of inquiry and knowledge (as contrasted with humanistic or craft-based forms). In the twentieth century, two schools of thought helped constitute these new colleges of education. One, led by John Dewey, emphasized pragmatic inquiry, philosophically informed but intimately tied to practice. Among his other achievements, Dewey (1896, 1929) both advanced the field of philosophy through his notions of pragmatism, and founded the first "lab school" in which teaching and learning concepts could be informed by practice. On the other hand, psychologist E. L. Thorndike (1910) propounded a view of the field as a by-product of psychological research in the behaviorist paradigm, with an emphasis on controlled experimentation, psychometrics, and animal studies. (To be fair, the differences between these two scholars were in emphasis; both recognized the importance of experimentation and both recognized the importance of listening to practitioners, but their relative emphases concerning these activities were starkly different.) These two perspectives—education as a practice-informed profession and education as a domain of psychology—competed throughout the twentieth century, but it is fair to say the psychological perspective dominated for much of the twentieth century. In many ways, the politics of the definition of the field centered on three key issues: the relationship between research and practice; the epistemology and fundamental assumptions of psychology as opposed to other social sciences; and the tension between modern, positivistic science as embodied in Thorndike's views and the postmodern perspective that somewhat parallel Dewey's perspective.

So given the diverse roots, what makes the learning sciences perspective different from the points of view that came before it? One element of the learning sciences is openness to multiple perspectives on learning. That openness is necessary because it takes multiple perspectives to understand the complex ecologies in which learning is situated. Just as traditional instructional designers work with stakeholders, learning scientists need practitioners and individuals who see the world from the perspective of sociology and anthropology as well as psychology. Thus, most often learning scientists operate as teams rather than individuals. Note, that even though learning scientists try to look to more than psychology when it comes to learning and instruction, they would welcome a psychological perspective as one window on learning.

A second element that is important is a commitment to building solutions to the problems in teaching and learning in school *and* out of school. Learning scientists want to have an impact on learning and that means taking on the real world and its complexities. This often means studying the meaning of these complex contexts for learners at different stages of socialization into these contexts to understand how expertise is developed in real world.

Yet a third element is that knowledge of learning and instruction that is generalizable and meaningful can be acquired by studying the design process and is not just the province of experimental basic research done in laboratory settings. What this means for instructional designers is that they, too, can potentially contribute to the knowledge base by documenting and reflecting on the design process, and using it as a means to collect information that can drive theory. Obviously, not every project an instructional designer engages in will provide such insights, but documenting and reflecting on design projects in meaningful ways can lead to the development of new insights into how people learn.

A fourth element of the learning sciences perspective is to recognize the value of informal and nontraditional instructional contexts. As Bell, Lewenstein, Shouse, and Feder (2009) note, if one looks at schooling in the context of the learning someone does over a lifetime, then it is clear that much more of someone's life span is spent outside of school contexts in work and other situations. There is obviously value in studying learning in those contexts.

The fifth element is that learning scientists look to how new tools and artifacts created from the available technologies we have can be used to help facilitate learning. Just as an engineer might use a new type of material to create buildings that are better able to withstand hurricanes, learning scientists are interested in how the technologies that we have available can transform how we teach and learn. That means not only fitting technologies and tools into already existing structures, but also radically transforming those structures or even creating new ones (Collins & Halverson, 2009).

Findings and Design Implications of the Learning Sciences

In the prior sections, we have seen how the learning sciences capitalized on the multiple theories of learning arriving in psychology, drew on disciplines outside of psychology that better addressed issues of learning contexts, and maintained a hands-on stance toward designing interventions for both formal and informal learning contexts. In this section, we summarize some of the findings from this work over the last thirty years as they apply to the work of instructional designers.

We can divide the major findings and implications into three areas: research on thinking, research on learning processes, and research on learning environments.

Research on Thinking and Knowing

Research on thinking has helped fulfill the promise of cognitive psychology: uncovering the architecture of the mind and its workings. An excellent summary that holds up well despite its age is Newell and Simon's unified theories of cognition (Newell, 1990). One of the strongest findings has been that the mind, while incredibly flexible, appears to have specific limitations in how it can process information, relying on relatively specialized systems in the brain for functions such as vision, attention, memory, motor skills, language, and planning. Key findings have been the role of short-term and long-term memory, language, and skill in knowledge, including a rich idea of what it means to know something. Rather than assuming knowledge to be the ability to correctly recall facts, modern learning scientists distinguish between propositional knowledge, skills, and deeper conceptual knowledge. Additionally, research on individual differences shows that many individuals may learn the "same" content differently (i.e., forming different representations of the ideas depending on their mental predilections). Useful instructional theories connect to this broader version of knowledge, including Bloom's taxonomy, which highlights the difference between shallow and deeper forms of knowledge (Anderson, Krathwohl, & Bloom, 2001). Similarly, the theory of multiple intelligences reflects how different people may encode their understandings very differently based on sensory or learning preferences (Gardner, 1993).

Another key finding from the learning sciences is insight into the properties of expert thinking (Chi, Glaser, & Farr, 1988). Studies of chess players have shown that expert chess players not only know more about chess strategies, but their perceptions of chess boards are qualitatively different than novices—they can see problems in a way that leads to more economical thinking about solutions and allows them to better remember the positions of pieces on a board quickly shown to them. Further studies have shown that, in contrast with novices, experts possess a number of strong mental resources in every discipline studied. Experts can improvise to find solutions to problems using so-called weak methods, but are often efficient at using known solutions. Many of the skills needed to solve problems are "automatized," meaning they can be executed easily without conscious thought (e.g., compare the mental effort required the first time to drive a car versus after years of driving). These automatic skills free up attention and memory for other parts of problem solving. In many cases, experts have not only knowledge, smart perception, and skills on their side, but also sometimes "mental models," which allow them to predict or simulate how things work in the world before attempting to solve problems. Finally, experts are often very good at monitoring their problem solving, and using reflection and planning to achieve their goals (Gentner & Stevens, 1983; Schoenfeld, 1983).

The primary implication of this research for instructional designers and teachers is to appreciate the complexity of expertise, and to deepen the ways knowledge is both shared and tested. An emphasis on factual recall is guaranteed to produce "brittle" knowledge; whereas a focus on the development of instructional interventions that develop complex pattern recognition, build knowledge structures that focus on "big ideas," and supporting metacognitive processes are more likely to yield more durable learning.

Research on Learning Processes

Perhaps one of the biggest breakthroughs in the learning sciences was the examination of conceptual change (Vosniadou, 2008). Researchers found that constellations of memories, skills, perceptions, and ideas determined how people think and solve problems. Rather than starting as a blank slate, learners use their initial conceptions to think through problems. While refining that understanding or tweaking it is rather easy, much learning required deep reorganizations of ideas and ways of thinking about the world; for instance, distinguishing the scientific notions of heat and temperature requires sophisticated new ideas about energy, and suppressing the idea that things with high temperature necessarily have high heat energy (Carey, 1985). This complicated rethinking was not easy and required a great deal of mental energy on the part of learners, as well as careful support from the teachers; and the shifts that took place often mirrored (or were mirrored by) shifts in language (Driver, Leach, Millar, & Scott, 1996).

Advances were also made in understanding how literacies play a role in learning. On the psychological side, research helped to show the processes by which, for instance, students might decode a text, and make it correspond to their ideas about the world (Kintsch, 1998); or might try to coordinate an understanding of the world from multiple sources such as images and text (Mayer, 1993). In other domains, learners might develop understanding hand in hand with developing literacy of another kind, namely picking up the specialized representations used by experts in a domain, like the notation of mathematics or chemistry (Kozma, Russell, Jones, Marx, & Davis, 1996). Learning these literacies is more than psychologically decoding materials; it is also a social process of sense making and meaning making (Schoenfeld, 1991). Over time, learners who use representations socially will start to converge on a shared understanding that has not only formal meaning, but also social meaning (Roschelle, 1992).

More recently, researchers have begun examining the relationship between literacies, the practices of these literacies in particular contexts, and interest and identity development. Identity and literacies help link what were more traditionally thought of as distinct research traditions on culture, context, and transfer. For example, Nasir (2002) examined the ways African American learners differentially developed practice-linked identities related to math in the context of basketball and playing dominoes, and later how practice-linked identities form differently with respect to formal school contexts versus on the basketball court (Nasir & Hand, 2008). This representation of learners as existing in a ecology of learning resources in which they have to develop identity in various cultural contexts has been explored with respect to technology learning (Barron, 2006), science learning (Brown, Reveles, & Kelly, 2006), teacher education (Luehmann, 2007), and as previously mentioned, games and sports (Nasir & Cooks, 2009; Nasir, 2002). Continuing work examines how identity can be viewed as a sociocultural phenomenon, an act of narrative creation, a psychological process of interest development, or some combination of the three (Renninger, 2009; Sfard & Prusak, 2005). As traced by Lee (2008), this linkage between culture, identity, and learning has a long heritage of research in education, but was not historically linked to the dominant cognitive models of learning or instructional design.

In many cases, this connection to real meaning can make or break learning. Researchers found that relevance and authenticity are crucial elements in this meaning-making process (Cognition and Technology Group at Vanderbilt, 1990). Students who work on problems that (a) mean something to them personally and (b) are rich and complex enough to invoke real expertise, are far more likely to learn. Without authenticity, students might be motivated to learn within the confines of toy problems, but then would have difficulty applying their knowledge to other domains, the so-called transfer problem (Bransford & Schwartz, 1999).

The instructional implications of this research on processes include focusing on relevant, authentic tasks for learners, and focusing on the difficult process of conceptual change. To foster conceptual change, learners need to deeply engage topics in ways that may radically shift their concepts, even while building on their existing conceptions; and the learning needs to take place through literacies and representations that allow the learners to make meaning individually and with others (Donovan, Bransford, & Pellegrino, 1999).

Research on Learning Environments

Understanding learning does not always mean knowing how to teach. The findings of the learning sciences in the 1980s and later often had to do with ways of understanding teaching in the new perspective of constructivism—either cognitive constructivism (focusing on the learner as performing a psychological learning process) or social constructivism (focusing on the learner as a participant in a sociocultural process of learning). Donovan, Bransford, & Pellegrino (1999) term this the "learner-centered classroom," although increasingly as educators think about both formal and informal learning, the term "learner-centered learning environment" may be more accurate.

Perhaps one of the more robust principles in the learning sciences is that one can structure supportive learning environments without resorting to direct instructionist transmission of information. The main metaphor used in the learning sciences to describe noninstructivist teaching is *scaffolding* (Wood, Bruner, & Ross, 1976). This term, like *constructivism*, has come to mean many things in practice, but the common idea is that, like training wheels on a bicycle, the learner is supported in some way that provides room for exploration and self-directed learning, while still constraining the possibilities so as to minimize unproductive floundering.

Scaffolding takes many forms, ranging from computerized tools that support tasks, to activity structures, to larger social structures that support learning. For instance, an intelligent tutoring system might permit a learner to make only certain moves as he or she advances through the process of an algebra proof. The computer might use a model of human cognition to "follow along with" the learner. When the computer senses that the learner is not following a reasonable problem-solving sequence, it can leap in with advice or simply limit the possible steps the learner might take (Koedinger, 1998). Or, an online lab notebook might use a combination of hints, visualizations, and structured step-by-step supports to help students make sense of a desktop experiment (Linn & Hsi, 2000); or, a scaffolding scheme might not use technology at all. For instance, a technique called "reciprocal teaching" is used in literacy education (Palincsar & Brown, 1984). Students take turns using strategies to comprehend text. Initially the teacher models these strategies, and over time students take the lead practicing them. Even such a simple technique was found by Palinscar and Brown (1984) to dramatically improve how well students learned reading skills. Finally, larger social structures can be used to support learning. One of the predominant theories in this area is "cognitive apprenticeship," with the idea that learners become apprentices (of a sort) to experts, who model how experts think, coach learners as they practice problems (in context) with feedback, and fade their support and feedback over time to help learners become more autonomous (Collins, Brown, & Holum, 1991; Collins, Brown, & Newman, 1989). Rather than specifying a particular activity, cognitive apprenticeship spells out a relationship between novices and experts that allows transfer of expertise and supports learning. Such theories can be used to design social settings in which learners are able to construct an understanding. For instance, "computer-supported intentional learning environments" are a particular structure for classrooms, in which learners generate their own questions, then create, extend, and validate a shared knowledge repository (similar to how scholars conduct and share research) with the guidance of a teacher. A key aspect of such environments is that a certain sort of social context must be established, and the means for doing so is often not prespecified, but rather determined by the interaction between existing cultures and social contexts, and the educator's goals and relationships to those cultures and social contexts (Tabak, 2004).

Current research in the learning sciences (Dillenbourg, 2013; Prieto, Wen, Caballero, & Dillenbourg, 2014; Roschelle, Dimitriadis, & Hoppe, 2013) has further studied orchestration of the multilayered interactions that occur in learning environments like classrooms. Dillenbourg (2013) points out that the failure of technology integration in classrooms often lies in the lack of fluidity of classroom interaction around technology. In several studies, and with a variety of technologies, Dillenbourg and colleagues have shown that effective pedagogical use of technology in classrooms requires teachers to efficiently "orchestrate activities in the classroom. If students are to be engaged in problem solving, critical thinking, and more complex cognitive activities, they cannot be disrupted by complicated or inefficient or dysfunctional technological tools. The activities need to be set up with the appropriate affordances to allow the activities to occur seamlessly in a student-centered classroom" (p. 491). The work Dillenbourg describes involves part classroom management (making sure that time is not wasted and instructional time maximized) and part the creation and use of functional technological tools that can be easily worked with by students and afford rich learning experiences without much down time.

The concept of orchestration can be useful in that instructional strategies that afford learning in student-centered instruction emerge from the synergy of activities. Unlike in teacher-centered classrooms, where the events of instruction are fairly predictable, ordered, and controlled by the teacher, instructional moments in student-centered learning environments are dependent on students being synchronized with the instructional activities that the teacher guides them to in the classroom. Technologies that keep students on task and in sync are the ones that are most likely to afford learning. For example, Prieto et al. (2014) describe work done with "augmented paper" where students interact with paper objects containing icons that interface with computers. One instance that was widely studied involved using paper to design logistical systems in warehouses. Another simple, but useful technological tool involved a lamp that alerted tutors concerning the wait time for students in need of help. The lamp system reduced the wait time for students by directing the tutors to the students who were waiting longest for help. Consideration of technology and pedagogical strategies that improve classroom logistics can be use of instructional designers as they build and implement instruction. Although designers are knowledgeable of instructional strategies for student-centered classroom, research or models in instructional design on how to orchestrate the successful implementation of student-centered instruction across people, tools, and resources are more nascent.

Conclusion

As stated, the goal of this chapter has been to describe the learning sciences perspective and provide some insights that may prove useful to instructional designers. *How People Learn* (Donovan et al., 1999) summarizes this for designers and educators as the need for classrooms to be learner centered, knowledge centered, feedback or assessment centered, and community centered. Sawyer (2006b) summarizes this as a focus on conceptual understanding, putting learning processes on par with teaching processes, aiming for authenticity, building on prior understanding, and providing opportunities for reflection.

For further reading, we recommend these journals: *Journal of the Learning Sciences, International Journal of Computer-Supported Collaborative Learning, Cognition and Instruction,* and *Mind, Culture, and Activity*; the excellent volumes *How People Learn* (Donovan et al., 1999), the *Cambridge Handbook of the Learning Sciences* (Sawyer, 2006a), and *Knowing, Learning, and Instruction: Essays in Honor of Robert Glaser* (Resnick, 1989). For more on the relationship between the learning sciences and instructional design, we recommend a special issue on the topic in *Educational Technology* (Chellman-Carr & Hoadley, 2004).

In summary, research in the learning sciences has implications for instructional design by deepening our ideas about thinking and knowing, by illuminating the learning processes individuals go through, and by highlighting how learning environments can be designed to support learning. Although this chapter cannot encompass everything, we have attempted to identify major insights that may be most useful.

Summary of Key Principles

1. **Learning must be understood as a multidisciplinary phenomenon rather than just a psychological one.**

2. **Our understanding of learning and instruction is not limited to that which we learn through experimental research studies conducted in laboratory settings.** The process of instructional design can yield artifacts, tools, strategies, and ideas that enable us to get a clearer understanding of how people learn.

3. **Much of learning is a social process where people interact with others; thus, learning contexts and their meaning to learners are as important to analyze as individual learner characteristics.**

4. **Vygotsky's concept of the zone of proximal development suggests that it is important for instructional designers to pay attention how interactions between experts and novices can be structured to support the development of novice learners.**

5. **Learning environments can be designed that structure and support learning through scaffolding without resorting to traditional lecture techniques that view teaching as just the transmitting of knowledge.**

6. **The creation of learning environments that are authentic and relevant, as suggested by situated learning theorists and embodied in approaches such as anchored instruction, is important to the development of expertise (not just factual or procedural learning) in students.**

7. **Technology (both computer technology and other forms) can be thought of as creating tools that can transform thinking and learning.**

8. **Exploring expertise within a field can yield important information about how to design instruction within it.**

Application Questions

1. As an instructional designer you are asked to design an apprenticeship program for electricians. What are some ways in which taking a learning sciences perspective can help you to carry out this task? Describe the elements of the learning sciences that would help you with this task. How would knowledge of how expertise develops help you to create an effective apprenticeship program?

2. The traditional ways we teach science in schools has been to teach children science concepts and vocabulary primarily through lectures. You have been hired by a school district to redesign their physical science curriculum for seventh grade. The school district wants something other than lectures and canned laboratory exercises, but also feels that just

giving students hands-on activities where they explore materials will not provide them sufficient experiences to learn. Use what you know about the learning sciences to describe the kind of curriculum you would develop. What are some principles of the learning sciences that you would apply to the curriculum? What kinds of instructional activities would you include? How would you design the learning environment? How would it differ from the traditional classroom environment?

3. One aspect of the learning sciences is that technologies are viewed as tools for distributing workload, intelligence, and facilitating learning. Pick a technological advance or tool and describe how it can help facilitate learning from the learning sciences perspective. Provide an example of a context where it has the potential to transform how one learns. Examples of possible technologies include e-mail, blogs, discussion groups, videoconferencing, interactive video, handheld computers, iPods, smartphones, and so on.

References

Anderson, J., Boyle, C., & Reiser, B. (1985). Intelligent Tutoring Systems. *Science, 228*, 456–462.

Anderson, L. W., Krathwohl, D. R., & Bloom, B. S. (2001). *A taxonomy for learning, teaching, and assessing: A revision of Bloom's taxonomy of educational objectives* (Complete ed.). New York: Longman.

Barron, B. (2006). Interest and self-sustained learning as catalysts of development: A learning ecologies perspective. *Human Development, 49*(4), 193–224.

Bell, P., Lewenstein, B., Shouse, A. W., & Feder, M. A. (Eds.). (2009). *Learning science in informal environments: People, places, and pursuits.* Washington, DC: National Academies Press.

Bransford, J., & Schwartz, D. (1999). Rethinking transfer: A simple proposal with multiple implications. *Review of Research in Education, 24*, 61–100.

Brown, A. L. (1992). Design experiments: Theoretical and methodological challenges in creating complex interventions in classroom settings. *Journal of the Learning Sciences, 2*(2), 141–178.

Brown, A. L., & Campione, J. C. (1994). Guided discovery in a community of learners. In K. McGilly (Ed.), *Classroom lessons: Integrating cognitive theory and classroom practice.* Cambridge, MA: MIT Press.

Brown, B. A., Reveles, J. M., & Kelly, G. J. (2006). Scientific literacy and discursive identity: A theoretical framework for understanding science education. *Science Education, 89*, 779–802. doi: 10.1002/sce.20069

Carey, S. (1985). *Conceptual change in childhood.* Cambridge, MA: MIT Press.

Carr-Chellman, A. A, & Hoadley, C. M. (Eds.). (2004). Learning sciences and instructional design [Special issue]. *Educational Technology, 44*(3).

Chi, M. T. H., Glaser, R., & Farr, M. J. (1988). *The nature of expertise.* Hillsdale, NJ: L. Erlbaum Associates.

Chomsky, N. (1959). Review of B. F. Skinner, verbal behavior. *Language, 35*, 26–58.

Cognition and Technology Group at Vanderbilt. (1990). Anchored instruction and its relationship to situated cognition. *Educational Researcher, 19*(6), 2–10.

Cognition and Technology Group at Vanderbilt. (1992). The Jasper series as an example of anchored instruction: Theory, program description, and assessment data. *Educational Psychologist, 27*, 291–315.

Cole, M., & Means, B. (1981). *Comparative studies of how people think: an introduction.* Cambridge, MA: Harvard University Press.

Collins, A. (1992). Toward a design science of education. In E. Scanlon & T. O'Shea (Eds.), *New directions in educational technology* (pp. 15–22). New York: Springer-Verlag.

Collins, A., Brown, J. S., & Holum, A. (1991). Cognitive apprenticeship: Making thinking visible. *American Educator*, 6–11, 38–46.

Collins, A., Brown, J. S., & Newman, S. E. (1989). Cognitive apprenticeship: Teaching the crafts of reading, writing, and mathematics. In L. B. Resnick (Ed.), *Knowing, learning, and instruction: Essays in honor of Robert Glaser* (pp. 453–494). Hillsdale, NJ: Erlbaum.

Collins, A., & Halverson, R. (2009). *Rethinking education in the age of technology: The digital revolution and schooling in America.* New York: Teachers College Press.

Cronbach, L. J. (1975). Beyond the two disciplines of scientific psychology. *American Psychologist, 30*(2), 116–127.

Design-Based Research Collective. (2003). Design-based research: An emerging paradigm for educational inquiry. *Educational Researcher, 32*(1), 5–8, 35–37.

Dewey, J. (1896, Spring). [Original letter to the Trustees of the University of Chicago arguing for the creation of a Laboratory School].

Dewey, J. (1929). *The sources of a science of education.* New York: H. Liveright.

Dillenbourg, P. (2013). Design for classroom orchestration. *Computers & Education, 69*, 485–492. doi:10.1016/j.compedu.2013.04.013

Donovan, S. M., Bransford, J. D., & Pellegrino, J. W. (Eds). (1999). *How People Learn: Bridging Research and Practice.* National Research Council, Washington, DC.

Driver, R., Leach, J., Millar, R., & Scott, P. (1996). *Young people's images of science*. Philadelphia: Oxford University Press.

Gardner, H. (1985). *The mind's new science: A history of the cognitive revolution*. New York: Basic Books.

Gardner, H. (1993). *Frames of mind: The theory of multiple intelligences* (10th anniversary ed.). New York: BasicBooks.

Gentner, D., & Stevens, A. L. (1983). *Mental models*. Hillsdale, NJ: L. Erlbaum Associates.

Greeno, J. G., & The Middle School Mathematics Through Applications Project Group. (1998). The situativity of knowing, learning, and research. *American Psychologist, 53*(1), 5–26. doi: 10.1037/0003-066X.53.1.5

Hoadley, C. (2007). Theories and methods from learning sciences for e-learning. In R. Andrews & C. Haythornthwaite (Eds.), *Handbook of e-learning research* (pp. 139–156). Thousand Oaks, CA: SAGE Publications.

Kintsch, W. (1998). *Comprehension: A paradigm for cognition*. Cambridge, MA: MIT Press.

Kirshner, D., & Whitson, J. A. (1997). *Situated cognition: social, semiotic, and psychological perspectives*. Mahwah, NJ: Erlbaum.

Koedinger, K. R. (1998). Intelligent cognitive tutors as modelling tool and instructional model: Position paper for the NCTM Standards 2000 Technology Conference. Retrieved September 6, 2000, from http://www.carnegielearning.com/nctm2000.html

Kolodner, J. L. (1991). The Journal of the Learning Sciences: Effecting changes in education. *Journal of the Learning Sciences, 1*(1), 1–6.

Kozma, R. B., Russell, J., Jones, T., Marx, N., & Davis, J. (1996). The use of multiple, linked representations to facilitate science understanding. In S. Vosniadou, E. De Corte, R. Glaser, & H. Mandl (Eds.), *International perspectives on the design of technology-supported learning environments* (pp. 41–60). Mahwah, NJ: Lawrence Erlbaum Associates.

Lagemann, E. C. (2000). *An elusive science: The troubling history of education research*. Chicago: University of Chicago Press.

Lave, J. (1988). *Cognition in practice: Mind, mathematics, and culture in everyday life*. Cambridge, MA: Cambridge University Press.

Lave, J., & Wenger, E. (1991). *Situated learning: Legitimate peripheral participation*. New York: Cambridge University Press.

Lee, C. D. (2008). The centrality of culture to the scientific study of learning and development: How an ecological framework in education research facilitates civic responsibility. *Educational Researcher, 37*(5), 267–279. doi: 10.3102/0013189X08322683

Linn, M. C., & Hsi, S. (2000). *Computers, teachers, peers: Science learning partners*. Mahwah, NJ: Lawrence Erlbaum Associates.

Luehmann, A. L. (2007). Identity development as a lens for science teacher preparationb. *Science Education*, 822–839. doi: 10.1002/sce.20209

Mayer, R. (1993). Illustrations that instruct. In R. Glaser (Ed.), *Advances in instructional psychology* (Vol. 4, pp. 253–284). Hillsdale, NJ: Lawrence Erlbaum Associates.

McGarrigle, J., & Donaldson, M. (1974). Conservation accidents. *Cognition, 3*(4), 341–350.

Nasir, N. I. S. (2002). Identity, goals, and learning: Mathematics in cultural practice. *Mathematical Thinking & Learning, 4*(2/3), 213–248.

Nasir, N. I. S., & Cooks, J. (2009). Becoming a hurdler: How learning settings afford identities. *Anthropology & Education Quarterly, 40*(1), 41–61. doi:10.1111/j.1548-1492.2009.01027.

Nasir, N. I. S., & Hand, V. (2008). From the court to the classroom: Opportunities for engagement, learning, and identity in basketball and classroom mathematics. *Journal of the Learning Sciences, 17*, 143–179. doi:10.1080/10508400801986082

National Research Council Committee on Learning Research and Educational Practice, Bransford, J., Pellegrino, J. W., & Donovan, S. (Eds.). (1999). *How people learn: Bridging research and practice*. Washington, DC: National Academy Press.

Newell, A. (1990). *Unified theories of cognition*. Cambridge, MA: Harvard University Press.

Palincsar, A. S., & Brown, A. L. (1984). Reciprocal teaching of comprehension-fostering and comprehension-monitoring activities. *Cognition and Instruction, 1*(2), 117–175.

Papert, S. (1980). *Mindstorms*. New York: Basic Books.

Pea, R. (1993). Practices of distributed intelligence and designs for education. In G. Salomon (Ed.), *Distributed cognitions: Psychological and educational considerations* (pp. 47–87). New York: Cambridge University Press.

Pea, R. D., Kurland, D. M., & Hawkins, J. (1985). LOGO and the development of thinking skills. In M. Chen & W. Paisley (Eds.), *Children and microcomputers: Research on the newest medium* (pp. 193–212); *Logo programming and the development of planning skills*. Thousand Oaks, CA: SAGE Publications.

Prieto, L. P., Wen, Y., Caballero, D., & Dillenbourg, P. (2014). Review of augmented paper systems in education: An orchestration perspective. *Journal of Educational Technology & Society, 17*(4), 169–185.

Renninger, K. A. (2009). Interest and identity development in instruction: An inductive model. *Educational Psychologist, 44*(2), 105–118. doi:10.1080/00461520902832392

Resnick, L. B. (1989). *Knowing, learning, and instruction: Essays in honor of Robert Glaser*. Hillsdale, NJ: Lawrence Erlbaum Associates.

Riesbeck, C. K., & Schank, R. C. (1989). *Inside case-based reasoning*. Hillsdale, NJ: L. Erlbaum.

Roschelle, J. (1992). Learning by collaborating: Convergent conceptual change. *Journal of the Learning Sciences*, 2(3), 235–276.

Roschelle, J., Dimitriadis, Y., & Hoppe, U. (2013). Classroom orchestration: Synthesis. *Computers and Education*, 69, 523–526. doi:10.1016/j.compedu.2013.04.010

Sawyer, R. K. (2006a). *The Cambridge handbook of the learning sciences*. Cambridge, MA: Cambridge University Press.

Sawyer, R. K. (2006b). Introduction: The new science of learning. In R. K. Sawyer (Ed.), *The Cambridge Handbook of the Learning Sciences* (pp. 1–16). Cambridge, MA: Cambridge University Press.

Schank, R. C., & Abelson, R. P. (1977). *Scripts, plans, goals, and understanding: An inquiry into human knowledge structures*. Hillsdale, NJ: L. Erlbaum Associates; New York: distributed by the Halsted Press Division of John Wiley and Sons.

Schoenfeld, A. H. (1983). Episodes and executive decisions in mathematics problem solving. In R. Lesh & M. Landau (Eds.), *Acquisition of mathematics concepts and processes* (pp. 345–395), New York: Academic Press.

Schoenfeld, A. H. (1991). On mathematics as sense-making: An informal attack on the unfortunate divorce of formal and informal mathematics. In J. F. Voss, D. N. Perkins, & J. W. Segal (Eds.), *Informal reasoning and education* (pp. 311–343). Hillsdale, NJ: Lawrence Erlbaum Associates.

Sfard, A., & Prusak, A. (2005). Telling identities: In search of an analytic tool for investigating learning as culturally shaped activity. *Educational Researcher*, 34(4), 14–22. doi:10.3102/0013189X034004014

Stokes, D. E. (1997). *Pasteur's quadrant: Basic science and technological innovation*. Washington, DC: Brookings Institution Press.

Tabak, I. (2004). Reconstructing context: Negotiating the tension between exogenous and endogenous educational design. *Educational Psychologist*, 39(4), 225–233.

Thorndike, E. (1910). The contribution of psychology to education. *Journal of Educational Psychology*, 1(1), 5–12.

Vosniadou, S. (2008). *International handbook of research on conceptual change*. New York: Routledge.

Vygotsky, L. S., & Cole, M. (1978). *Mind in society: The development of higher psychological processes*. Cambridge, MA: Harvard University Press.

Wood, D., Bruner, J. S., & Ross, G. (1976). The role of tutoring in problem solving. *Journal of Child Psychology and Psychiatry and Allied Disciplines*, 17(2), 89–100.

Chapter 9
Motivation, Volition, and Performance

John M. Keller

Florida State University

Markus Deimann

FernUniversität in Hagen

Ashley, a 24-year old student, is in her first semester of a new master's program in educational psychology. Her introductory course is in a blended mode with a kick-off phase at the campus, an occasional meeting during the semester, and a large amount of independent study. She is happy to discover that this course utilizes many innovative technologies such as Weblogs, E-Portfolio, and Wikis. She is loving all the innovative teaching methods and strategies and one day she comes across an even newer innovation. She finds that she has the opportunity to select and enroll in a massive open online course (MOOC) at no cost. She is excited by the opportunity to add an elective course of personal interest and to experience still another innovative approach to course delivery so she enrolls in one. Consequently, her motivation is very strong and she is able to manage her assignments without any problems. However, after a while the independent study assignments, especially in the MOOC, become more demanding, other courses require more attention, and she spends more and more time socializing with her new friends in the master's program. Thus, Ashley's motivation for this course is not as strong as it was and she gets behind her schedule. As she approaches the course deadlines she is still having motivational problems and she finds it difficult to maintain a strong level of effort to excel on her tasks even though she wants to do well.

Ashley's efforts to regain strong motivation, avoid the distractions that have developed during the semester, and focus on her work require a special form of energy which is different from motivation. Called *volition*, it is beyond motivation and targeted on overcoming obstacles and hindrances during the learning process. Knowledge of the concepts related to this "special form of energy" is highly relevant for instructional designers because these concepts offer detailed knowledge that supplements knowledge of motivational processes and how to maintain one's persistence and performance. The purpose of this chapter is to provide an overview of principles of motivation and volition, how they are incorporated in a systematic motivational design process, and how they relate to challenges to motivation and persistence faced by all students at one time or another.

Concerns for learner motivation and motivational design processes have been growing in instructional systems design since the publication of Keller's (1979) article, "Motivation and Instructional Design: A Theoretical Perspective." Certainly there was a large existing psychological literature on motivation, but it did not provide an adequate understanding of how to integrate motivational principles into design process. Since 1979, there has been a steady growth of interest in this topic as a result of the work of people such as Wlodkowski (1999), Brophy (1998), the continued work of J. M. Keller (1999, 2008b, 2010) and the inclusion of the concept of volition, or self-regulation, in motivational design investigations of factors that facilitate or impede learner persistence (Astleitner & Hufnagl, 2003; Deimann & Keller, 2006; Kim & Keller, 2008), especially in distance education (Deimann & Bastiaens, 2010).

Even though there has been this increased activity, it can still be difficult for an instructional designer to obtain a quick overview of this literature and its relevance. Consequently, we have formulated six questions that provide a structure for understanding the current situation; the major characteristics of motivation, volition, and motivational design; and trends in this area of activity.

1. What do I need to know about motivation and volition? Why should I have to know anything about it if my focus is on instructional design and technology?

Employers complain that instructional design and technology graduates who are well versed in the various authoring and graphics applications for designing computer-based and Web-based instruction often produce instruction that is pedestrian, if not actually boring, and not sufficiently effective. To produce high-quality products, instructional designers must be thoroughly grounded in the processes of both motivational and instructional design. Recognition of this is illustrated by several instructional design texts that now include a section on motivational design (Dick, Carey, & Carey, 2015; Medsker & Holdsworth, 2001; Smith & Ragan, 2005).

Another reason for developing competency in motivational design is the trend to move from the perspective of instructional design to the broader perspective of human performance technology (HPT). From this perspective, instructional designers must understand and be able to identify all of the factors that influence human performance, which certainly includes motivation.

2. What is motivation (and what isn't it—what is it different from)?

Most writers in the field of human performance technology (Gilbert, 1978; Porter & Lawler, 1968; Rummler & Brache, 1990) identify three major categories of influence on performance. These can be classified as capability, opportunity, and motivation (Keller, 2008b). *Capability* refers to a person's knowledge, skills, and aptitudes, which determine what a person is able to do. *Opportunity* refers to resources and information that are necessary for a person to perform a task. These can include clear statements of goals, instructional content and tests that are matched to the goals, availability of tools and equipment, sufficient time to perform the task, and guidelines for performing the job. Finally, *motivation*, in its broadest sense, refers to a person's desire to pursue a goal or perform a task, which is manifested by choice of goals and effort (persistence plus vigor) in pursuing the goal.

To design effective learning environments, or to develop holistic programs of human performance development, the instructional designer must understand and integrate all three of these components in relation to their influences on effort, performance, and satisfaction (Keller, 1983a, 2008b, 2010). The motivational element is particularly important because it pertains to a person's basic decisions as to whether to accept responsibility for a task and to pursue a given goal. Without this initiation of behavior, none of the other things matter.

3. What are some of the key issues regarding motivational design principles and processes?

Issues in the study of motivation

Three issues that pervade the study of motivational concepts are intrinsic versus extrinsic motivation, states versus traits, and the affective versus cognitive domains.

Intrinsic versus extrinsic motivation.   Intrinsic motivation (Deci, 1975) occurs when one engages in a task for which there is no apparent reward except the pleasure of the activity. In contrast, extrinsically motivated individuals engage in tasks for rewards associated with successful accomplishment. Naturally, there can be a mixture of the two elements in a given situation, but there can also be conflicts such that extrinsic rewards reduce one's intrinsic motivation for learning (Deci, 1971; Lepper, Green, & Nisbett, 1973; Lepper & Greene, 1978). However, extrinsic motivation, when carefully prescribed, can be used to build learners' intrinsic motivation (Kruglanski, Riter, Amitai, Margolin, Shabtai, & Zaksh, 1975). The effective use of feedback and reinforcement must consider these relationships.

Trait versus state.   Motivational characteristics, like other psychological characteristics, have been conceptualized as both traits and states (Brophy, 1998; Keller, 1983b; Rotto, 1994). A state is a condition brought on by a situational stimulus or process, whereas a trait is a stable psychological drive or motive. Berlyne (1965) indicates that curiosity, for example, can be a trait, but it also has state characteristics—that is, people differ in their stable, trait-level degree of curiosity, but some situations will awaken state curiosity more than others. Rotto (1994) made the same point in regard to intrinsic motivation and other motivational variables.

Affective versus cognitive domain.   Some theorists have considered motivation to be contained within the affective domain and call motivational factors "non-cognitive" variables (Messick, 1979). The affective domain does, indeed, include emotions that are an essential part of motivation (Astleitner, 2001). However, motivation also has cognitive components. For example, attributional theories of motivation (Rotter, 1966; Weiner, 1974) are primarily cognitive. These theories focus on people's interpretations of the causes of outcomes and their perceived value as a major influences on the goals they pursue.

Issues in the study of volition.   Volition represents an old variable in the study of human behavior, which can be traced back to the beginning of scientific psychology (James, 1890). It is targeted on explaining phenomena of goal-directed processes such as persistence. The ultimate purpose of volition is to help people stay on task and overcome difficulties. In this regard, volition has been conceptualized as several interrelated control processes that facilitate goal-striving behavior (Kuhl, 1984). One of them is attention control, or selective attention, which shields a current intention against other, competing stimuli. To illustrate this mechanism, we refer again to our student Ashley who needs to complete an assignment in her MOOC before the weekend or risk falling hopelessly behind, especially with all the deadlines in her campus courses. After logging into the MOOC, she starts with a few thoughts and gets absorbed by the interesting topic. Yet, after a while, she suddenly is thinking about the upcoming birthday party of her best friend. Ashley has promised to assist her friend because this will be a big event with a lot of people she has not seen in a while. This leads to an inner struggle between two highly valued goals: completing the assignment satisfactorily versus spending time for the preparation of the birthday party. This is the point when volition can come into play and help people overcome such kinds of conflicts by focusing their attention on task-relevant issues and blinding out irrelevant thoughts.

Another important characteristic in the analysis of volition pertains to the ego-depletion effect (Muraven & Baumeister, 2000). Based on empirical data, the exercise of volitional control is like exercising a muscle; it can be exerted with great energy for a limited period of time but then becomes fatigued and requires rest in order to regain strength. Thus, volitional actions should not be applied over a lengthy period of time. The actual degree is subject to individual differences; that is, there is no general specification such as, for example, "the volitional muscle can only work for three hours a day." The instructional designer must design learning materials and environments in such a way as to keep distractions at a minimum and thus reduce the load on volitional efforts. This is analogous to avoiding unnecessary complexity or ambiguity in learning materials in order to minimize extraneous, or nontask-oriented, cognitive load (Pass, Tuovinen, Tabbers, & vanGerven, 2003).

In summary, these motivational and volitional issues are present in much of the literature on these topics, but they do not provide a sufficient basis for motivational design. There are two major requirements for establishing a systematic approach to motivational design. The first is to understand the major elements of human motivation and volition, and the second is to employ a design process that assists in diagnosing learner's motivational requirements and prescribing appropriate tactics. The next two sections of this chapter provide a brief introduction to major concepts and theories of motivation and volition and give an overview of design approaches.

4. What are the major concepts and principles of motivation and volition, in particular the ones that will be useful for me to know?

There are many characteristics of human beings that must be considered in understanding motivation and volition, and it can be extremely challenging to comprehend the full array of them from a direct reading of the literature. There are several syntheses (Keller, 1983b; Keller & Burkman, 1993; Wlodkowski, 1999) and contemporary textbooks (Brophy, 1998; Pintrich & Schunk, 2002; Weiner, 1992) that are helpful, but one is still faced with a broad spectrum of concepts, theories, and research.

However, Keller (2008a) has proposed a set of "first principles" of motivation that were derived from a synthesis of motivational and volitional constructs. The first four of these were first introduced in 1979 (Keller, 1979) and were elaborated in 1983 (Keller, 1983b), but they were not called "first principles" at that time nor were they stated in the current manner (Keller, 2008a) as basic principles of motivation to learn. In the current formulation, there are five principles and each has a theoretical basis in key motivational and volitional concepts (Keller, 2010). The five principles are:

1. **Motivation to learn is promoted when a learner's curiosity is aroused due to a perceived gap in current knowledge.**
   Broadly speaking, curiosity is aroused by uncertainty or a desire to close a perceived gap in one's knowledge due to such things as unanswered questions or unresolved conflicts. One of the best known researchers in this area is Berlyne, who introduced a distinction between perceptual and epistemic curiosity (Berlyne, 1965). Perceptual curiosity is characterized by reflexive reactions to unexpected and intrusive stimuli such as a loud noise or unexpected movement detected in one's peripheral vision and it is resolved as soon as the cause of the stimulation is perceived and determined to not be dangerous. Epistemic curiosity refers to a desire to gain knowledge to explain the causes of gaps in one's understanding or why something is happening the way it is (e.g., "Why is my car engine making that noise?" or "What did Einstein mean by $E=mc^2$?" or "What technique can I use to remember the geographical locations that are likely to be on the test?").

   It is also necessary to understand the dynamics of boredom (Geiwitz, 1966; Vodanovich, 2003) in order to understand curiosity. Boredom is not necessarily the opposite of curiosity; boredom results from being in an environment that is filled with uniform, unchanging stimuli such as a warm classroom with an instructor lecturing in a soft uninflected voice. It is possible to be curious about the topic but so bored by the delivery method that sleep is inevitable. People differ in their needs for excitement and stimulation (Zuckerman, 1979): Those who have higher sensation seeking needs have higher levels of boredom susceptibility and will require more frequent changes of topic, instructional tactics, or media to remain engaged in the learning process.

2. **Motivation to learn is promoted when the knowledge to be learned is perceived to be meaningfully related to one's goals.**
   Goals can be of many types. They can be concrete and specific such as earning an A in a specific course, getting a job with an accounting firm, or driving from Tallahassee to Houston in fewer than eleven hours. Goals can also be nonspecific and even emotionally based, as in wanting to feel good about oneself, having opportunities to enjoy friendly interactions with other people, or being successfully engaged in challenging activities. All of these goals can become a source of creating feelings of relevance among students. This is in contrast to a frequently held assumption that instruction must be perceived to be useful in order for

students to consider it to have relevance. Perceptions of usefulness or "authenticity" in a learning task contribute to relevance, but they are not the only important components.

Relevance can also be achieved by creating meaningful challenges, especially for people with high needs for achievement, and giving them a measure of control over setting their goals and the means of accomplishing them (Alschuler, Tabor, & McIntyre, 1971; McClelland, 1984). A related factor is the more general concept of interest. As Dewey pointed out, effort by itself might lead to accomplishment but it does not lead to motivated goal pursuit unless there are high levels of interest (Dewey, 1913), which in his conceptualization was a type of intrinsic motivation. Among other factors that help produce relevance are activities that contribute to increases in a person's feelings of competence (White, 1959).

3. **Motivation to learn is promoted when learners believe they can succeed in mastering the learning task.**
A central concept related to building confidence in mastering learning tasks is that of control. The belief or actuality of having control over a situation underlies many of the psychological constructs in this category such as locus of control (Rotter, 1966) and attribution theory (Weiner, 1974). These concepts refer to the degree to which people believe their achievements are the result of their own abilities and effort versus luck or other uncontrollable influences. Another related concept is self-efficacy (Bandura, 1997), which refers to the extent to which people can plan and implement behaviors that will result in successful goal accomplishment.

When people do not have positive expectancies for success or when they have been unable to avoid failures and catastrophes over which they have no control, they can develop feelings of helplessness. Called learned helplessness (Seligman, 1975), this condition refers to people who absolutely believe that they cannot succeed at a task even though they could succeed if they exerted sufficient effort. This condition can be overcome with strategies that help students attribute the outcomes of their behavior to their abilities and skills instead of luck or uncontrollable factors (Dweck, 2006).

4. **Motivation to learn is promoted when learners anticipate and experience satisfying outcomes to a learning task.**
Feeling good about accomplishments and not feeling inappropriately bad when not successful is a result of several external and internal factors. External factors include the use of reinforcement contingencies that provide appropriate rewards for accomplishments. There is a long history of behavior management strategies (Gardner, Sainato, Cooper, Heron, Heward, & Eshleman, 1994) based on the systematic use of rewards and penalties in accordance with operant conditioning principles (Beck, 1990). Extrinsic reinforcement can sometimes have an undermining effect on intrinsic interest (Condry, 1977; Deci & Porac, 1978; Lepper & Greene, 1975). A primary reason for this might be that the use of reinforcement contingencies to manage another person's behaviors tends to take personal control away from that

person and put it in the hands of the performance manager (deCharms, 1968; Harlow, 1953; Hunt & Sullivan, 1974; White, 1959). Thus, it is usually best, with regard to maintaining motivation to learn, to use feedback that is informational instead of controlling. In other words, use of feedback that reinforces a student for successfully completing an optimally challenging task by including a congratulatory comment together with an internal attribution for success helps sustain intrinsic satisfaction (Brophy, 1981).

5. **Motivation to learn is promoted and maintained when learners employ volitional (self-regulatory) strategies to protect their intentions.**
It is questionable that learners always follow a direct, uninterrupted path from goal-setting to goal achievement. Instead, students pursue not one but multiple goals aimed not only at learning but also at a variety of positive experiences. Thus, different goals interact in complex ways and change over time. For example, there is one type of priority given to growth goals (e.g., to deepen one's knowledge base); another type of priority is given to maintain emotional well-being (e.g., to look smart and protect one's ego). In cases when those goals collide, volitional strategies can help students prioritize their goals and avoid being distracted by those that are less important at a given moment (Kuhl & Kraska, 1989). However, this requires that students have facility in using volitional strategies.

When it comes to applying volitional strategies and concepts to an educational context, three basic steps have appeared to be useful. The first step involves a comprehensive assessment of a person's motivational and volitional characteristics. The second step pertains to intervention and entails a careful inspection of the learners' motivational and volitional profiles. The third and last step is about the evaluation of the treatment (see Deimann & Bastiaens, 2009; Kuhl & Fuhrmann, 1998; Kuhl, Kazen, & Koole, 2006; McCann & Turner, 2004). This can be carried out in a relatively straightforward manner by comparing the persons' motivation and volition function prior to and following the treatment.

Positive effects of utilizing volitional strategies have been reported in numerous studies. Pintrich and Schunk (2002) stress the importance of volition for college students "who, when you talk to them, are very motivated and concerned about doing well, but often have a very difficult time enacting their intentions, given all the internal and external distractions they confront in college life" (p. 126f). In a similar vein, Wolters (2003) highlighted the usefulness of volition in explaining how students manage distractions or other problems that might interfere with the timely completion of academic work. In this regard, it has become clear that motivational beliefs (e.g., task value, learning goal orientation) can be used to explain volition regulatory strategies (e.g., environmental control, interest enhancement) (Wolters & Rosenthal, 2000).

A major purpose of this chapter is to highlight the distinction between motivation and volition. Although both refer to the same overall principle, which is to facilitate goal-directed behavior, there are noteworthy differences, especially with regard to their implications for instructional design.

5. How can I apply this knowledge of motivation and volition in the context of instructional design and human performance technology?

The effort to build applied models of motivation is not new, but the emphasis has changed. Whereas early models tended to focus on one specific motivational characteristic such as the achievement motive, more recent ones are trying to incorporate a broad variety of relevant concepts in a holistic approach.

To do this, one has to estimate learners' motivational characteristics, and then design the learning environment to match the students' motivational requirements. This implies that one must work holistically with motivation and not be limited to one or two specific motivational characteristics.

There are two well-published models of motivational design that are holistic: the time-continuum model of Wlodkowski (1999) and Keller's ARCS model (Keller, 1984). Wlodkowski's model contains categories of motivational tactics and prescribes when to use them during an episode of instruction. The questions of how many tactics or specifically what kinds of tactics to use are left to the teacher's judgment.

The ARCS model also contains categories of motivational strategies and tactics but it contains a systematic design process that includes an analysis of audience motivation to determine the number and types of appropriate tactics to include.

The full application of the ARCS design process has ten steps (Keller, 1987, 1999, 2010) ranging from analysis through design and development to evaluation and it integrates well with lesson planning and instructional design processes. The process begins with information about the lesson or course to be enhanced, the teachers (if it is an instructor-led course), and the students. It then proceeds to an analysis of the audience and current materials for the course. Based on this information, the designer or teacher can write motivational objectives, select or create motivational tactics, and then develop and test them (Keller, 2010).

Both models are similar in that they focus more on generating motivation than on ways of sustaining persistence until the learning process is finished. Research on student support has been done in the context of the ARCS model to help students sustain their efforts in the face of compelling distractions (Visser & Keller, 1990), but this research did not systematically incorporate ways of managing the motivational fluctuations that might be encountered. For instance, our student Ashley may realize that her upcoming assignment requires much more time and effort than she initially thought. This creates conflict and pressure on her and she starts wondering whether she will be able to master the task. As a result of this, her motivation wanes and she is having problems maintaining her effort. Such a situation is not very unusual when trying to concentrate on learning, especially in settings that require a high level of self-regulation such as MOOCs.

Models of motivational design tend not to adequately account for these situations. Therefore, it would be beneficial to integrate volitional conceptions into motivational design to have a more comprehensive framework that can effectively explain typical motivational problems (Deimann, 2007; Keller, 2008b). Major aspects of Deimann's (2007) approach to integration includes an instrument to assess volitional competence and a pool of volitional strategies that can be utilized based on the person's profile and the conditions of the learning environment.

6. What are the trends or future directions in motivational and volitional research and application to learning environment design?

Research and development with motivation and volition is a broad and seemingly growing area of interest based on the constantly growing number of articles in major journals on these topics. However, there are several trends that are specifically relevant to the field of instructional design and technology.

First, there continues to be growing interest and research on motivation in Web-based instruction, computer-based instruction, and distance learning. In most distance-learning contexts, the noncompletion rate is undesirably high and learner motivation problems are generally considered to be a primary cause; however, the number of formal studies is fairly small, although growing (Visser, 1998). With respect to computer-based instruction, Song (1998), building on the work of Astleitner & Keller (1995), demonstrated how one can produce motivationally adaptive, computer-based instruction. He embedded motivational self-checks in a lesson. Based on the learner's responses, the computer determined the amount and type of motivational tactics to use in the subsequent segment of the lesson.

Second, the most dominant trend that has emerged since the previous edition of this book pertains to the growing importance of MOOCs, or massive open online courses, and they have many motivational challenges. MOOCs are a form of the larger open education movement and provide open and cost-free access to the course and offer a learner-led approach, which means learners can decide where, when, and how long they want to study (this was also the case in previous e-learning formats, but they also provided some form of guidance). MOOCs, instead, assume the ideal of highly self-motivated learners and do little to help them to cope with motivational problems. It is thus not a big surprise that the dropout rates are between 90 and 95 percent (Haber, 2013) and has caused a heated debated. Despite the compelling argument that MOOCs are a self-driven concept—that is, learners are in charge of their success and not completing all the materials and assignments does not constitute a failure—much more attention should be directed to motivational issues. Most of the MOOCs are building on a Hawthorne effect, which assumes that learners are motivated by the fact that they are taking part in an innovative event. But as with every innovation there comes a time when learners get used to it revealing deficiencies in motivational design. Fortunately for Ashley, the professor of her MOOC and his assistant had implemented an innovative motivation management system incorporating some of the strategies listed earlier in this chapter. She received messages of support in time to reinforce her intentions and help her get back on track.

Third, there continues to be interest in the design of blended learning environments which have their own motivational challenges, especially in large enrollment courses. An approach that has been taken in this context has been to provide motivational and volitional support to students by using motivational messages delivered via email as part of the online portion of the course (Keller, Deimann, & Liu, 2005; Kim & Keller, 2005).

Conclusion

Even a casual comparison of today's instructional design and educational psychology literature with that of fifteen years ago illustrates a dramatic growth of attention to motivational and volitional (or self-regulatory) factors in learning and performance. As with any field of research on human learning and performance, there is much to be learned, but there is also much that has been learned. In the past, motivation was generally regarded as being too elusive and changeable to encompass in a holistic theory or model of explanation and prescription; however, as shown here it is possible to build valid, systematic approaches to understanding and influencing learner motivation and persistence and this contributes significantly to the larger pictures of learning environment design and human performance development.

Certainly the field of instructional design can benefit from current research and practices in motivation and volition. Inasmuch as what causes someone to learn is never a precise science with easy-to-follow guidelines, incorporation of motivational techniques is essential to maximize learning. As stated earlier, motivation is an internal construct embedded in personal experience and expectations. Instructional designers must not only be fully cognizant of the entire range of motivational methods and models available, but also must know how to integrate them into a variety of instructional situations. Even the most accurate content, related activities, and diligent preparation can be ineffective without the systematic incorporation of motivation and volitional strategies.

Summary of Key Principles

1. **Motivation to learn is promoted when the following occurs:**
   - A learner's curiosity is aroused due to a perceived gap in current knowledge.
   - The knowledge to be learned is perceived to be meaningfully related to one's goals.
   - Learners believe they can succeed in mastering the learning task.
   - Learners anticipate and experience satisfying outcomes to a learning task.

2. **Motivation to learn is protected and maintained when learners employ volitional (self-regulatory) strategies to protect their intentions.**

3. **Instructional designers and teachers can predictably influence motivation and volition in a positive way by applying a systematic process of design.**

Application Questions

1. You see a room where learners are smiling and happy and the instructor is entertaining. You go into the classroom next door and the learners have serious expressions on their faces and are hunched over their desks with pencils in their hands. Would you assume that the learners in the first room have positive levels of motivation to learn and the ones in the second room do not? What indicators (evidence) would you look for in addition to the ones mentioned above? What evidence would support a conclusion of high levels of motivation to learn in one or both of the classrooms? How do the concepts of engagement versus entertainment fit in here?

2. Do additional research on Wlodkowski's Time Continuum Model of Motivation and then describe two or more situations in which his model would provide useful guidance. When it is time to prepare a list of specific motivational tactics to use in a given situation, how would the decision making process be different with the ARCS model than with Wlodkowski's time-continuum model?

Clue: With the ARCS model, what is the process for determining what motivational tactics are appropriate?

3. Ashley is elated to be accepted into the LPN (Licensed Practical Nurse) program at her local state college. She is thrilled because she has held this goal for many years. Her intention is to successfully complete the program, but beyond that, she wants to finish in the top 5 percent of her class. She begins the semester with hurricane intensity and receives top grades on everything as well as the admiration of her instructors. Midway through the semester, she is invited to join the women's volleyball team after a friend observes her excellent skills during a "pick-up" game with friends. She is almost immediately added to the varsity team and finds the competition and field trips to games at other schools to be exciting and satisfying. What kind of effect might this new goal have on her previous goals regarding her LPN program? What can she do to protect her original intentions? Use key concepts from this chapter in formulating your answer.

4. Search the Web using these two descriptors: arcsmodel and "arcs model". Be sure to use quotation marks around the two words ("arcs model"). Find two examples of postings in which people describe the ARCS model, an instructional design application of it, or a research project incorporating it. Describe and critique each example with regard to how accurately and completely it incorporates the key elements of the ARCS model.

References

Alschuler, A. S., Tabor, D., & McIntyre, J. (1971). *Teaching achievement motivation: Theory and practice in psychological education*. Middletown, CT: Education Ventures, Inc.

Astleitner, H. (2001). Designing emotionally sound instruction—An empirical validitation of the FEASP-approach. *Journal of Instructional Psychology, 28*.

Astleitner, H., & Hufnagl, M. (2003). The effects of situation-outcome-expectancies and of ARCS-strategies on self-regulated learning with web-lectures. *Journal of Educational Multimedia and Hypermedia, 12*(4), 361–376.

Astleitner, H., & Keller, J. M. (1995). A model for motivationally adaptive computer-assisted instruction. *Journal of Research on Computing in Education, 27*(3), 270–280.

Bandura, A. (1997). *Self-efficacy. The exercise of control*. New York: Freeman.

Beck, R. C. (1990). *Motivation: Theories and principles* (3rd ed.). Englewood Cliffs, NJ: Prentice-Hall.

Berlyne, D. E. (1965). Motivational problems raised by exploratory and epistemic behavior. In S. Koch (Ed.), *Psychology: A study of a science* (Vol. 5). New York: McGraw-Hill.

Brophy, J. E. (1981). Teacher praise: A functional analysis. *Review of Educational Research, 51*, 5–32.

Brophy, J. E. (1998). *Motivating students to learn*. New York: McGraw-Hill.

Condry, J. (1977). Enemies of exploration: Self-initiated versus other-initiated learning. *Journal of Personality and Social Psychology, 35*, 459–477.

deCharms, R. (1968). *Personal causation*. New York: Academic Press.

Deci, E. L. (1971). The effects of externally mediated rewards on intrinsic motivation. *Journal of Personality and Social Psychology, 18*, 105–115.

Deci, E. L. (1975). *Intrinsic motivation*. New York: Plenum Press.

Deci, E. L., & Porac, J. (1978). Cognitive evaluation theory and the study of human motivation. In M. R. Lepper & D. Green (Eds.), *The hidden costs of reward*. Hillsdale, NJ: Lawrence Erlbaum Associates.

Deimann, M. (2007). *Entwicklung und erprobung eines volitionalen designmodells [Development and examination of a volitional design model]*. Berlin: Logos.

Deimann, M., & Bastiaens, T. (2009, April 13–17). *The role of volition in distance education: An exploration of its capacities*. Paper presented at the AERA Annual Meeting: "Disciplined Inquiry: Education Research in the Circle of Knowledge," San Diego, CA, USA.

Deimann, M., & Bastiaens, T. (2010). The role of volition in distance education: An exploration of its capacities. *International Review of Research in Open and Distance Learning, 11*(1), 1–16.

Deimann, M., & Keller, J. M. (2006). Volitional aspects of multimedia learning. *Journal of Educational Multimedia and Hypermedia, 15*(2), 137–158.

Dewey, J. (1913). *Interest and effort in education*. Boston: Houghton Mifflin Co.

Dick, W., Carey, L., & Carey, J. O. (2015). *The systematic design of instruction* (8th ed.). Boston: Pearson.

Dweck, C. S. (2006). *Mindset*. New York: Random House.

Gardner, R., Sainato, D. M., Cooper, J. O., Heron, T. E., Heward, W. L., Eshleman, J. W., et al. (Eds.). (1994). *Behavior analysis in education: Focus on measurably superior instruction*. Pacific Grove, CA: Brooks/Cole Publishing Company.

Geiwitz, J. P. (1966). Structure of boredom. *Journal of Personality and Social Psychology, 3*(5), 592–600.

Gilbert, T. F. (1978). *Human competence: Engineering worthy performance*. New York: McGraw-Hill.

Haber, J. (2013, November 25). MOOC attrition rates—running the numbers. Retrieved from http://www.huffingtonpost.com/jonathan-haber/mooc-attrition-rates-runn_b_4325299.html

Harlow, H. F. (1953). *Motivation as a factor in the acquisition of new responses*. Lincoln, NE: University of Nebraska Press.

Hunt, D. E., & Sullivan, E. V. (1974). *Between psychology and education*. Hinsdale, IL: Dryden.

James, W. (1890). *The principles of psychology* (Vol. 2). New York: Henry Holt.

Keller, J. M. (1979). Motivation and instructional design: A theoretical perspective. *Journal of Instructional Development, 2*(4), 26–34.

Keller, J. M. (1983a). Investigation of the effectiveness of a learned helplessness alleviation strategy for low aptitude learners. In G. Zeeuw, W. Hofstee, & J. Yastenhouw (Eds.), *Funderend onderzoek van het onderwijs en onderwijsleerprocessen* (pp. 191–202). Lisse, The Netherlands: Swets & Zeitlinger B.V.

Keller, J. M. (1983b). Motivational design of instruction. In C. M. Reigeluth (Ed.), *Instructional design theories and models: An overview of their current status*. Hillsdale, NJ: Lawrence Erlbaum Associates.

Keller, J. M. (1984). The use of the ARCS model of motivation in teacher training. In K. S. A. J. Trott (Ed.), *Aspects of educational technology* (Vol. XVII). London: Kogan Page.

Keller, J. M. (1987). The systematic process of motivational design. *Performance & Instruction*, *26*(9), 1–8.

Keller, J. M. (1999). Motivation in cyber learning environments. *Educational Technology International*, *1*(1), 7–30.

Keller, J. M. (2008a). First principles of motivation to learn and e3-learning. *Distance Education*, *29*(2), 175–185.

Keller, J. M. (2008b). An integrative theory of motivation, volition, and performance. *Technology, Instruction, Cognition, and Learning*, *6*(2), 79–104.

Keller, J. M. (2010). *Motivational design for learning and performance: The ARCS model approach*. New York: Springer.

Keller, J. M., & Burkman, E. (1993). Motivation principles. In M. Fleming & W. H. Levie (Eds.), *Instructional message design: Principles from the behavioral and cognitive sciences*. Englewood Cliffs, NJ: Educational Technology Press.

Keller, J. M., Deimann, M., & Liu, Z. (2005). Effects of integrated motivational and volitional tactics on study habits, attitudes, and performance. In *Proceedings of the Annual Meeting of the Association for Educational Communications and Technology*. Orlando, Florida.

Kim, C. M., & Keller, J. M. (2005). Using motivational and volitional messages to promote undergraduate students' motivation, study habits and achievement. In *Proceedings of the Annual Meeting of the Association for Educational Communications and Technology*. Orlando, Florida.

Kim, C. M., & Keller, J. M. (2008). Effects of motivational and volitional email messages (MVEM) with personal messages on undergraduate students' motivation, study habits and achievement. *British Journal of Educational Technology*, *39*(1), 36–51.

Kruglanski, A. W., Riter, A., Amitai, A., Margolin, B., Shabtai, L., & Zaksh, D. (1975). Can money enhance intrinsic motivation?: A test of the content-consequence hypothesis. *Journal of Personality and Social Psychology*, *31*, 744–750.

Kuhl, J. (1984). Volitional aspects of achievement motivation and learned helplessness: Toward a comprehensive theory of action control. In B. A. Maher & W. B. Maher (Eds.), *Progress in experimental personality research* (pp. 101–171). Orlando: Academic Press.

Kuhl, J., & Fuhrmann, A. (1998). Decomposing self-regulation and self-control: The volitional components inventory. In J. Heckhausen & C. S. Dweck (Eds.), *Motivation and self-regulation across the life span* (pp. 15–49). Cambridge, MA: Cambridge University Press.

Kuhl, J., Kazen, M., & Koole, S. L. (2006). Putting self-regulation theory into practice: A user's manual. *Applied Psychology: An International Review*, *55*(3), 408–418.

Kuhl, J., & Kraska, K. (1989). Self-regulation and metamotivation: Computational mechanism, development and assessment. In R. Kanfer, P. L. Ackermann, & R. Cudeck (Eds.), *Abilities, motivation and methodology. The Minnesota Symposium on Learning and Individual Differences* (pp. 343–374). Hillsdale, NJ: Erlbaum.

Lepper, M. R., & Greene, D. (1975). Turning play into work: Effects of adult surveillance and extrinsic rewards on children's intrinsic motivation. *Journal of Personality and Social Psychology*, *31*, 479–486.

Lepper, M. R., & Greene, D. (1978). *The hidden costs of reward: New perspectives on the psychology of human motivation*. Hillsdale, NJ: Lawrence Erlbaum Associates.

Lepper, M. R., Green, D., & Nisbett, R. E. (1973). Undermining children's intrinsic interest with extrinsic rewards: A test of the overjustification hypothesis. *Journal of Personality and Social Psychology*, *28*, 129–137.

McCann, E. J., & Turner, J. E. (2004). Increasing student learning through volitional control. *Teachers College Record*, *106*(9), 1695–1714.

McClelland, D. C. (1984). *Motives, personality, and society: Selected papers*. New York: Praeger.

Medsker, K. L., & Holdsworth, K. M. (Eds.). (2001). *Models and strategies for training design*. Silver Spring, MD: International Society for Performance Improvement.

Messick, S. (1979). Potential uses of noncognitive measurement in education. *Journal of Educational Psychology*, *71*, 281–292.

Muraven, M., & Baumeister, R. F. (2000). Self-regulation and depletion of limited resources: Does self-control resemble a muscle? *Psychological Bulletin*, *126*(2), 247–259.

Pass, F., Tuovinen, J. E., Tabbers, H., & vanGerven, P. W. M. (2003). Cognitive load measurement as a means to advance cognitive load theory. *Educational Psychologist*, *38*(1), 63–71.

Pintrich, P. R., & Schunk, D. H. (2002). *Motivation in education. Theory, research, and applications* (2nd ed.). Upper Saddle River, NJ: Merrill Prentice Hall.

Porter, L. W., & Lawler, E. E. (1968). *Managerial attitudes and performance*. Homewood, IL: Richard D. Irwin.

Rotter, J. B. (1966). Generalized expectancies for internal versus external control of reinforcement. *Psychological Monographs*, *80*(1, Whole No. 609).

Rotto, L. I. (1994). Curiosity, motivation, and "flow" in computer-based instruction. In M. R. Simonson (Ed.), *Proceedings of selected research and development presentations at the 1994 National Convention of Association for Educational Communication & Technology* (ERIC Document Reproduction Service No. ED373 774).

Rummler, G. A., & Brache, A. P. (1990). *Improving performance: How to manage the white space on the organization chart*. San Francisco: Jossey-Bass.

Seligman, M. E. (1975). *Helplessness*. San Francisco: Freeman.

Smith, P. L., & Ragan, T. J. (2005). *Instructional design* (3rd ed.). San Francisco: Jossey-Bass.

Song, S. H. (1998). The effects of motivationally adaptive computer-assisted instruction developed through the arcs model. Unpublished doctoral dissertation, Florida State University, Tallahassee.

Visser, J., & Keller, J. M. (1990). The clinical use of motivational messages: An inquiry into the validity of the ARCS model of motivational design. *Instructional Science*, 19, 467–500.

Visser, L. (1998). The development of motivational communication in distance education support. Unpublished doctoral dissertation, Educational Technology Department, The University of Twente, The Netherlands.

Vodanovich, S. J. (2003). Psychometric measures of boredom: A review of the literature. *The Journal of Psychology*, 137(6), 569–595.

Weiner, B. (1992). *Human motivation*. Newbury Park, CA: Sage Publications.

Weiner, B. (Ed.). (1974). *Achievement motivation and attribution theory*. Morristown, NJ: General Learning Press.

White, R. W. (1959). Motivation reconsidered: The concept of competence. *Psychological Review*, 66(5), 297–333.

Wlodkowski, R. J. (1999). *Enhancing adult motivation to learn* (Revised edition). San Francisco: Jossey-Bass.

Wolters, C.A. (2003). Regulation of motivation: Evaluating an underemphasized aspect of self-regulated learning. *Educational Psychologist*, 38(4), 189–205.

Wolters, C. A., & Rosenthal, H. (2000). The relation between students' motivational beliefs and their use of motivational regulation strategies. *International Journal of Educational Research*, 33, 801–820.

Zuckerman, M. (1979). *Sensation seeking: Beyond the optimal level of arousal*. Hillsdale, NJ: Erlbaum.

Chapter 10

Evaluation in Instructional Design: A Comparison of the Major Evaluation Models

R. Burke Johnson

Angelia Bendolph

University of South Alabama

One of the fundamental components of instructional design is evaluation. The purpose of this chapter is to describe several of the most influential and useful evaluation models.

In 1967 Michael Scriven coined the terms *formative* and *summative evaluation*. These concepts are still used today. Here are Scriven's (1991) definitions of formative and summative evaluation:

> *Formative evaluation* is evaluation designed, done, and intended to support the process of improvement, and normally commissioned or done by, and delivered to, someone who can make improvements. *Summative evaluation* is the rest of evaluation: In terms of intentions, it is evaluation done for, or by, any observers or decision makers (by contrast with developers) who need evaluative conclusions for any reasons besides development. (p. 20)

The evaluation processes described in early instructional design models incorporated two key features. First, testing should focus on the objectives that have been stated for the instruction. This is referred to as *criterion-referenced* (or *objective-referenced*) testing. The argument is made that the assessment instruments for systematically designed instruction should focus on the skills that the learners have been told will be taught in the instruction. The purpose of testing is not to sort the learners to assign grades, but rather to determine the extent to which each objective in the instruction has been mastered. Assessments, be they multiple-choice items, essays, or products developed by the learners, should require learners to demonstrate the skills as they are described in the objectives in the instruction.

The second feature is a focus on the learners as the primary source of data for making decisions about the instruction. Although subject-matter experts (SMEs) are typically members of the instructional design team, they cannot always accurately predict which instructional strategies will be effective. Formative evaluation in instructional design should include a SME review, and that of an editor, but the major source of input to this process is the learner. Formative evaluation focuses on learners' ability to learn from the instruction, and to enjoy it.

Defining Evaluation

To begin, we provide a formal definition of *evaluation*. Because of the prominence of Scriven's work in evaluation, we will use his popular definition (Scriven, 1991, p. 139): "Evaluation is the process of determining the merit, worth, and value of things, and evaluations are the products of that process." By *merit* Scriven is referring to the "intrinsic value" of the evaluation object or *evaluand*. By *worth*, Scriven is referring to the "market value" of the evaluand or its value to a stakeholder, an organization, or some other collective. By *value*, Scriven has in mind the idea that evaluation always involves the making of evaluative judgments. Scriven contends that this valuing process operates for both formative and summative evaluation.

Scriven (1980) also provides a "logic of evaluation" that includes four steps. First, select the criteria of merit or worth. Second, set specific performance standards (i.e., the level of performance required) for your criteria. Third, collect performance data and compare the level of observed performance with the level of required performance dictated by the performance standards. Fourth, make the evaluative (i.e., value) judgment(s). In short, evaluation is about identifying criteria of merit and worth, setting standards, collecting data, and making value judgments.

The Major Evaluation Models

Many evaluation models were developed in the 1970s and 1980s. These evaluation models were to have a profound impact on how designers would come to use the evaluation process. The models were used on projects that included extensive development work, multiple organizations and agencies, and multiple forms of instructional delivery. These projects tended to have large budgets and many staff members, and were often housed in universities. The projects had multiple goals that were to be achieved over time. Examples were teacher corps projects aimed at reforming teacher education and math projects that attempted to redefine what and how children learned about mathematics. These projects often employed "new" models of evaluation. Perhaps the most influential model of that era was the CIPP model developed by Stufflebeam (1971).

Stufflebeam's CIPP Evaluation Model

The CIPP acronym stands for Context, Input, Process, and Product. These are four distinct types of evaluation, and they all can be done in a single comprehensive evaluation or a single type can be done as a stand-alone evaluation.

Context evaluation is the assessment of the environment in which an innovation or program will be used, to determine the need and objectives for the innovation and to identify the factors in the environment that will impact the success of its use. This analysis is frequently called a *needs assessment*, and it is used in making *program planning decisions*. According to Stufflebeam's CIPP model, the evaluator should be present from the beginning of the project, and should assist in the conduct of the needs assessment.

The second step or component of the CIPP model is *input evaluation*. Here, evaluation questions are raised about the resources that will be used to develop and conduct the innovation/program. What people, funds, space, and equipment will be available for the project? Will these be sufficient to produce the desired results? Is the conceptualization of the program adequate? Will the program design produce the desired outcomes? Are the program benefits expected to outweigh the costs of the prospective innovation/program? This type of evaluation is helpful in making *program structuring decisions*. The evaluator should play a key role in input evaluation.

The third step or component of CIPP is *process evaluation.* This corresponds closely to *formative evaluation.* Process evaluation is used to examine the ways in which an innovation/program is being developed, the way it is implemented, the initial effectiveness, and the effectiveness after revisions. Data are collected to inform the project leader (and other program personnel) about the status of the project, how it is implemented, whether it meets legal and conceptual guidelines, and how the innovation is revised to meet the implementation objectives. Process evaluation is used to make *implementation decisions.*

The fourth component of CIPP is *product evaluation,* which focuses on the success of the innovation/program in producing the desired outcomes. Product evaluation includes measuring the outcome variables specified in the program objectives, identifying unintended outcomes, assessing program merit, and conducting cost analyses. Product evaluation is useful in making

summative evaluation decisions (e.g., "What is the overall merit and worth of the program? Should it be continued?").

Introduction of the CIPP model to instructional design changed the involvement of the evaluator in the development process. The evaluator became a member of the project team. Furthermore, evaluation was no longer something that just happens at the end of a project, but became a formal process continuing throughout the life of a project.[1]

Rossi's Five-Domain Evaluation Model

Starting in the late 1970s and continuing to today, Peter Rossi and his colleagues developed a useful evaluation model (Rossi, Lipsey, & Freeman, 2004). According to this model, each evaluation should be tailored to fit local needs, resources, and type of program. This includes tailoring the evaluation questions ("What is the evaluation purpose?" "What specifically needs to be evaluated?"), methods and procedures (selecting those that balance feasibility and rigor), and the nature of the evaluator–stakeholder relationship ("Who should be involved?" "What level of participation is desired?" "Should an internal or an external/independent evaluator be used?"). For Rossi, the evaluation questions constitute the core, from which the rest of the evaluation evolves. Therefore, it is essential that you and the key stakeholders construct a clear and agreed upon set of evaluation questions.

The Rossi model emphasizes five primary evaluation domains. Any or all domains can be conducted in an evaluation. First is *needs assessment,* which addresses this question, "Is there a need for this type of program in this context?" A *need* is the gap between the actual and desired state of affairs. Second is program *theory assessment,* which addresses this question, "Is the program conceptualized in a way that it should work?" It is the evaluator's job to help the client explicate the theory (how and why the program operates and produces the desired outcomes) if it is not currently documented. If a program is not based on sound social, psychological, and educational theory, it cannot be expected to work—this problem is called *theory failure.* Third is *implementation assessment,* which addresses this question: "Was this program implemented properly and according to the program manual?" If a program is not properly operated and delivered, it can't succeed—this problem is called *implementation failure.*

The fourth evaluation domain is synonymous with the traditional social science approach to evaluation, and the fifth domain is synonymous with the economic approach to evaluation. The fourth domain, *impact assessment,* addresses this question: "Did this program have an impact on its intended targets?" This is the question of cause and effect. To establish cause and effect, you should use a strong experimental research design (if possible). The fifth domain, *efficiency assessment,* addresses this question: "Is the program cost effective?" It is possible that a particular program has an impact but it is *not* cost effective. For example, the return on investment might be

---

[1]The CIPP model continues to be a popular evaluation model today. For more information about this model (including model updates), as well as some of the other models discussed here, go to the Evaluation Center website at Western Michigan, https://www.wmich.edu/evaluation/checklists.

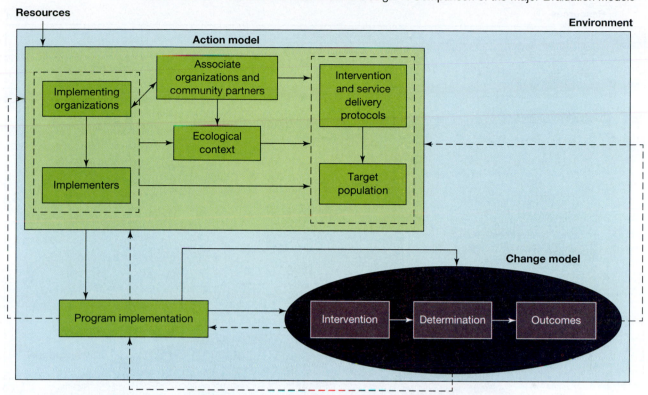

FIGURE 10.1   TDE program theory schema, including action model and change model (provided to B. Johnson by H. Chen, August 13, 2015).

negative, the costs might outweigh the benefits, or the program might not be as efficient as a competitive program. The efficiency ratios used in these types of analysis are explained in a footnote.[2] Because of the importance of *program theory* we next discuss Huey Chen's theory-driven evaluation.

Chen's Theory-Driven Evaluation Model

Theory-driven evaluation (TDE) is an evaluation approach where evaluators and stakeholders determine how and why an intervention/program works as an important part of the evaluation (Chen, 2015). The TD evaluator helps articulate, evaluate, and improve the *program theory*, which is the stakeholders' implicit and explicit assumptions about how a program responds to a problem and the actions required to solve the

problem (Chen, 2015). An advantage of theory-driven evaluation is that it uncovers and articulates the areas that "black-box evaluation" (which focuses only on desired outcomes and not the processes between input and output) and "method-driven evaluation" (which emphasizes prioritized research methods and focuses only on impact) do not.

The paradigmatic TDE program theory schema is shown in Figure 10.1. A program theory includes an action model and a change model. The program theory is used to drive the theory-driven approach for program planning and evaluation (Chen, 2015). An *action model* is the program's systematic plan for organizing resources, settings, staff, and support organizations to deliver intervention services and to reach the target population. An action model includes the following: (1) an intervention protocol and service delivery protocol (which details an intervention's operating procedures and perspective and includes the steps needed to deliver the intervention in the field), (2) implementing organization(s) (i.e., the organization(s) that allocates resources, recruits, supervises, and trains implementers and coordinates activities), (3) implementers (i.e., the persons who deliver services to clients), (4) associated organizations and community partners (i.e., interested interorganizational stakeholders, to establish collaboration between community partners and associate organizations), (5) ecological context (i.e., the segment of the environment that interacts directly with the program), and (6) the target population (i.e., the group of people receiving the intended services) (Chen, 2015). The action model includes a lot of useful information, and it is an important tool to be constructed and used during the planning and conduct of a TDE.

---

[2]In business, financial results are often measured using the *return on investment* (ROI) index. ROI is calculated by subtracting total dollar costs associated with the program from total dollar benefits (this difference is called *net benefits*); then dividing the difference by total dollar costs, and multiplying the result by 100. A ROI value greater than zero indicates a positive return on investment. A *cost-benefit analysis* is commonly used with governmental programs; this relies on the *benefit-cost ratio*, which is calculated by dividing total dollar benefits by total dollar costs. A benefit-cost ratio of 1 is the break-even point, and values greater than 1 mean the benefits are greater than the costs. Because it can be difficult to translate benefits resulting from training and other interventions into dollar units (e.g., attitudes, satisfaction), *cost-effectiveness analysis* is often used rather than cost-benefit analysis. To calculate the *cost-effectiveness ratio* the evaluator translates training program costs into dollar units but leaves the measured benefits in their original (nondollar) units. A cost-effectiveness ratio tells you how much "bang for the buck" your training provides (e.g., how much improvement in job satisfaction is gained per dollar spent on training).

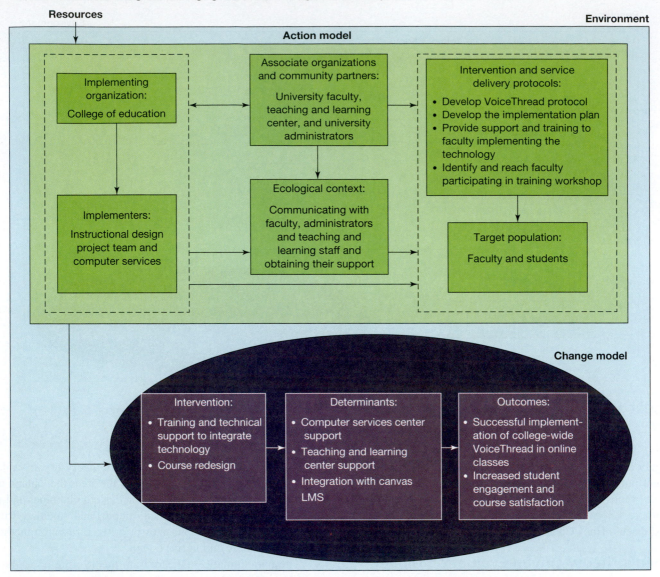

FIGURE 10.2 Program theory of VoiceThread software implementation.

The *change model* is the program's description of the causal processes and outcomes required to resolve the identified problem(s). A change model includes three major elements: (1) the intervention (i.e., activity aimed directly at changing a problem), (2) causal determinants (i.e., causes of the problem or leverages, moderator variables, and intervening variables), and (3) program outcomes (i.e., changes on targeted proximal and distal dependent variables) (Chen, 2015). As shown in Figure 10.1, appropriate implementation of the components of the action model is critical for the change model's transformation process to be activated (Chen, 2015).

We now provide a brief example of a TDE, illustrating the program theory for a technology integration program at a university in the southeastern United States.[3] Specifically, the

college of education at this university added VoiceThread to its campus learning-management-system toolkit. (VoiceThread is a software program that allows images, documents, and videos to be added to asynchronous discussion forums in online courses.) Figure 10.2 shows the program theory, including the action and change models. Take a moment now to examine the content in that figure.

The evaluation involved the following processes. The evaluator served as facilitator of the TDE process, helping outline the program theory and assumptions of the faculty and administration in the college of education and the computer center. The evaluator used the working-group-meeting process (Chen, 2015) to articulate and develop the program theory by interacting with representatives from the college of education, the instructional design project team, computer services, university faculty, the teaching and learning center, and university administrators. In this evaluation, forward reasoning was used to construct the action model

[3]This example is hypothetical and was inspired by Pacansky-Brock, M. (2012, January 12). *Integrating VoiceThread into Your Campus-Wide Toolkit*. Retrieved from http://blog.voicethread.com/webinars-all/

(i.e., general program goals were articulated to determine the action model); backward reasoning (i.e., movement from the change model to the action model to determine program goals) was used to construct the change model; and the two approaches were integrated to determine the overall program theory. Initial program implementation was evaluated using constructive evaluation, which included a troubleshooting strategy (specifically, formative evaluation and program review/development meeting) and a development partnership strategy (where program stakeholders and the program evaluator collaborated). This was intended for internal use to immediately address the problems in the program. Next, using a hybrid process evaluation, the evaluator collected data on how the intervention was implemented. Finally, outcome data were examined to determine whether implementation contributed to changes on the outcome measures. The evaluation included communicating with stakeholders on the procedures of the evaluation, the program plan and the action model, as well as collecting data using a combination of qualitative and quantitative methods (Chen, 2015). In this evaluation, results indicated that the program theory was sound and implementation produced the desired results on several outcome measures. The results and action plan were first presented to the dean of the college of education (who commissioned the evaluation) and then to the other stakeholders.

Kirkpatrick's Training Evaluation Model

Kirkpatrick's model was published initially in four articles in 1959 and is still frequently used today.[4] Kirkpatrick specifically developed his model for *training* evaluation. What he originally referred to as *steps* later became the *four levels* of evaluation. Evaluators might only conduct evaluations at the early steps or they might evaluate at all four levels. The early levels of evaluation are useful by themselves, and they are useful in helping one interpret evaluation results from the higher

levels. For example, one reason transfer of training (level 3) might not take place is because learning of the skills (level 2) never took place; likewise, satisfaction (level 1) is often required if learning (level 2) and other results (levels 3 and 4) are to occur.

Level 1: Reaction.   Kirkpatrick's first level is the assessment of learners' reactions or attitudes toward the learning experience. Anonymous questionnaires should be used to get honest reactions from learners about the training. These reactions, along with those of the training director, are used to evaluate the instruction, but should not serve as the only type of evaluation. It is generally assumed that if learners do not like the instruction, it is unlikely that they will learn from it.

Although level 1 evaluation is used to study the reactions of participants in training programs, it is important to understand that data can be collected on more than just a single *overall* reaction or customer satisfaction with the program (e.g., "How satisfied were you with the training event?") Detailed level 1 information should also be collected about training components and experiences (such as the instructor, the topics, the presentation style, perceived engagement, the schedule, the facility, the learning activities, and how engaged participants felt during the training event). We recommend also including open-ended items (i.e., where respondents respond in their own words): (1) "What do you believe are the three most important strengths of the training program?" and (2) "What do you believe are the three most important weaknesses of the training program?" It is usually best to use a mixture of open-ended items (such as the two questions just provided) and closed-ended items (such as providing a statement or item stem such as, "The material covered in the program was relevant to my job," and asking respondents to use a four-point rating scale, such as very dissatisfied, dissatisfied, satisfied, very satisfied).[5] The research design typically used for level 1 evaluation is the one-group posttest-only design (Table 10.1).

TABLE 10.1	**Research Designs Commonly Used in Training Evaluation**			
Design Strength	**Design Depiction**			**Design Name**
1. Very weak		X	O_2	One-group posttest-only design
2. Moderately weak	O_1	X	O_2	One-group pretest-posttest design
3. Moderately strong	O_1	X	O_2	Nonequivalent comparison-group design
	O_1		O_2	
4. Very strong	RA	O_1	X	O_2	Pretest-posttest control-group design
	RA	O_1		O_2	

Note: X stands for the treatment (i.e., the training event), O_1 stands for pretest measurement, O_2 stands for posttest measurement, and RA stands for random assignment of participants to the groups. Design 3 has a control group but the participants are not randomly assigned to the groups; therefore, the groups are to a greater or lesser degree, "nonequivalent." Design 4 has random assignment and is the gold standard for providing evidence for cause and effect. (For more information on these and other research designs, see Johnson & Christensen, 2014.)

---

[4]For more information on the Kirkpatrick model go to http://www.kirkpatrick-partners.com/OurPhilosophy/TheKirkpatrickModel.

[5]Kirkpatrick (2006) provides several examples of questionnaires that you can use or modify for your evaluations.

Level 2: Learning. In level 2 evaluation, the goal is to determine what the participants in the training program learned as well as their confidence that they can use it later and their commitment to use it later. By *learning,* Kirkpatrick (2006) has in mind "the extent to which participants change attitudes, improve knowledge, and/or increase skill as a result of attending the program" (p. 20). Training events will be focused on creating a combination of *knowledge* ("I know it"), *skills* ("I can do it"), *attitudes* ("I believe this will be worthwhile to do on the job"), *confidence* ("I think I can use it on my job"), and *commitment* ("I intend to use it later on my job").

In addition to the perceptions just listed, level 2 evaluation should always include measurement of what specifically was covered in the training event and listed on the learning objectives. The tests should cover the material that was presented to the learners in order to have a valid measure of the amount of learning that has taken place. Knowledge is typically measured with an *achievement test* (i.e., a test designed to measure the degree of knowledge learning that has taken place after a person has been exposed to a specific learning experience); skills are typically measured with a *performance test* (i.e., a testing situation where test takers demonstrate some real-life behavior such as creating a product or performing a process); and attitudes and perceptions are typically measured with a *questionnaire* (i.e., a self-report data-collection instrument filled out by research participants designed to measure, in this case, the attitudes targeted for change in the training event).

The one-group pretest-posttest design is often sufficient for a level 2 evaluation. As you can see in Table 10.1, this research design involves a pretest and posttest measurement of the training group participants on the outcome(s) of interest. The estimate of learning improvement is the difference between the pretest and posttest scores. Kirkpatrick appropriately recommends that a control group also be used when possible in level 2 evaluation because it allows stronger inferences about causation. This typically means that you will use the nonequivalent comparison-group design shown in Table 10.1 to demonstrate that learning has occurred as a result of the instruction. Learning data are not only helpful for documenting learning, but also for training directors in justifying their training function in their organizations.

Level 3: Behavior (transfer of training). Here the evaluator's goal is to determine whether the training program participants change their on-the-job behavior (OJB) as a result of having participated in the training program. Learning in the classroom or other training stetting is no guarantee that a person will demonstrate those same skills in the real-world job setting. The training director should conduct a follow-up evaluation several months after the training to determine whether the knowledge, attitudes, and skills learned are being used on the job.

Kirkpatrick (2006) identifies five environments that affect transfer of training: (1) preventing environments (e.g., where the trainee's supervisor does not allow the trainee to use the new knowledge, attitudes, or skills), (2) discouraging environments (e.g., where the supervisor discourages use of the new knowledge, attitudes, or skills), (3) neutral environments (e.g., where the supervisor does not acknowledge that the training ever took place), (4) encouraging environments (e.g., where the supervisor encourages the trainee to use new knowledge, attitudes, and skills on the job), and (5) requiring environments (e.g., where the supervisor monitors and requires use of the new knowledge, attitudes, and skills in the work environment).

To determine whether the knowledge, skills, and attitudes are being used on the job, and how well, it is necessary to contact the learners and their supervisors, peers, and subordinates. Kirkpatrick oftentimes seems satisfied with the use of what we call a *retrospective survey design* (asking questions about the past in relation to the present) to measure transfer of training. A retrospective survey involves interviewing or having trainees and their supervisors, peers, and subordinates fill out questionnaires several weeks and months after the training event to measure their perceptions about whether the trainees are applying what they learned. To provide a more objective indication of transfer to the workplace, Kirkpatrick suggests using designs 2, 3, and 4 (shown in Table 10.1). Level 3 evaluation is usually more difficult to conduct than lower level evaluations, but the resulting information is important to decision makers. If no transfer takes place then one cannot expect to have level 4 outcomes, which is the original reason for conducting the training.

Level 4: Results. Here the evaluator's goal is to find out if the training leads to "final results." Level 4 outcomes include any leading indicators and outcomes that affect the performance of the organization. Some desired organizational, financial, and employee results include reduced costs, higher quality of work, increased production, lower rates of employee turnover, lower absenteeism, fewer wasted resources, improved quality of work life, improved human relations, improved organizational communication, increased sales, few grievances, higher worker morale, fewer accidents, increased job satisfaction, and, importantly, increased profits.

Kirkpatrick acknowledges the difficulty of validating the relationship between training and level 4 outcomes. Because so many extraneous factors other than the training can influence level 4 outcomes, stronger research designs are needed (see designs 3 and 4 in Table 10.1). Unfortunately, implementation of these designs can be difficult and expensive. Nonetheless, it was Kirkpatrick's hope that training directors would attempt to conduct sound level 4 evaluations and thus enhance the status of training programs.

Brinkerhoff's Success Case Method

The next evaluation model is more specialized than the previous models. It focuses on finding out what about a training or other organizational intervention *worked.* According to its founder, Robert Brinkerhoff, the success case method (SCM) "is a quick and simple process that combines analysis of extreme groups with case study and storytelling . . . to find out how well some organizational initiative (e.g., a training program, a new work method) is working" (Brinkerhoff, 2005, p. 401). The SCM uses the commonsense idea that an effective way to determine "what works" is to examine successful cases and compare them to other cases. The SCM recognizes the organizational embeddedness of programs and seeks to explicate personal and contextual factors that differentiate effective from ineffective program use and results. This method is popular in human performance improvement (HPI) because it works well with training and nontraining interventions (Surry & Stanfield, 2008).

SCM follows five steps (Brinkerhoff, 2003). First, you (the evaluator) focus and plan the success case study. You must identify and work with stakeholders to define the program to be evaluated, explicate its purpose, and discuss the nature of the SC approach to evaluation. You must work with stakeholders to determine their interests and concerns and obtain agreement on the budget and time frame for the study. Finally, this is when the study design is constructed and agreed upon.

Second, construct a visual *impact model*. This includes explicating the major program goals and listing all impacts/outcomes that are hoped for or are expected to result from the program. The far left side of a typical depiction of an impact model lists "capabilities" (e.g., knowledge and skills that should be provided by the program); these are similar to Kirkpatrick's level 2 learning outcomes. The far right depicts "business goals" that are expected to result from the program; these are similar to Kirkpatrick's level 4 results outcomes. The middle columns of a typical impact model include behaviors and organizational and environmental conditions that must be present to achieve the desired business goals. These might include critical actions (i.e., applications of the capabilities) and key intermediate results (e.g., supervisory, environmental, and client outcomes). An impact model is helpful for knowing what to include in your questionnaire to be used in the next step.

Third, conduct a survey research study to identify the best (i.e., success) cases and the worst cases. Unlike most survey research, responses are *not* anonymous because the purpose is to identify individuals. Data are collected from everyone if there are fewer than 100 people in the population; otherwise, a random sample is drawn.[6] The survey instrument (i.e., the questionnaire) is usually quite short, unless you and the client decide to collect additional evaluation information.[7] Three key questions for the questionnaire are: (1) "To what extent have you been able to use the [insert name of program here] to achieve success on [insert overall business goal here]?" then (2) "Who

is having a lot of success in using the [insert program name]?" and (3) "Who is having the least success in using the [insert program name]?" The survey data can be supplemented with performance records and any other information that might help you to locate success cases (e.g., word of mouth, customer satisfaction reports).

Fourth, schedule and conduct in-depth interviews (usually via the telephone for approximately 45 minutes per interview) with multiple *success cases*. Sometimes you will also want to interview a few nonsuccess cases. The purpose of the fourth step is to gain detailed information necessary for documenting, with empirical evidence, the success case attributes and stories. During the interviews you should discuss categories of successful use and identify facilitating and inhibiting use factors. During the success case interviews, Brinkerhoff (2003) recommends that you address the following information categories:

a. What was used that worked (i.e., what information/strategies/skills, when, how, with whom, and where)?
b. What successful results/outcomes were achieved, and how did they make a difference?
c. What good did it do (i.e., value)?
d. What factors helped produce the successful results?
e. What additional suggestions does the interviewee have for improvement?

During nonsuccess case interviews, the focus is on barriers and reasons for lack of use of what was expected to be provided by the program. You should also obtain suggestions for increasing future use. During and after all interviews, it is important to obtain *evidence* and carefully document the validity of the findings.

Fifth, document and communicate the evaluation findings. In Brinkerhoff's words, this is where you "tell the story." The report will include detailed data and evidence as well as rich narrative communicating how the program was successful and how it can be made even more successful in the future. Again, provide sufficient evidence so that the story is credible. Brinkerhoff (2003, pp. 169–172) recommends that you address the following six conclusions in the final report:

1. What worthwhile actions and results, if any, is the program helping to produce?
2. Are some parts of the program working better than others?
3. What environment factors are helping support success, and what factors are getting in the way?
4. How widespread is the scope of success?
5. What is the ROI (return on investment) of the new program?
6. How much more additional value could be derived from the program?

Brinkerhoff emphasizes that success case evaluation results must be used if long-term and company-wide success is to result. The most important strategy for ensuring employee "buy-in" and use of evaluation results and

---

[6]For information on determining sample size, see Johnson and Christensen (2014) or Christensen, Johnson, and Turner (2014). A free program for determining sample size is provided here: http://www.gpower.hhu.de/en.html.

[7]Note that the *survey instrument* is not properly called "the survey." The "survey" is the research *method* that is implemented. Survey instruments include questionnaires (paper-and-pencil, web based) and interview protocols (used in-person, over the phone, or via technologies such as Skype or teleconferencing).

recommendations is to incorporate employee participation into all stages of the evaluation. For a model showing many of that factors that affect evaluation use, read Johnson (1998). Because of the importance of evaluation, the next and final evaluation model is constructed around the concept of evaluation use.

Patton's Utilization-Focused Evaluation

Evaluation process and findings are of no value unless they are *used*. If an evaluation is not likely to be used in any way, one should not conduct the evaluation. In the 1970s, Michael Patton introduced the utilization-focused evaluation (U-FE) model, and today it is in the forth book edition (which is much updated/expanded from earlier editions) (Patton, 2008). The U-FE model is "evaluation done for and with specific intended users for specific, intended uses" (Patton, 2008, p. 37). The cardinal rule in U-FE is that the utility of an evaluation is to be judged by the degree to which it is used. The evaluator focuses on use from the beginning until the end of the evaluation, and during that time he or she continually facilitates use, and organizational learning or any other process that helps ensure that the evaluation results will continue to be used once the evaluator leaves the organization. *Process use* occurs when clients learn the "logic" of evaluation and appreciate its use in the organization. Process use empowers organizational members to become internal evaluators.

The U-FE model follows several steps. Because U-FE is a participatory evaluation approach, the client and primary users will be actively involved in the structuring, conducting, interpreting, and using evaluation and its results. Here are the major steps:

1. *Conduct a readiness assessment* (i.e., determine if the organization and its leaders are ready and able to commit to U-FE).
2. *Identify the "primary intended users" and develop a working relationship with them* (i.e., primary intended users are the key individuals in the organization that have a stake in the evaluation and have the ability, credibility, power, and teachability to work with a U-FE evaluator in conducting an evaluation and using the results).
3. *Conduct a situational analysis* (i.e., examine the political context, stakeholder interests, and potential barriers and supports to use).
4. *Identify the "primary intended uses"* (e.g., program improvement, making major decisions, generating knowledge, and process use or empowering stakeholders to know how to conduct evaluations once the evaluator has left).
5. *Focus the evaluation* (i.e., identify stakeholders' high priority issues and questions).
6. *Design the evaluation* (one that is feasible and will produce results that are credible, believable, valid, and actionable).
7. *Collect, analyze, and interpret the evaluation data* (and remember to use multiple methods and sources of evidence).
8. *Continually facilitate evaluation use* (e.g., interim findings might be disseminated to the organization, rather than waiting for the "final written report"; U-FE does not stop with the final report, because the evaluator must work with the organization until the findings are used).
9. *Conduct a metaevaluation* (i.e., an evaluation of the evaluation, to determine (a) the degree to which intended use was achieved, (b) whether additional uses occurred, and (c) whether any misuses and/or unintended consequences occurred; the evaluation is successful only if the findings are used effectively).

Utilization-focused evaluation is a full approach to evaluation (Patton, 2008), but it also is an excellent approach to complement any of the other evaluation models presented in this chapter. Again, an evaluation that is not used is of little use to an organization; therefore, it is wise to consider the principles provided in the U-FE model.

To become an effective *utilization-focused evaluator*, we recommend that you take courses in human performance improvement, leadership and management, industrial-organizational psychology, organizational development, organizational communication, and organizational behavior. If you become a utilization-focused evaluator, it will be your job to continually facilitate use, starting from the moment you enter the organization. You will attempt to facilitate use by helping transform the state of the organization so that it is in better shape when you leave than when you entered.

Conclusion

Evaluation is important because it is a part of all major models of instructional design, it is a required skill for human performance technologists, it provides a systematic procedure for making value judgments about programs and products, and it can help improve employee and organizational performance. Some instructional designers will elect to specialize in evaluation and become full-time program evaluators. To learn more about evaluation as a profession, go to the website of the American Evaluation Association (http://www.eval.org/).

Stufflebeam's CIPP model focuses on program context (for planning decisions), inputs (for program structuring decisions), process (for implementation decisions), and product (for summative decisions). Rossi's evaluation model focuses on tailoring each evaluation to local needs and focusing on one or more of the following domains: needs, theory, process/implementation, impact, and efficiency. Chen's TDE model focuses on articulating a program theory so that one will know how and why a program operates well or poorly. Kirkpatrick's model focuses on four levels of outcomes, including reactions, learning, transfer of learning, and business results. Brinkerhoff's success case model focuses on locating and understanding program successes so that success can become more widespread in the organization. Patton's U-FE model focuses on conducting evaluations that will be *used*.

Summary of Key Principles

1. Evaluation is the process of determining the merit, worth, and value of things, and evaluations are the products of that process.

2. *Formative evaluation* focuses on improving the evaluation object, and *summative evaluation* focuses on determining the overall effectiveness, usefulness, or worth of the evaluation object.

3. Rossi shows that evaluation, broadly conceived, can include needs assessment, theory assessment, implementation assessment, impact assessment, and efficiency assessment.

4. Chen shows how an evaluator working with program staff articulates the program theory (includes an action model and change model) to facilitate development and evaluation of a program.

5. Kirkpatrick shows that training evaluations should examine participants' reactions, their learning (of knowledge, skills, and attitudes), their use of learning when they return to the workplace, and business results.

6. Brinkerhoff shows that organizational profits can be increased by learning from success cases and applying knowledge gained from studying these cases.

7. It is important that evaluation findings are *used*, rather than "filed away," and Patton has developed an evaluation model specifically focused on producing evaluation use.

8. One effective way to increase the use of evaluation findings is through employee/stakeholder participation in the evaluation process.

Application Questions

1. Current research indicates that most companies conduct level 1 evaluations, and many conduct level 2 evaluations; however, organizations infrequently conduct evaluations at levels 3 and 4. Describe problems with this practice, and provide reasons for it. Explain how you would attempt to increase the use of levels 3 and 4 evaluations.

2. Identify a recent instructional design or performance technology project on which you have worked. If you have not worked on any such project, interview someone who has. Describe how you did (or would) evaluate the project using one or more of the evaluation models explained in this chapter.

3. Using ideas presented in this chapter, construct *your own* "hybrid" evaluation model.

References

Brinkerhoff, R. O. (2003). *The success case method: Find out quickly what's working and what's not.* San Francisco: Berrett-Koehler.

Brinkerhoff, R. O. (2005). Success case method. In S. Mathison, *Evaluation* (pp. 401–401). Thousand Oaks, CA: Sage.

Chen, H. T. (2015). *Practical program evaluation: Theory-driven evaluation and the integrated evaluation perspective* (2nd ed.). Los Angeles: Sage.

Christensen, L. B., Johnson, R. B., & Turner, L. A. (2014). *Research methods and design* (12th ed.). Boston: Allyn & Bacon.

Johnson, R. B. (1998). Toward a theoretical model of evaluation utilization. *Evaluation and program planning: An international journal, 21,* 93–110.

Johnson, R. B., & Christensen, L. B. (2014). *Educational research: Quantitative, qualitative, and mixed approaches* (5th ed.). Los Angeles: Sage.

Kirkpatrick, D. L. (2006). *Evaluating training programs: The four levels.* San Francisco: Berrett-Koehler.

Patton, M. Q. (2008). *Utilization-focused evaluation: The new century text.* Thousand Oaks, CA: Sage.

Rossi, P. H., Lipsey, M. W., & Freeman, H. E. M. W. (2004). *Evaluation: A systemic approach.* Thousand Oaks, CA: Sage.

Scriven, M. (1967). The methodology of evaluation. In R. W. Tyler, R. M. Gagné, & M. Scriven (Eds.), *Perspectives of curriculum evaluation* (pp. 39–83). Chicago: Rand McNally.

Scriven, M. (1980). *The logic of evaluation.* Inverness, CA: Edge Press.

Scriven, M. (1991). Beyond formative and summative evaluation. In M. W. McLaughlin & D. D. Phillips (Eds.), *Evaluation and education: At quarter century* (pp. 19–64). Chicago: University of Chicago Press.

Stufflebeam, D. L. (1971). *Educational evaluation and decision making.* Itasca, IL: F. E. Peacock.

Surry, D. W., & Stanfield, A. K. (2008). Performance technology. In M. K. Barbour & M. Orey (Eds.), *The foundations of instructional technology.* Retrieved March 12, 2016, from http://projects.coe.uga.edu/itFoundations/

Chapter 11

Measuring the Return on Investment (ROI) in Technology-Based Learning

Jack J. Phillips

Patricia P. Phillips

Hope Nicholas

ROI Institute

It is difficult to imagine a world of learning and development without technology, and investment in technology continues to grow at astonishing rates. Its growth is inevitable and its use is predestined. But these investments attract attention from executives who often want to know if they're working properly. Does it make a difference? How does it connect to the business? Does it really add the value that we anticipated? Is it as effective as facilitator-led learning? These are some of the questions instructional design professionals must answer to show the impact learning technologies have on workplace learning and performance.

A Fundamental Change Is Needed

Learning technologies have been used in the workplace for more than twenty years, but it is only in the past few years that their impact could be described as a "fundamental change." More recent evolutions of learning technology bring significant change in how we grow and develop our current and future employees. These technological innovations include the following:

- Mobile learning
- Game-based learning
- Bring your own device (BYOD) programs
- Open educational resources
- Massive open online courses (MOOCs)
- Flipped classrooms

Technology, with its many forms and features, is here to stay. However, some concerns must be addressed about the accountability and success of technology-based learning. In the Association for Talent Development's (ATD) new book, Elkeles, Phillips, and Phillips explain how these types of programs can be evaluated with executive-friendly data (2014).

The Need for Business Results

Most would agree that any large expenditure in an organization should in some way be connected to business success. Even in nonbusiness settings, large investments should connect to organizational measures of output, quality, cost, and time—classic measurement categories of hard data that exist in any type of organization.

Udell (2012) makes the case for connecting mobile learning to business measures. He starts by listing the important measures that are connected to the business, including:

- Decreased product returns
- Increased productivity
- Fewer mistakes
- Increased sales
- Fewer accidents
- Fewer compliance discrepancies
- Increased shipments
- Reduced operating cost
- Fewer customer complaints

Udell goes on to say that mobile learning should connect to any of those measures, and he takes several of them in step-by-step fashion to show how, in practical and logical thinking, a mobile learning solution can drive any or all of these measures. He concludes by suggesting that if an organization is investing in mobile learning or any other type of learning, it needs to connect to these business measures. Otherwise, it shouldn't be pursued. This dramatic call for accountability is not that unusual in today's climate.

Credible Connections

Executives and administrators who fund budgets are adamant about seeing the connection between investing in learning technologies and business results. These executives realize that employees must learn through technology, often using mobile devices; and they know that employees must be actively involved and engaged in the process and learn the content. More importantly, however, employees must use what they have learned and have an impact on the business.

Unfortunately, the majority of results presented in technology case studies are void of measurements at the levels needed by executives. Only occasionally are application data presented—measuring what individuals do with what they learn—and rarely do they report a credible connection to the business. Even rarer are attempts to calculate the return on investment (ROI).

Evaluation of technology-based learning rests on five levels of data (see Table 11.1 later in the chapter) with ROI being at level 5. In a recent review of award-winning e-learning and mobile learning case studies published by several prestigious organizations (Elkeles et al., 2014), not one project was evaluated at the ROI level where the monetary value of the impact was compared with the program's cost. Instead, they used the concept of ROI to mean any value or benefit from the program. Defining ROI differently, as was the case in several of these projects, creates some concerns among executives, who are accustomed to seeing ROI calculated in a very precise way by the finance and accounting team. Only two of the award-winning projects were evaluated on the cost savings of technology-based learning compared with facilitator-led learning. Credible connections to the business were rare. Only one study attempted to show the impact of mobile learning using comparison groups. Even there, the details about how the groups were set up and the actual differences were left out. When the data are vague or missing, it raises a red flag.

Reasons for Lack of Data

In our analysis of technology-based learning programs, several major barriers to conducting adequate evaluations of technology emerged. These obstacles keep the proponents from developing metrics to the levels desired by executives:

- *Results are feared.* Although few will admit it, individuals who design, develop, or own a particular program are concerned that if the results are not good, the program may be discontinued and it will affect their reputation and performance.
- *Evaluations are not necessary.* Some designers and developers are suggesting that investments in technology-based learning should be measured on the faith that it will make a difference. After all, technology is absolutely necessary.
- *Measuring at higher levels is not planned.* When capturing the business impact and developing the ROI, the process

starts from the beginning, at the conception of the project or program. Unfortunately, evaluation is not given serious consideration until after the project is implemented, which is too late for an effective evaluation.
- *Measurement is too difficult.* Some feel it is too difficult to capture the data or that it's impossible to secure quality information.
- *Measurement is not the fun part of the process.* Technology-based learning is amazing, awesome, impressive, and fun. Gamification is taking hold. People love games. They're fun. However, measuring application, impact, and ROI is usually not fun (but it can be).
- *Not knowing which programs to evaluate at the ROI level.* Some technology proponents think that if they go down the ROI path, executives will want to see the ROI in every project and program. The challenge is to select particular projects or programs that will need to be evaluated at this level.
- *Personnel are not prepared to conduct these evaluations.* The preparation for designers, developers, implementers, owners, and project managers does not usually include courses in metrics, evaluation, and analytics.

Because these barriers are perceived to be real, they inhibit evaluation at the levels desired by executives; but they are myths, for the most part. Yes, evaluation will take more time and there will be a need for more planning, but the step-by-step process of the ROI methodology is logical.

The ROI Methodology

Return on investment is the ultimate measure of accountability. Within the context of measuring learning through technology, it answers the question, For every dollar invested in technology-based learning, how many dollars were returned after the investment is recovered? ROI is an economic indicator that compares earnings (or net benefits) to investment, and is expressed as a percentage. The concept of ROI to measure the success of investment opportunities has been used in business for centuries to measure the return on capital expenditures such as buildings, equipment, or tools. As the need for greater accountability in learning, demonstrated effectiveness, and value increases, ROI is becoming an accepted way to measure the impact and return on investment of all types of programs, including technology-based learning.

The counterpart to ROI, benefit–cost ratio (BCR), has been used for centuries. Benefit–cost analysis became prominent in the United States in the early 1900s, when it was used to justify projects initiated under the River and Harbor Act of 1902 and the Flood Control Act of 1936. ROI and the BCR provide similar indicators of investment success, though one (ROI) presents the earnings (net benefits) as compared to the cost, while the other (BCR) compares benefits to costs. Here are the basic equations used to calculate the BCR and the ROI:

$$BCR = \frac{\text{Program Benefits}}{\text{Program Costs}}$$

$$ROI\ (\%) = \frac{\text{Program Benefits} - \text{Program Costs}}{\text{Program Costs}} \times 100$$

What is the difference between these two equations? A BCR of 2:1 means that for every \$1 invested, \$2 in benefits is generated. This translated into an ROI of 100 percent, which says that for every \$1 invested, \$1 is returned after the costs are covered (the investment is recovered plus \$1 extra).

Benefit–cost ratios were used in the past, primarily in public sector settings, whereas ROI was used mainly by accountants managing capital expenditures in business and industry. Either calculation can be used in both settings, but it is important to understand the difference. In many cases the benefit–cost ratio and the ROI are reported together.

Although ROI is the ultimate measure of accountability, basic accounting practice suggests that reporting the ROI metric alone is insufficient. To be meaningful, ROI must be reported with other performance measures. These measures are included in the five-level ROI evaluation framework, which was developed in the 1970s and became prominent in the 1980s (Phillips, 1983). The framework is used to categorize results for all types of programs and projects, and includes the following five levels of evaluation:

- Level 1: Reaction and Planned Action data represent the reactions to the program and the planned actions from participants. Reactions may include views of the format, ease of use, convenience, facilitator effectiveness, and fit. This category must include data that reflect the value of the program content, including measures of relevance, importance, amount of new information, and participants' willingness to recommend the program to others.
- Level 2: Learning data represent the extent to which participants have acquired new knowledge about their strengths, development areas, and skills needed to be successful. This category of data also includes the level of confidence of participants as they plan to apply their newly acquired knowledge and skills on the job.
- Level 3: Application and Implementation data determine the extent to which professionals apply their newly acquired knowledge and skills from the learning program. This category also includes data that describe the barriers preventing application, as well as any supporting elements (enablers) in the knowledge and skill transfer process.
- Level 4: Business Impact data are collected and analyzed to determine the extent to which applications of acquired knowledge and skills positively influenced key measures that were intended to improve as a result of the learning experience. The measures include errors, rejects, new accounts, customer complaints, sales, customer returns, down time, cycle time, job engagement, compliance, absenteeism, and operating costs. When reporting data at this level, a step to isolate the program's effect on these measures is always taken.
- Level 5: Return on Investment compares the monetary benefits of the impact measures (as they are converted to monetary value) to the fully loaded program costs. Improvement can occur in sales, for example, but to calculate the ROI, the measure of improvement must be converted to monetary value (profit of the sale) and compared to the cost of the program. If the monetary value of sales improvement exceeds the costs, then the calculation is a positive ROI.

Each level of evaluation answers basic questions regarding the success of the program. Table 11.1 presents these questions.

Categorizing evaluation data as levels provides a clear and understandable framework to manage the technology-based learning design and objectives, and manage the data collection process. More importantly, however, these five levels present data in a way that makes it easy for the audience to understand the results reported for the program. While each level of evaluation provides important, stand-alone data, when reported together, the five-level ROI framework represents data that tell the complete story of program success or failure.

Case Study

The following case study, reported by Phillips and Phillips (2014), provides an example of how the five-level ROI evaluation framework was used to evaluate the effects of a technology-based learning innovation at all five levels of evaluation. In this case the project involved a mobile learning application for sales associates of a large software firm specializing in software solutions for the trucking industry. Sales associates were provided a mobile learning application for their iPads that was designed to teach them to describe and sell an upgrade to its most popular software product, ProfitPro. The application consisted of five learning modules.

Twenty-five people signed up to use the mobile learning application within three days of the program's announcement. Level 1 reaction data were collected after they completed the fifth module. Reactions were as expected, averaging 4.3 on a five-point scale. Level 2 learning seemed appropriate, and quiz scores were above targets. The average score was 20.8 out of a possible 25.0.

Level 3 application data seemed to be on track. The skills of identifying pricing options and explaining implementation and support were off a little, but overall the objectives were met. As expected, there were some barriers and enablers to success. The barriers were minimal. However, there was a concern that 9 percent of sales associates were not encouraged by their managers to use the program. The number one enabler was management encouragement.

TABLE 11.1	Evaluation Framework and Key Questions
Level of Evaluation	**Key Questions**
Level 1: Reaction and Planned Action	• Was the learning relevant to the job and role? • Was the learning important to the job and success of the participant? • Did the learning provide the participant with new information? • Do participants intend to use what they learned? • Would they recommend the program or process to others? • Is there room for improvement in duration and format?
Level 2: Learning	• Did participants gain the knowledge and skills identified at the start of the program? • Do participants know how to apply what they learned? • Are participants confident to apply what they learned?
Level 3: Application and Implementation	• How effectively are participants applying what they learned? • How frequently are participants applying what they learned? • Are participants successful with applying what they have learned? • If participants are applying what they learned, what is supporting them? • If participants are not applying what they learned, why not?
Level 4: Business Impact	• So what if the application is successful—what impact will it have on the business? • To what extent did application of knowledge and skills improve the business measures the program was intended to improve? • How did the program affect sales, productivity, operating costs, cycle time, errors, rejects, job engagement, and other measures? • How do you know it was the learning program that improved these measures?
Level 5: ROI	• Do the monetary benefits of the improvement in business impact measures outweigh the cost of the technology-based learning program?

Source: ROI Institute, Inc (2016).

The Level 4 impact data comparing the experimental group of twenty-five sales associates with the control group of twenty-two associates revealed that almost all of the control group members (nineteen of twenty-two) were selling the upgrade even though they did not participate in the program. But the difference between the two groups was impressive. For the control group, the average amount of monthly sales per associate was $3,700 and the average time to first sale was twenty-one days. Conversely, the experimental group members took an average of only eleven days to make their first sale and sold on average $7,500 per month—a difference of $3,800. The difference was then annualized, producing an improvement of $1.14 million.

Next, the fully loaded costs were included to make the ROI calculation credible. The benefit–cost ratio and ROI were then calculated. ROI was measured as 311 percent, which exceeded the objective. In addition to the tangible sales increase converted to money, several intangible benefits were connected to the program:

• Customer satisfaction increased.
• Brand awareness for ProfitPro increased.
• Job satisfaction of sales associates increased.
• Stress for sales associates decreased.
• Reputation of the company increased.

Other intangible benefits were connected to the program as indicated on a post-program questionnaire. Additionally, this questionnaire contained an extra question about the extent to which this program influenced these measures.

Tips for Increasing Impact from Technology-Based Learning

Unfortunately, many technology-based learning evaluations are revealing deficiencies with on-the-job success, making it difficult to convince management that e-learning or mobile learning is adding significant value. Learning through technology is convenient, timely, and in most cases, extremely low cost—sweet words to an executive; however, these same executives want results. They need assurance that learning through technology will drive application and impact. We know from our own experience that learning through technology can drive business impact. We have ROI studies to show this. Based on our experience here are some specific steps you might take to increase the business impact of technology-based learning innovations:

Develop application and impact objectives. Application objectives describe what the participant should do with what they are learning. The impact objective describes the consequence of the application. These are powerful objectives that link the program to the bottom line. Although rarely presented in e-learning or mobile learning, they can be developed in almost any learning process.

Develop content to reflect application and impact objectives. Because objectives have moved beyond learning, it is critical to position the content to focus on application and impact, essentially relaying the message that the program is not successful unless application occurs and there is a corresponding impact. This is reinforced with case studies, videos, demonstrations, exercises, games, and examples to help with application and impact.

Design for application and impact. As you design the programs, build application tools into the process. Include action plans, checklists, guides, templates, and other tools. This is critical to ensure that application and impact occurs. These tools facilitate the use of what participants are learning and suggest that application and impact are absolutely necessary.

Create an expectation for results. Sometimes it is simple to define success. Participants must know that success is not achieved when they have learned the content, but only if there is a corresponding application and impact. This effort goes beyond developing objectives and focuses on emphasizing and describing program success. Part of this may include defining responsibilities that shift the participant's responsibility beyond participating in the program. Yes, it is important to participate in the program, complete it, and learn what is necessary to be successful; but it is more important to actually apply it and have an impact. This is part of their responsibility. One organization included a statement of responsibilities at the beginning of each technology-based learning program that defined what the CEO saw as the participant's responsibility in the program.

Involve the participant's manager. Almost any research on the transfer of learning to the job will underscore the importance of the participant's manager in achieving results. For the most part, technology-based learning programs seem to ignore the manager. Sometimes, participants take programs on their own time and the manager does not know about it. Still, there are times when it is helpful to let managers know that their employees will be involved. Provide a few low-level activities to encourage manager involvement, both before participants actually become involved in the program and after they have completed it.

Apply the principles of learning transfer. Perhaps there is no area within learning and development that is as important as the transfer of learning to the job. Most typical actions work well in the learning-through-technology environment. Several valuable references on transfer strategies are available to ensure that learners use the learning on the job, such as *Beyond Transfer of Training: Engaging Systems to Improve Performance* (Broad, 2005) and *Making eLearning Stick: Techniques for Easy and Effective Transfer of Technology-Supported Training* (Carnes, 2012).

By following some prescribed steps, designers and developers can make a huge difference in the success of e-learning, pushing it to impressive levels of success for application and impact. When this is the case, then you can easily base the ROI on the cost savings generated when comparing learning through technology to a facilitator-led counterpart.

Summary of Key Principles

1. **Technology-based learning programs need to show results.** Executives and administrators who fund large amounts of technology-based learning and key stakeholders want to see the value of their programs and projects. Their definition of value is often application, impact, and ROI. The challenge is to move forward and accomplish this in the face of barriers that may get in the way.

2. **Connect technology-based learning to business needs in a credible way.** Within the context of measuring learning through technology, return on investment is the ultimate measure of accountability. ROI is an economic indicator that compares earnings (or net benefits) to investment, and is expressed as a percentage. Another indicator often used is benefit–cost ratio (BCR), which divides benefits by costs. ROI and BCR provide similar indicators, although ROI presents the net benefits as compared to cost and BCR compares only benefits to cost.

3. **The concept of the ROI methodology is a systematic logical process with conservative standards.** The process collects and generates six types of data: reaction, learning, application, impact, ROI, and intangibles. It includes techniques to isolate the effects of the learning on impact data, such as sales, productivity, new accounts, quality, costs, and time. The ROI methodology also requires communicating the results to a variety of key stakeholders.

4. **Evaluation of technology-based learning rests on a five-level ROI evaluation framework.** Frameworks serve as a way to categorize data, keep an evaluation on track, and represent the complete story of program success or failure. The five-level framework captures data that follow a logical flow moving from participant reaction (level 1), learning acquisition (level 2), application and implementation (level 3), impact to the business (level 4), and economic contribution or ROI (level 5).

5. **Take proper steps to increase the impact of technology-based learning.** Develop application and impact objectives. Design the learning content around these objectives, communicate expectations, involve managers, and create the tools that are necessary for the participant to be fully involved. A well-designed program combined with a participant who is motivated to learn will make achieving success a reality.

Application Questions

1. Sydney Mitchell has been serving as CEO for Global Communications for the past nine months. She has a reputation for being aggressive in meeting goals, yet is pragmatic and fair. In her previous organization, Sydney increased profits as well as customer satisfaction ratings while reducing staff and positioning the company as one of the best 100 companies to work for. Before making significant changes in the Global Communications organization structure, Sydney is giving each function the first year to make strides toward meeting strategic objectives. These strategic objectives focus on increasing profits, market share, customer satisfaction ratings, and employee engagement. Sydney has communicated these objectives very clearly throughout her first nine months and even holds monthly sessions with employees to help them understand the meaning and importance of each objective.

With three months remaining in the year, Sydney has been meeting with executives of each function to get a status report. She has been relatively pleased with the results in operations, engineering, marketing, human resources, and distribution functions. Today she is meeting with the head of GlobalCom University, which is the Global Communications corporate learning and development department.

Donald Hodges is the vice-president of GlobalCom University. He was selected by the past CEO and believes the university is making a difference. He always receives rave reviews from participants after each program. Donald is ready for Sydney. He has a very flashy PowerPoint presentation and the results of all of his program evaluations are ready to review.

Sydney enters the room.

Sydney: Hi, Donald. It's nice to see you. The place looks great and everyone seems really busy.

Donald: Yes, Sydney. We're developing twelve new programs and converting fifteen programs to e-learning.

Sydney: Really? What are these programs?

Donald: Well, we're developing a new communications program as well as revising our orientation program to include our new benefits package. We've also had requests from employees to offer programs they're interested in, including a personal development program, a time management program, and a business acumen program. And we're developing a leadership program similar to one I attended recently and really enjoyed. I think the managers will enjoy it as well. Six of the new programs are e-learning programs in sales and new product development. As for the e-learning conversions, most of them are in compliance, IT, and sales.

Sydney: Hmmmmm. How much time does it take to develop these programs?

Donald: Oh, not long. About a week for each day of training at the most. We have our four program developers working on three programs each. I estimate it will take a few months to develop all twelve programs. For e-learning we use external developers and the cost is about $5,000 for each hour of e-learning.

Sydney: I see.

Donald: Come on in the conference room, Sydney. I want to share our accomplishments thus far!

Sydney: Great, I'd really like to see your results.

Donald "boots up" the presentation. He goes through all the preliminary issues, and then presents the results of the past nine months.

Donald: In the past nine months we have developed ten new programs with six of them in the e-learning format. We offered 750 hours of training, had 1,500 employees attend training, and received an average of 4.6 out of 5.0 on the overall program satisfaction rating. So basically, we have developed new training, offered some of the new programs as well as some of the old favorites, and the employees attending training seem to think we're moving in the right direction.

Sydney: Well, I see you've been busy. Thanks for the update, Donald. Do we know about the success of these programs on the job?

Donald: No, not specifically, but we are confident that they are adding value.

Sydney: How do you know they are adding value?

Donald: Because of the feedback we receive.

Sydney: What kind of feedback do you receive?

Donald: Many of the participants tell us that they have been very successful with what they have learned.

Sydney: So, you've actually had a follow-up of each program?

Donald: No, not exactly. We just receive random comments.

Sydney: So you have no organized way of knowing about the success of your programs?

Donald: Well, it's not a formal follow-up, but we still receive good feedback.

Sydney: I see. Well, thanks, Donald. I'd like to meet with you next Monday to discuss your contribution to the organization.

Questions:

a. From Donald's perspective, how do you think the meeting went?

b. From Sydney's perspective, how do you think the meeting went?

c. Describe at least four types of data Donald and his staff should have tried to collect so that he could have made a stronger case for the "success" of the new programs GlobalCom University has created. Also describe some methods he and his staff could have used to collect that data.

2. In previous years many companies developed and implemented instructor-led or online programs for new product training, but these programs were costly. In a large organization, a one-day instructor-led class can cost $150 per participant to deliver. At this rate, sending 1,000 employees to a one-day course on a new product or product upgrade would cost the company $150,000, plus the cost of employees' time away from the office, travel, development, and coordination. Assuming a loaded cost of $300 per employee, this would add another $300,000 to the cost of training. So that one-day training event would carry a total cost of about $450,000—and that's not even factoring in overhead expenses.

Given the high costs of training and support, these companies searched for alternatives. E-learning was the cost-effective alternative with a total cost of $25 per participant plus the time away from work (many of them took the training at night or on weekends).

Questions:

a. What benefit does e-learning bring to this situation?
b. What's the ROI on the e-learning?
c. What questions might product managers ask?

References

Broad, M. (2005). *Beyond transfer of training: Engaging systems to improve performance.* San Francisco: Pfeiffer.

Carnes, B. (2012). *Making eLearning stick: Techniques for easy and effective transfer of technology-supported training.* Alexandria, VA: ASTD Press.

Elkeles, T., Philips, P. P., & Philips, J. J. (2014). *Measuring the success of learning through technology: A step-by-step guide for measuring impact and ROI on e-learning, blended learning, and mobile learning.* Alexandria, VA: ASTD Press.

Phillips, J. J. (1983). *Handbook of training evaluation and measurement methods.* Boston: Butterworth-Heinemann.

Phillips, J. J., & Philips, P. P. (2014). Measuring ROI in an upgrade selling program: A mobile learning solution. In T. Elkeles, P. P. Philips, & J. J. Philips (Eds.), *Measuring the success of learning through technology: A step-by-step guide for measuring impact and ROI on e-learning, blended learning, and mobile learning* (pp. 177–194). Alexandria, VA: ASTD Press.

Phillips, P. P., & Phillips, J. J. (2016). *Handbook of training evaluation and measurement methods* (4th ed.). London & New York, NY: Routledge

Udell, C. (2012). *Learning everywhere: How mobile content strategies are transforming training.* Alexandria, VA: ASTD Press.

Chapter 12

An Introduction to Learning Analytics

Beth Dietz

Janet E. Hurn

Thomas A. Mays

David Woods

Miami University

It is undeniable that we are living in a data-driven world. Amazon, iTunes, and Netflix seem to know what our favorite books, electronic gadgets, music, and movies are before we ourselves know. Google can predict what we are searching for before we even finish typing. And our grocery stores send us coupons for the exact products we purchase every week. In short, the amount of data we have at our fingertips is astonishing. So why not use that data to make instructional design decisions?

Data-informed decision making involves making use of data to inform judgments (Jones, 2012; Long & Siemens, 2011; Picciano, 2012). As an instructional designer, you make decisions about course design and delivery based on evidence. For example, you likely know that active-learning activities can lead to deeper processing of content, which can lead to deeper learning (e.g., Yoder & Hochevar, 2005). Evidence such as this leads to the creation and inclusion of active-learning activities in a course. Likewise, it would be helpful to make course-design decisions based on evidence from prior performance in the course or on student characteristics. Perhaps students who have certain skills or abilities or prior coursework perform better in the class or set of classes than those who do not. The use of data to make decisions about course design is one of the goals of learning analytics.

In this chapter, we provide a brief overview of learning analytics, including various tools to track, extract, and analyze data. We will also explore its uses and applications, goals, and examples. Furthermore, we discuss why instructional designers will want to make use of learning analytics. Any discussion of learning analytics is not complete without a thorough discussion of the issues and concerns with the use of this type of data, so we will discuss that as well.

An Overview of Learning Analytics

Although the term *analytics* is relatively new in the field of education, the concept is not. Analytics involves collecting and exploring data sets to search for meaningful patterns. For an educator, an example of this could be reviewing student attendance and grade data and observing that students with poor attendance often have poor grades. The discovery of these patterns may give insight into observed behavior and prompt actions to address problems or otherwise improve a situation. The growing interest in analytics is driven by the ubiquitous nature of modern technology and deluge of data it generates. An ever expanding range of tools and techniques are being developed to collect, organize, analyze, and visualize this data. With knowledge of these tools, instructional designers will be able to make use of learning analytics to improve learning experiences.

In education, learning analytics can be defined as "the measurement, collection, analysis, and reporting of data about learners and their contexts, for the purpose of understanding and optimizing learning and the environment in which it occurs" (Long & Siemens, 2011, p. 32). Learning analytics are being explored across all aspects of the educational environment. At the course and department levels, instructors and instructional designers look for insight on how students interact with course material provided in a learning management system (LMS), to explore ways to improve specific outcomes for individual activities within a class, for a class as a whole, or for a department or program.

Long and Siemens (2011) use the term "*academic analytics*" to distinguish analytics that focus on institutions and, more broadly, higher education, including recruitment and retention of students (Campbell, DeBlois, & Oblinger, 2007) and selection of courses and programs of study by students (Denley, 2014). While this narrows the focus, it still includes a wide range of practices, such as inspecting student data in a gradebook, examining student access information in a LMS, assessing adaptive learning (Feldstein, 2013), and other activities. To gain a sense of the use of and value of learning analytics, consider Puget's analytics landscape (Puget, 2015). It distinguishes four "maturity levels" (Table 12.1) and provides the instructional designer with a useful path for progressing from less complex uses of learning analytics to more mature and complex levels. When the course is first designed, the instructional designer can use best practices to focus on identifying the data that can be collected (descriptive analytics). After the course has been delivered (or even as the course is being delivered) the data can be explored to look for patterns that may explain observed outcomes (diagnostic analytics). These patterns can then be analyzed to explore and test predictive hypothesis that can be validated the next time the course is delivered (predictive analytics). If a hypothesis is found to have predictive power, then efforts can be made to identify students who need to be encouraged to take specific actions (prescriptive analytics).

Goals of Learning Analytics

Learning analytics can have multiple goals and can be pitched at several levels, including course, department, and institutional levels. Instructional designers should keep these goals in mind during course planning and design. Liñán, Alejandro, and Pérez (2015) suggest that the main goal of learning analytics is to "extract information from educational data to support education-related decision making" (p. 99). While institutions have access to data for improved reporting, educators can use learning analytics to improve the student learning experience. Larusson and White (2014) summarize the goals of learning analytics:

> Whether it be through the use of statistical techniques and predictive modeling, interactive visualizations, or taxonomies and frameworks, the ultimate goal is to optimize both student and faculty performance, to refine pedagogical strategies, to streamline institutional costs, to determine students' engagement with the course material, to highlight potentially struggling students (and to alter pedagogy accordingly) to fine-tune grading systems using real-time analysis, and to allow instructors to judge their own educational efficacy. (p. 1–2)

Of course, in practice, the goals of learning analytics should support student success. This can be accomplished through data-driven initiatives focused on monitoring and documenting student learning, identifying at-risk candidates for intervention, improving pedagogy and instruction, and streamlining institutional processes. By understanding the goals of learning analytics, the data to be collected, and how it can be utilized, instructional designers are better prepared to support student success through informed design.

Types of Data

As previously stated, the use of learning analytics serves many purposes and fulfills numerous academic and institutional goals. But what are these data and how does an instructional designer assist faculty in finding and using them? There are a number of different *data sources*. One type of data source is institutional (not course specific) in nature. In educational settings, there is a massive amount of institutional-type data to be mined and analyzed. Examples of such data include admissions data (e.g., SAT scores, high school GPA), proficiency and readiness data (e.g., online readiness scores), demographic data (e.g., demographic profile of students who dropout), and data on characteristics of successful students in the major. Instructional designers as well as faculty can make use of these data in the course design process. For example, Morris, Wu, and Finnegan (2005) found that high school GPA and SAT scores successfully predicted dropout (60 percent) and student completion (76 percent) rates in online courses.

Another type of data source, and the one most commonly used in learning analytics, is LMS data. In general, these data are not only readily available to faculty and instructional designers, but are very amenable to basic analysis. For example, the first column in Table 12.2 shows the type of data that are available in the LMS used at our institution (Canvas). For the most part, these data can be easily culled from the LMS and used in various analyses. For example, Smith, Lange, and Huston (2012) used such LMS data as login frequency, site engagement, student pace in the course, and assignment grades to predict course outcomes for individual students.

Instructor-generated data can also be a valuable source of data for learning analytics. The first column of Table 12.3 shows examples of the types of data that may or may not be available in a LMS, but that faculty and instructional designers can track and collect. For example, to determine the effects

TABLE 12.1	Puget's (2015) Analytics Landscape Applied to Learning Analytics	
Maturity Level	**Questions Answered**	**Possible Learning Analytics Question**
Descriptive analytics	What happened? What is happening?	Which students are accessing LMS content?
Diagnostic analytics	Why did it happen? What are the trends?	Which students have succeed in a specific assignment? Why?
Predictive analytics	What will happen?	Which students will succeed in the future?
Prescriptive analytics	What should I do? How can I make it happen?	How can I get students to engage in an activity I know predicts success in a course?

TABLE 12.2	Examples of Source and Purpose of Data in an LMS
Data Generated by LMS	**Purpose of Data (data may serves as an indicator of)**
Number of Page Views	Engagement; Retention
Date and Time of Page View	Engagement; Retention
Action Taken During Page View	Engagement; Retention
Number of Messages to Instructor	Engagement; Retention
Data and Time of Messages to Instructor	Engagement; Retention
Number of On-Time, Late, and Missed Assignment Submissions	Engagement; Retention; Learning
Assignment Outcomes	Retention; Learning
Grades	Learning

TABLE 12.3	Examples of Source and Purpose Type of Instructor-Generated Data
Instructor-Generated Data	**Purpose of Data (data may serves as an indicator of)**
Number of Emails Sent to Instructor	Engagement; Retention
Type and Content of Email Sent to Instructor	Engagement; Retention
Content Coded Discussion Board Contributions	Engagement; Retention; Learning
Social Network Analysis of Discussion Board Contributions	Engagement; Retention; Learning
Number and Type of Questions Asked in a Discussion Board	Engagement; Retention; Learning
Number of Contributions to a Google Doc	Engagement; Retention; Learning

of sending a "checking in" email to students in an online course, Dietz (2015) examined the number and types of email responses. She found that the number of replies were positively correlated with final grades.

When thinking about data sources, it is also important to be mindful of what purpose the data might help serve; in other words, it is important to think about the goals of each specific learning analytic activity. As noted in an earlier section of this chapter, from an instructional design or faculty perspective, the goals can be varied, but might include a desire to track student engagement, assess various forms of student learning (e.g., knowledge acquisition, critical thinking skills, inquiry skills), measure feelings of community, assess retention, and so forth. The second column of Tables 12.2 and 12.3 provide suggested purposes for each of the various data sources. For example, if an instructional designer or faculty member was interested in the factors predicting student engagement, he or she might perform a social network analysis of the discussion board posts (Shum & Ferguson, 2012).

How to Use Learning Analytics

Instructional designers now have a host of data available to improve the design of their courses at every level of the instructional design process. Course design is a continuous process, and a constant flow of incoming data allows for a solid foundation and improvement of courses and programs. Learning analytics adds another tool to the designer's tool box. Learning-analytic information can be used in the initial design of a course or program or for the continuous improvement of an existing course or program. Data can also be used to improve the achievement of learning outcomes. If there is evidence of limited instructor-to-student engagement, for example, then interventions can provide instructors with strategies for increasing engagement. If there is evidence that students are not engaging with the content, the design of the course can be altered to include scaffolded checkpoints to incorporate continuous course touchpoints with feedback.

When thinking of how to use learning analytics, we find it helpful to be mindful of the goals of learning analytics, which then determine the level of data that are necessary to achieve those goals. At the institutional level, an examination of data is useful for developing an appreciation of educational backgrounds, experiences, and life status of the audience for the course or program. Useful questions that can be answered with institutional and departmental data are, What is the educational background of the students entering this course? What are other factors in the lives of these students that might influence their ability to learn? Where does this course fall in the program progression for most students? What are the specific skill averages (reading, writing, math, technical level) of the students when they take this course? For example, students who have not yet taken a research methods course, or have limited writing skills, will often struggle with a research paper assignment. These students may require additional scaffolding with support to successfully reach a specific learning outcome.

A key to continuous program improvement is to examine and analyze data at the program level. For example, completion data is useful in discovering which courses students find to be the most challenging, which courses cause students to exit a program, and which courses serve as gateway course for the program. A simple adjustment to the design of a program might be to change the order in which students move through the required courses of study. Similarly, an examination of key assessments in a program can provide essential data to ensure that multiple sections of courses with different instructors are achieving the intended student learning outcomes. Programmatic data might demonstrate patterns based on key assessments which can be used to continuously improve the course and subsequent student performance.

Increasing amounts of data are also available at the course level through the LMS as well as from electronic versions of textbooks, if one is being used (Van Horne, Russell, & Schuh, 2015). When designing or redesigning courses, these data make it easier to determine necessary areas for improvement. Historical data from a course that is being redesigned can be compared to courses in which students are successful and are satisfied with their experiences.

Finally, it is wise to consider data at the national or higher education level. It is known, for example, that students who do well on the initial exam of most courses tend to do well on subsequent work (Brown, 2012). Similarly, a more personalized approach to learning often leads to greater achievement of student learning outcomes. For example, Bloom explained that students perform much better with one-on-one or one-on-two tutoring (Bloom, 1984). It is important to design courses that allow faculty to utilize real-time data to personalize the experience for each student or better yet, for the student to "choose their own adventure" through the course.

Case Studies and Tools

To gain a sense of the scope and ability of learning analytics, it is helpful to be aware of some case studies and tools. In this section, we provide examples of how institutions have used dashboards, institutional data, and database tools to improve student success and retention. Many institutions have created and/or used dashboard tools (see Verbert, Duval, Klerkx, Govaerts, & Santos, 2013, for a review). The goal of a dashboard is to provide a visualization of student progress and performance in a course (e.g., Baepler & Murdoch, 2010). Dashboards can be configured for students, instructors, or both. For example, Purdue University created SIGNALS, which extracts data and provides a dashboard for both students and faculty to track student progress.

There are also interesting examples of using institutional data to predict student success and retention. For example, Sinclair Community College developed their Student Success Plan (SSP) for advising and retention. Collection and analysis of these data allows them to track student development and improve student success. In a similar vein, the University of Maryland Baltimore Country makes use of a learning analytics tool built in to their institutions' LMS, which allows them to track student progress. Similarly, there are many examples of institutions that have successfully implemented student-focused learning analytics systems. These institutions use data to create a model of successful student behavior to which current students can be compared. When students deviate from the model, an intervention is triggered, and advisors, instructors, or other student services can be notified. Norris and Baer (2013) documented several institutions including Purdue, Rio Salado College, and Arizona State University that have implemented predictive analytics to identify at-risk students for intervention. The University of Michigan uses an intervention program that, at the time it was designed, was based on fourteen years of historical student data. The system uses this data to identify students and recommends study resources and strategies (Wright, Mckay, Hershock, Miller, & Tritz, 2014). These institutions have reported success in identifying and intervening with at-risk students.

Finally, there are a plethora of database tools that can be used to track student progress and predict student success. These include large databases such as dataTEL, DataShop, and Mucle (Verbert, Manouselis, Drachsler, & Duval, 2012) that have been or can be used for learning analytic projects. Social network tools include "Mzinga" or SNAPP (Social Networks Adapting Pedagogical Practice) can be used to quantify level of participation in a network of learners. Similarly, "Gephi" provides a visualization of social network participation.

Benefits of Using Learning Analytics

A well-designed learning analytics program comes with a host of benefits that can be realized at both the institutional and classroom levels. For institutional administrators, the benefits include the ability to provide a clearer picture of the institution's health, leading to more efficient resource allocation and improved productivity (Long & Siemens, 2011). In the classroom, benefits include identifying at-risk students, measuring classroom success, gaining insight into student learning, and informing pedagogical choices. Students benefit from an analysis of their learning activities, leading to the recommendation of specific resources (Long & Siemens, 2011), and the development of customized study plans (Bichsel, 2012). These benefits are not only advantageous to students, but they also can support predictive models of student behavior, enabling educators and academic advisors to intervene, and instructional designers to improve course design.

Learning analytics often uses a combination of longitudinal student data and LMS activity (Norris & Baer, 2013). In a case study on using learning analytics to engage in interventions, Smith et al. (2012) found that several kinds of student activities logged by the LMS correlated with course outcomes. By tracking log-in frequency, time spent in course, and other activity data, instructors can intervene early in a course to help students improve their academic behaviors (Smith et al., 2012). These interventions not only help students stay enrolled, they also benefit the institution by helping it meet its education mission.

Furthermore, the benefits of learning analytics extend to course design/redesign and pedagogy. Learning analytics can help educators identify and reinforce weak content areas as well as address student needs for additional instruction (Krumm, Waddington, Teasley, & Lonn, 2014). Not only can instructors monitor student progress, but both instructors and instructional designers can gain insight into the structure and content of their curriculum and make improvements in future course iterations

(Liñán et al., 2015). Another benefit comes from informing students about their own learning processes (Scheffel, Drachsler, Stoyanov, & Specht, 2014). By sharing these data with students, they can reflect on their learning activities and behaviors and make adjustments if necessary.

As the study and use of learning analytics matures, new kinds of benefits will be realized. For example, Norris and Baer's (2013) learning analytics framework not only involves the use of predictive analytics on campus, but extends data collection after graduation and into careers, leading to another potential area for applying student modeling. Additionally, academic advisors have become users of learning analytics systems, which have helped advisors keep track of advisees even when those students do not actively participate in the advising process (Krumm et al., 2014). The benefits of learning analytics impact the institution through improving the depth and richness of data reporting. Instructors and instructional designers benefit from gaining insight into student behavior as well as discovering areas for course improvements and pedagogical changes. Most important, students benefit with an improved learning experience based on a data-driven support structure.

Concerns/Issues

While learning analytics offers great promise for improving experiences and outcomes for students and instructors, there are several issues and concerns that need to be considered. Instructional designers should be aware of these concerns as they may be involved in addressing many of them. A fundamental set of concerns relates to culture and includes ethical, legal, and privacy matters. The globalization of education complicates these considerations by bringing together different national and cultural perspectives.

Ethically, analytics need to be seen as tools to support pedagogy rather than as an end in and of themselves (Greller & Drachsler, 2012). Learning analytics involve and impact human beings, so the ethical and legal constraints applied to research on human subjects should be considered (Belmont Report, 1979). Other cultural issues include concerns that learning analytics may be "Big Brother-ish" and lead to profiling of learners (Campbell et al., 2007), could reveal information before individuals wish to share the information (Duhigg, 2012), or lead individuals to feel that they are being monitored and manipulated for the benefit of others.

Questions about privacy are complicated by the fact that it is not often clear who has ownership of the data. The digital nature of data makes it easy to transfer data around the world, but legal protection for data changes at national borders. The nature of digital data also makes considerations of ownership difficult. If data is generated through a student's participation, does the student have rights over the data? While data rights are poorly defined in the United States, the European Union has clear protection for an individual's personal data (Council Directive 95/46/EC, 1995).

A related concern with learning analytics is that data used in analytics is often not collected specifically for use in the analytics process. For example, a LMS typically logs student actions like accessing a page or viewing a video. These data could be useful in learning analytics. However, typically all that is being recorded is that the student requested the page or video, not that the content was delivered. Similarly, apparent patterns in student participation in an online discussion may simply reflect the due dates for the assignment. This secondary use of data presents many challenges (Solove, 2008). A related issue involves the responsibility of acting on the data. If learning analytics can identify an intervention that will improve student success, is there an obligation for the institution to act? If so, who should act? Should the instructor or perhaps a dedicated learning support specialist respond? And who will be responsible for providing the resources to support necessary interventions?

The use of learning analytics broadens the skills and knowledge that instructional designers and instructors must understand. While detailed knowledge of data collection methods and statistical analysis may not be needed, instructional designers will need knowledge to understand that individual uses of learning analytics are appropriate for the context of a specific course. A special challenge here is that there can be wide variations in the number and demographics of students enrolled in a course. So, analytics that show good predictive power in one setting may have no predictive power in another setting. While this may seem daunting, many of the techniques used to introduce and support the use of technology in teaching could be applied to developing knowledge and promoting use of learning analytics.

A final concern is the current immaturity of learning analytics, which is to be expected for a new and developing field. One consequence of this is that before they can look for insights, instructional designers may need to be involved in data collection, management, and analysis. Instructional designers may spend more time finding or building tools, managing data, and resolving issues than they spend getting insights about how to improve a course. Adding to this challenge is that many of the tools and techniques developed for analytics outside the educational sector are intended for data sets several orders of magnitude larger than those from a class of twenty to one hundred students. A related aspect of this immaturity is that tools and data available often were not developed specifically for learning analytics. For example, data on student use of video content in a LMS may simply represent when the student requested the content, with no indication that the content was successfully displayed to the student, much less whether the student actually viewed the video. Similarly, a LMS may display the last time a student logged into the LMS, but from an analytics perspective, it would be more useful to display the elapsed time since the last login.

These issues and concerns will continue to evolve as learning analytics mature. Issues related to ethics, privacy, and use of data will be ongoing concerns at the institutional, national, and international levels. As the individuals most directly involved in designing and delivering learning experiences, instructional designers and instructors must be involved in discussing and addressing these concerns. Concerns about developing knowledge and tools to support learning analytics will also persist, but should diminish as research and exploration of learning analytics progresses.

Conclusion

There is no doubt that we increasingly live in a data-driven world of predictive data analytics. The ultimate goal is to use these data to improve the learning experiences of students through data-supported decision making and design. There are prescriptive analytics available at the course, program, institutional, and national levels that can be used in the initial design of a course as well as for continuous improvement of courses and programs. The potential benefits include better institutional and programmatic health and, of course, more successful students. Because learning analytics is still in the infancy stage, it might require a steep investment in planning, collecting, and analyzing data in order for the instructional designer to reap significant benefits. Care should be exercised in the collection, securing, and usage of all data to be sure that privacy and ethical issues are properly addressed. Learning analytics are here to stay and will soon be an expected part of the instructional designer's arsenal.

Summary of Key Principles

1. **The main goal of learning analytics is to use data-driven tools and procedures to improve student experiences.** Student experiences can be improved through using data to improve administrative efficiency, inform pedagogy and curriculum, and advance student learning.

2. **The sources and types of data amenable to learning analytics are many and varied.** Although most data for learning analytics applications are culled from learning management systems, data can also be obtained from institutional records, e-texts or other learning applications, course evaluations, national data, and the instructor.

3. **Learning analytics can be applied in design at the course, program, and institutional levels.** Data can be used to drive the initial design and redesign of courses and programs while also influencing institutional directions and decisions.

4. **To gain a sense of the utility and capability of learning analytics, consider modeling some of the tools or case studies described in this chapter.** Many institutions have developed their own tools for learning-analytic purposes or have exploited the features of their learning management systems for student alerts or for predictive purposes.

5. **Many stakeholders benefit from the application of learning analytics, most importantly students.** By developing tools that make effective use of learning analytics, behaviors can be modeled, at-risk students identified, and interventions implemented.

6. **Before making use of learning analytics, instructional designers should be familiar with concerns about ethics, invasion of privacy, and profiling that could impact learning and the relationship between instructors and students.**

Application Questions

1. The provost at your institution has recently expressed concern about retention in lower-division courses. Specifically, she has data suggesting that the retention rates for lower-division courses are about 10 percent lower than upper-division courses. She has asked for proposals to help study this issue, with the goal of providing recommendations for how the university can improve retention rates in lower-division courses. Given what you know about learning analytics, write a proposal that outlines the various ways that learning analytics can be used to study the issue, and how it can be instrumental in providing solutions.

2. At a recent department meeting, the department chair asked faculty and graduate students what they knew about learning analytics, as he had been reading about its use in higher education. For the most part, the ensuing discussion was positive—faculty mentioned that they, too, had been hearing more about learning analytics and how it could be used to improve student success. But a couple of faculty expressed serious concern about ethical issues, stating that learning analytics can lead to profiling and that its use violates FERPA. Being well versed on many of the controversies and concerns surrounding learning analytics, how do you contribute to this conversation? Describe how you can educate faculty and graduate students about the concerns and issues that have been articulated in the literature.

3. You are working with a faculty member to design an introductory online science course. The instructor argues that if the students read the book and do assigned homework problems, that should be sufficient to properly learn the material. How can you use what you know about learning analytics to explain why there should be more to the design of this course? What types of design alternatives would you suggest based on learning-analytic data from other successful science course designs? What type of data could be collected and analyzed after the course is designed to measure its "success" or "failure"?

References

Baepler, P., & Murdoch, C. J. (2010). Academic analytics and data mining in higher education. *International Journal for the Scholarship of Teaching and Learning, 4(2),* article 17.

Belmont Report. (1979). *The Belmont report: Ethical principles and guidelines for the protection of human subjects of research.* Retrieved from http://www.hhs.gov/ohrp/policy/belmont.htmlhttp://www.hhs.gov/ohrp/policy/belmont.html

Bichsel, J. (2012). *Analytics in higher education: Benefits, barriers, progress, and recommendations.* Louisville, CO: EDUCAUSE Center for Applied Research. Retrieved from http://net.educause.edu/ir/library/pdf/ERS1207/ers1207.pdf

Bloom, B. S. (1984). The 2 sigma problem: The search for methods of group instruction as effective as one-to-one tutoring. *Educational Researcher, 13*(6), 4–16.

Brown, M. (2012). Learning analytics: Moving from concept to practice. *Educause Learning Initiative,* 1–5. Retrieved from https://net.educause.edu/ir/library/pdf/ELIB1203.pdf

Campbell, J. P., DeBlois, P. B., & Oblinger, D. (2007). Academic analytics: A new tool for a new era. *EDUCAUSE Review, 42*(4), 40–57. Retrieved from http://er.educause.edu/articles/2007/7/academic-analytics-a-new-tool-for-a-new-erahttp://er.educause.edu/articles/2007/7/academic-analytics-a-new-tool-for-a-new-era

Council Directive 95/46/EC on the protection of individuals with regard to the processing of personal data and on the free movement of such data. (1995). *Official Journal of the European Communities, L281/31.* Retrieved from http://eur-lex.europa.eu/legal-content/EN/TXT/?uri=CELEX:31995L0046http://eur-lex.europa.eu/legal-content/EN/TXT/?uri=CELEX:31995L0046

Denley, T. (2014). How predictive analytics and choice architecture can improve student success. *Research & Practice in Assessment, 9*(Winter), 61–69.

Dietz, B. (March, 2015). *Immediacy behavior in the online classroom: Effects on student performance and engagement.* Poster presented at SoTL Commons, Savannah, GA.

Duhigg, C. (2012, February 16). How companies learn your secrets, *The New York Times Magazine.* Retrieved from http://www.nytimes.com/2012/02/19/magazine/shopping-habits.html

Feldstein, M. (2013, December, 17). What faculty should know about adaptive learning [Blog post]. Retrieved from http://mfeldstein.com/faculty-know-adaptive-learning/http://mfeldstein.com/faculty-know-adaptive-learning/

Greller, W., & Drachsler, H. (2012). Translating learning into numbers: A generic framework for learning analytics. *Educational Technology & Society, 15*(3), 42–57.

Jones, S. J. (2012, Spring). Technology review: The possibilities of learning analytics to improve learner centered decision making. *The Community College Enterprise,* 89–92.

Krumm, A., Waddington, R. J., Teasley, S. D., & Lonn, S. (2014). A learning management system-based early warning system for academic advising in undergraduate engineering. In J. A. Larusson & B. White (Eds.), *Learning analytics: From research to practice* (pp. 103–119). New York: Springer.

Larusson, J. A., & White, B. (Eds.). (2014). *Learning analytics: From research to practice.* New York: Springer.

Liñán, L. C., Alejandro, Á., & Pérez, J. (2015). Educational data mining and learning analytics: Differences, similarities, and time evolution. *RUSC. Universities and Knowledge Society Journal, 12*(3), 98–112.

Long, P. D., & Siemens, G. (2011). Penetrating the fog: Analytics in learning and education. *EDUCAUSE Review Online.* Retrieved from http://www.educause.edu/ero/article/penetrating-fog-analytics-learning-and-educationhttp://www.educause.edu/ero/article/penetrating-fog-analytics-learning-and-education

Morris, L. V., Wu, S., & Finnegan, C. (2005). Predicting retention in online general education courses. *The American Journal of Distance Education, 19*(1), 23–36.

Norris, D. M., & Baer, L. L. (2013). *Building organizational capacity for analytics.* Louisville, CO: EDUCAUSE. Retrieved from https://net.educause.edu/ir/library/pdf/PUB9012.pdf

Picciano, A. G. (2012). The evolution of big data and learning analytics in American higher education. *Journal of Asynchronous Learning Networks, 16*(3), 9–20.

Puget, J. F. (2015, September 21). Analytics landscape [Blog post]. Retrieved from https://www.ibm.com/developerworks/community/blogs/jfp/entry/Analytics_Models?lang=enhttps://www.ibm.com/developerworks/community/blogs/jfp/entry/Analytics_Models?lang=en

Scheffel, M., Drachsler, H., Stoyanov, S., & Specht, M. (2014). Quality indicators for learning analytics. *Educational Technology & Society, 17*(4), 117–132.

Shum, S. B., & Ferguson, R. (2012). Social learning analytics. *Educational Technology & Society, 15*(3), 3–26.

Smith, V. C., Lange, A., & Huston, D. R. (2012). Predictive modeling to forecast student outcomes and drive effective interventions in online community college courses. *Journal of Asynchronous Learning Networks, 16*(3), 51–61.

Solove, D. (2008). *Understanding privacy.* Cambridge, MA: Harvard University Press.

Van Horne, S., Russell, J., & Schuh, K. L. (2015). *Assessment with e-textbook analytics.* Retrieved from Educause website: http://net.educause.edu/ir/library/pdf/erb1501.pdf

Verbert, K., Duval, E., Klerkx, J., Govaerts, S., & Santos, J. L. (2013). Learning analytics dashboard applications. *American Behavioral Scientist*, *57*(10), 1500–1509. doi:10.1177/0002764213479363.

Verbert, K., Manouselis, N., Drachsler, H., & Duval, E. (2012). Dataset-driven research to support learning and knowledge analytics. *Educational Technology & Society*, *15*(3), 133–148.

Wright, M. C., Mckay, T., Hershock, C., Miller, K., & Tritz, J. (2014). Better than expected: Using learning analytics to promote student success in gateway science. *Change: The Magazine of Higher Learning*, *46*(1), 28–34.

Yoder, J. D., & Hochevar, C. M. (2005). Encouraging active learning can improve students' performance on examinations. *Teaching of Psychology*, *32*, 91–95.

Chapter 13
Onsite and Virtual Project Management

Brenda C. Litchfield

University of South Alabama

Experience shows that many new instructional designers, very early in their careers, are put in charge of an instructional design project. In other words, they become instructional project managers. The purpose of this chapter is to provide you with some suggestions to successfully perform that role.

Instructional project managers face a variety of unique situations with every project they direct. Although the topics and products are different, the skills needed to successfully manage them are the same. How would you react to each of the following scenarios? What would you do first, then second? As an instructional project manager what leadership and management skills do you need? What communication skills are required? How would you organize project components? How would you get these different teams motivated and moving in the same direction to complete the project on time and within budget? How will you manage a virtual team? Here are a few examples you may face as a project manager:

Scenario 1: You just received an e-mail from your supervisor. Your team was selected to create instruction for the administrative staff of the county license division. Instead of having the staff sit and listen to long classroom lectures for training, the director wants it all to be delivered as an online course. There are six separate topics that must be informative and interactive. You will be the project manager and a detailed plan is needed by next week for completing the project in four months. (Team members: 3)

Scenario 2: A contract was given to your organization to develop a comprehensive set of online courses for restaurant managers on topics such as dealing with employees, budgets, and general food service management. Eight online course developers who live in different locations in the United States were hired to design and develop courses. They must work with programmers, writers, and graphic artists. All courses must be in a similar format with the same look and feel. The project has a seven-month timeline. (Team members: 10, with 5 offsite)

Scenario 3: AAA has awarded you a grant to create a driver's safety course for teenagers. Everything has been planned—objectives, timelines, cost breakdowns, design specifications, content, evaluation procedures. As project manager, you will need to hire a staff to complete the project within a twelve-month time frame. (Team members: 20, with 10 offsite)

Each of these three scenarios is an example of a situation requiring instructional project management. These projects vary considerably in many aspects. One will have all the staff under one roof while another will use developers in different locations. Often, projects are a combination of both. Some have a complete design document specifying all procedures and deliverables. For others, it is up to you to do all the planning. One scenario involves three team members; others require a staff of up to twenty talented individuals. The timeline for one project is three months; another will take one year.

The common thread running through each project, regardless of scope and complexity, is your ability as project manager to manage, motivate, and lead your team. It is often thought that a small instructional development project is much easier than a large one. Not necessarily true. Regardless of size, you should be able to monitor progress, solve problems, motivate, and move your team forward by communicating your instructions and desires. All teams strive to accomplish the objectives of the project and meet the expectations of the project and client (Dinsmore, 2006). The clearer you can make your objectives and expectations, the better results you will achieve. All teams have personalities and are motivated by different payoffs as individuals and as a team. Your job is to find out what the desired payoffs and motivations are and use them to the project's advantage, as well as your own.

There are numerous books, articles, and guides on project management detailing how to budget, schedule, produce documents, and evaluate projects (Berkun, 2008; Craig, 2012; Greer, 2011; Hanley, 2015; Kerzner, 2013; Portny, 2013). This chapter will not focus on areas considered to be *tools* of project management, but will concentrate on the aspects of project management and leadership related to the basic personal qualities that can help make you an effective project manager and team leader while producing a quality instructional product. The areas considered especially important for successful project management are development of effective leadership skills, development of effective teams, and effective communication with your team.

Management and Leadership

There are different definitions of management. The most commonly reoccurring component of management definitions is that a manager is tasked with achieving certain organizational goals with a team or staff of individuals. Specific tasks are to be carried out and it is up to the manager to make sure they are accomplished. Hersey and Blanchard (2013) offer one definition encompassing many aspects of what a manager does: "Management is the process of working with and through individuals and groups and other resources (equipment, capital, technology) to accomplish organizational goals" (p. 5). Thus, strong interpersonal skills are paramount to the success of a manager.

Instructional project management employs many of the components of general management (e.g., program management, administrative management). It does, however, differ because of the nature of projects. As illustrated in the introductory scenarios, each project is different and can take on a life of its own. To see an instructional project through to completion, your personal management style will be a critical factor in ensuring the team meets deadlines and produces its deliverables.

Successful project management also requires leadership. The terms *management* and *leadership* are often used synonymously but are operationally two different sets of actions and philosophies. Leadership deals with a broader aspect of achieving goals and objectives. Leaders function more as innovators, visionaries, trust builders, and influencers of people. Effective leaders motivate their teams by bringing out the best in individuals (Wong, 2007) and integrating the team's energy, talents, and abilities to foster success (Duke Corporate Education, 2009). Leaders can also influence people through charisma and earned respect. Managers execute the plan, keep the closest goal in sight, and focus on production and deadlines. "Managers do things right, leaders do the right things" (Bennis, 1994, p. 12).

Because management skills (meeting deadlines, supervising staff, staying within budget, etc.) are usually understood more easily than leadership skills, some important aspects of leadership will be discussed. In the past, it was widely accepted that some people are "born leaders" and others were not. Today, however, it is possible for individuals to become successful leaders through work experience, opportunity, education, role models, and mentors. These situations can further be enhanced through positive personal characteristics such as competence, character, and emotional stability (Hill & Lineback, 2011).

According to Hersey and Blanchard (2013), leadership involves three interrelated competencies. These areas represent cognitive, behavioral, and process skills. Being able to diagnose the environment in terms of assessing the current situation and planning what can be done to solve a problem is considered a cognitive skill. Adapting behavior and other resources to match whatever actions are required to solve the problem is a behavioral skill. The process skill is communication. Being able to communicate with staff members and have them understand plans and goals while you listen and respond to their suggestions and concerns is the third essential competency of an effective leader.

Certainly, there are numerous aspects of diagnosing, adapting, and communicating, with each being worthy of further study. It is important to remember that, as an instructional project manager, you must integrate these skills in your daily routine because *you* are responsible for the ultimate success or failure of your project. You must always know the status of all aspects of the project(s) your staff and team members are working on. If they are behind schedule or do not understand project objectives, not only must you recognize this, but you must also be able to design a solution to remedy whatever the problem is, and communicate it effectively.

So, as a person in the position of directing an instructional project should you be more of a manager or a leader? You must be both. As an instructional project manager, you are in a unique position of using both management and leadership skills. In instructional projects such as the scenarios described at the beginning of this chapter, there may be as few as three people or as many as twenty on a project. Unless you are working for a large instructional design company or training organization where many teams and numerous projects run concurrently, you will probably work with a relatively small group of individuals. In these cases, as project manager, you will be responsible for meeting project goals, timelines, and budgets. At the same time you will be the person leading and motivating your team with your energy, insight, and encouragement.

The ability to influence your team depends heavily on your personality and behavior. Maslow (1998) posits that enlightened management can produce more well-rounded employees. If management is fair, rewarding, and understanding, then employees develop more positive actions among each other and with people they know. Barry (2015) surveyed participants in many of his project leadership courses about what they thought it took to be a successful project manager. Participants mentioned that such a person would have these ten essential traits: (1) a shared vision, (2) good communication, (3) integrity, (4) enthusiasm, (5) empathy, (6) competence, (7) the ability to delegate, (8) compose under pressure, (9) team-building skills, and (10) problem-solving skills.

From this list it is evident the skills considered most critical to successful project management were not the abilities to create schedules, define objectives, develop a budget, or conduct formative evaluation. They were interpersonal skills that direct and motivate a team. Certainly, technical skills are important—a project would ultimately fail if the project manager could not handle these aspects of the job—but the personality and behavior you exhibit toward your team is the underlying foundation that builds all relationships and determines whether you are respected or simply tolerated as a leader. You must be flexible and adapt to a variety of situations and people throughout the course of a project.

The Hersey and Blanchard situational leadership model (2013) is an important tool for project managers. It is based on three factors: (1) the amount of guidance and direction a leader gives, (2) the amount of socio-emotional support a leader provides, and (3) the readiness level followers exhibit in performing a specific task, function, or objective. From your basic personality and behavior you develop a leadership style. Different situations and people require different responses. Your leadership style should not remain consistent. This may seem like odd advice, but to treat all situations and all people exactly the same will result in your handling some situations effectively and others ineffectively. By adapting your leadership style and resources based on correctly analyzing specific situations you will be more effective.

Using the situational leadership approach involves a cycle of four phases based on the maturity of your project team. If your team was inexperienced and unsure (often at the beginning of projects) your leadership style (phase 1) would be directive, detailed, and supervisory without being overbearing or appearing to be demanding. As your team gains more confidence but is still learning (phase 2), you can move from a more directive role to one where you explain and clarify decisions and reward improvements in direction and knowledge. At this point you are securing the team's "buy in" of the process and product. The more team members learn, the more they can function on their own. Now your leadership role (phase 3) changes to focusing on results and making sure your team is rewarded for effort and production. The last stage (phase 4) involves less of your involvement as a director and more as a monitor. Your team has learned how to work together to produce a product and you can step back and let it work without the close supervision that was necessary in the beginning of the project.

In each of the four phases there are fine lines between being effective or ineffective in your management. For example, while you may see your decrease in direct, observable monitoring as an indication of your trust in your team, the team members may see it as a lack of interest on your part. What is important in each phase is how you communicate what you want to those involved in designing and producing the product.

Communication

Effective communication among all individuals is an essential skill that is becoming more important as we move to a wider base of workers and businesses. According to Meyer (2014), the increase in globalization, along with digital technologies, presents even more communication challenges. Communication with your team members, whether they are in the same building or located in different states or countries, can be challenging. Everyone requires concrete instructions as well as enthusiasm, motivation, and acceptance. Your team will want to know exactly what you expect, when you expect it, and what quality you expect. There is no room for errors in communication when *you* are ultimately responsible for deadlines, budgets, and products. Do not assume people know what you are thinking. Make it crystal clear—regardless of how many people you are communicating with. Often serious communication problems can arise when you are working on a small project with just a few people because it is easy to believe you are all thinking the same way.

Discipline problems among some team members are unavoidable in most projects. In numerous situations you will have to recognize inadequate or improper actions and have a serious meeting with some of your team members. How you handle these situations can have a strong bearing on other team members' perception of your leadership. To recognize a discrepant situation and not act quickly can make you appear to be uninterested, uninvolved, or showing favoritism. A classic in the field of management, *The One-Minute Manager* (Blanchard & Johnson, 1982), stresses the importance of "The One Minute Reprimand." Reprimand immediately, explain exactly what was done wrong and how you feel about it, focus on the action not the person, remind that you value the person, and end it. No overblown confrontations, just straight to-the-point communication.

As an instructional project manager, you will have to communicate with a variety of people individually and as groups. Figure 13.1 illustrates the typical communication pattern of a project manager. The arrow width indicates the frequency of communication with each individual or group. You will also have to negotiate and interpret communication between and among groups and individuals even though you may not attend meetings or interact with some individuals directly. In these cases you may act as a mediator between groups—an important function and one that is necessary to keep the project running smoothly and on time.

Team Communication

An instructional project development team usually consists of instructional designers, assistant project managers (large projects), writers, artists, and (in video/computer projects) videographers, scriptwriters, and other technical people such as programmers. The majority of your communication will be with the team itself. Your primary tasks with the team are to motivate and monitor progress. These are the individuals with whom you will be most involved over the term of the project. Whether you have a team of three or twenty, accurate, timely, and genuine communication with the team is the most critical element in successfully completing an instructional project. The

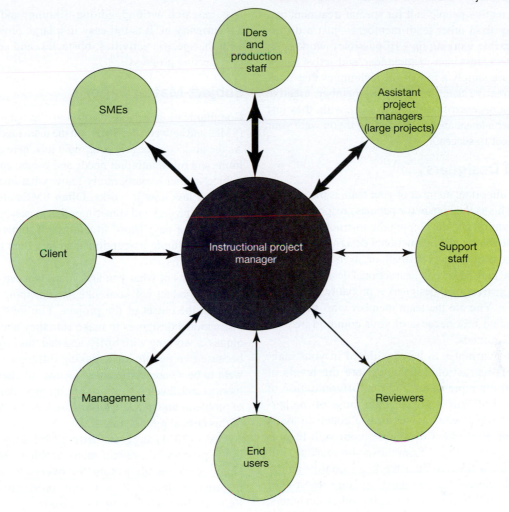

FIGURE 13.1 Communication pattern of an instructional project manager.

bulk of your communication with the team will focus on project direction and motivation. You should communicate your enthusiasm and monitor progress regularly. Even though these individuals are competent in their respective fields, the particular combination of personalities in a specific instructional project may present unique problems, all of which you will be expected to handle.

Production Staff

The production staff on a project may include writers, editors, graphic designers, artists, web designers, and other media specialists. Oftentimes, one of the most interesting challenges for an instructional project manager is working with the creative people who serve as members of the production staff. If you approach management of creative people the same way you approach traditional management, you may find resistance and misunderstanding. Most views of management are meeting deadlines, budgets, and so forth. Creative people are not often driven by the same goals.

Creativity on demand is difficult, if not impossible, to achieve. Often what is required with creative individuals is

flexible work hours and scheduling. Creative individuals often take their jobs very seriously because their egos are in each idea and presentation. Critiquing the work of a creative individual takes a bit more sensitivity because of these issues. To most employees, when something is not done to the supervisor's liking, it is easy for them to say, "That's what you told me to do." Not so with creative team members. They put themselves and their creativity on the line each time they explore a way to develop a lesson, create a page design, or produce a video.

Creative people are independent and can be unpredictable and risky (McGuinness, 2010). An important factor for many is an appreciation of their efforts, along with freedom to be creative without fear of being criticized for trying new ideas. Creative people should be approached with sensitivity and knowledge of the processes they go through to produce their "product" which they may consider to be a reflection of themselves. Sometimes the legendary temperamental and stubborn side of creative people actually comes from misunderstandings or feelings of being limited creatively. They have ideas about a design or an approach and at least want to be heard before you say it will not work or is totally in the wrong direction.

It is not that creative people call for special treatment and less responsibility than other team members—just a different approach. Flexible working time (if possible), working in teams, freedom to express ideas without fear, and active listening on your part are simply a few of the techniques that work well with your creative team members. Remember, creative individuals are not necessarily difficult to work with; they just require a bit of special care and understanding if you want your instructional project to succeed.

Instructional Designers

Perhaps the most important member of your team is the instructional designer. This is the person (or persons) responsible for researching, designing, and developing the instructional product. It may be that *you* are the instructional designer as well as the manager because the project is small, or, as in the case of a large project, there may be several instructional designers. Your relationship with instructional designers is probably the closest one you will have. You are the team member who should be able to communicate best because of your common instructional design backgrounds.

Two important variables to be considered in your management of other instructional designers are the levels of experience and skills represented and the differentiation of roles. If your level of skill is greater than those of the persons you are managing, you can serve as a coach to assist their development. Regardless of whether your skill level is greater, lesser, or just different from those you manage, it is your responsibility to review their work for quality and to provide feedback. Secondly, you must separate the role of manager from "doer." If you are managing other designers, it will be difficult to get used to the fact that their styles and products will be different from what you would have done, and you will be tempted to do it yourself whenever possible. However, it is vital to remember that you are responsible for their development, and you obtain the products you want by means of clear communication of expectations, coaching, and feedback, not by doing it yourself. Even though you are a designer, team members will still look at you as a manager or leader first and expect the guidance and direction that comes with that position.

Assistant Project Managers

If yours is a large project, multiple teams may be necessary, which will require assistant project managers (APMs). Your main focus with these individuals is to motivate, direct, and inform. They are responsible for communicating with their specific team members. Because directions and procedures are going through APMs, each communication should be especially clear and precise. It may be best to provide APMs with written directives and memos to ensure exact communication. Instructional development is particularly detail oriented; and those details must make it to the right person intact.

It is also helpful if you have APMs file a weekly report to you about the progress of their team and fill out a team status report. This consists of each of the development phases (e.g., research, writing, editing, filming) and what stage they are currently in. It is too easy in a large project to lose touch with the specific activities, obstacles, and achievements that are affecting progress.

Subject-Matter Experts

Communication between you and the subject-mater expert (SME) and between the SME and the team takes on many forms. As the project manager, your main jobs here are to explain the limits and roles, interpret needs and wants, and settle disputes. Subject-matter experts rarely know what instructional design is, much less how it works. Often SMEs are "appointed" to work on a project and sometimes this means extra work with no extra time or pay. These situations are sometimes challenging due to inaccurate perceptions and less than positive attitudes of some SMEs.

The limits of what you and your team can do, and what the finished product will look like, is something the SME should know at the outset of the project. You must work with your instructional designers to make sure they understand the techniques of working with SMEs and that this is often a trying task because two people are speaking different languages. SMEs want to be aware of the consequences of changes (more time, money) and develop specific sign-off procedures. Identification of problems and quick solutions are keys to careful monitoring of this critical relationship.

Greer (2011) suggests getting SMEs involved very early in the process, to prevent many problems later. In addition, Greer recommends asking for overviews of their field or information that will help you understand what they do. Requests for such information also make it clear you respect the SME's professional judgment. You want to develop a close relationship with SMEs because they are often vital to a project, especially as relates to reviews and meeting deadlines.

The Client

The amount of communication you have with the client actually depends on the size of the project. If the project is small, such as the county license project scenario (team of three members), you may have direct contact with the client. In contrast, in the case of the restaurant management scenario (staff of fifteen) or the AAA grant (team of twenty), there may be a separate project director who oversees the general components of the project while you run the daily operations. Sometimes the project director will have more direct contact with the client.

Assuming you have direct contact with the client, your tasks are to interpret ideas, explain limits, get approvals and sign-offs, and most of all, make the client happy. In an ideal project, you will not have much contact with the client if everything is going according to schedule. Your communications focus mainly on where you are in the schedule and what progress you are making. It is important to communicate to the client (as you did to the SME) that changes to the set plan are serious and can have time and money consequences. A solid, direct understanding about this early on will save many problems later. It is desirable at the beginning of the project to gain firm client commitment to supporting the project by providing *and motivating* SMEs and reviewers, and providing in a timely manner all other input information that will help the project.

You may also be required to mediate communication between the client and SME. If the SME gets upset about something the instructional designer cannot do, a meeting with the client often ensues. Then you may have the "them against me" situation you will have to interpret, analyze, and solve. Keeping a client happy involves good communication so there are no surprises. Nothing is worse than surprising a client with a statement such as, "We are going to require three extra weeks to finish this part," or "Because you changed this, I forgot to tell you it will cost $5,000 more" (as you hand over the bill). The secret with client communication is keeping it on a regular interval and filling it with pertinent details.

Management

Management in this context refers to your supervisor. Your communication with this person focuses on information about progress and problems with the client. Unless something goes wrong, these communications take the form of regularly scheduled meetings or status reports. Management does not need to know about specific problems with the team—these are yours to solve. The more you can handle yourself, the more capable you are. Management and the client tend to want the same information—that is, where you are in terms of progress.

Management should be consulted if something gets beyond your control, such as the client making unreasonable requests or wanting substantial changes. You may not have total authority to make these decisions depending, again, on the size of your project. If you do, make sure you get things in writing and have everyone sign off on the new schedule and process.

End Users

At first thought, it would seem that as an instructional project manager you would not communicate with the end users. Actually, communicating with them during the initial stages of the project is essential. If possible, at the initial stage conduct a face-to-face meeting. If this is not feasible, send out a questionnaire. The purpose of a meeting or questionnaire is to ascertain if the planned direction or approach is appropriate and realistic for this particular audience. Although your initial communication with end users may not be extensive, it can make a tremendous difference in the acceptance of your instructional product. After this point, the instructional designer carries out the majority of the interaction with the end user.

It is especially helpful for the instructional designer to communicate with the end user when planning and designing instruction. It is easy to get so involved in the design that the overall approach is overlooked and may not be something interesting to the audience. Audiences vary in many respects:

culture, age, education, interests, and backgrounds. For example, an adult designing for teenagers is tricky because you have the design skills but lack an understanding of relevant strategies and current trends that would capture teenagers' interest and keep them motivated.

Reviewers

The most difficult issue to communicate successfully to reviewers is the importance of timely turnaround. You will often not meet reviewers in person. Your contact with them is usually only through a cover letter or an e-mail explaining the process and what they are expected to do, such as how to fill out an evaluation form and what specific aspects of the program they will be addressing. Because everyone is busy and some reviewers are taking on this task in addition to their other work, you will rarely get all reviews back by the specified date. Others you may never get back. It is most helpful to gain support from the managers of the reviewers, especially when your client is their manager. This will help ensure the reviewers understand their timely cooperation is expected.

Some reviewers may need multiple requests for completion. As in all other instances of working with your team and staff, you must be assertive but not aggressive in your request. An important gesture with reviewers is to take the time to send a short thank-you note if they are doing the review without payment. They will not forget this and will be more likely to work with you in the future.

Support Staff

The support staff consists of a number of individuals such as editors, copyright specialists, and researchers who are essential to the timely function of the project. Although the support staff will mainly be communicating with the development team, you should make it a point to periodically check with the support staff to find out if things are progressing smoothly and on time. You will often be on a tight schedule and these individuals can make or break meeting deadlines. Support staff like clear, unambiguous instructions with enough time to do the job well. Do not underestimate the importance of communicating to establish and maintain good rapport with these individuals.

Building Productive Teams

As the instructional design projects become more complex and interrelated, teamwork becomes more of a necessity. As an instructional project manager you have to be a manager, a leader, and communicate well enough to get your team moving in the same direction, at the same time. An integrated, high-performing team can accomplish a great deal and make a project successful by being more innovative and solution oriented (Topchick, 2007). You have to guide team members to want to accomplish the goals and objectives you, the client, and management set forth. This is not an easy task with a diverse group of talented individuals. What motivates teams is a complex issue.

Keeping your team relaxed and happy amid deadlines and pressure is one way to make sure people are motivated to produce a quality product. Team members develop a much better understanding of team norms, roles, and goals if discussions related to these factors are held early on and throughout the project (Miller, 2011). Most workers are members of one or more work groups with whom they may interact more frequently than with members of their immediate family (Vroom, 1995). In addition to the usual project planning and formal communications, you must develop interesting ways to boost morale and engagement and keep everyone working well.

In addition to developing and nurturing the working relationship of a team, you, as project manager, must be able to "account for the culture, personality, and habits of the current team" (Berkun, 2008, p. 196). You must also be adept at leading your team through its growing stages. Your objective should be to get your team to work together effectively as soon as possible. This does not happen quickly. There are distinct but often overlapping stages in team development. Simply put, the stages are beginning, middle, and closure.

In the beginning, your job and how you handle yourself are most critical. You are responsible for setting the initial course and motivating your team. The project manager's ability to immediately take charge is extremely important (Portny, 2013). This sets the tone for the entire project. Roles must be defined and everyone should be clear about responsibilities. Not only must team members understand their own roles but they should also realize how all relationships in the entire organization interact and depend on each other.

Thinking back to our creative team members (who may have freelanced prior to this job) and first-time team members, they may not be cognizant of organizational relationships. This beginning stage can be confusing as personalities, new roles, and responsibilities come together for the first time. Professionals like to know what the ends are and to be given some control over the means. You will need to provide a great deal of guidance and monitor progress in a supportive manner without being overbearing, which is not an easy task.

In the middle of a project, team members are, hopefully, moving along and understanding their roles, the direction of the project, and developing their skills in accordance with project specifications. They will still need to be guided and monitored, but not as closely as in the beginning. At this point they should have a clear idea of what they are doing and how to do it. They are becoming more familiar with each other and the design and development task.

In the closure stage, the team is functioning at its upper limit and may neither require nor request much guidance from you. You must continue to diligently monitor and keep track of team progress and address any problems that arise. In some ways, your job has become easier now that team members know what to do, are producing products, and are taking pride in their work. But even though things are working well, there can be problems. The addition of new team members, changes in funding or direction, or not enough monitoring often result in new challenges. The most common project management mistake at this stage is to not pay enough attention to the team. It is important to monitor and motivate during both the drudgery and stress periods of a project. It is especially important as you approach the end of the project because this is often stressful, as everyone is struggling to meet deadlines and coordinate the final production of deliverables. Your interaction must be ever present but with a varying focus and level of direction throughout the stages of a project.

Virtual Instructional Project Management

One major area for the future of instructional project management is managing at a distance. With e-mail, instant messaging, and videoconferencing, you can select, direct, and manage a project and never meet your team members in person. Team members will be chosen for their knowledge and skills along with their computer and electronic skills. Managing at a distance can produce a whole new set of challenges for you as a manager, but it basically requires an extrapolation from in-person effective communication to effective electronic communications.

Virtual project management requires that managers and team members are aware of feedback systems and expend extra effort to communicate effectively. It is also important to develop methods where managers can detect early warning signs of potential problems. Managing at a distance can be a challenge for even an experienced project manager because the procedures and lines of communication are different. Leadership skills become e-mail based, communication can be impersonal, and development of effective teams takes place in cyberspace. Specific effort must be expended to make sure expectations are clear and all team members understand how to handle all aspects of a project, including conflict if it arises (Portny, 2013).

Hill and Lineback (2011) specify some critical challenges of managing virtual teams: specifying purpose, goals and team culture, developing trust among members, fostering interaction, and looking for evidence of interpersonal skills when hiring. Careful attention to these issues at the beginning can provide successful team development and communication with team members. It is important that you keep in close contact with all team members even if they are highly competent individuals. Often managers of virtual teams hire competent individuals and think they do not need much guidance. There is a difference between guidance and interaction. You can interact with team members without giving them guidance if they are truly competent and self-directed. Don't make the mistake of just leaving someone alone. You will still need to coach and communicate. Communication with offsite team members is essential. The encouragement, feedback, and recognition can be an essential part of building team confidence and cohesion.

Not everyone is skilled at or comfortable with giving feedback (Wong, 2007). It takes practice and you must be aware of your delivery and the receiver's perception of your message. Consistent, frequent feedback is critical. Unsolicited feedback is important and can be very motivational. Motivational feedback and developmental feedback are two different things and both are important and should be given often (Gardiner, 2005). Think of it as "walking" around the office and talking to your team. You can drop in via the computer just as you would in an office. Many virtual project managers keep in touch by way of videoconferencing. Some systems cost thousands of dollars but save even more in travel and lost productivity. Free downloads and an inexpensive camera can provide you with an economical way to "drop in" in real time.

Building trust and keeping virtual team members informed is even more critical than when working with a site-based team. Communicating with e-mail and instant messaging is efficient and fast but lacks the human interaction of site-based teams. Electronic messages also lack specific context in that they may be interpreted various ways (Mersino, 2007). For example, what may appear to be a joke can be taken as sarcasm by the receiver. You must be careful not to sound terse in messages. It is easy to send a quick one- or two-sentence response to a question without adding any other feeling or information. Try to avoid this. Always start by using the person's name in a salutation and ending the e-mail with your name. Sounds simple to do, but we get *many* messages that omit these short courtesies.

Planning every minute detail and controlling all processes can stifle a virtual team. This sounds counterintuitive to the project manager who likes to have everything organized and systematic. Keep in mind that you may have team members from different regions, cultures, and backgrounds. What works in Houston may not work in New York, Paris, or Tokyo. A virtual team is a fluid, dynamic entity that may have to change in response to customer needs. It's best to have a standard procedure with room for flexibility.

Just as with site-based teams, building group cohesion is an important component of virtual teams. Develop a team home page with photos and vitae. This will give everyone an idea about other members, who they are, and put a face with a name.

This does not have to be elaborate, just informational and informal. There are many techniques you can use to develop the sense of community and team spirit of a virtual team.

Regardless of new technology and managing offsite teams, virtual project management will always need the perception, sensitivity, and problem-solving skills required for a site-based project manager. If you can do these things effectively in person then you are well on your way to adapting them to managing at a distance.

Conclusion

Instructional project management is a complex human endeavor requiring psychology, management, science, and counseling. It would be impossible to say, "In this situation, do this." Management does not work this way because people are individuals and often unpredictable. This goes for team members as well as clients and management. At times you need to be a leader and at others a manager. You should be able to identify, diagnose, and solve problems with people and production in a manner that is sensitive and fair while being firm and directive.

Virtual leadership and management are becoming much more commonplace today. The skills you use onsite must be honed and adjusted to account for diversity and differences in culture and perspectives. Globalization is adding to the widespread occurrence of teams with many talented individuals from different cultures (Meyer, 2014). In many cases, the leadership styles that these team members have previously experienced are likely to differ greatly across individual team members. Given this diversity, electronic communication for virtual global teams although efficient, may not always be effective unless you pay close attention to wording and meanings.

So, how do you learn project management skills? Read, watch, talk, listen, and practice. Each instructional project is unique with different objectives, teams, and clients. Regardless of the differences, successful project managers should always lead by example while providing direction and motivation to their teams. It is the mastery of interpersonal skills, consideration of individual differences, and effective communication that enable instructional project managers to understand their teams and guide them to produce the best products.

Summary of Key Principles

1. **Leadership and management are different and require different skills.** Leaders motivate people through innovation, visions, trust, and influence. Managers execute the plan, keep goals in sight, and focus on production and deadlines.

2. **The most important skills in project management are your interpersonal skills that direct and motivate a team.** The abilities to create schedules, budgets, define objectives, and conduct evaluations are important but the interpersonal skills to lead a team are foremost.

3. **Managing creative individuals presents some interesting challenges.** If you approach management of creative people the same way you approach traditional management, you may find resistance and misunderstanding. They can take their jobs more seriously than others because their egos are in each idea and presentation.

4. **Virtual project management requires more specific skills.** Communication, direction, interaction, and motivation become more important when administered through electronic means. Culture and diversity must be considered and accounted for in all phases of the project.

5. **Effective communication with a diverse workforce requires careful consideration and practice.** Workers today are more diverse than in the past. Your team may be from different countries and cultures. You must be well versed in how to get your message across in the most effective, least offensive way. Sometimes brevity is not effective.

Application Questions

1. A $1 million project to develop an ten-course CBT program for bank branch managers has been limping along for six months and has already had two project managers. The project is behind schedule and the client is starting to complain. So far, nothing has been produced. The project team is floundering, individuals are not getting along, and there is little direction. You have just been hired as the third project manager. How will you approach this situation? What will you do in terms of the leadership skills you exhibit? What aspects of leadership will you focus on first, then second? How will you bring this team together to complete the project in time?

2. You have been hired as a project manager and have assembled a team of ten engineers to design and create a five-day orientation program for engineers hired at a large shipyard. Four of your team members are in town, three are one state away, and three are across the country. Some you will be able to meet with, some not. You have engineer SMEs, instructional designers, a writer, a graphic artist, and a programmer. How will you convey project objectives and enthusiasm? How will you monitor people and products? How will you give feedback? Finally, how will you celebrate the end of a successful project?

References

Barry, T. R. (2015). *Top 10 qualities of a project manager*. Retrieved from https://www.projectsmart.co.uk/top-10-qualities-project-manager.php

Bennis, W. (1994, November). The differences between leadership and management. *Manage*, 12.

Berkun, S. (2008). *Making things happen*. Tokyo, Japan: O'Riley.

Blanchard, K., & Johnson, S. (1982). *The one-minute manager*. New York: William Morrow and Co., Inc.

Chamorro-Premuzic,T. (2013). *Seven rules for managing creative but difficult people*. Retrieved from https://hbr.org/2013/04/seven-rules-for-managing-creat/

Craig, J. C. (2012). Project management lite. Dover, DE: CreateSpace Independent Publishing.

Dinsmore, P. C. (2006). Studies in human resource management: Interpersonal skills. In P. C. Dinsmore, P. C., & Cabanis-Brewin, J. (Eds.). *AMA handbook of project management* (pp. 144–154). New York: Project Management Institute.

Duke Corporate Education. (2009). *Building effective teams*. Chicago: Dearborn Publishing.

Gardiner, P. D. (2005). *Project management: A strategic planning approach*. New York: Palgrave.

Greer, M. (2011). *Project management the minimalist approach*. Amherst, MA: HRD Press.

Hanley, J. (2015). *Project management: Compact guide to the complex world of project management*. New York: Axellerata Publishing.

Hersey, P., & Blanchard, K. (2013). *Management of organizational behavior: Leading human resources*. Upper Saddle River, NJ: Prentice Hall.

Hill, L. A., & Lineback, K. (2011). *Being the boss*. Boston, MA: Harvard Business Review Press.

Kerzner, H. (2013). *Project management: A systems approach*. New York: John Wiley and Sons.

Maslow, A. H. (1998). *Maslow on management*. New York: Wiley and Sons.

McGuinness, M. (2010). *#25 Herding cats-managing creative people*. Retrieved from http://lateralaction.com/managing-creativity/

Mersino, A. (2007). *Emotional intelligence for project managers*. New York: AMACOM.

Meyer, E. (2014). *The culture map*. New York: Public Affairs.

Miller, M. (2011). *The secret of teams*. San Francisco: Berrett-Kolher Publishers, Inc.

Portny, S. E. (2013). *Project management for dummies*. (4th ed.). Hoboken, NJ: John Wiley and Sons.

Topchick, G. S. (2007). *The first-time manager's guide to team building*. New York: AMACOM.

Vroom, V. H. (1995). *Work and motivation*. San Francisco: Jossey-Bass.

Wong, Z. (2007). *Human factors in project management*. San Francisco: Jossey-Bass.

Chapter 14

The Development and Evolution of Human Performance Improvement

Harold D. Stolovitch

HSA Learning and Performance Systems

Human performance improvement (HPI)—what a wonderful sounding term! Is there anyone who does not wish to "improve" in some way? Is this also not the mission of so many personal and organizational development programs? What is special and unique about HPI? Where did it originate? How did it grow into the embodiment of a professional field that is currently making assertive noises throughout the world? How, through its origins and evolution, does it affect individuals and organizations seeking to achieve workplace success in our ever-increasingly complex world? Finally, is HPI just another fad in the long list of miracle cures we have all seen roar into our busy work environments, disrupt our routines, offer incredible promises, only to fade away like broken dreams into the mists of organizational forgetfulness? Or is this a concept that is here to stay? These are questions this chapter addresses.

Defining Human Performance Improvement

There is power in words, but only when their meanings are made manifestly clear. Numerous definitions of HPI have been published. Van Tiem, Moseley, and Dessinger (2012) provides a recent one that captures the HPI spirit: "the systematic process of linking business goals and strategies with the workforce responsible for achieving the goals" (p. xxix). However, to fully understand what this field of study and practice truly represents requires greater elaboration. What follows, then, is a more comprehensive definition of the term HPI from three perspectives: vision, concept, and desired end. Subsequently, we define the term by examining each of the words that constitute it.

HPI: Vision, Concept, and Desired End

The vision of HPI is relatively simple: achieve, through people, increasingly successful accomplishments that are valued by all organizational stakeholders: those who perform, their managers and customers, their peers and colleagues, shareholders, regulatory agencies, and ultimately society itself (Kaufman, 2006).

Conceptually, HPI is a movement with a straightforward mission—valued accomplishment through people. Via systematic means, from analysis of performance gaps; to design and development of appropriate, economical, feasible, and organizationally acceptable interventions; to implementation and long-term monitoring and maintenance of these interventions, HPI concerns itself with achieving organizational goals cost effectively and efficiently. Unlike other movements with similar missions, HPI draws from a unique parent field, HPT, which contains a formidable array of processes, tools and resources, a scientific base, and a history of precedents that document attainment of valued results.

With respect to its "end," valued accomplishment, HPI provides an operational definition. Gilbert (1996) has written extensively about what he has termed "worthy" performance (P_w), the ratio of valued accomplishment (A_v) to costly behavior (B_c):

$$P_w = \frac{A_v}{B_c}$$

In the HPI universe, the desired end is performance whose cost is considerably lower than the value of the result. In recent years, cost and value issues have markedly moved to the forefront with increasingly solid means for calculating these (Bassi & McMurrer, 2007; Echols, 2008; Hubbard, 2007).

HPI: What Does Each Word Mean?

Another way of examining the meaning of the term *human performance improvement* is to define each of the three words that constitute the term. Let's do so.

Human.   HPI is a professional field of endeavor centered on the efforts and results of people operating in work settings, although there are increasing examples of the principles of HPI being applied to educational and societal situations (e.g., Harless, 1998; Kaufman, 1995; Stolovitch & Keeps, 2006a).

Performance.   This word creates difficulties from two perspectives. Some people, when they first encounter it, think of performance in the theatrical sense. It therefore carries connotations of the theatrical stage rather than of substantive workplace issues (Stolovitch & Keeps, 1999, p. 4; Webster's Dictionary. (2014). *New college edition* (5th ed.). Nevertheless, *performance* is an appropriate term as it also denotes a quantified result, or the accomplishment or execution of something ordered or undertaken, including the accomplishment of work. Nickols (1977, p. 14) defines performance as "the outcomes of behavior. Behavior is individual activity whereas the outcomes of behavior are the ways in which the behaving individual's environment is somehow different as a result of his or her behavior." Outcomes, accomplishments valued by the system, or achievements—these are the focus of HPI (Hartt, 2008, p. 3; Stolovitch & Keeps, 1999, p. 4). The second difficulty with performance is that it is an almost uniquely English term. Many languages do not possess an exact, equivalent word for it. In applying various similar words or paraphrases to convey its precise meaning, something often gets lost in the translation. Despite this annoyance, its operational sense, as Gilbert (1996) has suggested, remains clear. Performance is the valued accomplishment derived from costly behavior. Lowering the behavioral (activity) cost and significantly increasing the valued result or benefit is what HPI is about (Corrado, Hulten, & Sichel, 2004).

Improvement.   The meaning of this word is almost self-evident. It refers to making things better. In the work environment, improvement is operationally defined in many ways: increased revenues and/or market share; greater speed to market; decreased wastage and/or costs; more successful conformance to regulatory requirements; and better safety and health data, to name only some of the more common ones (Robinson, Robinson, Phillips, Phillips, & Handshaw, 2015).

Taken together, these three words have created a major business movement—one that endeavors to bring about changes in such a way that organizations are improved in terms of the achievements they and all stakeholders value.

HPI: Why Its Time Has Come Now

A significant confluence of ideas and events has recently occurred to favor the growth of HPI. Among these are the renewed interest in human capital (see especially Mitchell, Ray, & van Ark, 2015, p. 6), the emergence of the field of human capital analytics (Bassi & McMurrer, 2007; Davenport & Harris, 2007; Fitz-enz, 2014; Pease, Byerly, & Fitz-enz, 2012), the recognition of the importance of systemic thinking, the dramatic surge in organizational complexity, and the focus on performance.

Human Capital

Nobel laureates Theodore Schultz (1981) and Thomas Becker (1993) established the importance of human capital at macroeconomic levels. They demonstrated with convincing data that as the knowledge and performance capabilities of populations improve, so, too, the economic successes of countries and their peoples. Corrado and colleagues (2004) have provided similar findings focusing exclusively on the United States. Keely (2007) presents a comprehensive and global examination of human capital and how it shapes people's lives. One need only investigate singularly successful smaller nations with limited natural resources and landmasses, such as Japan, Israel, Singapore, South Korea, and the Netherlands, to confirm the validity of this thesis. Their vast and varied accomplishments attest to the enormous power of leveraging human capital.

The power of human capital has also been demonstrated at the organizational level (Crawford, 1991; Davenport, 1999; Edvinsson & Malone, 1997; Fitz-enz, 2009; Halal, 1998; Pfeffer, 1998; Stewart, 1997). Bassi & McMurrer (2007), Bradley (1996), Lickert and Pyle (1971), and Stewart (1994) have empirically shown that human capital yields higher rates of return than physical capital in corporate settings. HPI has adopted at its core the maximization of human capital achievements.

Systemic versus Linear Thinking and Acting

There is a growing demand for systemic as opposed to linear thinking and acting in the workplace (e.g., Pourdehnad & Bharathy, 2004; Senge, 1990). General systems theory (e.g., de Rosnay, 1975) opened the business world to conceiving of organizations as organic entities with interacting subsystems. In the human resource and development arenas, individual types of interventions (e.g., scientific management, management by objectives, management by walking around) have yielded to more systemic and integrated approaches (e.g., quality circles, reengineering, teamwork, six-sigma). This has fostered movements such as HPI, which views performance outcomes as the end result of a number of interacting elements such as clear expectations, timely and specific feedback, access to required information, adequate resources, properly aligned policies, efficient procedures, appropriate incentives and consequences, targeted training, comprehensive selection systems, communication of values, knowledge sharing, varied management support activities, among others (e.g., Binder, 2009; Marker, 2007). The demonstrated ineffectiveness of single (aka "silver bullet") solutions—miracle interventions to improve performance—have bred mistrust for the next "flavor of the month" and a receptiveness to the systemic approach of HPI (Boardman & Sauser, 2013).

Growth in Organizational Complexity

As instantaneous communication across the world, global markets and 24/7 service availability become our realities, more of the burden of decision making and customer satisfaction falls upon the individual worker's shoulders. Companies no longer produce single products. Each product line has a shorter lifecycle than in previous eras. Workers and managers must access and share information and knowledge with extreme speed.

In this atmosphere of continuous pressure and upheaval, accompanied by frequent mergers and acquisitions of enterprises, people have to be supported by an environment that facilitates agility, encourages independent activity, and provides easy-to-use links to others for assistance, expertise, and reassurance. Here is where HPI stands out. The professional HPI practitioner—the performance consultant (PC) (Robinson et al., 2015; Rummler, 2004; Stolovitch & Keeps, 2004a)—is essentially an account manager, an investigator, and a valued consultant with close links to client groups (van Tiem et al., 2012). As changes are planned or occur, or as problems manifest themselves, the PC is there to identify gaps between desired and actual performance, analyze them, isolate the systemic factors affecting the gaps, and recommend an integrated set of suitable interventions to rapidly and effectively eliminate (or at least, significantly reduce) them. The PC's toolkit is the set of resources, processes, and job aids HPI provides (e.g., Rossett, 2009).

Focus on Performance

The impatience with training and other groups of single intervention specialists is that these focus on individual, isolated stimulus solutions rather than the package of necessary responses. Gilbert (1996) laid out a number of principles and theorems that at first sight appear counterintuitive until examined closely:

- If you pit the individual against the environment, the environment will ultimately win.
- Hard work, great knowledge, and strong motivation without valued accomplishment is unworthy performance.
- A system that rewards people for their behavior (e.g., hard work, knowledge, motivation) without accounting for accomplishment encourages incompetence.
- A system that rewards accomplishments without accounting for behavior invites waste.

These and other principles emphasize the need to account for the many environmental factors that affect how people perform their work, achieve their business-valued results, apply their work processes, and exhibit their behaviors. The growth in availability of alternative means for achieving business-driven success and the demand by management to demonstrate such success concretely (Van Buren & Erskine, 2002, p. 4) have paved the way for HPI to showcase its relevance.

The Relationship between HPI and HPT

There are several ways that one might view the relationship between human performance improvement and human performance technology. In one sense, HPI is what we wish to achieve and HPT is the means we use to achieve it. In another sense, however, the two terms can be viewed as being synonymous. The term *human performance improvement* is relatively new. In a strict sense, it is a euphemism (a less direct expression used in place of one considered offensive). It emerged in the 1990s, most likely because of its softer sound than human performance technology (HPT).

HPT is a field of professional practice that began to take form during the 1970s and became recognized in its own right in the 1980s. It is an offspring of general systems theory applied to organizations (Stolovitch & Keeps, 1999; Stolovitch & Keeps, 2006a, p. xvi). In the mid-1980s, Geis (1986) stated a number of assumptions underlying HPT that are still true today. Some of the key assumptions include the following:

1. Human performance follows specific laws and can often be predicted and controlled.
2. Knowledge of human behavior is limited (although growing rapidly), and so HPT must rely on practical experience as well as scientific research.
3. HPT draws from many research bases while generating its own.
4. HPT is the product of a number of knowledge sources: cybernetics, behavioral psychology, communications theory, information theory, systems theory, management science, and, more recently, the cognitive sciences and neuroscience.
5. HPT is neither committed to any particular delivery system nor confined to any specific population and subject-matter area. It can address human performance in any context, but it is most commonly applied within organizational, work, and social improvement settings.
6. HPT is empirical. It requires systematic verification of the results of both its analysis and intervention efforts.
7. HPT is evolving. Based on guiding principles, it nevertheless allows enormous scope for innovation and creativity.
8. Although HPT cannot yet pretend to have generated a firm theoretical foundation of its own, the theory and experience-based principles that guide it are molded by empirical data that have accumulated as a result of documented, systematic practice. In many ways, HPT shares attributes with other applied fields (e.g., management, organizational development, medicine, psychiatry).

It may be said that these assumptions hold true regardless of whether you prefer to use the term HPI or HPT to describe the field.

The notion that human performance technology and human performance improvement are terms that can be used interchangeably is further reinforced by examining some of the formal definitions of these two terms. Harless (1995, p. 75) defines HPT as "an engineering approach to attaining desired accomplishment from human performers by determining gaps in performance and designing cost-effective and efficient interventions." Stolovitch and Keeps (1999; 2006, pp. 59–148) have defined HPI in much the same way.

Related Fields

The preceding paragraphs may lead one to conclude that what has been said of HPI and HPT might just as easily be restated with respect to human resource development (HRD). This is largely true. As Gilley, Maycunich, and Quatro (2002) state, the traditional role of HRD professionals has mainly been a transactional one (p. 23), mostly focused on training interventions. They emphasize that these roles must change to become more transformational and performance focused. In their assertion that "the challenges facing organizations require HRD professionals to adopt a role that improves firm performance, enhances competitive readiness and drives renewal capacity and capability" (p. 25), they closely approach the goals of HPI.

This convergence is to be expected, given the evolving nature of enterprises. One sees a similar viewpoint emerging from the field of organizational effectiveness (OE), with growing emphasis on the ability of the organization to fulfill its mission through a blend of sound management, strong governance, and a persistent rededication to achieving results. This includes meeting organizational and shareholder objectives—immediately and long term—as well as adapting and developing to the constantly changing business environment. OE professionals focus on the overall functioning of an organization. HPI is about engineering effective human performance in specific ways. The link between the two is both evident and natural.

What is true for OE can also be said for organizational development (OD). While generally operating at the macro level of organizations, OD professionals serve a mission of increasing organizational effectiveness and health, through planned interventions in the organization's processes or operations. OD adopts less of an engineering emphasis than OE, and is characterized more by its communication and facilitation style. Nevertheless, its purpose, just as with HPI, is to deliver valued organizational results, largely through people. Both are concerned with improving human performance.

Early Precursors to Performance Improvement

In the beginning, there were apprenticeships. The master-apprentice model formed the basis for acquiring workplace performance capability. Whether the learner bore the official title of apprentice or some other nomenclature such as "page," "squire," or even "scullery maid," the idea was that a young person was taken into service and taught a trade. This person learned through observation, instruction, practice, and feedback, all of which were virtually continuous. It also took a long time.

With the introduction of workplace literacy, those youngsters who could read about their work gained a competitive edge. The Industrial Revolution of the nineteenth century gave rise to the need for literate workers. Public education arose to provide basic reading and calculation skills. Literate, mathematically capable workers tended to be more productive in the increasingly complex, industrial world. With the introduction of printed, illustrated texts, the combination of pictures and words made a great difference in the efficiency and effectiveness of learning.

This fed directly into the audiovisual movement. First photos and then projected images, films, and television brought to life what could not always be experienced directly. Educators were able to bring the world to the classroom. For industrial trainers, these additions made a dramatic difference. They could show objects, products, results, even processes, without the need to "be there" physically. More trainees could be formed and generally in less time than by older methods.

With the arrival of World War II and the need to train millions of soldiers rapidly, the audiovisual discoveries were combined with those of the rapidly growing field of behavioral psychology. The result was well-designed audiovisual training materials that structured and presented learning content in ways that facilitated the acquisition of new skills and knowledge. Learners were shown how things worked, were coached and prompted as they learned, and then were released and monitored as they performed.

By the end of the war, the use of behaviorally designed audiovisual training programs had also found adherents in the war-related industries. Then, as soldiers went back to school and to the general workplace, acceptance extended to schools, universities, and business organizations.

However, something was lacking. Audiovisual training materials were only perceived as training tools and aids. Their use was essentially tactical. When, in the 1950s and 1960s, general systems theory was discovered by the training community, a major shift occurred that gave birth to instructional technology. All of the pieces were now in place. By focusing on the array of elements affecting learning—learner characteristics, learning context, tasks to be mastered, clearly defined learning objectives, criterion measures, media and delivery systems—a more comprehensive view of learning systems arose. This fit with the surge in knowledge production and the evolution toward a global service and knowledge-based economy. Learning was no longer narrowly viewed as a prerequisite for obtaining a job position and functioning within it. It now became evident that lifelong, continuous learning was a workplace necessity for both worker and organizational survival.

Instructional technology led to the development of instructional systems design (ISD), which has evolved into the standard for engineering effective learning. The key advantage of this systematic and systemic approach was that it took into account the essential variables for learning. ISD provided a clearly defined and documented pathway for designing, developing, implementing, and evaluating learning—one that was replicable and transferable and that had a demonstrable record of success.

Yet within the very euphoria of having created an effective training-learning technology, one based on the best knowledge acquired from both human and physical sciences, there was disquiet in the professional training community. True, the newly engineered learning systems were demonstrating success. People learned. However, when the instructional systems designers verified whether the learning transferred to the job or the extent to which things changed or improved in terms of business criteria, they were frequently dismayed (Bhati, 2007; Esque & McCausland, 1997).

An Idea Is Born: HPT/HPI

Thomas F. Gilbert is generally considered to be the father of HPT. As a graduate student of B. F. Skinner, Gilbert was formed in the principles and practices of behaviorism. He became an ardent and able practitioner of programmed instruction, which Skinner had initiated through his research and development of teaching machines.

Taking Skinner's principles and venturing into the workplace arena, Gilbert soon developed a new science of *mathetics* (Gilbert, 1962), derived from the Greek *mathein,* "to learn." His *Journal of Mathetics* attracted the attention of a group of like-minded individuals, including many from learning research laboratories and the American military. They and others, fascinated with the possibilities offered by the science of learning, formed the National Society for Programmed Instruction (NSPI). Together with Geary Rummler, Gilbert soon progressed beyond issues of learning and by the mid-1970s had created his behavior engineering model (Gilbert,1996) that lays out six major categories of variables affecting workplace performance (Figure 14.1). These include environmental factors (e.g., Is relevant and frequent feedback available? Are work tools designed to meet performance needs? Are there adequate financial incentives that are contingent upon performance?) and individual factors (e.g., Are employees provided with systematically designed training to match the requirements of exemplary work performance? Are good employee selection and promotion processes in place? Is there adequate assessment of worker

motivation?). Gilbert's model was a significant milestone and is still used as a fundamental analytic HPI tool.

At approximately the same time, Joe Harless, a former student of Gilbert, was developing his own performance improvement process (PIP). In 1970, Harless published an interactive volume, *An Ounce of Analysis (Is Worth a Pound of Objectives),* in which he introduced his now famous front-end analysis methodology. This had a marked influence on practitioners of training, especially instructional designers. Harless had discovered, through follow-up evaluation posttraining, that "despite the training having been well-designed in accordance with the standards of the time" (Dean & Ripley, 1997, p. 94) and although students performed well on tests, the skills and knowledge were not being transferred to the workplace. His PIP model, which incorporated front-end analysis, laid the foundation for the numerous performance improvement models that were to follow.

Another slim, but immediately popular, publication by Robert F. Mager and Peter Pipe, *Analyzing Performance Problems or You Really Oughta Wanna* (1970) also appeared on the scene at this time. The Mager and Pipe volume had a tremendous impact on instructional designers, trainers, HRD professionals, and educators. The very sensible approach to solving workplace performance problems resonated clearly with both practitioners and training managers. It provided ammunition to stimulate significant changes in how human performance at work was viewed.

These models created an enormous stir (and support) among many, who were ill at ease with the lack of impact of their training–learning solutions in the workplace. Even more importantly, they helped effect two fundamental shifts in thinking. The first of these was opening the minds of training and HRD

	Information	Instrumentation	Motivation
Environment	*Data* 1. Relevant and frequent feedback about the adequacy of performance 2. Descriptions of what is expected of performance 3. Clear and relevant guides to adequate performance	*Resources* 1. Tools, resources, time and materials of work designed to match performance needs	*Incentives* 1. Adequate financial incentives made contingent upon performance 2. Non-monetary incentives made available 3. Career-development opportunities 4. Clear consequences for poor performance
Individual	*Knowledge* 1. Systematically designed training that matches the requirements of exemplary performance 2. Placement	*Capacity* 1. Flexible scheduling of performance to match peak capacity 2. Prosthesis or visual aids 3. Physical shaping 4. Adaptation 5. Selection	*Motives* 1. Assessment of people's motives to work 2. Recruitment of people to match the realities of situation

Reference: Dr. Thomas F. Gilbert, "Human Competence: Engineering Worthy Performance," 1978, 1996

FIGURE 14.1 Gilbert's behavior engineering model.

professionals to the fact that many human performance problems could be solved via means other than training; that there are an infinite array of possible interventions to improve human performance. Categories of interventions that can improve human performance in the workplace include offering new incentive systems, providing more timely and detailed methods of feedback, creating and making available the use of performance support tools, employing better worker selection and promotion procedures, improving job design and environmental conditions in the workplace, and a host of other performance improvement techniques. Somewhat frightened (After all, is this our concern? Are we the right people to involve ourselves in this?), yet excited and exhilarated, training and HRD professionals began to see their horizons expanding, their challenges increasing, and at the same time the possibility of having a much greater influence on bottom-line business results.

The second shift in thinking was the growing awareness that the HRD/training community could now offer stronger, more convincing arguments to senior management that what they were engaged in should be viewed as an organizational investment rather than a cost. This naturally led to an emphasis on evaluation, the demonstrable leveraging of organizational human capital and human performance, and return-on-investment calculations (e.g., Phillips, 2003; Stolovitch & Keeps, 2004b).

One of the most important milestones in the evolution of HPI was the appearance of another volume, *Improving Performance: Managing the White Space in the Organization Chart* (Rummler & Brache, 1995) that presented a comprehensive performance improvement model and set of practices that were more strategic and detailed than earlier approaches. Rummler and Brache approached the organization as a whole and identified key variables affecting performance at the organizational, process, and individual worker levels. Their model integrated all of these levels in a tightly integrated manner and with a single purpose: to engineer effective performance.

Stolovitch and Keeps (2004a) have produced an engineering effective performance model that is highly prescriptive and is accompanied by a large number of performance aids (Stolovitch & Keeps, 2006b). What is unique about their contribution are the very practical, procedural guidelines and tools they have produced, which make it relatively easy for training, OD, OE, or HRD professionals to apply. Their work has helped build momentum for the emergence of the PC in organizations.

To sum up the evolution of HPT/HPI, we present in Figure 14.2 a generalized HPT model (Van Tiem et al., 2012), which has probably had the most global exposure. This is the HPI/HPT model adopted and continuously refined by the International Society for Performance Improvement (ISPI), an organization that many HPI practitioners, worldwide, consider to be their professional home.

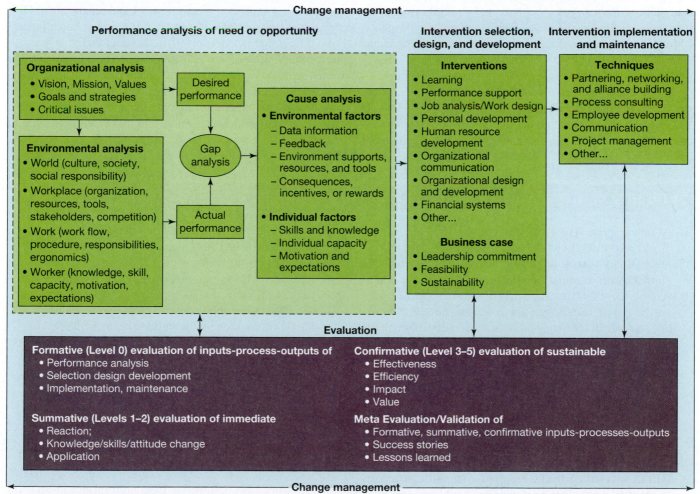

Source: From Fundamentals of Performance Improvement Optimizing results through people, processes, and organizations, by D.M. Van Tiem, J.L. Moseley, and Joan C. Dessinger, 2012. Used with permission from ISPIWiley.

FIGURE 14.2   HPT model of the International Society for Performance Improvement.

As Figure 14.2 illustrates, the model is divided into four major blocks: (1) analysis activities to identify performance gaps, determine reasons (causes) for these gaps, and isolate factors affecting the gaps; (2) selection, design, and development of appropriate, feasible, economical, and acceptable interventions along with the building of business cases; (3) implementation of selected performance interventions; and (4) ongoing monitoring and evaluation activities to verify intervention effectiveness and identify required improvements.

Armed with suitable tools and processes, the HPI professional applies well-documented steps that bring about desired performance improvement in both an orderly and systemic manner.

The Future of HPI

All signs point to a healthy, expanding future for HPI and its professional practitioners who are playing increasingly significant organizational roles. The most important indicator of this is the steady evolution and growth of HPI and HPT. It is not a field of practice that has suddenly appeared on the scene. It has emerged slowly, but forcefully, over the past fifty years to attain a position of prominence among those seeking to effect significant, bottom-line change through people. It is very present not only in North America, but also in Europe (see, for example, the *Performance Improvement* special issue highlighting the application of HPI in Europe and globally [Mueller & Voelkl, 2004]) and Asia, especially China with its dynamic and robust economy.

As attention focuses more and more on return on investment in learning and performance, (e.g., Bassi, Frauenheim, McMurrer, & Costello, 2011; Robinson et al., 2015; Stolovitch & Keeps, 2004a), the demand for HPI professionals will increase. From a career perspective, performance consultants are becoming highly visible in organizations and are thus paid significantly more for their contributions than "training practitioners." In a 2015 salary summary by Glassdoor, the average performance improvement consultant's salary in the United States amounted to $89,750. This compares with an annual average instructional designer salary of $63,000 (Indeed.com, n.d.) and a corporate trainer salary of $53,251 (Payscale.com, n.d.). All of this augurs well for the future of the field.

Conclusion

HPI is not a flavor of the month, radical departure, or off-the-wall movement. Rather, it is a natural evolution toward systemic alignment of human capital management with organizational requirements to meet tough and competitive demands. Its vision of achieving, through people, increasingly successful accomplishments that are valued by all stakeholders is appropriate to this moment in time.

Although HPI originated and has had its most dramatic developments in North America, it is not unique to this geography. The need for and interest in HPI is a worldwide phenomenon. Groups of training, HRD, OE, and OD professionals have come together in Australia, Europe, Asia, and the developing world to espouse the vision and practices of HPI.

This chapter has responded to the key questions raised at its outset. It has explained what is special and unique about HPI, recounted its beginnings, and how it has grown into a professional field that is asserting its message globally. It has also traced its origins and evolution demonstrating how it can assist individuals and organizations to achieve workplace success. Finally, it has demonstrated that HPI is not just another disruptive fad, but a rational and reasonable next step in building valued human performance—one that makes eminent sense in today's exacting world of work.

Summary of Key Principles

1. **At its core, the vision and mission of HPI is to effectively and efficiently achieve, through people, increasingly successful accomplishments that are valued by all organizational stakeholders.** In order to achieve these outcomes, a series of systematic processes are employed, resulting in the design and development of economical, feasible, and organizationally acceptable interventions that lead to improvements in workplace performance and business results.

2. **A desired end for HPI is "worthy" performance— defined as valued accomplishment derived from behavior whose cost is considerably lower than the value of the accomplishment.** As an HPI practitioner, demonstrate concretely both the cost and value to the organization of your proposed intervention.

3. **HPI involves the use of a series of systematic processes to identify workplace performance problems and to design and develop appropriate interventions to solve**
those problems. These processes include (a) analyzing desired and actual workplace performance activities to identify performance gaps; (b) determining reasons (causes) for these gaps and isolating factors affecting the gaps; (c) selecting, designing, and developing appropriate, feasible, economical, and acceptable interventions, along with building business cases; (d) implementing the selected performance interventions; and (e) conducting ongoing monitoring and evaluation activities to verify intervention effectiveness and identify required improvements.

4. **Gilbert's behavior engineering model, created in the 1970s, remains a fundamental analytic tool that lays out six major categories of variables affecting workplace performance.** These include environmental factors (e.g., Is relevant and frequent feedback available? Are work tools designed to meet performance needs? Are there adequate financial incentives that are contingent

upon performance?) and individual factors (e.g., Are employees provided with systematically designed training to match the requirements of exemplary work performance? Are good employee selection and promotion processes in place? Is there adequate assessment of worker motivation?).

5. **Many human performance problems can be solved via means other than training.** Categories of interventions other than training that can improve human performance in the workplace include offering new incentive systems, providing more timely and detailed methods of feedback, creating and making available the use of performance support tools, employing better worker selection and promotion procedures, improving job design and environmental conditions in the workplace, and a host of other performance improvement techniques.

Application Questions

1. Examine the HPT model presented in Figure 14.2, and answer the following questions:
   a. What seems to be the major purpose of the performance analysis phase of the process?
   b. Why is the cause analysis phase of this model crucial? Use some of the terms listed in that section of the model to support your point of view.
   c. Select three of the interventions (other than training and education) listed in the Intervention Selection, Design, and Development phase. Using other resources, locate definitions of three of these interventions, and write a definition for each. For each of the three, describe whether you feel an instructional designer would need extra training in order to adequately plan an intervention of that type. Explain why you feel that way.

2. Assume that the chairperson of an academic department is holding a discussion with the person responsible for handling all the paperwork associated with student applications for admission to the department. In explaining the reasons for the problems, the admissions clerk states, "The office manager never told me exactly what I was expected to do in this job, and she never gives me any help or tells whether I'm doing good work. She also has me answering phone calls that I think should be answered by our office receptionist. On top of that, I often have to walk to the other end of the office in order to fax copies of admissions forms to the university admissions office, and that takes up a lot of my time. Also, the faculty often ask me to copy textbook materials for them, and whenever they ask me to do so, I put down whatever else I'm working on so that I can get the copying done." Identify the categories of performance problems apparent in the clerk's statement. For each problem you identify, describe an appropriate solution.

3. Some students who are enrolled in instructional design and technology (ID&T) programs, upon first learning about human performance technology, feel that their training will not adequately prepare them to perform the many tasks listed in Figure 14.1. However, many graduates of ID&T programs now refer to themselves as performance improvement specialists, and/or engage in many of the activities listed in Figure 14.1. With the help of a faculty member, identify two graduates of your program who now consider themselves to have some expertise in HPT. Interview these individuals and try to ascertain (a) what HPT skills they employ, and (b) how they acquired those skills. Write a brief report describing your findings. Conclude the report by providing an assessment of how you think you might go about acquiring these skills.

References

Bassi, L., Frauenheim, E., McMurrer, D., & Costello, L. (2011). *Good company: Business success in the worthiness era.* Oakland, CA: Berrett-Koehler Publishing.

Bassi, L., & McMurrer, D. (2007). Maximizing your return on people. *Harvard Business Review, 85*(3), 115–123.

Becker, G. S. (1993). *Human capital: A theoretical and empirical analysis with special reference to education* (3rd ed.). Chicago: University of Chicago.

Bhati, D. (2007). *Factors that influence transfer of hazardous material training: the perception of selected firefighter trainees and supervisors.* Doctoral dissertation submitted in partial fulfillment of the requirements for the degree of Doctor of Philosophy, University of Central Florida.

Binder, C. (2009). *The six boxes approach: A fast on-ramp to HPT.* Paper presented at the annual conference of the International Society for Performance Improvement, Orlando FL.

Boardman, J., & Sauser, B. (2013). *Systematic thinking: Building maps for worlds of systems.* Hoboken, NJ: Wiley & Sons.

Bradley, K. (1996, October). *Intellectual capital and the new wealth of nations.* Lecture delivered to the Royal Society of Arts, London.

Corrado, C., Hulten, C. R., & Sichel, D. (2004). *Intangible capital and economic growth.* Washington, DC: National Bureau of Economic Research, Working Paper No. 11948.

Crawford, R. (1991). *In the era of human capital: The emergence of talent, intelligence and knowledge as the worldwide economic force and what it means to managers and investors.* New York: HarperBusiness.

Davenport, T. O. (1999). *Human capital: What it is and why people invest in it.* San Francisco: Jossey-Bass.

Davenport, T. O., & Harris, J. (2007). *Competing on analytics: The new science of winning.* Boston: Harvard Business School Publishing.

Dean, P. J., & Ripley, D. E. (1997). *Performance improvement pathfinders: Models for organizational learning systems* (vol. 2). Washington, DC: International Society for Performance Improvement.

de Rosnay, J. (1975). *Le macroscope, vers une vision globale.* Paris: Le Seuil.

Echols, M. (2008). *Creating value with human capital investment.* Wyomissing, PA: Tapestry Press.

Edvinsson, L., & Malone, M. S. (1997). *Intellectual capital: Realizing your company's true value by finding its hidden brainpower.* New York: HarperBusiness.

Esque, T. J., & McCausland, J. (1997). Taking ownership for transfer: A management development case study. *Performance Improvement Quarterly, 10*(2), 116–133.

Fitz-enz, J. (2009). *The ROI of human capital: Measuring the economic value of employee performance* (2nd ed.). New York: American Management Association.

Fitz-enz, J. (2014). *Predictive analytics for human resources.* Hoboken, NJ: John Wiley & Sons.

Geis, G. L. (1986). Human performance technology: An overview. In M. E. Smith (Ed.), *Introduction to performance technology* (vol. 1). Washington, DC: National Society for Performance and Instruction.

Gilbert, T. F. (1962). Mathetics: The technology of education. *Journal of Mathetics, 1*(1).

Gilbert, T. F. (1996). *Human competence: Engineering worthy performance* (ISPI Tribute Edition). Washington, DC: International Society for Performance Improvement.

Gilley, J. W., Maycunich, A., & Quatro, S. (2002). Comparing the roles responsibilities, and activities of transactional and transformational HRD professionals. *Performance Improvement Quarterly, 15*(4), 23–44.

Glassdoor. (2015). E-Y performance-improvement-consultant salaries. Retrieved from www.glassdoor.com/Salary/EY-Performance-Improvement-Consultant-Salaries-E2784_D_KO3,37htm

Halal, W. E. (1998). *The infinite resource: Creating and leading the knowledge enterprise.* San Francisco: Jossey-Bass.

Harless, J. (1970). *An ounce of analysis (is worth a pound of objectives).* Newman, GA: Harless Performance Guild.

Harless, J. (1995). Performance technology skills in business: implications for preparation. *Performance Improvement Quarterly, 8*(4), 75–88.

Harless, J. (1998). *The Eden conspiracy: Educating for accomplished citizenship.* Wheaton, IL: Guild V Publications.

Hartt, D. C. (2008). *Human performance improvement . . . the Coast Guard way.* Presented to the American Society for Training & Development, Annual Conference, Yorktown, VA.

Hubbard, D. (2007). *How to measure anything: Finding the value of "intangibles" in business.* Hoboken, NJ: John Wiley & Sons.

Indeed.com. (n.d.). Instructional designer salary. Retrieved from www.indeed.com/salary/Instructional-Designer.html

Kaufman, R. (1995). *Mapping educational success.* Thousand Oaks, CA: Corwin Press.

Kaufman, R. (2006). *Change, choices and consequences – A guide to mega thinking and planning.* Amherst, MA: HRD Press.

Keely, B. (2007). *OECD insights human capital: How what you know shapes your life.* Paris, France: OECD Publishing.

Lickert, R., & Pyle, W. C. (1971). Human resource accounting: A human organizational measurement approach. *Financial Analysis Journal,* 75–84, 101–102.

Mager, R. F., & Pipe, P. (1970). *Analyzing performance problems or you really oughta wanna.* Belmont, CA: Fearon Publishers.

Marker, A. (2007). Synchronized analysis model: Linking Gilbert's behavior engineering model with environmental analysis models. *Performance Improvement Journal, 46*(1), 26 – 32.

Mitchell, C., Ray, L. R., & van Ark, B. (2015). *The conference board CEO challenge 2015: Building innovative, people-driven organizations.* New York: The Conference Board.

Mueller, M., & Voelkl, C. (Eds.). (2004). Sustaining performance [Special issue]. *Performance Improvement Journal, 43*(6).

Nickols, F. W. (1977). Concerning performance and performance standards: An opinion. *NSPI Journal, 16*(1), 14–17.

Payscale.com. (n.d.). Corporate trainer salary. Retrieved from www.payscale.com/research/US/Jobs=Corporate-Trainer/Salary

Pease, G., Byerly, B., & Fitz-enz, J. (2012). *Human capital analytics: How to harness the potential of your organization's greatest asset.* Hoboken, NJ: John Wiley & Sons.

Pfeffer, J. (1998). *The human equation: Building profits by putting people first.* Boston: Harvard Business School Press.

Phillips, J. J. (2003). *Return on investment in training and performance improvement programs.* Burlington, MA: Butterworth-Heinemann.

Pourdehnad, J., & Bharathy, G. K. (2004). *Systems thinking and its implications in organizational transformation.* Proceeding for the Third International Conference on Systems Thinking in Management, Philadelphia, PA.

Robinson, D. G., Robinson, J. C., Phillips, J. J., Phillips, P. P., & Handshaw, D. (2015). *Performance consulting: A strategic process to improve, measure, and sustain organizational results* (3rd. ed). Oakland, CA: Berrett-Koehler Publishers.

Rossett, A. (2009). *First things fast: A handbook for performance analysis.* San Francisco: Pfeiffer.

Rummler, G. A. (2004). *Serious performance consulting—according to Rummler.* Silver Spring, MD: International Society for Performance Improvement.

Rummler, G. A., & Brache, A. P. (1995). *Improving performance: How to manage the white space on the organization chart* (2nd ed.). San Francisco: Jossey-Bass.

Schultz, T. W. (1981). *Investing in people: The economics of population quality.* Berkeley and Los Angeles, CA: University of California Press.

Senge, P. M. (1990). *The fifth discipline: The art and practice of the learning organization.* New York: Doubleday.

Stewart, T. A. (1994, March 10). Your company's most valuable capital: Intellectual capital. *Fortune,* 68–74.

Stewart, T. A. (1997). *Intellectual capital: The new wealth of organizations.* New York: Doubleday Dell Publishing Group.

Stolovitch, H. D., & Keeps, E. J. (1999). *Handbook of human performance technology: Improving individual and organizational performance worldwide.* San Francisco: Jossey-Bass.

Stolovitch, H. D., & Keeps, E. J. (2004a). *Training ain't performance.* Alexandria, VA: American Society for Training & Development.

Stolovitch, H. D., & Keeps, E. J. (2004b). *Front-end analysis and return on investment toolkit.* San Francisco: Jossey-Bass/Pfeiffer/Wiley.

Stolovitch, H. D., & Keeps, E. J. (2006a). Forward. *Handbook of human performance technology* (3rd ed.). San Francisco: Pfeiffer/Wiley.

Stolovitch, H. D., & Keeps, E. J. (2006b). *Beyond training ain't performance fieldbook.* Alexandria, VA: ASTD Press.

Van Buren, M. E., & Eskine, W. (2002). *State of the industry: ASTD's annual review of trends in employer-provided training in the United States.* Alexandra, VA: American Society for Training and Development.

Van Tiem, D. M., Moseley, J. L., & Dessinger, J. C. (2012). *Fundamentals of performance improvement.* San Francisco: Pfeiffer/Wiley.

Webster's Dictionary. (2014). *New college edition* (5th ed.). Boston: Houghton Mifflin Harcourt.

Chapter 15
Performance Support

Marc J. Rosenberg[1]

Marc Rosenberg and Associates

Imagine.

Imagine you lead a sales organization where the competition is brutal. Your company announces new products almost daily, requiring constant training. Your sales force spends almost 20 percent of their time in class, in manager briefings, or on conference calls trying to keep up. This time away from customers hurts your bottom line. To combat this, you build a mobile support solution that provides your sales team with instant information on new products and competitive positioning—available anywhere and anytime. What happens? Customer contact time and sales conversation quality goes up, as do sales.

Imagine your online business is booming, so much so that you are constantly hiring new reps for your expanding call centers. Initial training takes eight weeks and new product promotions require numerous staff briefings and refresher training. On top of this, you are in a regulated business, with all sorts of government requirements for customer interactions. Your solution: online support, embedded within the call center application, delivering on-demand and proactive guidance that streamlines much of your routine call center activities and provides tracking for compliance purposes. You significantly reduce your training time while continuing to satisfy regulatory requirements.

Now, use your imagination. Where else do you see opportunities to support learning and performance exactly where and when it is needed? How would you support:

First responders who need instantaneous information to make life-saving decisions?
Warehouse workers who must track constantly changing inventories and orders?
CEOs who need a real-time dashboard to monitor the health of their business?

Want to know more about the power of the unique and innovative strategies used to meet challenges like these? Read on.

Training, Learning, and Performance in Modern Organizations

We live and work in a knowledge-intensive world. New knowledge is growing exponentially, but the half-life of knowledge is decreasing dramatically. We must know more, but what we know has a shorter shelf life than ever. Also, work is more sophisticated. There's more to do, it's more complex and varied, and, if not done right, the consequences can be severe.

A single solution, more training, dominated our historical response to the knowledge explosion. But there are limits to what training can do. In our fast-paced, globalized work environment, traditional approaches to training and learning, well intentioned as they are, cannot, by themselves, meet the seemingly insatiable appetite modern workers have for new knowledge and capabilities. There are three major reasons for this, detailed next.

Costs matter. Training is expensive. Sometimes, it's worth it, but not always. Expenses for classroom facilities, instructors, and travel can mount up. E-learning saves on these costs,

---

[1]This chapter is excerpted, with permission, from the white paper, "At the Moment of Need: The Case for Performance Support," published by The eLearning Guild (www.elearningguild.com). Copyright 2013. Find and download the complete white paper at: http://bit.ly/wp-1306.

although development costs can be quite high. But, the biggest expense by far is time away from the job. Given this, how many hours, days, and weeks can you afford to take people off task to train them? Good training is critical to well-run organizations, but there is a limit to how much time employees, customers, or businesses can devote to it. New strategies to reduce this productivity hit are worth serious consideration.

Speed matters.   We know that classroom training is not highly scalable, especially with large learner populations, without incurring huge costs. E-learning enables simultaneous content delivery to vast numbers of people, but it often takes too long to create and update. When workers need to know something, or do something—right away—what are the costs of waiting? Do you have the luxury of months, weeks, or even days to get the information out or to update it? And, if the information is important but brief, do you want to spend all that time and expense packaging it in a course?

Sometimes, less is more.   Organizations have been looking to make work easier, simpler, and more efficient for as long as there has been work to do. If you can quickly get a tool or resource into the hands of workers in ways that help them do their jobs faster and better, with less training, shouldn't you do it?

Consider this: We can embed tools and resources within the work itself so people do not have to stop for training every time something is new or changed. The better the tools and resources that people have at their immediate disposal, the more productive they can be.

Work Is Learning; Learning Is Work

The line between working and learning is quickly disappearing—a good thing.

We want better performance as an outcome of better processes, tools, and resources.

We now focus on mobility, to assure we support workers anytime and anywhere.

We recognize the social nature of work, and use social media to share content and connect people with expertise, be it in the form of explicit content in an online resource, or peers and experts at the other end of a communications network.

We know that we cannot mandate a single strategy for all performance improvement. People pursue knowledge and skills in their own way, at their own pace. We must accommodate this.

We want to personalize knowledge and skill access so that workers get only what they need, when they need it. We do not want to put them in the position of trying to take in knowledge as if they are drinking from a fire hydrant.

We want to use new technology to make the complex simple, the lengthy brief, the disjointed systematic, and the obscure more obvious to all.

We now recognize solutions and approaches that provide direct support for human performance in the workplace as increasingly important in the overall learning and performance strategy of an enterprise. Collectively, we call this field performance support.

What Is Performance Support?

Performance support is a tool or other resource, from print to technology supported, which provides just the right amount of task guidance, support, and productivity benefits to the user— precisely at the moment of need.

Common to all performance support definitions is the focus on tools and resources, the emphasis on application, and the timing—"at the moment of need." In other words, you don't use performance support to learn about a task, but rather you use it directly in conjunction with the performance of the task. Its ultimate goal is to deliver the right support, at the right level of complexity or detail, to the right people, at precisely the right time they need it.

Although the concept of "tool" is important in understanding performance support, we cannot, in fact, consider all tools as performance support. Rossett and Schafer (2007) note that, "to qualify, the object [tool] must house valued information, processes, or perspectives that target a task or need." So a computer would not be performance support, but a software application might be. A hammer would not be performance support, but a laminated card that advises what type of nail to use for a particular job, might be as well.

To understand performance support better, it is helpful to differentiate it from training. Table 15.1 illustrates the major differences.

Differentiating Training from Performance Support

The role of training is to provide very-well-planned instruction with specifically defined objectives, structure, and activities to enable people to master specific skills and knowledge, in the classroom or online. On the other hand, the function of performance support is to get work done, to accomplish tasks directly (no learning objectives, just performance goals). Learning is incidental. Training requires stopping work to participate, then

TABLE 15.1	Differences between Training and Performance Support	
	Training	**Performance Support**
Purpose	Instruct	Perform
Workflow	Postpone work	Do work
Value of learning	Learning is structured	Learning happens incidentally
Goal	Gain skill and knowledge	Accomplish work tasks

TABLE 15.2	Types of Performance Support		
Gloria Gery	**Steve Foreman**	**Allison Rossett & Lisa Shafer**
External Stands alone, apart from the work, requiring the user to stop work to use the tool. Examples: user manuals, reference books	**Software help** Assists users of software products. Examples: online help systems, wizards	**Planners** Supports users getting ready for, or following up on, a task. Helps users think more robustly about the challenge. Examples: preflight checklist, recipes
Extrinsic Available within the performance system, a little closer to the work at hand but not integrated into the workflow. Example: online help systems	**Task and process support** Guides users more directly through complex tasks and end-to-end processes. Allows users to zoom out to gain insight into how the task fits into the bigger picture, and zoom in to detailed step-by-step guidance. Example: interactive flow charts	**Sidekicks** Supports users in the act of accomplishing a task. All about getting things done in the moment. Examples: online help, recipes again (Not all performance support tools are both planners and sidekicks, but there are many examples like this, where one does double duty.)
Intrinsic Completely embedded in the workflow, and practically impossible to differentiate the work from the support. Example: Wizards guide you through a software installation, hiding complexity, and guiding you through the process as you work.	**Diagnostic tools** Focuses on decision-making and problem-solving support. Includes scenario-based or "what-if" tools that may ask questions and propose recommendations. Examples: loan payment estimator, mobile phone plan calculator	

returning to work to apply what was learned. With performance support, workers use the solution in the flow of work.

The Moment of Need

Perhaps nothing expresses the uniqueness of performance support as the notion of the moment of need. Done right, performance support is often indistinguishable from the job itself.

At its core, the moment of need is a simple test: How are you enabling people to successfully accomplish their jobs tasks exactly when they need to do so? Performance support experts Gottfredson and Mosher (2010) provides a framework that can be very helpful. Their "five moments of need" model targets when to consider performance support. The first two moments focus on acquisition of knowledge and capability, preparing people for work, thus more closely and appropriately aligning them with training. The next three moments shift to application of knowledge and capability, emphasizing supporting people during work. Together, the five moments of need represents what Gottfredson calls the full journey people take from learning something new, to applying skills and knowledge to real-time challenges. Doing anything less short-changes the effectiveness of an entire performance strategy.

Types of Performance Support

There are many different ways to categorize performance support. One basic approach splits it into two categories: job aids and electronic performance support systems (EPSS). Job aids are often paper-based tools, like shopping lists, recipes,

and maps. EPSSs are centered and dependent on technology, from small apps to enterprise IT systems.

In Table 15.2, three more characterization schemes, from several experts, provide additional insight. How you approach performance support depends, in part, on how you see it.

Seven Characteristics of Good Performance Support

What makes performance support worth the effort? What is likely to lead to success? These seven characteristics of good performance support will point you in the right direction.

1. Good performance support makes work easier. This is a no-brainer. If using the tool or resource takes more effort, if it is more complex than the process or tool it replaced, you will never get to the tipping point of critical mass—where you reach the number of users you need to make the innovation self-sustaining. On the other hand, if users find their jobs easier because of the tool, adoption should soar.
2. Good performance support makes users—and organizations—more productive. Of course, easy does not necessarily mean worthwhile. Users, and the organization, need to see tangible business benefits in terms of efficiency, productivity, cost reduction, time saving, and so forth. Ease of use and productivity, together, are essential.
3. Good performance support integrates into the workflow. The closer performance support aligns with work, and the less time users are away from actual work tasks, the better.

The more you have to stop working, and remain in a nonworking mode in order to get support, the less efficient the performance support solution is.

4. Good performance support is cost effective. This is simple math. Performance support may make jobs easier and may increase productivity, but the bottom line is whether the gains exceed the investment. The real measure of success is bottom-line results.

5. Good performance support is easy to master. While the use of performance support is often intuitively obvious, it may require some initial training or coaching, justified by the return generated from using the tool down the road. But if the training is too expensive, frustrating, complicated, or lengthy, then users may not deem it worth their time.

6. Good performance support is easy to scale. Performance support's value proposition increases as the number of users increases. Making your solution available to all who need it is essential. Anything getting in the way can hurt chances of adoption by the critical mass of employees needed to generate the best cost-effective results.

7. Good performance support is easy to update. The knowledge explosion and constant organizational change demands tools and resources that can be updated, modified, improved, and redeployed quickly and efficiently. Performance support is keenly susceptible to abandonment if users sense that it is falling behind their needs.

The Rationale for Performance Support

Performance support offers great opportunities, but to be successful, gaining buy-in from sponsors, clients, and leadership is Task One. Why should you consider performance support? What's the business case? What are the risks and benefits?

Training, as a ticket to performance improvement, is often a bumpy road. Between classes, old habits creep back in and forgetfulness ensues. There is also, in training, the capability disparity of employees. Some need more learning time than others, but the course—especially an instructor-led course—is difficult to pace optimally for everyone. E-learning has helped, but when it comes time to apply what was learned, workers are often quite alone.

Does Training Produce Competence?

It's rare for people coming out of training to be fully competent. As shown in Figure 15.1, there is a myth that training brings people directly to competence (line 1), but in reality, the best that we can expect is to get people ready to continue building skills back on the job (line 2). Without posttraining support, the risk is that what they learned will atrophy (line 3). If that happens, and we do nothing about it, you will likely have to start over (very costly), and the next time you train expect more resistance from learners who wonder why they must go through the program again. However, using workplace support, including performance support, increases the likelihood that the learners will reach higher levels of competence, even mastery (line 4).

The advantages of this approach include:

- A lower overall cost of competence, with less retraining.
- Higher performance and productivity levels than could be achieved with training alone.
- Shorter training times as performance support in the workplace helps improve productivity in the context of doing the job. (The productivity of a worker in training is zero; any strategy getting people back to work quicker adds to the bottom line.)
- Less on-the-job performance degradation.

Opportunities for Performance Support

Successful performance-support initiatives rely on picking the right project or problem to begin with. If the problem is unique, highly experienced based, or if there is no explicitly definable set process or approach, performance support is

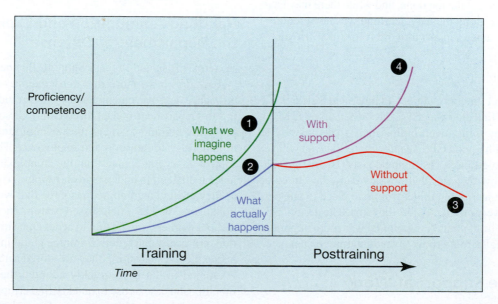

FIGURE 15.1   The role of support in getting to mastery.

likely not a good candidate. But many situations present great performance-support opportunities:

- When a task is clear and repetitive, performance support speeds up the work and removes some of the drudgery.

  When a task is complex, performance support hides some of the complexity, allowing the worker to focus on the most essential aspects of the work.
- When a task requires the application of a process, performance support turns conceptual information into productive outputs.
- When work processes, procedures, and/or outputs significantly change, performance support "coaches" users moving from the old to the new way of doing things.
- When you need standardized and reliable work outputs, performance support reduces deviations that can cause compatibility or consistency problems later.
- When you require work monitoring or record keeping, performance support tracks activities and generates reports that help run the business.

No doubt organizations have many performance-support opportunities; you just have to look around and listen for the cues. They are easier to spot than you think.

Performance Support in Daily Life

From tax software to satellite networks, performance support is everywhere in our daily lives.

Tax Software

(Extrinsic and Intrinsic, Task and Process Support, Sidekick)

Most people can't do their taxes. The mind-numbing forms and regulations, not to mention the math, can be daunting. What to do? Attend training to learn how to prepare a tax return; even learn bookkeeping or accounting. Or, hire a trained professional to do it. Or, use one of many tax software products like TurboTax, which guides users though the process, hiding the complexity. You get the job done, and while there may have been some learning along the way, learning was not a requirement. This performance support tool did it for (or with) you.

GPS

(Intrinsic, Task and Process Support, Planner and Sidekick)

How do people find their way these days when driving? Maps are so passé, many think, even online maps. The answer, of course, is GPS. With a good GPS, the likelihood that you will get where you want to go increases tremendously. But ask people who use a GPS how they got there. Many can't say. In other words, they didn't learn how to get from one place to another, but they got there very efficiently just the same. The desired performance (getting from point A to point B) was more important than the underlying learning (how to read/interpret maps).

Performance Support at Work

Performance support adds value to many roles and functions in many modern organizations.

Improving Workplace Support at a Technology Company

(Extrinsic, Task and Process Support, Sidekick)

When one uses e-learning for on-the-job reference, it is often fraught with problems because it's not designed for quick access, and finding small bits of information within the instructional program can be difficult. In many cases, reaccessing online training requires re-registration and a long transit through the course to find exactly what you are looking for—a huge time waster. This was the situation at a major high-tech company. Workers needing on-the-job support found the training materials ineffective in providing quick and accurate answers to job-related questions. Calls to the help desk increased, a cost that they could not sustain. By transitioning some of the content out of a courseware platform and onto a performance support platform, important information became more easily available to workers at the moment of need, and the training was refocused on the most critical skills. In four years, the performance support solution was accessed more than 400,000 times and the help desk saw savings of $7.6 million.

Adopting New Sales Software and Processes in Health Care Services

(Extrinsic and Intrinsic, Task and Process Support, Sidekick)

Introducing new software is hard; including a new sales process on top of it is even harder. When a major health care services company noticed its sales force using more than a dozen variations of their sales process, they knew they had to do something. Once the new sales-software package was in place, the company added sophisticated performance support directly into the software. Contextually aware, the solution monitors the salesperson's use of the tool and provides "how-to" support with little workflow disruption. This solution dramatically reduced costs and time off the job for training. First-year results showed almost 79,000 work hours saved, with a corresponding cost savings of more than $2.75 million.

Handling Ammunition and Explosives in the Department of Defense

(External, Task and Process Support, Planner and Sidekick)

Few jobs have more dire consequences than mishandling ordinance. A government agency that provides essential training to Department of Defense (DoD) personnel experienced problems helping learners master complicated tasks related to handling ammunition and explosives. They addressed the subject in several courses, but the complexity of the topic still made it difficult to understand and apply. To overcome this, the agency created a combined resource that works as an instructional game and as a field-based performance support tool. On the job, workers use the tool to access mission-critical information, protocols, and required storage guidelines for ammunition and explosives, ensuring they are stored safely and efficiently. Personnel in the field quickly adopted the tool, praising its mobility and ease of use to quickly find critical job information. The speed and ease of revising and redeploying the tool based on updates to government requirements, and overall lower costs

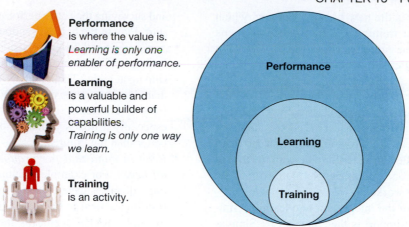

FIGURE 15.2   The relationship between training, learning, and performance.

of keeping the information up-to-date, also proved significant benefits.

Managing People in the Pharmaceutical Industry

(External, Task and Process Support, Planner)

Sometimes, you don't have to invest in new technology to achieve your performance support goals. Rather, the solution lies in using an existing tool in new ways. This was the case for a major pharmaceutical company that wanted to improve the "people management" skills of project managers. After six months of training, many of these managers were still having difficulty in doing supervisory tasks. Taking a novel approach to performance support, the company used Skype to establish a peer-based hotline and staffed it with volunteer managers who were successful in leading high-performance teams. The hotline significantly increased the availability of credible guidance and information to project managers at the moment of need. After four months, they observed marked improvement in supervisory performance, and within a year, 85 percent of the project managers were considered "effective contributors" in this area. In this case, the performance support solution didn't provide access to documents or other types of expert-created content. Instead, it provided direct access to the experts themselves.

Performance Support and Training: Working Together

Understanding how training and performance relate to one another is helpful in developing more comprehensive learning and performance support solutions, where each provides unique value commensurate with its strengths. Figure 15.2 illustrates this relationship. Training is one of many ways we learn. We also learn from our peers, through trial and error, through practice and coaching, from observing others, from a myriad of information resources, and more. And while learning is essential to performance, it is not the only way to get there. Incentives and rewards boost performance, as does the right work environment. And, of course, the right tools help tremendously. Here is where performance support stands out.

The New Blended Learning

Many people think of blended learning as the marriage of classroom and online training. While useful, this definition is woefully incomplete. Going forward, as illustrated in Figure 15.3, our toolbox of performance improvement solutions, including performance support, is expanding.

This model showcases new, informal approaches to workplace learning and performance, with an emphasis on doing

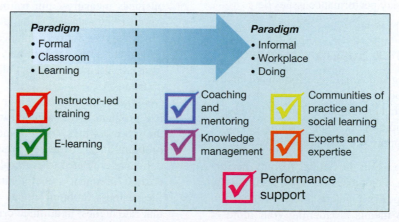

FIGURE 15.3   The expanding toolbox of performance improvement solutions.

rather than learning. This is the new blended learning, which does not diminish formal training's value; rather, it opens up new opportunities to be more successful and efficient in improving performance. Performance support is part of this new strategy.

Performance support can move with the learner from the training setting to the field. Training—classroom or online—can provide background knowledge to set the context for using the tool, and that training can also provide instruction and practice so that the user is skilled and comfortable with the tool in a work context. This approach helps people more seamlessly transition from learners to workers.

An excellent example of the integration of e-learning (simulation) and performance support is the "Save a Life Simulator" (www.heartrescuenow.com), which teaches when to use a defibrillator, not how. That's left to the defibrillator itself, which talks the user through the process at the moment of need. Can you imagine a person who has never done this before trying to make sense of a set of printed instructions when time is so critical? By having the defibrillator actually guide the user, errors and delays are minimized.

Each approach—training and performance support—is valuable in its own right. Choosing which to use (and as the defibrillator example illustrates both are often appropriate) requires an in-depth understanding of the performance environment in the workplace, the work to do, and the learning and performance requirements of the users. As such, performance support strategy and learning strategy are often interdependent, especially where needs assessment is concerned.

Dealing with Demands for More Training Time

Trainers and students often complain that there's just too much content in a course. The pressure to increase training time runs into resistance from the business due to cost and productivity issues. The pressures to cut content runs into resistance from SMEs who argue the essential nature of what they are teaching. By putting some content into performance support, available at the moment of need, precious training time is freed for additional, often more advanced, content deemed best delivered in a training mode.

Embracing performance support serves training professionals well as it provides a powerful entry into the workplace arena, where the real everyday performance issues lie.

Making Performance Support Happen

There's a lot about designing and building performance support that is common to any good project, but there are also some process steps and nuances that are unique to this solution type. Here are twelve areas to think about when selecting the right project for performance support and then seeing it through:

- *See the bigger picture.* This is critical for any performance support project. For those who have traditionally looked at workplace performance issues as primarily a training problem, this means broadening your mindset and surveying the entire performance landscape before you start. Play in the biggest sandbox, not the smallest.
- *Assess the need.* Select a business problem perceived as a "pain point" that must be addressed. Is it keeping leadership up at night? Then, narrow your selection to a problem that clearly requires ongoing support that training cannot fully or efficiently address. Don't overextend yourself, especially if this is your first project. Small victories are better than big failures.
- *Keep in mind that performance support can't address all needs.* For example, scenarios that are infrequent or unpredictable make creating a performance support solution impractical at best (the *Apollo 13* crisis is a classic example). Other scenarios include cases where instant reactions and flawless performance, the first time, is critical (think of an emergency room doctor or a soldier in combat). The response here may be to train the worker to better recognize and respond, without hesitation, to these unique situations. It's expensive to do, but consider the consequences of not doing it right.
- *Begin with the end in mind.* Too often, we begin with solutions and then try to find problems to solve. Only at the end do we think about whether we were successful. Better to start with the business or performance problem, which drives success criteria, and then, from that desired outcome, a performance support solution takes shape.
- *Build sponsorship.* Performance support is new thinking. No matter how much you feel it's the right thing to do, you can't get there on your own. Look for support from the owner of the "point of performance." This is the person who owns (not just manages) the specific work process to be addressed. Getting the right sponsor on board begins with talking their language and understanding their issues, then establishing credibility and demonstrating understanding of their problem, how they measure it, and how human performance most impacts it. Then, sell the concept by presenting a prototype or model of a proposed solution. Be clear and thorough when asking for what you need from the sponsor (i.e., funding, resources, and/or endorsement). When you roll out your solution, be sure you have cascading sponsorship from the top down, especially in the performers' organization.
- *Define the success criteria.* Doing this early sets clear expectations for the project. Focus on performance and business measures, not training or learning measures. Another key measure is that a critical mass of users must adopt a successful performance support solution. Without critical mass, the solution may have little impact on these measures. Remember to establish your critical-mass target up front.
- *Generate requirements.* Once you've identified the critical problem and associated measures, you then identify the job roles that have the most impact on the business problem and list the key areas of performance risks or deficiencies related to each role. Ask experts to rate those areas by frequency, complexity, and degree of impact on the business problem. Focus first on performance areas that rate highest in all three criteria and define the type of

performance support solution needed to enable effective performance in each area. Here is where initial design attributes will emerge.

- *Design for the work.* Designing performance support is primarily about understanding the nature of the work, the tasks that make up the work, and the approaches, capabilities, and styles of the workers performing the work. Collaborating with experts (subject-matter experts or master job performers) and novice performers (they'll provide different but equally important perspectives) is the key to designing and building the right tool. We call designing for the work, performance-centered design.

- *Get the technology right.* If your solution uses technology, getting it right is essential. Great technology alone will not make performance support successful, but bad technology will certainly kill it. Without a solid IT partnership, performance support will never go anywhere. You may own the "car," but they own the "road."

- *Test the solution.* You can catch and correct many mistakes before they become too costly by allocating enough time and resources to thoroughly test the solution. You should undertake three types of tests: prototyping, user testing, and quality assurance and system testing. Prototyping provides an opportunity to collect feedback on the concept and early design ideas from stakeholders. User testing engages a few users to try out the solution at various points in the development process to ensure its relevance and ease of use. You perform quality assurance and system testing at the final stages of development to ensure the technology works reliably and has the capacity to handle the expected number of users.

- *Promote user adoption.* Once performance support is built and ready for deployment, your mission is only half over. To reach the most users in the shortest amount of time, implement a long-term communications plan that focuses on buy-in, not just awareness, and be sure to provide solid training and support. Talk benefits, not features, and frame it as a solution to a problem rather than an "activity" or a "technology." Embed the performance support tool into case studies and simulations as part of initial training. Promote it with demonstrations and success stories until you reach critical mass in usage. Then, communicate progress toward your targeted business measures.

- *Reinvent and innovate.* The usability of performance support will certainly decrease over time, sometimes more quickly than expected, as new processes and knowledge come into play. Updating the tool will enhance its usability over a longer period, making the effort more cost effective. To keep your solution fresh, gather regular feedback from performers and leadership, and be sure to respond proactively. Develop a multiyear roadmap for expanding the content and functionality of the solution through a series of releases. Finally, build on the success of the solution and identify other problems to address with subsequent projects. Early successes will likely generate increased demand for performance support in other areas of the organization.

Performance support will never be a viable option if it's always approached as a learning or training solution; it's not. For some trainers and HR professionals, this can be outside their comfort zone. Changing mindsets extends to the line organizations as well, who may see training or other traditional approaches as the default solution, or the easy way out, when they should be looking closer to the work they manage. Shifting perspectives is not easy, but failure to do so can be devastating. You want fans, not just users.

The Future of Performance Support Technology

The future of performance support is very promising, not just because it makes so much sense in the workplace, but also because technology is making design, implementation, and distribution easier and less expensive.

Mobile

Like work itself, performance support is going mobile. The ubiquitous availability of high-speed networks makes accessing sophisticated tools, anytime and anywhere, not just possible, but very practical. When time is money, mobile workers need access to performance support quickly and on demand. Fast networks eliminate the lag time that once resulted in a predictably frustrating experience when working with mobile content. While a minute here and a minute there may seem trivial, as hundreds (or more) people use performance support multiple times every day, those minutes add up fast.

Mobile devices are finally portable enough and fast enough to support highly valuable and data-intensive performance support on the go. The proliferation of smartphones, and especially tablets (including increased support for "bring your own device" – BYOD programs), will provide a much more flexible platform for performance support than traditional laptops and desktop computers, at a cost low enough to equip everyone.

Apps

Just the idea of "apps" has a performance support ring. Of course, not all apps are performance support; for example, games, news, weather, and streaming music apps aren't. But many mobile apps do serve a performance support purpose, such as mortgage calculators, navigation (GPS) systems, medical self-diagnosis tools, and inventory control barcode scanners.

Apps are low cost to make and distribute, easily updatable, have very specific purposes, and are quick to build in response to new needs and challenges. App developers don't usually think they are building performance support tools, but if you look at their products, you will see that it's what they've been doing all along.

Apps will allow organizations to push new tools to the field far easier than much larger, more complex enterprise-wide solutions. Those won't go away, but simpler apps represent a huge growth opportunity for performance support.

For a great example of how mobile apps can serve a performance support role, check out the collection of mobile apps from the American Red Cross here: http://www.redcross.org/prepare/mobile-apps.

Social Media

An aspect of performance support that will have an increasing impact is the rise of social media. It's not just Twitter, Facebook, LinkedIn, and other popular social media services that are intriguing, but the emergence of specialized social apps that are customizable for an organization or industry. Think about opportunities for collaboration and performance support inside a business. For example, using microblogs to ask questions in online discussions, communities of practice and blogs to share insights, and wikis to build new knowledge, keeps the solution vibrant and timely.

Cloud Computing

Cloud computing is a boon for performance support. The cloud allows storage and management of vast amounts of accessible on-the-go data and information that is mobile and incorporated into low-cost apps. Without it, there would be too much content to store on mobile devices, making a mobile performance support future impractical. And if performance support can't go mobile, it's not going anywhere.

Equally important, the cloud allows better quality control of information from a knowledge management perspective. This single source significantly improves the accuracy, usefulness, and consistency of content as opposed to everyone downloading their own version of a content library and worrying about keeping it up to date.

Experience API (xAPI)

Training organizations use SCORM interoperability standards to track training activity. One of the frustrations of SCORM has been its inability to track non-instructional, on-the-job activities. Now, the Experience API (xAPI, also referred to as the "Tin Can" API) provides technical specifications for tracking a much wider variety of learning and performance experiences in the workplace. Done carefully, the Experience API will enable the capture and reporting of data related to performance support utilization.

Other Technology Advances

People are developing additional technologies in a variety of areas that can significantly aid the development, deployment, and use of performance support. Among these are:

- Crowdsourcing tools enable large numbers of users to provide input, ideas, new knowledge, and improvement suggestions to communities of practice.
- Augmented reality merges performance and job information with the physical workplace in virtual ways never done before. Integrating products like Google Glass with performance support is an example of the potential here.
- Inference engines bring a higher level of "intelligence" to performance support, helping the system "learn" user preferences and needs over time, making the performance support solution more personalized.
- Responsive design is a Web design approach that optimizes the content viewing experience on any device, making electronic performance support more easily accessible across platforms, including smartphones, tablets, and computers.
- DITA (Darwin Information Type Architecture) is an example of a new breed of "write once, use many times" XML data models that can make authoring content for different audiences and purposes easier and more efficient.
- Task management systems allow the performance support solution to monitor task progress, completion, and other activities associated with the work.
- Workflow support systems assist more complex performance support applications in managing the steps and processes inherent in the use of the tool.

Market intelligence firm IDC defines big data, one of the hottest topics in IT, as "a new generation of technologies and architectures, designed to economically extract value from very large volumes of a wide variety of data, by enabling high-velocity capture, discovery, and/or analysis." Getting better at extracting value from what IDC calls the digital universe has important implications for knowledge management and performance support.

Performance Support Gets Smarter

A final way to think about where we may be heading with performance support is what Gottfredson (2013) calls the performance support spectrum. There is sometimes a tendency to just put out a lot of content and let users try to find and make sense of it on their own. This may be useful to a few people, but for most it's often too frustrating and not worth the time. In the future, performance support will be more targeted, automated, and smart.

We'll embed targeted performance support in work processes, creating a direct link between content and work; only what's relevant is included.

Automated performance support will provide the right information and guidance in the context of the work being done without users having to ask for it, thus enhancing ease, accuracy, and efficiency.

Smart performance support will "learn" what users need, and "evolve" to support them based on their history with the tool, as well as their past job performance. These tools will adjust as users move from novice to proficient, then to experienced, and, ultimately, to expert. Smart performance support has the potential to dramatically shorten time to mastery.

As technology allows performance support to proliferate in multiple work domains (sales, IT, customer care, manufacturing, finance, HR, etc.) and in multiple work environments (office, home, on the road, and at client and customer locations) anywhere and anytime, its potential will become more prominent. The result will be increased confidence in choosing performance support as a first or primary response to a performance improvement opportunity, rather than as an afterthought.

Summary of Key Principles

1. **We live and work in a knowledge-intensive world.** New knowledge is growing exponentially, but the half-life of knowledge is decreasing dramatically. We must know more, but what we know has a shorter shelf life than ever.

2. **Performance support is a tool or other resource, from print to technology supported, which provides just the right amount of task guidance, support, and productivity benefits to the user—precisely at the moment of need.**

3. **Performance support offers great opportunities to improve performance, especially when the tasks are clear and repetitive, complex, applications of a process, representative of fundamental change, require standardized outputs, and when work monitoring and record keeping are required.**

4. **Advantages of performance support include a lower overall cost of competence with less retraining, higher performance and productivity levels than could be achieved with training alone, less on-the-job** performance degradation, and shorter training times as performance support in the workplace helps improve productivity in the context of doing the job. (The productivity of a worker in training is zero; any strategy getting people back to work quicker adds to the bottom line.)

5. **Performance support can move with the learner from the training setting to the field.** Training—classroom or online—can provide background knowledge to set the context for using the tool, and that training can also provide instruction and practice so that the user is skilled and comfortable with the tool in a work context. This approach helps people more seamlessly transition from learners to worker.

6. **The future of performance support is very promising, not just because it makes so much sense in the workplace, but also because technology is making design, implementation, and distribution easier and less expensive.**

Application Questions

1. Describe a hypothetical (or real) example of how a performance support system or tool might be (or is) used to support operations within one of the types of organizations listed (your example should be one other than those used in the chapter): (a) call center, (b) customer relations department, (c) government agency, (d) military organization, (e) human resources department, (f) consulting agency, or (g) sales department.

2. Identify a real (or hypothetical) performance problem that does (or might) exist in one of the types of organizations listed in question 1. Describe how performance support might be used to solve that problem, and the potential impact on current or planned training once performance support is introduced.

3. Assume that you are working for one of the types of organizations mentioned in question 1. Further assume that your supervisor is reluctant to approve the development of performance support for the organization. The supervisor has asked you to write a one-page memo describing three reasons why performance support should be useful to the company. Write the memo!

4. Imagine you are an instructional designer in the not-too-distant future, where the use of performance support is commonplace. How might these tools be used outside formal course instruction to enhance learning? How might these tools be integrated into a formal course design to enhance learning? How might performance support be used before or after the formal learning? Provide an example of each.

References

Gottfredson, C. (2013). From scattered information to transformational performance support: Where are you? Retrieved from http://www.learningsolutionsmag.com/articles/1156/from-scattered-information-to-transformational-performance-support-where-are-you

Gottfredson, C., & Mosher, B. (2010). *Innovative performance support: Strategies and practices for learning in the workflow*. New York: McGraw-Hill.

Rossett, A., & Schafer, L. (2007). *Job aids and performance support in the workplace: Moving from knowledge in the classroom to knowledge everywhere*. New York: Pfeiffer/Wiley. Associated web site and tool: http://www.colletandschafer.com/perfsupp/

Chapter 16
Informal Learning

Saul Carliner

Concordia University

Informal learning happens when visitors interact with exhibitions in a museum.

Informal learning also happens when a person goes online to investigate a medical condition associated with a recent diagnosis.

Informal learning happens, too, when a graduate student absorbs the work experiences that experienced professionals describe during a social event at a conference.

Informal learning occurs when one person helps another solve a computer problem.

Informal learning also happens when a worker suggests a procedural change to five different managers—and each says no.

But what is informal learning?

In this chapter, I provide an explanation. After defining informal learning and placing current interest in the subject among instructional designers into context, I describe opportunities for informal learning and considerations about the manner in which it happens, and close by suggesting how instructional designers can support informal learning in the organizations where they work.

About Informal Learning

This section provides a general background on informal learning. In it, I first define the term in general and then in the context of the workplace. Next, I suggest some of the motivations for recent interest in the topic, and close by identifying the most common forms of informal learning, especially in a work context.

Defining Informal Learning

Many definitions of informal learning focus on its learner-controlled nature. For example, in our book, *Advanced Web-Based Training: Unlocking Instructionally Sound Online Learning* (2005), Margaret Driscoll and I define it as a process in which learners set their own learning objectives and determine for themselves what successful completion looks like. This contrasts with formal learning, in which an instructor or instructional designer establishes the objectives and establishes a means to determine the criteria for successful completion.

Such definitions suggest that formal and informal learning are distinct from one another. However, as indicated by Victoria Marsick (2009), one of the leading researchers on informal learning, oftentimes "informal and formal learning interacts in important ways." In other words, oftentimes an informal learning activity includes some elements of formal learning. For example, a new employee might learn how to greet customers and operate the cash register through a series of on-the-job activities, without going to a formal class. In some sense, the learning is informal because it happens at the learners' convenience and at the learners' speed; but it is not completely informal because the employer determines the outcomes and designs a series of activities to facilitate learning.

In the workplace, learning activities that many label as "informal" have somewhat formal characteristics. In fact, the British government enlisted researchers Janice Malcolm, Phil Hodkinson, and Helen Colley (2003) to define informal learning. Their resulting definition likened informal learning to a series of levers, each providing a different type of control over the learning process. These "levers" include:

- *Process:* Who controls and assesses learning. In the most formal situations, learning is controlled and defined by the instructor, who establishes objectives and, through assessments, determines whether learners have achieved the objectives. In the least formal situations, learners establish their own objectives and criteria and determine when the learning is complete.
- *Location:* Where the learning occurs. In the most formal situations, learning occurs in a place intended for learning, such as a traditional or virtual classroom. In the least formal situations, learning occurs organically within the context of everyday life.
- *Purpose:* Whether learning is a primary or secondary goal of the learning activity. In the most formal situations, learning is the primary goal. In the least formal situations, learning is an accidental by-product.
- *Content:* Whether the topic of study is for immediate or long-term use. Acquisition of a body of content—such as the concepts underlying an occupation—tends to have long-term use and is considered more formal, while content about processes and procedures within a particular context has more immediate impact on the job—and in job performance—and is considered more informal.

Working on a similar project for the Canadian government, Wihak, Hall, Bratton, Warkentin, Wihak, and MacPherson (2008) added a fifth "lever":

- *Consciousness:* The extent to which learners are aware that learning has occurred. In the most formal situations, learners have a high level of awareness that learning has occurred (or that it should have occurred). In the least formal situations, learners may not even realize that they learned something until long after the experience.

This extended definition builds on the earlier notion that informal learning is linked to formal learning. It also encompasses a number of particular learning processes, including *nonformal learning*, which covers instruction that occurs in locations other than schools, universities, and the workplace; *incidental learning*, which refers to insights and facts unexpectedly gained through interactions with other people and experiences; and *self-directed learning*, which refers to an educational process that is carried out by the learner under a formal agreement with a mentor or instructor.

Motivations for the Recent Interest in Informal Learning

Admittedly, informal learning has existed as long as humans have passed knowledge from one person to another—intentionally and otherwise. Furthermore, researchers have explored various aspects of informal learning for well over a century. For example, museum researchers have explored ways that visitors learn from museum exhibitions and educational

researchers have explored ways that individuals learn on their own.

But interest in the subject has noticeably risen in the past twenty years. Some of the interest has come from practicing instructional designers. The adoption of the performance improvement paradigm (described in depth in Chapter 14) by most training groups generated interest in *transfer of training* to the job so as to improve worker on-the-job performance. Oftentimes, transfer of training focuses on the application of material learned in a formal class to the job. However, a preponderance of research evidence suggests that successful transfer results from providing a variety of informal learning opportunities and supports in the workplace so that learners receive practice and feedback as they attempt to apply in the "real world" the skills they were taught in the classroom environment, thus helping learners to expand the base of skills started in the formal class. Informal learning plays a central role in effective transfer, as workers receive guidance and coaching on their attempts to apply skills in the workplace, build confidence through repeated successes in the workplace, and expand the scope of work they can handle by observing coworkers and through online resources, such as reference and user materials, follow-up tutorials, and performance support systems. Performance support systems (which are discussed in depth in Chapter 15) are collections of resources that assist workers with the implementation of on-the-job tasks. In some cases, the systems perform tasks for workers; in others, the systems guide workers in performing the tasks. Informal learning plays a central role in effective performance support, too.

Another significant driver of interest in informal learning among instructional designers is the rise of the Internet, which provides workers with access to extensive repositories of information. In addition, social media—especially discussion boards and groups on social networking sites like LinkedIn—connect workers so they can exchange tips and techniques and, in the process, learning. As a result of such developments, instructional designers posit that workers are increasingly learning on their own.

But perhaps the most significant driver of interest in informal learning among instructional designers is the rise of dynamic, knowledge-based work. In addition to connecting users, computers provide decision makers with information more quickly, and with a pinpoint focus not otherwise feasible. This, in turn, has helped organizations develop sophisticated business strategies that let them better target their activities and respond more quickly to external events. This, in turn, has led to more flexible work assignments: (a) flexible work teams that bring together people with the expertise needed on a particular project and then disband when workers have completed the project and (b) shorter product development cycles (projects that once took one to five years now take three months to one year). This flexibility demands that workers become productive more quickly on projects. Because of the general challenge of scheduling formal classes in a timely way and, even when that's feasible, the need for highly specialized courses for which few qualified instructors exist, organizations increasingly rely on informal learning to prepare workers for projects.

The Most Common Forms of Informal Learning

Although informal learning can take many forms, some appear more commonly than others. In this section I describe those common forms, many of which are designed, developed, or facilitated by instructional designers.

Two categories of informal learning formats exist. The first promotes individual learning, through which people build awareness, knowledge, and skills on their own. Instructional designers can promote independent learning activities among workers by:

- preparing case studies. These studies are usually written or video-based descriptions of a particular challenge in a particular context, so people can see how others addressed the challenge and can transfer the knowledge gained to their own work environment.
- developing *content* or *documentation*. These terms refer to many types of informational materials that help workers perform their jobs and that workers usually check on the job, including user's guide, references, reports, and similar materials.
- designing *guided tours*. Guided tours provide quick overviews of a topic, familiarizing workers with a subject and helping workers determine whether they need to learn more about it.
- providing lists of *tips and tricks*. These are suggestions— usually offered automatically by a computer system—that advise workers on ways to effectively and efficiently use software and other products.
- developing *tutorials*. These are formal instructional programs that, in the context of informal learning, workers voluntarily take and, when feasible, at the learners' convenience. These tutorials help workers develop and practice skills needed on the job.
- creating *gaming and simulation activities* that model a particular environment or challenge (the simulation component) and provide participants with the opportunity to experience the benefits of good choices and the consequences of poor ones in the environment (the gaming component).
- providing opportunities for *on-the-job training* (OJT) in which workers perform tasks within the contexts of their everyday job assignments, receive feedback on their performance, and reflect on the experience so they can identify and apply what they learned the next time they perform the task.
- creating *performance support systems,* which provide workers with assistance with a task while workers do the task. Systems of this type are described in detail in Chapter 15 of this book.

Two additional powerful forms of individual informal learning usually occur without the involvement of instructional designers. The first is *trial and error*, in which workers attempt a task until they effectively perform it and, in the process of doing so, determine what they should not do when performing the task. The second is *developmental assignments*, which give workers new responsibilities within the context of their current jobs and that require the regular use of skills that workers either have not used or only use occasionally. Developmental assignments integrate many of the other forms of informal learning just mentioned; but managers usually devise developmental assignments for their staffs without the involvement of instructional designers.

The second broad category of informal learning promotes learning among two or more people. In these situations, learning is sometimes a by-product of events that might or might not have an agenda for learning. To encourage workers to interact with and learn from one another, instructional designers might:

- coordinate *lunch and learn programs*, typically sixty- to ninety-minute programs with an educational agenda and that occur in conjunction with a meal, usually lunch (hence, the name). Lunch and learn sessions typically feature a guest speaker presenting a topic of interest, but might also involve a group discussing a topic on its own with a moderator to ensure that the conversation stays on topic.
- tease out *insights arising from meetings about topics other than learning*. For example, a meeting leader might end a meeting by debriefing it. During the debriefing, participants might identify new insights or tips that can help them work more effectively.
- organize *seminars, symposia, conferences, and webinars*. These formal sessions are intended to provide participants with new insights and ideas either from a guest speaker who is an expert in a topic of interest to participants, a facilitated conversation within a group, or a combination of these activities. Instructional designers often organize the events, recruit speakers and facilitators, and provide them with guidance on what to cover and how to interact with the participants.
- set up *coaching programs*, in which workers who recently received new responsibilities perform their work under the guidance of a more experienced worker and receive feedback on that work. Instructional designers often prepare guidance for coaches and tips on providing feedback to learners.
- moderate *communities of practice*, groups of people who share a common interest and discuss it together, sometimes through social media groups like a LinkedIn group for higher education instructors or a Facebook page for a professional association for technical writers. These communities provide workers with answers to immediate questions and long-term socialization into a profession or organization, as well as help workers build their networks.
- develop and coordinate *mentoring programs*, in which an experienced worker provides ongoing job and career guidance to a protégé by listening to the protégé, helping the protégé devise solutions to immediate and longer term challenges, offering suggestions and insights, and, when feasible, linking the protégé with new opportunities.

Opportunities and Issues to Consider Regarding Informal Learning

This section first explores opportunities for informal learning, which is when people typically learn in the context of their jobs. Then it describes some characteristics of informal learning to consider when thinking about promoting the use of informal learning within an organization.

Informal Learning Opportunities throughout the Job Life Cycle

In a study of the ways that people develop expertise in their professions, researcher Michael Eraut (2000) found that the nature of the problems workers encounter changes the longer workers stay in their jobs. Early in their tenures, workers focus on determining which types of problems they need to solve, a process called pattern recognition. As workers become more experienced, the focus changes to understanding the broader situation in which they are working, a process called meta-cognition.

Research like this suggests that the life cycle of the job provides a framework that training and development professionals can use to anticipate the changing learning needs of workers throughout their job life cycles. Life cycle refers to the span of a worker's tenure in a given position, from the time the worker starts the job until he or she moves on to the next position or leaves the organization. Figure 16.1 identifies the key junctures during the life cycle of a job.

Throughout the life cycle, workers must address ongoing organizational initiatives such as change management programs, quality improvement initiatives, and revisions to policies, work standards, products, and processes. Each of the junctures, or phases, in the life cycle of a job also presents opportunities for learning. In most phases, external factors drive the learning process, such as when a worker is asked to assume additional responsibilities, start using a new software program, or adhere to a new policy or procedure. In many of these instances, employers often provide little formal training so workers have to figure out for themselves how to address these requests. As will be noted, informal learning can help develop workers at each of these phases:

- Orienting workers to the technical aspects of a job, such as ringing up a sale or using a special authoring tool to create e-learning programs. During this phase, on-the-job training is usually employed. Ideally, the learning is structured and an experienced worker coaches the new worker.

- Onboarding workers to the culture and values of the group, so workers can interact with others in a culturally appropriate manner. Much of this learning happens informally. At its best, formal mentoring and integration into a community of practice facilitates learning. At its worst, workers learn through trial and error.

- Expanding the scope of assignments a worker can handle (e.g., having a sales representative handle returned merchandise or having an instructional designer develop more complex materials). A variety of informal learning methods, such as tutorials, coaching, documentation, tips and tricks, and communities of practice help workers expand the scope of assignments they can handle.

- Building workers' proficiency, in which workers handle their current job responsibilities more effectively or efficiently. A simple example is moving from menu options to keyboard shortcuts when working with Microsoft Office. The same informal learning methods used to expand the scope of assignments also help workers build proficiency.

- Helping workers address undocumented challenges, such as complex customizations of computer systems and addressing interpersonal problems on work teams. Documentation provides some guidance in these instances, but communities of practice that let experts brainstorm ideas are often most effective at developing these skills.

- Helping workers choose career goals, which workers need to consider when they are ready to start a new job or circumstances compel it. Sometimes workers find their next job through personal study; other times, workers receive coaching and mentoring. In many instances, workers rely on a combination of the two to determine how to proceed in their careers.

- Preparing workers for their next jobs. Once workers decide which jobs they would like to move into, they often require formal learning, including degrees and certification programs. But tutorials taken informally, developmental assignments, coaching, and mentoring can also help workers prepare for their next jobs.

- Addressing ongoing organizational initiatives, such as a switch to a new reservations system. Although these initiatives usually involve the use of an entirely new software to perform old job tasks, they often involve a change to job responsibilities or work processes. Although organizations rely on formal programs to teach workers how to use the new systems and perform job responsibilities and processes, many workers skip the formal learning or resist the change, so organizations rely extensively on informal initiatives,

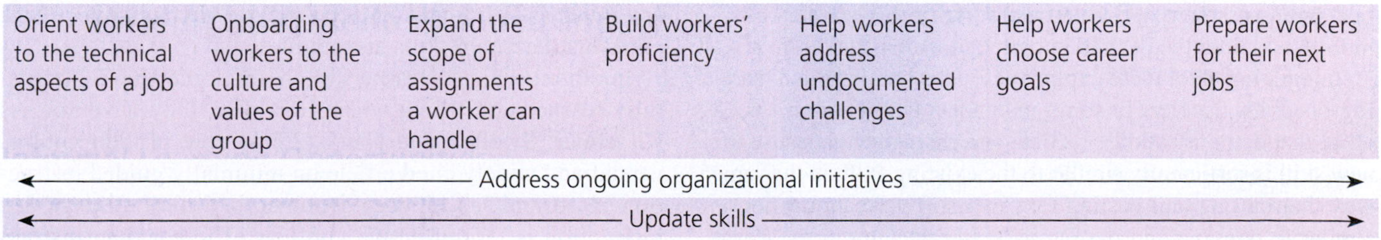

Orient workers to the technical aspects of a job	Onboarding workers to the culture and values of the group	Expand the scope of assignments a worker can handle	Build workers' proficiency	Help workers address undocumented challenges	Help workers choose career goals	Prepare workers for their next jobs

←———————————————— Address ongoing organizational initiatives ————————————————→

←———————————————————————— Update skills ————————————————————————→

FIGURE 16.1 Opportunities for learning during the life cycle of a job.

such as promotional messages to encourage people to try the new systems, responsibilities, and processes; tips and tricks to help workers easily make the transition; and coaches and mentors to help with the interpersonal side of the transition.

- Updating workers' skills and knowledge, in which workers try to perform their jobs using the most recent approaches and technologies. Mentoring and coaching help workers recognize they need to update their skills. Many of the means used to expand the scope of assignments and build proficiency also help workers update skills.

Characteristics of Informal Learning

The framework of the life cycle of a job suggests broad processes of informal learning—that is, what inspires people to learn informally and how they approach the learning at each phase of the job life cycle. A growing body of evidence from empirical studies provides insights into specific characteristics of informal learning and characteristics that affect its success.

Informal learning requires leadership to model it and to give permission to learn.   Studies have found that participation in informal learning is directly influenced by the behaviors of the top leaders of the organization. If top leaders set an example of engaging in informal learning and talking about it with their staffs—that is, modeling the behavior and encouraging their workers to engage in it—workers are more likely to engage in informal learning than if leaders merely suggest doing so. The unexpected results of a study into the informal use of e-learning programs on the job provides some insights into why this modeling is necessary. In that study, workers did not feel that they should be studying on work time as it was an unproductive use of work time, even if the studying directly related to an immediate on-the-job need.

Informal learning differs from information sharing.   In the course of a day, people share countless factoids—facts and details that might have immediate application but have no long-term benefit (at least, not at the time that users receive these factoids). Factoids are just information (e.g., news about a change in leadership in an organization is a factoid).

In contrast, instruction not only tells, but ultimately provides the opportunity to develop knowledge, skills, and attitudes. Knowledge, skills, and attitudes are ultimately demonstrated to third parties who, in turn, assesses whether the learner has developed competence. That's why, when teaching unfamiliar knowledge and skills, formal instruction often explicitly describes and demonstrates the material, and provides practice and assessment opportunities to verify that learners have, indeed, acquired the desired knowledge, skills, and attitudes.

Integrating all of these explicit activities into informal learning becomes trickier. In some instances, learners don't need all of that demonstration, practice, and assessment because the new skill is sufficiently similar to the existing skill, in the same way that cutting and pasting text in a software application is similar to copying and pasting text. In other instances, learners only find out whether they have successfully mastered new

knowledge, skills, and attitudes by performing them in the real world.

The point is, if learning represents a change in behavior, it only occurs when learners demonstrate a change in behavior; not merely when they become informed of factoids related to that behavior.

Informal learning is a social activity.   Just because learning does not happen in a formally scheduled class does not mean that informal learning needs to be a solitary activity. In fact, some of the most powerful online learning experiences are also social ones. For example, coaches help learners apply complex concepts in practical situations and strengthen performance of tasks. Similarly, mentors provide protégés with insights gained from their lived experience as well as advice tailored to the unique situation of the learner—gained through an ongoing and in-depth relationship.

But perhaps one of the most powerful means of social learning comes through communities. In the work world, they are called "Communities of Practice," a term coined by Jean Lave and Etienne Wenger (1991). Communities share news and ideas, discuss various ways to perform tasks, and provide support to their members. Communities can exist in face-to-face contexts, such as members of a department and a local actors' union, but can also exist online, through LinkedIn and Facebook groups, ongoing Twitter events like the weekly chats of instructional designers on #lrnchat, and dedicated websites like elearningguild.com. One of the benefits of communities is that they can help members apply ideas that are already documented (such as a particular policy or procedure) into practice, and speed members' development by helping them learn from other members' experiences. Communities are only effective at doing so if members are motivated to participate, the participation benefits the entire group more than it benefits the individual, and the discussions remain civil and relevant.

Informal learning is not always efficient or effective.   Although one of the great benefits of informal learning is the deep sense of ownership and pride that people feel in what they have learned, the practical reality is that informal learning is not always an effective or efficient means of learning.

In terms of effectiveness, part of the challenge is that people might not always realize that they need to initiate a learning sequence, as suggested by Marsick, Watkins, Callahan, and Volpe (2006). In a work context, for example, people might mistakenly believe they are performing a task correctly. This situation exists, in part because, as Sitzmann, Elly, Brown, and Bauer (2010) found, most people are often not effective at assessing their own skills and abilities.

In other instances, learners might think they have successfully learned something when, in reality, they have not. As Kirschner, Sweller, and Clark (2006) note in their controversial and widely cited article on minimally guided instruction in formal learning environments, "minimally guided instruction is less effective and less efficient than instructional approaches that place a strong emphasis on guidance of the student learning process" (p. 76). In a study of customer support representatives, for example, researcher Joe Downing (2007) found that they would conduct a Google search to solve customers' problems as quickly as possible. The representatives would suggest one of the first results as the fix to client problems. In many cases, however, the suggestion did not fix the problem, resulting in repeated calls and increasingly angry clients. The solution to the problem was a prescribed—or scaffolded—protocol to diagnose caller's problems that would solve 80 percent of the problems. If representatives needed to conduct a search after that protocol failed to solve a problem, representatives were trained in methods for conducting the search.

Facilitating Informal Learning

Although informal learning often happens without the direct involvement of instructional designers, we can provide the framework that makes high-quality informal learning available and support the learning process. In this section, I discuss several ways we can do so.

One way to facilitate informal learning is through technology. A variety of technologies support informal learning. Several categories of technologies do so, including computers (desktop and laptop) and mobile devices, tablets, smartphones, and e-book readers. Learners usually prefer one device or another for particular learning tasks. For example, learners might prefer using a desktop computer to practice complex calculations. However, oftentimes learners prefer to learn when the need or mood strikes, so learners will use whatever device is most convenient at the moment.

Several types of media deliver informal learning content to learners. These include:

- Classic or noncomputerized media, such as printed materials, classrooms and meeting rooms, and older recordings on records, film, and filmstrip.
- Core or Web 1.0 technologies, which share text, audio, and video with learners and include websites, online references and e-books, and online tutorials.
- Social media or Web 2.0 technologies, which encourage interaction among individuals (perhaps learners or learners and instructors) and include social networking sites like LinkedIn and Facebook, microblogging sites like Twitter, photo- and video-sharing sites like Flickr and YouTube, and virtual meeting spaces like Adobe Connect and Citrix GoTo Meeting.
- Enterprise learning systems, which distribute materials used for informal learning throughout an organization and track and report informal learning activities. Several classes of enterprise systems and include content management systems (which are primarily used to publish materials and track their use), learning management systems (which serve as electronic registrars and also link learners to learning materials), course management systems (which link learners to related materials), and talent management systems (which perform the tasks of a learning management system and digital all other human resource activities

within an organization such as payroll and employee information).

Providing people with access to as many of these technologies as possible helps facilitate informal learning. But more than providing access, the technologies need to be integrated into the work and personal lives of people so that learning occurs as seamlessly as possible. Professionals in our field can advocate for the value of these technologies, develop business cases to help organizations acquire or extend their use, and provide instructional support.

More than technology, however, learning professionals—including, but not limited to, instructional designers—can facilitate informal learning in these nine ways:

1. **Gaining executive support for informal learning efforts.** As noted earlier, successful modeling of informal learning behaviors by leaders, along with formal encouragement and permission to learn informally on the job, strengthens informal learning in the workplace. The same concept also applies in other environments. Students are more likely to learn beyond the classroom if the behavior is modeled by the role models in their lives, such as teachers, coaches, and of course parents.

   In workplaces, the training staff is the one invested in promoting the role of informal learning in the workplace, and therefore the one who should take leadership in petitioning top leadership of the organization to publicly demonstrate their support of informal learning. Support comes in several forms, including:

   - A statement in support of informal learning activities, which acknowledges that workers learn many aspects of their job informally and indicates that executives support such processes, promotes awareness of informal learning, and encourages workers to participate in it.
   - Approval of the use of work time for informal learning activities.
   - Approval of funding for proposed projects related to informal learning.
   - Sharing their own informal learning experiences with the staff of the organization when possible.

2. **Subscribing to external content to expand learning opportunities.** Although Google provides access to a lot of information, it does not provide access to all information, as most users have learned when they hit a content paywall (i.e., when they have to pay to see the content identified by Google). Furthermore, the information that is available for free is faulty: out-of-date content, incomplete content, or incorrect content. Or, the free resource might actually be a marketing tool and provide incomplete or misleading information.

   To facilitate informal learning from the highest quality content, organizations might therefore need to acquire copyrighted materials. These include:

   - Subscriptions to trade and professional magazines, and journals.

- Subscriptions to databases that provide access to several trade and professional magazines, and journals for a single fee.
- Tuition to individual webinars and online events sponsored by trade and professional associations and private organizations. In many instances, several workers can attend an event for a single registration, and people who register have access to recordings afterwards.
- Subscriptions to online tutorials provided by trade associations and professional associations, and private providers.
- Individual books or series of books.

Because most organizations do not hire a librarian, the training staff usually has responsibility for managing these resources. As a result, learning professionals need to take the responsibility for identifying and subscribing to these materials, promoting their availability, tracking their use, and overseeing renewal of the content.

In addition, learning professionals need to make sure that workers have access to them in the workplace. Many organizations limit workers' use of the Internet, whether for security reasons or to promote productivity. For example, some organizations block external files containing video. As a result, people will not be able to view the subscribed-to materials.

3. **Supporting people in their informal learning efforts.**
   As noted earlier, although it often happens individually, informal learning is not necessarily a fully independent activity. Learning professionals can support the process in a variety of ways, including:
   - When asked (or a need is sensed), helping workers establish or clarify their learning goals and the path toward their goals.
   - Linking workers to learning opportunities, by identifying learning options and how to take advantage of those options. Formal career development efforts used in some organizations help with this task. So do externally described career paths, which most medium and large organizations establish for their core job skills, and many professional associations offer for their professional programs.
   - Helping workers develop independent study and research skills. Specific services that learning professionals can provide include readiness assessments, which assess workers' preparedness to conduct independent study; workshops on assessing ones' own skills; workshops on searching for, and assessing, information on the Internet so workers recognize when the first Google result is useful and when it's not; individualized coaching and tutoring to assist workers should confusion or problems arise when learning informally; and providing signposts so informal learners can chart their progress in the learning process and assess unambiguously.

4. **Recognizing informal learning.** Partly because much of the learning occurs unconsciously, partly because the learning happens slowly over time rather than in a short, concentrated event like a training session, and partly because workers often focus on issues other than learning, neither the workers nor others around them (e.g., supervisors, other workers) realize that learning occurred, much less what they have learned. At the least, this failure to acknowledge informal learning prevents workers from recognizing how the new lessons affect their current behavior. At the most, this failure to acknowledge informal learning prevents workers from fully realizing the positive benefits, including externally recognized expertise, increased job responsibilities, and promotions.

   Formally recognizing informal learning first involves recognizing that learning occurred. This usually occurs through coaching processes, part of which involves coaches helping workers to identify and label what has been learned. Formally recognizing informal learning also involves crediting workers for their acquired expertise. This can occur less formally by updating an education record in an employer's human resources system. More formally, this occurs through certification processes—that is, getting a third party to recognize the acquired expertise.

5. **Supporting informal learning by fostering documentation efforts.** If managers and workers plan to leverage informal learning, they need material from which to learn. Although some of this material is "external" to the organization, more of it specifically pertains to the organization in which the learner works or participates. People typically turn to these types of documents for informal learning:
   - Policies, procedures, and processes, which typically exist for individual departments, functions (groups of departments), divisions, and entire organizations. The scope of this material broadens with the broadening scope of the document.
   - Guidelines
   - Standards
   - Marketing literature about current products and services
   - User documents about current products and services
   - Service documents about current products
   - Planning documents about future products and services
   - Service records
   - Customer records

   But one of the most persistent problems in organizations is that no one has ever documented this content or, if they have, it is inaccessible to workers who need it. In some cases, documents exist but have not been made available to others. They might be stored on the hard drive of an individual worker instead of in a shared folder that all workers can reach. In other cases, the documents are unreadable except to those who prepared them. They use codes and similar shorthand notations that only the author and perhaps a coworker or two might comprehend.

   Because instructional designers often apply this documentation in their formal programs—and, in some instances, create it—they can advocate for the creation of more complete documentation in their organizations as well as develop that content, when needed.

6. **Designing informal learning materials for "findability" and "usability."** As Marsick and Watkins (1990) noted, many people initiate informal learning activities to solve an immediate problem. But too often, they cannot find the desired material because the people who created it did not consider how people might look for the material and either used different terms to describe it or, more commonly, got buried in material they did uncover, but was actually about other subjects. In addition, when people do find the material on the topic they are looking for, oftentimes it remains marginally useful at best because the descriptions fail to take into account the actual use of the material in real-life circumstances.

Designing material so people can easily find it is called designing for "find-ability." Designing material so people can easily apply it is called designing for "usability." The nineteen principles of performance-centered design proposed by Gloria Gery in 1995 provide a framework for designing for findability and usability. More general principles of user-centered design, such as those advocated by Jakob Nielsen in his Alertbox blog (ongoing) and book, *Designing Web Usability* (2000), enhance this user-centric view of material and facilities learning.

7. **Developing templates to publish content.** Templates are like fill-in-the-blank forms that prompt people when writing and producing content, and as such they serve as informal learning tools. Many instructional designers use these to create online tutorials, but primarily use them to ensure that the look and layout of screens is consistent across materials.

In addition to indicating where to include information, templates can also prompt users to provide particular types of material in particular places and guide people in writing this material. As a result, even when subject-matter experts and users prepare content, it has a level of consistency with material developed by other subject-matter experts and users, and incorporates many of the find-ability and usability principles that an instructional designer would follow.

8. **Keeping content up-to-date.** If the material from which people learn informally is outdated, then so is the learning, too. Because instructional designers create or curate much of that material, we have responsibility for ensuring its ongoing accuracy. The problem is, although many instructional designers have great enthusiasm for developing new content like documentation, knowledge bases, tips and tricks articles, tutorials, similar types of resources used for informal learning, they have considerably less enthusiasm for keeping that content up to date.

To facilitate the ongoing maintenance of materials, organizations can include a publication date on all material it publishes. If the publication date seems like it's a bit dated, then people might initiate a search for more recent material on the same subject.

To get a better handle on the maintenance of content, however, organizations might use content management systems, which is software used throughout an organization to store and organize content in files, distinguish among different versions of the same file, and track the process of developing content—from inception through approvals to publication. One particular capability of some content management systems is identifying an expiration date. When content "expires," the person responsible for it receives a notification. That person reviews the material to determine if it remains current or requires updating.

9. **Continually promoting the availability of resources for informal learning.** People cannot take advantage of informal learning opportunities if they do not know they exist, especially those opportunities that involve a conscious learning effort. So organizations need to constantly promote the informal learning resources and opportunities available to workers. Because instructional designers create and curate many of these materials, we are in a particularly strong position to also create the materials that will be used to promote them.

At the least, instructional designers should prepare catalogs that identify the key categories of resources, and list and describe each learning resource available, and its intended or possible uses and audiences. Typically, organizations publish this material online through a learning portal or similar website.

At the most, instructional designers might prepare promotional materials, which provide short-term visibility to one or more informal learning resources or opportunities. Typical examples of promotional materials include:

- Announcement of a new resource, such as a subscription to a database like EBSCO or the availability of an updated standard operating procedure.
- Promotion of an individual set of resource to raise awareness of it, such as promotion of a series of tutorials on a new product line or a new program available through Coursera.
- General awareness of learning in the workplace, such as organizational events scheduled in conjunction with Learn@Work week sponsored by the Canadian-based Institute for Performance and Learning.
- Newsletter or webzine, a regularly published promotional vehicle that condenses several announcements into a single publication. In addition to promoting specific resources, these newsletters and webzines often include materials about how to make more effective use of informal learning in their newsletters and webzines.
- Social media posts, which call attention to many of the promotional efforts just described.

Conclusion

This chapter introduced you to informal learning, described the many forms it takes, explained how it happens—both in terms of the larger context of the job and the actual learning process that occurs—and suggested a number of ways to facilitate informal learning. As an instructional designer, note that informal learning supports the transfer of formal learning to the job. The coaching, documentation, trial-and-error, and similar forms help workers apply skills learned in formal programs as well as generate new insights about those skills and their value. As a professional, also note that informal learning is a tool you can use yourself to strengthen your skills as an instructional designer and develop your career in this field.

Summary of Key Principles

1. **The definition of informal learning varies depending on the context.** *True* informal learning is a process in which learners set their own learning objectives and determine for themselves what successful completion looks like. Because workplaces often prefer that people follow particular protocols and use accepted definitions of concepts, learners lose a bit of control over the learning process. As a result, the definition of informal learning in the workplace is a process in which learners have some control over the process, location, purpose, and content of learning, and may or may not be aware that learning has occurred. Both of these definitions contrast with formal learning, in which an instructor or instructional designer establishes the objectives and establishes a means to determine the criteria for successful completion.

2. **Although informal learning has been around as long as humans have, interest in this form of learning has grown extensively in the past twenty years.** Some of this interest has been fostered by the adoption of the performance paradigm in workplaces, interest in related topics such as transfer of training and performance support, and the rise of the Internet.

3. **Informal learning can take a variety of forms.** These forms include ones that are primarily individually focused such as experiences (like developmental assignments) and independent learning opportunities (like performance support), as well as ones that involve interactions with other people, including formal events (like symposia) and less formal interactions with people, such as conversations in the workplace.

4. **The act of informal learning is often triggered by a conscious or unconscious need for learning.** The nature of the material learned often varies depending on the phase in which someone is in the cycle of their job, from orienting workers to the technical aspects of their jobs to workers actively preparing for their next jobs.

5. **Effective informal learning also requires leadership to model it.** It should also give people permission to learn, recognizing that it differs from information sharing, a social activity, and that it is not always effective or efficient.

6. **Technology facilitates informal learning.** This technology includes the devices that permit learning to occur wherever learning is most convenient for learners.

7. **To facilitate informal learning, learning professionals have the responsibility to gain support for it.** They also should subscribe to external content to expand learning opportunities, support people in their informal learning efforts, and recognize informal learning.

8. **Also to facilitate informal learning, instructional designers, in particular, have a responsibility to help build an infrastructure of content that others can leverage for informal learning.** This includes designing those materials for "findability" and "usability," developing templates for people other than instructional designers to publish content, maintaining content, and continually promoting informal learning content.

Application Questions

1. Before considering how you might incorporate informal learning into your instructional designs, first consider how you might incorporate it into your own career. You recently completed your first year as an instructional designer with a boutique firm that specializes in designing and developing instruction for large organizations. During the past year, you assisted several of the more experienced instructional designers with pieces of the projects to which the others were assigned. You helped a couple with e-learning production, but also helped with the design of some job aids and concepts guides that supplemented one large program, the development of two modules of another e-learning program, and the design and development of one of five related webinars. You performed satisfactorily on each of these projects, and your colleagues feel that you are most effective on production assignments, where your knowledge of the most current authoring tools makes you a stand-out in your organization. But you enjoyed the design and development work the most. Some of your colleagues thought your design and development work was outstanding while others felt your design work was merely adequate, noting that the lessons primarily focused on lower-order skills, provided limited guidance in application, and tended to rely exclusively on rote multiple-choice questions for activities and interaction.

As you think about your second year—and your career beyond that—consider these issues:

- What learning goals do you establish for yourself? Why?
- How will you go about achieving these goals?
- How will you recognize that you have achieved them?
- From whom will you seek assistance? What type of assistance will you seek from them?

2. Now, consider how you might apply informal learning in your work. You are an instructional designer for the service center of a government employment agency. The center provides these services to the general public: applications for unemployment assistance, assistance with seeking a job (placement), assistance in determining which types of jobs are best suited to an individual (career counseling), and assistance with finding training and education to prepare one for a job, including guidance in locating financial assistance to pay for the training and education. Because of newly announced funding to address a spike in unemployment in your community, several workers from other centers will be transferred to yours to assist with the spike in traffic that the new legislation is expected to generate. Although all centers follow the same general approach, each has unique operating guidelines and addresses a slightly different clientele, as the economy in each community differs. Because the newly transferred workers will need to begin working with clients as soon as they start work in your center, they will not have time for much training, yet they need to learn how your procedures differ from those in other centers and learn about the unique economic issues in your community. As you think about integrating these new workers into your center, consider these questions:

- How can informal learning help address the needs of these recently transferred workers? In terms of the opportunities to learn in the lifecycle of a job, which phases does this type of learning address?
- What type of informal learning opportunities might you provide? Why did you choose these?
- Which characteristics of the informal learning process will you need to pay attention to when you design and curate informal learning for the recently transferred workers? Why? How will you address them?

References

Carliner, S. (2012). *Informal learning basics*. Alexandria, VA: ASTD Press.

Downing, J. (2007). Using customer contact centers to measure the effectiveness of online help systems. *Technical Communication, 54*(2), 201–209.

Driscoll, M., & Carliner, S. (2005). *Advanced web-based training strategies: Unlocking instructionally sound online learning*. San Francisco: Pfeiffer.

Eraut, M. (2000.) Non-formal learning and tacit knowledge in professional work. *British Journal of Educational Psychology, 70*(1), 113-136.

Gery, G. (1995). Attributes and behaviors of performance-centered systems. *Performance improvement quarterly, 8*(1), 47–93.

Kirschner, P. A., Sweller, J., & Clark, R. E. (2006). Why minimal guidance during instruction does not work: An analysis of the failure of constructivist, discovery, problem-based, experiential, and inquiry-based teaching. *Educational psychologist, 41*(2), 75–86.

Lave, J., & Wenger, E. (1991). *Situated learning: Legitimate peripheral participation*. Cambridge, UK: Cambridge University Press.

Malcolm, J., Hodkinson, P., & Colley, H. (2003). *Informality and formality in learning: A report for the Learning and Skills Research Centre*. Norwich, England: Learning and Skills Research Centre.

Marsick, V. J. (2009). Toward a unifying framework to support informal learning theory, research and practice. *Journal of Workplace Learning, 21*(4), 265–275.

Marsick, V. J., & Watkins, K. E. (1990). Informal and incidental learning in the workplace. Online submission.

Marsick, V. J., Watkins, K. E., Callahan, M. W., & Volpe, M. (2006). Reviewing theory and research on informal and incidental learning. Online submission.

Nielsen, J. (2000). *Designing web usability*, Indianapolis, IN: New Riders.

Nielsen, J. (Ongoing.) Alertbox. www.alertbox.com

Sitzmann, T., Ely, K., Brown, K. G., & Bauer, K. N. (2010). Self-assessment of knowledge: A cognitive learning or affective measure? *Academy of Management Learning & Education, 9*(2), 169–191.

Wihak, C., Hall, G., Bratton, J., Warkentin, L., Wihak, L., & MacPherson, S. (2008). *Work-related informal learning: Research and practice in the Canadian context*. Unpublished report. Ottawa, ON: Work and Learning Knowledge Centre of the Canadian Centre for Learning.

Chapter 17

Instructional Design in Business and Industry

Monica W. Tracey

Wayne State University, Detroit

Gary R. Morrison

Old Dominion University, Norfolk

One of the primary arenas for the practice of instructional design (ID) is within the private sector—primarily in business, industrial, health care, and military environments—that is likely the result of the ongoing need for employee training[1] as an integral part of most organizations. In the United States alone, the training industry was a $61.8 billion industry as reported by the Training Industry (2014). Remarkably, these data are only partially descriptive, because they reflect only the direct cost of formal training in organizations with 100 or more employees and ignore informal, on-the-job training, and training in smaller firms throughout the United States. Training payroll increased in 2014 as well, with companies spending $42.4 billion internally and $6.1 billion for outside consulting services and products. The investment in education and training in business and industry is not unique to the United States, but is duplicated to a great extent worldwide. While business and industry continues to expand globally, so does the demand for employee training.

This growth reflects an emphasis not simply on producing a more knowledgeable workforce, but increasingly on improving employee on-the-job performance and on solving organizational problems. Instructional design today encompasses much more than simply producing instruction. It is now associated with an overall design thinking approach, embraced by numerous companies in the United States and abroad.

In this chapter, we will expand on the nature of instructional design practice in the business environment today. We will discuss:

- the role of instructional designers and others on design teams in the design process;
- current constraints in instructional design in business and industry; and
- trends in corporate instructional design and development, including cross-cultural and design thinking.

The Nature of Instructional Design in Corporate Settings

There are numerous approaches to instructional design in the corporate sector. In this section, we will examine these approaches and some of the factors that can impact the design process.

Roles of Instructional Designers

There are traditionally three broad categories of roles that instructional designers may play in a corporate setting. These approaches vary by organization and by project. We begin this section with the examination of each of the traditional roles that instructional designers may play. Later in this chapter, we will introduce others who influence design in business and industry.

Sole designer.   Designers are change agents, with the goal of affecting knowledge, skill, and performance of the learner, team, and organization (Tracey & Boling, 2013). In the past, in some smaller companies and on small-scale projects, an instructional designer may have served as the only *permanent* team member. Today's instructional designers, in contrast, may find themselves in various organizational cultures as a sole designer

---

[1] We are not distinguishing here between the concepts of *education* and *training*. Consequently, under the umbrella of the term *training* we are including all types of professional development activities, from technical training to executive development.

on a project. In this case, a subject-matter expert (SME), working temporarily on the "team," typically provides the designer with the necessary content to develop the instructional materials and is involved only as needed (i.e., subject-matter review and revisions). Other employees in the company such as media developers, graphic designers, and computer programmers may be responsible for the production of all materials, while a facilitator or human resource manager may be responsible for scheduling, marketing, and the delivery and evaluation of the completed instructional intervention or product. Although others will contribute to the design, the designer may maintain overall control and responsibility or it may fall under the job of a project or account manager. The SME may also be the instructor, thus taking a greater interest and responsibility in the design and implementation of the intervention.

Team member/leader.
As instructional design has evolved in business and industry, a team including numerous members may be responsible for the design of an instructional product. The number of instructional designers on a team can vary from one to several, and the responsibility level can vary from that of the senior or lead designer to the instructional designer or technologist. Other members of the team will vary depending on the learners, the type of technology used for delivery, and the scope of the project. Table 17.1 provides a list of possible team members.

Teams themselves vary depending on the type of organization and the complexity of the project. Three of the more common types of work teams are virtual teams, cross-functional teams, and contractor-led teams.

With increased globalization and decentralization of organizations, instructional designers participating in or leading project teams in organizations are more likely to find themselves part of a virtual team, rather than a team located at the same physical site. Whereas a traditional team works in the same building and can physically meet together, members of a virtual team are located in different places. In some cases, the team members may be in the same general geographical area, but unable to physically meet. More common, however, are virtual teams with members in different time zones within one country, or in different countries around the globe. Virtual design teams must use forms of electronic communication for needs assessments, design reviews, and meetings. With the creation of communication tools including Skype, I-Chat, Google Docs, Microsoft's Net Meeting, and Adobe Connect, virtual team communication is inexpensive and efficient. The challenges of today's virtual team is working together across numerous time zones and on similar workdays for the various locations as instructional designers now find themselves working in extremely diverse cultures across the globe.

Collaboration is an important key to the success of a design team. Collaborative designers must possess behaviors that include expressing ideas, listening, and negotiating (Tracey, 2015). A design team's process of designing is as important as the final product, so instructional design team members and leaders encouraging productive collaboration produce more innovative designs. Some maintain that we must look at design as an opportunity to work *with* the stakeholders and end users, not *for* them (Brown, 2009). Collaborating with stakeholders and end users on a regular basis results in a product requiring fewer revisions during formative evaluations. If the design team is able to collaborate face to face, then they may experience a nurturing of relationships and inspiration allowing designers and team members to build on each other's ideas.

Design work in major companies is also outsourced to organizations or individuals offering design expertise. As a result, many instructional designers working particularly in large companies and in the military have experienced a shift in their role. Much of their time is now spent as project managers and supervising contractors with varying degrees of instructional design expertise. Coaching the external design team on the culture of the organization is an important role of the instructional designer in these situations.

External designer/consultant.
The external instructional designer/consultant is hired by the client company to produce a product or lead a project. The instructional design team can consist of all external members or can be made up of a combination

TABLE 17.1 Instructional Design Team Members	
Team Member	**Assignment**
Stakeholders	Duration of the project
Instructional designer(s)	Duration of project or design phase
Subject-matter expert	Begins with initial design planning meetings and stays through implementation
Evaluator	Duration or starts prior to conducting formative evaluation
Project manager	Duration, often starts prior to design planning phase
Text editor	Begins during production
Multimedia/computer programmer	Begins after strategy design or at start of production
Video/audio production	Begins at production phase
Scriptwriter	After strategies are designed or at production phase
Graphic artist	Begins with production phase
Translator	Begins with production phase
End users	Begin with design meetings and continue through formative evaluation

of internal members including developers, managers, and subject-matter experts as well as the designer and additional external members. Over the years in an effort to streamline services and become efficient, many organizations have reduced in-house training departments and increased the use of external consultants. Oftentimes, an external design consultant is hired for what the client may see as a *training* problem. The design consultant must then use excellent communication and observation skills to identify the root problem and its causes. The design consultant must communicate and educate the client by recommending the best solution, which may not align with the initial request. The skill set of the external design consultant must include the ability to build a relationship with the other players in the instructional design process, educate the client, and provide the best solution to the problem.

Roles of Other Players

Client. Numerous clients may be involved in a design project including the corporate employee who hired the instructional designer, other stakeholders in the company, the end users, and members of the internal design team if the instructional designer is an external member. In the simplest environment the client *owns* the problem, usually because this person is the supervisor or manager of the end user. It is important for the external design consultant to identify all of the clients immediately (Morrison, Ross, Kalman, & Kemp, 2013). For example, there may be two or more clients. First is the individual who is funding the project, who may be called the *stakeholder* and second is the *owner* of the project who may be the manager of the end users. An additional level of complication comes into play when one manager funds the project and another individual serves as project manager or *decision influencer,* who may be the primary contact throughout the project and the conduit between the design team and the *decision maker.* When we add the individual whose performance is expected to improve—or the *end user,* the client list grows to four! Some projects are even more complicated when one considers external subject-matter experts, additional internal design team members, or others who can influence design reviews or decisions. While each instructional design project will have at least one client, the designer must identify all of the clients who can influence the process and agree on the best method of communication and collaboration. Identifying the various clients and their responsibilities and expectations will help the designer to solve and to prevent problems. It is the role of the instructional designer and the design team to educate the client(s) on the entire process and the purpose and value of each step in the design process.

Subject-matter expert. Traditionally, identifying a subject-matter expert—who provides the necessary content for the designer to design and develop the instructional intervention—fell on the client. With the increasing complex problems designers are required to design solutions for, a broader pool of SMEs is needed. These may include someone who is expert on the content, another who is expert on the end users, another who understands the organizational culture, and one who provides expertise on the delivery system. Instructional designers must work with the stakeholder to identify and understand all of the

SMEs needed for the design product along with the amount of time each is able to commit to the design effort (Morrison et al., 2013). Once this requirement is determined, the designer must create a communication system that works with the SMEs rather than one that works with the designer. Each SME may have a different mode of sharing important information and the designer must be flexible, able to think critically, and ask the right questions to garner the information needed for a successful design. It is ideal if the SMEs are ongoing members of the design team. The designer along with the rest of the design team members will need to be flexible in their communication and design process to make sure this occurs.

End user. End users are the corporate employees, managers, and leaders who, with the goal of altering performance, use the designed product or intervention. Traditionally, instructional designers gathered end-user information through surveys, interviews, or other data-gathering methods. Today, more and more design teams are urging representatives of the end user to be ongoing members of the design team. This approach is in an effort to help designers emphasize with the end-user group by developing emotional connections and understanding, which can serve as a bridge between designer and end user (Kouprie & Visser, 2009).

Constraints in Instructional Design in Business and Industry

Gathering information is one of the first activities a designer performs when beginning a design project. It is during this time that initial constraints are often discovered if they have not been identified prior to the project beginning. Constraints are an integral part of any design project in business and industry. As a result of thinking that constraints inhibit or limit design, designers in the past often attempted to control or resolve constraints. Today, however, designers realize that constraints can actually bring possibilities to innovate, refine, and improve the design (Cross, 2011). Constraints are now viewed as helpful tools for designers in creating innovative, quality designed interventions and products.

Identifying and Embracing Constraints

Constraints go hand in hand with problem solving—a key design activity performed while designing. Design researchers have actually created models to support designers in their efforts to identify, embrace constraints, and solve problems while designing. For example, Lawson's (2006) model categorizes constraints along three dimensions. The first dimension considers who generates the constraints; this could be the designer, the stakeholder, the end users, etc. For example, the stakeholder can impose a time and resource constraint, limiting the time the design team would like to spend with the SME. The design team must then work to embrace this constraint and find alternative methods to communicate with the SME and gather the necessary information in order to design the best intervention. This dimension can also include designer constraints (e.g., design precedents such as experience with the client, the subject matter, or design in general). A designer may also bring a philosophical belief or theoretical perspective about how the end user learns and how the intervention should be created. These constraints will guide the design team's decisions and impact the final intervention or product.

Lawson's (2006) second dimension addresses constraints and context: Are they internal to the design such as content, delivery options, or multiple end users? Are they within the context of the design problem such as a perceived value to the organization, motivation of end users, perceived necessity of the instructional intervention? Although an organization may not completely understand the necessity of the design team's identified solution, the design team must understand and embrace the client's perception regarding the design problem. In turn, the team must not only understand and embrace the constraints the client and the design problem impose on the design solution but use these constraints to design an innovative solution.

The final dimension in Lawson's (2006) model focuses on the type of material for the design, the function, and practical application (i.e., a design team may want to design a multimedia intervention), but the content and end-user needs may require the use of a different delivery option. In these cases, the design team may not have the instructional design decision-making control they would like to have. Decisions regarding materials, function, and application may have been made prior to the team's involvement. In these cases, the team must quickly identify what decisions have been made and work within those constraints.

Lawson's (2006) model illustrates some of the numerous constraints designers must not only deal with but embrace during design. He also maintains that design problems are significantly composed of external constraints, over which the designer has little or no control. Although many might face these constraints with a sense of frustration, these are, in fact, the most important constraints designers must embrace and use to create innovative interventions and products.

Another constraint is the funding of the project. Although there are multiple ways of financing the development of instructional interventions, we can group these approaches into three broad categories (Morrison et al., 2013). The first is the fixed budget where the instructional design and (often) training departments receive a fixed amount that must last the year. Thus, the designers and managers must determine which projects they can complete based on budgetary constraints. For example, do they do one or two high-impact projects a year, or select several small projects that impact a greater variety of end users, but not necessarily a greater number. Second is the charge back system in which the cost of instructional design and training is part of corporate overhead and is charged back to the individual groups or divisions often as a hidden cost. Typically, with this system projects are taken on until all the design resources are maxed. Last is the profit-center approach. With this approach, the manager of the instructional design group approaches upper management with a project proposal for training that will generate income. If upper management views the proposal as viable—that is, it generates an appropriate return on investment—then the group receives a loan to cover development and initial implementation of the training.

Individuals who attend the training must pay tuition that is first used to pay back the loan and then any additional profit is used to fund future projects and to update existing projects. Thus, each form of financing the development of the training intervention comes with a number of constraints and opportunities.

Project Management versus Instructional Design

Projects with a significant budget, milestones, and personnel typically require someone to serve as project manager. Often, this responsibility is either delegated or assumed by the instructional designer, because this individual is often the de facto leader/manager of the project. The larger the project in terms of budget, timeline, or products, the greater is the project management responsibility. As this responsibility grows, the instructional designer is often faced with the dilemma of choosing between completing instructional design tasks or project management tasks. Neglecting the design process will affect the quality of the product. Neglecting the project management process will affect the schedule, personnel, production, and budget. To avoid this dilemma, very large projects often employ either a project manager specialist or delegate the full responsibility to one of the senior instructional designers who then concentrates on the management tasks. As organizations downsize, the responsibility for project management is often given to the instructional designer. In smaller organizations, a manager might assume all or most of the project manager responsibilities to free the instructional designers to focus on the design task.

Trends and Issues in Corporate Design and Development

Today, changes in business and industry regarding business practices in general and specifically workforce learning are forcing instructional designers to rethink how we work within and for corporations, military installations, and others in need of our expertise. Two examples of trends in business and industry include the growth and expansion of corporations beyond individual country boundaries and the implementation of specialized activities and habits of thought termed *design thinking* in daily business practices. As a result, instructional designers must address the issue of how to work cross culturally and integrate *design thinking* in their design activities.

Cross-Cultural Instructional Interventions

With the expansion of markets, communication methods, and globalization, cross-cultural instructional interventions are common in business and industry. Culture is the determining factor in all human expression (Barter, Jette, & Wiseman, 2003). When designing instructional interventions for a cross-cultural audience, designers and design teams must identify the societal and learner cultural factors.

Societal cultural factors.   In the past, when looking at cultural differences in business and industry, we focused on other countries. Today, however, demographic changes and trends show that the population is becoming more ethnically and culturally diverse both in the United States and abroad. When designing instruction for diverse cultures, understanding basic societal differences is a vital point of reference. Instructional designers must use SMEs, a comprehensive sample of end users, translators, and cultural experts to gather information that may impact the success of the instructional design process and final instructional intervention and product. Societal cultural factors that may impact instructional interventions include generational and social heritage or traditions; the ideas, values, and rules for learning; the way problems are solved; the interpretation of patterns, colors, and symbols; and the comprehension of ideas and behaviors. For example, in one instructional event, numerous societal cultural factors may be present in the representation of a cross-cultural workforce. The design team in this position must capitalize the cultural similarities while working closely with representative SMEs and end users to avoid culturally sensitive content and delivery.

Learner cultural factors.   Effective instructional design includes working with and understanding end users who bring their experiences to the instructional intervention. In cross-cultural instruction, the design team should become acquainted with representative end users early and develop a working relationship that spans throughout the entire design process. Although the SME will provide content accuracy, representative end users will bring the design team closer to their culture. Cultural factors in instructional interventions can impact how the design team approaches end user/instructor role expectation, the concept of time and the use of authentic activities, end user communication styles, and how end users approach interpersonal relationships. The transfer environment, where the end user implements what was learned in the instructional intervention, is also affected by cultural factors.

Designing instruction for a cross-cultural workforce.   When designing instruction for a cross-cultural workforce, instructional designers must observe the world through the lens of another culture other than their own while being aware of the extent to which their own culture determines how they practice instructional design. The values and worldview of the instructional designer determine the structure of the instructional materials and the context that the designer creates (Stevens, 1969; Zhang, 2001). To develop effective instructional materials for the global marketplace, one approach designers could employ is to internationalize the instruction by removing the cultural elements, and then localize the instruction by adapting it to each culture in a process similar to the localization of software applications such as word processors. Designers and design teams should consider how the cultural aspects of the information gathered to assist in the design might influence end-user attitudes toward instructional interventions, performance, and even learning itself. Sensitivity to the cultural impact the instructional materials may have, and the ability to accommodate within the design various cultural factors that may influence learning, include designing an instructional product that adheres to the cultural group beliefs in gestures, gender acceptance, and text conventions. The instructional

designer must be cognizant of not only word choices, but also subtle signals and cues in illustrations that convey different meanings in a different culture.

Design Activities in Business

A recent trend in business and industry is the infusion of specialized activities and habits of thought, termed *design thinking* (Cross, 2007; Lawson & Dorst, 2009). These concepts and activities have forced corporations to look at design principles as a comprehensive term affecting all levels and activities in an organization. Whereas we design instruction, companies including IBM (www.ibm.com/design/language/) are supporting managers who incorporate design thinking activities to support overall business growth. Design thinking is now being executed in numerous business actions. Although similar to many of the processes instructional designers employ, it is important to realize that, in business and industry, the understanding of the term *design* is now taking on new meanings. It is our responsibility as instructional designers to understand how business and industry are now embracing *design* and to educate our clients and stakeholders that we also employ design thinking, as we are designers first, and our product is instructional interventions. Our understanding of these concepts and activities will help us as we work in the culture of business and industry.

Design thinking.   Design thinking promotes activities that bring the creative approach of traditional design to business. The goal is to have employees, managers, and executives use the creative methods of designers to inspire original thinking, more creative strategic approaches, and better product innovation. Organizations including IDEO, Harvard Business School, and Stanford University teach interdisciplinary teams to embrace and integrate creative thinking (Ratcliffe & McNeil, 2012) and user-centered design (Baek, Cagiltay, Boling, & Frick, 2008) into their corporations to provide a better understanding of the value of the end-user experience (Ratcliffe & McNeil, 2012). This approach employs numerous methods instructional designers use including creative problem solving, context mapping, user observations, focus groups, persona development, fish-trap models, and interaction prototyping to look at a project within the context of the organization embracing complexity and systems thinking to produce sustainable solutions. There are numerous similarities with design thinking activities and instructional design in business. Design thinking emphasizes the needs of the customers or end users and stakeholders, identical to those emphasized in instructional design in business and industry. Design thinking is also highly collaborative and inclusive, promoting teams to work together to brainstorm numerous ideas and then refine those ideas involving end-user feedback before implementing the solution. Instructional design teams have conducted design activities in this manner for years. Organizations incorporating design thinking into their general activities will in turn have a greater understanding of instructional design and the work instructional designers do.

The designer as a researcher.   Although the instructional designer has numerous roles and responsibilities in business and industry, designers in these settings can make a unique contribution to the growing knowledge base of instructional design. Once thought of as purely a scholarly endeavor, research today may take on different forms including discovery, integration, application, and teaching (Boyer, 1997). The instructional designer is a problem solver, and reflection is a critical component in the problem-solving process (Schön, 1983; Schön, 1987). Plack and Greenberg (2005) suggest that reflection gives meaning to practice and encourages a deep approach to learning. As instructional designers reflect on designer decision making, they can reframe the problem, question their assumptions, and view the situation from different perspectives. Reflection in applied fields, including instructional design, can promote self and professional development while contributing to the research base in the field. The instructional designer's research is an example of integrating practice and scholarship, which can ultimately improve performance for the worker, the designer, and the organization.

Conclusion

The most prevalent applications of instructional design now occur in corporate settings. These complexities and pressures of these work settings shape not only the roles of designers, but also, in many cases, the design processes themselves. Demands for globalized instruction are stimulating the evolution of instructional design. As such, current instructional design focuses on complex problem solving with a strong end-user experience.

Summary of Key Principles

1. **One of the primary arenas for the practice of instructional design is within the private sector.** Since the 1980s there has been a steady growth of employee training in business, industrial, and military settings.

2. **There are three broad categories of roles that instructional designers may take in a corporate setting.** A designer may be a sole designer, a team member/leader of a design team, or an external designer/consultant.

3. **There are roles other players have in the design process that are critical to the success of the instructional intervention and product.** The client(s), subject-matter expert, and end user are critical players in the design process. Instructional designers must work to communicate and collaborate with these stakeholders.

4. **Constraints are an integral and important part of instructional design. The designer must identify and embrace the constraints of the project and use them in an effort to produce an innovative instructional intervention.** Constraints go hand in hand with problem solving—a key design activity. There are constraints generated by the designer, the stakeholder, and the end user; constraints within the context and constraints with the type of material for the design. Additionally, design problems may also have external constraints over which the designer has little or no control. All of these constraints can inhibit or enhance the design depending on how the designer and design team view them.

5. **There are many changes in the training industry including cross-cultural training and design thinking. Instructional designers in response to these trends ought to embrace the role of practitioner, educator, and researcher in an effort to identify, document, and execute best practices.** When designing instruction for a cross-cultural audience, the designer must identify the societal and learner cultural factors. Instructional designers today must also understand the infusion of design thinking in all areas of business and industry and educate clients and stakeholders on the alignment of design thinking activities and instructional design.

Application Question

An international corporation was building the largest shopping mall in the world. To ensure that this mall would be the cleanest mall and deliver world-class service, the corporation hired a U.S. instructional design consultant to work with a U.S. external cleaning company. The consultant was charged with assembling and supervising a team to design, develop, and deliver customized instruction for the cleaning staff implementing the mall cleaning system. The customer wanted the instruction designed to ensure that workers identified and executed their job tasks efficiently and increased their productivity. The workforce to clean the mall was comprised of multinational recruits from four different countries (India, Bangladesh, Nepal, and the Philippines), none of whom spoke a similar language. Reading skills of the workers were minimal or nonexistent and none had prior experience in cleaning a mall. All were immigrants brought in by the parent company. The learners were forty team leaders, identified from the initially hired workforce by the customer and 375 cleaning staff members.

Answer these questions:

1. What is the role of the external instructional designer?

2. What are the roles of the "other" players?

3. What are the contextual and designer-related constraints that may present themselves in this project?

4. As the designer, how would you attempt to prevent or overcome the contextual and designer-related constraints you have identified?

5. What questions would you ask to assist you in determining the societal and learner cultural factors?

6. How would you design instruction for this cross-cultural workforce?

References

Baek, E., Cagiltay, K., Boling, E., & Frick, T. (2008). User-centered design and development. In J. M. Spector, M. D. Merrill, J. Merrienboer, & M. P. Driscoll (Eds.), *Handbook of research on educational communications and technology* (3rd ed., pp. 659–670). New York: Lawrence Erlbaum Associates, Publishers.

Barter, Z. J., Jette, C., & Wiseman, D. (2003). Dancing numbers: Cultural, cognitive, and technical instructional perspectives on the development of Native American mathematical and scientific pedagogy. *Educational Technology Research and Development, 51,* 87–97.

Boyer, E. L. (1997). *Scholarship reconsidered: Priorities of the professoriate.* San Francisco: Jossey-Bass.

Brown, T. (2009). *Change by design.* New York: Harper Collins.

Cross, N. (2007). *Designerly ways of knowing.* London, UK: Springer-Verlag.

Cross, N. (2011). *Design thinking.* New York: Berg.

Kouprie, M., & Visser, F. S. (2009). A framework for empathy in design: Stepping into and out of the user's life. *Journal of Engineering Design, 20,* 437–448.

Lawson, B. (2006). *How designers think: The design process demystified* (4th ed.). Oxford, UK: Elsevier.

Lawson, B., & Dorst, K. (2009). *Design expertise.* Oxford, UK: Elsevier.

Morrison, G. R., Ross, S. M., Kalman, H. K., & Kemp, J. E. (2013). *Designing effective instruction* (7th ed.). Hoboken, NJ: John Wiley and Sons, Inc.

Plack, M. M., & Greenberg, L. (2005). The reflective practitioner: Reaching for excellence in practice. *Pediatrics, 116*(6), 1546–1552.

Ratcliffe, L., & McNeill, M. (2012). *Agile experience design: A digital designer's guide to agile, lean, and continuous.* Berkeley, CA: New Riders.

Schön, D. (1983). *The reflective practitioner: How professionals think in action.* London: Temple Smith.

Schön, D. (1987). *Educating the reflective practitioner.* San Francisco: Jossey-Bass.

Stevens, W. D. (1969). Sign, transaction and symbolic interaction in culture mediation. *AV Communication Review, 17,* 150–158.

Tracey, M. W. (2015). Design team collaboration with a complex design problem. In B. Hokanson, G. Clinton, & M. Tracey (Eds.), *The design of learning experience: Creating the future of educational technology.* Springer, NY: Educational Communications and Technology Series.

Tracey, M. W., & Boling, E. (2013). Preparing instructional designers and educational technologists: Traditional and emerging perspectives. In M. Spector, D. Merrill, J. Elen, & M. J. Bishop (Eds.), *Handbook of research on educational communications and technology* (4th ed., pp. 653–660). New York: Springer.

Training Industry. (2014, November/December). Training industry report. *Training Magazine, 51,* 16–29.

Zhang, J. (2001). Cultural diversity in instructional design. *International Journal of Instructional Media, 28,* 299–307.

Chapter 18

Instructional Design Opportunities in Military Education and Training Environments

Mary F. Bratton-Jeffery

Department of the Navy

The military forces of any nation, whether it be the United States Army, the British Royal Marines, the Royal Dutch Air Force, the German Bundeswehr, the Singapore Armed Forces, or the Australian Defence Force, are an integrated, dedicated, and astute group of individuals who share a camaraderie unmatched in the corporate world. Their culture is one born of the ever-present threat of war and the necessity to trust one another with their lives. Despite a common mission to protect the lives and fortunes of those at home and abroad and a responsibility to respond to that mission, those who comprise today's international military units are individuals with diverse interests and personal goals. An enhanced appreciation for the individual's needs has spurred a dynamic change in the military training of today. Those involved in that training—possibly YOU as an instructional designer—must produce training that meets the requirements of the military as well as the needs of the individual. Today's service personnel volunteer to serve their country, but they expect something in return.

Among the challenges to instructional designers working within a military environment are recognizing that ineffective instruction can have catastrophic consequences; creating training that addresses the needs of the military while considering the interests of the individual; designing for an environment that is constantly changing; using technology wisely when technology is evolving more rapidly than the ability to accommodate change; assuming the responsibilities dictated by one's role and relationship to the military (federal worker or contractor); and designing for individual projects, which may be repurposed into other training products or delivery environments.

Instructional designers play a significant role in the transformation to accommodate the needs of today's service members and move the military of today to the military of tomorrow. This role requires the following: knowledge of learning theories and instructional strategies and how to use them effectively; understanding how to apply technology at the optimal level to meet the needs of the user in a wide variety of learning environments; ability to create a blend of learning solutions; ability to work within budget; understanding and appreciation of the military culture both at home and abroad as well as the culture of international forces; and the ability to communicate with clients.

This chapter provides an overview of the major issues and challenges for instructional designers and developers in international military communities, from classroom to combat environment. Reading this chapter will help you gain insight into the roles and responsibilities of the instructional designers and developers who create training products for the military.

The chapter begins with an overview of the military culture and the role of instructional design and development within that culture. The following section addresses the changing roles and responsibilities of the military. Next, the chapter discusses the international military visions for the future. Finally, the chapter describes the role of instructional designers working with the military. A glossary has been included at the end of the chapter to assist with terminology unique to the military environment.

The Military Culture and the Role of Instructional Design and Development Within That Culture

Since the end of World War II, America's national protective force has evolved from national to global defense (Figure 18.1).

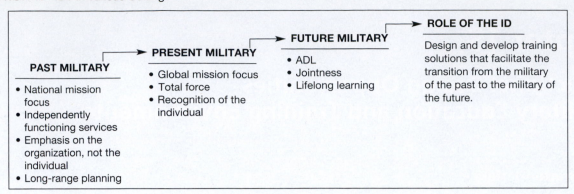

FIGURE 18.1 The evolving military culture.

In 1948 the United Nations Security Council established the United Nations Peacekeepers to oversee the fragile truce between the Arabs and Israelis (UN Peacekeeping Operations, 2012). Ten years following the end of the war, Germany became a member of the North Atlantic Treaty Organization (NATO). Recognizing the need to recruit and retain qualified personnel is a challenge for any military organization. General Volker Wieker, chief of staff, Bundeswehr, states, ". . . we must continue to offer competitive and attractive training programmes to prospective applicants who are seeking their first job. Among other things, I am talking about attractive qualification courses which help former soldiers starting a 'second career' after leaving the military" (Federal Ministry of Defence, 2010). In 2001, the United Nations Security Council authorized the establishment of an International Security Assistance Force (ISAF) comprised of military personnel representing nineteen countries. This joint force was tasked to assist the new Afghan Interim Authority with the provision of security and stability in Kabul (North Atlantic Treaty Organization, 2015). In 2009, the ISAF reaffirmed its commitment, not only to improved peacekeeping efforts, but to build a comprehensive, civilian-military approach in international communities. Reconstruction teams play significant roles in community engagement (NATO, 2008). This global military evolution demonstrates the increased logistical demand for training across cultures and around the world.

But winning wars and providing security is only part of the military mission. All of the NATO allies are committed to peacekeeping efforts as well as providing humanitarian relief assistance. These commitments require well-trained men and women, and it is within the realm of training that instructional designers will have an opportunity to apply their knowledge and skills.

To work effectively in the military environment, instructional designers must understand and appreciate the transitions the military will make in the years ahead. Military training will evolve alongside this transition, and the use of and emphasis on technology will have a significant impact on that training.

The military clients instructional designers work with are subject-matter experts (SMEs) in their occupational fields. They are not usually familiar with educational principles, learning theories, or instructional technology applications. Their knowledge of the classroom and learning is based on their personal experiences as students. Their knowledge of technology is through experience in the workplace. They place a great deal of trust in the instructional design team to provide them with the best recommendations for how and when to apply a theory or a technology in order to achieve optimal learning solutions and to help them stay within the financial and environmental constraints. Instructional designers must "know their stuff," and they are expected to keep abreast of the instructional technology field. Anything less is not in the best interests of the client or the design firm the team represents. Flawed designs or inefficient use of technology can result in hundreds of thousands of dollars wasted. Mistakes such as these will not enhance your company's reputation or lead to follow-on contracts.

The Changing Roles and Responsibilities of the Military

Over the years, the military in the United States and other developed nations have evolved into huge, technologically sophisticated, multifaceted, integrated organizations with an overwhelming number of responsibilities. Not only do the military of the various countries protect its own citizens, but they have assumed responsibility for protecting and defending the freedom of other nations. Additionally, with human trafficking and drug trafficking, and piracy on the open seas increasing, the United Nations Security Council has called on world navies to combat marine-based criminal gangs (UN Security Council Resolution 2077, 2012). Similarly, the Australian Defence Force is deployed in more than twelve international operations including border protection, UN and coalition operations, and third country deployments, as well as providing relief efforts to such devastating tragedies as Operational Nepal Assist 2015 and Operation Pacific Assist 2015 in Vanuatu. Their global reach is complicated not only geographically, but in communications and training with multinational forces, including the United States, Japan, China, Indonesia, Malaysia, Singapore, the Republic of Korea, India, and South Pacific countries (Australian Government, Department of Defence, 2015). These added responsibilities have altered the lives of each nation's soldier, sailor, or air personnel. These long-term global assignments impact personal lives and professional goals as never before. Instructional designers may be asked to provide learning solutions that will support training and learning opportunities both at home and abroad. Some of the major issues associated with the changing roles and responsibilities of the military and the role of the instructional designer with regard to those changes are discussed next.

Future Trends

The military of all nations will face a number of common challenges. Two of these challenges that may impact the role of a designer are:

- international responsibilities of a national or multinational military force; and
- new technologies.

The global corporate world thrives on international partnerships. Designers must recognize the cultural diversity of the clients and select training or learning solutions that can accommodate dissimilar audiences. Further complexities may be encountered when designing products that may be purchased by international forces. Many of the U.S. allies purchase American instructional products and access to the training as well as the weaponry. The German air force and navy combat jet crews and all surface-to-air missile operators are trained entirely in the United States and Canada (Halloman Air Force Base, 2016). Other countries offer exchange-training programs and support joint exercises at U.S. military training sites.

New technologies exist on every front, in every business, and in every home. Students share classroom experiences with children around the world via the Internet. Low-cost, digital communications have placed international friends and relatives within a finger's reach. These new technologies are also available to adversaries. Using secure networks and limiting the number of applications are just two ways in which the military tries to prevent illegal access. But these security solutions may cause instructional designers to adjust the design and delivery of training products. Designers must learn to work within the system.

Military Issues

Funding

The challenge for each service in any country is how to best utilize the money it has available for training. In most instances, trade-off decisions must be made in order to stay within budget. A low-tech training solution, such as a paper-based job aid, may not be the most desirable approach, but may well be the option selected to accomplish the training task and stay within budget. The desire to utilize all the capabilities of technology is a temptation that may be hard to resist, but using dollars injudiciously can quickly be the undoing of a design firm. For the instructional designer, suggesting new approaches to training using low- and high-tech methods incorporated with the mission equipment is an option that should be considered.

An instructional designer must be able to articulate carefully and accurately the cost of the training solution and provide alternative choices while keeping the project within budget. Whatever funds are applied to one project may be taken from another, and the designer must be able to help the client weigh the costs or trade-offs.

Technological Range

Instructional designers working with the military find themselves supporting the development of instructional products that range from the simplest paper-based, pocket-sized job aids to advanced, computer-based simulations and virtual training worlds. At the higher end of technology, the military employs the most sophisticated simulation in the world such as combat fighter pilot simulations and large-scale virtual command and control exercises. The range of technology available to training developers presents ever-increasing opportunities to improve training realism and effectiveness while also presenting an ever-expanding range of challenges for instructional designers as they work to adapt to the variety of instructional and performance requirements.

Delivery Environment

Like their civilian counterparts, members of the military must constantly learn new things to achieve professional success and survive in hostile environments. Unlike the civilian operational environment, training is always center stage. Except for new employee or new equipment training, training in the civilian environment is generally separated from the workplace or jobsite. In the military, training is part of the job and is integrated into the workplace, which means it represents a larger proportion of day-to-day activities than in the civilian environment. Because of this, training in the military is pervasive, and the quantity and diversity of training products tend to be much higher (Figure 18.2). Instructional designers recognize that training takes place in the classroom, in garrison, in base and shipboard environments, and wherever personnel are deployed—even in combat. This variable training delivery environment means training products must be adaptable to all environments.

Design Constraints

Large-systems design is an area that presents unique challenges to instructional designers. The larger and more widely dispersed the system, the greater the challenge. Designing for the military differs from designing for large corporations on a number of fronts: management, configurations, implementation, and expertise of training instructors.

The management philosophy within a large corporation generally follows a single directive from the board of directors. The military prides itself on the diversity and the mission scope of each of the independent services. Especially when working within the joint arena, the instructional design team may find itself trying to please a number of clients with strong, service-specific opinions.

The configuration component of any technology-based solution is probably the most difficult aspect of a project. Each service has its own network infrastructure(s) and equipment purchased over a number of years. In the majority of cases, designers will work with legacy (existing) systems and with integrating new hardware and software.

Once the project has been completed and beta-tested in an ideal setting, the instructional design team may assist with

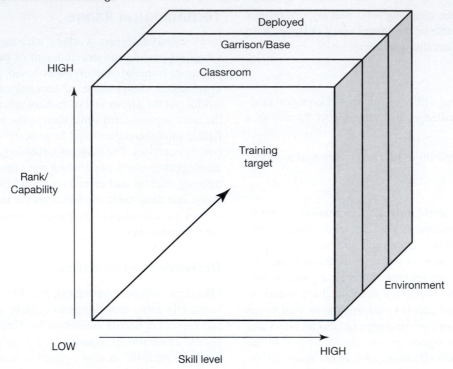

FIGURE 18.2 Full-spectrum use of training products.

implementation or provide instructions to the government's implementation team(s). Implementation presents unique challenges because it will more than likely be implemented in a variety of settings—in the field, aboard ship, and around the world as well as in the classroom.

Unlike major corporations that have training departments and professional instructors, the military uses subject-matter experts and provides them with instructional materials to assist them with "teaching." Instructional designers must create train-the-trainer materials that explain the lesson plans in a step-by-step manner and incorporate learning theory as well. The U.S. military recognizes master instructors, and while assignments are short lived (no longer than three years), instructors need materials that clearly explain all components of the learning package, including theories underlying the design.

People

The most critical challenge to all of the services is recruiting good people and retaining highly trained and skilled service members. The national defense planning documents of many of the allied nations address the need to recruit and retain highly qualified people (Australia's Force 2020, the U.K's. Future Strategic Context for Defence, the U.S. Joint Vision 2020). These plans also recognize the need to provide for quality of life, especially in the areas personal and professional growth.

Alternative Training Solutions

Instructional designers are accustomed to examining the skill and knowledge levels of the target audience in order to determine how to design the IDT instruction and what level of language to use. Particularly important is the ID's knowledge of learning

theories and instructional strategies. Historically, training has been designed for and delivered to the "group." Service members who did not achieve the desired performance during the first iteration of training were remediated until mastery was achieved. This remediation was often done in the manner in which the original instruction was presented.

In the case of remediation activities, rather than presenting the same information in the same format or the same information in a slightly different format, the instructional designer might recommend completely different instructional approaches. Allowing individual learners to select learning options allows for learner control that is a basic tenet of adult learning.

The technology options now available to instructional designers afford them an opportunity to recommend varied training solutions that address a variety of instructional challenges at the individual level. Take, for instance, a scenario in which a computer-based training product has been ordered to replace the resident classroom instruction for cooks in the Army. An examination of the ethnic composition of the client's cooks reveals that a large number of Hispanic/Latino soldiers are in that occupational specialty. Technology access studies indicate that members of that community come to the workplace with less computer experience than any other ethnic group (Katz & Levine, 2015; McGee, 2002). Hofstede's 1997 work (as cited in McGee, 2002) in cross-cultural theory is the basis of Web-based design identified by Marcus and Gould (as cited in McGee, 2002) that specifically addresses culturally based instructional considerations for this community. These include minimal emphasis on individual achievement; active learning; simple, straightforward design; consistent and repetitive visual cues; and an intimation of consequences before taking action or making decisions (McGee, 2002). The instructional designer might suggest to the client a blended solution that provides team-based review sessions or laboratory assignments or experiments. The computer software program or adjunctive materials would use minimal graphics and increased white space. Visual cues would orient the learner throughout the program and assist with intuitive navigation features. Finally, the program would allow the learner to select and access alternatives before making final decisions. Designing instruction such as this that adheres to the culturally based instructional considerations specific to the Hispanic/Latino community increases the likelihood that these learners will succeed.

The Military's Vision for the Future

Guiding Documents

Each country has a number of documents that are written by the military, which describe their vision and goals for the future and are submitted to their governing body. In the case of the United States, the *Quadrennial Defense Review* (required by Congress) articulates the military's posture for capabilities that will be needed in the future to protect the homeland, build security globally, and project power and win decisively (*Department of Defense, 2014*). This document establishes the vision for all efforts by each of the individual services. Each service must examine its current means of doing business and transform itself against the measures provided in the QDR. The vision statements written by each of the services in alignment with the QDR are excellent starting places when working as an instructional designer creating training for the military. A familiarity with the visions and plans of the particular branch of the military with which you are working will aid you in the quest to provide the best training solution possible.

Should you work with an international military service, you will be able to locate many of these planning documents via the Internet by visiting the country's department of defense website.

Long-Range Planning

By the time a plane or ship is designed, prototyped, and ordered, the technology has surpassed the original plans for the aircraft or ship. An instructional designer must be able to "look into the future" and provide input as to how technology and learning research may evolve and the impact this evolution will have on future training needs.

The key to the future of military training lies in three major areas: advanced distributed learning, jointness within a nation and internationally, and lifelong learning.

Advanced Distributed Learning

"The Advanced Distributed Learning (ADL) Initiative, sponsored by the U.S. Office of the Secretary of Defense (OSD), is a collaborative effort between government, industry and academia to establish a new distributed learning environment that permits the interoperability of learning tools and course content on a global scale. ADL's vision is to provide access to the highest quality education and training, tailored to individual needs, delivered cost-effectively anywhere and anytime" (ADL Mission, 2016).

Initially, a U.S. endeavor, ADL encompasses an international membership with ADL Partnership Labs in Canada, Korea, Latin America/Caribbean, NATO, New Zealand, Norway, Poland, Romania, Serbia, and the United Kingdom. For instructional design students, these co-labs provide international learning and professional growth opportunities.

Jointness

Maximum advantage of funding, acquisition, technology, and people can be attained through collaboration. The U.S. military and its allies fight as a combined force—an integrated whole of the service branches and the ally counterparts. This collaboration dictates that training be joint as well, necessitating training products that are developed to enhance the joint war-fighting skills of disparate forces. Inherent in this instructional design mission is recognition of the diversity of the force in terms of service perspective (i.e., Army, Air Force, Navy, and Marines), doctrine of allied forces (such as the case in NATO or UN coalitions with many different national armed forces and their associated war-fighting strategies and tactics), and even cultural diversity such as differences in language and religion.

Lifelong Learning

Military leadership supports and encourages learning beyond the military requirements for a number of reasons. Continued learning opportunities within the service improve the service member within his or her occupational specialty and open the doors to many opportunities for those who leave service. The U.K. offers advanced learning opportunities through its resident universities and the Open University. Its government has an established Lifelong Learning Policy and its military component is the Learning Forces Initiative that is open to all ranks (Serving Soldier, 2004).

The European Union (EU) has instituted Europe-wide educational reforms to allow students to "study without borders." The European Credit Transfer System (ECTS) simplifies accreditation between institutions. This open system allows military students to continue their personal learning goals while serving their countries abroad.

The words of the former U.S. Chief of Naval Operations, Admiral Vern Clark, evidence a respect for and recognition of the individual's learning goals:

> The people that make up our military decide that they are going to give of themselves. Every human being who puts on the uniform . . . makes tremendous sacrifices. . . . There should be a commitment from the leadership for the promise sailors make to us. I believe that promise has to be kept by people like me—to make sure people have the tools that they need to succeed. We've got to offer to them a chance to make a difference. They want us to give them a chance to show what they can contribute. They want a chance to grow and develop. (Kennedy, 2000)

The Role of Instructional Designers Working with the Military

The instructional design profession prides itself on creativity, ingenuity, and research. Thus, the instructional designer can and should suggest a number of innovative solutions. A novice instructional designer working with a military client might assume that the "bank" would have open doors for funding spectacular projects, but this is not the case. Limited funding will require trade-offs for every project. Using a technique similar to that of the quality function deployment model for instructional design (Bratton-Jeffery & Jeffery, 2003), the scenarios solution discussion matrix (Figure 18.3) suggests a systematic methodology for working through the trade-offs that

can serve as the basis of discussion between the instructional designer and the client.

As you examine the scenarios in this section identify what you know, make a list of questions to ask your client, and list possible solutions based on instructional technology practices and theories. Use the scenarios solution discussion matrix to guide your thinking. Be sure to consider areas in which the instructional designer will have been involved when reviewing the solutions.

Scenario 1: Degree Completion versus Deployment

Army Reserve Sgt. John King faces a twelve-month rotation overseas as a member of his Reserve unit. His unit along with

REMEMBER: When designing and developing training solutions for the military, the instructional designer must take into account design considerations as well as specific human- and technology-related issues unique to the military environment.

	Learning Theories	Technology Applications	Blended Solutions	Budget	Military Culture	Communication
Funding						
Long-Range Planning						
Joint Training						
Low-Tech vs. High-Tech						
Delivery Environment						
Alternative Training Solutions						
Design Constraints						
Motivation						
Cultural Diversity						
Knowledge Levels						
Skill Levels						
Learner Past Experiences						

(Column group heading: DESIGN CONSIDERATIONS. Row group label: DESIGN ISSUES)

FIGURE 18.3 Scenarios Solution Discussion Matrix.

a signal battalion from the state's National Guard will support coalition forces in promoting stability and safety in the war-torn region. Sgt. King's company will be part of a larger force designed to patrol and collect information.

Sgt. King currently works for a large corporation that has been paying for his college work in business management. In order to advance in the company, he must complete his degree. Unfortunately, the deployment will now interrupt his efforts and jeopardize his place in the company. The big question in Sgt. King's mind is what will happen to his personal goals as he takes time from his career to serve his country overseas.

Problem.   You are a member of an instructional design team that has been formed to address deployment and distance learning options. Identify strategies that will meet the needs of the individual service member while serving the requirements of the organization.

The Army's Solution.   Sgt. King is representative of the new Army in which soldiers are expected to be educated and technology-savvy enough to succeed in the missions and on the battlefields. The Army's training model is "train-alert-deploy-employ." Training, in addition to combat tactics, includes language, cultural awareness, and regional expertise education (Department of the Army, 2005). Individual services launched online learning opportunities in the late 1990s. In 2010, Defense Information Systems Agency, the Defense Acquisition University, and ADL launched Joint Knowledge Online (JKO) to support DoD training. JKO's goal is to produce immersive, media-rich training that stimulates cognitive, intuitive, innovating, and adaptive thinking for complex decision-making skills (JKO, 2010).

Scenario 2: Joint Training U.S. Forces

A joint task force has been formed with the mission to support port security activities at ports on the Gulf Coast. The task force comprises elements from the Air Force, Navy, and Coast Guard. The Coast Guard will have operational control and will coordinate with the Department of Homeland Security.

Proficiency in communications with civil agencies and aviation and marine assets has been identified as a training issue. While the Coast Guard members are well trained and experienced in the communications procedures of civil agencies such as the police and emergency services as well as commercial aviation and marine resources, the military services are not as familiar with these communications networks. Task force members from the armed services will receive training on these nonmilitary communications procedures in order to coordinate security activities.

Problem.   You are a member of an "assembled team" of representatives from each of the services as well as a number of design firms. The team has been charged with finding a means of training all of the forces as a single, ready-response unit.

What are the various methodologies that present the most realistic training scenario possible and would utilize technology advances both in weaponry and in evaluation of the training?

The Department of Defense's Solution.   The Department of Defense requires that every service be prepared to fight in an urban setting and to conduct humanitarian and peacekeeping efforts. Eglin Air Force Base, in the Panhandle of Florida, is the site of a $20 million urban combat and antiterrorism training center for Military Operations on Urbanized Terrain (MOUT). This facility replicates a city in which America's military and its allies train in all facets of this new type of warfare—switching from humanitarian to combat at a moment's notice (Blair, 2004). The Marines have recently opened a similar facility located at Quantico, Virginia. According to Capt. David Moon, commander, B. Company, "With the complexity of today's operating environment and the growth in large urban hubs this is the focus for the future. Although there is still importance on conventional warfare, a lot of the wars are fought in the urban environment" (Davis, 2015).

Conclusion

Although working as an instructional designer in a military environment is challenging, it provides an exceptionally rich opportunity for growth as a professional. The knowledge of learning theories and instructional strategies that will be needed can be employed in virtually any manner: instructor-led or instructor-facilitated classroom, informal self-study, formal online learning courses with synchronous and/or asynchronous options, or a blend of any or all of these.

Many of the challenges the instructional designer faces in a military environment, however, require skill sets that go beyond the basic information learned in either a formal or an informal study program. Perhaps most daunting of these is acquiring an understanding and appreciation for the military culture. There is a steep learning curve that encompasses everything from familiarity with ranks to military protocols—things that are not directly related to instructional design. Also, it is virtually impossible to "bend the rules" when working with the military, and designers face scheduling deadlines and budgeting constraints that require tremendous productivity in record time at a minimal cost to the taxpayer. This can make the ID's job particularly stressful.

A greater emphasis on the professional needs of the individual in tandem with the needs of the organization, budget limitations, and quickly evolving technologies are all challenges that make a career as an instructional designer in the military education and training environment difficult but rewarding. Instructional designers who work in the military environment are never bored and, given enough time, will have the opportunity to work in every aspect of instructional design from analysis to evaluation.

Summary of Key Principles

1. **Genuinely respect and appreciate the roles and responsibilities of your customers and the organization they support.** You'll find that military customers are generally very direct and decisive. At times, you may find yourself waiting on the SMEs to review deliverables. It can be frustrating, but know that your SMEs put mission first and all else is secondary. Developing backup plans and alternate approaches that can be implemented quickly should be standard tools in your ISD toolkit.

2. **Research the organization's vision and direction for the future.** Use your knowledge to help them ride the learning waves. Just as the SMEs are experts in their field, so are you in the realm of instructional design, learning strategies, and the use of technology to enrich the learning process. Your customers will rely on you to provide input about how to organize or convey information, how to select appropriate or implement strategies, and to help them understand the complex world of instructional technology. It is imperative that after you graduate, you continue your professional development.

3. **Use the language of the customer to convey or illustrate your strategies.** As instructional designers we pride ourselves on the ability to communicate. We learn the customers' jargon in order to develop the content, yet we expect the customer to learn our jargon to understand the terms of the contracts or the design approaches. Using analogies and metaphors the customer is familiar with goes a long way in team building and developing a common understanding.

Application Questions

1. You've been asked to assist an organization that is establishing computer-based training opportunities for the military system in a third-world nation. Prepare a short briefing paper (one to two pages) of the considerations and constraints for program implementation. Use the matrix in Figure 18.3 to assist you with framing your answer.

2. Your customer wants to use technology in its training program; however, the field of operation does not always provide electronic access. What are alternatives you might suggest for a successful program? Use the diagram in Figure 18.2 to guide your thoughts. Prepare a table that provides the learning outcome and a comparison of the technology-based strategy with one or more complementary alternatives including capability, skill level, the delivery environment, and development issues or constraints.

3. Humanitarian efforts are a major role for the military of many countries. Prepare a list of Web-based training materials to assist service members charged with learning how to conduct relief efforts. Consider checking websites for first aid, disaster or famine relief, wildfires, etc.

Glossary

Active duty. Service member is assigned to an active unit and serves full time as a member of the regular force.

Advanced distributed learning. A federal initiative that supports a collaboration of government, academia, and industry to provide a philosophy of accessibility, durability, interoperability, and reusability in network and software solutions.

Deployment. The active force moves from its standing residence within the United States to an overseas location for a designated period of operation.

Jointness. The term exemplifies the independent U.S. Services (Air Force, Army, Marine Corps, and Navy) operating as an integrated force sharing resources, personnel, and operational missions.

Joint Vision 2020. The military document that defines the vision and requirements of the Armed Forces in the future. The Joint Vision is published in ten-year increments (e.g., 2010, 2020, 2030).

Total Force. All those who work with the U.S. military including active duty, reserves, National Guard, and federal employees.

References

Advanced Distributed Learning. (2015). The power of global learning, partnerships. Retrieved from http://www.adlnet.org/partnerships.html

Advanced Distributed Learning: About Us–Our Mission. Retrieved July 5, 2016 from https://www.adlnet.gov/about-adl/

Australian Government, Department of Defence. (2015). Global operations. Retrieved from http://www.defence.gov.au/Operations/

Blair, K. (2004, January 13). Eglin plans for street fight: Proposed training facility would replicate city for urban warfare. *Pensacola New Journal*, 1A.

Bratton-Jeffery, M. F., & Jeffery, A. (2003). Integrated training requires integrated design and business models. In A. M. Armstrong (Ed.), *Instructional design for the real world: A view from the trenches* (pp. 218–244). Hershey, PA: Idea Group.

Davis, S. (2015, June 19). MOUT training, brilliance at the basics. Retrieved from http://www.barracks.marines.mil/News/NewsArticleDisplay/tabid/4206/Article

Department of the Army. (2005, June). FM 1: The army and the profession of arms. Retrieved from http://www.army.mil/fm1/chapter1.html#section6

Department of Defense. (2014, March). *Quadrennial defense review report*. Retrieved 6 July, 2016, from http://www.defense.gov/Portals/1/features/ defenseReviews/QDR/2014_Quadrennial_Defense_Review.pdf

Federal Ministry of Defence. (2010). Interview with General Wieker: "We need to think in terms of what is feasible." Retrieved from http://www.bmvg.de/portal/a/bmvg/kcxml/04_Sj9SPykssy0xPLMnMz0vM0Y_QjzKLd4k3cQsESUGY5vqRMDFfj_zcVP2g1Dx9b_0A_YLciHJHR0VFAFwAQBQ!/delta/base64xml/L2dJQSEvUUt3QS80SVVFLzZfRF80Rzk!?yw_

contentURL=%2FC1256F1200608B1B%2FW282TE2G049INFOEN%2Fcontent.jsp

Joint Knowledge Online. (2010, February). Courseware and capabilities. Retrieved from http://jko.jfcom.mil/catalog.pdf

Katz, V.S., & Levine, M. H. (2015). *Connecting to learn: Promoting digital equity among America's Hispanic families.* New York: The Joan Ganz Cooney Center at Sesame Street.

Kennedy, D. (2000, June 22). Clark will leave legacy of progress [Electronic version]. *The Flagship*. Retrieved from http://www.chinfo.navy.mil/navpalib/cno/covenant.html

McGee, P. (2002). Web-based learning design: Planning for diversity. *USDLA Journal*, *16*. Retrieved from http://www.usdla.org/html/journal/MAR02_Issue/article03.html

North Atlantic Treaty Organization. (2008, December). Final communique'. Retrieved from http://www.nato.int/cps/en/natolive/official_texts_46247.htm

North Atlantic Treaty Organization. (2015, September). ISAF's mission in Afghanistan (2001-2014). Retrieved 5 July, 2016, from http://www.nato.int/cps/en/natohq/topics_69366.htm

Serving Soldier. (2004). Education for personal development. Retrieved from http://www.army.mod.uk/servingsoldier/career/usefulinfo/epd/ss_cmd_epd_w.html

United Nations Department of Peacekeeping Operations and Department of Field Support (2012). Civil Affairs Handbook. http://www.un.org/en/peacekeeping/documents/civilhandbook/Civil_Affairs_Handbook.pdf

United Nations Security Council Resolution 2077. (2012). Recalling its previous resolutions concerning the situation in Somalia. Retrieved from http://www.un.org/en/ga/search/view_doc.asp?symbol=S/RES/2077(2012).

Chapter 19

Performance, Instruction, and Technology in Health Care Education[1]

Craig Locatis

National Library of Medicine

In this chapter, I review the role of technology in supporting performance and instruction in health care settings, especially as it relates to educating and training physicians and other health professionals. I emphasize medical education particularly, because many trends in medicine carry over to other health science disciplines. Although professional education is stressed, related areas, such as patient and consumer health education, also are addressed. My goals are to help readers understand the role of instructional design and technology in health care and provide them with sufficient context to determine whether they might want to explore working in the health care field.

The chapter begins with an overview of different health settings and a brief history of medical education. The latter is used to frame discussion of education and training in health care and the factors currently driving technology application. Clinical reasoning, problem-based learning, and evidence-based medicine are discussed and educational issues and methods important to the health science community are identified.

The Health Care Context

The health care field is very broad. It involves not just the delivery of health services, but also research. It includes the medical profession and its varied subspecialties plus the professions of veterinary medicine, dentistry, nursing, allied health, and public health. Biotechnology (the use of DNA and protein sequences to engineer biological substances) and medical informatics (the application of information and communication technology to support medical research, practice, and education) are also subspecialties.

The health field not only includes varied professions and specialty groups, but also embraces such related sciences and disciplines as anatomy, biochemistry, molecular biology, physiology, and psychology. In addition to academic institutions, hospitals, clinics, and research centers, the health care field also can include certain regulatory agencies, agencies and organizations that respond to disasters, and industries involved in drug manufacturing, genetic engineering, and medical instrumentation. When you take a pet to the vet, visit a pharmacy, eat in restaurant, or buy food at the grocery store, someone in the health sciences, either directly or indirectly, has affected your life.

Health care is comprised of varied subsettings that include (1) academic medical centers and health professions schools, (2) government agencies, (3) pharmaceutical and biotechnology companies and private foundations, (4) professional societies and health associations, and (5) hospitals, clinics, and other caregiving institutions. Each is involved to varied degrees with educating health professionals and paraprofessionals and providing consumer health education and continuing education.

The most obvious subsettings for education and training in health care are the professional schools. Medical schools have departments of medical education that evaluate students and courses and develop curricula; departments of biomedical communication that do medical illustration, photography, video, and multimedia; and academic departments in medical informatics doing teaching and research related to the application of computer and information technologies. They may have telemedicine offices for distance consultation and learning. Medical libraries provide computing and information resources supporting research,

[1]This work was completed as part of the intramural research program of the National Library of Medicine and National Institutes of Health.

practice, and education, and typically have learning resource centers and computer labs. Other health professional schools may have one or more similar departments, depending on size. Health profession schools not only offer courses, but develop interactive multimedia education programs on digital media or online, too.

Government health agencies, pharmaceutical companies, hospitals, and clinics train staff internally and often provide training to others. Some of the external training is geared to keeping public health and other professionals up to date, but much of it is focused on educating the general public and providing consumer health information.

Private foundations often underwrite development of health education programs and publish their own materials of interest to professionals and consumers. Professional associations are most actively involved in continuing education, holding conferences, publishing journals, producing tutorials and case studies, and offering virtual journal clubs where health professionals can discuss online the information appearing in publications. They also offer information to the general public.

Consumer health and continuing education cut across the other health education and training settings. Consumer health includes general education about wellness, health issues, and specific diseases as well as skills training (e.g., first aid) and patient education. Most health professionals are required to complete a certain number of hours of continuing education annually and almost every medical school and professional society has a continuing medical education (CME) program. Sometimes CME credit is provided for attending workshops and conferences, but it also can be obtained by documenting use of educational materials. Retraining or refresher training also is required for many paraprofessionals.

Medical Education: A Brief Overview

Physicians have key roles in providing health care and leading teams of other health professionals. This leadership extends to management and other areas outside the direct delivery of care (e.g., hospital administration and biomedical research). Trends and standards in medical education often spill over into other domains as a consequence. Because there tends to be more research and evaluation of medical education programs, much of the empirical evidence guiding education and training in health care emanates from medicine and other health professions that often mimic medicine's teaching methods. Nursing and public health schools, for example, have adopted many of the case-based teaching methods that are currently popular in medical schools.

In the United States, medical education does not commence until one has a baccalaureate degree. The medical education process can be divided into three phases: "undergraduate" education comprising the years in medical school, graduate education comprising time in residency, and postgraduate and continuing education to obtain knowledge and certification in additional areas or keep current.

Medical Education: A Brief History

The history of medical education also can be divided into three phases: a prescientific phase, a scientific or "Flexner" phase emphasizing selected disciplines and specialties, and a post-Flexner phase focusing on problem solving and cognition in addition to science.

Prescientific Phase

Educational technology has had a place in medicine from the time of Andreas Vesalius and Leonardo da Vinci. Their drawings, based on dissection of anatomical structures, were some of the first attempts to codify medical knowledge based on direct observation rather than speculation, superstition, or religious beliefs, and their drawings can be viewed as "research works" as well as teaching aids. Although "science" in medicine dates back to the Renaissance, it was not until the early 1900s that there was a concerted movement to develop a scientific foundation for the medical curriculum in the United States.

Scientific Phase

In 1910, a report to the Carnegie Foundation for the Advancement of Teaching by Abraham Flexner documented the evolution of medical teaching from apprenticeship to more formal education. The "Flexner Report" noted that the first medical schools in the United States in the late 1700s were university affiliated and devised to teach basic information preparing students for apprenticeship (Flexner, 1910). At the time of the report, most schools were independent, commercial enterprises emphasizing didactic instruction with minimal facilities and no hospital affiliation. Doctors could graduate by memorizing symptoms and doses (e.g., if fever, give quinine). Laboratories, except those used for dissection, were usually absent and there was very little emphasis on the biological sciences and new medical technologies (e.g., stethoscopes, thermometers, x-rays, and laboratory tests) that were revolutionizing medicine at the time.

The Flexner Report called for the reaffiliation of academic programs with colleges, universities, and hospitals, and the introduction of scientific rigor. The curriculum consisted of two years of basic science followed by two years of learning clinical disciplines. The scientific method was the glue holding the two parts of the curriculum together, because it was assumed that hypotheses testing and deductive reasoning in biomedical research also were employed for diagnosing and treating individuals.

Post-Flexner Phase

The Flexner Report established the concept of scientific medicine and created a curriculum that remained essentially unchanged for seventy years (Association of American Medical Colleges, 1984). Whether intentional or not, its categorization of laboratory and clinical science led to bifurcation of the medical curriculum that was challenged by the movement for problem-based learning (PBL) in the 1960s and 1970s.

PBL began as a reaction to what many perceived as the uncoupling of scientific and clinical content (Albanese & Mitchell, 1993). Its proponents endorsed learning content within a problem-solving context rather than applying knowledge to solve problems after it is acquired, arguing that the former approach lets students determine what they need to know and enables them to synthesize information from multiple disciplines, develop transferable problem-solving competence, and acquire effective self-study skills for lifelong learning. The methodology proposed for attaining these goals was to expose students to a rich array of real and simulated patient cases, often by having them work in groups (Barrows & Tamblyn, 1979).

Interest in PBL increased when the Association of American Medical College (AAMC) Panel on the General Professional Education of the Physician and College Preparation in Medicine issued *Physicians for the Twenty-First Century* in 1984 (Albanese & Mitchell, 1993). The *GPEP Report* endorsed PBL, the use of computer and information technology, and providing clinical learning experiences outside hospitals, since hospital patients do not reflect the patient population most physicians encounter in practice.

The AAMC issued another report, *Medical Education in the Information Age,* in 1986 that also impacted medical curricula by emphasizing the explosion of medical knowledge and amplifying the need to integrate information technologies, such as databases and decision support systems, to establish their habitual use for lifelong learning (Salas & Brownell, 1997).

Problem-Based Learning and Evidence-Based Medicine

Problem-based learning is supported by research on clinical reasoning indicating expertise is largely a function of previous problem-solving experience. Problem-solving expertise is dependent on the type of patient cases encountered, rather than applying general scientific methods and hypothetico-deductive reasoning as Flexner suggested (Norman, Young, & Brooks, 2007; Norman, 1985; Patel, Evans, & Groen, 1989). Instead, it depends on acquiring rich, elaborated conceptual information about particular diseases and illnesses (content-specific knowledge) that can be associated with problems patients present (Norman, 2008b, 2005).

As expertise develops, problem solving becomes automatic and more a matter of pattern recognition then formal deduction (Norman et al., 2007; Norman, 1985; Patel et al., 1989). Pattern recognition is important in clinical reasoning on several levels. It is mentally recognizing constellations of symptoms patients present as manifestations of different diseases and conditions, but also involves seeing physical patterns when examining patients, such as features of skin lesions, or interpreting images, such as abnormalities in x-rays (Norman et al., 1996).

Meta-analyses, literature reviews, and individual studies show PBL students perform as well or better than those in traditional programs on clinical reasoning tests, perform somewhat less well on basic science exams, have more favorable attitudes toward learning, are better able to transfer knowledge to different cases, and are superior self-directed learners (Albanese & Mitchell, 1993; Imanieh, Dehghani, Sobhani, & Haghighat, 2014; Norman, 2008a; Oh, Chung, & Han, 2015; Rideout et al., 2002; Vernon & Blake, 1993).

The evidenced-based medicine (EBM) movement is partially an outgrowth of problem-based learning. EBM involves formulating clinical questions, finding evidence in the medical literature that addresses the questions, critically appraising the evidence, and applying the evidence to specific patients (Craig, Irwig, & Stockler, 2001; Evidence-Based Medicine Working Group, 1992; White, 2004).

EBM has spawned meta-analyses and systemic reviews of research related to varied medical problems. Applying the methodology in the medical curriculum helps students become accustomed to consulting information sources to keep current (cf., Burrows, Moore, Arriaga, Paulaitis, & Lemkau, 2003; Finkel, Brown, Gerber, & Supino, 2003; Wadland et al., 1999; White, 2004), although implementing the methodology can be challenging (Greenhalgh, Howick, & Maskry, 2014).

Other Attributes of Health Science Education

Although problem-solving approaches to teaching and the use of evidence in the process of learning and providing care are paramount, risk, altruism and communication, sensory perception, science, and innovation are other important attributes of health care education.

Risk

What is taught and learned in health professions education can have life-threatening consequences. The health field is one area where errors in learning literally can be a matter of life or death. Moreover, the risks are not only for patients, but for health practitioners and students as well. Health professionals do not wear rubber gloves because they are trying to make fashion statements. They are exposed to contagious diseases and work with hazardous substances routinely. There are also emotional risks when dealing with difficult cases and communicating difficult information (Martin, Mazzola, Brandano, Zurakowski, & Meyer, 2015).

Altruism and Communication

The health professions are helping professions. The idea of healing and helping people is more than just rhetoric to those electing health care careers. The Hippocratic oath and guidelines published by professional associations and government agencies set standards for conduct. Since the work involves literally laying hands on others, interpersonal and communication skills are needed to build trust and address the psychosocial aspects of disease as well as to manage health care teams (Dimitrijevic et al., 2007; Farmer, 2015; Weiland et al., 2015).

Sensory Perception

The work of biomedical practitioners and researchers depends on making observations and reasoning about them. Some of the observations involve numerical data, such as pulse, blood pressure, or epidemiological plotting the spread of disease. Others involve sounds, such as listening to breathing and heart beat. Most involve images that can be visual representations of numerical values, such as EKGs, or "raw data," such as skin lesions viewed during physical examinations, cellular alterations and adaptations that pathologists identify with microscopes, and x-rays and other images that radiologists interpret. The sensory nature of the raw data dealt with by most health professions makes it hard to imagine how biomedical researchers and practitioners could learn without exposure to multimedia. A diagnosis literally can be seen in a biopsy specimen or a radiograph and there is probably no tougher or sensitive jury when it comes to judging image quality than health professionals.

Science

Those working with technology addressing performance and instruction in health care collaborate with subject-matter experts who are either scientists or practitioners having backgrounds in science, who see teaching as an outgrowth of their efforts to provide care or conduct research, and who are probably less likely than other academics to be egocentrically involved in their teaching. They are, however, unlikely to accept changes in education without evidence.

Innovation

A scientific mindset fosters willingness to experiment with new technologies and teaching methods. Some of the more innovative educational technology applications have been in health care, many of which were created by health science faculty and practitioners working intuitively on their own. Several of the earliest computer applications in the 1960s involving the development of databases, expert systems, and educational simulations were in the medical field (Blois & Shortliffe, 1990; Hoffer & Barnett, 1990) as were some of the earliest applications of interactive television and satellites for telemedicine and distance learning (cf., Foote, Parker, & Hudson, 1976).

Health Science Teaching Methodologies

Use of advanced computing and network technologies for consultation and education currently are active areas of health science research (Ackerman & Locatis, 2011). The entire adult human male and female anatomies have been digitized to provide an image library for creating educational objects and diagnostic applications (Ackerman, 1998; Dev & Senger, 2005; Kockro & Hwang, 2009), collaboratories, where scientist and teachers can work together and provide distance learning online, have been established (Cohen, 2002), and immersive, virtual reality environments using 3-D images and haptic feedback have been developed for surgical planning and training (Dev et al., 2002; Montgomery, Burgess, Dev, & Heinrichs, 2006; Sandrick, 2001).

Simulation and multimedia are two important and widely used methodologies in medical education. Simulations are needed to ensure students are exposed to a range of cases that they will likely encounter in real life, and multimedia are needed so educational experiences incorporate the kinds of information students need to process to be good problem solvers and practitioners.

There are three genres of medical simulations. First, case-based problem-solving simulations, usually presented by computer, take students through the process of history taking, examination and testing, formulating possible diagnoses, and choosing a most likely one. Some may also have students prescribe treatments (Association of American Medical Colleges & National Board of Medical Examiners, 2002). Second, mannequins and physical devices teach simple physical procedures, problem solving, or both. The simplest devices include the popular Resusci® Anne mannequin for learning and practicing cardiopulmonary resuscitation and models of the upper arm for practicing injection. More advanced simulators range from computerized systems with forced feedback for surgical training or learning endoscopy (Dev et al., 2002) to highly complex (and expensive) computerized mannequins that can breath and have heartbeats, dilating pupils, and veins that distend to mimic physical conditions. Mannequins and many computer problem-solving simulations are dynamic in that the state of the patient will change over time and by the actions students take. Finally, having trained persons as standardized patients for interpersonal skills training also is considered a form of simulation. There have been efforts to combine the use of actors with mechanical devices to provide a more realistic context for learning and applying skills (Kneebone & Baillie, 2008). For example, strapping an arm model for practicing injection to the arm of an actor makes the tasks more realistic, especially if the actor engages in distracting talk or complains like some patients might.

Simulations are used for team as well as individual training (Piquette & LeBlanc, 2015). Several computerized mannequins can be deployed to mimic an influx of patients from a disaster that students not only treat but have to triage to determine which mimicked conditions need more immediate treatment (Robertson et al., 2009). Similarly, 3-D virtual worlds can be used for training groups online. They are similar to public virtual worlds, such as Second Life, but they portray actual emergency rooms or entire hospitals (Hansen, 2008).

Almost all computer simulations today use multimedia to show lesions, radiologic images (CTs, MRIs, x-rays, sonograms), and video of patients talking or moving (for neurological exams, speech and gait analysis) as well as present audio of breath and heart sounds. Multimedia is incorporated into more didactic materials, too, and used in formal presentations that can be projected or shared with distance sites by videoconference. There is emerging evidence that 3-D images improve learning anatomical structures (Garg, Norman, Eva, Spero, & Sharan, 2002; Yammine & Violato, 2014) and that 3-D imaging helps surgical planning (Soria et al., 2009; Yoon, Catalano, Fritz, Hahn, & Sahani, 2009). Consequently, advanced simulations for teaching surgery and didactic programs for learning anatomy often incorporate 3-D imagery (Dev et al., 2002; Dev & Senger, 2005). The Association of American Medical Colleges has established an online medical education portal where multimedia programs and objects created by faculty can be deposited, reviewed, and shared (Reynolds & Candler, 2009). Additionally, the National Institutes of Health has established a 3-D Print Exchange where scientist can share 3-D models of biomedical objects that can be printed out. The combination of 3-D imaging and printing cannot only be used to print out educational artifacts, but to manufacture prosthetics and other medical objects for individual patients.

Factors/Issues Affecting Performance and Education

Some of the most significant factors affecting performance, the development of instruction, and the application of educational technology in health care are knowledge and research, costs and managed care, regulations and standards, and convergence.

Knowledge and Research

Knowledge advances rapidly in health care and its volume and timeliness has made information technology an important ingredient in education and practice (Salas & Brownell, 1997). As the cost of information technology continues to decline, its use becomes more feasible. The Internet makes it possible for anyone to search the National Library of Medicine's Medline database of the published medical literature for free and has put pressure on faculty and practitioners to keep it more up to date.

The ubiquity of health information on the Internet from varied sources has expanded the knowledge integrity and timeliness problem; however, especially with the development of Web 2.0 social tools, it is easier for anyone to author, edit, or vote on health science content. This has exacerbated the need to develop standards for health information and guidelines for helping nonprofessionals judge its quality and appropriateness (Bader & Braude, 1998; Robinson, Patrick, Eng, & Gustafson, 1998).

Costs and Managed Care

Education is a cost center, not a profit center, for health care institutions. These costs often are underwritten from income generated by hospitals and clinics. Attempts to cut care costs, especially through managed care, not only affect the delivery of health services, but professional education and training as well. There is more pressure on faculty to spend less time teaching and more time seeing patients and to limit the duration of individual patient encounters, further eroding the time faculty can coach students (Association of American Medical Colleges and National Board of Medical Examiners, 2002).

Faculty are interested in information technology as a way to lighten the burden of teaching, while others see it as a tool for patient and consumer health education. Ironically, while many health insurers see information and education

as a means to control costs (people knowledgeable about health tend need fewer services), many patients and laypeople view it as a way to ensure they are receiving appropriate care.

Regulations, Standards, and Licensure

Regulations and standards affect education and training because they dictate what has to be learned. The Health Insurance Portability and Accountability Act (HIPAA) establishes rights of access to medical information and sets standards for privacy that impacts how educators and researchers can use medical records (DiBenedetto, 2003). Mandated electronic medical records have increased the need for improved cybersecurity. Many of the substances and devices employed in health care and the procedures for their use are regulated and there are requirements for certification of health personnel and annual continuing education.

Convergence

As television, telephony, and computing come together, applications incorporating these varied modalities are emerging. It is possible to stream a video presentation and to simultaneously have a videoconference discussing the presentation's contents. The same conferencing hardware and software may allow physicians to consult each other at a distance and to share whiteboard and application software to discuss information about a case or provide consultation services directly to patients.

Students once used standalone computer-based instruction packages to learn content initially and then to access databases separately on CD-ROM or online to search for additional information. Now that educational and information resources are both online, they can be unified by simply establishing links. Linking to social network tools enables students to work together outside of class and to collaborate with colleagues at other institutions. The tools also have become mechanisms for health professionals to communicate with patients and consumers and patients to communicate with each other (Eysenbach, 2008).

The boundaries between educational and informational applications are becoming increasingly murky, especially in problem-based learning and evidence-based medicine where the use of information resources is part of the learning methodology. This convergence extends into practice where electronic medical records can be coupled with other systems assisting providers. For example, it is possible to link to a patient's record to databases and automatically conduct research literature searches related to a patient's condition or to link the record to expert systems providing advice about diagnosis and care or to knowledge bases that can provide alerts to interactions between drugs prescribed. Multimedia information can be included in many electronic medical record systems and devices are appearing that patients can use to collect their own health data (e.g., breath sounds, pulse, temperature, or throat, ear, and body images) and transmit it directly to physicians for evaluation.

Summary of Key Principles

1. **The health science enterprise is very broad, encompassing more than hospitals, clinics, and the practice of providing health care.** Many public, private, and nonprofit organizations are involved in providing care, promoting health, and doing biomedical research and development.

2. **The medical field has been the leader in developing performance and instruction methods that have been adopted by other health professions.** Medical education is better funded and the risks associated with poor education and training of physicians are greater. Consequently, there has been more educational research and evaluation in the medical field than other health care areas.

3. **Traditional medical curricula separate basic science from clinical practice.** This separation was an outgrowth of the philosophy that one learns biomedical science first and then applies it to practice and that hypothetico-deductive reasoning guides clinical problem solving.

4. **There is a movement from traditional to problem-based curricula in medicine and other health professions.** Basic sciences are taught in the context of clinical cases.

5. **Problem-based curricula are supported by research on medical expertise.** This research indicates that expertise is a function of previous problem-solving experience and that clinical problem solving is more a function of pattern matching than hypothetico-deductive reasoning.

6. **The sensory nature of clinical problem solving, the interpersonal skills needed to interact with patients, and the associated risks to patients and students have increased the use of simulation and multimedia as educational methods.** Computer simulations, manikins, and real people acting as standardized patients are used to provide a safe environment for learning clinical problem solving, medical procedures, and interpersonal skills.

7. **Simulations and multimedia enable students to work on cases they may not see in hospitals and clinics while in medical school and to process the rich content they will encounter in real-life problem solving.**

Application Questions

1. A general disaster plan has been released for the Washington, DC, area. The plan calls for victims in any mass medical emergency in the District to be evacuated first to Suburban Hospital and the National Navel Medical Center in neighboring Bethesda, Maryland. If these facilities reach capacity, the plan calls for victims not in immediate need of care (e.g., the walking wounded) to be directed to the Clinical Center at the National Institutes of Health which is located in between the other facilities. What general strategies would you propose for ensuring the three institutions are prepared for dealing with a mass natural or man-made disaster? What procedures and policies might need to be developed and how would one be confident that they really work?

2. A retrospective audit was done at a major hospital consisting of a randomly selected sample of patient charts for the last year. The review identified several sources of medical error which included insufficient documentation of patient current medications and possible interaction between previous medications and ones prescribed. A high percentage of entries were judged illegible and in ten percent of the cases duplicate medical tests were done, possibly because the results had not been entered into the chart at the time the patient was examined or because the provider could not find the test results in the chart. The hospital's medical director calls you in the office saying that it is obvious that the commercial off-the-shelf CD-ROM program on chart management and maintenance that he purchased and made available to staff didn't work. Consequently, he would like you to develop a custom training program that wouldn't consume too much staff time in the clinics and wards. How would you respond to the medical director's request?

References

Ackerman, M. (1998). The visible human project. *Proceedings of the IEEE, 86*(3), 504–511.

Ackerman, M., & Locatis, C. (2011). Advanced networks and computing in healthcare. *Journal of the American Medical Informatics Association, 18*(4), 523–528.

Albanese, M., & Mitchell, S. (1993). Problem-based learning: A review of the literature on its outcomes and implementation issues. *Academic Medicine, 68*(1), 52–81.

Association of American Medical Colleges. (1984). *Physicians for the twenty-first century.* Washington, DC: Association of American Medical Colleges.

Association of American Medical Colleges. (1986). *Medical education in the information age*. Washington, DC: Association of American Medical Colleges.

Association of American Medical Colleges and the National Board of Medical Examiners. (2002). *Embedding professionalism in medical education: Assessment as a tool for implementation*. Philadelphia, PA: National Board of Medical Examiners.

Bader, S., & Braude, R. (1998). "Patient Informatics": Creating new partnerships in medical decision making. *Academic Medicine, 73*(4), 408–411.

Barrows, H. S., & Tamblyn, R. M. (1979). *Problem-based learning in health sciences education*. (National Library of Medicine Monograph, Contract No. 1 LM-6-4721). Bethesda, MD: National Institutes of Health.

Blois, M., & Shortliffe, E. (1990). The computer meets medicine: Emergence of a discipline. In E. Shortliffe & L. Perreault (Eds.), *Medical informatics: Computer applications in health care*. Reading, MA: Addison-Wesley.

Burrows, S., Moore, K., Arriaga, J., Paulaitis, G., & Lemkau, H. (2003). Developing an "evidence-based medicine and use of the biomedical literature" component as a longitudinal theme of an outcomes based medical school curriculum: Year 1. *Journal of the Medical Library Association, 91*(1), 34–41.

Cohen, J. (2002). Embryo development at a click of a mouse. *Science, 297*(5587), 1629.

Craig, J., Irwig, L., & Stockler, M. (2001). Evidence-based medicine: Useful tools for decision making. *Medical Journal of Australia, 174*(5), 248–253.

Dev, P., & Senger, S. (2005). The visible human and digital anatomy learning archive. *Studies in Health Technology Information, 111*, 108–118.

Dev, P., Montgomery, K., Senger, S., Heinrichs, W. L., Srivastava, S., & Waldron, K. (2002). Simulated medical learning environments on the Internet. *Journal of the American Medical Informatics Association, 9*(5), 554–556.

DiBenedetto, D. (2003). HIPAA privacy 101: Essentials for case management practice. *Lippencott's Case Management, 8*(1), 14–23.

Dimitrijevic, I., Kalezic N., Ristic, J., Stefanovic, D., Millcevic M., Bumbasirevic, M., Subotic, D., Pavlovic, D., Vucetic, C., & Ivanovski, P. (2007). "I am sorry I have bad news . . . " – Principles in informing patients on the gravity of a disease and the treatment. *Acta chirurgica Iugoslavica, 54*(2), 95–100.

Evidence-Based Medicine Working Group. (1992). Evidence-based medicine: A new approach to teaching the practice of medicine. *Journal of the American Medical Association, 268*(17), 2420–2425.

Eysenbach, G. (2008). Medicine 2.0: Social networking, collaboration, participation, apomediation, and openness. *Journal of Internet Medical Research, 3*, e22.

Farmer, D. (2015). Soft skill matter. *JAMA Surgery, 150*(3), 207.

Finkel, M., Brown, H., Gerber, L., & Supino, P. (2003). Teaching evidence-based medicine to medical students. *Medical Teacher, 25*(2), 202–204.

Flexner, A. (1910). *Medical education in the United States and Canada: A report to the Carnegie Foundation for the Advancement of Teaching*. Boston, MA: Updyke. Reprinted in 1973 by Science and Health Publications, Bethesda, Maryland.

Foote, D., Parker, E., & Hudson, H. (1976). Telemedicine *in Alaska: The ATS-6 satellite biomedical demonstration; final report of the evaluation of the ATS-6 biomedical demonstration in Alaska*. Palo Alto, CA: Institute for Communications Research, Stanford University.

Garg, A., Norman, G., Eva, K., Spero, L., & Sharan, S. (2002). Is there any virtue in virtual reality? The minor role of multiple orientations in learning anatomy from computers. *Academic Medicine, 77*(10), S97–S99.

Greenhalgh, T., Howick, J., & Maskry, N. (2014). Evidence based medicine: A movement in crisis? *BMJ, 348*, g3725 (online only).

Hansen, M. (2008). Versatile, immersive, creative and dynamic virtual 3-D healthcare learning environments: A review of the literature. *Journal of Medical Internet Research, 10*(3), e26.

Hoffer, E., & Barnett, G. O. (1990). Computer in medical education. In E. Shortliffe & L. Perreault (Eds.), *Medical informatics: Computer applications in health care*. Reading, MA: Addison-Wesley.

Imanieh, M. H., Dehghani, S. M., Sobhani, A. R., & Haghighat, M. (2014). Evaluation of problem-based learning in medical students' education. *Journal of Advances in Medical Education and Professionalism, 2*(1), 1–5.

Kneebone, R., & Baillie, S. (2008). Contextualized simulation and procedural skills: A view from medical education. *Journal of Veterinary Medical Education, 35*(4), 595–598.

Kockro, P., & Hwang, P. (2009). Virtual temporal bone: An interactive 3-dimensional learning aid for cranial base surgery. *Neurology, 64*(5) (Suppl 2), 216–229.

Martin, E. B., Mazzola, N. M., Brandano J., Zurakowski, D., & Meyer, E. C. (2015). Clinicians' recognition and management of emotions during difficult healthcare conversations. *Patient Education and Counceling, 98*(10), 1248–1244.

Montgomery, K., Burgess, L., Dev, P., & Heinrichs, L. (2006). Project hydra—A new paradigm of Internet-based surgical simulation. *Studies in Health Technology Information, 119*, 399–403.

Norman, G. (1985). The role of knowledge in the teaching and assessment of problem-solving. *Journal of Instructional Development, 8*(1), 7–10.

Norman, G. (2005). Research in clinical reasoning: Past history and current trends. *Medical Education, 39,* 418–427.

Norman, G. (2008a). Problem-based learning makes a difference. But why? *Canadian Medical Association Journal, 178*(1), 61–62.

Norman, G. (2008b). The glass is a little full – of something: Revisiting the issue of content specificity in problem solving. *Medical Education, 42,* 549–551.

Norman, G., Brooks, L., Cunnington, J., Shali, V., Marriott, M., & Regehr, G. (1996). Expert-novice differences in the use of history and visual information from patients. *Academic Medicine, 71*(10), S62–S64.

Norman, G., Young, M., & Brooks, L. (2007). Non-analytical models of clinical reasoning: The role of experience. *Medical Education, 41,* 1140–1145.

Oh, S. A., Chung, E. K., & Han, E. R. (2015). The relationship between problem based learning and clinical performance evaluations. *Korean Journal of Medical Education, 27*(3), 195–2000.

Patel, V., Evans, D., & Groen, G. (1989). Biomedical knowledge and clinical reaoning. In D. Evans & V. Patel (Eds.), *Cognitive science in medicine.* Cambridge, MA: MIT Press.

Piquette, D., & LeBlanc, V. (2015). Five questions critical care educators should ask about simulation-based medical education. *Clinics in Chest Medicine, 36*(3), 469–479.

Reynolds, R., & Candler, C. (2009). MedEdPortal: Educational scholarship for teaching. *Journal of Continuing Education in the Health Professions, 28*(2), 91–94.

Rideout, E., England-Oxford, V., Brown, B., Fothergill-Bourbonnais, F., Ingram, C., Benson, G., Ross, M., & Coates, A. (2002). A comparison of problem-based and conventional curricula in nursing education. *Advances in Health Sciences Education, 7,* 3–17.

Robertson, B., Schumacher, L. Gossman, G., Kanfer, R., Kelley, M., & DeVita, M. (2009). Simulation-based crisis team training for multidisciplinary obstetric providers. *Simulation in Healthcare, 4*(2), 77–83.

Robinson, T., Patrick, K., Eng, T., & Gustafson, D. (1998). An evidence-based approach to interactive health communication: A challenge for medicine in the information age. *Journal of the American Medical Association, 280*(14), 1264–1269.

Salas, A., & Brownell, A. (1997). Introducing information technologies into the medical curriculum: Activities of the AAMC. *Academic Medicine, 72*(3), 191–193.

Sandrick, K. (2001). Virtual reality surgery: Has the future arrived? *Bulletin of the American College of Surgeons, 86*(3), 42–43, 63.

Soria, F., Delgado, M., Sanchez, F., Alona, A., Jimenez Cruz, J., Morell, E., & Uson, J. (2009). Effectiveness of three dimensional fluoroscopy in percutaneous nephrostomy: An animal model study. *Urology, 73*(3), 649–652.

Vernon, D., & Blake, R. (1993). Does problem-based learning work? A meta-analysis of evaluative research. *Academic Medicine, 68*(7), 550–563.

Wadland, W. C., Barry, H., Farquhar, L., & White, A. "Training medical students in evidence-based medicine: a community campus approach." *FAMILY MEDICINE-KANSAS CITY*-31 (1999): 703–708.

Weiland, A., Blankenstein, A. H., Van Saase, J. L., Van der Molen, H. T., Jacobs, M. E., Abels, D. C., Kose, N., Van Dulmen, S., Vernhout, R. M., & Arends, L. R. (2015). Training medical specialists to communicate better with patients with medically unexplained physical symptoms (MUPS). A randomized control trial. *PLoS One, 10*(9), e0138342 (online only).

White, B. (2004). Making evidence-based medicine doable in everyday practice. *Family Practice Management, 11*(2), 51–58.

Yammine, K., & Violato, C. (2014). A meta-analysis of educational effectiveness of three-dimensional visualization technologies in teaching anatomy. *Anatomical Sciences Education,* 1–14 (online only).

Yoon, L., Catalano, O., Fritz, S., Hahn, P., & Sahani, D. (2009). Another dimension in magnetic resonance cholangiopanreatography: Comparison of 2- and 3-dimensional magnetic resonance cholangiopanreatography for the evaluation of intraductal papillary mucinous neoplasm of the pancreas. *Journal of Computer Assisted Tomography, 33*(3), 363–368.

Chapter 20

Integrating Technology into K–12 Education

Anne Ottenbreit-Leftwich

Thomas Brush

Indiana University

Introduction

According to the 2010 U.S. National Education Technology Plan, "Technology is at the core of virtually every aspect of our daily lives and work, and we must leverage it to provide engaging and powerful learning experiences and content, as well as resources and assessments that measure student achievement in more complete, authentic, and meaningful ways" (Gray, Thomas, & Lewis, 2010 (p. ix). The availability of technology resources for both teachers and students in K–12 schools has been increasing for decades. For example, an Organisation for Economic Co-operation and Development (OECD) report (2015) found significant increases in the percentages of students engaging in weekly technology activities at school from 2009 to 2012. In a similar vein, a Project Tomorrow report indicated that in a comparison to 2013, in 2014 teachers in the United States were using more digital content, with an increase in teacher use of online videos (up 33 percent), Google for education (up 38 percent), and digital curriculum (up 55 percent) (Project Tomorrow, 2014a).

Given the increased availability and use of technology in K–12 settings and the increasing importance of technology in the everyday lives of most individuals, it is important to consider the most effective methods for integrating these tools and resources into instruction, with a particular focus on the tools and methods that support student learning and engagement. Thus, this chapter will focus on:

1. models and strategies that detail how to support instruction with technology,
2. current technology resources in K–12 settings, and
3. an overview of the issues associated with technology integration.

Supporting Instruction with Technology: Current Models and Strategies

Models of Technology Integration

There are several well-described models focusing on effective methods for integrating technology into instruction to support teaching and learning. The two most prevalent models in the literature are the SAMR model and the TPACK model. Both focus mainly on the teacher—that is, areas a teacher should consider in order to effectively integrate technology to support instruction.

The substitution, augmentation, modification, redefinition (SAMR) model, developed by Puentedura (Romrell, Kidder, & Wood, 2014), defines a progressive model in which each level represents a more effective means for integrating technology into instruction. At the initial level (substitution), technology functions as a direct tool substitute without changing the pedagogical approach. For example, the teacher could use the computer to create a printable worksheet that students would complete and hand in. At the second level (augmentation), technology is used as a direct tool substitute, but there is functional improvement. At this level, teachers could have students use an online resource as opposed to a print-based resource—functional improvements would include students now having the ability to easily search for key terms. The third level is modification, where technology enables the teacher to significantly redesign a task. At this level, teachers may have students collaborate together to create a book using an online publishing tool such as Google Docs. The fourth and highest level is redefinition, where the technology enables teachers to create new tasks that were previously inconceivable without technology. At this level, students could publish persuasive writing on public blogs and Skype with "live" experts on a particular topic/problem (Puentedura, 2013).

The technological pedagogical and content knowledge (TPACK) model is a framework for articulating and improving teachers' use of technology for teaching and learning (Mishra & Koehler, 2006). Researchers and teacher educators have adopted the TPACK model as a tool for understanding and advancing preservice and inservice teachers' ability to integrate technology into their instruction (e.g., Baran, Chuang, & Thompson, 2011; Graham, Cox, & Velasquez, 2009; Hughes, 2005). TPACK is depicted as three overlapping circles of knowledge (technological, pedagogical, and content). These three circles overlap to create seven distinct constructs of knowledge: content (CK), pedagogical (PK), technological (TK), technological pedagogical (TPK), technological content (TCK), pedagogical content (PCK), and technological pedagogical content knowledge (TPACK). It is suggested that if teachers have strong TPACK, they will be able to integrate technology into their instruction. In one example, more experienced teachers may have excellent PCK, but because their TK is weak, they would have difficulties with TPACK and therefore, technology integration.

In order to help teachers develop their TPACK and thus be able to integrate technology, teachers' current abilities of all seven distinct constructs should be assessed and action should be taken to address deficiencies. For example, if a teacher is weak in TK, professional development should focus on developing that teacher's technology skills. For example, Mishra and Koehler (2006) examined teachers' TPACK during a professional development activity. Teachers brought a lesson they wanted to work on and they were shown applicable technologies that could support that particular lesson. Although the model is strong conceptually and widely implemented (Koehler, Shin, & Mishra, 2012), some researchers question the validity of the model (Brantley-Dias & Ertmer, 2013; Graham, 2011; Kopcha, Ottenbreit-Leftwich, Jung, & Baser, 2014).

Technology Standards for Teachers and Students

In K–12 education, common standards for students are important in order to delineate a baseline by which to assess student progress toward meeting developmental goals. In the field of educational technology, the International Society for Technology in Education (ISTE) has provided six overarching standards that students should achieve in order to be technology literate: (1) creativity and innovation, (2) communication and collaboration, (3) research and information fluency, (4) critical thinking, problem solving, and decision making, (5) digital citizenship, and (6) technology operations and concepts. The most recent ISTE student standards were published in 2007 and will be updated soon.

ISTE also put forth ISTE teacher standards, which outlines five performance indicators for teachers to achieve in order to integrate technology into teaching and learning: (1) Facilitate and inspire student learning and creativity, (2) design and develop digital age learning experiences and assessments, (3) model digital age work and learning, (4) promote and model digital citizenship and responsibility, and (5) engage in professional growth and leadership. Other standards providing technology competencies for students and teachers have been designed by UNESCO (http://unesdoc.unesco.org/images/0015/001562/156210E.pdf) and the Partnership for 21st Century Learning (http://www.p21.org/our-work/p21-framework).

Enhancing Instruction with Technology

There are numerous enhancements to current instructional practices that are being proposed for K–12 settings, and technology is a key factor in many of these strategies. Suggestions for instructional enhancements that involve significant use of technology include fostering more inquiry-based learning, supporting personalized learning, engaging students in content via alternative strategies such as games, using online and blended learning strategies such as flipped learning, and providing "maker movement" design spaces that enable students to use digital technologies to create a variety of products. Each of these enhancements will be described in this chapter.

Supporting Inquiry-Based Learning

One area that is increasingly discussed focuses on inquiry-based learning methods, including project-based and problem-based learning (Brush & Saye, 2014). With both of these models, instructional activities are centered around an engaging, authentic problem. Students are provided resources and scaffolding in order to assist them with developing and defending a solution to the problem. With these models, technology can be used to support the inquiry process. For example, Saye and Brush (2007) provided students with authentic multimedia resources focusing on the African American civil rights movement of the 1960s in order to assist students with exploring problems and issues of social justice. They found that students believed the multimedia available to them assisted them in better understanding the struggles faced by African Americans. Ertmer and Ottenbreit-Leftwich (2013) describe an activity where students conducted research on energy sources. Students used technology to develop experiments, collaborate with another group of students across the United States, and present their results to a larger audience. Throughout this project, students used Web 2.0 tools to collaborate with other learners to develop a shared knowledge base.

Supporting Personalized Learning

Personalized learning focuses on utilizing different strategies and approaches to support individual, self-directed learning goals (Grant & Basye, 2014). Such approaches typically involve having students use their own strategies to learn and progress through learning goals at their own pace and demonstrate their knowledge in unique ways. Some of the common approaches to personalized learning include engaging students in blended learning environments, establishing individualized college and career readiness learning plans, and integrating competency-based models of instruction for students (Tanenbaum, Le Floch, & Boyle, 2013).

Some researchers have suggested that personalized learning can be easier for teachers to facilitate with the help of technology. For example, adaptive learning software can be provided to guide students through individualized programs with immediate formative assessment (Johnson, Adams Becker, Estrada, & Freeman, 2014).

Game-Based Learning

As one of the more popular trends, many are touting the importance of digital games in education. According to a recent report from the Joan Ganz Cooney Center, nearly 75 percent of classroom teachers surveyed indicated that they utilized digital games within their instruction, with over 45 percent stating that they used digital games at least once a week (Takeuchi & Vaala, 2014). Teachers often define digital games as both drill-and-practice activities with rewards and more sophisticated educational games that have rules and mimic mainstream games. A Project Tomorrow (2013) report indicates that "teachers who use games in class firmly believe in the power of those games to increase engagement. Five of ten teachers said they see a role for digital games in helping their students visualize difficult academic concepts . . . resulting in both improved student outcomes and an enhancement of their own personal productivity" (pp. 6–7).

Online Learning in K–12

One of the increasing trends in K–12 education has been online learning. In fact, a Project Tomorrow (2014a) survey found that whereas 24 percent of traditional students took at least one online course in 2006, 50 percent did so in 2013. Furthermore, the same survey revealed that twenty-nine states were operating full-time online schools. Picciano, Seaman, Shea, and Swan (2012) reported that district and high school administrators described the following as the main reasons for offering online courses; such courses provide access to courses that otherwise are not available (including advanced placement courses), permit students who failed a course to take it again, and provide for the needs of specific students.

While online learning at the K–12 level is growing widely in the United States, the growth of online and blended instruction in other parts of the world is quite uneven. For example, one of the challenges identified in a report on online learning in K–12 education around the world is that while blended and online learning is typically available to urban students from developed countries, students in other countries, such as Botswana, indicate that they lack access to technology and are unable to even consider online learning as an instructional option (Barbour et al., 2011). Typically, both local and national governments provide the funding for online learning; however, this report provided evidence that many countries around the world still lack not only funding, but also policies and plans for implementing online K–12 learning on a wide scale. Moreover,

these countries often fail to provide teachers with the necessary training and support to effectively implement online learning.

Flipped Learning

Flipped learning is a term used to describe an innovative pedagogy where (a) lectures are recorded and viewed, via technology, for homework and (b) students work on assignments and projects during class time, implementing the ideas they learned from their homework (Finkel, 2012). Some of the concerns about flipped learning have focused on student access to the materials they are expected to study for homework. For example, nearly half the teachers responding to a recent survey expressed concerns that their students would be unable to access online resources from home, thus making the implementation of the flipped model problematic (Project Tomorrow, 2014b). Finkel (2012) provided potential solutions for overcoming the issues associated with lack of access in lower-income populations: providing access to technology in the library before and after school, formatting content so students can view videos on their mobile devices or devices they can check out from the school library, and providing resources on DVDs or flash drives, which can also be checked out to students who do not have access to network resources from their homes.

Finkel (2012) further describes the advantages of flipped learning, stating that this approach greatly increases teachers' abilities to differentiate instruction. Advanced students can quickly view videos and watch other videos for extension activities, while students struggling with the content can pause and replay videos until they understand the concept. Another potential problem could be teachers creating their own videos, which could take extra time and effort. However, using existing open resources, such as those provided by the Khan Academy (http://khanacademy.org), can help teachers overcome this barrier. More resources that can be used to support flipped learning can be found at http://flippedclassroom.org/.

Maker Movement

The "maker" movement focuses on providing a design space for K–12 students to use computer programming, electronics, 3-D printers, robotics, and other technologies/materials to create a variety of products. Some popular products that children have constructed have included electronic jewelry, video games, cybernetic creatures, and interactive textiles (Blikstein & Krannich, 2013). Many maker spaces are appearing in libraries across the country, providing more than just information resources (Peppler & Bender, 2013). Peppler (2013) suggests that this type of "interest-driven arts learning" requires four practices of production: technical (coding, debugging, repurposing), critical (observing and deconstructing media, evaluating and reflecting, referencing, reworking and remixing), creative (making artistic choices, connecting multimodal sign systems), and ethical (crediting ownership, providing inside information, respectful collaboration and sharing). As Blikstein and Krannich (2013) pointed out, research on maker spaces and projects has not yet fully examined the learning implications of this curricular innovation; however, several projects, such as Barron (as cited in Peppler, 2013), have found that students involved in digital productions were more likely to display constructive dispositions (e.g., Internet skills, confidence in computing), critical dispositions (e.g., seek other sources to validate information), and social dispositions (e.g., create and share media with political messages).

Current Technology Resources in K–12 Settings

In recent years, new technology tools and resources have become available to schools on an increasing basis. As these tools become available, scholars have repeatedly advocated for more student-centered uses of technology (e.g., Ertmer & Ottenbreit-Leftwich, 2013). Following are several types of technology-based tools and resources that have emerged recently that provide promising abilities to support more student-centered learning approaches.

Mobile Devices

Mobile learning (which includes cell phones and tablets) has become increasingly popular in K–12 education. The educational affordances of mobile technologies include the ability to deliver content at any place, at any time. In addition, mobile devices provide the opportunity for immediate learning assistance and feedback (Lai, Yang, Chen, Ho, & Chan, 2007). Mobile technologies also provide the ability to access information and resources regardless of time or location, opening up the capacity to have students document and create artifacts based on their learning (Lai et al., 2007). With the increase in student ownership of mobile devices (cell phones and tablets), mobile learning is quickly becoming easier and more feasible for K–12 education. In a nationally representative survey, 37 percent of 802 smartphone users were age twelve to seventeen (Madden, Lenhart, Duggan, Cortesi, & Gasser, 2013). In addition, 74 percent reported that they accessed the Internet occasionally on a mobile device (cell phones or tablets), with one in four mostly using their cell phone to access the Internet (Madden et al., 2013).

When it comes to mobile technologies in the classrooms, reports have shown that tablet devices saw the greatest increase in classroom adoption (PBS, 2013). Out of the teachers using tablets, 71 percent reported apps as the most beneficial for teaching; 68 percent used the tablets at least once a week, with 29 percent using them every day (PBS, 2013). However, teachers have also indicated that although mobile devices can increase student engagement and motivation, classroom use of this technology can lead to difficulties, such as lack of equitable access to mobile devices and class disruptions (Thomas, O'Bannon, & Bolton, 2013).

K–12 students have also reported increases in access and use of mobile devices in classrooms. For example, in a recent survey (Project Tomorrow, 2013), almost a third of the 325,000 students surveyed indicated that they used a mobile device in school. The increase in popularity of these devices and their capabilities for student learning has led to an increase in 1:1 initiatives (one computing device per student). The 1:1 initiatives provide immediate access to learning for all students regardless of time and location (Wong & Looi, 2011). Unfortunately, not all schools are able to afford the cost of 1:1 initiatives (Ullman, 2011), with some districts using funds typically allocated for textbooks to purchase technology devices.

Many school districts have found it difficult to implement a 1:1 initiative because of issues with purchasing enough resources for their students and being responsible for the technical problems associated with those devices. To address this problem, many schools have begun turning to a BYOD (Bring Your Own Device) program, where students are allowed to literally bring in their own mobile devices and use them in class (Ullman, 2011). One elementary school in Hong Kong examined their one-year implementation of BYOD for seamless science inquiry. They found that students obtained knowledge beyond information available from their textbooks and reported positive attitudes toward seamless science inquiry (Song, 2014). However, there are difficulties associated with BYOD initiatives. As McCrea (2015) pointed out, wireless networks in schools need to be able to support the large number of users. To accommodate the wide range of devices, McCrea also recommends carefully selecting resources such as instructional apps that are available for a wide variety of devices and not proprietary to any one device. In addition, available IT support for the various devices that students will use is essential.

Digital Textbooks

Electronic/digital textbooks are a digital form of textbooks that can be accessed via mobile devices or computers. According to the Federal Communications Commission (FCC), U.S. schools spent over $7 billion on textbooks in 2012 alone. In addition, many of the textbooks in schools are seven to ten years old and contain outdated materials. To correct this problem, the FCC and the Department of Education have worked with the Digital Textbook Collaborative to create a plan to facilitate K–12 adoption of digital textbooks and increase bandwidth for schools and the community. Some countries, such as South Korea, have already begun transitioning all their students to digital textbooks.

There are both advantages and challenges to implementing digital textbooks in K–12 schools. Some of the advantages include the ability to store multiple e-books on one device, the provision of unique features provided by e-books such as annotation capabilities and integrated tools such as glossary and search functions, and the decreased cost of e-books compared to traditional textbooks. Challenges to using digital textbooks in K–12 environments can include the following: short loan periods for books, complex software, lack of technical support, poor user design (device, software, text alignment), limited classroom power sources, lack of teacher training, and lack of access to e-book devices (Gu, Wu, & Xu, 2015). Overall, it seems that many teachers and school leaders agree that digital textbooks have enormous potential for K–12 education (Embong, Noor, Ali, Bakar, & Amin, 2012; Lee, Mossam, & Kok-Lim, 2013), but specific strategies and continued efforts supporting design and development of both hardware and software need to be implemented (Gu et al., 2015).

Web 2.0 Tools

Web 2.0 is a term that began in popularity over a decade ago (Cormode & Krishnamurthy, 2008). Web 2.0 is considered to be an improvement over the original Internet. Initially, the Internet was primarily static, users would passively receive information from various Web pages; however, with Web 2.0, users are much more engaged, posting comments, uploading content, and interacting with other users. Many tools have been introduced that exemplify Web 2.0 collaborative characteristics: media sharing sites (e.g., Flickr, Instagram, YouTube), social networking sites (e.g., Facebook), blogging and microblogging sites (e.g., Tumbler, Twitter, Blogger), social bookmarking (e.g., Delicious), and collaborative knowledge development wikis (e.g., Wikispaces). Perhaps the most popular Web 2.0 example, Wikipedia, has become one of the largest reference websites. Individual users (over 76,000 active contributors) can create or update articles on virtually any topic (currently more than 34 million articles in 285 languages).

Web 2.0 tools have increased user interaction and engagement because these tools are simple enough for basic users (Hew & Cheung, 2013). Students in particular, are taking advantage of Web 2.0 tools and using them for both personal and learning purposes. Greenhow, Robelia, and Hughes (2009) reconsidered how the new advantages of Web 2.0 can impact teaching and learning. They suggested that "with technical expertise now serving as less of a barrier, and expanded Web access and contexts for learning, Web 2.0's affordances of interconnections, content creation and remixing, and interactivity might facilitate an increased research interest in learners' creative practices, participation, and production" (p. 249). In K–12 environments, more teachers and students are taking advantage of these affordances. However, some teachers and students have also expressed frustrations associated with using Web 2.0 tools. Teachers have reported that student papers and projects created with Web 2.0 tools may be more time consuming to grade and provide feedback, while students indicated that technical issues, poor time management, and Internet distractions made Web 2.0 assignments more challenging (Nair, Tay, & Koh, 2013).

In a review discussing the impact of Web 2.0 tools on K–12 student learning, Hew and Cheung (2013) suggested that any positive impacts on student learning were more indicative of how the Web 2.0 technologies were used, as opposed to the tools themselves. For example, using blogs for peer review or self-reflection, or using a podcast to review information, seemed to increase student achievement; however, the increased achievement may have had more to do with the instructional strategy used (i.e., peer feedback and review), than the use of the tools (blog and podcast). The Web 2.0 tools just made it easier and more efficient to implement the strategies (Hew & Chung, 2013). Thus, from an instructional standpoint, it may be more important to focus first on the instructional strategy that is most effective for meeting learning goals, and then examine the Web 2.0 tools available that can facilitate the implementation of that strategy.

Open Educational Resources

The use of educational resources (OER) and open content has become increasingly popular in K–12 education. OERs are teaching and learning materials that exist in the public domain or have been uploaded with a special copyright license allowing others to use and edit them. OERs can include a wide range of educational materials ranging from full courses to singular learning objects such as videos or images. Teachers and educational stakeholders advocate that OERs save schools money due to the saved time and resources required to develop new educational materials (Trotter, 2008). In addition to saving money, time, and resources, studies have shown that students using OERs have similar learning gains to those using traditional materials (Robinson, Fischer, Wiley, & Hilton, 2014).

Creative Commons (2015) is a nonprofit organization dedicated to assisting owners of creative works to legally share and distribute their materials. As of 2014, users had shared 882 million CC-licensed works. Teachers and educators around the world contribute to OER databases that exist on a number of different websites (Table 20.1).

TABLE 20.1	Open Educational Resources
Curriki	http://www.curriki.org
OER Commons	https://www.oercommons.org
EDSITEment!	http://edsitement.neh.gov
Federal Resources for Educational Excellence	http://free.ed.gov
CK–12 Foundation	http://www.ck12.org
Gooru	http://www.goorulearning.org
OpenEd	https://www.opened.io
Saylor Academy	http://www.saylor.org
HippoCampus	http://www.hippocampus.org
TED-Ed	http://ed.ted.com
Share My Lesson	http://www.sharemylesson.com
WatchKnowLearn	http://www.watchknowlearn.org
MIT Open Courseware for High School	http://ocw.mit.edu/high-school/

Issues Associated with Integrating Technology into K–12 Settings

Barriers and Enablers

Although there are many descriptions of how technology can be used to powerfully impact teaching and learning (e.g., Ertmer & Ottenbreit-Leftwich, 2013), scholars have indicated that the level of use is still not where they would like it to be. Many scholars have investigated this phenomenon and purported that the lack of technology integration in our K–12 schools is due to specific barriers. Hew and Brush (2007) found that the barriers to technology use in K–12 schools included the following:

- Resources (lack of technology, lack of access to technology, lack of time, lack of technical support)
- Knowledge and skills (lack of technology skills, technology-supported pedagogy skills, and technology-related classroom management skills)
- Institution (leadership, school schedules, lack of technology integration plan)
- Attitudes and beliefs (teacher attitudes and beliefs toward technology)
- Assessment (measuring student learning, high-stakes testing, perceived tension between using technology and traditional examinations)
- Subject culture (institutional practices and expectations surrounding a subject area)

Out of all of these factors, teachers typically report internal factors (e.g., knowledge and beliefs about technology) as the most influential for teacher adoption and use of technology. In order to integrate technology, teachers need to have general knowledge about technology (how to use both hardware and software), as well as how technology can be used to support teaching and/or learning. However, because technology is constantly updating, teachers need continuous professional development to keep their knowledge updated. For example, Ertmer, Ottenbreit-Leftwich, Sadik, Sendurur, and Sendurur (2012) found that even teachers who were award winners with regards to their technology use indicated that sometimes their knowledge was a barrier because they "still think there is always so much out there to learn and to discover, . . . especially with technology [because] it grows so fast" (p. 429).

Teachers beliefs also play a critical role with regard to teacher adoption and use of technology. For example, in the study cited earlier (Ertmer et al., 2012), teachers indicated that the attitudes and beliefs of their fellow teachers were the most impactful barrier on students' use of technology. If teachers do not view technology as important, then they are less likely to implement it and use it in their classrooms, regardless of mandates or resources.

Professional development experiences provide the opportunity to overcome both of the aforementioned barriers. Professional development opportunities should be directly related to teachers' beliefs, asking teachers to integrate technology into an existing lesson (Mishra & Koehler, 2006).

During the professional development, teachers should be introduced to technology that is directly relevant to their classroom. Because the teachers are comfortable with the pedagogical context, they develop knowledge around their own specific context and it integrates well with their existing beliefs.

Digital Divide

Since the advent of technology in education, stakeholders and researchers alike have voiced concerns about the digital divide and the impact on students. The digital divide refers to the differences in educational experiences resulting from students' technology exposure. The digital divide seems to be present within most developed nations, with the differences primarily being due to the socioeconomic status of students (Li & Ranieri, 2013). From an international perspective, the digital divide is also present between nations; across countries, student access available to technology is greatly dependent upon the wealth of the country (Mardikyan, Yildiz, Ordu, & Simsek, 2015).

Initially, the digital divide simply referred to the differences emerging between students that had technology in their schools versus those that did not have access to technology. Concerns arose that those students without access (who were typically from lower socioeconomic status areas) would be less prepared and skilled for the twenty-first-century workforce (Reinhart, Thomas, & Torskie, 2011). Therefore, more technology was purchased by schools in order to prevent their students from falling behind. However, more technology may not be able to result in student preparation for the twenty-first century.

Studies have shown that low socioeconomic status schools tend to be less likely to use technology in ways that promote higher-order thinking and are less likely to have technology facilitators. Reinhart and colleagues suggest that the lack of technology facilitators may lead to fewer professional development activities and less knowledgeable teachers. This is termed the second-level digital divide (Reinhart et al., 2011). Some also suggest a different theory of the digital divide (Hohlfeld, Ritzhaupt, Barron, & Kemker, 2008), stating that the digital divide exists on multiple levels: school infrastructure, classroom, and individual student.

Enabling Adoption

While many acknowledge the presence of the digital divide, some studies have indicated that even when there are limited resources, teachers that see value in technology use tend to overcome these barriers and integrate technology into their classrooms (e.g., Ertmer et al., 2012). For example, one teacher in this 2012 study brought in their own devices from home to compensate for the lack of resources, while another wrote grants to obtain more resources. Teachers can also utilize stations to make the most of limited resources or have students BYOD from home.

Many scholars have debated about which is the most effective and efficient way to facilitate large-scale technology adoption in K–12 schools. Typically, technology innovations are introduced through a top-down (administrator-driven) or bottom-up (teacher-driven) decision-making process. Petko, Egger, Cantieni, and Wespi (2015) examined four different types of decision-making and adoption processes of technology innovations: complementary (top-down and bottom-up), top-down, bottom-up, and optional (meaning teachers could decide whether or not to adopt). Petko et al. (2015) found that when schools had a combined top-down and bottom-up approach in which district initiatives were supported by both the administration and teachers, teachers and students reported using technology more in their classrooms. Entirely top-down was the next most successful model, followed by bottom-up.

Conclusion

Perhaps the most important consideration when deciding whether and how a particular technology might be employed in a particular classroom situation is to first think about whether the use of that technology will enhance teaching and learning. Sometimes, researchers and educators are quick to adopt new technologies without first focusing on how that technology may affect instructional practices and student learning. By keeping effective pedagogical practices and student learning as our focus, we can investigate the affordances of various technologies and determine how their use may support what we already know about effective pedagogy. When considering whether to use a new technology in an instructional situation, it is important to consider whether the affordances of that particular technology can help support good pedagogical practices and thus increase the likelihood that learning will be enhanced.

Summary of Key Principles

1. **Understanding technology integration is not simple.** Many have tried to define successful technology integration and what that looks like. Although there are several models and standards, we suggest that this can vary as long as it is positively impacting K–12 teaching and/or learning.

2. **Curricular and instructional practices can be enhanced with technology.** Several of the emerging innovative practices being implemented into K–12 schools (inquiry-based learning, flipped learning, personalized learning) can all be supported with the use of technology.

3. **New tools will constantly be introduced.** There seems to be a continuous stream of new technology tools and resources available to teachers. Before adopting a new tool, it's important to identify the educational affordances of that tool and how those affordances can be used to improve teaching and/or learning.

4. **Adoption of technology requires systemic support.** To enable successful technology adoption, districts need to understand all barriers and enablers to encourage and support technology integration.

5. **Teachers are the greatest asset for technology integration adoption.** If teachers believe technology is important and have the necessary support, technology adoption and use will be much more likely.

6. **Technology should only be used when beneficial for teaching/learning.** Before using any technology for teaching and learning, we should first ask ourselves, what's the benefit to teaching and learning?

Application Questions

A school district has recently decided to adopt a 1:1 iPad initiative for all students and teachers. They believe that iPads can help support a student-centered personalized instructional approach to learning where technology is utilized in meaningful ways. They hope that iPads will help improve student achievement, student engagement, collaboration, and communication. Although some teachers are excited about the initiative, many have concerns and questions about how they can use the devices in their classrooms. The school district would like you to help in several ways:

1. Provide the school district with ideas on helping with technology adoption. In other words, describe three or four ways in which the district can help support teachers (especially those with concerns and questions) adopt and successfully integrate technology.

2. Develop a workshop to provide teachers with ideas on how to use technology. Keep in mind that providing subject-specific examples can help connect with teachers and enable them to see practical ideas they can directly transfer to their classrooms. Describe the workshop.

3. The school would also like to investigate methods to keep the cost down. What recommendations could you make to help keep the cost of the program down?

References

Baran, E., Chuang, H. H., & Thompson, A. (2011). TPACK: An emerging research and development tool for teacher educators. *TOJET, 10*(4). Retrieved from http://www.tojet.net/ articles/v10i4/10437.pdf

Barbour, M., Brown, R., Hasler Waters, L., Hoey, R., Hunt, J. L., Kennedy, K., Ounsworth, C., Powell, A., & Trimm, T. (2011). Online and blended learning: A survey of policy and practice from K–12 schools around the world. *International Association for K–12 Online Learning*. Retrieved from http://files.eric.ed.gov/fulltext/ED537334.pdf

Blikstein, P., & Krannich, D. (2013, June). The makers' movement and FabLabs in education: Experiences, technologies, and research. In *Proceedings of the 12th International Conference on Interaction Design and Children* (pp. 613–616). Chicago: ACM.

Brantley-Dias, L., & Ertmer, P. A. (2013). Goldilocks and TPCK: Is the construct "just right?" *Journal of Research on Technology in Education, 46*(2), 103–128.

Brush, T., & Saye, J. (2014). Guest editors' introduction: Special issue on technology-supported problem-based learning in teacher education. *Interdisciplinary Journal of Problem-Based Learning, 8*(1).

Cormode, G., & Krishnamurthy, B. (2008). Key differences between Web 1.0 and Web 2.0. *First Monday, 13*(6).

Creative Commons. (2015). *Creative Commons licenses.* Retrieved from http://creativecommons.org/

Embong, A., Noor, A., Ali, R., Bakar, Z., & Amin, A. (2012). Teachers' perceptions on the use of e-books as textbooks in the classroom. *World Academy of Science, Engineering and Technology, 70*, 580–586.

Ertmer, P., & Ottenbreit-Leftwich, A. (2013). Removing obstacles to the pedagogical changes required by Jonassen's vision of authentic technology-enabled learning. *Computers & Education, 64*, 175–182.

Ertmer, P., Ottenbreit-Leftwich, A., Sadik, O., Sendurur, E., & Sendurur, P. (2012). Teacher beliefs and technology integration practices: A critical relationship. *Computers & Education, 59*(2), 423–435.

Finkel, E. (2012). Flipping the script in K12. *District Administration, 48*(10), 28.

Graham, C. R. (2011). Theoretical considerations for understanding technological pedagogical content knowledge (TPACK). *Computers & Education, 57*(3), 1953–1960.

Graham, C., Cox, S., & Velasquez, A. (2009). Teaching and measuring TPACK development in two preservice teacher preparation programs. In *Society for Information Technology & Teacher Education International Conference* (pp. 4081–4086). Retrieved from http://www.editlib.org/p/31297/

Grant, P., & Basye, D. (2014). *Personalized learning: A guide for engaging students with technology.* Eugene, OR: International Society for Technology in Education.

Gray, L., Thomas, N., & Lewis, L. (2010). *Teachers' use of educational technology in U.S. public schools: 2009* (NCES 2010-040). Washington, DC: National Center for Education Statistics, Institute of Education Sciences, U.S. Department of Education.

Greenhow, C., Robelia, B., & Hughes, J. E. (2009). Learning, teaching, and scholarship in a digital age Web 2.0 and classroom research: What path should we take now? *Educational Researcher, 38*(4), 246–259.

Gu, X., Wu, B., & Xu, X. (2015). Design, development, and learning in e-textbooks: What we learned and where we are going. *Journal of Computers in Education, 2*(1), 25–41.

Hew, K., & Brush, T. (2007). Integrating technology into K–12 teaching and learning: Current knowledge gaps and recommendations for future research. *Education Tech Research Development, 55*, 223–252.

Hew, K. F., & Cheung, W. S. (2013). Use of Web 2.0 technologies in K–12 and higher education: The search for evidence-based practice. *Educational Research Review, 9*, 47–64.

Hohlfeld, T. N., Ritzhaupt, A. D., Barron, A. E., & Kemker, K. (2008). Examining the digital divide in K–12 public schools: Four-year trends for supporting ICT literacy in Florida. *Computers & Education, 51*(4), 1648–1663.

Hughes, J. (2005). The role of teacher knowledge and learning experience in forming technology-integrated pedagogy. *Journal of Technology and Teacher Education, 13*, 277–302.

Johnson, L., Adams Becker, S., Estrada, V., & Freeman, A. (2014). *NMC horizon report: 2014* (K–12 Edition). Austin, TX: The New Media Consortium.

Koehler, M. J., Shin, T. S., & Mishra, P. (2012). How do we measure TPACK? Let me count the ways. In R. Ronau, C. Rakes, & M. Niess (Eds.), *Educational technology, teacher knowledge, and classroom impact: A research handbook on frameworks and approaches* (pp. 16–31). Hershey, PA: Information Science Reference.

Kopcha, T., Ottenbreit-Leftwich, A., Jung, J., & Baser, D. (2014). Examining the TPACK framework through the convergent and discriminant validity of two measures. *Computers and Education, 78*, 87–96.

Lai, C., Yang, J., Chen, F., Ho, C., & Chan, T. (2007). Affordances of mobile technologies for experiential learning: the interplay of technology and pedagogical practices. *Journal of Computer Assisted Learning, 23*(4), 326–337.

Lee, J., Mossam, C., & Kok-Lim, A. (2013). Can electronic textbooks be part of K12 education? Challenges, technological solutions, and open issues. *Turkish Online Journal of Educational Technology, 12*(1), 32–44.

Li, Y., & Ranieri, M. (2013). Educational and social correlates of the digital divide for rural and urban children: A study on primary school students in a provincial city of China. *Computers & Education, 60*(1), 197–209.

Madden, M., Lenhart, A., Duggan, M., Cortesi, S., & Gasser, U. (2013). *Teens and technology 2013*. Washington, DC: Pew Internet & American Life Project.

Mardikyan, S., Yıldız, E., Ordu, M., & Simsek, B (2015). Examining the global digital divide: A cross-country analysis. *Communications of the IBIMA*. Retrieved from http://www.ibimapublishing.com/journals/CIBIMA/2015/592253/592253.pdf

McCrea, B. (2015). 9 IT best practices for BYOD districts: Districts with successful bring your own device programs share their key strategies for rolling out and managing student-owned devices in school. *THE Journal (Technological Horizons In Education), 42*(1), 26.

Mishra, P., & Koehler, M. J. (2006). Technological pedagogical content knowledge: A framework for teacher knowledge. *Teachers College Record, 108*(6), 1017–1054.

Nair, S. S., Tay, L. Y., & Koh, J. H. L. (2013). Students' motivation and teachers' teaching practices towards the use of blogs for writing of online journals. *Educational Media International, 50*(2), 108–119.

OECD. (2015). *Students, computers and learning: Making the connection*. PISA: OECD Publishing.

PBS. (2013). Teacher technology usage. Retrieved from http://www.edweek.org/media/teachertechusagesurvey-results.pdf

Peppler, K. (2013). *New opportunities for interest-driven arts learning in a digital age* (Deliverable to the Wallace Foundation). Bloomington, IN: Indiana University.

Peppler, K., & Bender, S. (2013). Maker movement spreads innovation one project at a time. *Phi Delta Kappan, 95*(3), 22–27.

Petko, D., Egger, N., Cantieni, A., & Wespi, B. (2015). Digital media adoption in schools: Bottom-up, top-down, complementary or optional? *Computers & Education, 84,* 49–61.

Picciano, A., Seaman, J., Shea, P., & Swan, K. (2012). Examining the extent and nature of online learning in American K–12 Education: The research initiatives of the Alfred P. Sloan Foundation. *Internet and Higher Education, 15,* 127–135.

Project Tomorrow. (2013). The new digital learning playbook: Understanding the spectrum of student activities and aspirations. Retrieved from http://www.tomorrow.org/speakup/pdfs/SU13Studentsreport.pdf

Project Tomorrow. (2014a). Digital principals, digital teachers. Retrieved from http://www.tomorrow.org/speakup/downloads/PROJECT-TOMORROW-10-3-14.pdf

Project Tomorrow. (2014b). Speak up 2014 national research project findings: Flipped learning continues to trend for third year. Retrieved from http://flippedlearning.org/cms/lib07/VA01923112/Centricity/Domain/4/Speak%20Up%20FLN%202014%20Survey%20Results%20FINAL.pdf

Puentedura, R. (2013). SAMR first steps. Retrieved from http://www.hippasus.com/rrpweblog/archives/2014/11/13/SAMR_FirstSteps.pdf

Reinhart, J. M., Thomas, E., & Torskie, J. M. (2011). K–12 teachers: Technology use and the second level digital divide. *Journal of Instructional Psychology, 38*(3), 181.

Robinson, T., Fischer, L., Wiley, D., & Hilton, J. (2014). The impact of open textbooks on secondary science learning outcomes. *Educational Researcher, 43*(7), 341–351.

Romrell, D., Kidder, L., & Wood, E. (2014). The SAMR model as a framework for evaluating mLearning. *Online Learning, 18*(2), 1–15.

Saye, J., & Brush, T. (2007). Using technology-enhanced learning environments to support problem-based historical inquiry in secondary school classrooms. *Theory and Research in Social Education, 35*(2), 196–230.

Song, Y. (2014). "Bring your own device (BYOD)" for seamless science inquiry in a primary school. *Computers & Education, 74,* 50–60.

Takeuchi, L., & Vaala, S. (2014). Level up learning: A national survey of teaching with digital games. The Joan Ganz Cooney Center. Retrieved from http://www.joanganzcooneycenter.org/publication/level-up-learning-a-national-survey-on-teaching-with-digital-games/

Tanenbaum, C., Le Floch, K., & Boyle, A. (2013). Are personalized learning environments the next wave of K–12 education reform? American Institutes for Research: Education Issue Paper Series. Retrieved from http://www.air.org/sites/default/files/AIR_Personalized_Learning_Issue_Paper_2013.pdf

Thomas, K. M., O'Bannon, B. W., & Bolton, N. (2013). Cell phones in the classroom: Teachers' perspectives of inclusion, benefits, and barriers. *Computers in the Schools, 30*(4), 295–308.

Trotter, A. (2008). Educators assess open content movement. *Education Week, 27*(43), 8–9.

Ullman, E. (2011). BYOD and security. *Technology & Learning, 31*(8), 32–36.

Wong, L. H., & Looi, C. K. (2011). What seams do we remove in mobile-assisted seamless learning? A critical review of the literature. *Computers & Education, 57*(4), 2364–2381.

Chapter 21

Instructional Design in Higher Education

Brenda C. Litchfield

University of South Alabama

Numerous books have been published on teaching in higher education and how to be an effective instructor. Classics in the field (Bain, 2004; Filene & Bain, 2010) give an overall view of philosophy along with strategies in areas such as lecturing, discussion, assessment, and expectations when teaching in higher education. McKeatchie's book (Svinicki & McKeachie, 2014) is on its fourteenth edition and covers the abovementioned strategies along with distance education, active learning, technology, and diversity, among other topics. Barkley (2010) has compiled a wealth of student engagement activities to supplement college classroom instruction. Nilson (2010) has produced a concise, readable book of the basics of college teaching. What most books on college teaching are lacking is attention to systematic course design and basic instructional design. Wood (2009) comes close by specifying that course design should begin with creating goals, objectives, and assessment. Few books include instructional design and development as a starting point.

Articles and books about instructional design abound. Topics include skills of instructional designers (Allen, 2012), as change agents (Campbell, Schwier, & Kenny, 2009), as leaders (Shaw, 2012), as model implementers (Enkenberg, 2001), as strategy designers (Kagan, 2014), and what ID can do for higher education (Terlouw, 2014). What is missing from many articles and books on instructional design is how to specifically integrate instructional design into higher education teaching for graduate and undergraduate courses.

Quite a few instructional design models exist for a variety of purposes: Systems-orientated models (Branson, 1975; Dick & Carey, 2010; Smith & Ragan, 1993), and product development models (Bergman & Moore, 1990; Leshin, Pollock, & Reigeluth, 1990), and classroom orientation (Gerlach & Ely, 1980;

Kemp, Morrison, & Ross, 1994; Reiser & Dick, 1996), among others. These models are prescriptive and cover the basics of instructional design as a systematic process. The classroom orientation models come closest to designing for the higher education classroom but they are more suited to K–12 situations where the instructional event will be limited, the amount of resources will be low, it is an individual effort, the instructor will not be trained in instructional design, and materials will be selected and adapted instead of created (Gustafson & Branch, 1997).

Merrill's Pebble-in-the-Pond Model (Merrill 2013), discussed in Chapter 4 of this book, specifically addresses the instructional design phase of course development. Its analysis has been conducted and it is agreed the problem is one that can be solved with instruction. The model is useful for focusing on the instructional design part of course development and leads a designer through the following six phases : (1) problem to be solved, (2) progression of activities to solve the problem, (3) instruction to develop component skills, (4) enhance strategies, (5) finalize instructional design, and (6) design assessment and evaluation. While providing structural framework for each phase, the model does not address specifics of the learner and motivational factors.

The successive approximation model (SAM) by Allen (Allen, 2012) (see Chapter 4 and 5) streamlined the ADDIE model. It considers the fundamental characteristics of learning events to be meaningful, memorable, motivational, and measurable. These four characteristics appear to address learners and learner involvement, but the SAM model is more of a process development model and does not go into detail about how to achieve these results with learners in higher education.

While a number of instructional design models do a good job of providing guidance on how to develop instruction, there is a lack of attention to the learner and affective involvement in instruction. Used with developing training, they are effective. However, in most training situations, learners are there to gain a new skill they want or need. There is little need to convince them the instruction is necessary even if it is a mandatory training situation. Designing and developing courses in higher education is about more than just information. It is also about skills and attitudes, being involved with the content, becoming excited through involvement, and ideally a student choosing or changing a major based on a course experience. In the case of higher education we need to look further than the basic instructional design models that are effective and efficient in designing and developing instruction. We need a model that considers learners' knowledge, skills, and attitudes as essential components of the instructional design and development process and the ultimate development of the learner.

Significant Learning Model

A model that has excellent potential for use with higher education is one created by Fink (2013). According to Fink (2013), learning is defined in terms of change. "For learning to occur, there has to be some kind of change in the learner. No change, no learning. And significant learning requires that there be some kind of lasting change that is important in terms of the learner's life" (p. 34). For significant learning to occur, instructors must create learning experiences that will facilitate and encourage awareness, connection, integration, and commitment by learners.

Integrated Course Design

Creating instructionally sound, motivating, and active learning is not an easy task for instructors who are not trained in teaching methods. Many are familiar with and practice primarily content-centered rather than learner-centered teaching. Rather than being driven by how much content needs to be covered, instructors should focus on the skills and values students need to develop related to course content. The highest compliment an instructor can receive is that a student changed majors as a result of a relevant, meaningful, and fun course. The essential structure of integrated course design is a relationship of learning goals, feedback and assessment, and teaching and learning activities as determined from an analysis of situational factors (Figure 21.1).

For a course to be truly integrated, all four components must be aligned and interrelated. For example, if the instructor has the objective for learners to develop critical thinking skills in the subject area, then the teaching strategies must present critical thinking examples and activities for learners to practice these skills. Their competence in this area is then assessed and feedback is given on their success or need for improvement. If the instructor delivers mostly lecture, then it would be difficult for learners to develop critical thinking skills; hence, assessment cannot focus on critical thinking. If it does, this can cause frustration and lack of learner confidence. The problem

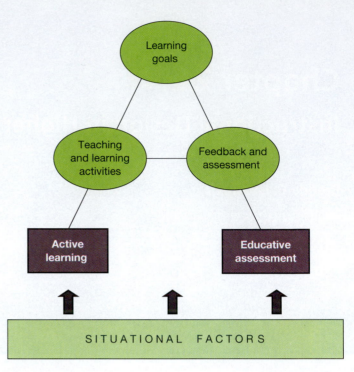

FIGURE 21.1   Key components of integrated course design.

is, many instructors are unaware of this essential connection between objectives and learning activities and assess critical thinking skills anyway even though classroom activities did not provide students with practice to develop them.

Taxonomy of Significant Learning

Fink describes his model as relational and interactive rather than hierarchical. As a whole, it is not radically different from other instructional design models. It has steps for design and development that can be followed easily. What is different is the integration of the categories of his taxonomy of significant learning into the overall design. These categories begin with the standard knowledge and application levels but move into additional categories that focus on the learners and their experiences with a course (Figure 21.2).

Interactive Nature of Significant Learning

What is important to consider is that the categories of the taxonomy are interactive and support each other. The support is not linear but instead it is interactive in that activities and assignments created for one category can lead to other types of learning. For example, guiding students with tips on how to remember content in the foundational knowledge category applies to the learning how to learn category. An assignment in the application category can help develop feelings, interests, and perhaps change values in the caring category (Figure 21.3).

The taxonomy categories form the basis for achieving integrated course design. Keeping these categories in mind, the next step is to progress through the twelve design phases and associated steps. Each step specifies the process and questions for designing a higher education course that is systematic, comprehensive, and provides students with experiences and

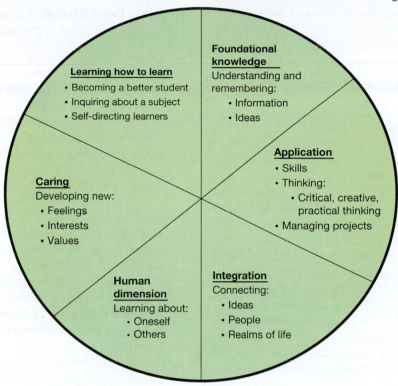

FIGURE 21.2   Taxonomy of significant learning.

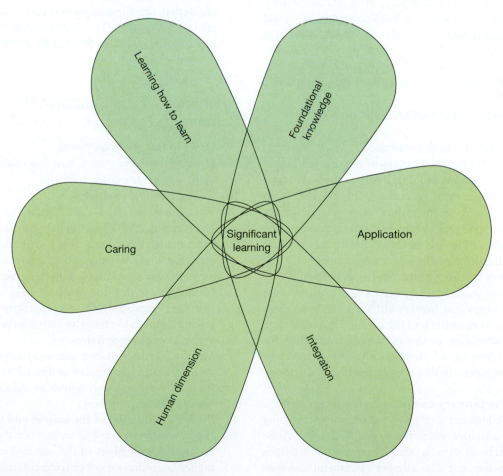

FIGURE 21.3   Interactive nature of significant learning.

activities that address the categories of the taxonomy. Each step is detailed in Fink's 2013 book. Following is a brief description of each step.

Initial Phase: Build Strong Primary Components

1. **Identify important situational goals.**

   In instructional design this is called the audience analysis, and includes information about student characteristics (prior knowledge, attitudes, experiences, out-of-class responsibilities, learning styles, etc.) as well as instructor characteristics (knowledge base, experience, skills, competence, etc.). What is the specific context of the teaching and learning situation such as number of students, level, location, delivery method? What are the expectations of external groups and how does this course fit into a program or major sequence and what is the nature of the subject? Finally, is there a special pedagogical challenge that challenges students? Are there any major misconceptions or misunderstandings that need to be cleared up to demystify the course content? Answers to these questions identify the audience and its needs and helps the instructor for the basic framework for the course.

2. **Identify important learning goals.**

   This step is the basis of sound instructional design and sets the expectation and guidelines for the course. What is it that students should be able to do after this course they could not do before? This is not just knowledge, skills and attitudes to be achieved at the end of the semester but also carried into the future. The taxonomy provides a framework for creating activities to address new knowledge, skills, and attitudes. Being specific at this point leads directly into the third step.

3. **Formulate appropriate feedback and assessment procedures.**

   What will learners do to demonstrate they have mastered the knowledge, skills, and attitudes of the course? This is obviously more than the usual quizzes, midterm and final exams. Assessment must be meaningful and align with course objectives. Assessment procedures relate directly to the activities in the taxonomy. Without frequent assessment, it is difficult to give relevant feedback and build learners' confidence regarding their achievement.

4. **Select effective teaching and learning activities.**

   Using learning goals and objectives as a guide, create or locate activities that involve students and keep them active. Variety is essential and the activities should relate directly to categories in the taxonomy. Activities for both in class and out of class should be designed. An easy way to accomplish this is by using Fink's castle-top template.

5. **Make sure the primary components are integrated.**

   The primary components of goals and objectives, teaching and learning activities, assessment, and feedback must be integrated and build on each other. There must be activities for each objective and then aligned assessment and constructive feedback for each activity.

Intermediate Phase: Assemble the Components into a Coherent Whole

6. **Create thematic structure for the course.**

   Most courses should have at least four and no more than seven important issues, topics, or themes (Fink, 2013). There are, of course, subtopics, but there should be a few major themes that form the basis for knowledge, skills, and attitudes about the subject.

7. **Select or create a teaching strategy.**

   A teaching strategy is different from a teaching technique. Types of techniques are lecture, discussions, group work, case studies, to name a few. These are specific activities instructors use. A strategy is a combination of techniques that, when used together, produce learning results. Think of team-based learning, cooperative/collaborative learning, and problem-based learning as strategies. Instructors can also create strategies by integrating and sequencing different approaches and activities.

8. **Integrate the course structure and the instructional strategy to create and overall scheme of learning activities.**

   Now that the strategies and techniques have been designed and developed, it is time to create an overall roadmap of what will happen in class and out of class. The important thing to think about is variety and what sequence is most effective. Two important questions here are, "How should this course begin?" and "How should this course end?" The answers to these questions will form what instructors create to get students off to a good start and how their knowledge, skills, and attitudes will be exhibited and assessed at the end.

Final Phase: Finish Important Remaining Tasks

9. **Develop the grading system.**

   Figure out what is graded, how it is graded, and when. Are there weights to certain activities?

10. **Debug possible problems.**

    What can go wrong? Is the timing for activities and assignments reasonable? Think through activities and assignments and calculate how much time it will take learners to complete them. Have a student read directions to make sure they are easy to understand. Is there too much or too little for learners to do? Too much to do is often a concern in first-time course development. Do learners have the appropriate resources to complete activities or assignments?

11. **Write the course syllabus.**

    Most universities have a standard template to use. If not, there are many examples online or available from colleagues. Note this part comes at the end of the process rather than the beginning.

12. **Plan an evaluation of the course and of your teaching.**

    If you want to improve as an instructor you have to evaluate your course. Many of the standard evaluations used in higher education do not provide enough specific information to make effective revisions in a course. Students can provide constructive feedback about the course because they have gone through it. If you want to find out if specific activities were effective, then ask questions about each activity. It is best to create an evaluation form that addresses your class, all activities, and components. You could also set up interviews and focus groups at the end of the course for more information. The more feedback you get, the more you can improve your course next time.

The twelve steps of the design phase are similar to other instructional design models and they need to be applied in a systematic manner. Each step builds on the next and is prescriptive. They are easy to follow and familiar to instructional designers. What sets Fink's model apart from others is the six categories of his taxonomy. For each category there is a set of questions an instructor should ask to frame the design and development of the course. The questions and their answers fall into steps 2 through 8. These are where the objectives, activities, and integration of the course are designed.

Integrating the Taxonomy and Asking the Right Questions

The significant learning model is comprised of six categories: foundational knowledge, application, integration, human dimension, caring, and learning to learn. Each category contains several additional types of learning and strategies that complement the category and extend learning for students. A brief description of each category and questions to ask for each one follows.

Fink's guiding question for developing significant learning experience is, "What do I want learners to do one or more years after the course is over?" This sets up a different thinking pattern for an instructor. It is not only important to think about a current semester, but also long-term knowledge, skills, and attitudes. What will the learners think about the course one year later? What will they remember? Will they remember anything? Will they change their major to or from that course?

Foundational Knowledge

This category is the mainstay of all instruction and the one that is most easily and widely used in the majority of higher education classrooms. It is the standard presentation of information and ideas that is often delivered via lecture, reading the text, or viewing videos and presentations. Foundational knowledge is essential for understanding a subject area and its concepts, ideas, and principles. Having a solid foundation in a subject area is critical for further study and progress. Most courses in higher education do a good job of implementing this through lecture, class time, and assessment; but the question becomes what is the most important information learners should remember? What ideas, concepts, principles, and relationships should learners recall? When you look at a college text it is filled with hundreds of pages of information. It can't all be equally important. What should learners remember long after the course is over? This is one of the first decisions an instructor should make when beginning to design a course.

Application

When foundation knowledge is strong it is then possible to move to application. In this category, learners use the information to develop the thinking abilities and skills associated with the subject. They should be able to think in three ways: critically, creatively, and practically. Each of these types of thinking is essential to be able to navigate and understand the full scope of a subject area. When learners are able to think in a variety of ways they are more likely to be able to participate successfully in complex projects that demonstrate what they have learned. In addition, they become more competent in communicating ideas, data, and results.

The major question to ask is if learners are developing critical, practical, and creative thinking skills. Many courses do include a fair amount; but with courses that rely heavily on multiple-choice testing this is rarely possible. For example, while writing this chapter, one of my doctoral students who took a test the previous day came in. I asked him how it went and he said there were ninety-three multiple-choice questions on the exam—and that was just one of four exams in the course—but there were also numerous article summaries and a final project. Does this meet the application level? Maybe, if the final project required learners to use knowledge and skills developed in the course. If the article summaries required critical, practical, or creative thinking, then maybe, but he said they were just summaries of what the article was about. The four multiple-choice tests were probably not application at all but more aligned with simply remembering foundational knowledge rather than thinking critically.

Integration

Integration is the natural extension of application, but many courses do not provide experiences in this category. It involves students being given opportunities through coursework to make connections among the course ideas, their learning experiences, and their lives. It requires creation of activities where students use their knowledge and skills to not only learn a specific subject, but also apply concepts and ideas to other areas of learning and life.

The integration category of the taxonomy is focused on connecting ideas, people, and relevance to life. This requires carefully crafted instructional activities and assignments so learners discover the relationships of the topic to their lives and/or its potential to help them in a career. This is where service learning activities are applicable. In addition, learners should be able to see the integration between the course and other courses in the subject area.

Human Dimension

The human dimension and the next two categories, caring and learning how to learn, are seldom integrated into higher education courses. This category relates to students learning about themselves and others, which is accomplished through a variety of ways: leadership opportunities, teamwork, self-authorship, service learning, and others. Experiences that use simulations, role playing, or observations can enable students to see and to interact in situations that require different points of view. By considering different points of view and reflecting on them they can learn more about themselves and others in the process.

Integrating the human dimension category into course design includes helping learners find out about themselves in relation to the subject area. How are they affected by it? What long-term ideas and practices will be remembered as a result of the course? How will they interact with others based on new knowledge and skills they have acquired? This may sound difficult to design but through projects, activities, classroom interactions, and group work learners can develop an appreciation for the subject and their relation to it now and in the future.

Caring

Caring is the logical progression from human dimension. If students have been able to see the connections to themselves and others, then they should be able to develop new feelings, interests, and values about themselves and the subject. This may be exhibited through increased motivation about the subject and additional time spent researching and working on projects. They may become more interested in working on service learning projects that provide direct experiences to learn more about a subject. At this level they may be making an actual commitment to participate more fully in activities and change their perspective toward the content and its value.

Caring is a category that is in the affective domain. Learners should develop an emotional connection with the subject area and its content, ideas, and principles. The question to ask here is, "What should learners' feelings, interests, and ideas be as a result of taking this course and participating in the activities?" In order for learners to have an emotional connection they should be guided and provided with activities where they can apply the knowledge and skills in a meaningful, relevant way that makes sense to them and changes their outlook.

Learning How to Learn

This final category is at the heart of significant learning and can be integrated throughout the course by the instructor. All faculty desire to have students become better learners and be more self-directed. In addition, it is important for students to become informed consumers and constructors of knowledge. These skills can be initiated at the foundational knowledge level and carried through the entire course. Although learning how to learn sounds like basic good study skills, it operates at a higher level that transcends all subjects a student may be involved in at a particular time and should be practiced and enhanced throughout a higher education experience.

The last category is also one that should be woven throughout the design process. In order for learners to be successful, most need help. This comes in the forms of modeling, encouragement, and direction. It begins in the foundational knowledge category and continues through all others. By asking the questions of how learners can become good students, good students in a certain subject, and how to become self-directed learners, instructors can plan how to guide learners to achieve these goals. Study tips, constructive feedback, examples, and enthusiasm can assist learners in appreciating a subject and directing their attention to achieve the maximum meaning and relevance from it.

Category Integration

There are no specific divisions between the categories and "achieving any one kind of learning simultaneously enhances the possibility of achieving the other kinds of learning as well" (Fink, 2013, p. 37). For significant learning to occur, each of these categories flows forward and backward with others. The learning experience is a fluid process rather than a linear one with steps.

An activity in one category that can enhance another would be an example of a service learning activity, an internship, student teaching, field work, and so forth. The experiences gained in any one of these can add to the caring category and learners can develop a strong connection with the course and content that affects a change in the learner. These categories are not progressive steps but more akin to a ribbon woven through each one that connects them to each other.

Conclusion

With accrediting agencies and university strategic plans broadening their expectations, institutions of higher education are looking at not only learning outcomes but also students, their well-being, and retention in uncertain economic times. The significant learning model can help develop courses that are based on solid instructional design and focus on learners and their experiences. The goal of instruction should be to develop the whole learner and not just one who is full of information. Instructional design models can provide the guidance for systematic course design and development. The significant learning model can extend the systematic design process to produce learners who are engaged and develop the knowledge, skills, and attitudes to get as much as possible out of a higher education learning experience.

Summary of Key Principles

1. Significant learning means designing a course with six major categories: foundational knowledge, application, integration, human dimension, caring, and learning how to learn.

2. Integrated course design is the interaction of learning goals, teaching and learning activities, feedback, and assessment guided by specific situational factors in the learning environment.

3. Situational factors influencing learning are specific context, expectations of others, and the nature of the subject, students, and teacher.

4. All learning is framed by learning goals, teaching and learning activities, along with feedback and assessment.

Application Questions

1. You have been hired as a consultant to redesign a course in higher education. Think about a course you have taken that could be improved. Answer the following questions with that in mind. Specify the course.

   a. Create eight to ten specific questions you would ask the professor to gather information about the situational factors in the course.

   b. What are three overall learning goals for your course that would answer the question, What should students be able to remember three to five years after completing the course?

   c. Design two service learning projects for students to complete.

   d. Briefly explain three assessments for your course. (Do not include tests, quizzes, and writing papers.) Be creative.

2. Evaluate the courses you are taking this semester. How do they fit with Fink's model? Which parts do they include, not include?

References

Allen, M. (2012). *Leaving ADDIE for SAM*. Davners, MA: American Society for Training and Development.

Bain, K. (2004). *What the best college teachers do*. Cambridge, MA: President and Fellows of Harvard College.

Barkley, E. F. (2010). *Student engagement techniques: A handbook for college faculty*. San Francisco: Jossey-Bass.

Bergman, R., & Moore, T. (1990). *Managing interactive video/multimedia project*. Englewood Cliffs, NJ: Educational Technology Publications.

Branson, R. K. (1975). *Interservice procedures for instructional systems development: Executive summary and model*. Tallahassee, FL: Center for Educational Technology, Florida State University. (National Technical Information Service, 5285 Port Royal Rd., Springfield, VA 22161. Document Nos. AD-A019, 486 to AD-A019 490)

Campbell, K., Schwier, R., & Kenny, R. (2009). The critical, relational practice of instructional design in higher education: an emerging model of change agency. *Education Technology Research & Development, 57*, 654–663.

Dick, W., & Carey, L. (2010). *The systematic design of instruction* (5th ed.). New York: Harper Collins College Publishers.

Enkenberg, J. (2001). Instructional design and emerging teaching models in higher education. *Computers in Human Behavior, 17*, 495–506.

Filene, P., & Bain, K. (2010). *The joy of teaching: A practical guide for new college instructors*. Chapel Hill, NC: University of North Carolina Press.

Fink, L. D. (2013). *Creating significant learning experiences: An integrated approach to designing college courses*. San Francisco: Jossey-Bass.

Gerlach, V. S., & Ely, D. P. (1980). *Teaching and media: A systematic approach* (2nd ed.). Englewood Cliffs, NJ: Prentice-Hall Incorporated.

Gustafson, K., & Branch, R. (1997). *Survey of instructional development models*. Syracuse, NY: ERIC Clearinghouse on Information and Technology.

Kagan, S. (2014). Kagan structures, processing, and excellence in college teaching. *Journal on Excellence in College Teaching, 25*(3-4), 119–138.

Kemp, J. E., Morrison, G. R., & Ross, S. M. (1994). *Designing effective instruction*. New York: Merrill.

Leshin, C., Pollock, J., & Reigeluth, C. (1992). *Instructional design: Strategies and tactics for improving learning and performance*. Englewood Cliffs, NJ: Educational Technology Publications.

Merrill, M. D. (2013). *First principles of instruction*. San Francisco: John Wiley & Sons.

Nilson, L. B. (2010). *Teaching at its best: A researched-based resource for college instructors*. San Francisco: Jossey-Bass.

Reiser, R., & Dick, W. (1996). *Instructional planning: A guide for teachers* (2nd ed.). Boston: Allyn and Bacon.

Shaw, K. (2012). Leadership through instructional design in higher education. *Online Journal of Distance Learning Administration, 15*(3).

Smith, P. L., & Ragan, T. J. (1993). *Instructional design*. New York: Macmillan.

Svinicki, M., & McKeachie, W. J. (2014). *McKeachie's teaching tips: Strategies, research, and theory for college and university teachers*. Belmont, CA: Wadsworth.

Terlouw, C. (2014). Instructional design for higher education. *Instructional Design: Volume II: Solving Instructional Design Problems, 341–354.*

Wood, B. (2009). *Lecture free teaching*. Arlington, VA: NSTA Press.

Chapter 22

Instructional Design in Europe: Trends and Issues

Jeroen J. G. van Merrienboer
Maastricht University

Begoña Gros
University of Barcelona

Helmut Niegemann
Saarland University

Introduction

In Europe, instructional design is nonexisting. In Europe, instructional design is a flourishing field. Strange enough, both statements are true. When searching the almost 22,500 master-degree programs offered in higher education in Europe, instructional design and educational technology are almost absent, with only a few exceptions (e.g., Utrecht University in the Netherlands, the University of Murcia in Spain, Saarland University in Germany). Yet, in the European Association for Research on Learning and Instruction (EARLI), the leading European scientific organization in the field of education, Instructional Design, is a popular and active special interest group. Thus, although educational programs with a focus on instructional design and educational technology are rare, researchers and practitioners from educational psychology, educational sciences, learning sciences, pedagogy, media studies, computer sciences, and other scientific disciplines share an interest in instructional design issues and meet each other in this special interest group as well as other organizations.

Yet, the position of instructional design in Europe is clearly different from that in the United States. In the United States, instructional design is a discipline of its own. Admittedly, it is a highly eclectic discipline that tries to apply theory from many different fields to instructional design practice in order to improve learning and produce more efficient instruction, yielding a very large number of instructional design models and approaches (at least more than 100), which greatly differ with regard to context, setting, underlying learning theory, preferred delivery mode, and so forth (Branch & Gustafson, 2002). Nevertheless, it is typically seen as *one* eclectic field

which differs, for example, from the learning sciences. Indeed, the differences and commonalities between instructional design and the learning sciences are a topic of debate in the United States, and some plea for a further integration of the two. In Europe, such a discussion is absent because instructional design is not seen as a discipline of its own, but as a diffuse scientific and practical field in which researchers from many different disciplines meet each other.

The aim of this chapter is to describe the main trends and issues that can be observed in this diffuse field. To make things even more complex, these trends and issues not only occur in a highly diffuse field, but also occur in fifty-one different countries, of which only twenty-eight countries are members of the European Union, and that all have their own educational systems, practices, and policies. Obviously, this chapter cannot do justice to the enormous variation found in these many different countries, and because the authors represent three countries, they describe trends and issues that are shared by the Netherlands, Spain, and Germany—without claiming that they can be found in all other countries in Europe. The forthcoming sections discuss trends and issues in, in order, training in business and industry, vocational education and training (VET), primary and secondary education, and higher education. In the final section, we discuss differences and similarities between the trends and issues in these different fields of application.

Training in Business and Industry

In European business and industry, instructional design is still an unfamiliar field and existing instructional design models and approaches are rarely used for the design of training programs, at least not in a systematic fashion. Training design is typically taken care of by content experts rather than instructional designers or training specialists. Traditionally, two approaches are prevalent: the short-course approach and the on-the-job training approach. The short-course approach is typically driven by emerging training needs that result from the development of new products, services, and technologies. In order to meet these needs, which are often assessed informally rather than through a careful training needs analysis, one or more content experts are invited to set up a course or workshop in which target learners are taught about the new product, service, or technology. The courses are typically short (ranging from a half day to one week) and given at a central location or provided through e-learning applications that focus on information transmission. A strong point of this approach is that it flexibly meets new training needs and provides information that is up to date and presented by true experts. Weaknesses include the often low quality of instruction, with its focus on presentation of new information and less eye for providing meaningful practice and feedback, and, even more important, a low transfer of what is learned from the course to the workplace (Van Wijk, Jansen, & Lyles, 2008).

The on-the-job training approach has its roots in the apprenticeship model, which dates back to the Middle Ages. It comes in different forms. At one extreme, employees learn by working under strict supervision. The supervisor is a content expert and models how the work tasks are performed, sets tasks that the learner can handle, stimulates the learner to explore different approaches to performing those tasks, provides guidance and feedback, and encourages the learner to reflect on his or her own performance and to articulate acquired skills and knowledge (cf. cognitive apprenticeship learning; e.g., Stalmeijer et al., 2013). Often, summative assessments are organized for making go/no-go decisions. This approach is common in fields where safety is important, such as medicine, aviation, and chemical industry. Then, supervision fulfills a dual role: It helps employees to learn but also prevents human errors than can have disastrous effects. At the other extreme, workplace learning can be largely unstructured but supported by some kind of performance appraisal process. That is, regular performance appraisals are organized, plans for improvement and personal development are made, and actions are determined to realize those plans. A coach or mentor, who is not necessarily a content expert, helps the employee to draw up and realize development plans (Swager, Klarus, van Merrienboer, & Nieuwenhuis, 2015). Needless to say, many companies and industries use forms of on-the-job training that are located somewhere between the two extremes.

For a long time, the short-course approach and the on-the-job training approach existed in parallel, with very little integration between the two. At best, a supervisor or coach would recommend a particular course to an employee because it was believed to contribute to his or her learning and development, but an integrated design of on-the-job training and course offerings was out of the question. This situation started to change when competency-based approaches became more popular in Europe in the 1990s. These approaches stress the joint development of job-related knowledge, skills, and attitudes (i.e., professional competencies) as well as the development of higher-order skills dealing with communication, ethics, critical thinking, information literacy, and so forth (i.e., generic competencies; Delamare Le Deist & Winterton, 2005). Working on real-life professional tasks is typically seen as the basis for the development of such competencies, and competency-based training programs often contain practice on professional tasks in both simulated task environments (e.g., role play, computer-based simulation, high-fidelity simulators, serious games) and the real on-the-job environment. Such an integrated approach where one common training design is underlying both on-the-job and off-the-job training had for a long time been limited to highly specific fields such as aviation, but became more and more common with the upsurge of competency-based learning.

Another, more recent trend contributing to the further integration of the short-course approach and the on-the-job training approach is blended learning (e.g., Spanjers et al., 2015). In the short-course approach, e-learning has never been a great success because it proved hard to replace the "real expert," but also because its relation to the workplace was often weak. In a sense, modern approaches can best be seen as "double blended," because they not only integrate e-learning with face-to-face learning, but also learning on the job with learning off the job. In such an integrated design, learners may work on real-life professional tasks in both simulated settings (giving them the opportunity to practice in a safe environment) and on the job. They may consult e-learning resources for information they need for performing these tasks and discuss those resources with peer learners and experts, and they may participate in face-to-face meetings in which they reflect on previously performed tasks and difficulties they encountered and plan future learning activities. In such a double-blended approach, new products, services, and technologies do not directly lead to new short courses with a focus on information transmission, but are first translated into new professional tasks, and the necessary information is taught only in the context of performing those new work tasks, either in a simulated or real professional environment (e.g., van Merrienboer, 2000).

Vocational Education and Training

Vocational education and training (VET) is far from being unitary or even standardized across European countries. While some countries have overriding vocational schools (full time) in different forms, in other countries such as Germany the preferential model for initial vocational education (I-VET) is a dual system. In this dual system, students have apprenticeship contracts with companies for two to three and a half years and, at the same time, are required to visit a state-funded vocational school, typically for 20 percent of their time (i.e., one day per week). This German model has influenced several other countries; for instance, in Spain, some schools have started to introduce the dual system. The quality of VET programs is controlled by the chambers of commerce or chambers of crafts; the curricula are elaborated in cooperation between employers' organizations and employees' organizations (mostly trade unions).

State-licensed certificates are awarded by the chambers after exams. In other countries school-based I-VET is preferred (e.g., in France and the Netherlands), although there do exist dual-system-like forms as there are school-based i-VET forms in Germany, Austria, and other countries with a preference for the dual-system approach.

The current aim of the European Union is not the standardization of the different forms of VET, but quality assurance of certificates as well as the compatibility and comparability of formal qualifications: The European Qualification Framework comprises eight common reference levels, described in terms of learning outcomes. Level 1 stands for "basic general knowledge, basic skills, and work or study under direct supervision in a structured context"; level 8 refers to "knowledge at the most advanced frontier of a field of work or study . . . ," "most advanced and specialized skills and techniques, including synthesis and evaluation . . . ," and "demonstrate substantial authority, innovation, autonomy, scholarly and professional integrity and sustained commitment to the development of new ideas or processes . . . " (European Commission, 2015). This corresponds to the popularity of competence-based approaches with a focus on integration of skills, knowledge, and attitudes. Instructional design approaches such as four-component instructional design (4C/ID; van Merrienboer & Kirschner, 2013) and the framework model DO ID (Niegemann et al., 2008), both of which focus on the integration of various types of outcomes, are quite popular in Germany and countries with a similar system. In VET, the focus is then on taking real-life *professional* tasks as the basis for the design of learning tasks.

While the problem of school-based I-VET is often the gap between the facilities, tools, and machines offered by the vocational school and those offered by companies, a problem of the dual-system approach is the fact that big companies often have much more possibilities to train their apprentices in the full range of competencies whereas small and medium companies (SMCs) are highly specialized and cannot offer this full range. For example, a small rural restaurant that does not offer high-level dishes cannot convey the same range of competencies as a big chain of high-class restaurants, and the same is true for a highly specialized supplier company that produces only specific car parts, compared to a larger company with a much wider range of products. Although there are sometimes centralized courses to compensate for the deficit of competencies, flexible forms of e-learning and blended learning are more often applied in big companies while actually the SMCs would need these methods much more urgently.

Partially in response to the aforementioned problems, several European countries, as well as the European Union, are offering programs to foster the use of multimedia learning environments in SMCs. The Lifelong Learning Program of the European Union granted several projects concerning simulations in VET, for example, in the domain of professional driving (Ball, 2015). However, although simulators cost often 1 million euros or more, the manufacturing companies mostly do not offer much support for the trainers who have to select and to sequence suitable sequences of simulator-based learning tasks. Moreover, database devices to administrate the simulated driving processes, assess failures, and recommend individualized task sequences based on instructional design principles are generally missing.

While outside driving and flying simulations of working tasks is much too expensive for the budgets available in VET, there seems to be a change due to the availability of virtual reality (VR) and augmented reality (AR) glasses (e.g. Oculus Rift®, Google™ Glass). A German project (Glassroom, granted by the federal government) will systematically design and evaluate instructional uses of VR and AR devices in the training of maintenance technicians. VR glasses allow the simulation of almost all technique-related activities without any risk. The focus of instructional design in this domain is on thorough task analyses. To assess critical situations (e.g., failure analyses in case of climate machines) a body cam is used and an experienced technician explains what he or she is doing without the presence of an instructional designer. The video is then analyzed using task analyses procedures (e.g., Jonassen, Tessmer, & Hannum, 1989) to generate authentic simulation tasks. The use of AR glasses should support novices during their actual work by providing necessary information to fulfill difficult tasks, for instance, to overhaul a high-tech agricultural machine the technician sees in the display of the AR glasses relevant parts of the wired plan.

Serious games, which could often be seen as a kind of simulation-based learning, are yet rarely used in VET. Despite many innovative projects in the European Union such approaches are not yet standard, neither in big companies nor in SMCs, mainly due to their high development costs. An interesting exception in Dutch senior vocational education is CRAFT: It offers a game-facilitated curriculum based on 4C/ID, in the field of mechatronics (van Bussel, Lukosch, & Meijer, 2014). CRAFT contains a simulated workplace with virtual machines that students can use to build all kinds of mechatronic products, and an amusement park in which they can build attractions from these products; these attractions can be shared with friends and family. CRAFT is not just a serious game but a tool to provide a game-facilitated curriculum: It sets learning tasks that students perform in the simulated workplace in the game, it sets learning tasks that students perform on real machines in the school setting, and it sets learning tasks that student perform as interns at the workplace. These learning tasks are either assessed by the game, the teacher, or the workplace supervisor, and *all* student assessments are fed back into the game. This offers the possibility to monitor student progress and to adapt the provision of learning tasks to the individual needs of students, yielding a highly flexible curriculum.

Primary and Secondary Education

Primary and secondary education comprise the period of compulsory education in all European countries, yet there are large differences in how it is organized in different countries (European Commission, 2014). In 2011, the International Standard Classification of Education (ISCED) was introduced, making it possible to collect statistical data for making comparisons. For primary and secondary education, relevant levels are ISCED 1 (primary education; legal age of entry is usually not below five years old nor above seven years old and its duration can range between four and seven years); ISCED 2 (lower secondary education; students typically enter this level between ages ten and thirteen, although age twelve is most common); and ISCED 3 (upper secondary education; students typically enter this level between ages fourteen and sixteen). There are three main models of organization:

1. *Single structure education.* Education is provided from the beginning to the end of compulsory schooling, with no transition between primary and lower secondary education, and with general education provided in common for all pupils (e.g., Norway, Sweden, Czech Republic, Hungary).
2. *Common core curriculum.* After successful completion of primary education, all children progress to lower secondary education where they follow the same general common core curriculum (e.g., United Kingdom, France, Spain, Italy).
3. *Differentiated lower secondary education.* After successful completion of primary education, children are required to follow distinct educational pathways in lower secondary education (e.g., Germany, the Netherlands, Austria, Lithuania).

Despite large differences in educational systems, Europe has succeeded in the policy of "school for all." With very rare exceptions, the rate of compulsory schooling attendance in European countries is 100 percent. In all countries, primary and secondary school curricula pay ample attention to language, foreign languages, mathematics and science, personal and life skills, and ethical values. Yet, the insight is growing that mastery of reading, writing, and arithmetic and, in secondary education, also other school subjects, is a necessary but not a sufficient condition for a successful adult life. As a result, more and more attention is paid to generic or twenty-first-century skills such as communication and teamwork, problem solving and reasoning, creative and analytical thinking, learning-to-learn, and so forth (Voogt, Erstad, Dede, & Mishra, 2013). The inclusion of twenty-first-century skills demands significant changes in the already overloaded curricula. Because it seems impossible to make room for new subjects or new content within traditional subjects, these changes are typically realized through the use of new instructional methods and assessment procedures.

Some schools try to integrate twenty-first-century skills across the curriculum in such a way that they underpin all different school subjects; other schools try to transform the traditional structure of school subjects in such a way that they can more easily be integrated with twenty-first-century skills. This transformation affects both the contents of the curriculum and the instructional methods used. With regard to the contents, there is a tendency to integrate school subjects in broader multidisciplinary themes; for example, secondary education in the Netherlands distinguishes the themes *Culture and Society*, emphasizing arts and foreign languages; *Economy and Society*, emphasizing social sciences, economics, and history; *Nature and Health*, emphasizing biology and natural sciences; and *Nature and Technology*, emphasizing natural sciences. With regard to instructional methods, there is a tendency to make increasing use of projects or other rich learning tasks, which require students to work on challenging multidisciplinary projects offering them the opportunity to learn knowledge and skills related to traditional school subjects in direct connection to twenty-first-century skills. For example, so-called *Technasia* in the Netherlands, which are schools for pre-university education with a focus on technology, have a central learning trajectory called "Research and Design," in which students work in small groups on technological projects formulated by companies and universities. This approach is consistent with holistic instructional design models such as Merrill's first principles of instruction (2013) and van Merrienboer's 4C/ID-model (van Merrienboer & Kirschner, 2013) that focus curriculum design around real-life tasks. Whereas in VET the real-life tasks are typically taken from the professions, in primary and secondary education they are typically taken from daily life, society, or science.

Although most European countries are heavily investing in the information and communications technology (ICT) infrastructure of primary and secondary schools, and stand-alone "drill-and-practice" applications for learning basic skills (math, spelling, etc.) are quite popular, until now ICT has not fundamentally changed teaching and learning processes. Yet, three recent developments might eventually lead to a breakthrough. First, the "flipped classroom" model is quickly gaining popularity in, especially, secondary education (Touron & Santiago, 2015). In this model, some or most of the direct instruction is no longer delivered by the teacher in front of the classroom, but made available using video lectures or other modes of online delivery. The freed-up time in class can then be used to work in smaller discussion groups and/or work on assignments and projects that also allow for the development of twenty-first-century skills. Thus, the flipped classroom nicely complements multidisciplinary project-based learning as previously described. Second, ICT-based systems for student monitoring are becoming increasingly popular in, especially, primary education (Tymms, 2013). Such systems provide the teacher with progress information of his or her students, so that instruction can be better tailored to the needs of individual learners (individualization) or subgroups of learners (differentiation). This need to tailor instruction to individual needs will increase when not all learners simultaneously listen to the same lecture or work on the same assignment, but work in small groups on different multidisciplinary problems. Third, new mobile technologies such as tablet computers support both of the aforementioned developments in "iPad schools" or "tablet classes," because they provide a flexible solution for studying multimedia information anytime anywhere, and can also provide the data necessary for student monitoring.

Higher Education

In the last decade, an important development in higher education in Europe has been labeled the "Bologna process," which refers to a series of meetings and agreements between European countries designed to ensure comparability in the standards and quality of higher education (cf. the European Qualification Framework in VET). This process promoted a strong emphasis on the development of structural reforms, such as one common European system of academic degrees (the bachelor-master or

BAMA system) and study credits (European Credit Transfer System or ECTS). At the same time, the learning and teaching process in higher education is undergoing important developments caused by rapid social changes, with much more student mobility between European countries, a higher share of non-European students, and the influence of ICT. Thus instructional design must take more complex learning scenarios into account, yielding a customized learning system that can be accessed from anywhere and at any time. Flexibility and personalization are becoming important elements in the design of learning in higher education.

Distance education pedagogy and e-learning have a strong influence on European higher education, creating new modalities of learning often involving a combination of face-to-face activities and online learning (i.e., blended learning). Anderson and Dron (2012) divide distance education pedagogy into three categories: cognitive behaviorism, social constructivism, and connectivism. Their definition of cognitive behaviorism refers to the pre-Web period of printed materials, television, and radio; social constructivism is defined as the Web 1.0 and teleconference period; connectivism refers to the communication and interaction processes provided by Web 2.0 and social networks. The connectivism approach promoted the initial development of massive open online courses (MOOCs), which enabled thousands of learners to participate in the same course, accessing the content and using tools for interaction with other course participants.

The Open Education Europa portal[1] indicates a very strong interest in MOOCs in Spain, the United Kingdom, France, and Germany. The Spanish UNED (National University of Distance Education) has a significant share of the nearly 300 MOOCs available in the Spanish language. The British platform FutureLearn, led by the British Open University, comprises twenty-six partners in total, including the British Library, the British Museum, and the British Council. In France, the government has launched France Université Numérique, the first French digital learning portal. Its MOOC platform is one of the eighteen actions in a five-year strategic plan for the digitalization of learning and teaching in France. The German platform for online teaching—iversity[2]—was founded in 2008 as an academic collaboration platform and incorporated in 2011. It offers MOOCs in the German and English language and has announced that two higher education institutions using its platform will award ECTS credits. With regard to the design of the MOOCs, we see a movement from traditional cMOOCS based on connectivism and stressing autonomy, diversity, interactivity, and openness (Downes, 2014) to so-called xMOOCS. According to Bates (2014), six design principles for xMOOCs include the use of (1) video lectures, (2) computer-marked assignments, (3) peer assessment, (4) supporting materials, (5) badges or certificates, and (6) learning analytics. In addition, research is being conducted on the use of small-group work in MOOCs. For example, Maastricht University in the Netherlands is a problem-based learning (PBL) university that also applies PBL principles, including the use of small-group activities, in its MOOCs.[3]

MOOCs fit in a broader development in which students' interests and preferences are becoming increasingly important. Some approaches have explored student participation in planning and designing the curriculum, considering that incorporating their perspective on teaching and learning could be beneficial for students and teachers. The "student engagement" approach considers that enabling students to participate may encourage them to take control, reflect and become more aware of their learning process, and foster the adoption of deep-learning approaches (Bain & Zimmerman, 2009). The "student voice" approach recognizes students' perceptions and experiences of their learning as unique and essential for improving education (Bovill, Cook-Sather, & Felten, 2011). Current research on incorporating students' voice has shown that providing more options, control, challenges, and opportunities to collaborate increases motivation and commitment (Toshalis & Nakkula, 2012). In higher education, students are also involved in academic research together with teachers and being considered as "producers" or "researchers." This makes students key agents in a radical transformation of higher education institutions, creating a new social institution in which values are revised and openness and knowledge sharing is promoted (Neary, 2012).

Discussion

This chapter made an attempt to discuss trends and issues in instructional design in Europe. Yet, the position of instructional design in Europe is different from its position in the United States, trends and issues in instructional design are markedly different between European countries, and they are also different between application fields such as business and industry, vocational education and training, primary and secondary education, and higher education. Thus, there are many more differences than similarities. If we nevertheless had to identify one trend, with regard to both instructional contents (What is taught?) and instructional methods (How it is taught?), it would be *integration*. With regard to contents, in business and industry, the teaching of job-related knowledge and skills is more and more integrated with the teaching of generic competencies; in primary and secondary education, traditional school subjects are increasingly integrated in broader themes including both subject-matter knowledge and twenty-first-century skills; in VET, professional competencies replace the traditional triple of knowledge, skills, and attitudes; and in higher education, students are increasingly involved in research and real-life projects, not only to develop their academic competencies but also to give them more control over their own learning trajectories. With regard to methods, in business and industry as well as in VET, we see a further integration of both face-to-face learning and e-learning as well as on-the-job and off-the-job learning (leading to "double-blended" programs); in primary and secondary education, we see a further integration of homework with schoolwork, where students prepare at home for (multidisciplinary) project work at school (flipped classroom);

---

[1]http://openeducationeuropa.eu/

[2]https://iversity.org/

[3]https://moocs.maastrichtuniversity.nl/

and in higher education, we see the integration of e-learning (especially, MOOCs) with campus-based work on projects and problems, leading to more flexible programs and open curricula.

In this chapter's introduction, we already indicated that the position of instructional design in Europe is different from that in the United States: It is not a discipline of its own, but together with educational technology it forms a more diffuse field in which researchers and practitioners from many different disciplines meet each other. What holds this field together is not only a common interest in instructional design and educational technology issues, but also European policies (reports, guidelines) that set common themes and create contexts that are becoming more and more similar between European countries. This is evident in business and industry, where open borders created a European market in which most companies operate in different countries but have one approach to training and development. In VET, steps are taken toward a European Qualification Framework to make certificates comparable and compatible with each other. In primary and secondary education, there is still a great diversity of systems but even the classification systems make it at least possible to collect data on a European scale and to make comparisons. In higher education, the Bologna process led to one academic degree system and a European Credit Transfer System that facilitates mobility of students between European countries.

Conclusion

To conclude, instructional design in Europe is a diffuse but lively field. Given the policies and trends in Europe we expect it to become even more important in the future. First, there is an increasing need for "complex learning" (e.g., van Merrienboer & Kirschner, 2013), aimed at either the simultaneous development and integration of knowledge, skills, and attitudes or the development of professional and generic competencies. Second, there is an increasing need for more flexible educational programs that use a rich media mix of e-learning and face-to-face learning as well as off-the-job and on-the-job learning. Powerful instructional design models and the expertise of instructional designers are badly needed to meet those needs.

Summary of Key Principles

1. **In Europe, instructional design is a diffuse scientific and practical field.** There are very few educational programs called either "Instructional Design" or "Educational Technology" in Europe. But there are active scientific and professional organizations dedicated to instructional design issues, with members from many different disciplines.

2. **Double-blended approaches are becoming popular in business and industry and in VET.** In double-blended approaches, educational programs not only combine face-to-face learning and e-learning, but also off-the-job learning and on-the-job learning (for VET: internships).

3. **Real-life professional tasks are increasingly used as the basis for the design of learning tasks in VET.** Although this nicely fits the use of simulated task environments, virtual reality, augmented reality, and games, their use is still curbed by the relatively high development costs.

4. **Traditional school subjects are more and more integrated and intertwined with twenty-first-century skills in primary and secondary education.** Multidisciplinary projects make such integration possible: Flipped-classroom models are becoming popular so that students study online-information at home and can apply this to multidisciplinary projects in school.

5. **Flexibility through the use of e-learning is an important aim in higher education.** Higher education aims to adapt more to individual learning needs of an increasingly diverse student population, and e-learning applications such as MOOCs play an important role in that.

6. **The main instructional design trend in Europe deals with integration.** This relates to the integration of contents and learning goals, for example, in multidisciplinary themes or professional and generic competencies; and it relates to the integration of instructional methods, such as online learning with face-to-face learning, off-the-job learning with on-the-job learning, and so forth.

Application Questions

1. A European company for electrical installations in buildings develops every year new technical products and solutions. The clients are about 100,000 crafts enterprises (e.g., companies active in lighting, heating and air conditioning, home electronics) in Europe. When a new product is released all clients have to be instructed in a very short time span. Additionally, there should be instructional materials for apprentices and students of vocational schools in different European countries. Imagine you are an instructional design consultant for this European company. Describe a possible solution to instruct all the target persons.

2. In 2015–2016, more than 1.5 million refugees will come to Europe from Syria and other countries in the Middle East. Most of them do not speak English or any other European language. In many cases, their vocational qualifications do not fully conform to the European standards. Expecting a longer stay in Europe, these refugees should be integrated into the European economies. Imagine you are a VET

consultant for the European Union. Develop a plan for integrating refugees from the Middle East into the European vocational systems.

3. In Europe, primary and secondary education can take the form of single-structure education, a common core curriculum, or differentiated lower secondary education. Which form does it take in the country where you live? Each system has its own challenges from an instructional design perspective. For example, individualized instruction might be especially effective in single-structure education because this systems deals with highly heterogeneous groups of students. Which trends do you see as particularly important in your country given its system of primary and secondary education?

References

Anderson, T., & Dron, J. (2012, September). Learning technology through three generations of technology enhanced distance education pedagogy. *European Journal of Open, Distance and E-learning*. Retrieved from http://www.eurodl.org/

Bain, K., & Zimmerman, J. (2009). Understanding great teaching. *Peer Review, 11*(2), 9–12.

Ball, C. (Ed.). (2015). *Proceedings of the Conference Transport Meets Education* (Potsdam/Germany 12.-13.02.2015). Stuttgart, Germany: etmServices.

Bates, T. (2014). *Comparing xMOOCs and cMOOCs: Philosophy and practice*. Retrieved from http://www.tonybates .ca/2014/10/13/comparing-xmoocs-and-cmoocs-philosophy-and-practice/#sthash.DOCQbLJN.dpuf

Bovill, C., Cook-Sather, A., & Felten, P. (2011). Students as co-creators of teaching approaches, course design and curricula: Implications for academic developers. *International Journal for Academic Development, 16*, 133–145.

Branch, R., & Gustafson, K. (2002). What is instructional design? In R. Reiser & J. Dempsey (Eds.), *Trends and issues in instructional design and technology* (pp. 17–25). Upper Saddle River, NJ: Pearson Education.

Delamare Le Deist, F., & Winterton, J. (2005). What is competence? *Human Resource Development International, 8*, 27–46.

Downes, S. (2014). The MOOC of one: Personal learning technologies. *INTED2014 Proceedings*, 4757-4757.

European Commission. (2014). *The structure of the European education systems 2014/2015: Schematic diagrams*. Brussels, Belgium: European Commission.

European Commission. (2015). Learning opportunities and qualifications in Europe. Retrieved from https://ec.europa.eu/ ploteus/search/site?f%5B0%5D=im_field_entity_type%3A97

Jonassen, D. H., Tessmer, M., & Hannum, W. H. (1999). *Task analysis methods for instructional design*. Mahwah, NJ: Erlbaum.

Merrill, M. D. (2013). *First principles of instruction*. New York: Wiley.

Neary, M. (2012). Student as producer: An institution of the common? [Or how to recover communist/revolutionary science]. *Enhancing Learning in the Social Sciences, 4*(3), 16–24.

Niegemann, H. M., Domagk, S., Hessel, S., Hein, A., Hupfer, M., & Zobel, A. (2008). *Kompendium multimediales Lernen* [Compendium of Multimedia Learning]. Heidelberg, Germany: Springer.

Spanjers, I. A. E., Konings, K. D., Leppink, J., Verstegen, D. M. L., De Jong, N., Czabanowska, K., & van Merrienboer, J. J. G. (2015). The promised land of blended learning. *Educational Research Review, 15*, 59–74.

Stalmeijer, R. E., Dolmans, D. H. J. M., Snellen-Balendong, H., van Santen-Hoeufft, M., Wolfhagen, I. H.A.P., & Scherpbier, A. J. J. A. (2013). Clinical teaching based on principles of cognitive apprenticeship: Views of experienced clinical teachers. *Academic Medicine, 88*, 861–865.

Swager, R., Klarus, R., van Merrienboer, J. J. G., & Nieuwenhuis, L. F. M. (2015). Constituent aspects of workplace guidance in secondary VET. *European Journal of Training and Development, 39*, 358–372.

Toshalis, E., & Nakkula, M. J. (2012). Motivation, engagement, and student voice. In N. Hoffman, A. Steinberg, & R. Wolfe (Eds.), *The students at the center series* (pp. 1–42). Washington, DC: Jobs for the Future.

Touron, J., & Santiago, R. (2015). Flipped learning model and the development of talent at school. *Revista de Education, 368*, 196–231.

Tymms, P. (2013). *Baseline assessment and monitoring in primary schools*. London, UK: Routledge.

van Bussel, R., Lukosch, H., & Meijer, S. A. (2014). Effects of a game-facilitated curriculum on technical knowledge and skill development. In S. A. Meijer & R. Smeds (Eds.), *Frontiers in gaming simulation* (pp. 93–101). Berlin, Germany: Springer.

van Merrienboer, J. J. G. (2000). The end of software training? *Journal of Computer Assisted Learning, 16*, 366–375.

van Merrienboer, J. J. G., & Kirschner, P. A. (2013). *Ten steps to complex learning* (2nd rev. ed.). New York: Routledge.

Van Wijk, R., Jansen, J. J. P., & Lyles, M. A. (2008). Inter- and intra-organizational knowledge transfer: A meta-analytic review and assessment of its antecedents and consequences. *Journal of Management Studies, 45*, 830–853.

Voogt, J., Erstad, O., Dede, C., & Mishra, P. (2013). Challenges to learning and schooling in the digital networked world of the 21st century. *Journal of Computer Assisted Learning, 29*, 403–413.

Chapter 23

Instructional Design and Technology in an Asian Context: Focusing on Japan and Korea

Katsuaki Suzuki

Kumamoto University

Insung Jung

International Christian University, Tokyo

In several Asian countries, such as South Korea, China, and Taiwan, governmental initiatives to support adoption of media and technology in education and training have stimulated the growth of instructional design and technology (IDT) as a specialized field. In this chapter, we focus on two distinctive contexts in Asia—Japan and South Korea (Korea hereafter). To Western eyes, Japan and Korea appear to have much in common. As observed by Latchem, Jung, Aoki, and Ozkul (2008), both have inherited Confucian, Buddhist, and other cultural manifestations from China and have become great industrial powers by adopting and adapting Western ideas and inventions. Both countries have highly sophisticated high-tech industries and highly developed digital infrastructures. Both highly value education and teachers, human contact, and both have attempted to reform their education systems for the twenty-first-century world. However, as shown in this chapter, when it comes to the application and development of IDT, Japan and Korea are quite different from Western countries and from each other. And each presents unique challenges. In this chapter, we take turns describing each of these settings in detail in order to provide insights into these differences, causes, and consequences.

The Case of Japan[1]

Introduction

As an industrialized country that shares a similar technological environment for teaching and learning with the rest of the industrialized world, Japan has long had a prominent position among the leaders in the world economy. However, the field of

IDT is different from the rest of the world because of Japan's unique way of combining rapid westernization with a long history of Asian culture. It may well depend on people, rather than technology. It may also depend on how an organization has been maintained: How is it different? How is it similar?

Japan has been a country of mystery to Western eyes. It is known as the country of Geisha girls and Shogun, Hara-kiri, and Sukiyaki song. It is also known as a country that once, before and during World War II, had a fascist regime and then became a democracy. The miracle comeback from postwar state to become a leading industrial country has attracted many researchers hoping to find out how it happened and to learn from it.

Total quality management, a technique invented in Japan but now exported from the United States back to Japan, is one of the results of such investigations. The bestselling book *Japan as Number One* (Vogel, 1980) and Prof. Nonaka, guru of knowledge management, with his theory of implicit vs. explicit knowledge (Nonaka, 1994), have caught much attention and are seen as clues to uncover the Japanese miracle.

Japan has thus been full of mystery and stereotypes. How is the practice of IDT in Japan different from that of the Western world? In this section, you will find out how the IDT situation in Japan may be different from or similar to the world you are acquainted with. We will look at the business and industry sector first and then proceed to the schools.

IDT Brought to Japan With the E-Learning Movement

Professionals called instructional designers or educational technologists have not been known in Japan until very recently.

---

[1]This case was authored by Katsuaki Suzuki.

IDT captured the interests of the human resource development (HRD) sector of the Japanese business and industry only with the emergence of e-learning.

The year 2000 is considered to have marked the beginning of e-learning in Japan. An important event in that context was the compilation and publication of the *E-Learning White Book* by the Advanced Learning Infrastructures Consortium (ALIC, 2001), an affiliated organization of the Japanese Ministry of Economy, Trade and Industry. Such training technologies as computer-based and web-based instruction, multimedia use, and Internet-based learning merged under the name of e-learning, a term that since got firmly established. IDT was seen as a "new technique" and a key tool to improve and assure the quality and effectiveness of e-learning.

IDT, as it emerged in the Japanese e-learning industry, meant at first no more than designing appealing and usable screens and providing structure to learning materials. The focus was on better screen layout, adequate use of fonts and colors, and easier navigation techniques. The purpose was to give the materials a professional look. The word "design" played a certain role in leading people to think of the "new technique" as having something to do with visual and artistic design of e-learning. However, they did not understand in what way IDT was different from usability design and visual design.

It took time before the focus shifted to the systematic process for bringing about effective results in education and training. Only after that happened, analyses of training needs, participants, contexts, and available resources were taught as essential steps of IDT. Examples of these included a two-day seminar to introduce the ADDIE model (Analysis → Design → Development → Implementation → Evaluation) to the development of instruction, a one-day workshop on how to use the *Instructional Designer's Tool Kit*, and a five-day workshop to become familiar with the basics of the design and development of e-learning material. Lee and Owen's (2000) *Multimedia-based Instructional Design* was translated into Japanese as the first major introductory text on IDT in 2003. Even so, it was still difficult for the Japanese readers to understand in what way IDT was different from project management.

The availability of IDT training materials in Japan grows slowly but steadily. The author of this section, for instance, wrote an introductory book in 2002, *Instructional Materials Design Manual*, based on the Dick and Carey model. The Japanese translation of the well-known Dick, Carey, and Carey (2001) book became available in 2004. In 2006, Japan's first online master's program in instructional systems was established at Kumamoto University to train e-learning professionals in business and industry. The Japan e-learning Consortium started its e-learning professional certification program in 2008. Several major works in IDT have been translated, including Gagné, Wager, Golas, and Keller's (2005) *Principles of Instructional Design* (5th edition in 2007); Keller's (2009) *Motivational Design for Learning and Performance* in 2010; and the third edition of this book (Reiser & Dempsey, 2011).

IDT that combines usability design, project management, and research-based instructional design principles is gradually becoming a recognizable consideration in business and industry. Nevertheless, another big step forward needs to be made. The idea that IDT, in the sense of the design and development of instructional materials, should be combined with notions of performance technology that connect training and a company's business strategies must gain greater popularity before a really big impact on the practice of HRD can be expected. Paradoxically, this process has gradually become noticed by the current decline in economic growth in Japan. The economic situation has attracted more professionals than ever to become interested in better quality of HRD, higher effectiveness of training, and the design of change processes to better prepare companies to play their part in the unclear and ever-changing world of the knowledge society. ASTD Japan was established in 2007, which has been translating ASTD global basic series into Japanese, including such topics as organizational development, human performance improvement, succession planning, leadership development, since 2011.

IDT Before the Advent of E-Learning

My earlier assertion that IDT only came to Japan with the advent of e-learning should not be interpreted to mean that media and technology were not used in training prior to that time. Although it has been and still is common for many training sessions to be conducted by live instructors in face-to-face group settings, media and technology have been used in many training scenarios. Especially after the CD-ROM drive became a standard part of all personal computers, ample learning materials for this medium entered the consumer and business market. With the advance of the Internet, many online learning materials also appeared on the market. This trend formed a strong basis for the development of an e-learning infrastructure.

On the other hand, the majority of media-based training materials have not yet fully utilized IDT research-based principles. Many of the available materials are no more than books or instructor lectures transformed into electronic media. The lack of analysis and design and an almost total dependence on experience-based rules of thumb can likely be identified as a major factor limiting IDT's adoption. The reason why IDT only appeared with the emergence of the e-learning movement is simple. There were no IDT specialists trained in Japan. At the time of this writing, we still have only one graduate program that produces IDT specialists in business and industry (Suzuki, 2009). Moreover, unlike the United States, there are almost no graduate programs in colleges of education geared toward training in business and industry. The focus in such schools has been on teacher education to prepare educational personnel for the K–12 school system. Yet another reason why IDT has not been fully employed in Japan can be gleaned from a more detailed look at the tradition of HRD in Japanese business and industry.

Non-IDT Characteristics of HRD in Japan

While there has been a long history of the existence of education and training sections in larger business firms in Japan, there has been little concern for the quality of the training or for adequate return on investment (ROI). Until the collapse of the economy in the late 1980s, the high-growth economy helped companies make profits without seriously training their employees. The major concern of companies was to produce as much as possible. The more they could produce, the more they could sell. Thus, HRD was solely concerned with productivity, not with the personal growth of employees.

The training function, consequently, has long been regarded as a way to reward employees for their daily good work. The thought behind it was that it is "nice to have a retreat from time-to-time from the daily chores." The expectation behind offering training was that it would refresh the employees by taking them to a remote training facility, letting them escape from the noise and hassle of their daily routine. Consequently, it was thought employees would come back to work with a revitalized state of mind. Major companies even tried to attract recruits by making them aware of their excellent training facilities in famous resort areas, rather than by reference to the content and effectiveness of their training programs for personal growth. The content of the training did not need to be readily applicable to the next day's duties, nor to building the employees' job-related competency. Training was merely expected to provide a mindset for the future, in rather indirect ways.

While comparing systems and traditional approaches, Hannum and Briggs (1982) pointed out that in traditional training (a) content comes solely from instructors' experience, (b) instructional strategies are experience based, (c) tests are full of surprises, (d) expected test results are normally distributed, and (e) should instruction fail, it is considered that the trainees need more time and effort. It is fair to say that the traditional approach as described by Hannum and Briggs still characterizes most of the training conducted in Japan today.

As a rule, Japanese companies do not consider their training divisions to be organizational entities made up of specialized professionals. Rather, they consider positions in a training division to be a temporary stopover for those who occupy them. People come and go as they advance along their career paths. So, it is rare for a person to stay more than, say, two or three years in a training division before moving on to another job assignment. It is equally rare for accumulated IDT-related knowledge and skills to remain within the training division. Even though organizations are responsible for the success of the training of new employees as well as for the follow-up training of employees who are in their second or higher year with the company, the provision of training remains largely intuitive and based on the commonsense principle that past experience can best be repeated. Trainers also take strong cues from how they were themselves taught in school during their childhood, especially the chalk-and-talk approach.

IDT in Japanese Schools

The emergence of a new technology has always been an opportunity for the IDT field to guide its introduction in the school context. This has been the case when audiovisual aids and personal computers first appeared. It holds equally true for the educational opportunities that result from the introduction of the Internet and the World Wide Web. Such challenges require teachers to think about how they can best integrate the new technology in their existing teaching repertoire and what implications this has for the redesign of their instruction.

The recent emphasis in Japan on the use of information communication technology (ICT) in the classroom may thus become an opportunity for IDT-related concepts and techniques to be disseminated amongst school teachers.

In April 2009, the Ministry of Education, Culture, Sports, Science and Technology Japan (MEXT) announced its initiative called "School New Deal Plan" to advance ICT in schools. Year 2009 marked another epoch in ICT education in Japan. MEXT published an expanded (second edition) version of the *Handbook for ICT Education*. No portion of the *Handbook* has been made available in English, but three aims of ICT education remain the same in the second edition of the *Handbook*, which were set forth in the first edition in 1990: (1) skills for information utilization, (2) scientific understanding of information, and (3) participatory attitude toward information society. With those purposes in mind, "Integrated Study" was introduced in curricula from grades 3 to 12 (three hours/week until grade 9) in 2002, and "Information" was created in 2003 as a compulsory new subject in high school curriculum (a single two-unit course in three years), both of which are still included in the curriculum.

More recently, one-to-one mobile devices have been tested in experimental schools (future school project) sponsored by the government during 2010–2013, resulting in proposed guidelines. The movement of flipped classroom has caught the attention of many innovative schoolteachers. MEXT has started advocating "active learning" to be introduced as the keyword for fostering the twenty-first-century skills, not only for universities, but also for K–12 school reform. The Japan Open Online Education Promotion Council (or the JMOOC for short, http://www.jmooc.jp/en/) was established in 2013, with two first courses offered as JMOOC Jr. for K–12 education in 2014.

Government has thus been offering teacher training in basic ICT-related skills and ICT-enhanced instruction as well as training seminars for school-based ICT leaders from early years (Akahori, Horiguchi, Suzuki, & Nambu, 2001). Many opportunities have been developed online for teachers to access ICT-related skill development and good practices and tips for their teaching. In addition, during preservice teacher training in teacher certificate programs at the college level, a two-credit 'ICT basics' course is required for all teacher licenses. However, reluctant or technophobic teachers may receive no further training once they have their licenses. There are no strong demands or regulations specifying how much ICT should be incorporated in the teaching of a particular subject area. So, those teachers who like to use ICT will try and become capable of effective ICT utilization, whereas those who do not use ICT now may remain nonusers for the rest of their career. Thus the digital divide may well grow among teachers (and those students who are in their classrooms), rather than be diminished.

Good Practices Continue: Where the Japanese Mindset Is Fostered

Although IDT has a weak tradition as a specialization, many Japanese schoolteachers have been creative enough to develop their own teaching styles. There are many methodologies that groups of teachers of a particular subject area have created and that they share as their traditions. This creative process is widely known as lesson study (e.g., Lewis, 2002). Through this process, the teaching tradition of Japan has thus formulated subject-matter-specific principles for the design of instruction. In other words, teachers can be regarded as instructional designers in the area of their own subjects.

Because the tradition in each subject area plays such an influential role among Japanese schoolteachers, teaching methods tend to be transmitted from the older to the younger generation. Until the late 1970s, the so-called "overnight alert," in which a small group of teachers stayed awake and engaged in informal communication late into the night, was part of teachers' duties. It is said that these late-night talks created good opportunities for sharing the wisdom of older teachers with younger ones. MEXT has since established a mentorship program for first-year teachers, to make such an informal sharing of traditions official, but it is difficult to say how much of the school traditions are simply transmitted with official training sessions and to what extent new ones are being created.

Becoming a schoolteacher is still a very competitive matter in Japan and the teaching profession still commands great respect. Local organizations of teachers in all subjects play an important role in nurturing the development of high-quality activities, even without the help of colleges of education and the government. Japan will continue to foster the younger generations' ability to learn effectively using various media and technologies, as schoolteachers maintain their creative and high-quality practices of teaching, widely known to the Western world as "lesson studies" (e.g., Fernandez & Yoshida, 2004).

The Case of Korea[2]

IDT in Corporations

To illustrate recent IDT practice in a Korean corporation, let us introduce you to Ms. Lee Youngmin, an experienced instructional designer who is chief project manager of a premier e-learning firm that has produced over 1,000 e-learning courses and programs for over 1,000 companies, government agencies, universities, teacher training institutions, and public organizations. Ms. Lee holds a master's degree in IDT and has over ten years of experience in corporate e-learning. She began her career in a small e-learning company spending hours doing extensive storyboarding. Many of her colleagues left the company after a couple of years—some to study graduate programs in IDT or HRD overseas, some to become teachers, some to join HRD units in large companies, and some to join e-learning or IDT centers in higher education institutions. But Ms. Lee persisted in her work, became a senior instructional designer five years later, and one of the chief project managers seven years after that. In the latter capacity, she manages several e-learning development projects, meets clients to assess their needs, talks with subject-matter experts and conducts task/content analysis, develops standardized storyboarding formats, and arranges multimedia production schedules. In addition, she supervises less experienced instructional designers and presents the final

e-learning products to the clients. She fully understands that IDT and e-learning needs to be of the highest quality and reflect theory and research but at the same time, she has limited time and funds to conduct proper needs and task analysis, and apply individualized or constructivist instructional strategies in e-learning design. Therefore, most of her e-learning courses follow the company's standardized templates for content presentation, apply similar screen design layouts illustrated by in-house graphic designers, and take the form of video-lectures-on-demand with some additional PowerPoint materials. But Ms. Lee also manages to develop at least one or two exemplary e-learning courses applying systemic IDT procedures more rigorously and she sometimes employs constructivist or other innovative approaches.

When we describe the kind of work you'd do as an instructional designer in Korea, it is important to realize that you might be called upon to perform in different roles in different contexts. In some settings, you might simply be expected to concern yourself with drawing up specifications for the instructional process before the actual development is undertaken by others. In others, you might be expected to see through the project in the role of course developer or as computer or web technology expert. In some cases, you might be involved at the needs assessment and task analysis stages, in others with graphic and screen layout design, and with yet others in actually evaluating the learning processes and outcomes. In some organizations, you might be the only instructional designer. In others you might be working with other instructional designers or in multidisciplinary course development teams. Your employers' expectations of your qualifications and experience may also differ as may their expectations of you as an instructional designer. You may need to bear these points in mind as we describe the role, work, and status of instructional designers in Korea.

Companies that develop and deliver e-learning courses or programs either employ in-house instructional designers or outsource the work to freelancers. As a newly appointed instructional designer with one of these companies, you could probably expect to spend most of your early years storyboarding. Rather than being involved in the kinds of exciting creative design activities you experienced during your formal studies, you would find that you were expected to conform to the requirements of the more senior instructional designers or content experts. You would work to the company's standardized templates for content presentation, apply the oft-repeated screen design layouts of the in-house graphic designers, and mainly employ video-lectures-on-demand and PowerPoint material. With the recent introduction of Web 2.0/Web 3.0 technologies and social media in education and training, you would occasionally be asked to develop bits-sized video-based content, promote virtual learning communities, apply AI (artificial intelligence) concepts in ID, promote user-created content development, all of which require the refinement and update of your IDT competencies (Lee, Park, & Song, 2014).

In general, you would be working under pressure on a number of projects and programs and would neither have the time nor the funds to apply systemic IDT procedures more thoroughly or employ the interactive and innovative principles

---

[2]This case was authored by Insung Jung.

you had been taught in your studies. Understandably, you would find such repetitive, low-level work boring and unfulfilling, and not surprisingly, about 50 percent of your fellow instructional designers would leave the company and be lost to the field of IDT forever. As they leave, you might well find that their positions tended to be filled with non-IDT majors, partly because there is such a shortage and such a high demand for instructional designers. Those of you who do stay on with the companies may eventually graduate to more interesting and challenging IDT work and enjoy closer working contact with the clients. With further experience or further studies in IDT, you may even move up to become a project manager.

As noted in several studies, e-learning has been more strategically targeted by the Korean government than has been the case in Japan and indeed many other countries. Bonk (2004) observed in the early 2000s that Korea had already entered the mass adoption stage, and Innovation Centre Denmark Seoul (2014) reports that with the continuous support from various ministries and agencies of the government, e-learning in Korea keeps growing. With the rapid growth of corporate e-learning in the late 1990s, the concept of IDT has been more intensely applied in corporate training in Korea. The larger companies are keen to employ instructional designers or HRD personnel who have majored in IDT. They tend to appoint those holding master's or doctoral degrees in IDT to senior instructional design or training positions. Instructional designers, HRD specialists, and training managers are highly regarded and well rewarded in such large companies as Samsung, LG, SK, and Hyundai, where they collaborate in multidisciplinary teams with trainers from management, marketing, sales backgrounds, or outside training firms.

Lim (2007) attributes the exponential growth of e-learning in corporations to the expansion of the Employment Insurance Act, which provided financial support for e-learning in corporations since 1999. In order to be eligible for funding, corporations must accept regular evaluation of their e-learning programs by an external monitoring team commissioned by the Ministry of Labor who assesses the quality of the content, IDT, and learner support. This policy has led Korean corporations to engage instructional designers in e-learning development and delivery.

As an instructional designer in corporations in Korea, you may well find that you are in great demand. In 2009, when the prior edition of this chapter was prepared, it was indicated that IDT programs in the universities, particularly at the undergraduate level, were failing to produce enough really competent instructional designers for the fast growing e-learning market. Unlike the United States and other Western countries, several universities in Korea offer an IDT program at the undergraduate level and produce around 150 graduates each year. Their program covers various aspects of IDT, including IDT models and theories, e-learning design and development, educational media, motivational design, learning theories and IDT, human resources development, and computer skills. However, employers feel that the graduates of these undergraduate programs are not well enough prepared to handle IDT for quality e-learning development. Song (2009) estimates that of those involved in e-learning design, less than 5 percent can confidently handle the whole systemic IDT process from needs assessment to evaluation, about 30 percent can carry out major IDT activities but with low confidence, and the remaining 65 percent have difficulties in engaging in the IDT process. However, more recently, continuous efforts have been made by IDT academic programs to offer needs-based courses and develop their students' competencies for the fast changing e-learning field, and as a result, the quality of graduates of those IDT programs has been significantly improved.

To supply qualified instructional designers to the Korean e-learning market and promote training in IDT, the Korea Institute of Electronic Commerce (KIEC), a government-supported organization established to promote e-commerce, created a national level "E-Learning Instructional Designer" certification test in 2008. This assesses the IDT knowledge and skills considered necessary to design quality e-learning courses at introductory and advanced levels. So far, the contribution of this certification system to the development of IDT and quality in e-learning is in general positive.

IDT in Higher Education

The proliferation of e-learning in higher education has also led to enhanced job opportunities for IDT personnel. Whereas for-profit corporations including e-learning companies were the major employers of IDT graduates in the late 1990s and early 2000s, higher education institutions are now hiring more IDT graduates. Twenty-one private non-profit cyber universities and colleges and online graduate schools employ IDT majors as instructional designers, instructors, or e-facilitators. Almost all conventional universities in Korea have centers for teaching and learning (CTLs) or e-learning support units and hire IDT graduates as instructional designers or ICT specialists (Leem & Lim, 2007; Korean Association of Centers for Teaching and Learning, 2011). The extensive application of IDT principles in e-learning has raised the quality of courses and teaching and learning, and led to more interactive approaches (Kim & Eom, 2014). While a majority of the so-called e-learning courses offered by conventional and cyber universities are video lectures, some recent e-learning courses focus on improving higher-order thinking skills.

Korean educational technologists have persuaded legislators to include "instructional systems design effort" in the e-learning evaluation system that periodically accredits and evaluates the e-learning courses or programs offered by the cyber universities and online graduate schools.

Latchem et al. (2008) note that many Korean educational technologists and e-learning researchers and developers have, as a result of government policy, studied overseas, majored in IDT, and see e-learning or other innovative forms of learning as driven by sound educational principles. This contrasts with Japan, where the majority of educational technologists have majored in electronic engineering or computing, regard technology as the main mover, and treat the IDT aspects somewhat superficially. If you are well qualified in IDT in Korea, there are quite a number of career routes open to you. Possible careers include academic staff or instructors in universities, researchers in such centers as the Korea Education and Research

Information Service (KERIS), Korea Research Institute for Vocational Education and Training (KRIVET) or Institute of Distance Education at the Korea National Open University, or instructional designers in university centers for teaching and learning (CTLs), cyber training centers for government officials or the Korean Air Force.

Since 2003, the Korean government has supported the establishment of CTLs in all universities including the cyber universities. If you have a master's or doctoral degree in IDT, you might be able to gain a full-time position in one of these centers. Your role would be to conduct workshops, seminars, and online courses for staff and students and help faculty members in planning, implementing, and evaluating their teaching and learning programs and applications of ICT, in contrast to Japan where few such support systems exist. You might also be expected to undertake or engage in research and publication. This, of course, goes hand in hand with being recognized as a member of the academic community and not simply a technician.

IDT in Schools

The term "instructional design" began to gain currency about fifteen years ago when the Internet opened up the potential in corporate training and higher education. However, IDT has its origins in the 1950s with the introduction of audiovisual media in Korean schools, the 1960s and early 1970s with the concept of "educational technology" as systematic planning for educational improvement based on research and development (Morgan & Chadwick, 1971), and the 1980s and 1990s with ICT integration in K–12 education (Mizukoshi, Kim, & Lee, 2000). Korea's policy on sending young teachers and scholars overseas in the 1960s and 1980s to enroll in master's and doctoral programs in IDT also helped to promote the concepts and applications of IDT in formal education.

With the introduction of ICT and e-learning across the curriculum and in teacher training programs, more and more Korean teachers have accepted the notion that linking the principles of IDT to the capacity of ICT can achieve higher levels of learner satisfaction, participation, and performance. As UNESCO Bangkok (Farrell & Wachholz, 2003) and UNESCO Institute for Statistics (UIS, 2014) observe, Korea has set national e-learning policies and plans and provided adequate budgets for their implementation. Curricula are being revised to make the most of e-learning. Pedagogical recommendations exist for integrating ICT across the curricula and at most grades. Computers and Internet connectivity are commonplace as are low student–computer ratios in classrooms. If you are a principal, head of department, or teacher, there is an expectation that you will continually receive training, not only in ICT skills but in e-learning development, online collaboration, IDT, and knowledge community building. As a teacher, you are expected to upgrade your technical and pedagogical knowledge and ICT skills every three years. Specific performance indicators are used to monitor your capacities in these areas and you are supposed to ensure that, whatever subject or age group you teach, at least 10 percent of the classroom activities are ICT based (Latchem & Jung, 2009). Inservice training is increasingly provided online and acquiring and updating your knowledge and skills by these means gives you a very good idea of what it is really like to learn through e-learning and blended learning.

IDT in Policy Studies and Research Institutes

If your interests lie in such areas as national-level policy studies, research, evaluation, best practice studies, the potential of cutting-edge technologies in education, or train-the-trainer programs, you may be able to gain employment in KERIS, an organization mandated to provide the impetus, planning, infrastructure, resources, and incentives for e-learning in K–12, teacher training, and higher education sectors. Or you may be able to work in KRIVET, which evaluates and audits e-learning in the corporate sector. Or in the Korea Education Development Institute (KEDI), which develops research-based educational policies. Or in the National Institute for Lifelong Education, which develops and supports lifelong learning programs including Korea's massive open online courses (K-MOOCs) for all citizens. All of these institutes make good use of IDT majors with master's or doctoral degrees.

Bridging the Research-Practice Divide in IDT

While it can be shown that IDT is an accepted, specialized field in education and training in Korea, you may well find that as far as the academic community is concerned, it has still some way to be regarded as a professional field or discipline in its own right. You may also begin to find that there can be some conflict between the Western concepts of IDT and the long-held reverence for the teacher, lecture, face-to-face contact, and exam in Korean culture. You will still find lecturers. Teachers and parents, and even some in the corporate sector, contend that instruction is best delivered via lectures by teachers or content experts. This is why, as Lim, Leem, & Jung (2003); Jang, Jang, Seo, Lee, and Leem (2003); and Lim (2007) report, most corporate e-learning takes the form of one-way informational texts or video lectures-on-demand and provides little opportunity for interaction, problem solving, or higher-order thinking. You will also find when examining so-called e-learning programs provided by institutions such as the Korea National Open University, that the streaming video or broadcasts are often in the form of video lectures. It is found that the students prefer recorded face-to-face communication by the teacher or content expert to the more impersonal online text. This may be because they can see what their lecturers look like and replay the recordings until they feel they understand the lectures and are ready for the exam (Latchem & Jung, 2009). It is also important to them because context, nonverbal communication and the status of the speaker are all important in Korean communications and of course these are still present in the video recordings. Similarly, you may find that the students are less ready to discuss and disagree with the content of the video lectures. This is partly due to the normal anxiety on the part of learners not to fail but also because Korean society traditionally has been much more hierarchical than Western societies and the textbook, teacher, and older person are therefore to be respected and not challenged.

Unfortunately, such cultural differences in instruction have not been the main focus of research by Korean educational technologists. Koreans are more interested in seeking global or generalizable ways of carrying out research and development in IDT while their Japanese counterparts look for Japan's unique way in IDT. Lim and Yeon (2009) found that only 15 percent of the articles on IDT theories, published in the Korean *Journal of Educational Technology* between 1994 and 2006, focused on context-specific developmental research; whereas the remaining 85 percent discussed general IDT theories and models. A recent study by Lim, Yoo, and Chung (2014) revealed that a majority of studies on IDT were interested in theoretical discussions and ignored IDT-applied practices. If the potential of IDT is to be fully realized in Korean education and training, more research into varying cultural circumstances is needed. Overreliance on IDT theories and models from Western countries, particularly the United States, may inhibit Korea from contributing more to the world knowledge network in the field of IDT. Maybe it is time that Korea develops a "producing culture" in IDT, as Sinlarat (2007, p. 166) puts it, acknowledging the large pool of wisdom and experience that Korea can contribute to the world's IDT literature.

Conclusion

In this chapter we have shown that there are exciting expansions and encouraging trends in IDT implementation in Japan and Korea. While circumstances may greatly vary from place to place, as they do between the settings discussed in this chapter, we have found that education and training institutions and governments need clear visions, strategic plans, commitment, and an implementation capability to achieve the potential of IDT. Likewise, it is important to consider the culture, to train and support educators and trainers, and to avoid techno-determinism in applying IDT in education and training.

Summary of Key Principles

1. **IDT is now recognized as an integral part of educational and training practices in Japan and Korea.** E-Learning development has accelerated the application of IDT principles in education and training in both countries.

2. **Even though Japan and Korea have much in common, IDT is more firmly integrated and specialized in Korea than in Japan due to the government policy to** support IDT professionals and equip teachers with IDT knowledge and skills.

3. **Korean scholars are more interested in seeking global or generalizable ways of carrying out research and development in IDT while their Japanese counterparts look for Japan's unique way in IDT.** If the potential of IDT is to be fully realized in Asian education and training, more research into varying cultural circumstances is needed.

Application Questions

1. Imagine that you are an instructional design manager from Western Europe or North America. Use the Internet or the library to locate cultural factors that are important to consider in creating materials implemented in either Japan or Korea. Prepare a rubric that evaluates the cultural sensitively of these factors.

2. Consider the cases of Japan and Korea discussed in this chapter. Prepare a table indicating parallels or contrasts from both cases (Japan and Korea), as well as with your own experiences in your own country. In a narrative that uses your table as a reference point, discuss how these similarities and differences may affect the way IDT professionals carry their job roles in these settings.

References

Advanced Learning Infrastructures Consortium. (2001). *E-Learning whitebook 2001/2002*. Tokyo: Advanced Learning Infrastructures Consortium (ALIC).

Akahori, K., Horiguchi, H., Suzuki, K., & Nambu, M. (2001). Development and evaluation of Web-based in-service training systems for improving ICT leadership of school-teachers. *Journal of Universal Computer Science, 7*(3), 211–225.

Bonk, C. J. (2004). The perfect e-storm: emerging technology, enormous demand, enhanced pedagogy and erased budgets. *The Observatory on Borderless Higher Education*. Retrieved from http://www.publicationshare.com/part2.pdf

Dick, W. Carey, L., & Carey, J.O. (2001). The systematic design of instruction. (5th Edition). New York, NY: Longman. Upper Saddle River, NJ. Pearson Education, Inc.

Farrell, G., & Wachholz, C. (Eds.). (2003). *Meta-survey on the use of technologies in education in Asia and the Pacific*. Bangkok: UNESCO. Retrieved from http://unesdoc.unesco.org/images/0013/001349/134960e.pdf

Fernandez, C., & Yoshida, M. (2004). *Lesson study: A Japanese approach to improving mathematics teaching and learning*. New York: Routledge.

Gagné, R. M., Wager, W. W., Golas, K. C., Keller, J. M., & Russell, J. D. (2005). *Principles of instructional design*.

Hannum, W. H., & Briggs, L. J. (1982). How does instructional systems design differ from traditional instruction? *Educational Technology, 22*(1), 9–14.

Innovation Centre Denmark Seoul. (2014*). E-Learning in Korea: Overview of E-Learning sector in Korea.* Seoul: Embassy of Denmark, Innovation Centre Denmark Seoul.

Jang, I., Jang, S. J., Seo, Y. K, Lee, K. S., & Leem, J. H. (2003). *A monitoring report of cyber universities.* Seoul: Korea Education Research and Information Service.

Jung, I. S. (2009). The emergence of for-profit E-Learning providers in Asia. *TechTrends, 53*(2), 18–21.

Keller, J. M. (2009). *Motivational design for learning and performance: The ARCS model approach.* Springer Science & Business Media.

Kim, H., & Eom, W. (2014). A case study on action learning program for faculty development. *Korean Journal of Educational Technology, 30*(4), 839–878.

Korean Association of Centers for Teaching and Learning. (2011). *University education whitebook.* Seoul: Korean Association of Centers for Teaching and Learning. Retrieved from http://www.kactl.org/default/whitepaper.pdf

Latchem, C., & Jung, I. S. (2009). *Distance and blended learning in Asia.* New York and London: Routledge.

Latchem, C., Jung, I. S., Aoki, K., & Ozkul, A. E. (2008). The tortoise and the hare enigma in e-transformation in Japanese and Korean higher education. *British Journal of Educational Technology, 39*(4), 610–630.

Lee, J., Park, E., & Song, H. (2014). An exploratory study on the competencies of E-Learning instructional designers in the age of Web 3.0. *Korean Journal of Human Resource Development Quarterly, 16*(1), 143–168.

Leem, J. H., & Lim, C. (2007). The current status of E-Learning and strategies to enhance educational competitiveness in Korean higher education. *The International Review of Research in Open and Distance Learning, 8*(1). Retrieved from http://www.irrodl.org/index.php/irrodl/article/view/380/763

Lewis, C. C. (2002). *Lesson study: A handbook of teacher-led instructional change.* Research for Better Schools.

Lim, B., Leem, J. H., & Jung, I. S. (2003). Current status of cyber education in Korean higher education and quality control: The year of 2002. *Korean Journal of Educational Research, 41*(3), 541–569.

Lim, C. (2007). The current status and future prospects of corporate E-Learning in Korea. *The International Review of Research in Open and Distance Learning, 8*(1). Retrieved from http://www.irrodl.org/index.php/irrodl/article/view/376/761

Lim, C., & Yeon, E. (2009). Review of current studies in instructional design theory in Korea: Major trends and future directions. *Asia Pacific Education Review, 10*(3), 357–364.

Lim, H., Yoo, Y., & Chung, J. (2014). The comparison analysis of domestic research trends of educational technology in last decade. *The Journal of Educational Information and Media, 20*(2), 137–159.

Mizukoshi, T., Kim, Y. S., & Lee, J. Y. (2000). Instructional technology in Asia: Focus on Japan and Korea. *Educational Technology Research and Development, 48*(1), 101–112.

Morgan, R. M., & Chadwick, C. (1971). *Systems analysis for educational change: The Republic of Korea.* Tallahassee, FL: Learning Systems Institute, Florida State University.

Nonaka, I. (1994). A dynamic theory of organizational knowledge creation, *Organization Science, 5*(1), 14–37.

Reiser, R. A., & Dempsey, J. V. (2011). *Trends and issues in instructional design and technology.* Upper Saddle River, NJ. Pearson Merrill Prentice Hall.

Sinlarat, P. (2007, October 23-25). Reglobalizing Thai higher education: The path for future. Paper presented at The 8th International Conference on Education Research, Seoul National University, Seoul, Korea.

Song, S. (2009, July 18). E-mail interview.

Suzuki, K. (2009). From competency list to curriculum implementation: A case study of Japan's first online master's program for E-Learning specialists training. *International Journal on E-Learning, 8*(4), 469–478

UNESCO Institute for Statistics (UIS). (2014). *Information and communication technology (ICT) in Asia.* Retrieved from http://www.uis.unesco.org/Communication/Documents/ICT-asia-en.pdf

Vogel, E. F. (1980). *Japan as number one.* Tokyo: Tuttle.

Chapter 24

Getting an Instructional Design Position: Lessons from a Personal History

Robert A. Reiser

Florida State University

The purpose of this chapter is to describe some lessons that I learned when I was looking for my first position in the field of instructional design. By describing these lessons, I hope to provide some useful information to those of you interested in obtaining an instructional design position.

Because I am in an instructional design frame of mind, I will now restate the purpose of my chapter in terms that should please those of you who are firm believers in "traditional" instructional design practices. (Friendly note to constructivists: Please do not read the remainder of this paragraph; you may find it offensive.) The objectives of this chapter are as follows: Given a copy of this chapter, the reader will:

a. choose to apply the lessons described herein, and
b. obtain a desirable position in the field of instructional design.

Before I begin to describe the lessons I learned, I would like to briefly describe some of the conditions under which I learned them. First, I learned the lessons back in prehistoric days, in 1975, to be exact. As many people are fond of saying, "times were different then," but the times weren't all that different! Second, at the time I learned these lessons, I was looking for a faculty position in academia. Although a few of the lessons may apply primarily to those individuals looking for a similar position, I believe most of the lessons apply regardless of the type of instructional design position you are seeking. Third, I learned many of these lessons when I was a doctoral student. Some of the lessons I will describe may be geared toward doctoral students, but I think most of them should be of value to anyone interested in obtaining a position in our field.

Now that I have masterfully handled any concerns you may have had about the external validity of my findings, let me take you back to those thrilling days of yesteryear . . . the lowly graduate student (me) plods along again!

The Journey Begins

In the first half of the 1970s, a frequently used expression was "the light at the end of the tunnel," and in January 1975 I finally began to see that light. I realized that within a few months I would most likely graduate from Arizona State University's doctoral program in instructional design. At that point, I decided I should start looking for a position I could move into upon my graduation. Thus began my job search.

The first source I turned to during my search was the loose-leaf job book that was maintained and updated by the faculty members in my doctoral program. As I looked through that job book, I was reminded of a song that was popular back then, "Is That All There Is?" Needless to say, the number of faculty positions in academia listed in the job book was considerably less than I had expected. Thus, I decided to turn to other sources in order to find out about position openings. This leads me to the first lesson:

Lesson #1: Use a Wide Variety of Sources to Find Out about Instructional Design Job Openings

In today's world, job seekers often turn to the Internet to find out about jobs that are available in their field of interest, and doing so should be one of the primary strategies you employ as you seek a position in the field of instructional design. Popular job search websites such as Indeed.com, Monster.com, LinkedIn .com, and many others often list hundreds of instructional design positions that are available in a wide variety of types of organizations, including large and small businesses and institutions of higher education. Many instructional design positions in higher education, faculty positions as well as as administrative and staff openings, can also be found at ChronicleVitae. com, the job search website maintained by *The Chronicle of Higher Education*. Federal government positions in instructional design can be found online by visiting USAjobs.gov.

Job openings are also listed on the websites of many of the professional associations affiliated with the field of instructional design (Chapter 26 provides a comprehensive list of these associations). In addition, almost all of these associations operate *career centers* at their annual conferences. Career centers at conferences provide organizations with the opportunity to post jobs that are currently available, enable job seekers to post their resumes, and provide meeting areas where job interviews and informal discussions about job opportunities can take place. Many professional organizations offer these career center services year-round, with much of the activity taking place online.

The faculty members in your academic program are also excellent sources of information about job openings. They often will receive information about job openings from their colleagues at other institutions, as well as from program alumni and professional acquaintances. Thus, it is often wise to ask your faculty members about the job opportunities they may be aware of. Later in this chapter, I will discuss some related ideas about having job discussions with your professors.

As should be obvious by now, most of the sources of information about jobs I have mentioned so far are accessed via the Internet, but unfortunately, back in the days when I was job hunting there was no Internet. However, contrary to some of the rumors you may have heard, at the time I was looking for a job the printing press had indeed been invented! Thus, I was able to review the openings listed in various professional journals and posted at professional meetings and, as I looked through those job listings, I learned several useful lessons.

Lesson #2: Most Instructional Design Positions Are in Business and Industry

Although this lesson was a bit surprising to me back in 1975, it shouldn't be surprising to anyone today. While the number of instructional design positions in higher education has greatly expanded in recent years (Berrett, 2016), the majority of positions in the field of instructional design are in business and industry (e.g., Sugar, Hoard, Brown, & Daniels, 2012). And this was even more the case when I was seeking a position. Thus I found lesson #2 to be a bit disheartening. It was not as disheartening, however, as the next lesson I learned.

Lesson #3 (Also known as "the Faculty Members' Lament"): Most High-Paying Instructional Design Positions Are in Business and Industry

This lesson still holds true today. Many of the masters-level graduates of the instructional design program where I work

(Florida State University) begin their careers in business and industry at salaries that are comparable to those of new faculty members with doctoral degrees. Average annual salaries for instructional designers working in business and industry can be found in variety of online sources, such as PayScale.com, Salary.com, and Glassdoor.com.

Lesson #4: Learn How Businesses Operate

In light of lessons #2 and #3, you may decide that a job in business and industry is in your best interest. If that is the case, it is important that you acquire a clear understanding of how businesses operate. At Florida State, many students have acquired this knowledge by taking a graduate-level business and management course, such as organizational development, offered by the college of business. A similar course at your university should prepare you to better understand the business environment in which you may be working.

Lesson #5: Acquire a Strong Set of Media Production Skills

As I proceeded through the listings of job openings, I also noticed that many prospective employers were looking for instructional designers with a strong set of media production skills. Today this situation exists to an even greater degree. Over the years, the media that are frequently used to deliver instruction have changed (is it really true that the slide-tape presentations are no longer in high demand?), but organizations are still seeking to hire instructional designers who possess a strong set of media production skills, especially in such areas as e-learning and multimedia production (Sugar et al., 2012). Most programs in our field offer a wide variety of courses that focus on such skills. My advice is to take several such courses.

Unfortunately, when I was a graduate student, I did not take many media production courses, and I believe that my lack of skills in that area worked against me when I was being considered for several of the positions I applied for. Fortunately, the instructional design skills and experience I acquired while I was a student and graduate assistant at Arizona State did help me get several job interviews. This leads me to the next lesson.

Lesson #6: Acquire a Strong Set of Design (and Analysis!) Skills

I believe lessons #5 and #6 go hand in hand. Although media production skills are likely to help you acquire a job, I believe it is essential to have a strong set of design skills, ranging from being able to describe goals and objectives, all the way through to being able to conduct formative evaluations and revise instruction based upon the data that is collected. Moreover, with the recent emphasis on performance improvement, and particularly on front-end analysis, I believe it is also important to have a strong set of analysis skills, including skills in the areas of needs assessment, job task analysis, and instructional analysis.

Speaking of analysis, if your analysis of the skills you have (or don't have!) has led you to be concerned about the type of position you will be qualified for, let me assuage your fears—don't worry, you'll manage. And you can take the last part of the preceding statement quite literally. As was the case when I was looking for a position, many current job announcements call for skills in the management of instructional design projects. So, we come to the next lesson.

Lesson #7: Acquire Some Management Skills

Many graduates of instructional design programs have indicated that shortly after they obtain a position, they are thrust into some type of management role. Many graduate programs in our field offer courses and/or experiences in this area, and I believe it is to your definite advantage to gain some skills and experience in the management of instructional projects and personnel. Chapter 13 in this book focuses on these types of skills.

Lesson #8: Develop a Strong Set of Communication Skills

To be an effective instructional designer or manager, you need to be able to clearly communicate with others, both in your written work and in your oral communication. Moreover, you need to be a good listener; you need to be able to clearly understand what subject-matter experts and other members of a design team are stating. Oftentimes, in order to so, you will need to ask questions that will help clarify points that are not clear. You also need to be a good note taker. As I have discovered, and as many of my former students have confirmed, these communication skills are essential to success in our field.

Of course, being a good communicator is also a vital skill during your job search. As I began applying for positions, I tried to use my writing ability to prepare letters of inquiry that I felt would result in my being selected as a strong candidate for at least some of those positions. Working away at the old typewriter (this was during the pre-word-processing age), I sent off many letters of inquiry. And before I knew it, I received my first reply, which leads me to the next lesson.

Lesson #9: Don't Be Discouraged if You Don't Get the First Job You Apply For

As you can tell from this lesson, I did not get the first job I applied for. Unfortunately, the same thing is likely to happen to you, so be prepared for it! With this piece of advice in mind, instead of dwelling on the rejection letter I had received, I waited eagerly for a response from the second potential employer I wrote to. And before I knew it, it came. And with that response, came the next lesson.

Lesson #10: Don't Be Discouraged if You Don't Get the Second Job You Apply For

I could go on listing many similar lessons, but rather than dwelling on misfortune, let's just say I had a long string of bad luck. But my luck finally changed, and it did so when I joined the Association of Educational Communications and Technology (AECT). This leads me to the next two lessons.

Lesson #11: Join One or More Professional Organizations

Joining a professional association was one of the most important steps I took early in my career. Doing so, and then attending the annual AECT conference, gave me the opportunity to meet many other people in the field, including students and faculty in other academic programs and many instructional design professionals working in other settings (e.g., business and industry, government, K–12 education, the military). Thus, without even realizing it, I started establishing a network of professional acquaintances who would help me grow professionally throughout my career. And I am confident that the same thing can happen to you if, as a starter, you join a professional association, especially if you do so near the start of your career, when you are still a student (joining now will get you on the right path sooner, not to mention the fact that membership rates are lower for students!).

Which associations should you join? Read about them in Chapter 26 of this book and get an initial feeling for which ones are of interest to you. Also be sure to talk to your professors about your professional goals, and get their opinions as to which associations they think are well suited for you. Then proceed to join one or two. Now on to the next lesson.

Lesson #12: Become Active in One or More Professional Organizations

After I joined AECT, I attended their annual conference, which was held in Dallas that year. During the conference, I registered with the job placement service, gave several paper presentations, spoke with faculty from several universities (in spite of the fact that my professors kept trying to keep me hidden), and volunteered to work on a committee of one of the subgroups within AECT. In other words, in today's parlance, I kept a high profile. And for once in my life, my profile (no, I am not talking about my nose), paid off; being active at the conference helped me get invited to two universities for job interviews.

So, how can you become active within a professional association? One of the ways you can do so is by delivering one or more presentations at the annual conference. Many months prior to its annual conference, an organization will send out a message to all of its members, inviting them to submit proposals to deliver presentations at the conference. When you receive such a request, don't be shy; go ahead and submit a proposal, perhaps teaming up with a fellow student or one of your professors in order to do so (working with others on such tasks is often a good idea; it provides you the opportunity to share ideas and responsibilities; but be sure to work with someone who takes his or her responsibilities seriously!).

A second good way to become active in a professional association is to volunteer to do some work for a subgroup (often called a *division* or *special interest group*), within the organization. How do you begin? I suggest that when you attend a conference, that you attend the business meetings of several subgroups that are of interest to you. The dates and times of these business meetings, which typically last for about sixty to ninety minutes, usually are listed in the conference program and are open to everyone. When you attend one of these meetings you are likely to hear of some the activities that particular subgroup is planning. If the activity sounds even somewhat interesting to you, volunteer to help (in my case, I volunteered to organize an awards program within one of the AECT divisions). Then do a good job. When you do so, colleagues within the organization will recognize it and start respecting your initiative and your abilities. You will then be well on your way to moving on to bigger and better things. As indicated, my initial involvement in AECT led to two job interviews, and my continued involvement in the organization throughout my professional life has furthered my career in ways too numerous to mention.

Although my activities at the AECT conference led to invitations to two university job interviews, there was another contributing factor as well. By the time I attended the convention, several manuscripts I had written for class assignments or co-authored for research projects had been approved as conference presentations or were accepted for publication in a journal. Because I was seeking a position in the world of "publish or perish," my presentation and publication record did not go unnoticed. Thus, my next lesson.

Lesson #13: Publish, Don't Cherish

The dictionary indicates that *cherish* means "to cling fondly to something." Instead of clinging to (or flinging out) the papers and reports you have written for classes or projects, my suggestion is to submit them to be presented at conferences and/or to be considered for publication in a professional journal.

To which journals should you submit your papers and reports? Again, Chapter 26 provides a list of periodicals in our profession that are publication possibilities. Review the types of articles found in those publications and submit your manuscripts to the journals for which they seem best suited. Because I am a strong believer in practicing what I preach, I would like to point out that I have submitted manuscripts to many of the journals listed in Chapter 26. Notice, however, that I used the words *submitted to*, not *published in*. On rare (well, maybe not so rare!) occasions, my manuscripts have been rejected—which leads me to the next lesson.

Lesson #14: Don't Be Dejected if Your Manuscript is Rejected

Even if your manuscript is rejected, you are likely to get some valuable feedback from those who reviewed it. If the feedback indicates that the manuscript has some redeeming qualities, I suggest that you use the feedback to revise your manuscript. After you do so, submit the revised manuscript to another journal, or perhaps resubmit it to the same journal. If you follow this strategy it is likely that your manuscript eventually will be published, but don't be surprised if you receive some more rejection notices first!

Speaking of rejection, let me get back to my story. When we last left me, I was about to go off to job interviews at two universities. The first of these interviews was at the University of Toledo. I mention the name of that university for two reasons. First, it is to point out that when I told my wife that I was to be

interviewed there, her only reply was "Holy Toledo!" Second, it is to turn your attention to the next lesson.

Lesson #15: Develop an Area of Expertise

Oftentimes, organizations seeking to hire an instructional designer are looking for someone who has some expertise in a particular area within our field. Such was the case at the University of Toledo in the mid-1970s. At that time the College of Education at Toledo was in the midst of developing and implementing a competency-based teacher education program. Fortunately for me, competency-based instruction was an area in which I had developed a good deal of competency! Indeed, during the time I had been a graduate student at Arizona State I had worked with a faculty member in designing a course on competency-based instruction and I had taught the course several times. I had also delivered a conference paper describing my work in that area and had assisted two of my professors on an early draft of what would eventually become a popular textbook on the topic (i.e., Sullivan & Higgins, 1983). Thus, for someone who was still in graduate school, I had developed a good deal of expertise in the area of competency-based instruction. Having that expertise certainly was a major factor in my being called in for an interview at a university seeking help in the development of a competency-based program.

The lesson to be learned here is that by developing an area of expertise while you are a student, you are likely to increase your chances of standing out from the rest of the crowd when you apply for certain jobs. Of course, it is important that the area of expertise that you decide to develop is one that is likely to be in high demand within our field for many years to come. Moreover, it is important that while you are developing your expertise in that area, you produce some tangible evidence (such as instructional materials you develop, courses you teach and papers you present) that demonstrate your skill and experience. My vita provided such evidence, and was clearly a factor in my being invited to the University of Toledo to interview for the position. My experience during that interview leads me to my next lesson.

Lesson #16: When Preparing for a Job Interview, Find Out as Much as You Can About Your Potential Employers

I remember my interview at University of Toledo quite clearly. Everyone I met there was very nice and many of them were very interested in me and my work. One faculty member, let's call him Professor X, was particularly interested in one area in which I had professed some expertise (although I don't recall the area, let's say it was mastery learning). Indeed, Professor X himself had done some research in that area, and he asked me if I had read an article he had recently written about the topic. I responded by indicating that I had not read his paper. "Well," he said, "have you read Jones's outstanding literature review on mastery learning?" Again, I had to respond that I had not read the paper of reference. The conversation continued to proceed in this fashion and, as it did, I became more and more certain that I would not get the job. For once, I was right: I didn't get the job, but I did learn that when an organization invites you to participate in a job interview it is important to find out as much as you can about that organization and the people you are likely to be meeting.

If it is unclear as to who you will be meeting with, ask the person who has contacted you to send you an interview schedule (they are likely to do so anyhow). This schedule is likely to contain the names of some of the people you will be meeting (e.g., the name of a department head), and will also list the groups with whom you will be meeting (e.g., "meet with the search committee"). In the latter case, you may need to do some detective work to figure out who is a member of which particular group. In many cases, it may well be worth it to do so!

If I had taken the time to find out more about the interests and expertise of the faculty members at the University of Toledo, I most likely would have discovered that Professor X was interested in a topic area in which I was interested. By taking time before the interview to look at his work in that area, I would have been well prepared to mention and discuss his work before he questioned me. I'm sure that would have created a much better impression of me than the one he had of me after my interview. You can learn from my mistake by taking some time to find out about your potential employers. Then, during the interview you will be able to demonstrate that you know a good bit about them and their organization. These actions will not only increase the chances that you will get the job for which you are interviewing, but will also increase your knowledge about the organization. That way you can decide whether you want to work there or at one of the many other places craving to hire you!

Lesson #17: Keep Up with the Literature in Your Areas of Interest

As revealed by my University of Toledo anecdote, I had not kept up with the literature in at least one of the areas in which I thought I had some expertise. How do you keep up with the literature in the areas of our field that are of particular interest to you? A good way to start is by regularly examining the most recent issues of several of the journals in your area of interest. Ask your professors which ones they think are the most important for you to skim through.

After you have identified the journals in which you are most interested, skim through a few of them on a regular basis (preferably every few months, but even once or twice year is okay, at least by my standards!). Now that most journals are available online, accessing most journals should be fairly easy. When you do so, look at the titles of the articles in each issue, and read the abstracts of the articles whose titles interest you. If you are still interested in an article after having read its title and abstract, you should electronically file it for future reference (if you are really ambitious, you may even choose to read the article before you place it in an electronic folder!).

One folder I could have filled up back in 1975 would have been of unsuccessful interview experiences. I did not get the job at the University of Toledo, nor did I obtain the faculty position at the next university where I was interviewed. Shortly thereafter I had a job interview at a research and development center, but once again I failed to get the job! This failure was particularly disappointing—I was the only person who was interviewed! I did feel better, however, when I was told that the

only reason I was not hired was because there had been an unexpected budget cutback (at least that's what they told me!).

At this point, I decided to talk to my professors at Arizona State to see if they could give me some advice. This decision turned out to be a wise one because instead of advice, my professors gave me a job; they hired me as a faculty member in their department! This occurrence leads me to two further lessons:

Lesson #18: Let Your Professors Know You Are Looking for a Job

Lesson #19 (Prerequisite to Lesson #18): Demonstrate to Your Professors That You Do Good Work

Lesson #18 is important because your professors may be aware of job opportunities that you are not aware of. But lesson #19 is even more important because it is unlikely that your professors will recommend you for a position, or even inform you of some possibilities, if you have failed to demonstrate to them that you do good work. If, on the other hand, your work is good, your professors are likely to go out of their way to help you attain a good position. Because recommendations from professors often are a critical factor in determining whether a recent graduate obtains a particular job, I suggest that if you are still a student you should pay careful attention to lesson #19. (Would you expect a professor to say otherwise?)

When my professors hired me as one of their colleagues, it was with the understanding that if another good job opportunity arose, I would pursue it. Thus, I would be able to broaden my horizons and share the wisdom I had acquired at Arizona State with faculty members and students at other institutions. Besides, the contract money with which I had been hired wasn't expected to last forever!

Fortunately, well before Arizona State ran out of the contract money that was being used to pay me, I came across an announcement regarding an instructional design position that was available at Florida State University. Unfortunately, although the position sounded very interesting, the position announcement indicated that applicants were expected to have skills in a number of areas in which I had no experience or training. Nonetheless, I decided to apply for the position. And, sure enough, I got the job! Which brings me to the last lesson.

Lesson #20 (Also known as "the formative evaluator's advice"): If the Job Doesn't Fit, Revise It. Apply for Jobs That Interest You, Even if You Don't Have the Exact Qualifications Advertised

As I previously indicated (see lesson #15), oftentimes organizations in our field are seeking to hire someone who has expertise in a particular area and are likely to identify that area in their job announcement. While it is certainly to your advantage if you have expertise in that area, my experience, and indeed those of many of my former students, tells me that it is often worthwhile to apply for a position even if you don't possess all of the specific skills called for in the job announcement. Why would an employer hire someone who does not have several of the skills the employer is looking for? Two reasons: They may not find a suitable candidate who possesses the skill set the employer was seeking and/or they may find that another candidate's skill set is equally or more appealing. So, as long as the set of skills specified in a job posting is not too far removed from the set of skills you possess, I encourage you to apply for the position.

In my case, when I was offered the job at Florida State, I was told that the fact that I was strong in some skill areas, more than outweighed the fact that I lacked some of the skills they had emphasized in their job announcement. Fortunately, as those who hired me at Florida State had hoped, I was able to acquire some of those other skills once I obtained the job.

Now, more than forty years after I first learned the lessons described in this chapter, I'm still at Florida State and I'm still learning. I hope that by following the lessons I have described, you will be able to obtain a position that has been as enjoyable as mine has been. Good luck!

Summary of Key Principles

1. **Having a broad range of skills is likely to increase your chances of employment.** Make sure to develop a strong set of communication skills, as well as skills related to each of the phases of the instructional design process, including analysis, design, development (media production), implementation, evaluation, and management.

2. **Develop an area of expertise within the instructional design field, making sure that the skill set you decide to focus on is one that is currently in high demand and is likely to remain so for some years.**

3. **Most instructional design positions, including higher-paying ones, are in business and industry.** If you are interested in working in that environment, be sure to acquire a clear understanding of how businesses operate. Taking one or more business courses may prove to be very helpful.

4. **Starting while you are a student, become an active of member of the instructional design profession.** Joining a professional organization and becoming active in it (e.g., helping with the work of the organization, delivering papers at conferences, and submitting papers for publication) will increase your visibility and help you establish a professional network that will help you find a job and advance in your career.

5. **Be proactive when you are searching for a job.** Search a wide variety of sources that post job openings, ask your professors for advice and assistance, and don't be hesitant to apply for a wide variety of jobs within the field, including those that call for a set of skills that don't quite match yours.

6. **When you apply for jobs (or submit proposals for conferences presentations or papers for publication) you are likely to receive some, perhaps many, rejections.** Don't become dejected by these rejections! Keep on trying! If you do so, there is an excellent chance that you will succeed.

Application Questions

1. Assume that you are currently seeking a job in our field (perhaps you really are!). Examine at least three of the sources of job openings identified in this chapter and find at least six position announcements that describe jobs that are of interest to you. List the specific skills most frequently mentioned as being required for these jobs. Analyze the degree to which you possess each of those skills and list specific steps you might take to improve your abilities in the areas where you feel improvement is necessary.

2. Interview at least two of the recent graduates of your program who have obtained positions similar to the type of position you are interested in. Ask each graduate to discuss the factors that they felt were instrumental in helping them obtain their job. Use the list of lessons contained in this chapter as a prompt, asking the interviewees to indicate which of the lessons describe factors that were important in their successful job search effort.

References

Berrett, D. (2016). Instructional design: Demand grows for a new breed of academic [article in special section]. *Chronicle of Higher Education, 62*(25), B41–B42.

Sugar, W., Hoard, B., Brown, A., & Daniels, L. (2012). Identifying multimedia production competencies and skills of instructional design and technology professionals: An analysis of recent job postings. *Journal of Educational Technology Systems, 40*, 227–249.

Sullivan, H. J., & Higgins, N. (1983). *Teaching for competence.* New York: Teachers College Press.

Chapter 25
Performance Consulting

Catherine Tenzca

Tencza Designs

Judith Hale

Hale Associates

Introduction

Dr. Judith Hale and Catherine Tencza are both career performance consultants with more than a half century of experience between them. Performance consultants work with clients to solve issues related to helping people do their jobs better, especially when it comes to making sure they are equipped with the right skills and knowledge to succeed. While Judy and Cathy are from different areas of the country, have different degrees, and have worked on different types of projects, they both have enjoyed success in running small consulting companies, and they share a common vision of what it takes to be successful. In this chapter, Judy and Cathy—together and separately—tackle some of the questions people commonly have about consulting in our field.

Q: What is an independent consultant? How is this role different from that of a contractor? A subcontractor? An internal consultant?

Judy says . . .

Independent consultants have their own professional training and instructional design practices. They offer their expertise, at a price, to help organizations in the public and private sectors design, develop, deliver, and evaluate learning solutions. Their expertise consists of both work-for-hire and advice. The work-for-hire component may include analyzing performance data to identify learning needs, producing instructional and performance support materials for live or online distribution,

delivering training, facilitating meetings, and evaluating the effectiveness of programs. The advice component includes offering informed suggestions on issues such as selecting delivery technologies, interpreting data, sequencing content, and sharing information. It is the advice component that distinguishes someone as a consultant compared to a contractor. Without the advice component, you are a temporary worker doing what you are told.

The title "subcontractor" means a person is work-for-hire. Subcontractors may or may not be contracted to provide advice. Whether they operate as an extra set of hands or consultants depends on their relationship with whoever hired them.

Internal consultants, too, contribute professional and technical expertise on how to build workforce capacity. However, they are not independent businesses so they do not engage in the business management and business development activities that independent consultants do.

Q: What does a performance consultant really do?

Cathy and Judy say . . .

A performance consultant defines and helps solve problems related to people having the ability to do their jobs well. On any given day, each of us might have two or three client meetings—typically virtual—that involve some balance of structured listening, project management, and solution presentation.

Cathy says . . .

Let's look at a typical day—yesterday, in fact.

8:30	Pre-conference call with a project team in advance of a client call. The project was a medium-sized one and involved a handful of people on the client side and on the consulting side. We talked about where we were in the project, timeliness, roles, and upcoming activities, all while looking at the detailed project plan. We talked about the key items to discuss with the client, how we wanted to approach these items, and who would take the lead on each part of the discussion.
10:00	Follow-up call with the same client, a hospitality company. In this particular case, I took the lead, managing the call and making sure we got through our agenda items and got resolution on any issues.
10:45	Read the paper and had a cup of tea (I love being my own boss!)
11:30	Call with a long-time client about a potential new project related to teacher training. I asked questions about the project goals, the key stakeholders, the timeline, and the client's vision. I did an informal SWOT (strengths, weaknesses, opportunities, and threats) analysis in my head. I paraphrased what the client said and confirmed that I understood the need. I said that I could help and promised to get back to her with a plan.
12:30	For the next few hours, I answered email (a 24/7 job), surfed the Internet, procrastinated on working on the proposal, had lunch, worked on the proposal, and threw in a load of laundry.
2:30	Virtual meeting in which my client (an IT company) and I presented a training program we developed for my client's client, a federal agency. We walked through a list of their requirements, our recommendation, and the draft product—a three-day instructor-led training program. We were careful to tie everything we did to their needs. My role was to be primary presenter (and salesperson) on the solution and then to stay mostly quiet on responding to agency feedback so that my client could decide what was in scope for any additional requests.
3:30	Follow-up meeting from 2:30 call to determine next steps.
4:00	Thinking time. I mused a bit about possible solutions for a different client who needs to figure out how to efficiently onboard people for a highly technical, high-paid job with low turnover and low numbers. I often try to think a bit about problems at the end of the day, because then ideas seem to bubble up in my mind during the evening or while I sleep.

That really is typical—a lot of phone calls and web meetings around project management and presenting solutions and some time for thinking and writing.

The dark side. And then there are the days that end around 10:00 p.m. . . . It's pretty much the same as the schedule just provided, minus any time for thinking because:

- A client suddenly moved up a deliverable date.
- A new deliverable was added to an existing project.
- Unexpected, major feedback arrived.
- Somebody on the team had a personal emergency and I had to cover.
- I had a personal emergency.
- Meetings ran over allotted times.

On days like those, it is hamster-wheeling throughout business hours, leaving any thought or personal action items for the evening. This is real life for me.

Q: What does a consultant career path look like?

Cathy and Judy say . . .

Phase 1: Get experience. A lot of instructional designers work with large or medium-sized consulting companies before striking out on their own. Others work as internal consultants in a corporate or other environment and then start a consulting practice. Both of these are good options because they provide an opportunity to learn and get experience with very little risk. After two or more years as employees, career consultants decide to take the plunge and go out on their own.

Phase 2: Strike out on your own. Another typical step on the path to consulting is to establish one bread-and-butter client to sustain income during any initial one- or two-year startup period. A lot of people use that one client—and a lot of hard work—to develop new business. This stage takes patience and perseverance, as it may take months or even years to see the results of networking and marketing. A lot of aspiring consultants change their paths at this point, due to income or family pressures or because the work or lifestyle isn't what they had envisioned.

Phase 3: Look at long-term goals. OK, let's assume that the work is flowing in and the consultant is happy and successful in the role. At some point, prosperous consultants will have more work than they can handle alone, and they'll have to decide to (1) stick to projects that one person can handle, (2) form a network of subcontractors and/or partners to take on larger projects, (3) grow from an independent consultant to a small-business owner, with employees to perform the work, or (4) leverage the knowledge and experience gained to take on new challenges as an leader in an organization. All of these are valid options and the right choice depends on individual goals and ambitions. This chapter primarily focuses on consultants who work alone or in collaboration with subcontractors.

Each path is unique. Some people have a very well-planned career plan that they execute. Many people, though, have to make it up as they go along, based on good fortune, bad breaks, and family considerations.

Cathy says . . .

In my case, some decisions I pretty much fell into, and others were quite deliberate. To build a résumé, I took on some subcontracting while I was in graduate school that grew and continued past graduation, and I decided that I liked having some amount of control over the work I did, the people I worked with, and my work environment. Most importantly, I loved the challenge of working with new industries and content all the time. I was lucky to have full-time work pretty much immediately. As the amount of work grew, I had to make a decision about whether to grow the business by hiring people. I talked with several senior consultants who had faced the same decision. In the end, I decided that I was happy with my current level of income and also that I didn't want the stress of having to bring in business to support multiple salaries. I have been a general contractor with others subcontracting to me, a subcontractor to others, and an independent consultant working alone with clients. I have been working like this for thirty years. I anticipate someday transitioning to part-time consultant and spending time doing other things I enjoy.

Judy says . . .

I made the decision to grow my business. Even though my business was classified as a sole proprietorship, I had eleven full-time employees for more than twenty-five years. Today I have a corporation and I work through two Communities of Practice made up of independent consultants with expertise in performance improvement, school improvement, credentialing, and evaluation.

Q: What are the key foundational design skills a consultant needs?

Cathy says . . .

This question focuses not on consulting skills, but on the technical instructional design/performance improvement skills that are our core competencies. Choosing just a few key ID skills is hard, but here are some that seem to separate good consultants from those who should choose a different path:

1. **Design basics.** A performance consultant must be able to demonstrate fluency in an instructional design model, such as the Dick and Carey model, which helps you have a systematic approach to your work. This means having deep knowledge of the processes/tactics and the theory behind your model(s).

   Advanced practitioners are usually grounded in multiple models and theories and are able to apply different models and recommend different approaches based on individual project needs. Advanced practitioners also have ability to translate theory into practice and to translate "ID talk" into language that the client understands and appreciates. But the foundation skill here is fluency in at least one model, so you have an organized way to approach the work.

   For example, let's think about a familiar process-oriented model—ADDIE (analysis, design, development, implementation, and evaluation). Most people who work in and around training are familiar with the ADDIE model, so that is a good starting point when working with others. When it comes to phase one, analysis, all consultants should be able to advise the client on a strategic approach to the analysis based on the goals to be accomplished, discuss the rationale behind a variety of different data gathering methods (e.g., interviews, observations, focus groups, surveys, review of extant data, etc.), and facilitate each of those methods.

2. **Translation.** A performance consultant must be able to explain how a given performance solution will make a difference that matters to the client.

   Let's say you have completed an awesome analysis, and you have a great proposed solution. It might be simple or complex. Either way, you have to be able to sell that solution to the client in terms that are meaningful to them. They really don't care about skill building or even improved human performance unless you can show that the improvement will lead to something that they care about—which might be increased market share for a private company or a decrease in population obesity for a public health agency.

   As a consultant you really need to have a combination of deep technical expertise and sophisticated communication skills to help the client see the logical flow from problem to solution to results. You must be able to tell the story for them so that not only do they understand, but they can champion it for you as well.

3. **Writing objectives.** A performance consultant must be able to generate a set of instructional objectives that clearly tie to work behaviors.

   So much of our work is competency based, and good designers all have the ability to build a logical path from results to job behaviors to terminal objectives (instructional goals) to enabling objectives (subordinate skills and knowledge). Great designers can quickly write very meaningful objectives, which may take one of many forms. For example, you might write three-part (i.e., behavior, conditions, and criteria) objectives and you might use a specific and meaningful (to designers) taxonomy of verbs, such as those by Gagné or Bloom. In any case, skilled designers make a clear link between what the learner must master and the job performer must do. Failure to do so can lead to all sorts of issues down the line, including project management and scope creep issues.

4. **Designing to objectives.** Given a set of objectives, a performance consultant must be able to develop a design plan that includes appropriate instructional strategies.

   Once the instructional designer/performance consultant has a good set of objectives, the next step is to create a design plan that specifies how the instruction will help learners master the objectives. A foundational skill is identifying the most efficient path to whatever level of mastery you have specified. Almost anybody in a training organization can fill in a design plan with objectives, topics, instructional strategies, instructional time, and assessment, but somebody who is going to be successful as a consultant must do so with elegance—combining sound theory with creative and engaging approaches and lean, targeted content.

A good consultant has enough depth to accomplish this no matter what learning methods or technologies exist. For example, if a new technology were developed tomorrow that enabled people to learn in a completely new way, a good performance consultant would be able to figure out how, when, and why to leverage that technology most effectively.

5. **Developing solutions.** Experienced consultants listen to their clients' needs and have a toolbox of solutions to meet those needs.

Consultants ask and answer a lot of questions. In fact, "asking and answering questions" is a pretty good job description for a consultant. What is driving performance? Is this a training problem or not? What part of this problem can be solved through improved training? Given all the factors that are driving performance in this situation, what interventions are likely to be most effective and efficient? Why? What are our options, considering our organizational strengths and weaknesses?

A good consultant should be able to answer all these questions and provide examples of various types of solutions. An experienced performance consultant can do so from their own wealth of experience, and a newer consultant can do so from case stories that he or she has researched.

Judy says . . .

Over time, consultants may choose to expand their toolbox in response to client needs. For example, some consultants add the capability to redesign work processes and incentive systems, or provide advice on learning management systems, to their services of developing online and instructor-led training. Others choose to hone their expertise in a few select tools, and specialize, like I have, in evaluation and certification.

Q: What are the key non-ID skills a consultant needs?

Judy says . . .

The key non-ID skills a successful independent consultant must have fall into four categories:

1. Building brand
2. Financial and business management
3. Project management
4. Life management

Building brand is done through a marketing and communications plan. Marketing is any activity designed to make you appear credible, influential, and successful. Communications is how you tell your compelling story that associates you with quality, value for the money, efficiency, innovation, and so on. A marketing plan includes who you want to reach, your budget, and the metrics you will use to judge your success. What is often overlooked is how you plan to build market awareness of your services and communicate your value proposition. Communication channels are the vehicles you will use to explain and promote your products and services so potential clients can find you. Vehicles include:

- Print, including business cards, ads, postcards, flyers, letters, and articles
- Electronic, such as a website, webinars, mobile apps, and social media
- Affiliations, such as membership in associations, volunteer work, and participating on taskforces
- Speaking, such as being on professional panels, conducting workshops, giving presentations, and emceeing events

Some tips for building your brand:

- Learn associations' calendars as the call for speakers can be nine months in advance.
- Learn publication calendars because it may take nine months to one year between the time a manuscript is accepted for publication and the time it is actually published. Also be sure to check requirements related to format, length, citations, and reading level, and have someone edit your document before you submit it.
- Look for ways to establish yourself as an expert such as speak, get quoted, serve on panels, offer to emcee or facilitate events, publish, and serve on taskforces.
- Take advantage of opportunities to be known to potential clients in a safe and un-threating way by volunteering to serve on committees and always deliver on your promises and give others credit.
- Keep your messages up to date on your website and social media.
- Turn your activities and accomplishments into promotional material by announcing new contracts, being selected to speak, hosting a panel, or serving on a committee.

Business and financial management is mostly about the discipline of separating your personal and professional finances and setting priorities. For example, you should set up a separate bank account to deposit your earnings and pay business expenses, and get a credit card just for your business expenses. A good piece of advice is to always put aside at least 45 percent of your earnings for taxes, insurance, and infrastructure expenses. It is also important to seek advice from accountants that specialize in small businesses and consulting firms.

Project management is about coordinating your activities so your deliverables are on time. You also need to exercise oversight of your subcontractors and sometime your clients. Clients always remember when you come in late and forget they failed to complete their review on time. Creating a project charter, posting a timeline with agreed on delivery dates, and putting in frequent project status review dates help keep everyone on track.

Life management is about taking care of yourself physically and emotionally, and continuously learning in the process. Some tips:

- Believe you can learn how to be a good businessperson and how to be successful. It's a skill, not innate.
- Learn from your interactions—build an understanding about how to stand on the balcony and interpret what is going on.
- Manage your emotions in a healthy manner.
- Always communicate in a respectful way—a truly respectful way.
- Treat people with dignity and respect—even if they are stabbing you in the back, etc. (I'm still working on refining this skill!).
- Patience—know that it takes time to build a solid reputation.
  It also takes a long time for your networking to pay off. Just, again, be patient.
- Be willing to work long hours. Do right by your client.

Q: How do you get started as a businessperson? How do you get consulting work?

Judy says . . .

When I'm asked this question, I tell people to be clear about what their motivation is for wanting to be a consultant. The motives may be both personal and professional. On the personal side, it might be the desire to expand or reduce travel; have a more flexible work schedule, or to feel more in control of their lives. On a professional level, it might be to do more exciting work or to be their own boss. Unfortunately some expectations may be unrealistic.

Next, I ask them to define what exactly it is that they want to sell. I probe further by asking, What can you offer that is commercially viable so that potential clients will associate you with meeting a need or solving their problems? I remind them that there are many ways to distinguish yourself, for example it might be:

- Your scope of services. Some consultants specialize in development or delivery. Others do everything from the needs analysis, design, development, delivery, and evaluation.
- The quality of your work. Some consultants market themselves on the basis of the quality of their work and support their claims with testimonials.
- The efficiency of your methods. For example, I have well-documented processes and can compete on the basis of my shorter cycle times.
- The value you bring. You can add value by doing what clients are unable to do, do not want to do, or do not have the time to do.
- The way you operate and your philosophy of life.
- Next, I ask them to differentiate the activities they will engage in from what clients want.

For example:

- You may describe yourself as a skilled facilitator but clients pay you to get consensus on an issue or to get agreement by the team on roles and responsibilities or a course of action. So talk about what clients gain from your facilitation skills.
- You may develop online courses, but clients want employees to learn better, faster in ways that are less costly. So mention that employees can apply your content on the job.
- You may deliver instruction, but your clients want a more capable workforce, or to build bench strength across a work unit. So emphasize that clients are more confident in their employees' ability as a result of your work.

My intent is to get them to think about what differentiates them from other consultants. The goal is to be better than the norm.

Q: Compare and contrast a career as a consultant versus one working as an instructional designer for an employer.

Cathy says . . .

My husband and I met at orientation for grad school in the instructional systems program at Florida State. We were both sitting in the back row trying to look cynical, which was about as edgy as we got. Before we graduated, we were married and had a baby on the way. I went into consulting; he went to work as an employee for various organizations, including state and federal agencies. It worked for both of us for some years, as one person could provide strong income and flexibility for parenting stuff while the other provided steady income and employee benefits.

Then there was a layoff, and suddenly we had two performance consultants in the family—one of the dyed-in-the-wool type, and the other one a consultant by necessity. For five years we worked together and lived together, until he decided to go back to being an employee, his current status.

So we have had a lot of time in our family to talk about the difference between being a consultant and working for an employer. People often come to us and ask, "Which path is better?" Luckily, we both think we made the right choice for ourselves. In Table 25.1, there are some questions we suggest you answer for yourself before choosing a path or deciding to make a change.

We have found that a strong preference for novelty or for stability is a huge difference between those who flourish as consultants and those who flourish as employees.

Q: How is consulting different now than from ten years ago? Where do you see it going in the future?

Cathy and Judy say . . .

The number of "accidental consultants" has increased. In the past ten years, the job market has had some ups and downs, and many instructional design professionals have found themselves out of work. Suddenly, they show up on LinkedIn

TABLE 25.1	**Should You Consider Consulting?**

1. I prefer to:
   a. Meet new people all the time and form an ever-expanding network.
   b. Have a group of trusted colleagues and a stable team of people I understand.
2. I prefer to:
   a. Learn new things all the time and explore new industries and subject areas.
   b. Get comfortable with my subject matter so I have a deep understanding of what people in my organization need to know.
3. I prefer to:
   a. Sell the work.
   b. Do the work.
4. I prefer to:
   a. Bounce from one project to another; I crave new challenges but tend to become bored if I work on one thing for too long.
   b. Build relationships and expertise over time so I feel relaxed and comfortable; I don't like the pressure of always starting something new.
5. I think risk is:
   a. Invigorating.
   b. Frightening.
6. Monday morning I have to present some new ideas to a group of decision makers. This makes me feel:
   a. Very confident in presenting myself and my ideas to new people.
   b. Stressed out.
7. The idea of having to report to someone and conform to organizational policies makes me feel:
   a. Panicked; I need to control what I do.
   b. Relaxed; why should I mind?
8. Pick one:
   a. Job titles don't mean much to me. I like the idea of making my own career path.
   b. I like the idea of getting promoted and earning greater responsibility throughout my career.

Every situation is different, but in general, if you lean toward the "a" answers, your personality is probably suited to consulting, while "b" answers are generally more compatible with a career as an employee (or as a contractor with only one client).

as "consultants." There is a difference between somebody who is doing freelance work between positions and someone who is building a professional consultancy.

There is a bifurcation in compensation. There is an increasing pool of freelance developers who can create training programs using the latest rapid development tools. The skill level in this pool varies significantly, but the sheer number of people drives the pay down. Performance consultants with a broad and deep skill set who can work at the strategic level are always in demand, and they can command high compensation. So, you have low pay and increased competition at the "developer" level, and high pay and greater demand at the "strategy" level.

People are becoming a bit more specialized. Instructional design has always been a specialty, but now there are subspecialties in e-learning, learning strategy, sales training, among other. Whether it is in a content area or a learning technology, many consultants are seeking niches in which to be successful.

Rapid development is showing its ugly side. Having the latest training toys has always been attractive. Thirty years ago, clients were determined to get laser discs for training. Twenty years ago, the possibilities for computer-based instruction were tantalizing. Today, we are likely to hear our clients say, "I want a MOOC" (even if they have no idea what one is) or "let's do mobile learning" (even if all their employees sit at workstations where they access everything on computers). All these things have their purposes and appropriate uses, but

none is the solution to all problems. In the past, the high cost of getting the infrastructure in place to develop new delivery systems often meant that people had to put some thought into their appropriateness. While it is great that many technologies are available with low capital investment, the ugly side is that a lot of very poor instruction gets developed that then puts a black eye on the technology and the profession. We have heard clients say, "e-learning doesn't work," and that's a shame, because we think that a truer statement is, "e-learning that is poorly done or not the right solution to the problem doesn't work."

Conclusion

Judy says . . .

We hope the information we have shared gives you a better understanding of what it means to be an independent consultant. The suggestions throughout this chapter are intended to help you be better prepared should you decide to venture out on your own or changes in your employment decide for you. Our intent is for you to avoid the more troublesome pitfalls and not fear embracing challenges that you may not have anticipated. The journey wherever it takes you will bring you new insights about yourself and the world of entrepreneurism. When in doubt reflect on the mantra: competence leads to confidence which leads to courage.

Cathy says . . .

Choosing to become a consultant is a career decision, not a temporary gig between full-time jobs. Some days you can do a happy dance—when you see big positive results in a project that you led, when your clients are singing your praises, or just when you get to plan your own day and be your own boss. Other days are frustrating and demanding, but even then, you are the master of your destiny. If this sounds appealing, the life of a consultant might be a good choice for you.

Summary of Key Principles

1. **A true performance consultant is a professional with deep expertise in instructional design as well as well-honed consulting skills.**

2. **Consulting is a business, and it requires careful decision making**—whether to become one at all, how to get started, and how to grow and maintain your business.

3. **A consultant must be self-driven in many ways,** because he or she must develop new clients and nurture existing ones, drive his or her own learning, network constantly, and run a business.

4. **Smart consultants follow good business practices.** They separate their personal and business expenses, set aside money for taxes and insurance, and work with an accountant who understands financial practices relative to consulting.

5. **Market-savvy consultants build brand through a well-thought-out marketing and communications plan and they tell their story over and over.**

6. **It takes a combination of business and technical savvy and interpersonal skills—along with an entrepreneurial spirit—to be a happy and prosperous performance consultant.**

Application Questions

1. You will be moving to another state in eighteen months. The reason for the move is your spouse is being promoted, requiring a relocation to another office. You see this as an excellent opportunity to start your own consulting business. To prepare you for this career change, develop a marketing communications plan. In the plan:
   a. Describe the services you want to offer and not offer.
   b. Describe your services in a way that will set you apart from the competition.
   c. Identify the people, positions, or groups you want to inform of your services.
   d. Draft a series of messages to each.
   e. Identify the communications media you will use.
   f. Create a calendar indicating what you will communicate with each, when, and how.

2. You are an employee who has often toyed with the idea of venturing out on your own. There has been a change in management. You know you can stay, but you decide to seriously reconsider starting out on your own. Set time aside and reflect on the choice and use your insights to develop a plan of action even if that means staying employed for now. Use the following questions to guide your reflection:
   a. What do I expect will be different about my life if I decide to go it alone?
   b. Do I have the personal discipline to manage my time when there is no work and when faced with project deliverables? My finances?
   c. Am I willing to continuously reach out and market my services? Create a support system I can trust? Find advisors who are committed to my well-being?
   d. Do I have the skills and fortitude to negotiate terms that are in the best interest of my clients and myself?
   e. How much ambiguity can I tolerate? Am I comfortable working with people who resist my advice?

Chapter 26

Getting Involved in Instructional Design and Technology: Recommendations for Professional Development[1]

James D. Klein

Florida State University

Nick Rushby

British Journal of Educational Technology

Competent professionals in instructional design and technology (IDT) are expected to stay current in areas such as learning, instruction, performance improvement, media, and technology (Klein, Spector, Grabowski, & de la Teja, 2004; Koszalka, Russ-Eft, & Reiser, 2013; Richey, Fields, & Foxon, 2000). To stay abreast of recent developments in the field, scholars and practitioners join professional organizations, attend conferences, participate in formal and informal networking activities, read journals, conduct research, publish their results, and contribute to scholarship by reviewing work produced by others. While these last activities are often considered to be the province of professionals working in academia, practitioners in other work settings can also benefit greatly by reading, reviewing, and publishing.

This chapter will provide information about joining professional organizations, as well as using and contributing to publications in IDT. Our aim is to help you make informed decisions as a consumer and, hopefully, as an active member of the field. The chapter opens with a brief overview of the factors to consider when deciding about an organization or publication followed by specific details about twenty professional organizations and fifty-five publications of interest to members of the IDT community. We will respond to common questions. How do you know which organizations to join? Which conferences

should you attend? Which social networks should you spend your time on? We will also look at which publications to read and discuss the business of scholarly writing.

Joining a Professional Organization

Most professional organizations have a clearly stated mission geared toward the interests of a particular segment of a field. These organizations focus on a variety of areas such as educational technology, performance improvement and training, information technology and computers, or scholarly inquiry. Furthermore, they are aimed at a wide range of professionals from academics in higher education to practitioners in business and industry.

The decision to join a professional organization should be based in part on whether its focus matches your career goals and interests. For example, if your goal is to work as an instructional designer in a business setting, then you should consider joining a professional organization that focuses on performance improvement or training. If you plan to become a faculty member in higher education, you should think about joining an organization that has a mission related to scholarship and research.

The decision to join a professional organization should also be based on the specific benefits provided to its members. These may include annual meetings and conferences, employment assistance, journal subscriptions, and professional development opportunities. These benefits are important because they help you become an active and informed member of the field. For

[1]The authors wish to acknowledge Yasin Yalcin and Duke Lorr for their assistance in collecting information about the journals and professional organizations described in this edition of the chapter.

example, conferences provide you the opportunity to keep up with the latest trends, share ideas and problems, and network with others by forming professional relationships and contacts. In addition, a subscription to a journal or magazine published by an organization can help keep you informed of the latest theories, research, or techniques being employed by others.

The benefits of joining any professional organization should be weighed against the cost of membership. Annual dues can range from a small, nominal fee to several hundred dollars. The cost of conference fees and journal subscriptions can also be expensive. Since most professional organizations have special rates for graduate student members, you should consider joining a few groups while in school to see which are most appropriate for you.

Joining an Online Forum or Social Networking Site

A relatively new phenomenon is the plethora of online forums and social networking sites that have emerged in recent years. Today, these forums and social networks are being used to support communities of practice in many professional fields including IDT. At their simplest, an online forum may be no more than a loose grouping of people sharing some common interests, posting and discussing their ideas on the Internet. These tend to be ephemeral groups, forming, storming, and falling into neglect over a relatively short period of time. However, some are more robust. True social networking sites are structured. Some, like Facebook, are primarily intended for social contacts but are being used by professional networks. Others, such as LinkedIn, have been designed for professional networking from the outset. The best networks are expertly moderated so that discussion is nurtured.

You should be very cautious of the information and materials that you upload to online forums and social networking sites. Read the terms and conditions carefully to see what you may be giving away by accepting them. At least one site has attempted to claim ownership of all the material, photographs, and other items uploaded to their site. Other sites make it difficult (or even impossible) for you to delete personal details if you try to resign from the site. Some employers look at entries on social networking sites as part of their selection and recruitment process. Again, think carefully before you upload anything to a social networking site.

A good place to look for online forums and social networking sites is at the websites' professional organizations or by talking to like-minded colleagues at conferences you attend. A social network is only as good as its active members. Think about why you want to join a site. Is it to keep in touch with developments by lurking or participating in some of the discussions? Is it to get support from your peers by posting questions? Is it to build your reputation in the field by posting observations and insights that will mark you as a leader? Select just one or two social networking sites and focus your efforts on those. Active participation can accelerate the development of your professional network. Make sure not to underestimate the time you will have to devote to keep your network up to date.

The rapid rate of technological evolution means that more and different forms of online forums and social networking sites will be developed in the near future. Making effective use of them requires a careful look at personal cost effectiveness. You should ask, How much effort does it take to contribute and how much do I get in return?

Deciding What Conferences to Attend

Professional conferences that specifically focus on your interests are good places for meeting up with old friends, confirming existing ideas, and hearing colleagues preaching to the choir. Nevertheless, progress usually happens because people make connections between apparently unrelated ideas. Sometimes you need to be jolted out of established paths through contact with new ideas from another branch of IDT or even another discipline. It is sometimes very enlightening to attend a conference that is not directly focused on your field.

Conferences and exhibitions are learning events. As an informed learner you should go with clear learning objectives and plan in advance how you intend to achieve them (after all, you are an instructional technologist). Most conferences have a website that you can use to help you plan your visit. Identify the sessions you want to attend. Papers by recognized authorities are usually worth attending but don't ignore the less well known presenters who may have something important to say about the field.

Furthermore, many companies demonstrate learning materials at their exhibit booths. This provides you the opportunity to critique cutting-edge products. Ask questions (e.g., Would you have designed it like that? Do the materials work for the intended audience? How could they be improved?). Don't be hesitant about spending time talking to exhibitors and working through their materials. The exhibitors will feel flattered and you will learn from the experience.

Professional Organizations in IDT

This section of the chapter provides details about twenty professional organizations of interest to the IDT community. Many associations hold annual conferences or sponsor online forums and networks. The list contains a few organizations that were not included in previous editions of this chapter. Updated information was obtained by examining the website of each group. Keep in mind that like IDT itself, professional organizations are constantly evolving. New groups form, association names change, or organizations disband altogether.

American Educational Research Association (AERA) is concerned with improving education by encouraging scholarship and by disseminating research results. Members include educational researchers, administrators, evaluators, professors, and graduate students from a wide variety of disciplines. AERA consists of twelve divisions and approximately 155 special interest groups that enable members with a common interest in a specialized issue to exchange information and ideas. Individuals with an interest in IDT often belong to Division C: Learning and Instruction and to the Instructional

Technology Special Interest Group. AERA sponsors an annual meeting with several thousand presentations on a broad range of topics. Individuals seeking employment in academia will find the job placement center at the annual meeting and an online listing of job openings particularly helpful. AERA publishes several journals such as *American Educational Research Journal, Educational Researcher,* and *Review of Educational Research.*

Association for Educational Communications and Technology (AECT) is for professionals with an interest in the use of educational technology and its application to the learning process. Members include professors and graduate students, school library media specialists, researchers, and instructional developers from business and industry. The association has several divisions and councils to address the specific interests of its members. Individuals with an interest in IDT often join divisions focused on instructional design and development, research and theory, and training and performance. AECT also includes a graduate student assembly as a means to provide community, networking, and eventual transition into AECT and the profession at large. AECT sponsors an annual international convention with several hundred presentations and a job placement center, a summer conference focused on specialized topics, and an online job center. AECT publishes several journals including *Educational Technology Research & Development, Quarterly Review of Distance Education, TechTrends,* and *The Journal of Applied Instructional Design.*

Association for Talent Development (ATD), formerly the Association for Training and Development (ASTD), is an organization for individuals interested in workplace learning and performance. Members work in multinational corporations, midsize and small businesses, government, academia, and consulting firms. ATD has local chapters in several regions of the world that provide an opportunity to network with training professionals at the local level. The organization sponsors various professional conferences each year and an online job bank to assist members who are seeking employment in the training and performance field. ATD also offers eligible practitioners an opportunity to become a Certified Professional in Learning and Performance. ATD publishes *TD Magazine,* an annual state of the industry report, and several online newsletters of interest to its members.

Association for the Advancement of Computing in Education (AACE) is an international organization dedicated to the improvement of knowledge, theory, and quality of learning and teaching with information technology. Members include researchers, developers, practitioners, administrators, policy decision makers, trainers, adult educators, and others with an interest in information technology in education. AACE sponsors international conferences each year including ED-MEDIA (World Conference on Educational Multimedia), E-Learn (World Conference on E-Learning in Corporate, Government, Healthcare, and Higher Education), and Global Learn (Global Conference on Learning and Technology). AACE publishes several journals including the *Journal of Interactive Learning Research, Journal of Educational Multimedia and Hypermedia, International Journal on E-Learning,* and *Journal of Online*

Learning Research. The organization also hosts a sizable digital library with access to over 100,000 journal articles, abstracts and conference proceedings, and an online career center.

Australasian Society for Computers in Learning in Tertiary Education (ASCLITE) is for professionals involved in tertiary computer-based education and training, including educational interactive multimedia. It holds an annual conference and promotes cooperation with other organizations that have a similar focus and publishes the *Australasian Journal of Educational Technology.*

British Institute for Learning and Development (BILD) provides opportunities for networking and access to the collective expertise of its members by maintaining links with key organizations in the United Kingdom and worldwide.

Canadian Network for Innovation in Education (CNIE) is a community of educators, administrators, and practitioners who work to promote research and advance practice in distance education through the use of educational technologies. It holds an annual conference and publishes journals including the *Canadian Journal of Learning and Technology* and *Journal of Distance Education.*

Distance Education Association of New Zealand (DEANZ) fosters development, research, and practice in flexible, open learning systems for education. The association is made up of individual and institutional members mainly from within New Zealand but also from the Pacific Rim.

Educational Research Association of Singapore (ERAS) promotes the use of educational research to enhance the quality of education and facilitates close ties with the international research community. The group is one of the original, formative members of the World Educational Research Association.

E-Learning Network (ELN) is an organization for users of technology in training in the United Kingdom. Its aim is to be a source of information and best practice on technology-based learning and development in the workplace.

European Association for Research on Learning and Instruction (EARLI) is an organization for scholars from Europe and other parts of the world to discuss ideas on instructional and educational research. EARLI sponsors a biennial conference and publishes *Learning and Instruction, Educational Research Review,* and *New Perspectives on Learning and Instruction.*

Hong Kong Association for Educational Communications and Technology (HKAECT) was formed to promote educational technology and research both in Hong Kong and the international community. HKAECT sponsors a conference and publishes the *Journal of Communication and Education.*

International Council for Educational Media (ICEM) was formed to promote best practices in the use of educational technology. It sponsors an annual conference and publishes *Educational Media International.*

International Society for Performance Improvement (ISPI) is focused on improving performance in the workplace through the application of human performance technology. Members include performance technologists, training directors, human resource managers, instructional technologists, and organizational consultants. ISPI has an international network of local and regional chapters across the United States as well as in Canada, South America, Europe, Middle East, Australia, and New Zealand. The organization sponsors an annual international conference and exposition and several institutes each year. It also offers eligible individuals an opportunity to become a Certified Performance Technologist and a Certified School Improvement Specialist. ISPI provides information on employment opportunities through an online career center and publishes *Performance Improvement Journal, Performance Improvement Quarterly,* and *PerformanceXpress.*

International Society for Technology in Education (ISTE) provides leadership and service to improve teaching and learning by advancing the effective use of technology in K–12 education and teacher education. Members include teachers, administrators, technology coordinators, media specialists, and teacher educators. ISTE supports several special interest groups and is responsible for recommending guidelines for the accreditation of programs in educational computing and technology teacher preparation. The society sponsors the National Educational Computing Conference and a blog that addresses topics such as technology integration in the classroom. ISTE publishes *Journal of Computing in Teacher Education* and *Journal of Research on Technology in Education.*

Korean Society for Educational Technology (KSET) is focused on helping scholars and practitioners improve teaching and learning by creating educational technology solutions. Members include researchers, developers, and practitioners in academia, corporations, and government agencies. KSET sponsors an annual international conference on issues related to educational technology.

Malaysian Educational Technology Association (META) provides educators the opportunity to collaborate and exchange ideas related to educational technology. It publishes the *Malaysian Journal of Educational Technology.*

Open and Distance Learning Association of Australia is a professional association for individuals interested in the practice and administration of distance education and open learning. Its objectives are to advance the practice and study of distance education in Australia, foster communication between distance educators, and maintain links with other associations in distance education. It publishes the journal *Distance Education.*

Society for Information Technology and Teacher Education (SITE) promotes research, scholarship, and collaboration for professionals interested in the use of information technology in teacher education. Members are individual teacher educators and affiliated organizations of teacher educators in all disciplines. SITE sponsors an annual international conference and publishes *Journal of Technology and Teacher Education* and *Contemporary Issues in Technology and Teacher Education.*

Society of International Chinese in Educational Technology (SICET) supports the application of educational technology in China. It promotes international connections and exchanges for Chinese scholars who study educational technology for teaching and learning. It sponsors two conferences and publishes two online journals.

Reading, Reviewing, and Writing: The Three Rs for the IDT Professional

In addition to becoming actively involved in an organization, your own professional development can be enhanced by reading and writing about the latest trends and issues in the IDT field. The decision to spend time reading a specific professional publication should be based on whether its focus matches your interests. Like professional organizations, publications have a specific purpose aimed at a particular audience. Some are scholarly academic journals that publish reviews and articles on research and theory; others are magazines that publish about current practices. Publications of interest to the IDT community are focused on a wide variety of topics, including cognition and instruction, distance education, instructional development, multimedia, training, and performance improvement. The journals that you read are your telescope, providing information about the latest research and developments in the field.

The value or quality of a journal depends in part on the interests of readers. A journal that practitioners in business and industry might find very useful may be considered of little value to researchers in the field or IDT professionals working in school settings. Some factors to consider when the issue of quality is addressed are whether submissions are peer reviewed, the rate of acceptance versus rejection of submissions, the impact factor, and the reputation of the editor and editorial board.

In recent years, there has been an increase in the number of electronic journals found on the web. E-journals can be a good source for you to find information on the latest trends and issues in IDT. While some e-journals apply the same rigorous standards used by peer-refereed print journals, others are less careful about the accuracy of information they publish. As an educated consumer of information, you should critically analyze the content of what you read regardless of where it has been published.

If you are working in academia (or plan to in the future), a natural step in your professional development is to conduct research and submit your work for publication. For those who work in other settings, scholarly journal publication is less common. A number of editors value a practical point of view and some journals and magazines listed later in this chapter are specifically aimed at IDT practitioners.

The competition to get published can be tough and only a small percentage of submitted papers are accepted. Some scholarly journals accept less than 10 percent of all submissions. While there is not room in this chapter to provide all the details about how to get your work published, we list some of the key things to consider here.

First, think about what is already known about the topic, what your contribution will add to that knowledge, and what you want people to do differently after reading your article. You must be sure of your focus and the existing literature before you start writing. If your work does not add anything to the literature, then you should ask yourself these two questions: Why am I writing it? If I do not have ambitions for people to do something differently as a result of reading my paper, then why should I spend any time writing it? You may find it helpful to make a few concise, bulleted lists addressing these questions and post it where you can see it every time you sit down to write.

Second, research the journals that you think might be appropriate for your ideas. Understand what kinds of articles they publish, read the directions for contributors, and be sure to meet their requirements for style, format, and length. Many IDT journals publish in English. If English is not your first language, get some help from someone who is a native English speaker to polish your grammar and idiom. The editor and the reviewers must to be able to understand what you are trying to communicate. Furthermore, make your work interesting. You have to sell it to the editor, to the reviewers, and then to the readers. Not all topics are a good read but if you can hold your readers' attention, you have a much better chance of being published.

Next, submit only original work and do not plagiarize your own previously published work or that of other authors without careful attribution. There are established rules governing how much of another published work can be incorporated as fair use but it must be carefully attributed and referenced. There are also ethical considerations about listing coauthors and acknowledging others who have contributed to the work. We strongly encourage you to read and follow guidelines developed by the American Psychological Association (APA) or other professional groups.

Finally, use your colleagues to help polish your paper. Polish it until it gleams! Ask them to review and comment on your work and offer to review their writing in return. Make sure that your paper is as good as it can be before you submit it for review. Don't be discouraged if your early attempts are rejected. Every author (including those listed in this book) has experienced rejection.

Reading a variety of journals will help you identify examples of what makes a good paper. Another way to build your skills in this area is to become a reviewer for one or more journals. This role is not reserved for only the most experienced individuals in the field. Your views are valuable and the benefits for your own personal development can be enormous. In addition to the experience you will get from reading articles in the submission process, you will also get to read about trends and issues in IDT several months before they are published for others to read. If published journals are your telescope, then reviewing is your over-the-horizon radar. Select journals of interest and offer your services!

Professional Publications in IDT

This section provides specific details about fifty-five professional publications in IDT and related fields. The list includes the most recent information available for each journal and some newer periodicals that were not included in previous editions of this chapter. Information about each publication was obtained from either the journal itself, its website, or from one of the following *Cabell's International Directories:* Educational Technology & Library Science, Educational Curriculum & Methods, or Educational Psychology & Administration (see

www.cabells.com). Acceptance rates for each journal are provided when that information was readily available.

American Educational Research Journal publishes peer-reviewed articles that report on theory and research in education. A section on teaching, learning, and human development contains articles of particular interest to scholars in instructional design and technology. Acceptance rate is 13 percent.

American Journal of Distance Education is a peer-reviewed journal that publishes articles on research, theory, and practice of distance education. The journal is aimed at educators who develop and deliver training and educational programs at a distance and administrators of these systems. Acceptance rate is 11 to 20 percent.

Australian Journal of Educational Technology is a refereed journal that publishes articles focused on educational technology in settings such as higher and further education, lifelong learning, and training.

British Journal of Educational Technology publishes peer-reviewed articles on the theory, application, and development of learning technology and communications. The journal is targeted to an international audience of academics and professionals in education, training, information technology, and communications. Acceptance rate is 10 percent.

Canadian Journal of Learning and Technology is a peer-reviewed journal that focuses on the use of technology for learning. Topics include learning theory and technology, cognition and technology, instructional design theory and application, online learning, computer applications in education, simulation and gaming, and other aspects of the use of technology in the learning process. Acceptance rate is 20 percent.

Computers in Human Behavior is a peer-reviewed journal that publishes theoretical articles, research reports, and literature reviews examining the use of computers from a psychological perspective. The journal addresses human interactions with computers and the psychological impact of computer use on individuals, groups, and society. Acceptance rate is 30 percent.

Contemporary Educational Technology is a peer-reviewed, international journal focusing on research, theory, and application of educational technology and instructional design in various educational contexts. Acceptance rate is 30 percent.

Distance Education is a peer-reviewed international journal that publishes research and scholarly articles in the field of distance, open, and flexible education. Acceptance rate is 21 to 25 percent.

Educational Researcher contains scholarly articles of general interest to educational researchers from a wide range of disciplines. The journal has a features section that publishes peer-reviewed articles that report, synthesize, or analyze scholarly inquiry in education. Acceptance rate is 6 to 10 percent.

Educational Technology is a professional magazine that publishes nonrefereed articles interpreting research and practical applications of scientific knowledge in education and training environments. The magazine covers a variety of topics related to the educational technology field.

Educational Technology and Society publishes peer-reviewed articles on the issues affecting the developers of educational systems and educators who implement and manage such systems.

Educational Technology Research and Development is a peer-reviewed journal that publishes research reports, literature reviews, theoretical and conceptual articles, and descriptions of programs, methods, and models. The focus of the journal is on research and development in educational technology. Acceptance rate is 10 percent.

Electronic Journal for the Integration of Technology in Education is an online, refereed journal that features research findings and practical articles on technology integration.

Instructional Science is a peer-reviewed, interdisciplinary journal focused on understanding the theory and practice of instructional processes and how they relate to learning. Recent articles reflect a learning science perspective. Acceptance rate is 21 to 30 percent.

Interactive Educational Multimedia is an online journal that publishes peer-reviewed and invited articles related to research, implementation, and design of multimedia. The journal covers subjects related to educational multimedia, hypermedia, learning, design, teaching, and evaluation of new technologies when applied in education.

Interdisciplinary Journal of Problem-Based Learning is a peer-reviewed, online, open-access journal that includes articles focused on analysis, research, and practice related to all aspects of implementing problem-based learning in K–12 and postsecondary classrooms.

International Journal of Educational Technology is a refereed online journal that publishes research articles in the area of educational technology. It is published online twice each year and is available without an access charge.

International Journal of E-Learning & Distance Education publishes scholarly articles and research papers that focus on issues related to e-learning and distance education. Its objective is to promote and encourage scholarly work on those topics and provide a forum for the dissemination of international scholarship. Acceptance rate is 35 percent.

International Journal of Learning Technology publishes peer-reviewed articles related to theory, design, implementation, effectiveness, and impact of learning technologies. Acceptance rate is 30 percent.

International Journal of Online Pedagogy and Course Design focuses on developments in online course design and teaching methods to improve teaching and learning. Acceptance rate is 20 percent.

International Journal of Technology and Design Education publishes research and development articles related to issues such as the preparation of technology teachers, the assessment of technological competence, and the relationship of technology to other curriculum elements. Acceptance rate is 21 to 30 percent.

International Journal of Training and Development is a refereed journal that publishes theoretical, conceptual, and methodological research articles focused on training. The journal is aimed at an international audience from the academic and corporate communities, as well as those engaged in public policy formulation and implementation.

International Journal of Training Research publishes peer-reviewed articles that focus on research studies and reviews of research related to training and vocational education in Australia and internationally. Acceptance rate is 55 percent.

International Journal on E-Learning publishes peer-reviewed articles on research, development, and practice of e-learning. The journal is targeted to an international audience of educators and trainers in corporate, government, health-care, and higher education settings. Acceptance rate is 10 to 19 percent.

International Review of Research in Open & Distance Learning is a refereed, open access e-journal that includes articles about projects and programs in the area of open and distance learning. It provides documented research into the ways in which learning occurs via flexible delivery modes. Acceptance rate is 40 percent.

Journal of Applied Instructional Design is a peer-reviewed, online journal focused on the study and practice of instructional design. The objective of the journal is to encourage reflective practice and collaboration between academics and instructional design practitioners.

Journal of Applied Learning Technology is a peer-reviewed, online journal focused on issues, problems, and applications of applied learning technologies in education, training, and job performance. It is aimed at trainers, professionals, and educators across a broad spectrum of business, industry, and the military; administrators and executives; and academia.

Journal of Computer Assisted Learning is a peer-reviewed journal that focuses on the use of information and communication technology to support learning and knowledge exchange. It is aimed at an international audience of researchers and practitioners and addresses topics such as collaborative learning, knowledge engineering, and open, distance, and networked learning.

Journal of Computer-Mediated Communication is a refereed e-journal focused on research related to communicating with computer-based media technologies. The journal publishes original research articles and meta-analyses of prior research.

Journal of Computing in Higher Education is a peer-reviewed journal that publishes original research, literature reviews, implementation and evaluation studies, and theoretical, conceptual, and policy papers that contribute to the understanding of the issues, problems, and research associated with instructional technologies and educational environments. The journal provides perspectives on the research and integration of instructional technology in higher education. Acceptance rate is 10 to 12 percent.

Journal of Digital Learning in Teacher Education is a refereed journal that offers a forum to share information about using technology in teacher education among departments, schools, and colleges of education.

Journal of Educational Computing Research publishes peer-reviewed articles that focus on educational computing applications, design and development of computer hardware and software to be used in educational environments, and computer-based education. Acceptance rate is 11 to 20 percent.

Journal of Educational Multimedia and Hypermedia publishes peer-reviewed articles that discuss research, development, and applications of multimedia and hypermedia in education. The journal focuses on the theory and practice of learning and teaching using technological tools that allow the integration of images, sound, text, and data. Acceptance rate is 11 to 19 percent.

Journal of Educational Psychology is a peer-reviewed journal that publishes original psychological research pertaining to education at all levels. The journal occasionally publishes theoretical and review articles related to educational psychology. Acceptance rate is 17 percent.

Journal of Educational Research publishes peer-reviewed articles that describe or synthesize research on educational practices in elementary and secondary school settings. The journal gives special consideration to variables that can be manipulated in educational settings. Acceptance rate is 18 percent.

Journal of Educational Technology Systems publishes articles on the use of computers and web-based instruction as an integral component of an educational system. The journal examines the design and development of interactive computer-based systems, techniques and curriculum that utilize technology in educational systems, and classroom practices and experimentation with technology. Acceptance rate is 70 percent.

Journal of Interactive Learning Research is a refereed journal that publishes articles related to the theory, design, implementation, effectiveness, and impact of interactive learning environments in education and training. Types of articles include theoretical perspectives, research reports, literature reviews, and descriptions of learning environments. Acceptance rate is 10 to 19 percent.

Journal of Interactive Media in Education publishes articles on theory, research, and practice of interactive media in education. The journal uses an open peer-review approach where reviewers are named and accountable for their comment, authors have the right of reply, and readers have the chance to shape a submission before it is published. Acceptance rate is 16 percent.

Journal of Interactive Online Learning publishes manuscripts, critical essays, and reviews that encompass disciplinary and interdisciplinary perspectives in regard to issues related to higher-level learning outcomes. It is a peer-reviewed e-journal that publishes articles on theory, research, and practice related to interactive online learning. Acceptance rate is 6 percent.

Journal of Learning Design is an online, open-access, peer-reviewed journal concerned with the systematic study of pedagogy and learning design in higher education with a focus on the innovative use of technology. Acceptance rate is 40 percent.

Journal of Research on Technology in Education publishes refereed articles that report on research studies, system or project descriptions and evaluations, syntheses of the literature, and theoretical or conceptual positions that relate to instructional uses of educational technology. The journal is aimed at an international audience of teachers, teacher educators, technology coordinators, educational policy makers, and industry leaders. Acceptance rate is 17 percent.

Journal of Technology and Teacher Education is a peer-reviewed journal that publishes articles about the use of information technology in teacher education. The journal covers preservice and inservice teacher education, as well as graduate programs in areas such as curriculum and instruction, educational administration, staff development, instructional technology, and educational computing. Acceptance rate is 15 percent.

Journal of Technology, Learning, and Assessment is a peer-reviewed, scholarly online journal that provides an interdisciplinary forum where initiatives that combine technology, learning theory, and assessment are shared.

Journal of Visual Literacy is a refereed journal that publishes articles exploring the empirical, theoretical, practical, or applied aspects of visual literacy and communication. The journal focuses on the effective use of visuals in a wide variety of fields. Acceptance rate is 40 percent.

Learning and Instruction is a peer-reviewed journal that publishes empirical research studies, theoretical and methodological articles, and literature reviews on learning, development, instruction, and teaching. The focus of the journal is on European work in the field. Acceptance rate is 13 percent.

Open Praxis is a peer-reviewed open access journal that publishes scholarly papers and provides information on worldwide developments in the field of open, distance, and flexible education.

Performance Improvement is a nonrefereed professional magazine aimed at practitioners of human performance technology in the workplace. The journal deals with all types of interventions and all phases of the HPT process and publishes hands-on experiences with models, interventions, how-to-guides, and ready-to-use job aids, as well as research articles.

Performance Improvement Quarterly is a peer-reviewed journal that publishes literature reviews, research studies, and other scholarly articles in the field of performance improvement and human performance technology. The journal seeks to integrate and expand the methods, processes, and findings of other disciplines as they relate to solving problems and realizing opportunities in performance improvement.

Quarterly Review of Distance Education is a peer-reviewed journal that publishes articles, research briefs, reviews, and editorials related to theory, research, and practice of distance learning. The journal frequently examines issues related to the design of online instruction. Acceptance rate is 50 percent.

Research in Learning Technology publishes peer-reviewed papers concerning the use of technology in learning and teaching in education and industry. Acceptance rate is 35 percent.

Review of Educational Research is a peer-reviewed journal that publishes critical, integrative reviews of research literature related to education. The journal contains reviews that interpret and synthesize educational research from a wide range of disciplines. Acceptance rate is 8 percent.

TD Magazine publishes non-peer-reviewed articles that provide useful information on current best practices through case studies, share new technologies and their applications, report emerging trends, and address relevant and pivotal issues to the field of talent development. The magazine is aimed at practitioners in business, government, academia, and consulting.

TechTrends publishes peer-reviewed articles that focus on the practical applications of technology in education and training. Topics include the management of media and programs, the application of instructional technology principles and techniques to education, corporate, and military training settings. The journal is aimed at professionals in the educational communications and technology field. Acceptance rate is 25 percent.

Training Magazine publishes non-peer-reviewed features such as interviews and profiles of industry leaders, special reports, original research, opinions, and the latest trends in training and workforce development.

Turkish Online Journal of Educational Technology is a peer-reviewed e-journal that publishes articles on educational technology use in the classroom, the impact of educational technology on learning, and the perspectives of students, teachers, and administrators on educational technology. Acceptance rate is 35 percent.

Conclusion

IDT is a rapidly evolving field. On the surface, trends in the field appear to be driven by advances in technology. However, there continues to be progress in learning and performance that underpins the design and delivery of instruction and other interventions. Competent professionals invest significant amounts of time in their own continuing development by joining organizations, attending conferences, reading relevant publications in the field, and contributing its knowledge base. Social and professional networks are born, flower, and die so frequently and quickly that it requires conscious effort to keep abreast of them. As a professional in the field of IDT, you must apply this knowledge to yourself and develop your own strategies for making effective use of these channels. Getting actively involved in the instructional design and technology field will contribute to your own professional development.

Summary of Key Principles

1. **Professionals in the IDT field are expected to stay current in areas such as learning, instruction, performance improvement, media, and technology.**

2. **To stay abreast of recent developments in the field, scholars and practitioners join professional organizations, attend conferences, participate in formal and informal networking activities, read journals, conduct research, publish their results, and contribute to scholarship by reviewing work produced by others.**

3. **The decision to join a professional organization or read a particular journal should be based on whether its mission matches your career goals and interests.**

4. **The benefits of joining any professional organization should be weighed against the cost of membership.**

   Benefits may include journal subscriptions, annual meetings and conferences, employment assistance, and networking opportunities.

5. **Active participation in online forums and social networking sites can accelerate the development of your professional network.** Making effective use of these resources requires a careful examination of personal costs and benefits.

6. **Conferences and exhibitions are learning events. You should attend with clear learning objectives and plan in advance how you intend to achieve them.**

7. **As an educated consumer of information, you should critically analyze the content of what you read regardless of where it has been published.**

Application Questions

1. Select a topic of interest and conduct a search of the publications listed in this chapter to identify those that have published articles on the topic. Read a few articles related to the topic (preferably from different publications) and explain which journals provided the best source of information.

2. Write an action plan for your next conference, listing your learning objectives, how you expect to meet those objectives, the preparation you will need to do, and other

resources you may need to achieve your objectives (it is easier if you select a specific conference rather than choosing some abstract event).

3. Contact the editor of one or more of the journals listed in this chapter. Ask about the requirements for becoming a reviewer and volunteer if you qualify. If not, examine your own skills related to these requirements and make a plan for meeting those you currently lack.

References

Klein, J. D., Spector, J. M., Grabowski, B., & de la Teja, I. (2004). *Instructor competencies: Standards for face-to-face, online, and blended settings.* Greenwich, CT: Information Age Publishing.

Koszalka, T. A., Russ-Eft, D. F., & Reiser, R. (2013). *Instructional designer competencies: The standards.* Charlotte, NC: Information Age Publishing.

Richey, R. C., Fields, D. C., & Foxon, M. (2000). *Instructional design competencies: The standards* (3rd ed.). Syracuse, NY: ERIC Clearinghouse on Information and Technology.

Chapter 27

E-Learning and Instructional Design

John V. Dempsey

University of South Alabama

Richard N. Van Eck

University of North Dakota

When we wrote this chapter for the first edition we argued that instructional designers could play a critical role in guiding the development of quality online programs. That has proven true in many areas, perhaps most dramatically at universities, where forms of e-learning have become as accepted as classroom learning once was, and where many instructional designers now routinely work in centers for learning technology. What has continued to change is the notion that there is a big divide between learning that is delivered online and learning that is not. Learning, as instructional designers have long argued, is the result of good instructional design, regardless of the modality, although certainly the modality embeds itself in the instruction. Virtual communities of practice and the ubiquitous nature of personal media have impacted all but the most recalcitrant educators and administrators. Convergence, virtual social learning communities, and personal technologies are and will continue to be primary drivers of e-learning, but to focus on the technology alone is myopic.

As with any learning environment, our efforts must always center on efficiently achieving learning outcomes, arranging creative and robust design, working in development and production teams, and administering workable learning support systems. Understanding what this means for e-learning today requires knowing where we have been with technology and distance education to be sure, but it also requires a kind of paradigm shift in our approach to learning in the twenty-first century. This raises many questions: Do we truly understand the concept and functionalities of e-learning as it exists today? Perhaps more importantly, do we have the conceptual models to adapt to this shifting landscape? Now that institutions are making greater investments in promoting high-quality instruction (online or not), do instructional designers have the skill sets to train faculty in best practices design or to conduct that design themselves on a large scale? Or, are we headed toward obsolescence? What changes to the training of instructional designers will be required by these advances in technology and delivery? In this chapter, we will address the core concepts that will help to answer these questions and, in the process, update concepts that are changing and outline some of the new challenges that exist in this exciting environment today and may appear in the future.

What Is E-Learning?

Over the last several years, *e-learning* has emerged as a broad term that encompasses all learning that involves technology in any way whatsoever. For years, we have attempted to separate learning by modality (computer-based instruction, multimedia, blended and online learning), by geography (distance, face-to-face, hybrid), by time (synchronous versus asynchronous), and various combinations of each (e.g., blended–hybrid). We had some success with this initially, but the pace of change has quickly made a mockery of such orthodox distinctions. Where online once meant asynchronous text, some images, and a rare video, it has evolved into a wonderful (if sometimes chaotic) mix of video, audio, animation, and interactivity.

Consider further how the terms *e-learning, online learning, Internet-based instruction,* and *distance learning* are often used interchangeably. Institutions casually apply different specifics to what the terms mean in practice (i.e., distance learning at one institution or learning environment may look very different at another). The contexts of these definitions create design constraints and affordances for the learning environment, yet designers and developers rarely work through the implications of these parameters. Learners today may interact synchronously (in real time), asynchronously (at different times), or both within a given course. Learners may interact with each other, with a learning management system (LMS), or both, and they may do so from the same or different geographic locations. These instructional experiences may be facilitated by cell phones, phone systems, dedicated audiovisual sites, LMS systems, multimedia computing, social media platforms, the Web and, soon, virtual reality headsets. Just as the technologies involved are varied and not always under the control of the designer or instructor, the instruction itself may be formal and intentional (e.g., designed learning experiences such as courses or training seminars), informal (e.g., social computing and networking), or even entirely incidental (e.g., noneducational computer games). Where, once upon a time, we might have had instruction that combined two or three of these features or aspects, e-learning today may combine any or all of them, do so at a moment's notice, and add or drop them as dictated by the needs of the moment. These descriptions only scratch the surface of the immense complexity in e-learning environments caused by e-learning designers' routine failure to think through the implications and parameters of modern-day e-learning. To borrow another metaphor, we mistake the forest (a simple word that implies uniformity) for the trees (the diverse organisms that make up a forest). We need look no further than the latest discussions about massively open online courses (MOOCs) to find evidence of our (instructional designers) abdication of responsibility. While MOOCs have tremendous potential for democratizing educational access, the public assumed them to be equivalent to "online" learning scaled up to reach thousands instead of dozens of students. The flurry of activity and debate about whether MOOCs "work" or not was, for those trained in instructional design, settled before it began. MOOCs rarely have mechanisms for providing meaningful guidance and feedback based on learner performance—two of Gagné's nine hallmarks of good instructional practice. Can they work? Yes, but only if designed and developed with a full understanding of the implications of technology, learner, outcomes, etc.

Because technology is so much more powerful, easier to use, and prevalent, we have been able to mix and match content, media, instructional methods, and modalities in the same way we had once hoped to combine learning objects. Combined with instructional design research and the rich laboratory of e-learning in higher education and corporate training today, this increase in power and its ease of use has led to highly effective learning that has proven to be every bit as effective as prior learning modalities and approaches (Shachar & Neumann, 2010; United States Department of Education, 2009). As the distinctions between asynchronous or synchronous and face-to-face or distance have faded, so has the need for their definitions and labels faded. Learning is learning, and e-learning simply involves electronic technology in what was once referred to as a transmission/reception/feedback cycle. The implications of convergence of time, space, and technology extend far beyond evolving learning paradigms and current trends. Contrary to popular opinion, it is not merely a matter of learning about "new technologies," but about the profound need to reinterpret our views of instructional design and our professional competence as instructional designers.

Analysis and Triangulation of Learning Outcomes

The richest learning experiences are those that go beyond simple acquisition of knowledge. As Merrill (1997) and others have long contended, information is not instruction. The most useful conceptual frameworks in instructional design are as appropriate for e-learning as they are for other functional architectures. Neither Gagné's nine events of instruction (1985) nor Keller's ARCS (attention, relevance, confidence, and satisfaction) model (1983) limit the nature of the instructional or motivational strategies. Rather, these models provide a framework by which instructional designers can actively approach course topics in intentional learning environments. The models created by Allen (see Chapter 5), Fink (2013) (see Chapter 21), and Lewis and Sullivan (see Chapter 37), for example, further this work by acknowledging the importance of the instructional context and culture for which the learning is designed.

Usually the instructional designer's job is to arrange for intentional learning outcomes. The marketplace continues to expect basic instructional design skills like the ability to use taxonomies of learning outcomes (e.g., Bloom, 1956; Gagné, 1985) and to conduct an analysis to achieve intentional learning outcomes. The methodology required for classifying learning outcomes and conducting learning or instructional analysis is well established and taught in a number of the leading instructional design texts in our field, as are other basic skills such as learner analysis, criterion-referenced assessment, and formative evaluation of instructional materials.

What is often less emphasized, yet critically important in intentional learning environments, is *triangulated alignment*. Triangulated alignment means that the objectives, assessment, and learning activities of the desired learning outcome are aligned, informed by each other, and interdependent. One of the most common examples of NOT achieving triangulated alignment is in situations where higher-order learning outcomes such as problem solving (intellectual skills) are desired, perhaps even precisely expressed in learning objectives, and then the assessment and/or the learning activities focus on verbal knowledge (a completely different variety of learned capability). Common nonexamples of triangulated alignment can even occur when the learning activities are creative and powerful but do not match the intended objectives, or when the learning activities do match the objectives, but the learner is confronted with assessments that are totally out of alignment with both. All three components must be aligned with and inform each other in a strong instructional design. With e-learning, the tools sometimes constrain the process. For example, the abundance of integrated, high-quality testing software in e-learning these days may tempt an instructor or instructional designer to prepare multiple-choice items that are not aligned with the stated learned capability outcomes. While it is fairly straightforward to prepare an objective which, after all, is simply a technical expression of a learning outcome, developing and aligning strategies and assessments can be much harder. Meaningful learning activities, particularly involving small groups in asynchronous environments, require more creativity and preparation than simple threaded discussions and reflection papers, so even when they are the most appropriate strategy for a given outcome, designers may be loath to take the time to design and develop them.

Adequately aligning meaningful assessments and learning activities with the learning outcome is tough work. In almost all situations, this requires some iteration of revision of the objectives, assessments, and learning activities until the three are highly associated (aligned) with each other and the desired learning outcome. This is a skill set in which instructional designers are well trained. Yet e-learning environments are also delightfully saturated with opportunities for informal or incidental learning outcomes, which are often underemphasized in formal IDT instruction. More than any other disruptive technology so far, the Internet allows for serendipity in acquiring or expanding knowledge. For instructional designers, this may be e-learning's most powerful and uncultivated feature. Without question, incidental learning and informal learning (see Chapter 16) on the Internet is a rich area for systematic exploration and research by university faculty, corporate research and development groups, and graduate students. What we learn parenthetically is often the spark that fires a burning interest in more sustained learning activities. Pedagogical philosophies such as constructivism, connectionism, and situated learning address incidental learning more steadfastly than what some individuals refer to as "objectivist" learning approaches, such as the Dick and Carey (1990) model. But while it therefore seems logical that instructional designers should use such conceptual approaches to systematically design for both intentional and unintentional learning outcomes when generating e-learning environments, many educators already believe instructional design is too cumbersome to be practical for intentional learning, let alone incidental learning.

Instructional design professors will tell you quite candidly that some alumni of well-established ID graduate programs cannot reliably conduct instructional analyses of even intentional learning outcomes. Although we believe learning to use traditional instructional analysis approaches is an important part of an instructional designer's education, it is unrealistic to expect nonpractitioners to apply such cumbersome approaches to instructional analysis. The speed at which e-learning materials must be created and the lack of training of many course developers or instructors also makes using taxonomies of learning in traditional instructional analyses unlikely in many situations.

Integrated Frameworks, Iteration, and Elemental Learning

One alternative to using the more abstract traditional taxonomies of instructional design can be found in integrated frameworks that consider learning outcomes in a more general sense. Rather than considering taxonomic levels as discrete,

decontextualized learning outcomes, we can consider them from the perspective of situated learning and authentic contexts. Most commonly that is how we humans learn—by relying on experience and real-world knowledge AND iteratively refining our learning experiences to achieve our goals.

For instance, the *elemental learning* (Dempsey, 2010) and the SAPS (Van Eck, 2015) approaches rely on more integrated alternatives to using formal taxonomies for design and assessment of learning outcomes. The model, based on learning analysis and direct measurement of learning, is iterative, as opposed to a front-end-only approach. Iterative models encourage triangulated alignment (objectives, assessment, and learning activities) by building in the important process of analyzing within the context of actual or simulated learning environments, reflecting on their impact, hypothesizing areas for improvement, and revising the intended learning outcomes, assessments, and learning activities to be more efficacious.

The *elemental learning* approach (Figure 27.1) differentiates between elemental learning (real-life outcomes and those that closely simulate real life) and *synthetic learning outcomes* (usually decontextualized procedures, concepts, and knowledge). In other words, actual and simulated elements involve assessing or learning a real-life task or a simulation of that task—synthetic learning outcomes do not. Instructional design education often provides more emphasis and focused practice on synthetic learning outcomes—the very ones non-ID practitioners find more burdensome and challenging. Influenced by the notion of folk taxonomies in biology and anthropology as well as Bruner's (1960) spiral curriculum, this approach gives primary consideration to elemental learning (actual or simulated real-life) outcomes and *integrates* synthetic learning outcomes (procedures, concepts, related knowledge) in a naturally occurring iterative process. This model also allows for an easier use of the uncanny intuition that creative content experts often demonstrate. These kinds of simpler, more immediate models of instructional design and learning analysis that concentrate on what occurs in the "real world" are most likely to be adopted and to proliferate in e-learning, and it behooves ID practitioners to become more fluent in their use and dissemination.

E-Learning Functional Architectures

Just because the landscape of e-learning has changed does not mean that the relationship of learning to instructional design has changed. We still use instructional design to create learning environments and products, regardless of the medium. The processes, or *functional architectures* involved in our work, however, are changing rapidly as a result of technology and its impact on human cognition and interaction. By *functional architecture*, we mean the various functional entities and components involved in an instructional system and the collaborations and interactions among them. Many of these are most certainly influenced by new technologies, but it is the means by which these technologies promote new ways of thinking and interacting that are perhaps the most significant. The use of texting on mobile phones, for example, shows how the functional architecture of learning environments can be influenced. While for

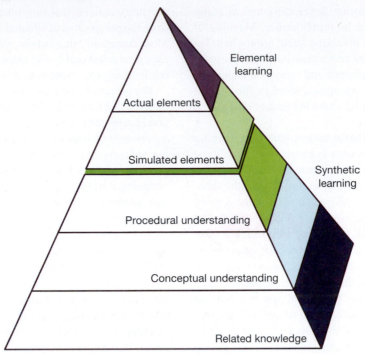

FIGURE 27.1 Elemental learning pyramid culminating in actual elements. The top two levels are elemental learning outcomes. The bottom three learning outcomes are viewed as synthetic.

many years people commonly used only voice to communicate on telephones, most now use text and voice. This, in turn, has expanded the capabilities of the functional architecture and how instructional systems can use this interactive technology (texting reminders to work on homework assignments, real-time group data reporting, etc.). We argue that it is necessary to understand and embrace changes in the functional architectures of instructional design, not just the technologies themselves, if we are to continue to play a meaningful role in the future of learning.

The Impact of Social Interaction on Design

The most consistent impact on e-learning since the turn of the century has been the strength of community and the use of social learning technologies for purposeful learning activities. The scenario of the solitary student working alone at her computer late into the night with little or no contact with her peers still exists, but many current and future learning systems will emphasize shared experience features. Designers have only to look at the meteoric rise of social learning tools such as Facebook and Twitter in the latter part of the first decade of the twenty-first century to see how the convergence of these technologies and e-learning experiences means we are not just "adding" technology, but changing the very nature of the learning experience—the functional architecture of learning.

If social constructivism has one true champion in circumstance, it is the shared construction of learning assignments—an inherently social activity. Many e-learning designers are coming to see the information they incorporate as a product along a continuum of permanence (a textbook, an e-book, a wiki, a Web conference, an informal mashup). Likewise, e-learning is a process of a learning group in action among an increasing array of learning options and shared experiences.

This requires a shift in our thinking as instructional designers akin to the strategies adopted by reality television shows and alternate reality games, in which designers must monitor, adapt, and coauthor the instructional narrative while keeping the short- and long-term goals in mind. More frequent instances of instructional designs with learners as designer teams, peer tutoring, and other collaborative designs indicate that this emphasis on product AND process may be one of the agreeable strengths of e-learning. Participation and creativity not available in conventional classes are commonplace in well-designed online environments. Effectively structured (but not rigid) e-learning group processes, such as those described by Johnson and Johnson (see Chapter 32), describe how teams can be structured and led, what authority the team leader has, what responsibilities other members of the team assume, how team projects are graded, and the role of the instructor in arbitration. These are the rules of the social game. These make learning communities eminently viable and joyfully fluid, and instructional designers will need to understand and navigate these and other changes in functional architecture if they wish to create or add value to meaningful e-learning environments.

Media versus Technics[1]

The functional architectures of e-learning also require us to change our conceptualizations regarding learning technologies as "mere media" modes of delivery or components of our

---

[1] Technics here is used in a more modern context than that experienced by Lewis Mumford, but is similar in that technology is viewed as "that part of human activity wherein . . . man controls and directs the forces of nature for his own purposes." (1952, p. 15)

courses. While our field has studied the role that technology plays in supporting cognition and learning, our terminology is probably insufficient to capture the complexity of technology, instructional design, and cognition that makes up e-learning. So, at the risk of introducing even more technical jargon into our field, we refer to the unique learning tactics made available by e-learning technologies as "technics." *Instructional technics*, then, are activities or tactics that use technology designed or selected to attain specific learning outcomes. They are influenced or driven by instructional strategies and, in some cases, the need for cost reductions. Technics are not strategic in the sense of the "big picture" of *what* or *when* to teach or learn in order to achieve elemental learning outcomes. Rather, they are the new tools in our instructional design toolbox, to be adopted or retired as learning environments evolve. They vary by circumstance and media. In effect, technics are the designer's toolkit used in the context of the e-learning functional architecture.

Instructional technics could include any combination of on-campus lectures, computer-based training modules, online seminars, reference websites, e-books, DVDs, threaded discussions, videoconferences, Weblogs, simulations, performance support systems, and numerous other elements by which learning is accomplished. E-learning can likewise be *synchronous* (takes place "in real time"), *asynchronous* (does *not* take place "in real time") or a mixture of both. As such, technics allow us to conceptualize (and design) instruction based on learning outcomes, "cognitively relevant characteristics" of media, the types of learners, the environment, and whatever constraints are present technically or in the learning culture.

Technics versus Trucks

Some thirty years ago, Richard Clark fostered a healthy debate in the instructional design world when he argued that media "do not influence student achievement any more than the truck that delivers our groceries causes changes in our nutrition" (1983, p. 446). This is often referred to as the "mere vehicle" argument. As far as it goes, this line of reasoning is hard to refute in statistical comparisons.[2] The follow-up assumption was that learning is "delivered" to learners (the method) and that the delivery vehicle itself (the medium) is not particularly important. In his equally well-known response, Kozma counterargued that "media are distinguished by cognitively relevant characteristics of their technologies, symbol systems, and processing capabilities" (1991, p. 179) and,

> Clark creates an unnecessary schism between medium and method. Medium and method have a more integral relationship; both are part of the design. Within a particular design, the medium enables and constrains the method; the method draws on and instantiates the capabilities of the medium. (p. 205)

In other words, not all trucks are equal: A water truck could carry watermelons, but they would have to be pureed in order to be stored in the truck efficiently, thus changing the experience of consumption. It is perhaps easier to see the logic of this stance when considering more advanced media such as online simulation games. While many have argued that games promote problem solving, closer inspection of different types of gameplay and different types of problems makes it clear that some gameplay types will be better for certain kinds of problems than others (e.g., Hung & Van Eck, 2010; Van Eck, 2015) (also see Chapter 33). The takeaway from this stimulating academic argument reinforces (for us) that it is not profitable to ask which aspects of a designed e-learning environment are more important than others, but instead to consider them as components of the overall design. Artful design incorporates prior knowledge in a way that transcends controlled experimental comparisons of one "kind" of learning versus another. Increasingly, instruction is not "delivered" or even intentionally designed; we learn attitudes from role models who may be unaware of their effect on us and acquire incidental learning outcomes by interacting with entertainment media. Design of any sort has the function of creating order. Instructional design at its best simply creates order in the sense of creating a rich environment where learning can take place. Good design does not presuppose a highly controlled delivery method that is quantitatively measurable in short-term learning outcomes. Method (delivered, constructed, or incidental) and media shape learning outcomes, but neither has an exclusive license to influence long-term learning within a rich, well-designed environment.

This distinction becomes particularly important as we continue to shift away from instructional design as a means of *creating* instruction and toward the *design* of learning experiences within which learners are themselves architects of their own learning. While our models and core tenets remain relevant in the design of e-learning, how we think about outcomes, objectives, media, and the learning experience itself must evolve. So what will this look like in practice?

Functional Architecture, Technics, and Elemental Learning

Combining the concepts of functional architecture, technics, and elemental and synthetic learning outcomes provides a road map for designing the kinds of e-learning environments that reflect current conceptions of learning as a constructed experience. Focusing on authentic, contextualized tasks as they occur in the real world (elemental outcomes) accomplishes several things. It helps us design cohesive, meaningful, and complex e-learning *environments* rather than contextually sterile and simplistic learning *containers*. This is not an entirely new approach within instructional design, of course; we have often begun our design with the real-world learning outcomes foremost in our minds (see Chapter 35). But it does allow an improved way of conceptualizing the learning environment as the dynamic interaction of the learner and the world in which knowledge will be applied. It is no longer a matter of thinking about how to transfer learning to the real world; we must design environments that overtly support connections to the complex and context-laden real world versus decontextualized synthetic learning.

---

[2] The outcomes of many comparative media-type and distance education studies have in the past generally resulted in no significant differences (Russell, 2001), although a huge U.S. Department of Education meta-analysis on which Clark was an advisor found that, on average, students in online and blended learning conditions performed better than those receiving face-to-face instruction (United States Department of Education, 2009).

Likewise, it is preferable to think of e-learning technologies not as a platform (e.g., a learning management system employing such and such media) but as parts of a functional architecture combining technics in designed experiences that support learners' reception or (preferably) construction of knowledge, skills, and attitudes. We ID folk are not providers of technology tools but designers of environments that allow for the use of technology in intended and unintended ways, including the important functions of assessing and documenting evidence of learning. There is a tendency to "stake out" the territory our learners cover by defining the platform, time, place, and tools learners will use. This makes our e-learning environments more artificial, less flexible, less relevant, and less long-lived. That reinforces the "mere vehicle" argument and, in some cases, can even diminish learning outcomes.

Rather than making assumptions about all online learners (e.g., they cannot attend campus classes and find synchronous learning too difficult), we should be selecting technics (and allowing learners to do so) in order to create rich, flexible environments that reflect elemental outcomes, support necessary synthetic outcomes, and provide connections to the world outside the e-learning environment. If the learning outcomes require interaction, synchronous sessions via Web conferencing and in-person attendance can be specified but also recorded for later viewing via Web, iPod, or cell phone playback. Where collaboration is needed, small groups of learners should be able to self-select from a variety of tools such as instant messaging, texting, wikis, and conferencing technology. Where interaction in real-world environments is important, secure Web conferencing tools and virtual worlds should be available for discussion, meetings where presence is desirable, or role-playing. Certainly, the proliferation of all of these technologies contributes to anxiety for learners and instructors. The bottom line is to consider the learning outcomes possible (intentional and informal) along with the affordances of various technology combinations and then create an instructional design that takes advantage of these factors in an artful, flexible, and theoretically appropriate fashion.

The Field of Instructional Design and E-Learning

E-learning environments are more complex and more demanding of skilled instructional designers than ever before, and the unprecedented rate at which ever more complex e-learning systems emerge can be mystifying. Times are good in ID because the field in which we labor is increasingly difficult to plow, making our roles even more important. Organizations need the help of instructional designers who have a good theoretical background AND a designer's grasp of the use of e-learning technologies. However, instructional designers will always be a high-cost item to an organization, and if we are not seen as essential to the e-learning development process, decreased demand and remuneration will threaten our continued existence or at least squash the potential of our contribution.

We suggest, therefore, that our field should revisit the concept of certification. While previous efforts have sometimes been contentious and unproductive, times have changed. Many schools are now moving to "certify" e-learning design through their own internally developed checklists and professional development, and instructional designers have absented themselves from the conversation. As with e-learning in the 1990s and 2000s, we are ceding the territory to those who do not understand instructional design principles and practices. We have seen checklists that focus on the presence of standard elements (e.g., announcements, syllabus, discussion board, wikis) without regard to the functional architectures or learning outcomes. We may feel it is too difficult to agree on what it means to be an instructional designer, but higher education does not find it difficult to define the field for us, at least as it relates to e-learning design. If we want a place at the table, we have to join the conversation.

Certification in essential instructional design and e-learning skills would at least suggest that an individual instructional designer has a basic level of competence in the field. As certification requirements tend to drive professional schools, certification would also ensure that university programs do not neglect basic instructional design skills in the pursuit of the latest fashions in educational psychology. Although there is little widespread consensus in the field about standards for certification, there are standards such as those proposed by the International Board of Standards for Training, Performance and Instruction (Koszalka, Russ-Elf, & Reiser, 2013) that could form a starting point for such certification efforts. Coupling efforts like this with accreditation requirements of universities and various professional societies would result in some reliability in the professional practice of instructional design. Standards and certification are one of the hallmarks of a rigorous profession, and we should get serious about these discussions or risk watching our window of opportunity close.

Summary of Key Principles

1. **E-learning has emerged as a broad term that encompasses all learning involving technology in any way whatsoever.** Distinctions such as hybrid, blended, and distance learning have been made largely irrelevant by the advances in technology, not just in its power, but also in ease of use. To a certain extent, this also makes distinctions of time (synchronous, asynchronous), place, and platform mode (e.g., mobile, Web, face-to-face) less relevant.

2. **E-learning is characterized by two phenomena:** (a) functional architectures that employ various collaborative or interactive functional entities and components, and (b) technics that use technology designed or selected to reach learning outcomes.

3. **Concentrating on elemental learning outcomes encourages a simpler, integrated, and iterative approach to learning analysis and assessment that**

helps guide the use of media, platform, location, and time. Although it is very important to analyze the learning outcomes of both intentional and incidental learning, traditional instructional analysis techniques are cumbersome.

4. **Neither media nor method (delivered, constructed, or incidental) exclusively influences long-term learning within a well-designed e-learning environment.** Instructional design, like all design, has the function of creating order.

Application Questions

1. If you were to design an undergraduate program in IDT, describe how you would reconceptualize the curriculum. What would move from the master's level down to the undergraduate level? How and where would certification come into play? How would master's degree work differ? What would be the relationship between master's and doctoral programs?

2. If you were to design an introductory IDT course for an e-learning format, how would you decide which technics to include? Use the terminology and concepts discussed in this chapter (e.g., elemental versus synthetic learning outcomes, selection of technics), and consider what it might mean to design functional architectures and select appropriate technics FOR learners versus designing to allow learners to do so for themselves. What impact might that have on the design process?

3. Assume you have been told to design a "Twenty-First-Century Learning Course" that incorporates the full range of technics and technologies that are used today (social networking, collaboration, Facebook, etc.). What are the key characteristics for which you would design, and how would you design for intentional versus unintentional learning?

4. Assume you have been hired as a consulting instructional designer to help an international corporation set up a virtual training network. Describe what steps you would take and what questions you would ask in evaluating the feasibility of this network and in developing your proposed system.

5. Using the Internet, find ten examples of distributed learning. Try to find examples of each of the following (one example may fit within several of the categories):
   a. Corporate distributed learning
   b. Academic distributed learning
   c. Distributed resource support
   d. Hybrid classes
   e. Virtual classes
   f. Distributed learning based at physical locations
   g. Distributed learning via virtual institutions
   h. For-profit distributed learning
   i. Free distributed learning
   j. Skills-based training (e.g., computer skills training)
   k. Knowledge-based learning (e.g., World War II history, introduction to psychology)

References

Bloom, B. S. (Ed.). (1956). *Taxonomy of educational objectives*. New York: D. McKay.

Bruner, J. (1960). *The process of education*. New York: Vantage.

Clark, R. E. (1983). Reconsidering research on learning from media. *Review of Educational Research, 53*(4), 445–459.

Dempsey, J. V. (2010). Elemental learning and the pyramid of fidelity. In R. Van Eck (Ed.), *Gaming and cognition: Theories and practice from the learning sciences* (pp. 82–107). Hershey, PA: IGI Global.

Dick, W., & Carey, L. (1990). *The systematic design of instruction* (3rd ed.). New York: Harper Collins.

Gagné, R. M. (1985). *The conditions of learning and theory of instruction* (4th ed.). Fort Worth, TX: Holt, Rinehart and Winston.

Hung, W., & Van Eck, R. (2010). Aligning problem solving and gameplay: A model for future research and design. In R. Van Eck (Ed.), *Interdisciplinary models and tools for serious games: Emerging concepts and future directions* (pp. 227–263). Hershey, PA: IGI Global.

Keller, J. M. (1983). Motivational design of instruction. In C. M. Reigeluth (Ed.). *Instructional design theories and models: An overview of their current status* (pp. 386–434). Hillsdale, NJ: Lawrence Erlbaum Associates.

Koszalka, T. A., Russ-Eft, D. F., & Reiser, R. (2013). *Instructional designer competencies: The standards* (4th ed.). Charlotte, NC: Information Age Publishing.

Kozma, R. B. (1991). Learning with media. *Review of Educational Research, 61*(2), 179–211.

Merrill, M. D. (1997, Nov/Dec). Instructional strategies that teach. *CBT Solutions,* 1–11.

Mumford, L. (1952). *Art and technics*. New York: Columbia University Press.

Russell, T. L. (2001). *The no significant difference phenomenon: A comparative research annotated bibliography on technology for distance education*. Montgomery, AL: IDECC.

Shachar, M., & Neumann, Y. (2010). Twenty years of research on the academic performance differences between traditional and distance learning: Summative meta-analysis and trend examination. *Journal of Online Learning and Teaching*, 6(2), 318.

United States Department of Education. (2009). Evaluation of evidence-based practices in online learning: A meta-analysis and review of online learning studies. Edited by B. Means, Y. Toyama, R. Murphy, M. Bakia, & K. Jones. Washington, DC: U.S. Department of Education Office of Planning, Evaluation, and Policy Development Policy and Program Studies Service.

Van Eck, R. (2015). SAPS and digital games: Improving mathematics transfer and attitudes in schools. In T. Lowrie & R. Jorgensen (Eds.), *Digital games and mathematics learning: Potential, promises and pitfalls*. New York: Springer.

Chapter 28

Social Media and Instructional Design

Vanessa P. Dennen

Florida State University

Social Media Overview

Social media are Internet-based tools that allow users to build networks through which they may then communicate and share information with each other. Social media have rapidly become a prominent feature of contemporary life. The majority of American adults are social media users (Perrin, 2015), as are most adults in Western Europe (Office for National Statistics, 2013). Rates of use in other countries vary, but they have been continuously trending upward. Although use is widespread across all population sectors, higher rates of use have been found among youth and increased with level of education and income (Perrin, 2015).

Social media use has spread through all facets of life. Through social media people build online networks that support and maintain relationships and provide information. These networks have for many become an indispensible part of everyday life, guiding activities both at work and at home and connecting individuals with other people and information on an as-needed basis (Rainie & Wellman, 2012). People look to social media for information about topics ranging from the news (Barthel, Shearer, Gottfried, & Mitchell, 2015) to health care (Fox & Duggan, 2013) and for activities ranging from participation in civic life (Smith, 2013) to seeking dating partners (Smith & Duggan, 2013) to education (Tess, 2013).

Within education, social media is considered an emerging technology, which means that its place in the field is still evolving, sometimes with associated hype, and its best uses are likely neither fully understood nor realized at this time (Veletsianos, 2010). At the institutional level, social media's reach extends well beyond learning. For example, it has been used to support marketing and recruitment, student outreach, and extracurricular activities. In the learning context, social media use may be institutionally prompted or encouraged, or initiated by the individual instructor or instructional designer. Some of the forces driving the push for social media integration include the desire to capitalize on technologies that many people already use in other realms of life, the desire to engage in current instructional trends, and the belief that social media will motivate students. However, simply deciding that social media should be used to support learning in a particular environment or context does not mean that the shift to design and teach with social media will be a smooth or successful one—even when individuals are already regular users of social media.

The following two scenarios are modeled from real situations facing instructional designers and instructors who design their own courses. They highlight the current cultural climates and expectations surrounding social media use in support of learning.

Scenario 1: *Stacey is an instructional design manager working for a major corporation in the insurance industry. She's been tasked with leading a team that will revise continuing education materials for field agents. The task might be relatively straightforward if all Stacey and her team were doing was updating content. However, they've been given a larger challenge—to engage their learners using social media or social media–like interactions. Stacey was told that the reason behind this revision was twofold: First, the corporation was hoping to capitalize on social media as a learning trend, appealing to some of the newer members of their workforce and* striving to be an innovative leader in their field. Second, the corporation hoped that incorporating social media into mandatory training would help promote greater use of the company's online communication tools and social media sites by employees. Upon receiving her assignment, Stacey immediately had a number of questions: Would social media be used to disseminate content only, or to interact with learners? Would her team be able to control the learning content and uphold quality standards when using social media? Would all of the targeted employees be ready and willing to learn via social media?

Scenario 2: *Todd is a faculty member at a public university. He's felt a lot of pressure lately to incorporate social media and related technologies in his classes, because he's read a lot about how social media appeals to millennials, but he's not sure how to begin. His learning management system has some integrated social media tools, and he's heard about other faculty using popular tools like Facebook and Twitter. He feels like his classes are already pretty well designed, and he doesn't know what he should be using social media for—to share information with his students, to communicate with his students, to have students work in groups? He's also a bit worried that his students will get inaccurate information via social media and that students might engage in uncivil online behavior that he's not entirely sure how to manage or regulate.*

Stacey and Todd's scenarios represent real opportunities and challenges facing current instructors and instructional designers. While Stacey's situation is driven by an organizational mandate and Todd's is simply in reaction to institutional pressure, both recognize that that effective integration will require careful needs assessment, instructional design, and facilitation. Both see that there are many ways in which social media might be used, some of which are more interactive than others. Finally, both worry about issues like content, quality, and participation. As they work through their instructional design processes, they will both need to identify appropriate social media-based learning activities, engage in a tool selection process, and directly confront some challenges posed by the use of online, often public, user-centered learning technologies.

Overview of Social Media Tools and Educational Uses

The landscape of social media tools is one that rapidly changes. New tools are developed and existing tools are discontinued or absorbed into other tools with great frequency. Even among the well-established tools with large user bases, change is common, with regular unveiling of new functions, features, and terms of service. Each of the tools appearing in Table 28.1 is commonly used by individuals for personal and professional purposes, and

TABLE 28.1   Popular Social Media Tools and Their Educational Uses

Tool	Brief Description	Common Educational Uses
Facebook	Facebook is a social network that provides individual users with a profile where content may be shared, liked, and commented upon by the user's connections, called "friends." Facebook also allows the creation of group spaces.	Facebook groups may be used to enable communication and sharing among class members.
Blogs	Blogging tools allow users to publish a series of posts (text, images, and video) to a Web page, with posts appearing in reverse chronological order. Readers can then comment on or share individual posts.	Individual student blogs can serve as a reflective writing forum or an online portfolio of class work. Instructors may maintain a blog to communicate with students and encourage commenting.
Twitter	Twitter is a microblogging tool that allows users to broadcast brief messages. Messages can include images and URLs. Twitter can aggregate messages by user or by hashtag (e.g., #socialmedia).	Shared hashtags enable chats among multiple users in real time or asynchronous resource sharing. Students can follow experts and key information sources.
LinkedIn	LinkedIn is a professional networking tool that allows users to create searchable profiles highlighting their education and experience. LinkedIn also supports open and closed groups, providing space for discussion and sharing.	Not commonly used to support formal learning, but informal learning occurs in group discussion areas.
YouTube	YouTube is a social media tool that focuses on video sharing. Users may post their own videos and view videos shared by other users. They can create their own channels, allowing other users to subscribe and receive notifications whenever new videos are posted.	Watch videos created by others (e.g., lectures, tutorials). Upload and share instructor lectures. Upload and share student projects.
Wiki	Wikis are Web pages that allow multiple users to edit them. Wikis record a complete edit history, and also include discussion tools so contributors can discuss their editorial work that is being done on the front-facing Web page.	Wikis have been used to facilitate collaborative brainstorming, peer writing, and editing.

has particular features that may make it attractive to support learning and professional development.

In addition to the writing and discussion-focused activities described in Table 28.1, social media tools are heavily used to share, collect, and curate information. Although many tools include features that foster these activities to varying degrees, some tools have been developed specifically to facilitate the collection and sharing of Internet-based information. Tools in this category include Delicious, Diigo, Pinterest, ScoopIt, and Storify. These tools encourage users to bookmark or collect items from websites or other social media channels, and then engage in activities such as grouping, tagging, annotating, and sharing. Users may form groups and collaborate in these bookmarking and curation activities.

The items listed here constitute a less-than-exhaustive list. There are myriad other social media tools that may be used by educators (see Table 28.2 for additional examples of learning activities). Some tools have been designed specifically for educational use, modeled off mainstream tools but with additional privacy, security, and instructor oversight features. For example, edublogs is a blogging platform created specifically for educator and class use, and edmodo is a multifaceted social network with private class spaces and a variety of short messaging and file sharing tools. Other social networks, like Flickr, the photo-sharing network, are focused on specific media.

Instructional Uses and Advantages

Social media, when used as an instructional tool, has the potential to open up classroom experiences, making them more learner centered and expanding the potential content base of the class. Using social media, both instructors and learners can tap into a vast array of learning resources and experts. Additionally, social media can be used to support learning interactions among members of a class or with people outside of a class, and can be used to seek feedback and critique from a wide audience. Table 28.2 presents a few common types of learning activities, summarizing how they may differ when conducted with or without social media.

Note that social media enhance learning in different ways in each of these activities. In some instances the use of social media may be instructor driven, designed directly into the class activity; and in other instances it may be student driven, and integrated into the activity without the instructor's prior planning and perhaps without their knowledge. Social media tools can be used to enable greater within-class communication, such as the backchannel that allows students to connect with each other in meaningful ways while the instructor speaks or the creation of work-sharing spaces where collective comments may be provided.

Social media tools also can help extend the boundaries of the classroom. Instructors can easily connect to a broad network of experts who might be invited to participate in online class activities. The authors whose work is being read in a class might be queried for additional information via social media. Students in different sections of the same course or learning the same topic at different institutions might be connected with each other, expanding the breadth of people with whom the resources related to or discussion on the course topic might be shared. Additionally, class members can seek a connection with an authentic population. For example, if learners are taking a class on social work, they might interact with actual

TABLE 28.2	Learning Activities, with and without Social Media	
Activity	**Without Social Media**	**With Social Media**
Lecture	Instructor lectures to students who sit in a classroom and listen. Online students may watch a video of the lecture.	Whether the lecture is live or video based, students can communicate with each other via a social media backchannel during a lecture, asking and answering questions and sharing relevant resources. Instructors can later review these communications to determine if additional learning assistance is needed.
Guest lecture	Limited to people within the class members' existing social spheres. Typically requires a formal, scheduled talk.	Easy to identify and contact a vast array of experts to seek participation, whether at the level of a full lecture, or for more casual and loosely scheduled interactions.
Readings and discussion	Students complete readings as assigned by their instructor. Students save questions to ask during class, or ask privately via e-mail or office hours. Discussion occurs during class time and is limited to course participants.	Students complete readings as assigned, but if they have questions along the way they may seek assistance from their instructor, classmates, or knowledgeable others by posting them online. Discussion may occur during class time and in class space, or outside of class in an online venue with non-class participants.
Critique	Students share their work with classmates during a class session and receive feedback. Alternately, students may exchange papers and provide each other with written feedback.	Students share their work with classmates or a wider audience via a social media tool and receive feedback. Feedback providers can typically see each other's comments.
Research projects	Students conduct research at the library and write up and submit reports to their instructor.	In addition to using library-based resources, students may search for relevant materials or may seek feedback on their developing ideas via online networks.

social workers to help them better understand the relationship between theory and practice. If they are learning about graphic design or advertising, they can get feedback from their target audience.

The self-archiving nature of social media content and actions along with the availability of user analytic data means that instructional designers might also take a fresh look at assessment. Learners in a social media environment may be assessed not only based on a final product, but also on the processes in which they engaged to develop that final product. Evidence such as number and types of interactions with both content and other people can show the breadth of effort expended by the learner, while the content and nature of those interactions and the specific path of creation and revision can shed light on the depth of the learner's processes.

Instructional Challenges

Designing instruction that incorporates social media poses some new challenges for instructional designers, as can be seen in the above scenarios. Instructional designers typically have experience working with subject-matter experts to collect learning content and organizing that content into logically sequenced chunks, with practice activities and assessments interspersed at appropriate intervals. Although practice activities may interject an element of the unknown in the classroom (no matter how directive or tightly prompted a practice activity is, learners may have a unique response), instructional designers typically are responsible for preparing the instructor to identify the target behavior and facilitate student movement toward that point. Situations that fall outside the bounds of the expected student response are left for the instructor to handle. However, social media technologies have a decentralizing effect in education, shifting the locus of control away from a single point and dispersing it across participants (Hoffman, 2009), meaning that unexpected events may extend beyond the scope of what an instructor expects to handle. Additionally, instructional designers need to rethink their pedagogical approach in order to fully take advantage of social media's decentralizing effect in a learning context.

Another challenge facing instructional designers in this area can be the pressure to incorporate social media into learning activities and assessments. As these tools and the networks they support become an increasing part of everyday life, many learning organizations want to adopt them. However, the driving force behind social media adoption in educational settings should be the learning objectives and context, not external pressures. Instructional designers may have to push back on these pressures when social media is not the best choice, or find other, nonpedagogical ways to support organizational use of social media.

Finally, social media can be a disruptive force within an educational setting. One study found that personal social media use in an educational context may not be desirable, diminishing learner performance and happiness and raising technostress (Brooks, 2015). In another study, learners were found to engage in frequent task switching, moving between the learning task and an unrelated social media interaction (Rosen, Mark Carrier, & Cheever, 2013). These findings raise questions as to the value of using social media to support learning, since learners may struggle with keeping themselves focused on the learning task at hand. For instructional designers, the challenge is to find ways to minimize the stress on learners by helping them learn how to use social media effectively, and to both leverage social media's disruptive qualities (e.g., use social media in ways that support just-in-time knowledge needs) and avoid social media when the disruption would harm productivity.

Tool and Service-Based Issues

Some of the very characteristics that make social media attractive to educators—the openness, the ease of sharing, the self-archiving nature of the media, and the pervasiveness throughout many parts of life—are the same characteristics that require careful consideration prior to adoption. Instructional designers should consider the risks to and perspectives of the learning organization as well as the instructors and learners who will be following the curricula and using the learning materials that they create. These instructors and learners may not be well prepared for or savvy about social media use, or they may not be comfortable learning in a social media environment. Thoughtful planning on the behalf of instructional designers can help mitigate or lessen the concerns of various learning stakeholders when social media are used.

Privacy is one concern that many social media users have, with fears that sharing too much information on social media will make them vulnerable to embarrassment or crime. In the United States, the Family Educational Rights and Privacy Act (FERPA) has provisions that govern the privacy of educational records. Although this act does not altogether prohibit use of social media for educational purposes, it does limit the types of student information that might be shared and the types of student interactions that an instructor might conduct in a public, online setting. To overcome privacy concerns, instructors might use secure tools with social media–like features or encourage students to use pseudonyms when interacting online for class. These solutions help lessen the likelihood that the student will create a digital footprint related to the educational experience. In other words, an Internet search for the student's name should not yield artifacts related to the coursework if all work is done under a pseudonym or is password protected with limited access (see Dennen, 2015, for greater discussion of learner privacy concerns in a distance learning context).

The ease with which digital information can be posted and then shared online also creates intellectual property concerns, which are magnified in a social media environment with its built-in sharing tools and culture. Instructional designers should be concerned with intellectual property rights on multiple fronts when designing for social media learning environments. Proprietary content is likely best kept from social media altogether, meaning that some topics should be addressed via other means. Learners may not be sufficiently aware of or concerned with intellectual property issues, and may either share course material with others or share outside materials with course members in a manner that violates someone's intellectual property rights. Additionally, the intellectual property rights of learners should be considered since asking them to share their intellectual work in a public setting can make them vulnerable.

Privacy and intellectual property rights both can be complicated by terms of service agreements. Terms of service agreements dictate the rights for both the social media network or tool provider and the end user and are determined by the provider. Users must agree to the terms of service when creating their accounts, although many users do not read the terms carefully, if at all, and the terms tend to be lengthy and written in complex language (see Fiesler & Bruckman, 2014, for an overview of social media terms of service, their language, and intellectual property rights). Typical topics covered in terms of service agreements include how user accounts may be used, what types of content may be hosted or shared using the service, by whom user-contributed content is owned and how it may be used, and how disputes between users and the service will be handled. These agreements tend to give a broad span of rights to user data—content intentionally shared, demographic information, and user actions—to the service provider and allow the service provider to cut off access to the service and the user's stored content at will. For many users, terms of service pose a latent problem. In other words, the potential for conflicts to arise remains and could be disruptive in an educational context.

For instructional designers, terms of service agreements create two levels of concern. First, instructional designers must determine if the terms of service are consistent with the learning organization's mission, internal policies, and intellectual property rights. Second, the instructional designer should consider if the terms of service of the selected tool or service will cause discomfort for any learners. For example, Facebook's terms of service dictates that users should have only one Facebook account and that account must use their real identity. For people who wish to keep personal and educational or professional activities separate, or who wish to minimize their digital footprint, using Facebook or other social media tools with similar policies in support of learning or professional development may be undesirable.

To promote greater comfort among learners, instructional designers can do three things. First, they can select tools or services carefully, considering how widespread existing use or acceptance is among the learner population, as well as whether there is any notable dissent among the population regarding the tool or service. Note that high current penetration and low dissent in other contexts does not necessarily mean that a tool or service will be embraced for learning purposes, and shifting to a tool that is not currently used for other purposes and that has a combination of social media features and strong privacy controls may be the best option in some contexts. Second, instructional designers can provide learning materials, including job aids, to help learners better understand the terms of service agreements and how to use these tools, including how to adjust privacy settings within the tools and other ways to maintain one's privacy (e.g., use pseudonyms, do not share personal information, do not accept contact requests from unknown persons). Third, although this diminishes the educational benefits of using social media, instructional designers can develop means of passive engagement with the content and interaction shared by others or alternate learning assignments for individuals who are not comfortable using the medium. This last option is imperfect, because it may result in a diminished or less interactive learning experience for learners who choose it.

International Considerations

When designing instruction for an international audience, additional considerations may be necessary. Although major social media tools such as Facebook and Twitter experience wide global use, they are not readily accessible to individuals in all countries. For example, China has blocked access to most internationally used social media tools; however, this does not mean that Chinese citizens and residents do not have access to social media. Instead, the Chinese government has fostered the development of Chinese social media tools and networks. At times, other countries have sought to limit or ban use of social media tools, especially when they have been used to speak out against the government.

Social Media and Other Trends

The use of social media to support learning has been buoyed by a number of other trends, most notably mobile learning, open educational resources, learning communities, and personal learning networks. Mobile phones have promoted greater anytime-anywhere access to social media networks and resources. Open educational resources are freely shared among online social networks. Learning communities use social media tools to connect and communicate online, and individuals can build and maintain their own learning networks via social media.

Conclusion

Social media use has become a standard part of everyday life, and the education sector is no exception. Social media provides another means through which content can be delivered to learners and members of learning communities can interact. For many individuals, content access and learning interactions are already happening informally as they engage in daily knowledge-seeking activities. Instructional designers, however, are tasked with determining when and how to best make use of social media in a formal learning context. This challenge requires careful consideration of many contextual factors. Some of these factors, such as learner characteristics and learning objectives, are familiar to instructional designers, but others such as privacy, intellectual property, disruptiveness, and learner comfort take on new twists in a networked online learning setting. As time passes, instructional designers will surely become savvier at not only using social media for their own professional development but also integrating social media into their learning designs. At the same time, it seems likely that the tools themselves will continue to evolve, creating new interaction opportunities along with new challenges for designing functional, safe, and pedagogically sound learning environments.

Summary of Key Principles

1. **Social media is an emerging technology, and one that is developing alongside related technologies such as mobile learning.** Instructional designers working in this area should maintain flexibility and expect both social media tools and practices to be dynamic.

2. **Social media can be used to develop dynamic learning communities and facilitate the sharing of knowledge in online environments.**

3. **Social media should not be used for its own sake. It should only be adopted in a learning environment when it is a good fit for the learners and the learning objectives.** Instructional designers should reject pressure to integrate social media into their learning designs just to keep current.

4. **Instructional designers need to consider privacy and intellectual property concerns for their organization and their learning participants prior to selecting public social media tools and networks for learning activities.**

5. **Three things instructional designers can do to maximize success when designing for social media are (1) select tools with the learners and context in mind, (2) provide opportunities and assistance for the learners to become familiar with and use the tools effectively, and (3) provide alternate options for learners who are uncomfortable using social media.**

Application Questions

1. Choose a social media tool with which you are already familiar. Explore the various features of the tool, including individual profiles, public, group and private communication options, and file sharing. Make a list of learning activities for which you believe the tool might be well suited, and a list of learning activities for which you believe it would not be well suited.

2. Locate a lesson plan online with learning objectives that you think could be met with the assistance of social media. Redesign the lesson plan to incorporate social media. Include guidelines that instructors and learners will need in order to successfully use social media to support learning and examples of anticipated social media interactions that instructors and learners might have.

3. Think of an organization with which you've been involved in the past. What social media tools might become an effective part of this organization's learning toolbox? For what learning activities might social media be used? What might be the privacy and intellectual property concerns? Create a presentation that you might give to the organization's leadership outlining the relative advantages and disadvantages of using social media, with recommendations for when and how it might be used.

References

Barthel, M., Shearer, E., Gottfried, J., & Mitchell, A. (2015). *The evolving role of news on Twitter and Facebook*. Washington, DC: Pew Research Center. Retrieved from http://www.journalism.org/2015/07/14/the-evolving-role-of-news-on-twitter-and-facebook/

Brooks, S. (2015). Does personal social media usage affect efficiency and well-being? *Computers in Human Behavior, 46*, 26–37. doi:10.1016/j.chb.2014.12.053

Dennen, V. P. (2015). Technology transience and learner data: Shifting notions of privacy in online learning. *Quarterly Review of Distance Education, 16*(2), 45–60.

Fiesler, C., & Bruckman, A. (2014). *Copyright terms in online creative communities*. Paper presented at the CHI '14 Extended Abstracts on Human Factors in Computing Systems, Toronto, Ontario, Canada.

Fox, S., & Duggan, M. (2013). Pew Internet and American Life Project. *Health Online 2013*.

Hoffman, E. S. (2009). Social media and learning environments: Shifting perspectives on the locus of control. *Education, 15*(2), 23–38.

Office for National Statistics. (2013). *Social networking: The UK as a leader in Europe*. London: Office for National Statistics. Retrieved from http://www.ons.gov.uk/ons/rel/rdit2/internet-access---households-and-individuals/social-networking--the-uk-as-a-leader-in-europe/sty-social-networking-2012.html

Perrin, A. (2015). Social networking usage: 2005–2015. Retrieved from http://www.pewinternet.org/2015/10/08/2015/Social-Networking-Usage-2005-2015/

Rainie, L., & Wellman, B. (2012). *Networked: The new social operating system*. Cambridge, MA: The MIT Press.

Rosen, L. D., Mark Carrier, L., & Cheever, N. A. (2013). Facebook and texting made me do it: Media-induced task-switching while studying. *Computers in Human Behavior, 29*(3), 948–958. doi:10.1016/j.chb.2012.12.001

Smith, A. (2013). *Civic engagement in digital life*. Washington, DC: Pew Research Center. Retrieved from http://pewinternet.org/Reports/2013/Civic-Engagement.aspx

Smith, A., & Duggan, M. (2013). *Online dating & relationships*. Washington, DC: Pew Research Center. Retrieved from http://pewinternet.org/Reports/2013/Online-Dating.aspx

Tess, P. A. (2013). The role of social media in higher education classes (real and virtual)—A literature review. *Computers in Human Behavior, 29*(5), A60–A68. doi:http://dx.doi.org/10.1016/j.chb.2012.12.032

Veletsianos, G. (2010). A definition of emerging technologies for education. In G. Veletsianos (Ed.), *Emerging technologies in distance education* (pp. 3–22). Athabasca, Canada: Athabasca University Press.

Chapter 29
Mobile Learning

Clark Quinn

Quinnovation

Introduction

Why mobile learning? The real question is why *not*? The devices are here; in fact they're here, there, and everywhere! And they're in use. You'd be hard pressed to go anywhere in the world and not see people on their devices. Can you name the last time you went somewhere where there weren't people with their heads in a device?

There's a reason for this ubiquity: These devices make people more effective. So, for example, we see these sorts of uses:

- Searching for the definition of a term used in a meeting
- Looking up product features
- Calculating a tip or splitting a bill
- Doing unit conversions (e.g., Fahrenheit to Celsius)
- Setting a reminder to not miss an appointment or event
- Checking the calendar to find an available time for a conversation
- Putting in a reminder to do something when back at the office
- Taking notes from a book or a presentation
- Looking up the contact details of someone
- Taking a picture of a parking space or a hotel room
- Sending an e-mail, text message, or tweet
- Making a phone call
- Getting directions to a location
- Finding a restaurant nearby

This is just a partial list of activities you probably have done and do regularly. Taking advantage of this opportunity specifically to meet organizational learning and performance needs is a core focus of m-learning. However, to properly address this opportunity, we need to have some clarity. We need some definitions and frameworks to move forward.

Devices

To start, let us be clear: What is a mobile device? Is it a feature phone, smartphone, tablet, or a laptop? How do we make sense of this? What can we use as a baseline for mobile devices?

It used to be easy; there were PDAs and there were laptops. When that first occurred, research by Palm (PalmSource, 2003) demonstrated a striking difference between the usage patterns: Mobile devices were used frequently for short bursts of times (a few minutes) whereas laptops were used less frequently but for considerably longer periods of time. This distinction provided a clear-cut differentiation.

With the growth in form factors for mobile devices, the differentiation is more challenging. When we're seeing wearables, phablets, netbooks, and more, the boundaries are blurring.

In an early report, we defined a mobile device (as part of a broader definition of mobile learning) to be "a compact digital portable device that the individual carries on a regular basis, has reliable connectivity, and fits in a pocket or purse" (Wexler et al., 2007). Is this sufficient?

It helps to consider what the likely device is. Which device is with people *always*? Increasingly, that is a phone. While smartphones are becoming ubiquitous (perhaps more properly called an "app phone"), feature phones are pretty well equipped with some base capabilities, cameras, and Web browsing, so thinking of a mobile phone is a good baseline. So the "regular basis" makes sense.

So, too, does "regular connectivity." While that can mean access whenever a cellular signal is available, it can also refer to wi-fi or even cabled syncing with a device when in proximity.

However, the "fits in a pocket or purse" is beginning to not be sufficiently detailed. When considering tablets, laptops, and other such things on the larger side, we need a principled answer. In the search for a relatively unambiguous definition, I have decided to consider that a mobile device is one that can be used *naturally* while standing or walking. Smartphones all too obviously fit this criterion, and tablets certainly can. Laptops, however, while able to be used while standing by using hunt-and-peck typing, are not naturally designed for use without support. Thus, on a principled basis, we can exclude laptops.

Then the question becomes: Where do tablets fit in? The pattern of usage of tablets differs from that of more pocketable devices. They tend to be used closer to the ways laptops are— that is, for longer periods of time; and they certainly aren't as easy to access and put away. However, the greater screen real estate means that they are capable of representing more data, a powerful value when interpreting data is required, such as diagnosing patients from their historical data, current symptoms, test results, and medications. They also can be used in situations where mobility isn't as expected or limited, such as airplane cockpits or hospital, office, or warehouse floors. Finally, they are far better suited for sharing with others, such as demonstrating to clients. Such considerations should be examined when determining what devices to use.

The more general situation, however, is to determine what devices are already being used. It is better to go to where people are than to try to direct them elsewhere. Thus, the smartphone is the prototypical mobile device; it's the one you have with you almost all the time, not just when expected, but at the store, at home, even at a party. Tablets should be considered as special purpose devices, and be matched to need.

M-Learning

If this is what characterizes mobile devices, then what characterizes mobile learning? Typically, we think of preparing people beforehand, the so-called "just in case" learning. However, the type of learning where we take people away from work, get them ready, and then return them to work is not aligned with the mobile experience.

As an overriding mental framework, consider that our goal is not "learning." We learn to be able to *do* things differently in ways that we cannot do now. Sometimes, learning is not the solution. For example, the field of performance consulting (a desirable predecessor or superset of instructional design), in addition to an initial gap analysis to identify the core problem, conducts a root cause analysis to figure out why the performance is not as desired.

As part of root cause analysis, the determination is made whether the problem is (a) lack of skills, indicating a need for training; or (b) lack of knowledge, in which case it's better to put knowledge "in the world" (in other words, provide

performance support to the learner). If it is the latter, then our goal should be creating successful performance by using the right tool for the job and looking at all the ways we can support that performance.

With that framework, and considering the natural usage of mobile devices as quick access mechanisms, the natural niche for m-learning is more closely aligned to performance support than formal learning. In regard to formal learning, m-learning makes more sense as a means of augmenting and extending formal learning than serving as a core delivery mechanism. To go further, we need to explore the inherent nature of mobile devices more deeply.

Models

For the basis of pragmatic design, as a practical basis for thinking about how to support learning and performance, I refer to four specific affordances of mobile devices, what I called the 4 Cs of mobile: *content, compute, communicate,* and *capture* (Quinn, 2011):

- *Content* is the individual accessing content or having content ready for consumption. This can be any media, whether text, graphics, images, audio, videos, or animation.
- *Compute* is a mixed-initiative process where the user interacts with the device in a dialectic process to achieve an outcome. So a calculator, or a software wizard, or a form with various options that computes an outcome are all examples.
- *Communicate* is, not surprising, connecting with others. That can be voice, video, or text; any way in which people can interact.
- *Capture* is capturing the current context. This can be via a camera, an audio recording via a microphone, or even the user taking notes via a keyboard or writing app. It includes any other data available about the current context such as time, location, or more.

Note that, by and large, none of these is unique to mobile. Certainly content, compute, and communicate are desktop capabilities as well. Even desktops can know what app you're using and let you grab the current state of the computer and even an audio or video image.

However, a mobile device takes it much further. It can capture your current location via that camera, but also detect location, motion, or ambient signals. In short, mobile can help you remember things exactly that your brain can't. And one more thing . . .

When we combine capture and compute, we get a new, and uniquely valuable, capability: contextualization. If we know where (and when) you are, we can do things specifically *because* of that. We can bring in relevant information that takes your current situation and turns it into a learning or performance opportunity that might not otherwise be available. Mobile learning is about a much tighter cycle between learning and life than has previously been possible without an ever-present personal mentor.

Two specific uses of contextualization include augmented and alternate reality. Augmented reality is when additional information is made available in a context that wouldn't ordinarily be available. Screens can take the image from a camera and add additional detail (e.g., from the underpinning workings of a device or associated troubleshooting information, or connections to nearby options for food or learning) in order to reveal otherwise hidden connections between elements. Such information can be added via text or audio, too. Alternate reality is when a separate world and story is created that doesn't really exist, but via technology can manifest itself in the world and be made concrete. And just as games have been leveraged for serious learning, so too can alternate reality games be used for serious outcomes (c.f. Pagano, 2013).

Uses

So how are these capabilities being leveraged? The answers span K–12, higher education, corporations, and more. The uses take advantage of the 4 Cs, providing information to supplement formal learning or as performance support, computational capabilities for general or specific reasons, ways to communicate and collaborate, and to capture performances or contexts for reflection and sharing. Contextualized uses are still relatively new but are being seen in more and more contexts.

In K–12, m-learning has some significant advantages. For younger kids, the smaller size of the device makes a more natural form factor, and a touch screen is more direct than a mouse as a pointing device. The devices can serve to deliver information such as shared videos or diagrams with learners, provide essentially unlimited practice through canned applications, serve as computational adjuncts for specific learning requirements, provide question and response capabilities, and serve as data collection and annotation devices. Moreover, the ability to provide contextual information is becoming easier, from identifying leaves to history, architecture, and more. A limitation is currently the lack of a standard for annotation of the existing world.

Several initial explorations of mobile technology in classrooms have not succeeded. One initiative using the One-Laptop-Per-Child platform did not succeed as it neglected to prepare and support teachers (Warschauer, 2011). Similarly, an exercise in using iPads in the Los Angeles Unified School District failed when the intended software did not deliver as promised. However, other initiatives that focus on natural integration of mobile functionality are succeeding, such as at St. Mary's City Schools (Gray, 2011).

Higher education similarly can leverage m-learning to serve classroom functions like information presentation, practice, and surveys. Note and picture taking can augment classes, as can information searching. Additional studying can be accomplished while commuting as well. Moreover, m-learning can be used in higher education to provide administrative capabilities such as submitting assignments, checking on grades, even searching the library and communicating with faculty and other students (Quinn, 2012). There have been some experiments in using contextualized learning opportunities, leveraging open source distributed mobile systems (e.g., ARIS; see arisgames.org), but the area is still in research as opposed to systematically available.

In higher education, the use of platforms has been more successful. Abilene Christian University has successfully integrated iPhones or iPod Touches as delivery platforms, and Duke University had a successful launch of iPods as well. A number of universities now provide iPads to students.

Corporate uses of m-learning are taking off. If we consider that mobile-accessible versions of enterprise software (software designed to meet the needs of an organization) are increasingly available, the performance support version of m-learning is well advanced. More typically, organizational m-learning is still in the stage of "courses on a phone," but increasingly we are seeing mobile adjuncts that extend the learning experience.

Equipping workforces, whether a sales team or an entire organization, with mobile devices is losing ground to an approach of "bring your own device (BYOD)," where solutions are being developed and delivered to the devices people have instead of trying to get them to accommodate to a new platform. It is becoming a safe bet that individuals have devices, and while initially providing them with an organization-provided one made sense, it increasingly is unnecessary, as software exists to manage solutions across devices.

Designing M-Learning

With this framework, we are ready to consider how to design m-learning solutions. The mobile picture goes beyond ID, and so too does the design process. Here I eschew the ADDIE model and use instead a four-part model consisting of analysis of the need, specification of solutions, development of those solutions, and evaluation of the outcomes.

Analysis

When you are designing for mobile devices, there are more factors to consider than when designing for the desktop. The devices, the contexts, and the needs are all likely to be different. And, if we take the above to heart, our design process needs to look more like performance consulting than instructional design.

While this is not, or should not, be different for mobile, the starting point should be asking the question: "What's the problem?" What is the performance gap, and why? Ideally, there are metrics: What isn't happening fast enough is occurring with too high an error rate, or is not occurring with sufficient success rate. This could be in sales, customer services, operations, or elsewhere. However, we should be specific and quantitative, otherwise how will we know when we've succeeded?

In addition to the usual information, there is mobile-specific data needed, such as the devices; while desktop devices are typically controlled, with the mobile devices there is a strong potential for BYOD conditions, and a likelihood that individuals will try to access the solution on a personal mobile device regardless. This can be simpler once a mobile strategy has been developed, identifying supported platforms, but regardless the solution space needs to be identified.

Similarly, the context of performance needs to be considered. If it's not at the desk, is it in the office or physical plant (e.g., meeting rooms or shop floor)? Or are targeted individuals "on the go," in any possible location whether vehicle, transportation hub, or client or public space? What are the connectivity, security, and mobility constraints in these locations? Are there others involved?

The determinants of success should be identified, too. What changes in those metrics would be considered a viable intervention? There should be a reality check here: Will what it takes to provide a solution have a promising relationship to the desired outcome? Of course, we should also be asking: Is this really a mobile learning situation? Would it be better served with contextualized resources rather than user-carried ones?

We should be asking ourselves a number of questions:

- Are people in motion or in shifting or constrained spaces?
- Do they have devices with them, and what ones?
- Would media or interactivity be valuable?
- Do they need to communicate with others?
- Is there a need to capture information?

The result of the analysis phase should have a clear proposition: There's a specific need that a mobile solution would address, with an expected cost and an expected benefit. When we have that proposition, we are ready to proceed.

Specification

Once we have identified the problem location and nature, as well as the available devices, we can start specifying solutions. We should be aiming to achieve a design that meets the need under pragmatic constraints. There are several considerations to keep in mind, particularly scope, alignment, and media.

One of the first principles that comes into play for mobile is the *Least Assistance Principle*, where the goal is to provide the least support that will allow the person to proceed successfully. This makes sense for a couple of reasons. First, it makes sense given the limited memory, power, and size of a mobile device. Second, most people just want to get back to what they're doing, particularly when they're on the go. Palm (PalmSource, 2003) advocated a sweet spot for mobile development that met 80 percent of the needs with 20 percent of the features (2003), which is still good advice.

Minimalism plays out particularly in media. Extra effort should be made to winnow down text and diagrams, to trim and compress audio and video, and to avoid extraneous interactive features. For example, you don't need full sentences. File size is an issue onboard, and bandwidth is an issue for remote content. Less is more when it comes to m-learning.

The second major principle is to design the solution first, before worrying about implementation. The point is to determine the best cognitive augment, whether to support learning or performance, creating the overall experience, before figuring out just how it is to be delivered. Focus on what you want them doing first.

Also, consider using the right channel and medium. We can often forget that mobile devices are possessed of multiple channels: SMS (aka text messages), voice, e-mail, and Web, as well as apps. We can send video, audio, and static documents, and we can have interactivity. Similarly, there are a number of ways users can communicate with the device, including touch, gestures, speaking, taking pictures, recording audio, and more. You should, however, look to minimize using text. If possible, have them point to the answer, not type it. Consider how you want the interaction to flow: What do you want from your users, and what should they get?

As mentioned, a useful way to think about it is from the perspective of augmenting our capabilities. Our brains are good at pattern matching, but not good at remembering rote or arbitrary information, nor performing complex calculations. Digital technology is the opposite, and with the complementary skills we are more powerful when coupled with such capability. The suggestion, then, is to look for the gaps in our cognition that technology can solve. We can make information available for easy lookup, such as product or package features, rather than expecting learners to remember them. Checklists help overcome our tendency to skip steps. Calculators can take the burden off of making paper and pencil calculations or returning to the office to make quotes. The list goes on, the goal is to find ways to supplement our capabilities that produce the highest likelihood of success.

Another useful design principle is to explicitly consider the context. Increasingly, we can identify the user, context, and need, and do things specific to this situation. What can we do *because* of where and when the user is? Can we provide local guidance? With an event, can we prepare them before, support them during, and afterward consolidate outcomes for both performance and learning? Who or what is nearby? Let's not do generic if we can do specific.

Once we have detailed what experience we want, then we can consider our development options. The capabilities continue to increase as development tools get more powerful, so we should not limit our designs to what we have previously experienced and we should be willing to imagine an ideal world first and see how close we can come.

Development

There are a surprising number of delivery options available, once an experience is designed. The considerations should be based upon evaluating the tradeoffs, as while it is easy to immediately imagine an application, there may be a better case for mobile Web or other solutions.

There is a fairly straightforward progression in development options, with associated tradeoffs. The easiest to develop and deploy is mobile Web: creating a Web application optimized for mobile delivery. With so-called *responsive design* (a suite of Web techniques that allow designs to adapt to whatever screen is available), we can create solutions that work across devices. And, if things change, it's easy to change solutions, with little additional technical knowledge required.

At the other end, the most expensive solution is a custom application, written in the development environment for that platform. This solution may provide the greatest user experience, and allows taking the greatest advantage of specific hardware. On the other hand, any changes have to be disseminated. While you can write the application to get data from the network, any changes to functionality or the interface will require a mechanism for updating the device with the new version of the software.

An intermediate approach is to use software packages that "wrap" mobile Web with platform-specific containers so they run locally on the device. These packages have more ability to leverage hardware, but in a more generic way, and they are not as fast and polished as a custom application. Criteria for making a determination of "wrap or app" is whether the user experience needs to be optimal (say, for instance, if you're selling the m-learning solution) or whether you need advanced hardware access to use things like unique sensors for specific contextualizations.

Another solution that works for content (e.g., with limited interactivity) is the ebook. Content can be made available for access via the ebook standards, and the authoring process is more like word processing than coding. Such resources are easily deployed, though updating requires the mobile device management solutions that are also recommended for apps.

Any of the platform devices can get data from servers, so there is not necessarily any reason to use Web development just to adapt to changes. With good design and development, the new information can be accessed when needed. That is, when there is connectivity, places that have no available networks, such as remote geographic locations such as mines and wilderness, will require a fixed solution.

Prototyping and testing is an essential part of development, which broaches the issue of evaluation.

Evaluation

Like any initiative, mobile interventions should have desired outcomes, and should be evaluated to determine whether they are achieving those outcomes or not. There is little specifically unique to mobile that comes into play, though the testing needs to be more broadly validated.

Just as with other learning or performance initiatives, mobile should be focused on measurables as determined in the analysis phase. Do individuals equipped with your solution have the desired performance? Specific issues to mobile include connectivity speeds, room on the devices for your solution, and ability to use "on the go."

As such, your testing has to sample representative contexts of use, not just where convenient. Test in locations and use cases that reflect what individuals will actually be doing. Are things easy enough to read in those conditions? Can the users interact? Do they get what they need?

With testing and revision (and do assume some cycles of revision), mobile solutions can be developed and deployed.

From M-Learning to M-Strategy

Mobile learning is somewhat misnamed; it's not really about learning, but performance. Another mistake is to think m-learning is a tactic, meeting an immediate need, when m-learning really is a strategy as it provides a platform upon which many initiatives may be delivered. Overall, however, m-learning is here to stay, and the opportunity is quite literally in the palm of our hand.

When we think of augmenting ourselves, we take a perspective that can honor our nature, and empower us rather than enslave us. The key is to start from using technology in human ways. This has strategic ramifications in several ways.

First, your first mobile initiative will establish expectations around what else can be done. If you produce an app as a tactic, the audience will continue to expect apps; and they will expect all the quality that they see in other apps. Also, whatever devices you initially support will constrain the solutions that are expected. Anticipate and be prepared for emerging expectations. Thus, your choices implicitly define your strategy, and it is better to choose your first mobile tactic in ways that line up with where you want to go in the longer term.

Second, the focus on using technology beyond courses is an opportunity to bring that broader perspective back to the desktop; and stop thinking about courses as the only role for learning and development. In this sense, mobile is a potential catalyst for change. It may well bring in new perspectives on potential roles for technology. This should be understood and factored into the overall plan. How can a mobile initiative be harnessed for successful organizational change?

Mobile also is more than just the device. Whatever development option you choose, there are technology implications. Management of mobile devices, security issues, and more come into play. Ideally, mobile takes a content engineering approach (Udell, 2012), which focused on tighter and more discrete definitions of content. This has implications for other areas, including e-learning. It should require a productive partnership with the information technology group.

Finally, the perspective of focusing on finding the right balance between what we have people do and what we have technology do can be the trigger to reevaluate the ways tasks are designed beyond mobile. This is not a bad thing, but should not be ignored. How can we successfully use mobile to conduct a shift in work process?

It is strongly recommended that you take a strategic approach to m-learning rather than treat it as a tactic. Figure out where you want to be, so that your first mobile move is a step in that direction as well as meeting a real need. Any initial mobile initiative will have repercussions, and these should be anticipated and planned for.

Mobile learning is the opportunity to empower people beyond the desktop, but it is also much, *much* more. That is a valuable situation to be in, so go forth and mobilize.

Summary of Key Principles

1. **M-learning is more than mobile e-learning.** It's not about courses on a phone as much as *everything* else: performance support, social, and informal learning. It's pull more than push.

2. **Design to augment our capabilities.** Extend learning, don't be the fount of it; and extend our brains by providing the assistance in areas we lack.

3. **Apply the Least Assistance Principle.** Minimalism is good practice in all forms, but it is critical in mobile design.

4. **Leverage context.** One of the ways to achieve minimalism is to wrap learning around the work, and use the preexisting context. Also look to what useful support you can provide *because* of where and when the performer is.

5. **Take a platform approach.** Recognize that mobile is a platform, and recognize that in terms of developing your strategy and architecture.

Application Questions

1. A census happens every ten years, whereby the country looks to identify all the individuals and their household status (as well as some other demographic information if possible). You are tasked with finding a mobile solution to the needs of a census enumerator; those who go door-to-door for people and places that have not answered the survey. These people are out and about interviewing people at their homes, and also documenting the homeless in their various enclaves. Ideally, there would be a large screen area to facilitate logging the data. On the other hand, prominent devices can intimidate many citizens. Describe a balanced implementation, including mobile devices, that facilitates the data collection process without intimidating the populations surveyed. Discuss how you would address privacy issues.

2. Patriot Insurance Services provides varying coverage packages via field representatives that work out of local offices. The packages combine plans across health, life, house, and disability and regularly change based upon region, market pressures, and regulations. They currently use training programs in a few training centers across the nation. They have started contracting out e-learning courses to a provider, and the provider has suggested that owing to the "on the road" nature of the audiences, the e-learning could be adapted for mobile delivery at an additional price. They have brought you in to assist them in developing a mobile strategy. What would be your suggestion for the use of mobile technology for their field people?

References

Gray, L. (2011). Small size, big potential: Mobile learning devices in school. *CoSN Compendium 2011, 9*(3).

Pagano, K. O. (2013). *Immersive learning: Designing for authentic practice.* Alexandria, VA: ASTD Press.

PalmSource. (2003). *Zen of Palm.* Retrieved from http://www.cs.uml.edu/~fredm/courses/91.308-fall05/palm/zenofpalm.pdf

Quinn, C. N. (2011). *Designing mlearning: Tapping into the mobile revolution for organizational performance.* San Francisco: Pfeiffer.

Quinn, C. N. (2012). *The mobile academy: mLearning for higher education.* San Francisco: Jossey-Bass.

Udell, C. (2012). *Learning everywhere: How mobile content strategies are transforming training.* Alexandria, VA: ASTD Press.

Warschauer, M. (2011). *Learning in the cloud: How (and why) to transform schools with digital media.* New York: Teachers College Press.

Wexler, S., Schlenker, B., Brown, J., Metcalf, D., Quinn, C., Thor, E., Van Barneveld, A., & Wagner, E. (2007). *360 research report mobile learning: What it is, why it matters, and how to incorporate it into your learning strategy.* Santa Rosa, CA: eLearning Guild.

Chapter 30

The Emergence and Design of Massive Open Online Courses

Curtis J. Bonk
Indiana University

Mimi Miyoung Lee
University of Houston

Thomas C. Reeves
The University of Georgia

Thomas H. Reynolds
National University

During the past two decades, the Internet has made available a wealth of interactive learning resources, unique forms of social interaction and collaboration, and novel types of content and course delivery. Among the more exciting new ways of learning delivery is the massive open online course (MOOC). The MOOC, while certainly controversial, has arguably brought online learning to the attention of the public at large like nothing before. Though the term itself is less than a decade old, dozens of MOOC vendors and software companies as well as a barrage of reports, announcements, courses, and programs related to MOOCs have emerged during the past few years. There are growing numbers of MOOC developers and instructors, MOOC participants or "learners," MOOC researchers, MOOC books and journals, and MOOC lists (for an historical perspective on MOOCs, including key events leading up to them, see Moe, 2015). As inevitably occurs with a new phenomenon of this kind, there are enthusiastic MOOC advocates as well as skeptical critics.

MOOCs Defined

The term *massive online open course* was coined by Dave Cormier from the University of Prince Edward Island, Canada. Cormier came up with this term when he noticed that his colleagues, George Siemens, at the time, from the University of Manitoba, and Stephens Downes, from the Canadian Research Council, had opened their online course titled "Connectivism and Connective Knowledge" well beyond the twenty-five enrolled and tuition-paying students to more than 2,200 learners who participated for free (Downes, 2011). As such, the MOOC descriptor is basically an attempt to provide unlimited participation in an educational experience via the Web, typically for free. Aside from the increased enrollment numbers and open access to course content, MOOCs often include both traditional instructional components and those more typically found in online courses, such as discussion forums and interactive exercises.

There is some controversy regarding what actually constitutes a MOOC. For example, some argue that MOOCs are not truly open since the content is often not available for reuse, such as when it is taken down once the course is over (Wiley, 2015). For others the word "massive" is misleading or difficult to pin down—at what point do we consider the enrollment massive? Other courses may be miscategorized as MOOCs since they may not actually be open to anyone, as with Google's offering MOOCs internally to company employees and not the outside world in its G2G (Googler to Googler) initiative on topics like public speaking, parenting, Python programming, data visualization, mindfulness, and meditation (Kessler, 2013). Clearly, such internal offerings do not meet openness criteria. Concerns have also been expressed about the degree to which MOOC offerings are overrepresented by elite U.S. institutions such as Harvard, MIT, and Stanford, and whether the MOOC movement perpetuates the perceived hegemony of Western culture and the English language to less developed parts of the world.

cMOOCs, xMOOCs, and pMOOCs

As noted, the MOOC trend began when several instructors in Canada taught courses that were free and open for outside participation and connections (Moe, 2015). Given that Stephen Downs and George Siemens tested ideas related to an emerging

TABLE 30.1	Differences among Three Types of MOOCs		
Type of MOOC	**cMOOC**	**xMOOC**	**pMOOC**
Learner Role	Active	Passive	Active
Instructor Role	Co-learner	Sage on video stage	Guide on the side
Learning Theory	Connectivism	Behaviorism	Constructivism
Primary Pedagogy	Knowledge integration	Knowledge duplication	Knowledge production
Metaphor	"We link movies"	"We watch movies"	"We make movies"
Development Approach	Learning design	Instructional design	Educational design research
Primary Type of Assessment	Self-assessment	External and/or peer assessment	Self- and/or client assessment
Funding Source	Seat of the pants funding	Large external funding	Moderate client-provided funding

(Reeves & Hedberg, 2014)

learning theory called "connectivism" when they taught their first MOOC, courses based on their ideals have come to be known as connectivist or cMOOCs (Kop, Fournier, & Mak, 2011).

In a cMOOC, fostering greater social interaction through sharing and negotiation of meaning is encouraged. Importantly, everyone in such courses has the potential to be a vital co-instructor or source of knowledge. For instance, each participant may have a blog to reflect on a course module or on resources shared by others, as well as provide some resources of their own. Others might post links to such blogs using various social media tools including Facebook, Twitter, Pinterest, and LinkedIn. In fact, participants will often mark their Twitter posts with a hash tag related to the course, thereby expanding as well as uniquely connecting course content resources (Kop et al., 2011). There might also be a course wiki in the MOOC for accumulating resources, in addition to tools for visualizing participant contributions and aggregating resources. Active participation through the production of digital artifacts related to the course often exceeds course expectations and can help participants reflect on their creative processes (Kop et al., 2011).

It was not long, however, before other individuals and institutions envisioned the possibilities for greater access to content. By 2010, for instance, universities such as Stanford, MIT, Harvard, Duke University, the University of Edinburgh, the University of Pennsylvania, and many other well-established institutions were experimenting with the notion of a MOOC. In the fall of 2011, Stanford offered several MOOCs that reached over 100,000 enrolled learners. Most of these massive courses were in the fields of computer science and engineering. Not surprisingly, such courses relied on traditional models of instruction, including the use of streamed or prerecorded lectures as well as discussion forums and online tests graded by computing technology. These types of MOOCs were labeled xMOOCs. Needless to say, not all such courses can rely solely on objectively scored exams; some xMOOCs, in fact, have experimented with peer assessment as well as with different forms of certification or badging for course completion.

The widely publicized intent of xMOOCs was the delivery of content to masses of people with the hope of democratizing education. However, many issues arose and arguably continue with the xMOOC instructional approach—related to a perceived lack of individualization, limited feedback, a sense of isolation or loneliness among learners, and weak forms of assessment. Many participants report significant difficulties keeping up with the pace of these online offerings while working full time or fulfilling other personal and professional commitments. Accordingly, the attrition rates in xMOOCs are often reported at 90 percent or above.

Beginning in 2013, the pMOOC model began to emerge (Reeves & Hedberg, 2014). In a pMOOC, participants collaborate online to complete a project (e.g., design a memorial) or address a problem (e.g., develop a plan for urban renewal of a declining area of a town or city). For example, in a pMOOC focused on open educational resources (OER), preservice or inservice teachers might be called upon to work together to produce OER that could be used by themselves and other teachers. Table 30.1 outlines the differences among cMOOCs, xMOOCs, and pMOOCs.

Additional Types of MOOCs

What has become clear in the short history of MOOCs is that benefits of MOOC participation depend on how it is delivered and the extent to which it meets audience needs and expectations. Increasingly, MOOCs are finding their way into lifelong learning and professional development situations such as those intended for K–12 teachers (Laurillard, 2014), health care personnel, or business leaders. Such MOOCs are referred to as "professional development" MOOCs (i.e., PD-MOOCs) (Bonk, Lee, Reeves, & Reynolds, 2015). These PD-MOOCs vary in length from a few days of meetings to several months. Some colleges and universities are catering to their extensive alumni and donor base with these types of MOOCs; in effect, bringing prior students and supporters back to the campus, albeit virtually. As might be expected, PD-MOOCs often are designed to upgrade the workplace skills of their participants—such as learning about a new statistical software tool, regulatory procedure, mortgage lending practice, or management style. Importantly, participants can sign up from their computers or mobile devices and participate in a PD-MOOC to quickly access the course content from wherever and whenever it is convenient. No longer must a person apply for admission, find funding, and then travel to a campus for several months for classes. With a MOOC, the course is online and typically without direct costs, although those who desire some sort of official recognition for MOOC completion may be required to pay a fee.

In addition to PD-MOOCs, other types of MOOCs have emerged during the past few years. For instance, remedial MOOCs are designed to help students who have fallen behind academically or lack sufficient skills or competencies to move to the next level. Remedial MOOCs often respond to the lack of sufficient reading, writing, mathematical, or general study skills among first-time college entrants (Bandi-Rao & Devers, 2015). Other types of MOOCs may be aimed at learners who want to take advanced placement (AP) tests. For example, learners can enroll in courses from edX's High School Initiative (edX, 2014b) with more than forty high school and AP exam preparation courses in such areas as calculus, computer science, biology, Spanish, introductory psychology, and physics.

In addition to professional development, job reskilling, remediation, and advanced placement, there are still other types of MOOCs or MOOC-like derivatives. Among these MOOC-like forms are BOOCs (big open online courses), MOOD (massive open online discussion), SPOCS (small private online courses) (Watters, 2013), and DOCCs (distributed open collaborative courses) (Bonk, Lee, Reeves, et al., 2015). Not surprisingly, many visions and plans for MOOCs, especially those that focus on requirements related to certification of completion or competency, presently lag behind in their implementation as institutions work to codify and align MOOC experiences with traditional forms of accreditation. As with any new instructional delivery system, much remains to be sorted out when it comes to MOOCs and the general use of open educational resources (OER) and open courseware (OCW). Nevertheless, the wide array of MOOC-related terms and their associated forms of organization and delivery fuels the discussion between those supporting and those arguing against the long-term potential of MOOCs as a type of transformative and, for many, disruptive delivery mechanism.

MOOC Vendors and Lists

Many people complain that they have trouble locating high-quality online contents (Bonk, Lee, Kou, Xu, & Sheu, 2015). Others cannot find the MOOCs or open educational resources that they need. Fortunately, there are lists of MOOCs from each MOOC vendor such as Udacity, edX, NovoEd, Coursera, and Udemy in the United States as well as from companies in the online learning and course management space which have begun offering MOOCs, such as Blackboard and Canvas. In addition to these U.S.-based entities, there are initiatives such as Mirada X in Latin America, Open2Study in Australia and New Zealand, FutureLearn from the Open University of the UK, iversity from Berlin, and the OpenupEd project from Europe. There are also summary lists across the MOOC providers such TechnoDuet, the MOOC List, Class Central, and Open Culture. Which of these lists will assume prominence in the coming years is difficult to forecast. It is likely that one or more additional services will emerge to better aggregate, advertise, and even manage MOOC courses and programs.

MOOC Business Plans

A common question related to MOOCs and other forms of open education is if these resources or courses are free, then what is the business model? Just how are they sustainable? A number of ideas to sustain MOOCs as a learning delivery vehicle have been discussed in the past few years. Some of these are listed here:

1. Require a course entry fee.
2. Establish a small and flexible program application fee (though it remains free or inexpensive for those from developing parts of the world).
3. Assign a fee for graded work, secured assessments, or examination processing (e.g., the University of the People).
4. Prove a certificate of completion or licensure fee option. [Note: The certificate option is highly common across MOOC vendors; MOOC providers like Coursera has a "signature track" whereas Udacity refers to this as a "nanodegree" (Schroeder, Cook, Levin, & Gribbins, 2015); it might also be referred to as a microcredential, or microlearning (Grovo, 2015).]
5. Charge tuition fees for those seeking course credit.
6. Charge a course enhancement fee for learners who desire more sophisticated or extensive content.
7. Sell data analytics derived from MOOC participants.
8. Provide a free initial MOOC experience in a certificate or degree program (i.e., what the business world would call "a loss leader").
9. Sell instructional support services and ancillary services (e.g., tutoring, study preparation, etc.) around MOOCs.
10. Recruit advertisers to underwrite courses and degrees.

Other ideas for generating income from MOOCs include revenue sharing schemes, membership or subscription services, donation models, corporate sponsorship, talent location fees and commissions, and content leasing and licensing. Recently, some universities like Georgia Tech University are experimenting with lowering the cost of traditional degree programs such as those in computer science by offering courses via MOOCs and removing or significantly reducing fees associated with being on campus (DeMillo, 2015). Clearly, there are various ways to support the giving away of educational services such as a MOOC. Additional business plans and models related to free and more open forms of education will likely emerge in the coming years. For now, it is important to learn from the experiences of those using one or more of the ideas listed in this section.

Why Should Instructional Design and Technology Professionals Care About MOOCs?

There are numerous reasons why instructional designers and other professionals in the field of instructional design and technology should be aware of MOOCs. First of all, they currently represent a scalable and disruptive form of educational delivery; as such, they are gaining the attention of educational administrators as well as instructors, parents, learners, and even politicians. Consequently, instructional designers and other educational technology practitioners are increasingly asked to design, develop, and evaluate MOOCs. Second, a wide array of organizations and institutions are experimenting with MOOCs and other forms of open education. As a result, there are many job opportunities for those who have experience with aspects of these new forms of educational content and delivery; especially those who have assumed leadership positions on MOOC-related projects and initiatives. Third, while the jury is still out on MOOCs, those involved in designing and offering MOOCs have a unique opportunity to impact the lives of people around the world that they will likely never meet. Involvement in MOOCs, therefore, might be highly meaningful work. Fourth, as a fast emerging form of educational delivery, MOOCs are testing the limits of technology, instruction, and learning. Those involved in such experiences would likely to be piloting unique approaches to instructional delivery including the use of emerging technologies that might have relevance in other forms of online learning. Fifth, many resources have been allocated to MOOC ventures. Given these and many other reasons, we recommend that those interested in instructional design and technology at any level seriously consider gaining experience related to MOOCs.

As mentioned, MOOCs have been employed for a vast array of learning needs and situations from remedial skill development to advanced learning at the secondary or higher education levels to skill upgrades and retooling for the general public. Notably in 2014, the company ALISON offered MOOCs to help with the Ebola crisis, while at about the same time, FutureLearn from the Open University in the UK offered a MOOC related to the Scottish referendum on independence (Reynolds, Reeves, Lee, & Bonk, 2015). Even more recently, Arizona State University partnered with edX to create the Global Freshman Academy that directly addresses the escalating costs of higher education by providing MOOCs as a low-cost option for introductory college courses (Lewin, 2015; Stripling, 2015). Along these same lines, as indicated earlier, Georgia Tech is unbundling the costs of its master's program in computer science to provide a much more competitively priced degree program for those who select the MOOC option (DeMillo, 2015).

In the corporate training world, there is more attention being given to MOOCs, as well (Hilger, 2014). For instance, engineers at Yahoo! can now obtain certificates via MOOCs (Meister, 2013). In this same vein, corporate MOOC provider Udacity has formed the Open Education Alliance to help educate the workforce of tomorrow by providing "nanodegrees" in areas like Web design, coding, interactive 3D graphics, and data analysis (Waters, 2015). Similarly, Aquent Gymnasium offers free technology courses for creative professionals in Web design, coding, JavaScript, and related skill areas. Yet another example is SAP, which now offers "OpenSAP" for its partners and various developers of SAP technologies to educate them in its technologies (Bersin, 2013).

Quality Concerns for Instructional Design and Technology Professionals

While it is obvious that MOOCs are opening up many new ways to learn online, the issue of quality has not been adequately addressed to the satisfaction of most critics of this unique educational development. First of all, no widely accepted means for accreditation of MOOCs has emerged to date. Second of all, some critics point to the low completion rates among MOOC enrollees (only 2 to 10 percent) as a sign of their poor quality. Keep in mind, however, as previously noted, such data often stems from studies of xMOOCs, not cMOOCs, pMOOCs, or PD-MOOCs. Moreover, there are new ways to look at actual engagement and course completion, such as following those who participate beyond the first week signup. Stated another way, many potential participants have good intentions when signing up but often forget about the course or lack sufficient time to devote to it.

Quality can be examined using criteria other than course completion (edX, 2014a; Reeves & Bonk, 2015). For instance, an investigation of the degree to which instructional design principles were represented in seventy-six randomly selected MOOCs (twenty-six cMOOCs and fifty xMOOCs) found very weak evidence of these principles across both types of MOOCs (Margaryan, Bianco, & Littlejohn, 2015). Although we know of no research to verify this, we speculate that relatively few MOOCs have been designed systematically with the aid of skilled instructional designers; instead, most MOOCs appear to have been assembled by a mix of subject-matter experts and computer programmers using persisting instructional materials.

A third obvious quality issue relates to the assessment of learning in MOOCs, especially when a specific MOOC involves topic areas that are difficult to objectively assess and score. There is also widespread concern voiced about the acceptability of MOOC credit by potential employers. Still other issues include (a) the extent to which MOOCs are truly open or full-fledged courses, (b) the capacity to transfer MOOC credits into other educational systems, (c) the English dominance in MOOCs, (d) issues of online plagiarism and verification of competence, (e) the use of copyrighted material, (f) adequate instructor training, and (g) various problems of equity and access, especially in regard to MOOCs that are, by intent and design, not free.

Despite these assorted issues and concerns, MOOCs and various by-products of MOOCs will most likely be around for some time into the future. As such, instructional designers, learning center directors, human performance technologists, and many others need to be aware of what a MOOC is or represents as well as their potential for extending and enhancing learning opportunities. Additionally, we encourage instructional designers or those in instructional design and technology programs to enroll in several different types of MOOCs to gain direct experience of their quality (or lack thereof).

MOOC Challenges and Barriers for Instructional Design and Technology Professionals

Beyond the array of issues mentioned, MOOC instructors, instructional designers, and other instructional technology professionals face many other challenges and barriers related to MOOCs and open education. Among these key barriers is finding and organizing quality content for use with thousands of participants. Given the wealth of online content available today, it is not only difficult to ascertain if one has located the most effective, current, useful, and accessible resource, but it is often equally challenging to produce an instructional strategy or set of strategies that aligns with and best implements the content within the problems, needs, and interests of diverse MOOC learners from different global regions and with unique expectations. Simply put, even though MOOCs are a liberating and disruptive technology, they represent a form of technology that is severely constrained and challenged by the immensity and complexity of its undertaking.

To this end, instructional designers who have traditionally organized instruction around accepted and canonical accounts of knowledge using behavioral or cognitive approaches to learning and instruction may be compelled to extend their designs and invite broader models of both learning and teaching to inform their efforts. For example, forms of feedback and assessment that extend across cultural, linguistic, and social boundaries present huge challenges; especially when they must align with various standards of practice. The massiveness of each MOOC course makes it extremely difficult, if not impossible at times, for the instructor to provide timely and accurate feedback to all of the diverse learners enrolled in the course. Yet another issue relates to creating sufficient instructional supports so that the open education aspects of MOOCs are not burdening the learner with too much content or choices. Opening up access, while important in offering learners a sense of autonomy and control, can seem chaotic and easily overwhelm the cognitive capacity of participants involved in the course experience.

MOOCs and the corollary distribution of open resources hold promise to advance cultural understanding and interaction, but this potential will not be realized in the present form of MOOCs and other types of open education. Some critics maintain that MOOCs are a twenty-first-century form of digital colonialism whereby the cultural practices, systems, and knowledge of the developed world are delivered to the developing and less developed world via MOOC platforms with little attention paid to learning needs across cultures and languages (Portmess, 2013). As such, MOOC-based instructional design approaches—perhaps more than other forms of instruction—require that participant voices and personal forms of agency be included in instructional considerations. More than ever before, instructional design and technology professionals need to discuss viable ways for MOOC participants and learners

to evaluate and deal with culturally offensive or hegemonic open resources. However imposing these challenges might be, there remain unique opportunities to formulate educational reforms that promote culturally thoughtful and respectful instructional designs that reduce or perhaps even eliminate such types of learner impediments and barriers.

Designing MOOCs: Some Guidelines

In some ways, designing a MOOC is similar to designing any type of online course experience; and, yet, in many ways, it is different. The design principles, however, will depend on the intended type of MOOC experience and content area. Some general guidelines and principles for the creation of MOOCs are listed next.

1. **Plan for the experience.** Perhaps the most important instructional design principle is to plan ahead for the MOOC experience. Naturally, some activities will evolve during the MOOC and be in response to learner needs. However, given the scale of a MOOC, there is much that must be designed and produced before the first class, including any video lectures; most, if not all, of the course tasks or activities; and the course assessments and examinations. In regard to the course tasks and activities, it is especially important for clearly designed participation opportunities such as discussion summarizer, content aggregator, annotator, and cultural interpreter (Bonk & Khoo, 2014).

2. **Build in feedback for each experience.** Feedback is critical in online environments; it is even more so in a MOOC. Feedback can come from other participants or learners (i.e., peers), the instructor(s) or instructional staff, self-evaluation, tutors and mentors (including prior learners of the MOOC), and the computer system. Feedback provided by computer algorithms is more often associated with xMOOCs. Other approaches involve peer review and different forms of group collaboration and evaluation.

3. **Create interactivities.** To increase retention, it is vital to create interactive sessions in a MOOC such as polling questions in a synchronous session or debates, role plays, discussion forums, and surveys. Participants want to know that their voices are being heard.

4. **Provide variation and choice.** Choice and variation of tasks is not only possible online, it is essential (Bonk & Khoo, 2014). Offer various types of tasks including self-initiated groups and collaborations with others as well as personal reflection activities. Embed the possibility to modify previously created learning objects using combination, permutation, substitution, deletion, and other strategies. Be sure to place learning objects into open resource collections and repositories.

5. **Combine synchronous and asynchronous experiences.** There is an increased social presence with synchronous experiences; however, combining both synchronous and asynchronous experiences in a MOOC provides opportunities for reflection as well as interaction.

6. **Segment video and other course components.** Short video clips of under twenty minutes are favored by MOOC participants over longer episodes. The technology tools to segment video are increasingly available (e.g., TubeChop), as are tools to annotate such video content as well as assess the learning from watching shared online video lectures and other content.

7. **Design responsive and interactive learning communities.** There are many forms of social media (e.g., blogs, Facebook, Twitter, Pinterest) and collaborative technologies (e.g., wikis, Adobe Connect, Skype, Google Hangouts) for developing and building an online community of learners. Although certainly present to some degree in other MOOC formats, the creation of learning and sharing communities is often associated with cMOOCs.

8. **Build in moments or opportunities for self-reflection and team reflection.** Given the thousands of potential MOOC participants, individuals need to reflect on their own personal learning journeys and accomplishments.

9. **Provide weekly recaps and updates.** With all the various resources provided and shared within a MOOC, a weekly summary of shared resources helps participants cope with information overload.

10. **Personalize the experience or activity where possible.** Addressing learners by name or location will foster more learning connectedness, as will linking to various social media sites or course profiles that include information that might promote personalization.

11. **Engage in resource sharing.** Often the MOOC participants will have knowledge and experience that the MOOC instructor(s) lack. Finding ways to share such experiences and resources will expand the course resources and learning possibilities.

12. **Be willing to change midstream.** There are myriad people relying on the MOOC experience. If the course seems to be lacking in quality or participation, consider changing the delivery, assignments, evaluations, or other variables.

Conclusion

The emergence of the Web as an educational delivery mechanism has brought with it the development of MOOCs. There is much criticism and caution as well as hope and opportunity about MOOCs and open education. Clearly, a range of issues related to training, attrition, language, accreditation, design, and assessment still need to be explored further. Along these same lines, the quality of MOOC content and delivery remains a fundamental challenge and concern. While much is already known about the effective design of a MOOC, many instructional design considerations and practices for MOOCs and MOOC-related spinoffs will continue to unfold during the coming years.

It is likely that you will encounter MOOCs both in your professional lives as instructional design and technology professionals as well as in your personal lives as self-directed online learners, whether in early adulthood or much later in your career or even in your retirement years. Massive open online courses related to your personal interests as well as your job responsibilities are being offered each day. We sincerely hope you enjoy the new opportunities that MOOCs bring to satisfy your internal curiosity about a particular topic and overall thirst for learning. Hopefully, this chapter offered you some insights in designing, as well as participating in, a high-quality MOOC experience.

Summary of Key Principles

1. **There are many types of MOOCs.** As detailed in this chapter, MOOCs provide educational content to large quantities of people, typically for free. They include standard course delivery xMOOCs, more socially oriented cMOOCs, those entailing the completion of projects as in pMOOCs, and courses aimed to upgrade the skills of those in the workforce with professional development—namely, PD-MOOCs.

2. **Business models for MOOC sustainability abound.** There are many business plans related to MOOCs; among the most promising are those with fees for secured assessments and certifications of completion, various subscription models, and those that utilize paid advertisement.

3. **MOOCs can no longer be ignored as a passing fad.** Instructional designers and technology professionals should care about MOOCs since they represent an emerging form of instructional delivery that has gained much traction during the past few years. There is much resource allocation and experimentation underway related to MOOCs and open education in which instructional designers will play a key role in the ultimate success. MOOCs are testing the limits of instructional technologies and pedagogical approaches to potentially change people's lives. They are serving an increasing role in secondary schools, higher education, and corporate training. With nanodegrees and certificates, there will be additional inroads made in this field in the coming years.

4. **Many complex issues underpin MOOC quality.** As might be expected, there are many quality issues related to MOOCs. Some concerns relate to the means and types of assessment, whereas other issues include low completion rates—especially for xMOOCs. At least one large-scale research study on MOOCs indicates that the application of instructional design principles in MOOCs is particularly weak (Margaryan et al., 2015). Other issues related to quality include assessment, learner plagiarism, limited instructor training, and the use of copyrighted materials.

5. **There are immense challenges and barriers to effective use of MOOCs.** The challenges facing those intending to utilize MOOCs include finding and organizing high-quality content that is accessible to individuals of varying technological capacity and cultural opportunity. Personalizing the learning experience across the wide cultural, linguistic, and social boundaries of a MOOC is extremely difficult. Another issue relates to knowing what instructional strategies or approaches might benefit the needs and interests of the majority of MOOC participants. Not too surprisingly, the instructional designer is often tasked with creating the instructional supports for MOOC learners that can help them navigate through myriad resources without being overwhelmed.

6. **Instructional design principles are beginning to unfold.** While MOOCs are a recent phenomenon, there are many solid instructional design principles that are already proven to foster success. Among them are designing multiple ways for participants to offer feedback on peer work as well as receive feedback from others, designing responsive learning communities, building in interactive and engaging learning experiences, recapping course events and support materials, and designing ways to share resources among participants.

Application Questions

1. You work as an instructional designer in the flagship university in a state that is known to rate low on national rankings of health and fitness. You and a team of public health and online education experts have successfully written a grant proposal to a large foundation to address this concern in your state. The governor's office heard the exciting news and invited you to attend a major press release that makes the headlines in several newspapers; you even get to briefly meet with the governor before departing back to your university about an hour or two away. A week after you return, you find out that the university in which you work has just inked a deal with a major vendor to offer MOOCs. Unfortunately, it is not the MOOC vendor with which you are familiar and your team has planned for. You and your team are charged with helping design courses on meditation and mindfulness, fundamentals of human nutrition, digital fitness training, exercise physiology, physical and mental health, marathon training, rethinking aging, and sustainable healthy diets; the first two of which are supposed to roll out in three short months. To your surprise, thousands of people in your state are already pre-enrolling for these courses. Regrettably, however, due to downsizing by your university, one of the two key people from the School of Public Health with whom you were initially planning to work is no longer employed by your university. Your reputation is at stake. In this scenario,

   a. What are two or three major issues that you feel must be addressed in this situation in order to ensure that the project is a success? What key steps might be undertaken to resolve them?

   b. What types of instructional design features or interactive components might you embed in these MOOCs on health and fitness to help them succeed? Are there specific pedagogical activities that can enhance these types of courses?

   c. What resources might you turn to in order to learn more information about health and fitness MOOCs and health and fitness in general?

   d. How might you evaluate the degree of success in this project? What are your criteria or goals? How might you sell your assessment approaches to management?

2. You work for a private, enrollment driven university that is trying to improve its Latin American market share through offering an E-Teaching and Learning master's degree specialization utilizing four MOOC-based courses. This new degree program will generate revenue by offering the for-credit program at a reduced cost in Latin America. It will also charge for completion certificates. As such, instructional activities and strategies that will be built into it must not only answer to the needs and standards of practice of the program, institution, and professional society, but it must do so in a way that responds to the cultural, linguistic, and political differences between the United States and Latin American countries. You and your instructional design team have been selected by the university leadership to address this new initiative. The university president's office is enthusiastic about the potential enrollment driven revenue that will be generated when the new program is fully implemented. To expedite the rollout of the MOOC-based e-teaching and learning specialization, the president has formulated a task force that will handle the program promotion as well as administer the course enrollments and address technological issues. However, the curriculum and instructional activities and strategies are being left to your group of instructional designers and subject-matter experts. You and your team are charged with designing courses on (1) the history and current trends in e-learning, (2) learning theories and instructional approaches in e-learning, (3) assessment and evidence of competence in e-learning, and (4) cultural and linguistic accommodation in e-learning.

   a. How will you manage this project? What policies and practices will you put in place to ensure success?

   b. What types of instructional design features might you embed in these MOOCs to help them succeed?

c. How will you ensure that the collaboration between the subject-matter experts and instructional designers is productive?

d. How might you evaluate the degree of success in this project overall, as well as the specific MOOC courses you have been charged with designing?

References

Bandi-Rao, S., & Devers, C. (2015). Developing MOOCs to narrow the college readiness gap: Challenges and recommendations for a writing course. In Special Issue: MOOCs and Open Education. *International Journal on E-Learning, 14*(3), 265–277.

Bersin, J. (2013, November 20). The MOOC marketplace takes off. *Forbes.* Retrieved from http://www.forbes .com/sites/joshbersin/2013/11/30/the-mooc-marketplace-takes-off/

Bonk, C. J., & Khoo, E. (2014). *Adding some TEC-VARIETY: 100+ activities for motivating and retaining learners online.* OpenWorldBooks.com and Amazon CreateSpace. Retrieved from http://tec-variety.com/

Bonk, C. J., Lee, M. M., Kou, X., Xu, S., & Sheu, F.-R. (2015). Understanding the self-directed online learning preferences, goals, achievements, and challenges of MIT OpenCourseWare subscribers. *Educational Technology and Society, 18*(2), 349–368. Retrieved from http://www .ifets.info/journals/18_2/26.pdf

Bonk, C. J., Lee., M. M., Reeves, T. C., & Reynolds, T. H. (2015). Preface: Actions leading to "MOOCs and open education around the world." In C. J. Bonk, M. M. Lee., T. C. Reeves, & T. H. Reynolds (Eds.), *MOOCs and open education around the world* (pp. xxx–xlii). New York: Routledge. Retrieved from http://publicationshare.com/moocsbook/ and http://www.moocsbook.com/free.php

DeMillo, R. (2015). Unbundling higher education and the Georgia Tech online MS in computer science: A chronicle. In C. J. Bonk, M. M. Lee, T. C. Reeves, & T. H. Reynolds (Eds.), *MOOCs and open education around the world* (pp. 147–156). New York: Routledge.

Downes, S. (2011, August). *Free learning: Essays on open educational resources and copyright*: Retrieved from http://www.downes.ca/files/books/FreeLearning.pdf

edX. (2014a, January 21). *Harvard and MIT release working papers on open online courses.* edX blog. Retrieved from https://www.edx.org/blog/harvard-mit-release-working-papers-open/#.VOEnbo1TFjs

edX. (2014b). *We are launching a high school initiative.* edX press release. Retrieved from http://blog.edx.org/we-are-launching-high-school-initiative/

Grovo. (2015). Training the trainer: How to create microlearning. Technical Report. Retrieved from https://www .grovo.com/microlearning

Hilger, C. (2014, September 8). Putting MOOCs to work recap [Infographic 7 ways that corporations are using MOOCs]. Extension Engine. Retrieved from http://extensionengine.com/putting-moocs-to-work-recap-infographic/#.VHKBnGd0zX4

Kessler, S. (2013, March 26). Here's a Google perk any company can imitate: Employee-to-employee learning. *Fast Company.* Retrieved from http://www.fastcompany .com/3007369/heres-google-perk-any-company-can-imitate-employee-employee-learning

Kop, R., Fournier, H., & Mak, J. S. F. (2011, November). A pedagogy of abundance or a pedagogy to support human beings? Participant support on massive open online courses. *International Review of Research on Open and Distance Learning (IRRODL), 12*(7). Retrieved from http://www.irrodl.org/index.php/irrodl/article/view/1041/2025

Laurillard, D. (2014, December 30). *Anatomy of a MOOC for teacher CPD.* University College London: Institute of Education. Retrieved from http://www.lkl.ac.uk/cms/files/jce/reports/anatomy_of_a_mooc_for_teacher_cpd_ucl-ioe.pdf

Lewin, T. (2015, April 22). Promising full college credit: Arizona State University offers online freshman program. *The New York Times.* Retrieved from http://www .nytimes.com/2015/04/23/us/arizona-state-university-to-offer-online-freshman-academy.html?_r=0

Margaryan, A., Bianco, M., & Littlejohn, A. (2015). Instructional quality of massive open online courses (MOOCs). *Computers & Education, 80,* 77–83.

Meister, J. (2013, August 13). How MOOCs will revolutionize corporate learning and development. *Forbes.* Retrieved from http://www.forbes.com/sites/jeannemeister/2013/08/13/how-moocs-will-revolutionize-corporate-learning-development/

Moe, R. (2015). The brief and expansive history (and future) of the MOOC: Why two divergent models share the same name. *Current Issues in Emerging eLearning, 2*(1), Article 2. Retrieved from http://scholarworks.umb.edu/ciee/vol2/iss1/2/

Portmess, L. R. (2013). Mobile knowledge, karma points and digital peers: The tacit epistemology and linguistic representation of MOOCs/Savoir mobile, points de karma et pairs numériques: L'épistémologie tacite et la représentation linguistique des MOOC. *Canadian Journal of Learning and Technology/La Revue Canadienne de L'apprentissage et de la Technologie, 39*(2). Retrieved from http://cjlt.csj .ualberta.ca/index.php/cjlt/article/viewFile/705/360

Reeves, T. C., & Bonk, C. J. (2015). MOOCs: Redirecting the quest for quality higher education for all. In Special

Issue: MOOCs and Open Education. *International Journal on E-Learning, 14*(3), 385–399.

Reeves, T. C., & Hedberg, J. G. (2014). MOOCs: Let's get REAL. *Educational Technology, 54*(1), 3–8.

Reynolds, T. H., Reeves, T. C., Lee. M. M., & Bonk, C. J. (2015). Open options: Recapping this book with eyes on the future. In C. J. Bonk, M. M. Lee., T. C. Reeves, & T. H. Reynolds (Eds.), *MOOCs and open education around the world* (pp. 327–341). New York: Routledge.

Schroeder, R., Cook, V. S., Levin, C., & Gribbins, M. (2015). Alternative models of MOOCs. In C. J. Bonk, M. M. Lee., T. C. Reeves, & T. H. Reynolds (Eds.), *MOOCs and open education around the world* (pp. 275–285). New York: Routledge.

Stripling, J. (2015, April 24). The making of a higher-ed agitator: Michael Crow's prescription for colleges divides and inspires. *The Chronicle of Higher Education.* Retrieved from http://chronicle.com/article/The-Making-of-a-Higher-Ed/229619/

Waters, J. K. (2015, August 5). How nanodegrees are disrupting higher education. *Campus Technology.* Retrieved from http://campustechnology.com/articles/2015/08/05/how-nanodegrees-are-disrupting-higher-education.aspx

Watters, A. (2013, November 29). Top ed-tech trends of 2013: MOOCs and anti-MOOCs. *Hack Education.* Retrieved from http://hackeducation.com/2013/11/29/top-ed-tech-trends-2013-moocs/

Wiley, D. (2015). The MOOC misstep and open education. In C. J. Bonk, M. M. Lee, T. C. Reeves, & T. H. Reynolds (Eds.), *MOOCs and open education around the world* (pp. 3–11). New York: Routledge.

Chapter 31
Using Rich Media Wisely

Ruth Colvin Clark

Clark Training & Consulting

Richard E. Mayer

University of California, Santa Barbara

How can you use rich media—such as animation, video, and audio—to help people learn in multimedia training environments? Consider three approaches to a lesson on how lightning forms. Version A includes simple visuals using line drawings described by on-screen text. Version B uses animated visuals of the lightning process described by audio narration. Because some might experience the topic of lightning formation as somewhat dry, Version C adds several stories with video to invoke interest. For example, one story describes the effects of lightning strikes on airplanes, including a visual of an airplane hit by lightning. Versions B and C use rich media including animation, audio, and video; Version A uses static graphics rather than animation or video and printed text rather than audio. In addition, Versions A and B stick to just the facts, whereas Version C adds some interesting stories about lighting to the factual descriptions. Which of these three lesson versions do you think is more effective for learning? Take a minute now to select one of the following choices.

Best learning would come from:

_____ A. Lesson Version A because it uses simpler media than the other lessons

_____ B. Lesson Version B because it uses animation and audio to illustrate a scientific process

_____ C. Lesson Version C because interesting stories would motivate learning about lightning formation

_____ D. There would be no difference in learning as all three lessons include the same content about how lightning forms

Which features of rich media promote learning and which features either detract from learning or do not add cost benefit? These are the questions that we explore in this chapter.

In 2013 American business invested over $150 billion in workforce learning (Association for Talent Development [TAD], 2014). To gain maximum return on this significant investment, instructional program developers are wise to consider evidence of what works as they make multimedia design decisions. To illustrate our argument, we will primarily focus on the research-based theory and research evidence for best use of basic instructional modes of still graphics, animation, audio, and text. Although we could have selected different instructional methods such as games and simulations, we will focus on evidence-based use of text, audio, and graphics as all instructional environments make use of some combination of these modes and there is a healthy body of research available to guide your decisions.

Technology-Centered versus Learner-Centered Instruction

Given the breathtaking advances in computer and communication technology, it may be tempting for instructional designers to ask, "How can we use rich media to design instruction?" This reflects a *technology-centered approach* to instructional design because we begin with the capabilities of technology (such as the availability of rich media) and design instruction to accommodate these capabilities. For example, in taking a technology-centered approach, we may seek ways to design a lesson using the capability of incorporating video and animation.

Let's take a brief look at the disappointing history of the technology-centered approach throughout the twentieth century

(Cuban, 1986, 2001). In the 1920s, motion pictures were touted as a cutting-edge technology that would revolutionize education. In the 1930s and 1940s, radio was promoted as a way to bring the world's experts into the classroom. In the 1950s, educational television was offered as the key to the future of education—combining the benefits of movies and radio. In the 1960s and 1970s, there were claims that computer-based programmed instruction would soon replace teachers. In each case, the cycle of events was similar: strong claims that a cutting-edge technology would transform education, followed by enthusiastic implementation in some educational settings, and ultimately, the conclusion that the new cutting-edge technology had not succeeded.

What is wrong with the technology-centered approach to instructional design? The main problem is, it does not take the learner into account, including what is known about how people learn. In contrast, in a *learner-centered approach* to instructional design, the focus is on how to facilitate the learner's natural learning process. Rich media must be adapted to serve the needs of learners, rather than the other way around. In short, in taking a learner-centered approach we ask, "How can we adapt rich media to aid human learning?"

A major theme of this chapter is that rich media should be used (or not used) in ways that are consistent with what we know about how people learn and with research evidence concerning instructional effectiveness (i.e., instructional designers should take a learner-centered approach to the use of rich media). Taking a learner-centered approach involves designing instruction that fosters learning. An important aspect of this approach is a commitment to *evidence-based practice*—the idea that instructional practice should be based on research evidence. We define an evidence-based approach as the judicious use of current best evidence in making decisions about the design, development, and delivery of learning environments (Clark, 2015). Although there are several types of evidence readily available, we favor experimental studies that involve random assignment of learners to treatments and a control group.

What is the rationale for evidence-based practice? Instructional decisions can be based on opinions, fads, ideology, advice, testimonials, or untested best practices. The problem with such approaches is that there is little reason to believe that they will lead to effective instruction. In contrast, in taking an evidence-based approach, we seek to use instructional methods and modes that have been shown to work for the kinds of learners and learning objectives at hand.

How People Learn

How does learning work? This is the key question addressed in the science of learning, which is the scientific study of how people learn (Mayer, 2011). According to this approach, learning is a change in the learner's knowledge caused by the learner's experience. Consequently, the science of instruction is concerned with instructional methods that help people learn (Mayer, 2011). Thus, instructional methods should be grounded in an understanding of how learning works.

As summarized in Figure 31.1, learning occurs within the learner's information processing system, which consists of three memory stores: sensory memory, working memory, and long-term memory. As you can see, information from the outside world—such as instructional words and graphics—impinges on the learner's eyes and ears and is held in for a fraction of a second as a visual or auditory image in sensory memory. If the learner attends to some of this fleeting incoming information, it is transferred to working memory where it can be organized into a cognitive representation.

Working memory is the center of all conscious thinking including deliberate learning, but it is limited in capacity. Learners can process only a few elements at any one time in working memory, as was popularized by Miller's (1956) review setting the limit at seven plus or minus two chunks of information. Therefore, a primary challenge of instructional design is to accommodate the learner's limited capacity for processing information in working memory.

In contrast, long-term memory is a permanent, large-capacity repository of information, including organized knowledge structures called schemas. During learning, prior knowledge in long-term memory, such as a schema, is activated and integrated with incoming information in working memory. There is an interaction between working memory and long-term memory in which existing knowledge in long-term memory can be used to chunk the material in working memory, allowing for more material to be processed. This is

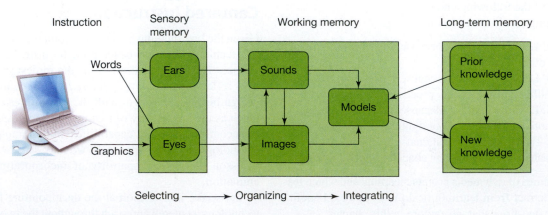

FIGURE 31.1 A model of human learning processes.

why novice learners with little related knowledge in long-term memory are much more susceptible to cognitive overload than are more experienced learners. Thus, differences in relevant prior knowledge is recognized as the perhaps the single most important individual differences feature to be considered when designing instruction.

Also as summarized in Figure 31.1, there are three cognitive processes needed to convert the instructional input into new knowledge and skills in long-term memory:

Selecting. The arrows from sensory memory to working memory indicate that the learner pays attention to some of the incoming information and transfers it to working memory for further processing.

Organizing. The arrows within working memory indicate that the learner is mentally organizing the incoming material into coherent verbal and visual representations.

Integrating. The arrows from long-term memory to working memory indicate that the learner is mentally integrating new knowledge representations with each other and with relevant prior knowledge activated from long-term memory to form new knowledge and skills.

Finally, the arrow from working memory to long-term memory indicates storing the newly constructed knowledge in long-term memory for later use.

Meaningful learning occurs when the learner engages in appropriate selecting, organizing, and integrating during learning. These processes are partially controlled by the learner's *metacognitive knowledge*—knowledge of how to manage learning—and the learner's *motivation*—which initiates and maintains goal-directed activity.

Another aspect of the information processing system is that there are separate channels for processing visual/pictorial information and for processing auditory/verbal information, each with its own cognitive load limits. Graphics are processed in the visual/pictorial channel. Spoken words are processed in the auditory/verbal channel. Printed words are processed initially in the visual/pictorial channel and then may be converted for processing in the auditory/verbal channel.

The amount of mental work imposed on working memory during learning is called *cognitive load* (Mayer, 2009; Sweller, Ayres, & Kalyuga, 2011). The major challenge of instructional

design is to promote appropriate cognitive processing—selecting, organizing, and integrating—without overloading working memory. Three forms of cognitive load are summarized in Table 31.1—extraneous processing, essential processing, and generative processing.

Poor instructional design can create *extraneous processing*, which saps limited processing capacity needed for meaningful learning, so an important instructional goal is to reduce extraneous processing. The complexity of the to-be-learned material can demand a high level of *essential processing* needed to mentally represent the incoming material (i.e., mainly selecting and initial organizing), so an important instructional goal is to help the learner manage essential processing. Finally, the learner must be motivated to exert the effort needed for making sense of the incoming material—that is, to engage in *generative processing* (mainly organizing and integrating)—so a final instructional goal is to foster generative processing.

Overall, instructional designers seek instructional programs that reduce extraneous processing, manage essential processing, and foster generative processing. Many recent studies (Clark & Mayer, 2011; Clark, Nguyen, & Sweller, 2006; Mayer, 2009, 2014; Sweller et al., 2011) have examined specific instructional methods aimed at reducing extraneous processing (such as adding signaling or placing printed text next to corresponding graphics), managing essential processing (such as breaking a lesson into segments or providing pretraining in key components), and fostering generative processing (such as using conversational style or assigning relevant practice activities).

Three research-based principles about learning that are particularly relevant for instructional designers are:

Limited capacity principle. People can process only a small amount of information in each channel at any one time.

Dual-channels principle. People have separate channels for processing visual/pictorial information and auditory/verbal information.

Active learning principle. Meaningful learning occurs when the learner engages in appropriate cognitive processing during learning, including attending to relevant aspects of the incoming information, mentally organizing the material into a coherent cognitive representation, and

TABLE 31.1	Three Types of Cognitive Load in Instructional Design	
Type of Load	**Description**	**Example**
Extraneous	Irrelevant mental load imposed by poor instructional design decisions	Using overly complex visuals with extraneous details to illustrate a process such as how blood circulates
Essential	Mental load aimed at representing the material and caused by the complexity of the instructional content	Presenting material that is complex for the learner (i.e., requiring the simultaneous manipulation of multiple elements in memory)
Generative	Relevant mental load aimed at making sense of the material and dependent on the learner's efforts to organize and integrate the content	Using explanatory visuals that help learners understand content meaning Assigning practice activities that help learners achieve the instructional objectives

mentally integrating it with existing knowledge activated from long-term memory.

To illustrate our suggestion that you consider evidence and human learning processes as you develop workforce learning programs, we focus on several questions regarding the best use of visuals and words in multimedia training.

Question 1: Do Visuals Improve Learning?

Visuals—including still graphics, animation, and video—can be difficult to generate and can add time, cost, and bandwidth to lesson development and delivery. Is there any benefit to an investment in visuals? Let's take a look at the evidence. Mayer (2009) has compared learning from multiple lessons that communicated with words alone to lessons that communicated the same content with both words and visuals. For example, in Figure 31.2 you can see a text-only lesson segment contrasted with a text plus graphic segment.

Learners were randomly assigned to each version and tested after learning. In eleven studies that focused on brakes, pumps, generators, lightning, and mathematics, the versions with visuals promoted better learning. The learning benefit of adding visuals was high with a median effect size of 1.39. That means that on average the scores of a group studying a lesson with text, will improve by nearly one and a half standard deviations if an appropriate visual is added. The psychological reason for the learning power of visuals relates to the dual channel features of working memory we discussed previously. Lessons with words and visuals offer the brain two opportunities to build meaning—one from the words and the second from corresponding images—and encourage learners to make connections between them.

Question 2: Are Visuals More Effective for Some Learners Than Others?

We saw that adding a visual to a textual description of how pumps work improved learning. Do some learners gain more from visuals than others? Some trainers believe there are visual and verbal learning styles that affect how an individual learns best. Do you believe that you are a visual learner or an auditory learner?

In fact, some learners do benefit more than others from visuals, but these individual differences have little to do with learning styles. Consider this experiment. Two versions of a judge's instructions to a jury in a self-defense trial were tested by Brewer, Harvey, and Semmler (2004). One version was the audio-only version traditionally given by judges. The second version added visuals such as flow charts and illustrations to the audio. Two different types of learners were randomly assigned to one of the two versions: legal novices similar to most juries and law students. After reviewing either the audio or the audio-visual version, individuals were tested for comprehension. The results are shown in Figure 31.3.

Take a look at the graph in Figure 31.3 and select the conclusion(s) most warranted:

_____ A. Novices benefitted most from visuals

_____ B. Experts benefitted most from visuals

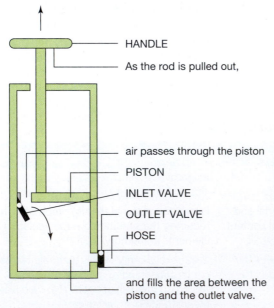
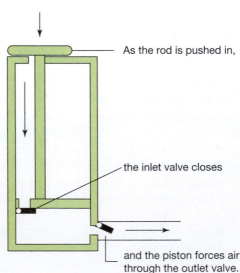

FIGURE 31.2 Two versions of a lesson on how bicycle pumps work.

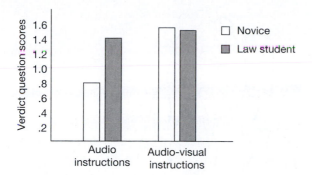

FIGURE 31.3 The effect of visuals on novice and expert learners. (Adapted from data reported by Brewer, Harvey, & Semmler, 2004)

_____ C. Both experts and novices benefitted from visuals

_____ D. Novices were boosted to expert levels by access to visuals

Novices benefitted the most from visuals and, in fact, their comprehension of legal instructions with visuals reached just about the same level as that of law students. Because of their prior knowledge, the law students were able to comprehend the audio instructions effectively without visuals. The answers to the questions about the data shown in Figure 31.3 are A and D.

Research studies reported by Mayer and Gallini (1990) and by Kalyuga, Chandler, and Sweller (1998, 2000) have been the basis for what Kalyuga (2014) calls the _expertise reversal effect_. The expertise reversal effect refers to the fact that an instructional mode or method that is helpful to novices does not help experts and in some cases can actually depress expert performance. As mentioned, the learner's prior knowledge is the most important individual difference to consider in instructional design.

What about the idea of learning styles? Kratzig and Arbuthnott (2006) asked learners to assess their own learning style (visual, auditory, or kinesthetic), tested each learner with standard learning styles inventories, and tested their visual, auditory, and kinesthetic memories. The research team then looked for correlations or relationships among the self-assessment, the inventory assessments, and the memory tests. They found no relationship among any of the measures. In other words, learners who classified themselves as visual learners did not test as visual learners on a learning style inventory nor did they exhibit higher visual memory. The report concludes, "In contrast to learning style theory, it appears that people are able to learn effectively using all three sensory modalities" (p. 241). A subsequent review of learning styles by Pashler, McDaniel, Rohrer, and Bjork (2008) concludes, "The contrast between the enormous popularity of the learning-styles approach within education and the lack of credible evidence for its utility is, in our opinion, striking and disturbing. If classification of students' learning styles has practical utility, it remains to be demonstrated" (p. 117).

Question 3: Are Richer Visuals Better for Learning?

A rich visual is one that is relatively more detailed or more complex. For example, a visual with 3D perspective like the one shown in Version B of Figure 31.4 is a richer illustration of blood circulation through the heart than the simple line drawing shown in Version A.

An animated depiction of how lightning forms as described in our introduction is richer than a series of still drawings. An animation incorporates a great deal of transient visual information which often plays under program control. In contrast still visuals display only a few key frames and are viewed by the learner at their own rate. A video of a classroom session is richer than an animation of the same classroom that omits extraneous background visual information. Recent advances in authoring and graphics software has made the production of rich visual displays such as animations and video easier. What evidence do we have about the effectiveness of rich graphics?

A. Line Drawings versus 2D Drawings

Butcher (2006) compared comprehension of how circulation flows through the heart from three lesson versions: text only, text with simple line drawing, and text with a more complex diagram rendered in a 3D perspective, as shown in Figure 31.4.

Similar to the bicycle pump experiment, Butcher found that adding a visual to text improved understanding of circulation—both simple and complex visuals were more effective than text alone. When comparing the two visuals, however, the simpler line diagram was more effective than the more complex graphic—especially for novice learners (Butcher, 2006). She recommends, "Especially for novice learners, removing nonessential details from visual representations may be advisable" (Butcher, 2014, p. 182).

B. Still Graphics versus Animations

Like many instructional methods, the debate between still versus animated graphics can best be answered with: _It depends_. Animated graphics (video or computer generated) can illustrate processes that could not be observed otherwise, such as seed germination or the flight pattern of a hummingbird. At the same time animations can impose a great deal of mental load by displaying a large quantity of visual information that is transient.

It seems intuitive that when teaching a process that involves moving physical elements such as lightning formation, animation would be more effective; however, when comparing several lesson topics (e.g., how brakes work, how toilets flush, and how lightning forms) in which learning from an animated version was contrasted with learning from a series of still graphics, Mayer, Hegarty, Mayer, and Campbell (2005) found that a series of still frames resulted in learning that was as good as or better than the animated versions.

Whether to use an animation or a series of stills will depend on (1) the purpose of your visual representation, (2) the cognitive match between the visual and the learner, and (3) specific features in the animation such as cueing (Hegarty, 2014; Lowe & Schnotz, 2014). For example, in one experiment the goal was to teach identification of the locomotion phases of a hopping kangaroo. The research team found that the animated representation resulted in poorer performance than a series of still representations because the still visuals allowed learners to carefully compare each phase against the other (Lowe, Schnotz,

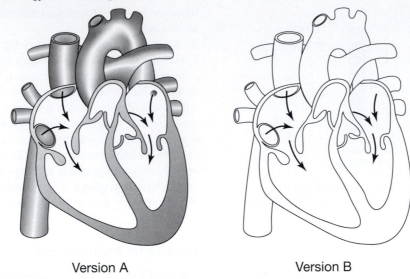

Version A   Version B

FIGURE 31.4 A simple and detailed diagram of blood circulation in the heart. (Butcher, 2006)

& Rasch, 2011). The transient nature of the animated images degraded the opportunity to distinguish subtle differences in the body alignments during movement.

Perhaps more relevant to educators is the value of an animation as a performance aid. If your goal is to guide workers to complete an assembly task, which representation would be more effective? A text description, still diagrams (with no words), or animations (with no words)? Watson, Butterfield, Curran, and Craig (2010) compared build time of a device requiring thirty-three steps over five trials with instructions provided in these three formats. The animated directions resulted in fastest build time for the first build. For the second build, there was no difference between animated and still graphics. By the fifth build, all three representations resulted in the same build time—perhaps the steps had been learned by that point. These results suggest that if your performance environment will involve one-time builds, animations will result in fastest performance; however if the same individuals will perform the build more than once, there is little difference between stills and animations.

This study reinforced the value of animations as reference support for performing motor tasks. Similar results have been reported for learning of other motor skills. For example, Ayres, Marcus, Chan, and Qian (2009) and Wong, Marcus, Ayres, Smith, Cooper, Paas, & Sweller (2009) found better learning of physical tasks such as knot tying or origami paper folding from an animated display than from a series of stills. Thus, when the task involves motor performance using the hands, animation can be more effective than still graphics.

Conditions for Effective Animations

When you determine that an animation is the best display for your performance support or instructional goal, consider ways to balance the mental load imposed by a complex transient display. First, consider cueing devices to draw attention to relevant aspects of the animation. In some situations the

important movements involve smaller elements of the display, which may be overshadowed by larger moving elements. In other cases, you may want to direct attention to multiple simultaneous sequences of movements. Recent research has shown that cueing devices that work well with static graphics such as arrows are not as effective with animations. Instead, consider use of color flows (i.e., progressive path cueing) to direct the eye to the most relevant phases of the animation (Boucheix & Lowe, 2010). Audio narration can also be used as a cueing device to guide learner attention to the relevant aspects of the display. Second, include tools allowing learner control over the display of the animation. For example, a slider bar offers learners a means to view an animation in a flexible manner (Lowe & Schnotz, 2014).

C. Computer-Generated Animations versus Video

Suppose you want to illustrate some interpersonal skills such as how to sell a product or how to manage a disruptive student in the classroom. You could show examples using text narratives, animation, or video. Moreno and Ortegano-Layne (2008) compared how student teachers learned teaching principles from classroom examples displayed in three formats: narrative text descriptions, computer animations, and video. Consistent with the research we've discussed so far, they found both visual formats (i.e., animation and video) resulted in better learning and higher student ratings than text descriptions.

Your decision to use animation or video may depend on several practical as well as instructional factors. For example, you may have technology to support video recording and editing rather than creation of animation or vice versa. Another factor to consider is volatility of your visual content. One very expensive video production focusing on military leadership skills was rendered obsolete in months because the military service changed uniforms. Video captures all visible elements in the scene and therefore may offer information of higher visual fidelity compared to animated drawings. However, it is less selective and flexible than animations. In contrast, animations are drawn and allow a number of visual affordances, including elimination of irrelevant details, dynamic illustration of an object from different perspectives, illustration of processes and events not readily depicted in alternative formats (Lowe & Schnotz, 2014).

Conditions for Effective Video

Video has been used extensively in teacher education and many of the lessons learned can be applied to goals involving interpersonal skills such as sales and customer service. In teacher education, video is used to illustrate teaching principles as described previously. Repositories of video cases are available that are edited specifically for various topics of problem-based learning lessons for teachers. Finally, teachers themselves may video their own work to be submitted as part of a portfolio or for critique and discussion.

Derry, Sherin, and Sherin (2014) recommend several techniques to manage cognitive load in video. One method is segmenting the video allowing stop, start, and revisiting of specific segments. The segmenting can be done by the class facilitator or can be built into an online program. The segmenting can be accompanied by textual cues guiding learner attention to relevant aspects of the video. For example, guidance prior to the video may ask viewers to pay special attention to how the teacher rewards desired behaviors and manages undesired behaviors. Another load management technique is pretraining in which the concepts to be illustrated in a video are presented first in text. Beitzel and Derry (2009) found better learning when a reading preceded a video compared to when the same reading followed the video. Third, Derry et al. (2014) recommend editing out footage irrelevant to the instructional goal.

Question 4: Do Visuals Added for Motivation Improve Learning?

Sometimes rich media elements are added for motivational purposes. Since workforce learning topics often tend to be rather dry, adding interesting stories and visuals may appeal to the younger generation raised on high-end media. For example, rather than stick with the basic description of lightning formation described in the introduction, the lesson can be spiced up with visuals and stories about lightning such as the one about airplanes struck by lightning. Does adding rich media in the form of stories or graphics improve learning?

In the early 1990s, Garner and her colleagues (Garner, Alexander, Gillingham, Kulikowich, & Grown, 1991; Garner, Brown, Sanders, & Menke, 1992) identified the negative effects of what they termed *seductive details*. In their studies seductive details consisted of textual information inserted into instructional materials that were intended to arouse interest. Seductive details in lessons are typically related to the general topic but are irrelevant to the main instructional goal. Harp and Mayer (1997) evaluated the learning effects of adding both seductive text as well as seductive visuals to multimedia lessons. For example, throughout a lesson on how lightning forms, they incorporated

brief discussions such as what happens when lightning strikes a golfer and the effect of lightning on airplanes. Learners rated the lesson versions that contained the seductive vignettes as more interesting than the lessons that omitted these details; however, these spiced-up lessons depressed learning dramatically. In six different studies, lessons that *omitted* seductive information showed a median learning gain of 105 percent with an effect size of 1.66, which is high, as compared to lessons with seductive information.

Sung and Mayer (2012) compared learning and student ratings from four lesson versions: text only, text plus decorative visuals, text plus seductive visuals, and text plus relevant visuals. Learners gave higher ratings to all three versions with visuals. In spite of learner preferences, the version with relevant visuals resulted in best learning. In fact, the version with seductive visuals resulted in scores lower than the lessons with text alone. In this study, we learn again the negative effects of seductive visuals; however, we also see that learners like visuals and generally do not discriminate between visuals that impede learning and visuals that boost learning. Your challenge is to visualize your content in ways that are both motivational and effective for learning.

An emerging approach to graphics intended to enhance motivation while also improving learning is called *emotional design* (Um, Plass, Hayward, & Homer, 2012; Mayer & Estrella, 2014). In lessons on how the immune system works (Um et al., 2012) and how a virus causes a cold (Mayer & Estrella, 2014) graphics presented in color and incorporating humanoid features such as expressive eyes improved learning outcomes as compared to black-and-white illustrations without humanlike features.

Question 5: Is Learning Better from Visuals Explained by Words in Audio or in Text?

In the previous sections we reviewed multiple research studies showing the benefit of adding a relevant visual to words. What evidence do we have about the benefits of describing a visual with audio versus on-screen text?

Explain Complex Visuals with Brief Audio Narration

In the 2009 version of this chapter, we summarized evidence showing that learning usually is better from visuals described by audio narration than by on-screen text. As we update our discussion, we have even more evidence about the benefits of audio narration as well as some boundary conditions regarding its use.

So many research studies have compared learning from visuals that are described by words presented in text to learning from visuals that are described by words presented in audio narration that we now have even stronger evidence for our recommendation. Reviews of research on this issue published by Ginns (2005), Lowe and Sweller (2005), Moreno (2006), and Mayer and Pilegard (2014) are consistent in their findings that learning usually is more effective when visuals are explained by audio narration. Instructional research psychologists call this finding the *modality effect*. Mayer and Pilegard (2014) review more than sixty published experimental comparisons between learning in groups that received graphics explained by printed text versus graphics explained by narration. The modality effect has been observed with a wide variety of content including mathematics, electrical engineering, lightning, brakes, an environmental science game, and with explanations from pedagogical agents (Mayer, 2009). Of thirty-three foundational studies, all yielded positive effects with a median effect size of 0.88, which is high. Further, the modality effect has been documented in actual classroom field tests (Harskamp, Mayer, Suhre, & Jansma, 2007).

If you recall our discussion of the dual channel features of working memory, you can see why audio narration can be more effective. As we summarized in Figure 31.1, working memory has a verbal (auditory) and visual channel. When pictures are explained by words in audio format, the information is divided between the audio and the visual channels of working memory and in that way optimizes the capacity limits of working memory. In contrast, when graphics are described by words presented in text all the content is directed toward the visual center of working memory and leads to overload.

Current research has revealed the following conditions under which the modality effect is most pronounced: (1) Learners have lower prior knowledge, (2) the narration is brief, and (3) the lesson plays outside of learner control such as in a typical animation. Mayer and Pilegard (2014) conclude in their review that "overall across a wide variety of learning situations, the preponderance of evidence shows that people tend to learn better from graphics and spoken text than from graphics and printed text, with a median effect size of 0.76" (p. 336).

As a practitioner, keep in mind the following issues as you plan the use of text and audio in e-learning. Information that is presented in an auditory mode is transient. In some situations, on-screen text is more appropriate for memory support. For example, when giving on-screen directions for a training exercise, text is more effective because the learner can refer to it over time as they work the exercise. In addition, whenever audio narration is used to describe visuals, the opportunity to review it should be provided via a replay button. New technical terms may benefit from both text and audio. Finally, the modality effect assumes fluency in the language used in the audio narration. Nonnative speakers may find narration adds more cognitive load than on-screen text.

Technology-Centered versus Learner-Centered: The Bottom Line

From social media such as wikis or Twitter to virtual worlds such as Second Life, each new technological innovation spawns a plethora of highly optimistic learning claims. However, the lessons from the last sixty years of media evolution and the evidence we have summarized here suggest a more constrained view. The first theme that we see through the threads of research we have summarized in this chapter is: *Less is often more and leaner media can be more effective for learning than rich media.* Why? The human brain has evolved an architecture that is easily overloaded. Secondly, the goals of learning unlike the goals of advertising or the goals of video games rely on effortful processing of information to build new knowledge and skills.

The second theme recommends a number of techniques, such as cueing or learner control, you can apply to rich media to minimize extraneous processing and manage essential processing. In short, we recommend that you adopt a learner-centered view of instruction that accommodates the learner's limits on information processing and leverages the strengths of human memory. It makes sense to maintain a skeptical perspective on the learning panaceas claimed for the latest technological innovation.

As you consider your options for displays that are leaner or richer, keep in mind your instructional goal, the learner background knowledge, your implementation of your display along with pragmatic issues of time, budget, and technological resources. Rather than advocate for any specific instructional method, we suggest you weigh your options based on current best evidence, the psychology of learning, and pragmatic constraints of your instructional environment.

Summary of Key Principles

1. **When designing multimedia instruction, consider the strengths and limits of human memory as well as evidence as you plan your use of visuals, text, and audio.**

2. **Use relevant visuals to support learning of novices.**

3. **When your goal is building understanding of a process, use simpler visuals such as line drawings or stills rather than more complex renditions such as 3D visuals or animations.**

4. **Consider animated displays for communicating procedural information about motor skills using** one's hands and for some of the unique effects that animations can generate.

5. **When using animated displays (computer generated or video), manage potential cognitive overload through progressive cueing in computer-generated animations, segmenting, learner control tools, and pretraining with computer-generated animations or video.**

6. **Explain visuals with brief audio narration except in situations where cognitive load is low and/or using audio will add cognitive load (e.g., when learners are not native speakers).**

Application Questions

1. Suppose you wish to help people learn how to carry out a fitness exercise routine using workout equipment. Would it better to use a series of still diagrams, an animation, or a video? Would it be better to use printed text or spoken text or no text? Justify your answer in terms of research evidence and a cognitive theory of learning.

2. Suppose you wish to help people learn how a virus causes a new flu strain. You develop a set of PowerPoint slides depicting the six steps in the process, along with on-screen text. Your supervisor suggests that the lesson should include some interesting stories about viruses to help spice up an otherwise dry presentation. Based on the research evidence and your understanding of how learning works, how would you respond to your supervisor?

3. What differences in the use of visuals, text, and audio might you consider for a lesson on how to use exercise equipment versus how a virus causes the flu? What differences might you consider for learners who are new to the concept of viruses versus learners with background on that topic? Compare and contrast instructional treatments based on differences in the desired learning outcomes and learner backgrounds based on the evidence we have discussed.

4. Suppose you plan to use computerized animation to illustrate multiple simultaneous movement of equipment parts. Describe how you might manage extraneous load imposed by the animation.

References

Association for Talent Development (ATD). (2014). *State of the industry report 2014.* Alexandria, VA: Association for Talent Development.

Ayres, P., Marcus, N., Chan, C., & Qian, N. (2009). Learning hand manipulative tasks: When instructional animations are superior to equivalent static representations. *Computers in Human Behavior, 25,* 348–353.

Beitzel, B., & Derry, S. (2009). When the book is better than the movie: How contrasting video cases influence text learning. *Journal of Educational Computing Research, 40,* 337–355.

Boucheix, J. M., & Lowe, R. K. (2010). An eye tracking comparison of external pointing cues and internal continuous cues in learning with complex animations. *Learning and Instruction, 20,* 123–135.

Brewer, N., Harvey, S., & Semmler, C. (2004). Improving comprehension of jury instructions with audio-visual presentation. *Applied Cognitive Psychology, 18,* 765–776.

Butcher, K. R. (2006). Learning from text with diagrams, promoting mental model development and inference generation. *Journal of Educational Psychology, 98,* 182–197.

Butcher, K. R. (2014). The multimedia principle. In R. E. Mayer (Ed.), *The Cambridge handbook of multimedia learning* (2nd ed., pp. 174–205). New York: Cambridge University Press.

Clark, R. C. (2015). *Evidence-based training* (2nd ed.). Alexandria, VA: ATD.

Clark, R. C., & Mayer, R. E. (2011). *E-learning and the science of instruction – Proven guidelines for consumers and designers of multimedia learning* (3rd ed.). San Francisco: Pfeiffer.

Clark, R. C., Nguyen, F., & Sweller, J. (2006). *Efficiency in learning.* San Francisco: Pfeiffer.

Cuban, L. (1986). *Teachers and machines: The classroom use of technology since 1920.* New York: Teachers College Press.

Cuban, L. (2001). *Oversold and underused: Computers in the classroom.* Cambridge, MA: Harvard University Press.

Derry, S. J., Sherin, M. G., & Sherin, B. L. (2014). Multimedia learning with video. In R.E. Mayer (Ed.), *The Cambridge handbook of multimedia learning* (2nd ed., pp. 785–812). New York: Cambridge University Press.

Garner, R., Alexander, P., Gillingham, M., Kulikowich, J., & Grown, R. (1991). Interest and learning from text. *American Educational Research Journal, 28,* 643–659.

Garner, R., Brown, R., Sanders, S., & Menke, D. (1992). Seductive details and learning from text. In K.A. Renninger, S. Hidi, & A. Krapp (Eds.), *The role of interest in learning and development* (pp. 239–254). Hillsdale, NJ: Erlbaum.

Ginns, P. (2005). Meta-analysis of the modality effect. *Learning and Instruction, 15,* 313–332.

Harp, S. F., & Mayer, R. E. (1997). The role of interest in learning from scientific text and illustrations: On the distinction between emotional interest and cognitive interest. *Journal of Educational Psychology, 89,* 92–102.

Harskamp, E., Mayer, R. E., Suhre, C., & Jansma, J. (2007). Does the modality principle for multimedia learning apply to science classrooms? *Learning and Instruction, 18,* 465–477.

Hegarty, M. (2014). Multimedia learning and the development of mental models. In R. E. Mayer (Ed.), *The Cambridge handbook of multimedia learning* (2nd ed., pp. 147–158). New York: Cambridge University Press.

Kalyuga, S. (2014). The expertise reversal principle in multimedia learning. In R. E. Mayer (Ed.), *The Cambridge handbook of multimedia learning* (2nd ed., pp. 576–597). New York: Cambridge University Press.

Kalyuga, S., Chandler, P., & Sweller, J. (1998). Levels of expertise and instructional design. *Human Factors, 40,* 1–17.

Kalyuga, S., Chandler, P., & Sweller, J. (2000). Incorporating learner experience into the design of multimedia instruction. *Journal of Educational Psychology, 92,* 126–136.

Kratzig, G. P., & Arbuthnott, K. D. (2006). Perceptual learning style and learning proficiency: A test of the hypothesis. *Journal of Educational Psychology, 98,* 238–246.

Lowe, R., & Sweller, J. (2005). The modality principle in multimedia learning. In R. E. Mayer (Ed.), *The Cambridge handbook of multimedia learning* (pp. 147–158). New York: Cambridge University Press.

Lowe, R. K., & Schnotz, W. (2014). Animation principles in multimedia learning. In R. E. Mayer (Ed.), *The Cambridge handbook of multimedia learning* (2nd ed., pp. 513–546). New York: Cambridge University Press.

Lowe, R., Schnotz, W., & Rasch, T. (2011). Aligning affordance of graphics with learning task requirements. *Applied Cognitive Psychology, 25,* 452–459.

Mayer, R. E. (2009). *Multimedia learning* (2nd ed.). New York: Cambridge University Press.

Mayer, R. E. (2011). *Applying the science of learning.* Boston, MA: Pearson.

Mayer, R. E. (Ed.). (2014). *The Cambridge handbook of multimedia learning* (2nd ed.). New York: Cambridge University Press.

Mayer, R. E., & Estrella, G. (2014). Benefits of emotional design in multimedia instruction. *Learning & Instruction, 33,* 12–18.

Mayer, R. E., & Gallini, J. K. (1990). When is an illustration worth ten thousand words? *Journal of Educational Psychology, 82,* 715–726.

Mayer, R. E., Hegarty, M., Mayer, S., & Campbell, J. (2005). When static media promote active learning: Annotated illustrations versus narrated animations in multimedia learning. *Journal of Experimental Psychology: Applied, 11,* 256–265.

Mayer, R. E., & Pilegard, C. (2014). Principles for managing essential processing in multimedia learning: Segmenting, pretraining, and modality principles. In R. Mayer (Ed.), *The Cambridge handbook of multimedia learning* (2nd ed., pp. 316–344). New York: Cambridge University Press.

Miller, G.A. (1956). The magical number seven plus or minus two: Some limits on our capacity for processing information. *Psychological Review, 63,* 81–97.

Moreno, R. (2006). Does the modality principle hold for different media? A test of the methods-affects-learning hypothesis. *Journal of Computer Assisted Learning, 22,* 149–158.

Moreno, R., & Ortegano-Layne, L. (2008). Do classroom exemplars promote the application of principles in teacher education? A comparison of videos, animations, and narratives. *Educational Technology Research and Development, 56,* 449–465.

Pashler, H., McDaniel, M., Rohrer, D., & Bjork, R. (2008). Learning styles concepts and evidence. *Psychological Science in the Public Interest, 9,* 105–119.

Sung, E., & Mayer, R. E. (2012). When graphics improve liking but not learning from online lessons. *Computers in Human Behavior, 28,* 1618–1625.

Sweller, J., Ayres, P., & Kalyuga, S. (2011). *Cognitive load theory.* New York: Springer.

Um, E. R., Plass, J. L., Hayward, E. O., & Homer, B. D. (2012). Emotional design in multimedia learning. *Journal of Educational Psychology, 104,* 485–498.

Watson, G., Butterfield, J., Curran, R., & Craig, C. (2010). Do dynamic work instructions provide an advantage over static instructions in a small scale assembly task? *Learning and Instruction, 20,* 84–93.

Wong, A., Marcus, N., Ayres, P., Smith, L., Cooper, G.A., Paas, F., & Sweller, J. (2009). Instructional animations can be superior to statics when learning human motor skills. *Computers in Human Behavioral, 35,* 339–347.

Chapter 32

Social Interdependence Theory and the Design of High-Quality Learning Experiences

David W. Johnson

University of Minnesota

Roger T. Johnson

University of Minnesota

Changing Role of Instructors

The role of instructors is changing from the presentation of information to the design of learning processes, environments, and experiences (Johnson, Johnson, & Smith, 2006). The influences behind this change include (a) the growing awareness that learning experiences should be active in ways that maximize student engagement, (b) the evidence that careful design of instructional experiences makes students' acquisition of knowledge and competencies more efficient, effective, and appealing, and (c) the impact of technological advances on student acquisition of information. *Instructional design* is defined as the teacher/instructor or instructional developer planning how to structure learning situations to maximize student acquisition of information and skills and inculcation of the attitudes and values needed to be a member of a community of practice and society as a whole. Frontward instructional design includes (a) determining the current state and needs of the learner, (b) defining the desired outcomes of instruction, and (c) structuring experiences for students that help them move from where they are to where they aspire to be. Backward instructional design, on the other hand, includes (a) identifying the desired outcomes of instruction (What should learners know, understand, be able to do as a result of instructional experiences?), (b) identifying the evidence needed to know that instruction was successful (How will we know if the learners achieve the desired outcomes and what will be accepted as evidence of learners' understanding and proficiency?), and (c) planning how to structure the learning experiences (What activities will provide learners with the needed knowledge and skills and what materials and resources are needed?).

There are at least three shortcomings to the frontward and backward design sequences. The general guidelines of frontward and backward design do not tell instructors how to create learning activities that overcome passive learning. Second, they give instructors few criteria to determine the most effective active learning activities to design and implement. Third, they provide no guidelines on how to modify their current or favorite existing assignments in order to optimize active learning. The template for planning lessons we include in this chapter provides specific guidelines for creating more active and engaging lessons as well as modifying existing activities to increase engagement.

In addition to being too general and vague, the forward and backward instructional design guidelines suffer from being atheoretical. What would advance the field of instructional design considerably would be a theoretically based set of guidelines that gave specific advice in how to structure lessons. In this chapter we will present such a template, derived from social interdependence theory and empirically verified by hundreds of studies with considerable internal and external validity.

The Basic Requirements of Well-Designed Lessons

Well-designed lessons require students to be active (not passive), induce student engagement (not disengagement), and have criteria-based assessment. These three aspects of lessons overlap so that often if you get one, you get the other two. Each of these aspects is discussed in this section.

Active Learning

The first requirement for designing a learning experience is to ensure students are active rather than passive. Passive to active is actually a continuum, as no learning experience is entirely passive (even sleep has actual components, so the only really passive behavior is being dead). The question is the degree to which a learning experience is structured to make students active or passive. Near the passive end of the continuum, learning is typically listening to the instructor or individually reading information with or without taking notes and highlighting key passages. Characteristics of passive learning are that the student is silent, isolated (working separately from others), and under the direction of others. Near the active end of the continuum, learning occurs when students construct, discover, and transform their own knowledge. Active learning requires students to engage meaningfully, cognitively, and emotionally with other students, the task assigned, and the materials or resources used to complete the task. Characteristics of active learning are that students are talking with others (i.e., engaged in dialogues), interacting with others (i.e., member of a pair, triad, group of four, etc.), generating new ideas and cognitive structures (i.e. discovering their own insights and meaning from the learning activities), and determining their own direction (i.e., coordinating with groupmates as to the direction and speed of the work). Active learning typically requires a learning partner or a small group in which the information being learned is analyzed, synthesized, and evaluated during discussions. In a discussion, students construct new cognitive structures or access their existing ones to subsume the new information and experiences.

There are many types of active learning. Some examples are as follows (Johnson, Johnson, & Smith, 2014).

Cooperative Learning

Cooperation is working together to accomplish shared goals (Johnson & Johnson, 1989; Johnson et al., 2014). Within cooperative situations, individuals seek outcomes that are beneficial to themselves and to all other group members. *Cooperative learning* is the instructional use of small groups so that students work together to maximize their own and each other's learning. It may be contrasted with *competitive* (students work against each other to achieve an academic goal such as a grade of A that only one or a few students can attain) and *individualistic* (students work by themselves to accomplish learning goals unrelated to those of the other students) learning. In cooperative and individualistic learning, you evaluate student efforts on a criterion-referenced basis, whereas in competitive learning you grade students on a norm-referenced basis. While there are limitations on when and where competitive and individualistic learning may be used appropriately, any learning task in any subject area with any curriculum may be structured cooperatively.

Problem-Based Learning

Problem-based learning may be defined as giving students a problem to understand and solve with the goal of having students learn relevant information and procedures (Allen & Duch,

1998; Barrows & Tamblyn, 1980; Smith, Sheppard, Johnson, & Johnson, 2005). Solving the problem correctly is less important than participating in the process of gathering and learning the information and procedures relevant to solving such problems. Problem-based learning was developed for small groups of students to work together. It is sometimes known as cooperative problem-based learning or problem-based cooperative learning.

Team-Based Learning

Team-based learning is an instructional strategy using learning teams to enhance the quality of student learning (Michaelsen, Watson, Cragin, & Fink, 1982). The instructor assigns students with diverse skill sets and backgrounds to permanent groups of five to seven members. Students are individually accountable for homework assignments and for contributing to team efforts in class. Significant credit is given for in-class team activities and application exercises. These in-class activities are aimed at promoting both academic learning and team development and are structured to give students frequent and timely feedback on their efforts.

Collaborative Learning

Collaborative learning has its roots in the work of Sir James Britton and others in England in the 1970s (Britton, 1990). Based on the theorizing of Vygotsky (1978), Britton notes that just as the individual mind is derived from society, a student's learning is derived from the community of learners. This community is developed by the students. Britton recommends placing students in groups and letting them generate their own culture, community, and procedures for learning. Britton believed in *natural learning* (learning something by making intuitive responses to whatever efforts produce) rather than *training* (the application of explanations, instructions, or recipes for action).

Peer-Assisted Learning

Peer-assisted learning may be defined as students acquiring knowledge and skills through active helping among equal classmates (Topping & Ehly, 1998). It subsumes reciprocal peer tutoring, which involves same-age student pairs of comparable ability whose responsibility is to keep each other engaged in constructive academic activity (Fantuzzo & Ginsburg-Block, 1998). Peer-assisted learning is different from traditional peer tutoring, which tends to involve students of different ages or different achievement levels.

Student Engagement

The second requirement for designing a learning experience is to ensure students engage intellectually and emotionally in the learning activities (Johnson et al., 2014). This continuum has disengagement at one end and engagement at the other. Student *disengagement* is defined as off-task behaviors and negative emotions as well as a lack of such indicators of learning as focus, interest, effort, curiosity, persistence, and use of cognitive strategies. Disengaged students are less likely to be graduated from high school or continue on to higher education.

Student *engagement* is the interest in and attention and focus on the learning activities and task, resulting in efforts to complete the task. Engagement is sometimes divided into behavioral engagement (attending class, doing homework), cognitive engagement (effort to understand information and master complex skills), and emotional engagement (positive reactions to classmates, academic task and materials, teachers, and so forth). Engagement is induced by involving students in group discussions in which they work together to complete a learning assignment.

One essential aspect of student engagement is the emotional involvement in the learning tasks. The more information and experiences invoke emotions the better they are remembered. An easy way to generate emotion is to structure group discussions in which students interact with each other. A discussion with classmates tends to generate more emotions than a lecture. Discussions add emotion to content learning, making the content more memorable.

Summary

Instructors as well as instructional designers need to design lessons in which students will be active and engaged. To do so, instructors need a theoretical foundation from which a template for planning lessons can be derived. The theories that provide that foundation are structure-process-outcome theory and social interdependence theory.

Structure-Process-Outcome Theory

Based on the theorizing of Kurt Lewin (1935), Watson and Johnson (1972) formulated a theory whose basic premise is that the way a situation is structured determines the process individuals engage in to complete the task, which in turn determines the outcomes of the situation. Outcomes, in other words, result from the processes of effort, not the structure of the situation directly. This theory is directly related to instructional design, as it focuses instructors on creating a structure that results in desired processes of interaction among students and between the students and the instructor. Once the desired processes occur, desired outcomes will almost automatically result (Johnson & Johnson, 1989, 2005). In other words, assessment should focus on the nature of the processes, not on the outcomes of learning.

Social Interdependence Theory

Theorizing on social interdependence began in the early 1900s, when one of the founders of the Gestalt School of Psychology, Kurt Koffka, proposed that groups were dynamic wholes in which the interdependence among members could vary. One of his colleagues, Kurt Lewin, refined Koffka's notions in the 1920s and 1930s while stating that (a) the essence of a group is the interdependence among members (created by common goals) which results in the group being a "dynamic whole" so that a change in the state of any member or subgroup changes the state of any other member or subgroup, and (b) an intrinsic state of tension within group members motivates movement toward the accomplishment of the desired common goals. For interdependence to exist, there must be more than one person or entity involved, and the persons or entities must have impact on each other in that a change in the state of one causes a change in the state of the others. From the work of Lewin's students and colleagues, such as Ovisankian, Lissner, Mahler, and Lewis, it may be concluded that it is the drive for goal accomplishment that motivates cooperative and competitive behavior. In the late 1940s, one of Lewin's graduate students, Morton Deutsch, extended Lewin's reasoning about social interdependence and formulated a theory of cooperation and competition (Deutsch, 1949, 1962). His work has been expanded primarily by one of his students, David W. Johnson and his brother Roger (Johnson & Johnson, 1989, 2005.).

Social interdependence theory posits that there are two types of social interdependence, positive (cooperative) and negative (competitive). *Positive interdependence* (i.e., cooperation) exists when individuals perceive that they can reach their goals if and only if the other individuals with whom they are cooperatively linked also reach their goals. *Negative interdependence* (i.e., competition) exists when individuals perceive that they can obtain their goals if and only if the other individuals with whom they are competitively linked fail to obtain their goals. *No interdependence* (i.e., individualistic efforts) exists when individuals perceive that they can reach their goal regardless of whether other individuals in the situation attain or do not attain their goals.

A basic premise of social interdependence theory is that the type of interdependence structured in a situation determines how individuals interact with each other and that, in turn, largely determines outcomes (Deutsch, 1949, 1962; Watson & Johnson, 1972). Positive interdependence tends to result in promotive interaction; negative interdependence tends to result in oppositional or contrient interaction; and no interdependence results in an absence of interaction. Depending on whether individuals promote or obstruct each other's goal accomplishments, there is substitutability (i.e., the degree to which actions of one person substitute for the actions of another person), cathexis (i.e., an investment of psychological energy in objects outside of oneself, such as friends, family, and work), and inducibility (i.e., the openness to being influenced and to influencing others) (Deutsch, 1949). In cooperative situations, students' actions tend to substitute for each other, students invest positive emotions in each other, and students are open to being influenced by each other. In competitive situations, students' actions do not substitute for each other; competitors invest negative emotions in each other; and competitors are resistant to being influenced by each other. In individualistic situations, there is no substitutability, cathexis, or inducibility. The relationship between the type of social interdependence and the interaction pattern it elicits is assumed to be bidirectional. Each may cause the other. Positive interdependence, for example, tends to result in collaborators engaging in promotive interaction (i.e., helping, sharing, encouraging each other), and patterns of promotive interaction tend to result in cooperation. Social interdependence theory has served as a major conceptual structure for this area of inquiry since 1949. It has generated hundreds of research studies.

From social interdependence theory, three types of cooperative learning have been derived (Johnson, Johnson, & Holubec, 2013): formal cooperative learning, informal cooperative learning, and cooperative base groups. Cooperative learning groups may be used to teach specific content (formal cooperative learning groups), to ensure active cognitive processing of information during a lecture (informal cooperative learning groups), and to provide long-term support and assistance for academic progress (cooperative base groups).

Formal cooperative learning consists of students working together, for one class period to several weeks, to achieve mutual learning goals and complete jointly specific tasks and assignments such as solving a set of problems, completing a curriculum unit, writing a report or theme, conducting an experiment, or reading a story, play, chapter, or book (Johnson et al., 2013). Any course requirement or assignment may be restructured to be cooperative. In formal cooperative learning groups, the instructor:

1. Specifies the objectives for the lesson (at least one academic and one social skill)
2. Makes a series of decisions about how to structure the learning groups (what size groups, how students are assigned to groups, what roles to assign, how to arrange materials, and how to arrange the room)
3. Teaches the academic concepts, principles, and strategies that the students are to master and apply, and explains the (a) task to be completed, (b) criteria for success, (c) positive interdependence, (d) individual accountability, and (e) expected student behaviors
4. Monitors the functioning of the learning groups and intervenes to (a) teach collaborative skills and (b) provide assistance in academic learning when it is needed
5. Evaluates student performance against the preset criteria for excellence, and ensures that groups process how effectively members worked together

Informal cooperative learning consists of students working together to achieve a joint learning goal in temporary, ad hoc groups that last from a few minutes to one class period (Johnson et al., 2013). During a lecture, demonstration, or film they can be used to focus student attention on the material to be learned, set a mood conducive to learning, help set expectations as to what will be covered in a class session, ensure that students cognitively process the material being taught, and provide closure to an instructional session. During direct teaching, the instructional challenge for the teacher is to ensure that students do the intellectual work of organizing material, explaining it, summarizing it, and integrating it into existing conceptual structures. Informal cooperative learning groups are often organized so that students engage in three- to five-minute *focused discussions* before and after a lecture and three- to five-minute *turn-to-your-partner discussions* interspersed throughout a lecture.

Cooperative base groups are long-term, heterogeneous cooperative learning groups with stable membership in which students provide one another with support, encouragement, and assistance to make academic progress (attend class, complete all assignments, learn) (Johnson et al., 2013). Members also help one another develop cognitively and socially in healthy ways, as well as hold one another accountable for striving to learn. Base groups meet daily (or whenever the class meets). They are permanent (lasting from one to several years) and provide the long-term caring peer relationships necessary to influence members consistently to work hard in school. They formally meet to discuss the academic progress of each member, provide help and assistance to each other, and verify that each member is completing assignments and progressing satisfactorily through the academic program. The larger the class or school and the more complex and difficult the subject matter, the more important it is to have base groups.

When used in combination, cooperative formal, informal, and base groups provide an overall structure for school learning.

The numerous *outcomes of cooperative efforts* may be subsumed within three broad categories: effort to achieve, positive interpersonal relationships, and psychological adjustment. Because research participants are varied as to economic class, age, sex, and cultural background, because a wide variety of research tasks and measures of the dependent variables have been used, and because the research has been conducted by many different researchers with markedly different orientations working in different settings and in different decades, the overall body of research on social interdependence has considerable generalizability (Johnson & Johnson, 1989, 2005).

Working together to achieve a common goal produces higher achievement and greater productivity than does working competitively or individualistically (Johnson & Johnson, 1989, 2005). This is so well confirmed by research that it stands as one of the strongest principles of psychology. Cooperation also tends to result in more higher-level reasoning, more frequent generation of new ideas and solutions (i.e., *process gain*), and greater transfer of what is learned within one situation to another (i.e., *group to individual transfer*) than do competitive or individualistic learning. Individuals care more about each other and are more committed to each other's success and well-being when they work together cooperatively than when they compete to see who is best or work independently from each other. This is true when individuals are homogeneous and it is also true when individuals differ in intellectual ability, handicapping conditions, ethnic membership, culture, social class, and gender. Cooperating on a task also results in more task-oriented and personal social support than do competitive or individualistic efforts. Finally, working cooperatively with peers, and valuing cooperation, results in greater psychological health and higher self-esteem than competing with peers or working independently.

Social interdependence theory (and structure-process-outcome theory) specifies that structuring positive interdependence into a situation will result in promotive interaction, which results in the desired outcomes of higher achievement, more positive and supportive relationships, and greater psychological health. In operationalizing active learning (primarily cooperative learning but also problem-based learning and others), five essential aspects of structuring an active learning situation that induces student engagement have been identified (Johnson & Johnson, 1989, 2005). They are positive interdependence, individual accountability, promotive interaction, appropriate use of social skills, and group processing. These five elements of effective instruction result in a template for instructional design (Figure 32.1).

Subject Area: _____ Date: _____

Lesson: _____

Objectives: _____ Academic _____ Social Skills _____

Group Size: _____ Method of Assigning Students: _____

Roles: _____ Materials: _____

Academic Task:	**Criteria for Success:**

Positive Interdependence:	**Individual Accountability:**	**Social Skills:**

Monitoring: _____ Teacher _____ Students _____ Visitors

Behaviors Observed: _____

Assessment of Learning: _____

Small Group Processing:	**Goal Setting:**	**Whole Class Processing:**

Celebration: _____

FIGURE 32.1   Template for Active Learning Lesson Planning.

Template for Instructional Design

From social interdependence theory and structure-process-outcome theory a template for designing instructional situations can be derived. The template consists of five basic elements that need to be included in any instructional experience that includes active student participation and high levels of student engagement (Johnson & Johnson, 1989, 2005; Johnson et al., 2013).

First, the heart of active learning is positive interdependence, the perception that you are linked with others in a way so that you cannot succeed unless they do (and vice versa) and that groupmates' work benefits you and your work benefits them (Deutsch, 1949; Johnson & Johnson, 1992). Positive interdependence includes mutual goals, mutual rewards, divided resources, and different roles.

Second, each group member has to be individually accountable, which means completing one's share of the work and facilitating the work of other group members (Johnson & Johnson, 1989). Individual accountability exists when the performance of each individual student is assessed and the results given back to the group and the individual. The purpose of active learning is to make each student a stronger individual in his or her right. Students learn together so that they can subsequently perform higher as individuals. Individual accountability may be structured by (a) giving an individual test to each student, (b) having each student explain to a classmate what he or she has learned, or (b) observing students as they work together and documenting the contributions of each member.

Third, students need to promote each other's success by helping, assisting, supporting, encouraging, and praising each other's efforts to learn (Johnson & Johnson, 1989, 2005). Doing so results in such cognitive processes as orally explaining how to solve problems, discussing the nature of the concepts being learned, teaching one's knowledge to classmates, challenging each other's reasoning and conclusions, and connecting present with past learning. It also results in such interpersonal processes as modeling appropriate use of social skills, supporting and encouraging efforts to learn, and participating in joint celebrations of success.

Fourth, students need to use social skills appropriately (Johnson & Johnson, 1989, 2005). Contributing to the success of a cooperative effort requires interpersonal and small group skills. Leadership, decision-making, trust-building, communication, and conflict-management skills have to be taught just as purposefully and precisely as academic skills. Procedures and strategies for teaching students social skills may be found in Johnson (2014) and Johnson and Johnson (2013).

Fifth, students need to engage in group processing, the examination of the effectiveness of the process members use to maximize their own and each other's learning so that ways to improve the process may be identified (Johnson & Johnson, 1989, 2005). Instructors need to focus students on the continuous improvement of the quality of the processes students are using to learn by asking group members to (a) describe what member actions are helpful and unhelpful in ensuring that all group members are achieving and maintaining effective working relationships and (b) make decisions about what behaviors to continue or change. Group processing may result in (a) streamlining the learning process to make it simpler (reducing complexity), (b) eliminating unskilled and inappropriate actions (error-proofing the process), (c) improving continuously students' skills in working as part of a team, and (d) celebrating hard work and success.

Implementing these five essential elements of an active lesson enables instructors to (a) structure any lesson in any subject area with any set of curriculum materials for active learning; (b) fine-tune and adapt active learning to their specific circumstances, needs, and students; and (c) intervene to improve the effectiveness of any group that is malfunctioning (see Figure 32.1). These five essential elements form a template for structuring any lesson for student activeness and engagement. For example, simply placing students in a group and giving them a problem to solve does not mean that problem-based-learning will actually take place. Students must perceive that they are positively interdependent, that each is accountable to do his or her fair share of the work, that they are to promote each other's learning and success, that appropriate use of social skills is required, and that after the lesson is over they will examine the processes of learning in order to improve them. It is only when these five aspects of an effective active lesson are carefully structured in a lesson that it becomes active and induces student engagement.

Ways Technology Can Enhance Active Learning

There are many ways that technology can enhance active learning and increase student engagement (Johnson & Johnson, 2014).

When used effectively, technology can bring students together into a joint effort, focus their attention on each other and their coordinated actions, increase student engagement in joint assignments, and enhance the overall student experience. First, technology can facilitate the active nature of reading the same or related material. Electronic devices as well as social media allow members of a learning group to share with each other passages out of the books they are reading, highlight passages so others can note what one thought was important in the text material, and make notes for the other members of their group to read and make responses.

Second, through Google Docs and similar programs technology can facilitate learning how to write while working together in producing one document authored by the whole group. A group of students can see and make changes to the joint document in real time, commenting on the document as a whole, or commenting on specific parts of the document.

Third, discussions can continue indefinitely as students have the ability to communicate with each other at any time. Through the use of texting, social media sites, or videoconferencing, group members can conduct discussions about what happened in class.

Fourth, technology can allow visual elements to be added to any group product. Image hosting and editing programs allow members of a learning group to upload photos and share them with the group, class, or even the world.

Fifth, technology allows learning groups to combine a variety of media to improve the quality of projects and presentations. Presentations can include videos, animations, slide shows with music and narration, plays or dances to music and narration, and so forth, all of which may be posted on YouTube.

These are only a few of the ways in which technology can facilitate active learning and student engagement without isolating students or requiring them to work alone.

Conclusion

Instructors should be more designers of instructional experiences than presenters of information. A goal of instructional design is to ensure students are actively engaged in their learning experiences. To do so, instructors need a theoretical foundation from which a template for planning lessons can be derived. The theories that provide that foundation are social interdependence theory and structure-process-outcome theory. Both theories note that the way learning situations are structured determines the processes students engage in to learn, which in turn determine the outcomes. Teachers and instructions should be focused on creating the desired processes of learning so that the desired outcomes can result. They do so by implementing five essential elements in every learning situation: positive interdependence, individual accountability, promotive interaction, appropriate use of social skills, and group processing. These five essential elements create the processes that lead to increased achievement, more positive and supportive relationships among students and between students and the faculty, and greater student psychological health.

Summary of Key Principles

1. **The role of instructors is changing.** They must design learning and assignments with student engagement in mind so students participate in active learning situations.

2. **The three basics of well-designed lessons are active learning, student engagement, and criteria-based assessments.**

3. **Structure-process-outcome theory and social interdependence theory provide a solid theory base for active lesson design.**

4. **The five essential elements for cooperative learning are positive interdependence, individual accountability, promoting each other's success, social skills accountability, and group processing.**

5. **Technology can increase student engagement by students working together in a joint effort to solve problems and create solutions.**

Application Questions

1. Select a topic of interest and conduct a search of the publications listed in this chapter to identify those that have published articles on the topic. Read a few articles related to the topic (preferably from different publications) and explain which journals provide the best source of information.

2. Write an action plan for your next conference listing your learning objectives, how you expect to meet those objectives, the preparation you will need to do, and other resources you may need to achieve your objectives (it is easier if you select a specific conference rather than choosing some abstract event).

3. Contact the editor of one or more of the journals listed in this chapter. Ask about the requirements for becoming a reviewer and volunteer if you qualify. If not, examine your own skills related to these requirements and make a plan for meeting those you currently lack.

References

Allen, D., & Duch, B. (1998). *Thinking toward solutions: Problem-based activities for general biology*. Fort Worth, TX: Saunders.

Barrows, H. S. & Tamblyn, R. M. (1980). *Problem-based learning*. New York: Springer.

Britton, J. (1990). Research currents: Second thoughts on learning. In M. Brubacher, R. Payne, & K. Richett (Eds.), *Perspectives on small group learning: Theory and practice* (pp. 3–11). Oakville, Ontario: Rubicon.

Deutsch, M. (1949). A theory of cooperation and competition. *Human Relations, 2*, 129–152.

Deutsch, M. (1962). Cooperation and trust: Some theoretical notes. In M. R. Jones (Ed.), *Nebraska symposium on motivation* (pp. 275–319). Lincoln, NE: University of Nebraska Press.

Fantuzzo, J., & Ginsburg-Block, M. (1998). Reciprocal peer tutoring: Developing and testing effective peer collaborations for elementary school students. In K. Topping & S. Ehly (Eds.), *Peer-assisted learning* (pp. 121–145). Mahway, NJ: Lawrence Erlbaum.

Fredricks, J., Blumenfeld, P., & Paris, A. (2004). School engagement: Potential of the concept, state of the evidence. *Review of Educational Research, 74*, 59–109.

Johnson, D. W. (2014). *Reaching out: Interpersonal effectiveness and self-actualization* (11th ed.). Boston: Allyn & Bacon.

Johnson, D. W., & Johnson, F. (2013). *Joining together: Group theory and group skills* (11th ed.). Boston: Allyn & Bacon.

Johnson, D. W., & Johnson, R. T. (1989). *Cooperation and competition: Theory and research*. Edina, MN: Interaction Book Company.

Johnson, D. W., & Johnson, R. T. (1992). *Positive interdependence*. Edina, MN: Interaction Book Company.

Johnson, D. W., & Johnson, R. T. (2005). New developments in social interdependence theory. *Genetic, Social, and General Psychology Monographs, 131*(4).

Johnson, D. W., & Johnson, R. T. (2014). Using technology to revolutionize cooperation. *Frontiers in Psychology, 5*, article 1156, 1–3.

Johnson, D. W., Johnson, R. T., & Holubec, E. J. (2013). Cooperation in the classroom (9th ed.). Edina, MN: Interaction Book Company.

Johnson, D. W., Johnson, R. T., & Smith, K. (2006). *Active learning: Cooperation in the college classroom* (8th ed.). Edina, MN: Interaction Book Company.

Johnson, D. W., Johnson, R. T., & Smith, K. (2014). Cooperative learning: Improving university instruction by basing practice on validated theory. In N. Davidson, C. Major, & L. Michaelsen (Eds.), Small-group learning in higher education: Cooperative, collaborative, problem-based and team-based learning. *Journal on Excellence in College Teaching, 25*(3/4), 85–118.

Lewin, K. (1935). *A dynamic theory of personality*. New York: McGraw-Hill.

Michaelsen, L. K., Watson, W. E., Cragin, J. P., & Fink, L. D. (1982). Team-based learning: A potential solution to the problems of large classes. *Exchange: The Organizational Behavior Teaching Journal, 7*(4), 18–33.

Smith, K., Sheppard, S., Johnson, D. W., & Johnson R. (2005). Pedagogies of engagement: Classroom-based practices. *Journal of Engineering Education, 94*, 1–15.

Topping, K., & Ehly, S. (Eds.). (1998). *Peer-assisted learning*. Mahwah, NJ: Lawrence Erlbaum.

Vygotsky, L. (1978). *Mind and society*. Cambridge, MA: Harvard University Press.

Watson, G. B., & Johnson, D. W. (1972). *Social psychology: Issues and insights*. Philadelphia: Lippincott.

Chapter 33

Leveling Up: Game Design Research and Practice for Instructional Designers

Richard Van Eck

University of North Dakota

Lloyd Rieber

University of Georgia

Valerie J. Shute

Florida State University

Anyone who makes a distinction between games and learning doesn't know the first thing about either.

– Marshall McLuhan

Introduction

Games have been used for learning since at least the Middle Ages, when chess was used to teach war strategy (Institute of Play, n.d.), and they formed the basis of early childhood education with the founding of the Play and Activity Institute by Friedrich Fröbel in 1837 (Friedrich Fröbel, n.d.), later to be termed Kindergarten. So, in a sense, we have been using and researching the power of games for learning for centuries. When games made the leap from analog to digital (first, as arcade machines, then computers, and finally consoles), however, research on their efficacy picked up in earnest. Seminal publications like Patricia Greenfield's *Mind and Media* in 1985 and Jim Gee's *What Video Games Have to Teach Us About Learning and Literacy* (2003) promised to usher in an era of research practice founded on sound theory and experimental design. Unfortunately, despite these important signposts on the road to a new discipline, much research focused on the medium itself rather than the instructional theory that accounted for the potential for learning through games. As a result, the demand for guidance on designing games and integrating them into formal learning now exceeds our ability to supply it. There remain critical gaps in our understanding of games and learning, including what kinds of problem solving are supported by what kinds of games (e.g., Hung & Van Eck, 2010), the role of player experience in making meaning (e.g., Gajadhar, 2012), validated models for integrating commercial games into the classroom (e.g., Van Eck, 2008), and the conditions under which games may or may not promote aggressive behavior (e.g., the work of Craig Anderson and Christopher Ferguson). These gaps present a serious challenge to the advancement of our understanding of games as formal and informal learning tools. We will leave the bulk of this challenge to you, the reader, as you enter the field and begin your own career. There are some signposts we think can help guide you on this journey, however, which is why we have written this chapter.

We believe that games are very effective learning tools. We believe this to be true for the same reason we believe that any mode of instruction, when designed using instructional design principles and processes, is effective. A recent meta-analysis of games found, among other things, that game-based instruction resulted in a .33 standard deviation improvement in learning when compared to non-game-based instruction in general and, more importantly, that theoretically augmented (well-designed) games accounted for a .37 standard deviation in increased learning compared to nonaugmented games used in instructional settings. To wit: well-designed games promote learning (Clark, Tanner-Smith, & Killingsworth, 2014).

We recognize the potential circularity of stating that well-designed games work because they are well designed. Yet, the number of published studies that fail to account for design (game and instructional) makes it clear that this is a point that cannot be made too often. Instructional design mandates that we analyze a given medium for its ability to support desired strategies and outcomes. One of the possible results of such analysis is the decision NOT to employ the given medium. There are plenty of examples of studies that purport to answer whether games are or are not effective for learning, but that is not the central question for any instructional medium. It is far more important to ask when, where, and for whom are they effective, and with what mechanisms can they achieve different learning outcomes. Games are not appropriate for all outcomes, all learners, in all venues, and at all times, any more than textbooks, video, or lecture-based instruction are. As with all media and modalities, games are effective when they align with instructional outcomes and strategies within the constraints of the medium, a given environment, and a set of learners. Why, then, is so much of the discussion about games and learning still centered on *if* games can teach rather than how they can best be *designed* to teach? We argue that three critical explanations, which will form the structure of this chapter, will be helpful in understanding the answer to this question.

In Part I of this chapter, we discuss how games involve play and how Western culture devalues play as a serious activity, which is one reason so many remain skeptical about "if" games can teach. In Part II, we discuss how many "serious games" end up being Frankensteinian mashups of game and context rather than true manifestations of games as a medium, thus contributing to the doubt about the *ability* of games to teach. Also in Part II, we argue that the true power of games may lie in their ability to promote higher-order intellectual skills like problem solving.

Finally, in Part III, we discuss a key challenge facing learning game designers, and one we are happy to report is beginning to be met: assessment. Assessing performance (and its close cousins, eliciting performance and providing feedback) requires us to know how the problem is solved incrementally, over time, and through the application of specific enabling skills (e.g., rules, defined concepts, concrete concepts). This means that we cannot just let students play a learning game and then give them a test—we have to know how knowledge is developed and demonstrated throughout the instruction (game) itself. This need has been met by an assessment design framework called evidence-centered design (ECD; see Mislevy, Steinberg, & Almond, 2003), which we argue is critical for instructional designers who want to work with games.

Part I: Games and Play Theory

The question of what makes a game fun to play is similar to the question of what makes a joke funny. On one level, we all know the answer, but articulating it well, if at all, is surprisingly difficult. In one episode of the television show *Star Trek: The Next Generation*, Commander Data decided to confront the question, "What makes something funny?" As an android who aspired to become human, this question perplexed him, and he set about answering it as a programmed machine or an analytical engineer might, by breaking the construct "funny" into all of the conceivable rules. Data erroneously tried to come up with a grand "if/then" tree for "funny" (i.e., if I say this, then say that, in this way, etc., *then* it is funny). In contrast, the best answer, to paraphrase Garrison Keillor, is that something is funny simply because people laugh. We can chuckle at Data's misguided attempt, but many people in the ISD field seem to be following a similar rule-based "engineering" path to try to understand how to design a game that is fun and also leads to learning. Similar to Keillor's definition of funny, a game is fun to play if people enjoy playing it. More specifically, we

argue that a game is engaging, or fun to play, if it triggers the play phenomenon in the player. So, we must take some time to understand the play phenomenon. Fortunately, much research has been done on play from a multitude of disciplines such as education, psychology, sociology, and anthropology.

Making play an objective of an educational game requires a paradigm shift for most designers—one that is learner centered and constructivist in nature. To understand this paradigm, you need to understand the difference between merely playing a game and being "at play." The former can be mandated by a teacher to students or a trainer to a group of employees, and these participants can dutifully "play the game." That is, one can watch and track their behavior or performance from beginning to end and even declare that one or more has won the game. However, these individuals may never have been "at play," meaning that they never entered the conceptual cognitive or cultural space in which play occurs (Huizinga, 1950).

So, what is play? Everyone reading this chapter already knows what play is, and you yourself have probably experienced it within the last 24 hours, even though you may resist, as many adults do, using the word "play" to describe it. It probably happened during your leisure time, although if you are fortunate enough to love your job, it may have happened at work. It was definitely something you wanted to do, and you would say that you did it voluntarily. You found the activity intrinsically motivating and so you were not concerned about "getting something" out of it. You were also doing something actively and possibly physically. Finally, you were likely in a state where you were not conscious of yourself or of your place in the world but rather felt wholly absorbed in the activity. This state also carried a feeling of being free from risks. You felt free to try new things or to experiment with different ways of doing or thinking—after all, it was only play. Your awareness of time likely disappeared, and you were probably surprised by how much time had passed when the activity had ended (see Pellegrini, 1995; Rieber, 1996; Sutton-Smith, 1997 for formal definitions and attributes of play). Some of you may have experienced play while engaged in a hobby such as gardening, woodworking, photography, painting, or some craft. Others may have experienced it while caring for a son or daughter and enjoying each other's company. Yet others experienced it while reading a book, playing a musical instrument, or playing a video game. A lucky few have experienced it while writing a chapter in a book!

Educators and other educational stakeholders (e.g., parents, state legislators) are quick to ask—"What good is play? Does it lead to some productive outcome or result?" The seminal work of Jean Piaget remains an important starting point for such questions (Phillips, 1981; Piaget, 1951). Piaget felt that play and imitation were core and innate human strategies for cognitive development. With play, children can rehearse a newly formed concept to make it fit within what they already knew and understood (assimilation). As children experience or encounter new events, activities, ideas, or rituals, they use imitation to build entirely new mental models (accommodation). The child continues in this way to achieve an orderly balanced world while constantly confronting a changing, shifting environment. Just as the mental processes of assimilation and accommodation continue throughout life, so too do play and imitation remain important cognitive tools for people from childhood through adulthood.

There are other examples of research literature, while not overtly aligning with play, that are clearly in the same camp. The research on self-regulated learning (Zimmerman, 1990, 2008) is one example, especially with its emphasis on an individual actively working toward goals within intrinsic motivating activities. However, the attributes of flow theory proposed by Csikszentmihalyi (1990) are the most similar to that of play, especially in the context of game design. For example, flow theory specifically addresses the need to optimize challenge, so as to continually avoid anxiety and boredom. Activities that induce flow have clear goals, coupled with clear and consistent feedback about whether a person is reaching these goals. Another important attribute of flow is that it takes effort to attain a state of flow, requiring a clear and deliberate investment of sustained attention.

The psychologist Brian Sutton-Smith (1997) has proposed many ways to think about play—what he calls the rhetorics of play. Among the most alluring of these rhetorics for educators is the idea that play leads to something productive (i.e., play as progress). However, Sutton-Smith refers to the ambiguity of play in being able to "deliver the goods." Although there are tantalizing reasons for believing that play is by and large a good thing, one should be careful in attributing positive results directly to it. There is evidence that positive outcomes and play go together (i.e., correlational effects), but much of that evidence is anecdotal rather than empirical, making it challenging to say that play *caused* these outcomes. Another ambiguity of play is that experiencing it itself may be its own reward and that the goal of getting something out of play is misguided. But, the presence of the play state may at least be evidence that the person is in a good state for subsequently experiencing cognitive and social growth, and this alone may be good enough reason to make play a goal for any learning environment.

David Elkind's (2007) theory of play further elucidates the relationship of play and work. He posits three instinctual drives that are the root of all human cognition and behavior throughout a person's lifetime: love (a person's disposition to express one's desires, feelings, and emotions), work (a person's disposition to adapt to the demands of his or her physical and social worlds), and play (a person's need to adapt the world to one's self and create novel learning experiences).

To become a well-adjusted person living compatibly within a complex social system, one must balance the demands and goals of each of these three elements in ways that change throughout life. In early life, play dominates, but gives way in early elementary years, when work dominates and love and play take on a supporting role. Love dominates as we enter adolescence, and all three become fully separate in adulthood, although each can be manifested in combination with the others. Bringing love, work, and play into harmony with each other at points throughout one's life is an important goal and one that parents and teachers (and instructional designers) should work to facilitate. Unfortunately, for many adults, play is often seen as the opposite of work, making the goal of achieving a balance between love, work, and play elusive.

Elkind's focus on balancing love, work, and play is similar to Csikszentmihalyi's concept of psychological growth during flow (1990), where an individual becomes more complex or advanced by balancing the need to be a unique individual with a unique identity (differentiation) while at the same time feeling connected to other people and social groups (integration). Furthermore, Elkind's theory of the relationship between love, work, and play can even be mapped onto the current interest in twenty-first-century skills (e.g., work productively within diverse teams, identify and solve complex problems with innovative solutions, communicate effectively, think critically, use technology efficiently, understand system dynamics, and engage in evidence-based reasoning).

This chapter is about digital, or computer, games for learning. Among those conducting research in this area, the prevailing interest tends to be focused on the immersive games, such as massively multiplayer online role-playing games, or MMORPGs. The technology underlying these highly visual, persistent virtual worlds is impressive, and the technical sophistication of these "high-tech" gaming environments can only increase, leading to new game genres and models of interaction which we cannot even imagine now. Would-be educational game designers, however, would do well to consider low (i.e., nondigital) and middle-tech (i.e., the span of digital games up to high-tech examples) approaches to gaming in addition to the high-tech games, if only to understand that the fundamentals of a game extend outside of the specific technology of any single game. Regardless of the degree of technology infusion in the game, we believe that the play phenomenon is always eager to emerge.

Having laid a theoretical foundation for learning and play in relation to educational games, we next examine architectural issues, viewed through the lens of instructional design. Specifically, we discuss a model for thinking about immersive game design that incorporates sound learning theory in a framework that is compatible with both learning and game design.

Part II: Blended Theories, Frameworks, and Problem Solving

As we've shown in the last section, there are many theories that inform game research and design. When examining the literature from the mid-1990s through today, however, this has not always been obvious. One of the key pitfalls awaiting new scholars in this area lies in mistaking the medium for the message—in assuming that "new" video games can only be explained by "new" theories. This is not to say that theories from different disciplines are not relevant, nor that the intersection of different disciplines will not produce new theoretical approaches to understanding how games work. The field is evolving rapidly, and our tools must keep up with our evolving understanding. The maxim is that all good research and theory builds upon prior research and theory. Therefore, it behooves the new and experienced scholar to have a core set of theoretical tools at his or her disposal. So, how do we know which theories are most relevant, and how do we synthesize them into a framework for research and design? The answer is, of course, that it depends. Principles of behaviorism (e.g., schedules of reinforcement, stimulus-response latency, and association) help us understand how Jeopardy-style games work for factual information. Constructivist principles (e.g., social negotiation of meaning) help us understand how people make meaning of their experiences in open worlds and MMORPGs. Sociocultural learning theory helps explain how culture mediates and situates knowledge; and of course, many other things like motivation, locus of control, and self-efficacy help predict how people will experience and perseverate (or not) in game worlds. Those we choose to apply and combine in our design and analysis of games depends on our outcomes, learners, and constraints. The promise of games to promote deep learning of more complex intellectual skills (defined concepts, rules, and problem solving) as well as attitudes and cognitive strategies, is among the most cited benefit of games, yet many who make such claims do not use (or report using) the theoretical tools that lead to such learning outcomes.

A recent report by the Joan Ganz Cooney Center at the Sesame Workshop (Takeuchi & Vaala, 2014) that surveyed 694 teachers from across the United States found that nearly 75 percent of K–8 teachers reported using digital games in their classrooms, and that more than 40 percent were doing so to meet local, state, and national standards. Yet, the vast majority of K–8 teachers are using what have sometimes been described as "drill and kill" games that focus on lower-level taxonomic outcomes (verbal information and concepts, in Gagné's taxonomy [Gagné, Wager, Golas, & Keller, 2004], and knowledge and application in Bloom's taxonomy [1984]) that can be accomplished in a single classroom session. There is nothing wrong with this in and of itself, of course, yet we would argue that there are many instructional strategies and modalities that can address lower levels of learning just as effectively. The true advantage of games as a medium is their potential to address higher levels of learning (e.g., rules and problem solving, or synthesis and evaluation) along with other outcomes (e.g., attitudes, metacognitive skills) that are traditionally difficult to address.

The design of immersive games that promote problem-solving outcomes can be driven by many theories, but there are three primary theories that we think are critical to designing any game for such outcomes. The first is based on situated cognition (e.g., Brown, Collins, & Duguid, 1989; Lave, 1988), which is commonly referred to as situated learning. Situated learning embeds learning and assessment in real-world environments. By "real-world," we mean environments that mimic the real-world contexts in which the goals of the instruction would normally be observed and demonstrated.

The second key concept is that the environment and tasks must also be authentic. This means that the actions *taken* within that real-world context reflect the actions and processes that would normally occur when *demonstrating* that knowledge in the real world. It also means that the environment *behaves* authentically, in that actions taken by the learner result in the kinds of responses by the environment (and the people, tools, and resources within it) that would happen in the real world. This is not to say that the world must be a fully realized simulation of the real world, of course. There are many aspects of the real world that do not apply to a given learning situation

(e.g., one need not experience a virtual world with gravity in order to learn how to react to angry customers in customer service training), and research on simulations has suggested that irrelevant details (seductive details) interfere with learning (e.g., Harp & Mayer, 1997). Even relevant information may be problematic if the learner's level of expertise is insufficient (e.g., Adcock, Watson, Morrison, & Belfore, 2010). It is important only that the key elements of the content and process outcomes are replicated in the environment.

While "real world" and "authentic" may sound like synonyms, there are important distinctions between them. Asking a student to solve a word problem about dividing up a *Pokémon* card collection is not a real-world example; it is a problem *about* a real-world problem. Putting kids in groups with actual *Pokémon* cards and telling them to work out a fair way to divide them so each person has the same value is *almost* a real-world problem—about as close as we can get in school settings. Having those students solve the problem by filling in worksheets or matrices based on provided values is *not* an authentic way of solving the problem; having them decide on the process to use, determine what a fair arbiter of true value is, and build their own value charts *is* as authentic as we can get in the formal educational environments. Research has shown that instruction built on these principles is effective in promoting initial and long-term learning as well as increasing the likelihood of transfer of learning to new contexts.

The third theoretical area is, of course, the research into problem solving itself. As an instructional outcome, problem solving refers to the ability to synthesize multiple rules and defined concepts and apply them to problems that do not have a known solution. It is generally believed that the only way to promote problem solving is, therefore, to present the learner with multiple problems to solve within a given domain. This is often done in the context of instructional strategies that scaffold problem solving, sometimes called problem-centered or problem-based learning. Thus, problem solving may be thought of as both a strategy and an outcome, yet problems are always at the heart of the instruction.

Obviously, formal education cannot create real-world problems for every topic, which is why video games are among the most effective means of providing situated learning environments for promoting problem-solving outcomes. Rather than asking students to "pretend as if" they are in the real world, video games *provide* that "real" world. That world can also be programmed to respond authentically in the context of the desired learning outcomes. Problem solving is an oft-cited benefit of video games but one that is routinely oversimplified. For example, it is important to recognize that there are many different kinds of problems that vary in their cognitive composition, degree of structuredness, and required domain knowledge. Jonassen (2000) has proposed a typology of eleven different types of problems, each of which requires specific design and instructional strategies to promote. It follows that if we must teach (and if learners must bring specific prerequisite knowledge to) each problem in a specific manner in face-to-face instruction, then we must also differentiate and do so for the problems we hope to embed in games designed to promote specific problem-solving skills. Space does not permit a more detailed discussion of problem-solving; see Hung and Van Eck (2010) for more on aligning problem types and game types.

This is hardly a full treatment of any of these areas, of course, but good resources are widely available for those who want to study them further. It is also not necessary to make use of every theory when designing games—as with all instructional design, our strategies rely on our learners, environment, content, and context. There are many different ways to blend these different approaches. One way to do so is a framework called situated, authentic problem solving (Van Eck, 2015), but there are other models that have been used with success as well (e.g., Barret & Johnson, 2010; Borchert et al., 2010).

We have articulated some of the theories and models that we feel can help guide the design of games for learning, but there are many others. We remind readers that this list is not exhaustive and that a large body of literature on games and learning exists and should be consulted. Our purpose in this chapter is to illustrate some of the key truths we believe must underlie all such models and frameworks. These key truths can be synthesized into several propositions, which we present next.

Learning Should Be Goal-Oriented. According to Jonassen (2002), all good problems share two characteristics. First, they have some kind of goal, or unknown. The goal/unknown requires the generation of new knowledge. Second, all problems should have some value to the learner in solving them. Like problems, games have a goal/unknown which requires the learner to generate new knowledge. Games (at least, good ones) also have a value to the learner in achieving the goal. So a game that focuses on problem solving will, by definition, be goal oriented.

Learning Should Be Active and Interactive. Problems in the twenty-first century, like the challenges in games, are solved in a distributed, iterative fashion. Such problems are often ill structured and nonlinear, and require data gathering from a variety of sources. Problems themselves are also rarely presented in a complete fashion but instead often have several elements missing. The problems for a game should be designed as a complete case first, then have key elements removed. Those missing pieces should be distributed across multiple resources. Solving the problems should require that the player seek out different resources throughout the game. Resources provide different types of information depending on where the player has been and what information he or she currently possesses. Thus, the game should provide multiple opportunities for interaction and require active participation for the player to solve the problem. This is a common feature of successful commercial games and ensures that the learner is an active participant.

Learning Should Provide Adaptive Challenge and Support. In order to provide varying levels of challenge and support according to different levels of expertise, designers should carefully organize the problems/scenarios in the game into levels of increasing complexity and decreasing support. Like the problems themselves, support should also be distributed and contextualized. Scaffolding can take many forms within the game, including dialog, interactions with mentor/advisor characters, etc. Challenge and support should also be adaptive in the sense that behavior patterns and actions (like the evidence model that we refer to in the final section of this chapter does) within the game may trigger support or challenge options. For example, too much elapsed time since the last action and repeatedly exploring dead-end branches of the game may trigger (authentic!) intervention.

Learning Should Incorporate Feedback. Every action in the game should result in some form of feedback, but the nature of that feedback should again be contextualized and authentic. Speaking to characters should always result in some form of response, either as additional information (in which case the player knows he or she is on the right track) or a canned response, like "I don't have anything to add to what I've already said" (in which case the learner knows that it is time to move on). What is key is that the feedback provides contextualized hints and prompts rather than direct answers or instruction, and it is contextually sensitive to the game narrative, problem, and environment.

Part III: Stealth Assessment and Evidence-Centered Design in Games

In games, as players interact with the environment, the values of different game-specific variables change. For instance, getting injured in a battle reduces health and finding a treasure or other object increases your inventory of goods. In addition, solving major problems in games permits players to gain rank or "level up." One could argue that these are all "assessments" in games—of health, personal goods, and rank. But now consider monitoring educationally relevant variables at different levels of granularity in games. In addition to checking health status, players could check their systems-thinking, creativity, problem-solving, and teamwork skills, where each of these competencies is further broken down into constituent knowledge and skill elements. If the values of those skills were to get too low, the player would likely feel compelled to take action to boost them.

One main challenge for educators who want to employ or design games to support learning is making *valid inferences* about what the student knows, believes, and can do—at any point in time, at various levels, and without disrupting the flow of the game (and hence engagement and learning). One way to increase the quality and utility of an assessment is to use evidence-centered design (ECD), which informs the design of valid assessments and yields real-time estimates of students' competency levels across a range of knowledge and skills (Mislevy et al., 2003). Accurate information about the student can be used as the basis for (a) delivering timely and targeted feedback, as well as (b) presenting a new task or quest that is right at the cusp of the student's skill level, in line with flow theory and Vygotsky's zone of proximal development. ECD will be described in more detail, shortly.

Given the goal of using educational games to support learning in school settings (and elsewhere) we need to ensure that the assessments are valid, reliable, and also pretty much invisible (to keep engagement intact). That's where "stealth assessment" comes in (see Shute, 2011; Shute & Ventura, 2013;

Shute, Ventura, Bauer, & Zapata-Rivera, 2009). During game play, students naturally produce rich sequences of actions while performing complex tasks, drawing on the very skills or competencies that we want to assess (e.g., creativity, persistence, spatial abilities). Evidence needed to assess the skills is thus provided by the players' interactions with the game itself (i.e., the processes of play), which lies in stark contrast to the norms in educational and training environments, where the product(s) of an activity are the main focus.

Making use of this stream of evidence to assess students' knowledge, skills, and understanding (as well as beliefs, feelings, and other learner states and traits) presents problems for traditional measurement models used in assessment. First, in traditional tests, the answer to each question is seen as an independent data point. In contrast, the individual actions within a sequence of interactions in a game are often highly dependent on one another. Second, in traditional tests, questions are often designed to get at one particular piece of knowledge or skill. Answering the question correctly is evidence that one may know a certain fact: one question—one fact. By analyzing a *sequence* of individual actions within a quest (where each response or action provides incremental evidence about the current mastery of a specific fact, concept, or skill), we are able to make inferences about what learners know about the instructional outcome overall. Now, because we typically want to assess a whole cluster of skills and abilities from evidence coming from learners' interactions within a game, methods for analyzing the sequence of behaviors to infer these abilities are not as obvious. As suggested earlier, ECD can address these problems.

The fundamental ideas underlying ECD came from Messick (1994) and were then formalized by Mislevy and colleagues (e.g., Mislevy, Almond, & Lukas, 2004; Mislevy & Haertel, 2006; Mislevy et al., 2003). A game that includes evidence-based assessment must be able to elicit behavior from the students that bears evidence about the targeted knowledge and skills (i.e., the competencies), and it must additionally provide principled interpretations of that evidence in relation to the purpose of the assessment. Figuring out these variables and their interrelationships is a way to answer a series of questions posed by Messick (1994) that get at the very heart of assessment design generally, and ECD specifically. In short, the framework requires an assessor to (a) define the claims to be made about learners' competencies (competency model), (b) establish what constitutes valid evidence of a claim and how to measure that evidence (evidence model), and (c) determine the nature and form of tasks or situations that will elicit that evidence (task model).

In games with stealth assessment, the competency model for a given student dynamically accumulates and represents belief about the targeted aspects of skill, expressed as probability distributions for competency-model variables (Almond & Mislevy, 1999; Shute et al., 2009). Evidence models identify what the student says or does that can provide evidence about those skills (Steinberg & Gitomer, 1996) and express in a psychometric model how the evidence depends on the competency-model variables (Mislevy, 1994). Task or action models express situations that can evoke required evidence.

One effective tool that has been used in such competency and evidence modeling efforts is Bayesian networks (e.g., Pearl, 1988).

That is, Bayes nets may be used within learner models (i.e., competency models tied to a particular learner) to handle uncertainty by using probabilistic inference to update and improve belief values (e.g., regarding learner competencies). Examples of Bayes net implementations for student models are numerous (Behrens, Mislevy, DiCerbo, & Levy, 2010; Conati, Gertner, & VanLehn, 2002; Kim & Shute, 2015; Shute & Ventura, 2013; Shute & Wang (in press); Shute, Graf, & Hansen, 2005; VanLehn et al., 2005).

Using ECD and Bayes nets to craft stealth assessments embedded directly in the game along with automated data collection and analysis tools can not only collect valid evidence of students' competency states but can also reduce teachers' workload in relation to managing the students' work (or "play") products. If a particular game was easy to employ and provided integrated and automated assessment tools, then teachers would more likely want to utilize the game to support student learning across a range of educationally valuable skills. Stealth assessment is intended to help teachers facilitate learning, in a fun and engaging manner, of educationally valuable skills not currently supported in school. It is also, of course, intended to facilitate the flow state for students engaged in game play.

Conclusion

Our goal for this chapter was to begin to connect the dots between games and learning. Toward that end, we first described how well-designed games provide an environment in which people are more receptive to learning, especially as compared to traditional environments like the classroom (see earlier discussion on Piaget's and Sutton-Smith's theories). Then we articulated the need for sound theoretical models and frameworks for game design that tap the true power of games for learning. We suggested that situated, authentic problem solving was one such framework. Our final section on stealth assessment was intended to highlight the need for accurate, dynamic assessment and diagnosis of educationally valuable skills during game play. We discussed how stealth assessment can support instructional decisions while operating beneath the radar in terms of monitoring and measuring these competencies.

In conclusion, well-designed games are a potentially powerful vehicle to support learning, particularly in relation to new competencies not currently embraced by our educational system but needed to succeed in the twenty-first century. There are simply too few experimental studies examining the range of effects of gaming environments on learning (e.g., Van Eck, 2007). We believe that the new games-for-learning research stream is highly relevant and important to the field of ISD, which can both inform and be informed by the research.

We close as we began with a relevant quote:

> *Games are thus the most ancient and time-honored vehicle for education . . . We don't see mother lions lecturing cubs at the chalkboard; we don't see senior lions writing their memoirs for posterity. In light of this, the question, "Can games have educational value?" becomes absurd. It is not games but schools that are the newfangled notion, the untested fad, the violator of tradition."*

– Chris Crawford

Summary of Key Principles

1. **Games-for-learning research should account for prior research on learning in general rather than reinventing the wheel.**

2. **Good games trigger the play phenomenon in the players.**

3. **Situated, authentic problem solving is an effective way to ensure that games can support problem solving.**

4. **There are many kinds of games, and many kinds of problems, and they must be aligned carefully.**

5. **Assessment of learning in games requires a fundamental shift in our thinking about assessment, from responses to external "test questions" to embedded actions and patterns within games.**

6. **Good games for learning can use the information from ongoing stealth assessments to provide timely**

and targeted feedback to players and present new game tasks that suit the student's current skill level.

7. **Good games for learning, like all good learning activities, should be active, goal-oriented (with goals valued by the players), contextualized, and designed with adaptive challenge and support.**

8. **The fundamentals of designing a good game for learning extend beyond any specific technology for a single game.**

9. **Principles of instructional design and problem-based learning can support and inform the design of good games for learning.**

10. **The ability to work creatively and effectively with others toward a common goal is an important twenty-first-century skill that is emphasized in good games.**

Application Questions

1. Design a nondigital game with everyday objects found in your home or classroom (e.g., paper cups, paper clips, ping pong balls). Ask friends to play it, then ask them if they think the game is any fun. Ask them for ideas to improve the game. Using any of their ideas, and others you thought of, redesign the game and ask another group of friends to play this new version. Is the game more fun? Try to list or chart out the design process you experienced. Does the game have any value for learning? If not, what is missing?

2. Choose a learning theory that you feel is compatible with games. What kind of game (MMORPG, puzzle game, adventure game, first-person shooter, etc.) do you think it would be most compatible with? Why? What are the design implications of adopting that theory for a given

game? Name one example of a specific design element in a game that was designed according to your theory.

3. Identify an instructional outcome at the level of problem solving and try to develop a narrative description of a game that could promote that outcome. How would you make it situated? Authentic? Where would it take place, who would be involved, and what would it look and feel like?

4. Using the game idea from question 3, or for another game idea/outcome of your choice, describe an approach to stealth assessment that could be built into that game. Be specific in addressing how it aligns with your learning outcome, how you would measure it, how you could integrate it surreptitiously, and how it could be used for assessment, to modify game performance in some way, or both.

References

Adcock, A. B., Watson, G. S., Morrison, G. R., & Belfore, L. A. (2010). Effective knowledge development in game-based learning environments: Considering research in cognitive processes and simulation design. In R. Van Eck (Ed.), *Gaming and cognition: Theories and perspectives from the learning sciences* (pp. 152–168). Hershey, PA: IGI Global.

Almond, R. G., & Mislevy, R. J. (1999). Graphical models and computerized adaptive testing. *Applied Psychological Measurement, 23*(3), 223–237.

Barrett, K. A., & Johnson, W. L. (2010). Developing serious games for learning language-in-culture. In R. Van Eck (Ed.), *Interdisciplinary models and tools for serious games: Emerging concepts and future directions* (pp. 281–311). Hershey, PA: IGI Global.

Behrens, J. T., Mislevy, R. J., DiCerbo, K. E., & Levy, R. (2010). *Evidence centered design for learning and assessment in the digital world* (Report No. 778). Washington, DC: National Center for Research on Evaluation, Standards, and Student Testing. Retrieved from http://files.eric.ed.gov/fulltext/ED520431.pdf

Bloom, B. S. (1984). *Taxonomy of educational objectives book 1: Cognitive domain*. White Plains, NY: Longman.

Borchert, O., Brandt, L., Hokanson, G., Slator, B. M., Vender, B., & Gutierrez, E. J. (2010). Principles and signatures in serious games for science education. In R. Van Eck (Ed.), *Interdisciplinary models and tools for serious games: Emerging concepts and future directions* (pp. 312–338). Hershey, PA: IGI Global.

Brown, J. S., Collins, A., & Duguid, P. (1989). Situated cognition and the culture of learning. *Educational Researcher, 18*, 32–42.

Clark, D. B., Tanner-Smith, E. E., & Killingsworth, S. (2014). Digital games, design, and learning: A systematic review and meta-analysis. Menlo Park, CA: SRI International.

Conati, C., Gertner, A., & VanLehn, K. (2002). Using Bayesian networks to manage uncertainty in student modeling. *User Modeling & User-Adapted Interaction, 12*(4), 371–417.

Csikszentmihalyi, M. (1990). *Flow: The psychology of optimal experience*. New York: Harper & Row.

Elkind, D. (2007). *The power of play: How spontaneous, imaginative activities lead to happier, healthier children.* Cambridge, MA: Da Capo Lifelong.

"Friedrich Fröbel." (n.d.). In *Wikipedia*. Retrieved from http://en.wikipedia.org/wiki/Friedrich_Fröbel

Gagné, R. M., Wager, W. W., Golas, K. C., & Keller, J. M. (2004). *Principles of instructional design* (5th ed.). Belmont, CA: Wadsworth/Thomson Learning.

Gajadhar, B. (2012). Understanding player experience in social digital games: The role of social presence [Dissertation]. Oisterwijk, Netherlands: Uitgeverij BOXPress. ISBN 978-90-8891-391-4

Gee, J. P. (2003). *What video games have to teach us about learning and literacy*. New York: Palgrave Macmillan.

Greenfield, P. M. (1985). *Mind and media: The effects of television, video games, and computers*. Cambridge, MA: Harvard University.

Harp, S. F., & Mayer, R. E. (1997). The role of interest in learning from scientific text and illustrations: On the distinction between emotional interest and cognitive interest. *Journal of Educational Psychology, 89*, 92–102

Huizinga, J. (1950). *Homo Ludens: A study of the play element in culture*. Boston, MA: Beacon Press.

Hung, W., & Van Eck, R. (2010). Aligning problem solving and gameplay: A model for future research & design. In R. Van Eck (Ed.), *Interdisciplinary models and tools for serious games: Emerging concepts and future directions* (pp. 227–263). Hershey, PA: IGI Global.

Institute of Play. (n.d.). History of games and learning. Retrieved from http://www.instituteofplay.org/about/context/history-of-games-learning/

Jonassen, D. H. (2000). Toward a design theory of problem solving. *ETR&D, 48*(4), 63–85.

Jonassen, D. H. (2002). Integration of problem solving into instructional design. In R. A. Reiser & J. V. Dempsey (Eds.), *Trends and issues in instructional design & technology* (pp. 107–120). Upper Saddle River, NJ: Merrill Prentice Hall.

Kim, Y. J., & Shute, V. J. (2015). The interplay of game elements with psychometric qualities, learning, and enjoyment in game-based assessment. *Computers & Education, 87*, 340–356.

Lave, J. (1988). *Cognition in practice: Mind, mathematics, and culture in everyday life*. New York: Cambridge University Press.

Messick, S. (1994). The interplay of evidence and consequences in the validation of performance assessments. *Education Researcher, 32*(2), 13–23.

Mislevy, R. J. (1994). Evidence and inference in educational assessment. *Psychometrika, 59*, 439–483

Mislevy, R. J., & Haertel, G. D. (2006). Implications of evidence-centered design for educational testing. *Educational Measurement: Issues and Practice, 25*(4), 6–20.

Mislevy, R. J., Almond, R. G., & Lukas, J. F. (2004). *A brief introduction to evidence-centered design* (CSE Report 632). Washington, DC: Center for Research on Evaluation, Standards, and Student Testing. (ERIC Document Reproduction Service No. ED483399)

Mislevy, R. J., Steinberg, L. S., & Almond, R. G. (2003). On the structure of educational assessment. *Measurement: Interdisciplinary Research and Perspective, 1*(1) 3–62.

Pearl, J. (1988). *Probabalistic reasoning in intelligent systems: Networks of plausible inference*. San Francisco: Morgan Kaufman.

Pellegrini, A. D. (Ed.). (1995). *The future of play theory: A multidisciplinary inquiry into the contributions of Brian Sutton-Smith*. Albany, NY: State University of New York Press.

Phillips, J. L. (1981). *Piaget's theory: A primer*. San Francisco: W. H. Freeman.

Piaget, J. (1951). *Play, dreams, and imitation in childhood*. New York: W. W. Norton & Company.

Rieber, L. P. (1996). Seriously considering play: Designing interactive learning environments based on the blending of microworlds, simulations, and games. *Educational Technology Research & Development, 44*(2), 43–58.

Shute, V. J. (2011). Stealth assessment in computer-based games to support learning. In S. Tobias & J. D. Fletcher (Eds.), *Computer games and instruction* (pp. 503–524). Charlotte, NC: Information Age Publishers.

Shute, V. J., & Ventura, M. (2013). *Measuring and supporting learning in games: Stealth assessment*. Cambridge, MA: The MIT Press.

Shute, V. J., & Wang, L. (in press). Assessing and supporting hard-to-measure constructs. To appear in A. Rupp & J. Leighton (Eds.), *Handbook of cognition and assessment.*

Shute, V. J., Graf, E. A., & Hansen, E. (2005). Designing adaptive, diagnostic math assessments for individuals with and without visual disabilities. In L. PytlikZillig, R. Bruning, & M. Bodvarsson (Eds.), *Technology-based education: Bringing researchers and practitioners together* (pp. 169–202). Greenwich, CT: Information Age Publishing.

Shute, V. J., Ventura, M., Bauer, M. I., & Zapata-Rivera, D. (2009). Melding the power of serious games and embedded assessment to monitor and foster learning: Flow and grow. In U. Ritterfeld, M. Cody, & P. Vorderer (Eds.), *Serious games: Mechanisms and effects* (pp. 295–321). Mahwah, NJ: Routledge, Taylor and Francis.

Steinberg, L. S., & Gitomer, D. H. (1996). Intelligent tutoring and assessment built on an understanding of a technical problem-solving task. *Instructional Science, 24,* 223–258.

Sutton-Smith, B. (1997). *The ambiguity of play.* Cambridge, MA: Harvard University Press.

Takeuchi, L. M., & Vaala, S. (2014). Level up learning: A national survey on teaching with digital games. New York: The Joan Ganz Cooney Center at Sesame Workshop. Retrieved from www.joanganzcooneycenter.org

Van Eck, R. (2007). Six ideas in search of a discipline. In B. Shelton & D. Wiley (Eds.), *The educational design and use of computer simulation games.* Boston: Sense.

Van Eck, R. (2008). COTS in the classroom: A teachers guide to integrating commercial off-the-shelf (COTS) games. In R. Ferdig (Ed.), *Handbook of research on effective electronic gaming in education.* Hershey, PA: Idea Group.

Van Eck, R. (2015). SAPS and digital games: Improving mathematics transfer and attitudes in schools. In T. Lowrie & R. Jorgensen (Eds.), *Digital games and mathematics learning: Potential, promises and pitfalls.* New York: Springer.

VanLehn, K., Lynch, C., Schulze, K., Shapiro, J. A., Shelby, R., Taylor, L., Treacy, D., Weinstein, A., & Wintersgill, M. (2005). The Andes physics tutoring system: Lessons learned. *International Journal of Artificial Intelligence and Education, 15*(3), 1–47.

Vygotsky, L. S. (1978). *Mind in society: The development of higher mental processes.* Cambridge, MA: Harvard University Press.

Vygotsky, L. S. (1987). *The collected works of L. S. Vygotsky.* New York: Plenum.

Zimmerman, B. J. (1990). Self-regulated learning and academic achievement: An overview. *Educational Psychologist, 25*(1), 3–17.

Zimmerman, B. J. (2008). Investigating self-regulation and motivation: Historical background, methodological developments, and future prospects. *American Educational Research Journal, 45*(1), 166–183.

Chapter 34

Problem-Based Learning: Essential Design Characteristics

Peggy A. Ertmer

Purdue University

Krista D. Glazewski

Indiana University

Introduction

Problem-based learning (PBL) represents a student-centered instructional approach, designed to facilitate students' active construction of knowledge through deep engagement with meaningful problems (Hmelo-Silver, 2004). The PBL model was formalized in medical education during the 1960s as a way of responding to problems of inert knowledge (Whitehead, 1929) and low motivation among medical students (Gijselaers, 1996). More specifically, medical faculty had observed that previously learned information could not be enacted or applied at the moment of patient diagnosis and treatment (Barrows, 1996). By engaging students in authentic, relevant medical problems from the start of their professional education, faculty aimed to foster student motivation, professional knowledge, and clinical skills, and more than fifty years of research has demonstrated success toward these student outcomes (Dochy, Segers, Van den Bossche, & Gijbels, 2003; Gijbels, Dochy, Van den Bossche, & Segers, 2005; Strobel & van Barneveld, 2009; Walker & Leary, 2009).

According to Barrows and Tamblyn (1980), PBL comprises "the learning that results from the process of working toward the understanding or resolution of a problem" (p. 18). In general, the goals in problem-based learning are twofold: (1) to promote deep understanding of subject-matter content, while (2) simultaneously developing students' higher-order thinking skills (Barrows, 1996). More specifically, PBL employs *real-world problems* as vehicles to stimulate student motivation, contextualize disciplinary content, and facilitate the growth of higher-order thinking skills. Students learn to analyze these problems, using authentic tools of the discipline (e.g., primary source documents, graphing calculators, scientific probes), in order to identify what information they need, how to integrate facts and concepts from different disciplines and sources, and how to evaluate the strength of their proposed solutions. Furthermore, the curriculum is structured to foster group work, self-directed learning, critical thinking, and self-reflection (Hmelo-Silver & Barrows, 2006).

In response to recent calls by educators, legislators, and policy makers to develop "innovators and inventors" (Bonamici, 2013; Educate to Innovate, n.d.; Wagner, 2012), PBL has been gaining in popularity in both K–12 and higher education contexts (American Institutes for Research [AIR], 2014; Ravitz, 2009). Although less common, PBL is also used as a training approach in the workplace, particularly when training goals comprise the development of decision-making or problem-solving skills. For example, PBL was used to introduce school personnel and emergency managers to critical decision-making processes when faced with severe weather outbreaks (Stalker, Cullen, & Kloesel, 2015). In a similar manner, the U.S. Air Force Research Laboratory (Andrews, Hull, & Donahue, 2009) used PBL to teach decision-making processes to aeronautical management trainees, preparing them to "draw on a decision process tied to issues of working through complex events with high stakes outcomes" (p. 13) when faced with a serious airplane malfunction.

According to Barrows (1986), PBL implementations exist along a continuum from short, isolated implementations on the one end to full curricular integration on the other. Bereiter and Scardamalia (2000) referred to these various levels of implementation as *uppercase PBL* and *lower-case pbl*.

In general, uppercase PBL comprises "a distinctive, well documented instructional approach that originated in medical education" (p. 185), whereas lowercase pbl refers to "an indefinite range of educational approaches that give problems a central place in learning activity" (Bereiter & Scardamalia, 2000, p. 185). As such, an examination of learning outcomes from PBL should be accompanied by a critical review of the implementation description to determine the extent to which the approach reflects signature elements of PBL pedagogy. This will prevent readers from drawing incorrect inferences about PBL that should, in reality, be attributed to other problem-centered methods.

Problem-Centered Methods: Similarities and Differences

Teachers, instructional designers, and other educators often question the similarities and differences between PBL and other forms of problem-centered instruction. In general, we view these methods as all falling under the broad classification of inquiry-based learning (IBL). According to Healy (2005), IBL is an instructional approach that "mimics, as closely as possible, the actual pattern of inquiry in the discipline being studied" (p. 68). As such, IBL is characterized by complex, relevant, and authentic learner experiences, which are driven by real or realistic problems (Edelson, Gordin, & Pea, 1999). Under the IBL umbrella, a variety of problem-centered practices exist. In addition to PBL, two of the more common methods include case-based instruction (CBI) and project-based learning (PjBL).

Differences between approaches are often quite subtle, but we argue that the distinctions generally fall along four dimensions: authenticity of problem (e.g., realistic versus real); purpose, as well as timing, of problem introduction (e.g., knowledge application versus knowledge building; introduced before or after all the relevant knowledge is gained); problem type/degree of structuredness in the problem (e.g., well structured versus ill structured), and type of final product produced (e.g., case analysis versus project artifact versus problem resolution). Table 34.1 illustrates these differences across the three approaches. In this chapter, we use the term PBL to refer, specifically, to the learning approach represented by the last row of the table.

More specifically, PBL is defined here as a student-centered instructional approach that incorporates the following features: (1) use of authentic ill-structured problems that are introduced before all the relevant content is learned; (2) support for, and facilitation of, self-directed student learning; (3) scaffolding of students' knowledge building; (4) cooperation and collaboration among students, teachers, and community members; and (5) authentic assessment of both process and product, including evidence-based recommendations for problem resolution (Ertmer & Glazewski, 2015; Ertmer & Simons, 2006; Grant & Hill, 2006). It is important to note that while these five components are considered key features of PBL, they are not necessarily unique to PBL. For example, scaffolding, collaborative learning, and authentic assessment are typically included within PjBL and CBI approaches as well. In this chapter, however, we focus specifically on how these features are reflected within a PBL approach. We discuss each component in more detail next.

TABLE 34.1	**Dimensions of Difference between Three Inquiry-Based Learning Practices**			
	Authenticity of Problem	**Problem Purpose; Timing of Problem Introduction**	**Problem Type / Structuredness**	**Type of Final Student Product**
Case-Based (CBI)	Realistic	Application of complex and general disciplinary knowledge. Students engage with problems that typically have been experienced by practitioners in the field. Typically introduced after concepts are learned with the expectation that students will *apply* prior knowledge.	Complex Scenario / Semi-Structured. *Example: Students are asked to consider the issues that practicing engineers face, related to stakeholders and design considerations, when tasked with building a better cast saw.*	Analysis and recommendations relevant to issues in problem situation (typically written and reflecting knowledge application).
Project-Based (PjBL)	Realistic	Application of complex and cross-disciplinary knowledge. Introduced after concepts are learned with the expectation that students will *apply* prior knowledge.	Complex / Semi or Well-Structured. *Example: Build a better cast saw.*	Project artifact (poster, plans, brochure, presentation, or other artifact).
Problem-Based (PBL)	Real or realistic	Integration of prior knowledge with new content knowledge; opportunities for additional knowledge building. Introduced before all relevant knowledge is acquired.	Complex / Ill-Structured. *Example: What can be done to reduce incidents of injury and litigation resulting from cast-saw injuries?*	Evidence-based problem resolution (typically a solution or recommendation).

Use of Authentic Problems

In a PBL approach, problems, rather than topics or subjects, are used to anchor the curriculum (Stepien & Gallagher, 1993). Typically, the learning process begins when learners are confronted with an authentic problem, query, or puzzle they wish to solve (Boud, 1985). Furthermore, as noted by MacDonald and Issacs (2001), "the problem comes before the knowledge (in the broadest sense) needed to solve or resolve it" (p. 317). This, then, is one of the defining characteristics of PBL – prerequisite disciplinary content knowledge is not introduced or mastered prior to asking students to apply that knowledge to solve real-world problems. As such, the problems drive the curriculum (Edutopia, 2014), and it is through solving these problems that students acquire content knowledge (Barrows, 1983; MacDonald & Issacs, 2001).

Problems in PBL comprise complex, ill-structured situations or dilemmas, which generally allow for multiple workable solutions as well as multiple paths to those solutions (Jonassen, 2011). Typically, the problem is presented to students in the form of a driving question (Table 34.2) that quickly engages students' interests and inspires a "need to know." According to Larmer and Mergendoller (2012), a good driving question "captures the heart of the project in clear, compelling language, which gives students a sense of purpose and challenge. The question should be provocative, open-ended, complex, and linked to the core of what you want students to learn" (p. 2). For example, a ninth-grade biology teacher developed a PBL unit that revolved around the question, "Should there be a meat tax?" which immediately provoked strong responses among his students and motivated them to engage (Brush et al., 2014).

Thus, the question brings purpose to the activities students undertake as part of the PBL unit, connecting their efforts under a unifying goal. Without a good driving question, learning efforts may not seem worth the hard work required. That is, students may lose sight of the authentic reason for their work and end up placing emphasis on a series of interesting, but not very relevant, activities (e.g., "We're making a poster.").

Self-Directed Student Learning

Self-directed learning (SDL) is defined as learner processes that involve " . . . diagnosing their learning needs, formulating goals, identifying human and material resources, choosing and implementing appropriate learning strategies, and evaluating learning outcomes" (Knowles, 1975, p. 18). These processes of SDL are critical to success in PBL. Barrows (1983) advocated for small groups of students to establish topics that required further exploration, divide topics among the group members, and devote time to individual research before reconvening to discuss findings. He observed that students initially tended to resist expectations of SDL, but quickly experienced success. Barrows attributed their success to the social pressure to appear proficient in front of peers, combined with the fact that continual practice of the skills led to greater competence. Once groups reassembled, they reported findings, revisited earlier hypotheses, brainstormed and critiqued new ideas, and developed a treatment plan. Barrows concluded that while self-directed processes are not easy for most students, they are critical to PBL and can be developed given practice and guidance. Blumberg (2000) came to similar conclusions regarding student self-direction. In a review of research studies, she examined

---

TABLE 34.2   Sample Driving Questions and Associated Disciplines/Content Addressed by Each

Primary Discipline	Driving Question	Primary Content Covered
Science	• How can biological methods be used to meet our energy needs? • How do drugs impact your body, your family, your community and your world?	Biology: Cellular processes Chemistry, math, humanities
Social Studies	• When are nations justified in using military force against other countries?	Persistent issues in history
Science/Social Studies	• Who is responsible for ensuring a safe food/water supply in our community?	Thermodynamics, water treatment, water rights
Math	• How can we, as concerned citizens, determine if the speed limits in Ripley County need to be changed to make them safer? • How much of the Earth's surface can be seen from the International Space Station?	Algebra: Linear equations Geometry: Circle formulas
Social Studies/Mathematics	• Why should kids care about price of gas?	Cost-benefit analysis, Political science
Engineering	• How is a new electrical product developed, engineered, and marketed for the public? • How can we design, build, and test a water purification system?	Physics, engineering, marketing Engineering design; science: water systems
Technology	• How can we plan, design, and model a biomass conversion plant in our community • What makes something strong?	Technology as a system Structural and material properties

Source: Adapted from Mong and Ertmer (2013).

evidence of SDL along three dimensions: learning processes, strategies, and tasks involving application or transfer. Student self-reports and faculty observations of students were consistent: Both groups reported that skills toward effective SDL were developed over time, and, in some cases, participants perceived that PBL was more effective at fostering these skills than were conventional curricula.

However, this is not to imply that self-direction learning is a skill that automatically occurs in PBL, but, rather, that it should be modeled, cultivated, and fostered. In some cases, this may involve a considerable time investment, as observed by van den Hurk, Wolfhagen, Dolmans, and van der Vleuten (1999). The authors reported that during multiyear PBL experiences, students in the first year tended to narrowly pursue the identified learning issues but in later years, many students allowed their learning to take diverse directions according to personal interests. Results suggested that those who engaged with diverse, personal interests tended to perform better in the courses.

In other cases, nurturing SDL may require directly teaching active learning strategies to students. In one study, in order to tackle problems of "PBL fatigue," researchers taught students a four-stage SDL cycle: (1) sensitization, or activation, of prior knowledge; (2) exploration of available resources and direct relevance to future professional goals; (3) integration of ideas across disciplines; and (4) application of knowledge through papers, public forums, and reflection (Czabanowska, Schröder-Bäck, Meijer, Moust, & Roebertsen, 2012). Students responded the most positively to the first and last phases of the cycle, as those were perceived to most directly interest them or benefit their learning. However, students struggled with the exploration and integration phases, finding the workload to be taxing and noting a lack of resources available to support their efforts to make cross-disciplinary connections. The authors concluded that students may need more assistance, especially during early exposures to PBL, which is why scaffolding represents such a critical component of the PBL learning environment.

Scaffolding of Student Knowledge Building

While there is growing evidence that problem-based learning activities promote the development of higher-order skills such as critical thinking and problem solving (Strobel & van Barneveld, 2009; Swan et al., 2013; Tiwari, Lai, So, & Yuen, 2006; Wirkala & Kuhn, 2011), there are difficulties associated with supporting student-centered learning. From the student's perspective, succeeding within problem-based activities requires multiple self-directed tasks: setting meaningful goals for completing the activities, assuming more responsibility for meeting those goals, and monitoring progress in order to determine if the strategies being used are effective (Barrows, 1983; Blumberg, 2000; Ertmer & Glazewski, 2015; Hmelo-Silver, Duncan, & Chinn, 2007).

These issues have led to the suggestion that additional guidance, or *scaffolds*, be used to assist students and teachers engaged in this type of learning (Ertmer & Simons, 2006; Wood, Bruner, & Ross, 1976). Scaffolds can take many forms, but serve to support and guide students in attaining a higher level of understanding than would be possible if students worked on their own, especially given the complexities of the PBL process (Hmelo-Silver et al., 2007).

Saye and Brush (2002) conceptualized two forms of support: soft and hard scaffolds. *Hard scaffolds* represent static supports that can be anticipated and planned in advance, based upon known, or anticipated, student difficulties with a task. These support structures are typically embedded within learning environments to provide students with support while they are actively engaged with a problem (Belland, Glazewski, & Richardson, 2011; Sandoval & Millwood, 2011; Simons & Klein, 2007; Wu & Pedersen, 2011). For example, Belland et al. (2011) developed an online system, the *Connection Log*, to support middle school students in organizing information, sharing content, and developing evidence-based arguments as they made decisions about uses of human genetic information. The researchers noted that the system benefited all learners, not only on their team project, but also on a transfer task that required individual evidence-based arguments. Furthermore, students with the highest gains were low-achieving learners, supporting the hypothesis that such forms of hard scaffolding can contribute to success for a wide range of learners.

In contrast, *soft scaffolds* are dynamic, situation-specific supports provided by a teacher, trainer, or peer. Such scaffolding requires facilitators to consistently monitor learner understanding and provide targeted support at critical moments (Saye & Brush, 2002). For example, in a community health fair context, a health care educator asked parents to bring the various information sources they used to inform their decisions about getting their children vaccinated to an FAQ session. She then facilitated a discussion to help them discern bias in the accounts from pro- and anti-vaccine groups. As the parents discussed their sources, the health care educator scaffolded their thinking by asking questions such as: "Who wrote this piece? Why do you think the author uses the word _____? Do the authors use evidence based on research or anecdote?" Once parents attained deeper understanding of the biases that existed in different media accounts, the health care educator referred them to other sources that provided research-based evidence related to the use of vaccines among children.

Of course, not all forms of scaffolding fall precisely into "hard" or "soft" categories, and for these reasons Puntambekar and Kolodner (2005) employed the term "distributed scaffolding" to capture the range of supports that may be available across the instructional setting. Furthermore, Pea (2004) noted the need to blend forms of scaffolding within a learning environment: "It seems possible to imagine 'mixed initiative' designs of scaffolding processes in which people and machines join together in helping someone learn something in the sense that certain scaffolding activities can be the responsibility of the teacher . . . and other scaffolding activities provided by the software" (p. 444). Thus, it is important for instructors and designers to consider which supports are best provided by software and which are best provided by the teacher to optimally facilitate problem solving among students. For example, to help students who may struggle with integrating evidence into a broader problem context, the teacher might conduct discussion sessions with each small group as they are deciding how to use evidence to support their solutions (Saye & Brush, 2002), a strategy that would be difficult to provide as a hard scaffold. In addition, we suggest that designers consider blending the two scaffolding designs. For example, some hard scaffolds may serve as intermediate structures that support teachers in the task of soft scaffolding by creating time for reflection before a response is required. In this way, we scaffold teacher thinking by providing a thinking space between the occurrence of a student's initial response and the teacher's supporting response (Saye & Brush, 2002).

Cooperation and Collaboration among Students, Teachers, and Community

Collaboration is another key component of PBL environments, as it allows students, or trainees, to draw on each other's perspectives and talents in order to devise well-conceived, effective solutions for the problem(s) at hand (Mergendoller & Thomas, 2005). Furthermore, working in groups provides an important opportunity for learners to practice and master key communication and interpersonal skills, as well as time management and self-directed learning skills.

While students typically enjoy group work, group time is not always used productively and teachers need to enlist strategies to ensure that relevant content is addressed. According to Larmer and Mergendoller (2012), a teacher in a PBL environment must explicitly teach and assess collaboration skills, as well as provide frequent opportunities for students to assess themselves. The use of frequent checkpoints and record-keeping devices (e.g., group folders, design diaries, goal charts) can keep students focused and provide opportunities for reinforcement or redirection. These techniques also serve motivational purposes as they allow students to observe their ongoing progress (Ertmer & Glazewski, 2015).

Establishing a collaborative classroom or training culture requires instructors to assume a facilitative, rather than directive, role. As such, instructors engage with learners through a variety of modeling and scaffolding techniques: asking good questions, demonstrating productive thinking patterns, providing just-in-time resources, leading debriefing sessions, and facilitating whole-group and individual reflection (Ertmer & Glazewski, 2015). In general, instructors may require a period of transition, and lots of practice, before they feel truly comfortable assuming this type of facilitative role (Grant & Hill, 2006).

Finally, one of the hallmarks of authentic work is that it engages multiple stakeholders; furthermore, stakeholder perspective-taking occurs at many points throughout the work. For example, teachers may invite a community member into the classroom to introduce the problem, or once students are engaged in the problem, experts may be accessed who can shed light on different aspects of the problem. Often, community members (parents, political representatives, etc.) are invited to attend a public presentation of students' final products or suggested solutions. This increases the authenticity of students' work (i.e., presenting to a "real" audience) and also can lead to increased involvement in, and engagement of, the community.

As an example, in an online environment, designers used interactive branching videocases to prepare U.S. Army personnel for emergency decision making as first responders to an incident on a military base (Glazewski, Benson, Rutledge, & Zeisset, 2009). Participants selected roles consistent with their current military assignments, and worked online in teams of three to rank order potential choices and decide the best solution path. The branching nature of videocases allowed teams to engage with the scenario more than one time, selecting different solution paths and experiencing the outcomes associated with each path. At the end of the case, participants collaboratively completed an after-action review in which they evaluated their team decisions and reflected on the outcomes.

Authentic Assessment of Process and Product

In PBL approaches, instructors commonly rely on a wide range of assessment practices, with most instructors using a variety of methods within each problem-based unit. In a study of student experiences in PjBL, Grant (2011) noted some of the acquired learning was unseen by the teacher, and concluded that it was unreasonable to expect artifacts to represent, completely, all that was learned. Generally, assessment practices can be divided into three broad categories: (1) enroute, for the purpose of monitoring student progress and assessing the learning process, (2) culminating, for the purpose of observing students' direct responses to the problem under investigation, and (3) individual, for the purpose of determining individual student mastery of targeted content. Table 34.3 illustrates how these three types of assessment might play out in different contexts and disciplines.

The first form of assessment comprises *enroute* tasks such as papers, journals, whole or small group debriefings, reflections, models, or other representations of learning, primarily for the purpose of monitoring student progress. Research suggests that students perform better when these types of enroute benchmarks are in place. In one study, researchers observed two groups of law students, some of whom voluntarily completed six enroute tasks and others who did not (Gijbels, van de Watering, & Dochy, 2005). These tasks comprised additional deep application of the learning material from any of the course topics or resources. Those who completed the additional tasks performed better on the final exam and reported greater course satisfaction than those who did not complete the tasks. The authors attributed students' successful outcomes to increased time spent in meaningful and productive enroute work outside of class, which served to deepen individual learning.

A second form of assessment is the *culminating* activity, which represents a direct response to the problem or question under investigation. The culminating activity is an essential component of PBL; without it, the problem-centered approach being implemented would not be classified as "true" PBL. This relates, specifically, to the fact that PBL instructors are most interested in implementing strategies and assessments that reflect complex problem solving (Gijbels et al., 2005). Barrows (1986) noted that assessment methods direct how students study, and therefore must reflect problem-solving,

TABLE 34.3	Examples of Assessment Approaches in Three Different PBL Contexts			
Context	**Driving Question**	**Enroute**	**Culminating**	**Individual**
K–12 science	Should there be a meat tax?	• Team milestones for debate preparation (e.g., argument development, gathering supporting evidence) • Draft of PP slides for feedback	• Stakeholders' debate	• End of unit assessment • Policy proposal
Medical education	What is the best treatment plan for Mrs. Garcia?	• Presentations to group members on identified learning issues • Use of KWL chart (What do we **Know**? What do we **Want** to know? What have we **Learned?**)	• Differential diagnosis and treatment plan	• End of unit assessment • Board exams covering specific content knowledge
Engineering education	What can be done to reduce incidents of injury and litigation resulting from cast-saw injuries?	• Preliminary design documents	• Detailed design documents • Prototype of proposed new cast saw	• End of course test

clinical reasoning, and self-directed learning: "Without these assessments, the educational objectives for PBL are weakened as students will not honour [SIC] them in their study. The teacher will never know whether the students are meeting these objectives" (p. 485). In medical education, a typical assessment is directly linked to the problem; that is, students develop a recommendation for the patient-case examination, as illustrated by the following example (adapted from Barone & Sattar, 2009):

> [Mrs. Garcia] A 30-year-old Hispanic woman, who speaks little English, is brought to the emergency department because of her agitated and restless behavior. The patient's history indicates she delivered a healthy baby boy at your medical school's obstetrics and gynecology clinic last month. She had been attending the prenatal clinic on a regular basis. Her previous labs are attached. The patient is not willing to stay in bed. She is very agitated, loud, and swearing at people around her. She is afraid and looking behind herself constantly. She is refusing to allow the nurse to examine her or draw blood (p. 35).

As students work through the case, a tutor facilitates the learning process, which culminates in diagnosis and a treatment plan.

Culminating activities can take on many other forms depending, foremost, on the nature of the driving question. In the meat tax example, students were assigned to stakeholder teams (e.g., farmer, parent, ecologist, or medical doctor), and then asked to present, in a culminating class debate, a reasoned, well-supported position from their assigned stakeholders' point of view (Brush et al., 2014). In addition, the teacher also had students complete a second, individual culminating assessment that required a written policy recommendation reflecting their own positions on the issue supported by strong science- and sociology-based arguments.

A third form of assessment comprises an individual measure, which is typically an exam or position paper reflecting the identified content objectives. Depending on the organization of the learning experience, this could be an end-course exam composed of learning objectives across the full semester or it might be a unit-based assessment reflecting targeted goals. For example, the teacher from the meat tax unit developed specific learning objectives to be tested at the end of the unit, four of which included:

• Describe the role of photosynthesis in the food web.
• Determine ecological/energy significance of eating foods at different levels of the trophic pyramid.
• Graph and hypothesize causes and effects for human population changes.
• Predict outcomes of antibiotic use in meat production based on natural selection.

The teacher developed a criterion-referenced exam to administer to each student individually, which informed both knowledge of individual performances and patterns of performance in meeting the state standards aligned with the objectives.

As noted previously, most PBL implementations involve more than one form of assessment, as it is impossible to represent all that is learned in a single artifact or measure of performance (Grant, 2011). Additionally, PBL instructors often include opportunities for students to engage in both peer and self-assessment, in order to examine, more clearly, how students are approaching the learning process itself, including the use of SDL skills. In many instances, an additional "community" assessment is included via a public presentation of students' work. Given the multiple goals of PBL (i.e., content learning and development of higher-order thinking skills), the use of multiple assessment measures enables teachers to better gauge how students are progressing toward mastery of both content and SDL skills throughout the PBL process.

Conclusion

A wide variety of problem-centered methods are being used in classrooms and professional training contexts today, including those that focus primarily on projects, cases, or problems. Problem-based learning encompasses a distinct variety of problem-centered instruction—that is, PBL comprises the use of authentic complex problems that are introduced through an engaging driving question before all the prerequisite disciplinary knowledge has been gained. The learning experience culminates in a final demonstration or application of that knowledge, and may involve a public venue attended by interested stakeholders.

Educators and researchers who promote the use of PBL stress that students' engagement with the problem itself deepens the motivation students need to do the hard work of complex problem solving (Wirkala & Kuhn, 2011). Thus, identifying and crafting an engaging driving question is a critical responsibility of a PBL instructor. However, PBL entails much more then devising an engaging problem. Instructors or designers should not expect to furnish a rich context and hope that is enough. As noted by Hmelo-Silver et al. (2007) and highlighted in this chapter, considerable planning is directed toward the implementation details, which includes how to promote and support collaboration among students and stakeholders, how

to provide the appropriate type and level of hard and soft scaffolds, and how to devise and implement assessment measures that capture both individual and team learning details (Ertmer & Glazewski, 2015).

In summary, this chapter provides a brief overview of the tenets and practices of problem-based learning; however, given the brevity of this chapter, we recommend that it be regarded as an introduction only. We certainly do not intend to give the impression that this chapter presents all the required information needed to design or implement a true PBL unit. As any PBL adopter will attest to, the degree of planning required, at least at first, is substantial (Czabanowska et al., 2012; Ertmer et al., 2009; Grant & Hill, 2006). Still, given the potential rewards in terms of both student engagement and learning (American Institutes for Research, 2014; Dochy et al., 2003; Swan et al., 2013), these initial investments of time and energy appear to be more than warranted. As our readers move forward, we encourage them to (1) build on the knowledge gained here by accessing additional, available resources that detail PBL implementation strategies, and (2) critically examine the research that documents evidence-based outcomes, with specific attention to the description of the environment in order to understand the essential elements that contribute to a robust, meaningful learning experience.

Summary of Key Principles

1. **The goals of PBL are twofold:** These goals are to promote students' deep understanding of discipline-based content and to support the development of higher-order thinking skills.

2. **Authentic complex problems are used to anchor the curriculum.** Within a PBL unit itself, a driving question provides both the purpose and motivation for students' learning—that is, it makes the hard work of complex problem solving worth the effort.

3. **PBL is distinguished from other problem-centered approaches, such as project- and case-based learning, in a variety of ways.** These include (1) its use of authentic, real (as opposed to realistic) problems; (2) its engagement of students in multidisciplinary problem solving *before* all the relevant knowledge is learned; (3) its employment of ill-structured nature of the problem to be solved; and (4) its focus on the development of a recommendation/solution for addressing the problem (as opposed to the development of single artifact).

4. **There are five main characteristics of PBL.** These include (1) the use of authentic ill-structured problems that are introduced before all the relevant content is learned; (2) the support for, and facilitation of, active self-directed student learning; (3) scaffolding of students' knowledge building; (4) cooperation and collaboration among teachers, students, and community members; and (5) authentic assessment of both process and product, including evidence-based recommendations for problem resolution.

5. **Scaffolds play an important role in supporting students' efforts during complex problem solving.**

6. **No one artifact can completely capture what is learned in PBL; multiple forms of assessment are needed.**

7. **Use of a PBL label does not necessarily equal a true PBL approach.** Given the wide variety of PBL implementations, consumers of PBL literature must pay close attention to authors' descriptions of the goals, context, and manner in which the implementation took place.

Application Questions

1. Consider the following descriptions, then classify each as an example of problem, project, or case-based learning and explain why you think it represents that approach.
   - Based on the assigned readings, choose one of the primary contributions of the Human Genome Project and create a representation detailing how that contribution came about.

   - Based on last week's work, read the account of how this genetic counselor advised the couple in this example, as well as their reactions to his advice. Provide a specific recommendation for the family, taking into account their unique risks for genetic disorders. Provide a list of pros and cons for your recommendation.

- As you will read, the plaintiff accuses the defendant of intentionally injecting her with HIV. What forms of evidence matter most? As a sitting jurist on this case, how would you use that evidence to influence your vote? (Adapted from Regassa, Cheeptham, & Shuster, 2013)

2. The roles that teachers and students play in a PBL context look different than they do in a traditional classroom environment. Create a chart that contrasts what a teacher/instructor does in a PBL classroom versus in a traditional classroom. As a starting point, consider the different characteristics of a PBL approach (see \#4 of the PBL principles) and then outline what a PBL teacher/instructor would need to do to successfully facilitate each component.

3. Consider the following scenario of a high school teacher who implemented a PBL unit in his ninth-grade biology class. Make recommendations for how Mr. Kaynor might improve the results obtained on the final assessment.

    To introduce his biology students to the topic of genetics, Mr. Kaynor designed a PBL unit around the question, "Should organizations be allowed to use personal genetic information to make decisions?" To ensure that different perspectives were considered during the unit, students were asked to assume the roles of different stakeholders (e.g., parent, lawyer, scientist, or religious leader). The final culminating activity was structured as a debate, with groups of students arguing the position of their assigned stakeholders. Results of the unit showed that students were highly engaged in the unit, and that, as a class, students performed significantly better on the teacher-created posttest than on the pretest. However, students who started with higher levels of previous knowledge didn't gain as much as those who started with lower levels, even though there was plenty of room for growth. In talking to Mr. Kaynor about this result, he thought that perhaps the culminating activity was not too effective and proposed eliminating this in the future.

    What are the potential pros and cons to this decision? What other strategies might the teacher consider for future implementations? How can Mr. Kaynor stay true to the PBL approach while assuring better learning outcomes?

4. Describe an inquiry-based approach that you have observed or experienced and classify it as problem-, project-, or case-based learning. Explain why it fits the category you selected.

References

American Institutes for Research. (2014). *Does deeper learning improve student outcomes?* Washington, DC: Author.

Andrews, D. H., Hull, T. D., & Donahue, J. A. (2009). Storytelling as an instructional method: Definitions and research questions. *Interdisciplinary Journal of Problem-Based Learning, 3*(2), 6–23. Retrieved from http://dx.doi.org/10.7771/1541-5015.1063

Barone, E., & Sattar, P. (2009). *Two problem-based learning cases: Methamphetamine.* National Institute on Drug Abuse. Retrieved from http://www.drugabuse.gov/sites/default/files/methamphetamine_0.pdf

Barrows, H. S. (1983). Problem-based, self-directed learning. *Journal of the American Medical Association, 250*(22), 3077–3080. Retrieved from http://dx.doi.org/10.1001/jama.250.22.3077

Barrows, H. S. (1986). A taxonomy of problem-based learning methods. *Medical Education, 20,* 481–486. Retrieved from http://dx.doi.org/10.1111/j.1365-2923.1986.tb01386.x

Barrows, H. S. (1996). Problem-based learning in medicine and beyond: A brief overview. *New Directions for Teaching and Learning, 68,* 3–12. Retrieved from http://dx.doi.org/10.1002/tl.37219966804

Barrows, H. S., & Tamblyn, R. M. (1980). *Problem-based learning: An approach to medical education.* New York: Springer.

Belland, B. R., Glazewski, K. D., & Richardson, J. C. (2011). Problem-based learning and argumentation: Testing a scaffolding framework to support middle school students' creation of evidence-based arguments. *Instructional Science, 39,* 667–694. Retrieved from http://dx.doi.org/10.1007/s11251-010-9148-z

Bereiter, C., & Scardamalia, M. (2000). Process and product in problem-based learning research. In D. H. Evensen & C. E. Hmelo (Eds.), *Problem-based learning: A research perspective on learning interactions* (pp. 185–195). Mahwah, NJ: Erlbaum.

Blumberg, P. (2000). Evaluating the evidence that problem-based learners are self-directed learners: A review of the literature. In D. Evensen, & C. E. Hmelo (Eds.), *Problem-based learning: A research perspective on learning interactions* (pp. 199–226). Mahwah, New Jersey: Lawrence Erlbaum Associates.

Bonamici, S. (2013). *Reps. Bonamici and Schock announce bipartisan congressional STEAM caucus.* Retrieved from http://bonamici.house.gov/press-release/reps-bonamici-and-schock-announce-bipartisan-congressional-steam-caucus

Boud, D. (Ed.). (1985). *Problem-based learning in education for the professions.* Sydney: Higher Education Research and Development Society of Australasia.

Brush, T., Glazewski, K., Shin, S., Shin, S., Jung, J., & Hogaboam, P. (2014). Iterative implementation of socio-scientific inquiry in high school biology: A teacher's perspective. Paper presented at the annual meeting of the Association for Educational Communication and Technology, Jacksonville, FL.

Czabanowska, K., Schröder-Bäck, P., Meijer, A. W. M., Moust, J. H. C., & Roebertsen, H. (2012). Problem-based learning revisited: Introduction of active and self-directed learning to reduce fatigue among students. *Journal of University Teaching & Learning Practice, 9*(1), 1–13.

Dochy, F., Segers, M., Van den Bossche, P., & Gijbels, D. (2003). Effects of problem-based learning: A meta-analysis. *Learning and Instruction, 13,* 533–568. Retrieved from http://dx.doi.org/10.1016/S0959-4752(02)00025-7

Edelson, D. C., Gordin, D. N., & Pea, R. D. (1999). Addressing the challenges of inquiry-based learning through technology and curriculum design. *Journal of the Learning Sciences, 8,* 391–450. doi:10.1080/10508406 .1999.9672075

Educate to Innovate. (n.d.). *Education: Knowledge and skills for the jobs of the future.* Retrieved from http://www.whitehouse.gov/issues/education/k-12/ educate-innovate

Edutopia. (2014). *Building rigorous projects that are core to learning.* Retrieved from http://www.edutopia.org/video/ core-to-learning-keys-pbl-series-2

Ertmer, P. A., & Glazewski, K. D. (2015). Essentials for PBL implementation: Fostering collaboration, transforming roles, and scaffolding learning. In A. Walker, H. Leary, C. Hmelo-Silver, & P. A. Ertmer (Eds.), *The essentials of problem-based learning: Exploring and extending the legacy of Howard S. Barrows* (pp. 89–106). West Lafayette, IN: Purdue University Press.

Ertmer, P. A., Glazewski, K. D., Jones, D., Ottenbreit-Leftwich, A., Goktas, Y., Collins, K., & Kocaman, A. (2009). Facilitating technology-enhanced problem-based learning (PBL) in the middle school classroom: An examination of how and why teachers adapt. *Journal of Interactive Learning Research, 20*(1), 35–54.

Ertmer, P. A., & Simons, K. D. (2006). Jumping the PBL implementation hurdle: Supporting the efforts of K–12 teachers. *Interdisciplinary Journal of Problem-based Learning, 1*(1). Retrieved from http://docs.lib.purdue .edu/ijpbl/vol1/iss1/5

Gijbels, D., Dochy, F., Van den Bossche, P., & Segers, M. (2005). Effects of problem-based learning: A meta-analysis from the angle of assessment. *Review of Educational Research, 75*(1), 27–61. Retrieved from http://dx.doi .org/10.3102/00346543075001027

Gijbels, D., van de Watering, G., & Dochy, F. (2005). Integrating assessment tasks in a problem-based learning environment. *Assessment & Evaluation in Higher Education, 30*(1), 73–86. Retrieved from http://dx.doi .org/10.1080/0260293042003243913

Gijselaers, W. H. (1996). Connecting problem-based practices with educational theory. *New Directions for Teaching and Learning, 68,* 13–21. Retrieved from http:// dx.doi.org/10.1002/tl.37219966805

Glazewski, K. D., Benson, J. B., Rutledge, D., & Zeisset, M. (2009, April). Designs for authentic engagement in virtual case study environments. Poster presented at the American Educational Research Association Annual Meeting, San Diego, CA.

Grant, M. M. (2011). Learning, beliefs, and products: Students' perspectives with project-based learning. *Interdisciplinary Journal of Problem-based Learning, 5*(2), 37–69. Retrieved from http://dx.doi.org/10.7771/1541-5015.1254

Grant, M. M., & Hill, J. R. (2006). Weighing the risks with the rewards: Implementing student-centered pedagogy within high-stakes testing. In R. Lambert & C. McCarthy (Eds.), *Understanding teacher stress in the age of accountability.* Greenwich, CT: Information Age.

Healy, M. (2005). Linking research and teaching: Exploring disciplinary spaces and the role of inquiry-based learning. In R. Barnett (Ed.), *Reshaping the university: New relationships between research, scholarship, and teaching* (pp. 67–68). New York: McGraw Hill/Open University Press.

Hmelo-Silver, C. E. (2004). Problem-based learning: What and how do students learn? *Educational Psychology Review, 16,* 235–266.

Hmelo-Silver, C. E., & Barrows, H. S. (2006). Goals and strategies of a problem-based learning faciliatator. *Interdisciplinary Journal of Problem-based Learning, 1*(1), 21–39. Retrieved from http://dx.doi .org/10.7771/1541-5015.1004

Hmelo-Silver, C. E., Duncan, R. G., & Chinn, C. A. (2007). Scaffolding and achievement in problem-based and inquiry learning: A response to Kirschner, Sweller, and Clark (2006). *Educational Psychologist, 42*(2), 99–107.

Jonassen, D. (2011). Supporting problem solving in PBL. *Interdisciplinary Journal of Problem-based Learning, 5*(2), 95–110. Retrieved from http://docs.lib.purdue.edu/ ijpbl/vol5/iss2/

Knowles, M. S. (1975). *Self-directed learning: A guide for learners and teacher*s. New York: Association Press.

Larmer, J., & Mergendoller, J. R. (2012). *Eight essentials for project-based learning.* Buck Institute for Education. Retrieved from http://bie.org/object/ document/8_essentials_for_project_based_learning

MacDonald, D., & Isaacs, G. (2001). Developing a professional identity through problem-based learning. *Teaching Education, 12,* 315–333. Retrieved from http://dx.doi .org/10.1080/10476210120096579

Mergendoller, J., & Thomas, J. W. (2005). *Managing project-based learning: Principles from the field.* Retrieved from http://www.bie.org/tmp/research/ researchmanagePBL.pdf

Mong, C., & Ertmer, P. A. (2013). Addressing STEM education needs: The case for adopting a PBL approach. *Educational Technology, 53*(3), 12–21.

Pea, R. D. (2004). The Social and Technological Dimensions of Scaffolding and Related Theoretical Concepts for Learning, Education, and Human Activity. *Journal of the Learning Sciences, 13*(3), 423–451.

Puntambekar, S., & Kolodner, J. L. (2005). Toward implementing distributed scaffolding: Helping students learn science from design. *Journal of Research in Science Teaching 42*(2), 185-217.

Ravitz, J. (2009). Introduction: Summarizing findings and looking ahead to a new generation of PBL research. *Interdisciplinary Journal of Problem-based Learning, 3*(1). Retrieved from http://docs.lib.purdue.edu/ijpbl/vol3/iss1/2

Regassa, L., Cheeptham, A., & Shuster, M. (2013). *Murder by HIV? Grades 5-8 Edition*. National Center for Case Study Teaching in Science. Retrieved from http://sciencecases.lib.buffalo.edu/cs/collection/detail.asp?case_id=672&id=672

Sandoval, W. A., & Millwood, K. A. (2011). The quality of students' use of evidence in written scientific explanations. *Cognition, 23*(1), 23–55. doi: 10.1207/s1532690xci2301_2

Saye, J. W., & Brush, T. (2002). Scaffolding critical reasoning about history and social issues in multimedia-supported learning environments. *Educational Technology Research and Development, 50*(3), 77–96. http://dx.doi.org/10.1007/BF02505026

Simons, K. D., & Klein, J. D. (2007). The impact of scaffolding and student achievement levels in a problem-based learning environment. *Instructional Science 35*(1), 41–72.

Stalker, S. L., Cullen, T., & Kloesel, K. (2015). Using PBL to prepare educators and emergency managers to plan for severe weather. *Interdisciplinary Journal of Problem-Based Learning, 9*(2). Retrieved from http://dx.doi.org/10.7771/1541-5015.1441

Stepien, W., & Gallagher, S. (1993). Problem-based learning: As authentic as it gets. *Educational Leadership, 50*(7), 25–28.

Strobel, J., & van Barneveld, A. (2009). When is PBL more effective? A meta-synthesis of meta-analyses comparing PBL to conventional classrooms. *Interdisciplinary Journal of Problem-based Learning, 3*(1), 44–58. Retrieved from http://dx.doi.org/10.7771/1541-5015.1046

Swan, K., Vahey, P., van 't Hooft, M., Kratcoski, A., Rafanan, K., Stanford, T., Yarnall, L., & Cook, D. (2013). Problem-based learning across the curriculum: Exploring the efficacy of a cross-curricular application of preparation for future learning. *Interdisciplinary Journal of Problem-based Learning, 7*(1). Retrieved from http://dx.doi.org/10.7771/1541-5015.1307

Tiwari, A., Lai, P., So, M., & Yuen, K. (2006). A comparison of the effects of problem-based learning and lecturing on the development of students' critical thinking. *Medical Education, 40*(6), 547–554. Retrieved from http://dx.doi.org/10.1111/j.1365-2929.2006.02481.x

van den Hurk, M. M., Wolfhagen, I. H., Dolmans, D. H., & van der Vleuten, C. P. (1999). The impact of student-generated learning issues on individual study time and academic achievement. *Medical Education, 33*(11), 808–814.

Wagner, T. (2012, August 14). *Graduating all students innovative ready*. Retrieved from http://www.tonywagner.com/resources/tonys-latest-ed-week-commentary-graduating-all-students-innovation-ready-now-available

Walker, A., & Leary, H. (2009). A problem-based learning meta analysis: Differences across problem types, implementation types, disciplines, and assessment levels. *Interdisciplinary Journal of Problem Based Learning, 3*(1). Retrieved from http://dx.doi.org/10.7771/1541-5015.1061

Whitehead, A. N. (1929). *The aims of education: And other essays*. New York: Macmillan.

Wirkala, C., & Kuhn, D. (2011). Problem-based learning in K–12 education: Is it effective and how does it achieve its effects? *American Educational Research Journal, 48*(5), 1157–1186. Retrieved from http://dx.doi.org/10.3102/000283121141949

Wood, D., Bruner, J. S., & Ross, G. (1976). The role of tutoring in problem solving. *Journal of Child Psychology and Psychiatry and Allied Disciplines, 17*, 89–100. Retrieved from http://dx.doi.org/10.1111/j.1469-7610.1976.tb00381.x

Wu, H-L., & Pedersen, S. (2011). Integrating computer- and teacher-based scaffolds in science inquiry. *Computers & Education, 57*, 2352–63. Retrieved from http://dx.doi.org/10.1016/j.compedu.2011.05.011

Chapter 35

Keep It Real: The Benefits of Authentic Tasks in Contemporary Learning Environments

Jan Herrington

Murdoch University

Thomas C. Reeves

The University of Georgia

Introduction

Spelling out in sufficient detail the learning design principles that instructional designers, performance technologists, and others can apply to develop and implement more effective learning environments for various educational and training purposes is a formidable task. There are many different instructional design models (Branch & Kopcha, 2014) as well as numerous learning designs (Beetham & Sharpe, 2013) to assist with this challenge. In this chapter, we identify the key elements of authentic learning environments, and then further explore the most critical of those elements—the design of authentic tasks—in greater depth. Task-based learning designs can enable and support powerful learning experiences allowing contemporary students and trainees, indeed all learners, to achieve a fuller range of cognitive (knowing), affective (caring), conative (willing), and psychomotor (performing) outcomes.

A Model of Authentic Learning

A pedagogical model of authentic learning, originally published in *Educational Technology Research and Development* in 2000 (Herrington & Oliver, 2000), and in subsequent years refined and published in the book *A Guide to Authentic e-Learning* (Herrington, Reeves, & Oliver, 2010) presented nine critical elements to guide the design of authentic learning environments. The research drew on the seminal work of key authors in situated learning and situated cognition, and other approaches based on constructivist philosophies such as anchored instruction (e.g., Brown, Collins, & Duguid, 1989; Cognition and

Technology Group at Vanderbilt, 1990; Lave & Wenger, 1991; McLellan, 1996). The framework is based on the proposition that usable knowledge is best gained in learning settings that feature the following characteristics (Herrington & Oliver, 2000). Authentic learning designs:

1. Provide authentic contexts that reflect the way the knowledge will be used in real life
2. Provide authentic tasks
3. Provide access to expert performances and the modelling of processes
4. Provide multiple roles and perspectives
5. Support collaborative construction of knowledge
6. Promote reflection to enable abstractions to be formed
7. Promote articulation to enable tacit knowledge to be made explicit
8. Provide coaching and scaffolding by the teacher at critical times
9. Provide for authentic assessment of learning within the tasks (Herrington et al., 2010, p. 18)

In further research, we investigated the second element of this model, authentic tasks, in more detail, determining ten specific learning design principles related to the design of authentic tasks (see Herrington et al., 2010; Herrington, Reeves, Oliver, & Woo, 2004 for cited research). These principles are:

1. **Authentic tasks should have real-world relevance.** The learning tasks set for learners should match as nearly as possible the real-world tasks of professionals in practice, rather than decontextualized or academic tasks.

2. **Authentic tasks should be ill defined, requiring learners to define the specific actions needed to complete the task, rather than use an existing rubric to do so.** The problems or tasks that learners are challenged to undertake should ideally be anchored in a context that approximates the complexity of the real world.

3. **Authentic tasks should require learners to investigate and accomplish them over a sustained period of time.** Tasks developed for learners should require work over days, weeks, and months rather than minutes or hours, thereby requiring significant investments of time, effort, and intellectual resources.

4. **Authentic tasks should provide opportunities for learners to examine the task from different perspectives, using a variety of resources.** The use of a variety of resources rather than a limited number of preselected materials requires students to distinguish relevant from irrelevant information and thus develop higher levels of information literacy as well as the enhanced technological fluency they will need to tackle new authentic tasks.

5. **Authentic tasks should provide the opportunity to collaborate.** Collaboration should be integral to the tasks that learners are challenged to complete because developing the ability to lead and work in groups is essential.

6. **Authentic tasks should provide the opportunity to reflect.** Tasks should be designed to enable learners to make choices and reflect on their learning both individually and socially by fostering self-reflection, meta-cognition, and self-regulated learning.

7. **Authentic tasks should ideally be integrated and applied across different subject areas and lead beyond domain-specific outcomes.** Tasks should be designed to encourage interdisciplinary perspectives and enable learners to play diverse roles, thus building robust expertise rather than knowledge limited to a single well-defined field or domain.

8. **Authentic tasks should be seamlessly integrated with assessment.** Assessment of how learners perform in the face of an authentic task should be seamlessly integrated with that major task in a manner that reflects real-world assessment, rather than separate artificial assessment removed from the nature of the task, and encompassing rich descriptions of the cognitive ("I know how to do this"), affective ("I desire to do this"), conative ("I am committed to doing this"), and psychomotor ("I physically can do this") progress made by these learners.

9. **Authentic tasks should encourage the development of polished products valuable in their own right rather than as preparation for something else.** The tasks set for learners should culminate in the creation of a whole product rather than an exercise or substep in preparation for something else, and ideally these products should contribute to society at large.

10. **Authentic tasks should allow competing solutions and diversity of outcomes.** Authentic tasks should allow a range and diversity of outcomes open to multiple solutions of an original nature, rather than a single correct response obtained by the application of specific rules and procedures; solutions should be subject to expert, peer, self, and public review, rather than subject to a predefined scoring scheme.

The authentic learning environment model originally developed by Herrington and Oliver (2000) provides an alternative learning design (or instructional model) that can be contrasted with a systems-oriented model such as Gagné's well-known "Nine Events of Instruction" model (Gagné, Briggs, & Wager, 1992). The Nine Events model arguably provides adequate guidance for the design and development of straightforward instruction with reference to a well-defined learning domain. But many important learning domains encompass higher-level objectives that require the capacity to solve ill-defined problems, and these types of complex objectives in turn call for the design and implementation of complex and realistic learning tasks within the learning environment.

Fortunately, tasks with the ten characteristics just listed do not have to be instantiated in the real world to be authentic. Herrington et al. (2010) delineate in great detail how these design principles can be extended to e-learning environments. Indeed, they can be delivered in a variety of ways including serious games, online learning simulations, mobile learning, and through other types of interactive learning environments. When these principles are applied successfully, the tasks will be perceived as "cognitively real" (Herrington, Reeves, & Oliver, 2007; Smith, 1987). Simulations and scenario-infused learning environments can effectively be presented as realistic contexts for the investigation of complex problems through authentic tasks.

Figure 35.1 illustrates the types of tasks that can be set in courses in relation to dimensions of task authenticity and setting (such as a real workplace or an on-campus classroom).

Most typically, tasks in universities sit in quadrant 1 (decontextualized tasks in an academic settings), where teachers set questions, essay topics, exercises, quizzes, and tests for students to complete in the educational setting. In quadrant 2, tasks are generally set by the teacher, and they are completed in a real setting, such as a worksheet on an excursion to a factory or on a field trip. Most practicums and internships occur in quadrant 3, where preservice professionals engage in the practices of the profession in the real workplace (authentic tasks in real settings).

Authentic tasks, as we define them here, inhabit quadrant 4 (authentic tasks in university settings), where the tasks that are created for students are not real responsibilities and jobs performed in a workplace setting, but they are "cognitively real" tasks (Smith, 1986; Smith, 1987). Smith (1987) in a review of research related to simulations concluded that the physical fidelity of the learning environment is of less importance than realistic problem-solving processes, a process Smith described as the "cognitive realism" of the task. In this sense, authentic tasks are realistic and complex tasks that can be completed in classrooms and educational institutions, giving students important opportunities to think as if in real problem-solving situations. Well-designed tasks create opportunities for students to think as if they were professionals faced with complex problems, where they need to reflect and decide how to act and behave.

Because authentic tasks yield realistic and polished products as outcomes, these learning environments usually require

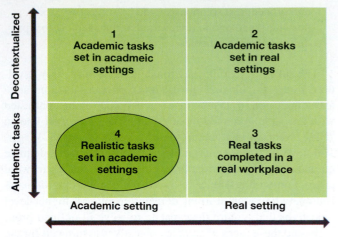

FIGURE 35.1 Types of tasks across dimensions of *authenticity* and *setting*.

considerable intellectual effort of learners working in collaboration with one another, as well as diligent on-task behavior. The investment of time and effort in these tasks exceeds the normal levels required by de-contextualized or academic exercises and tasks (Herrington & Herrington, 2006), and therefore some learners, especially those accustomed to being rewarded for their success on traditional tests and exams, may initially resist authentic task-based learning environments that require collaboration (Herrington, Oliver, & Reeves, 2003). But once they perceive the value of the kinds and depths of learning they are accomplishing, their resistance will fade away.

How Designers Go about Creating Authentic Learning Environments

Authentic learning environments and tasks can be designed in two key ways to ensure that important characteristics are not neglected. Firstly, the learning environment can be designed from scratch, where the scope of the curriculum is determined and authentic elements are designed from the beginning. The second method is to take an existing course of study, and redesign it to be more authentic. Each of these approaches is described in more detail in this section.

Designing a New Authentic Learning Environment

Designing a new authentic course can readily be accomplished using the following guidelines:

1. Determine the curriculum and scope, and the *aims and objectives* of the course. These steps are often completed in the planning and approval stages of a course, and are necessary to ensure that a course aligns with the overall program of study.
2. Use the *nine authentic learning elements* to act as a checklist for the design.
3. The most important element is *the design of the task* that students will complete. Use the design elements of authentic tasks provided earlier to guide the design. Don't

see the task as a separate kind of activity to test whether students have learned knowledge and skills that you will teach them, but as a vehicle for their own self-directed learning. Creating a task that can effectively "carry" all the aims of a course is a very difficult thing to do, but it is at the heart of the effectiveness of authentic learning because the pedagogy effectively resides in the task itself.

4. Ensure the *authentic context* is appropriate for the task. For example, the task might be for students to complete an occupational health and safety report, where the authentic context might be a simulated version of a workplace such as a restaurant, a laboratory, a building site, or an office. Or the task might be to complete a portfolio of works, where the authentic context might be an exhibition of art, an annotated collection of historical works, a series of mathematical proofs, or a sequence of activities for preschool children. The depiction of the context can range from the simple to the elaborate, from a paragraph description of the environment to a detailed simulated or computer-based representation.

5. When providing for *multiple perspectives* in the design of the learning environment, provide the opportunity for students to access a variety of resources to complete the task. This is readily accomplished with the vast array of resources available on the Internet, where an excess of resources is more likely to be the problem rather than a lack of them. Provide seminal resources as an indication of key relevant resources, but resist the temptation to assign chapters of the course textbook as the only resource students need. Students must be able to select resources themselves.

6. Access to *expert performance* can be provided for in a variety of ways, including the use of existing Internet expertise. However, this element may also include local resources—the teacher, and other students in the class who are perhaps only a little more knowledgeable than the target group. The more traditional lecture is a very appropriate example of expert performance, particularly if it is presented more in the style of a keynote address or TED talk (Gallo, 2015) than an instructional sequence.

7. In designing your learning environment, ensure that there are ample opportunities for students to *collaborate* on joint projects, to *articulates* their growing understanding—through speaking, defending their ideas, and writing—and to *reflect*, both in action (as they are engaging with the task) and on action (after the task is done) (Schön, 1987), as they complete their learning tasks.

8. When planning classes, ensure that there are opportunities for *scaffolding student learning* as they complete tasks. This needs to include one-to-one or one-to-group support so that assistance can be provided principally at the metacognitive level, rather than straightforward exposition of how to achieve a result.

9. *Authentic assessment* ensures that students are assessed on the products that they create rather than through separate testing. Shute (2011) calls this "stealth assessment," described as "a quiet, yet powerful process by which learner performance data are continuously gathered during the course of playing/learning and inferences are

made about the level of relevant competencies" (p. 504). Ensure that the task requires the creation of a polished and professional product that has value in its own right, and that these products can be shared, either through public display or dissemination on site, or through publication on Web 2.0 platforms. If marking or assessment by the teacher is the *only* life a learning product has, then the assessment is not truly authentic.

Such considerations will enable a more nuanced approach to the design of an authentic learning environment. In contrast to a systems approach to instructional design, the pedagogy resides not so much in the determination of the scope and sequence of a course and task analysis, but in the design of an authentic and meaningful task that determines the actions and approach—and essentially the learning—of students.

Revising an Existing Course for Authenticity

An existing course of study can be restructured to incorporate authentic elements, and often this can be achieved in a quite straightforward and effective way. A course that comprises weekly activities (often presented through a course learning management system, or LMS), together with lectures, recommended resources and a textbook, can form the basis of an authentic learning environment, but only if an authentic context, authentic task, and authentic assessment are added. In particular, an all-encompassing major task (or two or three substantial tasks) can be designed to provide a reason and purpose for instructional resources and events that already exist. Instead of weekly activities, grouped resources can be reorganized to support the more substantial tasks.

Case Studies

Examples of the application of authentic tasks as a defining pedagogy of an interactive learning environment can be found in many fields. For example, in the health field, Vesper, Herrington, Kartoğlu, and Reeves (2015) described how a twelve-week online course for public health personnel in developing countries was developed as an authentic task-based e-learning environment focused on managing the cold chain for vaccines and other perishable pharmaceuticals. Also in the health field, Sprod, Agostinho, and Harper (2009) used social networking, Web 2.0, and emerging communication technologies to support authentic self-management education for children living with type 1 diabetes. In business entrepreneurship, Lindsay and Wood (2015) used authentic tasks to facilitate creative problem-solving abilities. In the military, Ashford-Rowe, Herrington, and Brown (2014) describe how authentic assessment design principles were applied to military training. And in a professional development context, an authentic online course for higher education practitioners was designed and implemented aligning an authentic approach with the development of Garrison, Anderson and Archer's (2000) community of inquiry model (Parker, Maor, & Herrington, 2013).

The application of authentic tasks as a pedagogical approach has occurred in many other disciplines as well. Oh, Liu, and Reeves (2014) describe the application of authentic task design principles to the development and implementation of a graduate-level e-learning evaluation course. In history, Morrissey's (2006) *Not just a name on the wall* site, has students learn the history of World War I by researching a real soldier whose name is taken from a local memorial tower or plaque. In literature, students create a real online journal on *North American Fiction and Film* where they write, edit and review each other's papers (Fitzsimmons, 2006). In language learning, students learn the target foreign language of English (EFL) through the creation of a newsletter (Ozverir & Herrington, 2011). Authentic learning has also been used and researched across multicultural contexts in an examination of the use of authentic tasks across five countries (Leppisaari, Herrington, Vainio, & Im, 2013).

Educational and emerging technologies act as major facilitators in accomplishing the goals of authentic learning. Bozalek et al. (2013) describe how South African higher educators are using emerging technologies to achieve the characteristics of authentic learning.

An extended example of an authentic learning environment, where educational technologies are used as cognitive tools, has been implemented in a first-year preservice teacher course offered online and on campus (Herrington & Parker, 2013). In this fourteen-week semester course in an initial teacher education program, there is no attempt to explicitly teach students educational technologies and applications that may be useful in their future roles as teachers. Instead, students create genuinely useful products using educational technologies, and those technologies vary depending on the product that the student creates. Initially, all students create a website as a space to feature the products of the authentic tasks they undertake in the course, together with a personal blog to reflect on their learning throughout the course. The major authentic tasks focus first on the safe, responsible, and ethical use of the Internet; and second, on the creation of an authentic learning environment on a topic of their own choice. In the first task, students research responsible use of the Internet with particular reference to safe use by school-age children. They create a Web page to feature the findings of their research, and a poster suitable for displaying in a classroom. The second task requires students to choose a year level and subject for the creation of an authentic learning project. Students create the environment in a wiki, together with guidelines for teachers on how to implement it, and they make a short movie to describe the project they have produced.

Throughout the semester, students collaborate using the course learning management system (LMS), and through wikis, Skype chat, and a Diigo social bookmarking site. They principally access open educational resources (OERs) as almost all resources are outside the bounds of the LMS, which will be closed to students once they complete the course. All the products are shared on a website to allow the students access to a growing number of searchable authentic tasks when they are in teaching roles in practicums or in schools after graduation. These resources are not the typical assignments that have only a fleeting life during a period of study and are then assigned to the attic or the trash bin—they continue to provide inspiration to teachers over the years.

More and more courses are introducing authentic learning environments and tasks, as the benefits to students and teachers as learning partners become more evident. However, as discussed in the next section, there are some impediments to their widespread adoption.

Conclusion

A natural question that arises when we share our learning design ideas related to authentic tasks is: "If this approach is so powerful, why aren't more learning environments designed around authentic tasks?" Despite the intuitive appeal of authentic task-based learning environments, and the considerable evidence that they are effective in promoting learning (Herrington et al., 2010), developing an effective interactive learning environment with these characteristics may appear too complex or overly demanding for subject-matter experts as well as instructional designers. The promotion and support of authentic learning tasks in education and training may involve enhancing their visibility through providing appropriate representations of these learning designs online (such as the extensive resources provided at http://authenticlearning.info/).

The development of authentic tasks also requires teachers to adopt a less didactic, teacher-centered approach that can sometimes sit uncomfortably with their established roles. On first implementing the approach, the requirement to provide appropriate scaffolding is paramount, but at times teachers simply provide detailed advice without allowing students to experience the decision making and reflection that goes with establishing the path forward. De Bruijn and Leeman (2011, p. 699) suggest it is difficult to maintain a balance between guidance and letting students find their own way. At times, teachers respond too quickly to feedback on the challenging nature of the task by providing more detailed, step-by-step instructions on how to complete a task. Teräs and Herrington (2014) warn against such "jumping from the frying pan to the fire" in task design. In such circumstances, it is better to examine and adjust the level and nature of the scaffolding and support, rather than capitulate to a more "instructivist" solution.

In addition to these pedagogical considerations, more and better learning design research is needed. Although instructional designers per se may not be incentivized to conduct research on their own, faculty who teach in educational technology graduate programs certainly are. A relatively new approach called "educational design research" or "design-based research" encourages educational technology professors to collaborate with practitioners such as instructional designers and performance technologists to develop robust interactive learning environments while at the same time identifying reusable design principles (Reeves, Herrington, & Oliver, 2005). McKenney and Reeves (2012) provide detailed guidance for educational researchers and practitioners who seek to collaborate to develop effective, authentic, task-based learning environments and simultaneously refine the design principles underlying their designs.

Summary of Key Principles

1. **"Keep it real" is more than just a slogan.** It should serve as a reminder of the importance of infusing the design of learning environments with authentic tasks whenever possible.

2. **Realism rests more in the mind of the learner than in the media incorporated into the learning environment.** It is more important to focus on creating tasks and environments that are "cognitively real" (e.g., simple descriptions and images of realistic problems) rather than trying to recreate realistic and immersive computer-based simulations and serious games.

3. **Authentic tasks foster both "hands on" and "heads in" learning.** It is not enough just "to do" in order to learn. Reflection and meta-cognition must be encouraged by the design of the task-based learning environment.

4. **Authentic tasks require more time and dedication than traditional academic learning environments.** Time on task is critical to learning because despite what some pundits have claimed, "Learning is not easy or automatic." Meaningful learning requires commitment and effort. But if the tasks are truly authentic, most learners will be willing to invest the necessary level of effort.

5. **Assessment should be such a well-integrated part of the learning environment that learners perceive very little difference between when they are learning and when their work is being assessed.** Ensure that the learning task produces a professional product that is valuable in its own right, and that can be shared beyond the learning environment within which it was created.

Application Questions

1. The recidivism rate in America's prisons is extremely high, with more than three quarters of released prisoners imprisoned for new crimes within five years of release (Durose, Cooper, & Snyder, 2014). A major contributor to the recidivism rate is the lack of preparation for reentry into society experienced by most inmates. Many parolees lack basic literacy skills, marketable job skills, and the attitudes and intentions required for even the minimum-wage types of employment. Imagine that you work for an e-learning startup company that wants to apply for a $3 to $5 million grant from the U.S. Department of Justice to develop educational programming for prisoners with less than twelve months' time left on their sentences that will enhance core literacy competencies, provide key

skills for entry-level positions in information processing, and encourage the development of desirable work habits (e.g., showing up on time, exhibiting on-task behaviors, and the capacity to receive feedback concerning the need for improving job performance). How would you use the learning design principles related to authentic learning environments or, more specifically, tasks (presented at the beginning of this chapter) to prepare a high-level design plan for inclusion in your company's application for a grant from the U.S. Department of Justice?

2. When massive open online courses (MOOCs) first started making headlines in 2011–2012, it was predicted that people who lacked the financial or temporal means to avail themselves of traditional approaches to higher education would rush to take advantage of these free online courses in large numbers (Bonk, Lee, Reeves, & Reynolds, 2015). However, there is ample evidence that most of the people who successfully complete MOOCs are already highly educated (Emanuel, 2013; Jordan, 2014). Many of the MOOC providers such as edX and Coursera have their roots in elite higher education institutions such as Harvard, M.I.T., and Stanford (Pomerol, Epelboin, & Thoury, 2015). Suppose you are an instructional designer at a public community college that wants to begin providing MOOCs that will more successfully meet the professional development and learning needs of its population. The initial MOOC will be focused on "writing for business communications." Rather than a traditional writing course that focuses on grammar and mechanics, you and your design team desire to develop a highly engaging "authentic e-learning" environment for this MOOC. Prepare a preliminary design document that spells out how the design principles of authentic e-learning would be applied in this MOOC. In particular, propose several scenarios for how the MOOC could attain a desirable level of "cognitive realism" as described by Smith (1987).

3. Imagine that you are an instructional designer—on a large team together with faculty, designers, and developers—working on a project to redesign a course in research ethics. The course is currently offered across disciplines in master's programs at a large university, and it comprises a number of weekly modules based on readings and discussions. The course is assessed with an essay and a final examination. It has been running for many years without revision, but the university now wants a major overhaul to incorporate modern educational technologies. It wants the course to become a showcase for the university. As instructional designers for the project, how would you redesign the course as an authentic learning environment? Prepare an instructional design plan and presentation to put to the team at a planning day seminar.

References

Ashford-Rowe, K., Herrington, J., & Brown, C. (2014). Establishing the critical elements that determine authentic assessment. *Assessment & Evaluation in Higher Education, 39*(2), 205–222.

Beetham, H., & Sharpe, R. (2013). *Rethinking pedagogy for a digital age: Designing for 21st century learning* (2nd ed.). New York: Routledge.

Bonk, C. J., Lee, M., Reeves, T. C., & Reynolds, T. (Eds.). (2015). *MOOCs and open education around the world.* New York: Routledge.

Bozalek, V., Gachago, D., Alexander, L., Watters, K., Wood, D., Ivala, E., & Herrington, J. (2013). The use of emerging technologies for authentic learning: A South African study in Higher Education. *British Journal of Educational Technology, 44*(4), 629–638. doi: 10.1111/bjet.12046

Branch, R. M., & Kopcha, T. J. (2014). Instructional design models. In *Handbook of research on educational communications and technology* (pp. 77–87). New York: Springer.

Brown, J. S., Collins, A., & Duguid, P. (1989). Situated cognition and the culture of learning. *Educational Researcher, 18*(1), 32–42.

Cognition and Technology Group at Vanderbilt. (1990). Anchored instruction and its relationship to situated cognition. *Educational Researcher, 19*(6), 2–10.

de Bruijn, E., & Leeman, Y. (2011). Authentic and self-directed learning in vocational education: Challenges to vocational educators. *Teaching and Teacher Education, 27,* 694–702.

Durose, M. R., Cooper, A. D., & Snyder, H. N. (2014). *Recidivism of prisoners released in 30 states in 2005: Patterns from 2005 to 2010.* Washington, DC: Bureau of Justice Statistics.

Emanuel, E. J. (2013). Online education: MOOCs taken by educated few. *Nature, 503*(342). Retrieved from http://www.nature.com/nature/journal/v503/n7476/full/503342a.html

Fitzsimmons, J. (2006). Speaking snake: Authentic learning and the study of literature. In A. Herrington & J. Herrington (Eds.), *Authentic learning environments in higher education* (pp. 162–171). Hershey, PA: ISP.

Gagné, R. M., Briggs, L. J., & Wager, W. W. (1992) *Principles of instructional design* (3rd ed.). Fort Worth: Harcourt Brace Jovanovich.

Gallo, C. (2015). *Talk like TED: The 9 public speaking secrets of the world's top minds.* New York: St. Martin's Griffin.

Garrison, D. R., Anderson, T., & Archer, W. (2000). Critical inquiry in a text based environment: Computer referencing in higher education. *The Internet and*

Higher Education, 2(2-3), 87–105. doi: http://dx.doi .org/110.1016/S1096-7516(1000)00016-00016

Herrington, J., & Herrington, A. J. (2006). Authentic conditions for authentic assessment: aligning task and assessment. In A. Bunker & I. Vardi (Eds.), *Proceedings of the 2006 Annual International Conference of the Higher Education Research and Development Society of Australasia Inc (HERDSA): Critical Visions: Thinking, Learning and Researching in Higher Education*, Volume 29 (pp. 141–151). Milperra, NSW: HERDSA.

Herrington, J., & Oliver, R. (2000). An instructional design framework for authentic learning environments. *Educational Technology Research and Development, 48*(3), 23–48.

Herrington, J., Oliver, R., & Reeves, T. (2003). Patterns of engagement in authentic online learning environments. *Australian Journal of Educational Technology, 19*(1), 59–71.

Herrington, J., & Parker, J. (2013). Emerging technologies as cognitive tools for authentic learning. *British Journal of Educational Technology, 44*(4), 607–615. doi: 10.1111/ bjet.12048

Herrington, J., Reeves, T. C., & Oliver, R. (2007). Immersive learning technologies: Realism and online authentic learning. *Journal of Computing in Higher Education, 19*(1), 80–99. doi: 10.1007/BF03033421

Herrington, J., Reeves, T. C., & Oliver, R. (2010). *A guide to authentic e-learning*. New York: Routledge.

Herrington, J., Reeves, T. C., Oliver, R., & Woo, Y. (2004). Designing authentic activities in web-based courses. *Journal of Computing in Higher Education, 16*(1), 3–29.

Jordan, K. (2014). Initial trends in enrollment and completion of massive open online courses. *The International Review of Research in Open and Distributed Learning, 15*(1). Retrieved from http://www.irrodl.org/index.php/ irrodl/article/view/1651

Lave, J., & Wenger, E. (1991). *Situated learning: Legitimate peripheral participation*. Cambridge: Cambridge University Press.

Leppisaari, I., Herrington, J., Vainio, L., & Im, Y. (2013). Authentic e-learning in a multicultural context: Virtual benchmarking cases from five countries. *Journal of Interactive Learning Research, 24*(1), 961–970.

Lindsay, N., & Wood, D. (2015). Facilitating creative problem solving in entrepreneurship curriculum through authentic learning activities. In V. Bozalek, D. Ng'ambi, D. Wood, J. Herrington, J. Hardman & A. Amory (Eds.), *Activity theory, authentic learning, and emerging technologies: Towards a transformative higher education pedagogy* (pp. 92–101). New York: Routledge.

McKenney, S. E., & Reeves, T. C. (2012). *Conducting educational design research*. New York: Routledge.

McLellan, H. (Ed.). (1996). *Situated learning perspectives*. Englewood Cliffs, NJ: Educational Technology Publications.

Morrissey, P. (2006). Not just a name on the wall. Retrieved from http://www.notjustanameonawall.com/

Oh, E., Liu, Y., & Reeves, T. C. (2014). Supporting adult learners' authentic learning experience by optimizing collaborative group work in distance learning courses. In A. P. Mizell & A. A. Piña (Eds.), *Real life distance education: Case studies in research and practice* (pp. 139–158). Charlotte, NC: Information Age Publishing.

Ozverir, I., & Herrington, J. (2011). Authentic activities in language learning: Bringing real world relevance to classroom activities. In T. Bastiaens & M. Ebner (Eds.), *Proceedings of EdMedia 2011* (pp. 1423–1428). Chesapeake, VA: AACE.

Parker, J., Maor, D., & Herrington, J. (2013). Authentic online learning: Aligning learner needs, pedagogy and technology. *Issues in Educational Research, 23*(2), 227–241.

Pomerol, J. C., Epelboin, Y., & Thoury, C. (2015). *MOOCs: Design, use and business models*. New York: John Wiley & Sons.

Reeves, T. C., Herrington, J., & Oliver, R. (2005). Design research: A socially responsible approach to instructional technology research in higher education. *Journal of Computing in Higher Education, 16*(2), 96–115.

Schön, D. (1987). *Educating the reflective practitioner:Toward a new design for teaching and learning in the professions*. San Francisco: Jossey Bass.

Shute, V. J. (2011). Stealth assessment in computer-based games to support learning. *Computer Games and Instruction, 55*(2), 503–524.

Smith, P. E. (1986). *Instructional simulation: Research, theory, and a case study*. ERIC Document Reproduction Service No. 267 753.

Smith, P. E. (1987). Simulating the classroom with media and computers. *Simulation and Games, 18*(3), 395–413.

Sprod, R., Agostinho, S., & Harper, B. (2009). A dialogic approach to online facilitation. In *Same places, different spaces: Proceedings ascilite Auckland 2009* (pp. 1008–1012). Auckland, NZ: Ascilite.

Teräs, H., & Herrington, J. (2014). Neither the frying pan nor the fire: In search of a balanced authentic e-learning design through an educational design research process. *The International Review of Research in Open and Distance Learning, 15*(2). Retrieved from http://www.irrodl .org/index.php/irrodl/article/view/1705

Vesper. J. L., Herrington, J., Kartoğlu, U., & Reeves, T. C. (2015). Initial design principles for establishing a learning community for public health professionals through authentic e-learning. *International Journal of Continuing Engineering Education and Life-Long Learning, 25*(2), 241–257.

Chapter 36

Professional Ethics: Rules Applied to Practice

Sharon E. Smaldino

Northern Illinois University

Mary Herring

University of Northern Iowa

J. Ana Donaldson

University of Northern Iowa

Oftentimes, professionals in a particular field are unaware or do not have a clear picture of the code or rules that govern professional behavior in their field. In order to address this problem, many profession organizations have generated *ethical codes* by which they expect their members to practice. "The code of ethics provides direction for daily practice and a basis for understanding and interpreting the ethical implications of a variety of issues which may confront today's practitioner" (Seels & Richey, 1994, p. 107).

One of the key ideas supported by Clark (1995) is the need for an open dialog regarding ethics. Ethical considerations need to be incorporated into IT programs of study and need to go beyond limiting discussion to the legality of copyright and fair use issues. As IT professionals we are bound to the ideal of balancing our knowledge of new and advanced technologies with the integrity of design and implementation criteria (Lucivero, Swierstra, & Boernink, 2011). In a dynamic technology environment, it is easy to become a faceless individual without consideration of the consequences surrounding the moral, legal, and social issues surrounding a professional (Tavani, 2013).

When learning about IT responsibilities, Clark (1995) has suggested several elements necessary for developing and understanding ethical competencies. The initial step is defined as identifying the pitfalls that may be encountered when dealing with situations that include ethical issues. An example of an ethical dilemma might address the situation of a professor posing as a student to encourage discussion in an online course. The pitfall is that the professor's intention may be perceived as a way to encourage students to engage in a dialog, but is actually a misrepresentation of himself to his students. Sometimes

we can learn best by the examples of how not to do something. Clark encourages the use of unethical examples to foster further awareness. The aforementioned scenario of the professor posing as a student is an example of the use of this type of strategy.

The Association for Educational Communications and Technology (AECT) has generated a definition of the field that serves to guide the association's influence in professional practice. Refer to Figure 36.1 for the full AECT Code of Ethics. In examining the evolution of the definition of the field, ethics has been a term repeated over time, but until recently had not been included within the actual definition, although it has been expected within the practice of member professionals. The most recent iteration of the AECT Definition (AECT Definitions and Terms, 2008) has included ethical practice in the definition: "Educational technology is the study and *ethical practice* of facilitating learning and improving performance by creating, using, and managing appropriate technological processes and resources" (p. 1). However, even before the addition of the specific reference to ethical practice, the association has been a leader in establishing and supporting the implementation of a code of ethics by which members are expected to engage in their IT practice.

It is with this idea of an organizational code of professional ethics in mind, that in this chapter you will have the opportunity to review examples of ethical dilemmas in our profession. and reflect upon how the implementation of the AECT Code of Ethics can influence your practice in each situation. The AECT Code of Ethics includes three sections: Commitment to the Individual, Commitment to Society, and Commitment to Profession. In this chapter, each section will be introduced by a thought-provoking scenario. Questions to initiate discussion

Preamble

1. The Code of Professional Ethics contained herein shall be considered to be principles of ethics. These principles are intended to aid members individually and collectively in maintaining a high level of professional conduct.
2. The Professional Ethics Committee will build documentation of opinion (interpretive briefs or ramifications of intent) relating to specific ethical statements enumerated herein.
3. Opinions may be generated in response to specific cases brought before the Professional Ethics Committee.
4. Amplification and/or clarification of the ethical principles may be generated by the Professional Ethics Committee in response to a request submitted by a member.
5. Persons with concerns about ethical matters involving members of AECT should contact the Chair.

Section 1—Commitment to the Individual

In fulfilling obligations to the individual, the member:

1. Shall encourage independent action in an individual's pursuit of learning and shall provide access to varying points of view.
2. Shall protect the individual rights of access to materials of varying points of view.
3. Shall guarantee to each individual the opportunity to participate in any appropriate program.
4. Shall conduct professional business so as to protect the privacy and maintain the personal integrity of the individual.
5. Shall follow sound professional procedures for evaluation and selection of materials, equipment, and furniture/carts used to create educational work areas.
6. Shall make reasonable efforts to protect the individual from conditions harmful to health and safety, including harmful conditions caused by technology itself.
7. Shall promote current and sound professional practices in the use of technology in education.
8. Shall in the design and selection of any educational program or media seek to avoid content that reinforces or promotes gender, ethnic, racial, or religious stereotypes. Shall seek to encourage the development of programs and media that emphasize the diversity of our society as a multicultural community.
9. Shall refrain from any behavior that would be judged to be discriminatory, harassing, insensitive, or offensive and, thus, is in conflict with valuing and promoting each individual's integrity, rights, and opportunity within a diverse profession and society.

Section 2—Commitment to Society

In fulfilling obligations to society, the member:

1. Shall honestly represent the institution or organization with which that person is affiliated, and shall take adequate precautions to distinguish between personal and institutional or organizational views.
2. Shall represent accurately and truthfully the facts concerning educational matters in direct and indirect public expressions.
3. Shall not use institutional or Associational privileges for private gain.
4. Shall accept no gratuities, gifts, or favors that might impair or appear to impair professional judgment, or offer any favor, service, or thing of value to obtain special advantage.
5. Shall engage in fair and equitable practices with those rendering service to the profession.
6. Shall promote positive and minimize negative environmental impacts of educational technologies.

Section 3—Commitment to the Profession

In fulfilling obligations to the profession, the member:

1. Shall accord just and equitable treatment to all members of the profession in terms of professional rights and responsibilities, including being actively committed to providing opportunities for culturally and intellectually diverse points of view in publications and conferences.
2. Shall not use coercive means or promise special treatment in order to influence professional decisions of colleagues.
3. Shall avoid commercial exploitation of the person's membership in the Association.
4. Shall strive continually to improve professional knowledge and skill and to make available to patrons and colleagues the benefit of that person's professional attainments.
5. Shall present honestly personal professional qualifications and the professional qualifications and evaluations of colleagues, including giving accurate credit to those whose work and ideas are associated with publishing in any form
6. Shall conduct professional business through proper channels.
7. Shall delegate assigned tasks to qualified personnel. Qualified personnel are those who have appropriate training or credentials and/or who can demonstrate competency in performing the task.
8. Shall inform users of the stipulations and interpretations of the copyright law and other laws affecting the profession and encourage compliance.
9. Shall observe all laws relating to or affecting the profession; shall report, without hesitation, illegal or unethical conduct of fellow members of the profession to the AECT Professional Ethics Committee; shall participate in professional inquiry when requested by the Association.
10. Shall conduct research using professionally accepted guidelines and procedures, especially as they apply to protecting participants from harm.

First adopted in 1974, adherence to the AECT Code became a condition of membership in 1984. This version was approved by the AECT Board of Directors on November 2007. Persons with concerns about ethical matters involving members of AECT should contact the Chair Professional Ethics Committee (Code of Professional Ethics, n.d., p. 1).

FIGURE 36.1 Code of Professional Ethics.

prior to review of the section are provided. The chapter concludes with an overview from the Code of Ethics, offering you the opportunity to again consider each situation through the lens of the professional code.

Commitment to the Individual

Angela was at a loss as to which way to turn. She was the most recently hired instructional designer to the firm and didn't want to make waves; however, something just didn't feel right to her. Her boss, Cecil Wright, had come back from a lunch meeting with his favorite vendor and showed her his new tablet that had been given to him. Cecil was convinced that this new type of tablet was the answer to all the recurring problems within the accounting department staff who were dealing with outdated and slowly responding desktop computers. When Angela timidly asked about the advantages of this technology, Cecil stated the vendor had provided him with all their research reports stating the value of the new tablets. He ordered Angela to begin writing the justification document for ordering twenty-four of the new tablets.

What Should Angela Do?

What are the ethical issues that might be involved in this situation? What are some of the questions that Angela might ask? What approach might be the best for Angela at this time?

The first section in the AECT Code of Ethics, which addresses the commitment to the individual from a professional perspective, provides some guidance that might be useful in this situation. The nine indicators in this section can be grouped into three encompassing categories in relationship to the IT professional: technology and resources, diversity, and personal rights.

Technology and Resources. As IT professionals, we are often requested to make decisions regarding the technology and resources that are implemented as part of the ID process. As expected, the ethical code also addresses issues related to choices regarding the selection, implementation, and evaluation of technology and related educational resources. Questions to be considered might include: Does this selected resource ensure that the learner can meet the stated instructional goals? Have all alternatives for technology use been considered? Have the evaluation results been accurately reported, and have they led to suggestions for revisions? When dealing with technology, health and safety concerns are of paramount importance. It is important to ensure that all learners in an instructional setting have a safe environment in which to learn. Some ethical issues have included the need for ergonomically correct work stations, CRT screens that do not induce seizures, and safety instructions for meeting the needs of color-blind students, to name just a few.

Diversity. In today's world of cultural influences and technological change, diversity goes beyond the recognition of our place as a profession within the global community. The concept of diversity also extends to how we learn and how we design and create instruction. The ethical code encourages the practice of allowing individuals to acquire knowledge on their own terms from a variety of resources. It is important to keep in mind that the journey to reach a learning goal may have many paths to the final destination. An example of this concept is the obligation to create a learning situation that allows for an open discussion of various ideas that may differ from those held by the instructor. Another area of awareness regarding diversity is the concept of avoiding the use of images or discussions that negatively stereotype individuals.

Personal Rights. The third category of indicators within this section looks at the various aspects of what can be termed "personal rights." One way of thinking about personal rights is to consider them in terms of the individual within the field as well as the professional rights of other colleagues and those of our "clients." The IT professional needs to treat all individuals regarding privacy within the framework of personal integrity. And above all else, the IT professional will not behave in a manner that will infringe upon another's individual rights within our diverse profession and global community.

Commitment to Society

Donald and LaShandra are collaborating on the preparation of a grant, which involves working with area school districts as part of the requirements of the proposal. In addition, there is the expectation that at least one corporate sponsor be a participant in the grant activities. Donald has a good friend who works for XYZ Company, a distributor for technology in the region. He suggests to LaShandra that because of his connections he can get a "good deal" from that company, which will help them in putting together a budget. His idea is that they won't have to spend as much of the budget on technology and can use that amount of money for their own stipend as grant preparers. He is also sure that his friend can arrange to provide some additional materials for free if the grant is awarded.

What Should LaShandra Do?

Referring to the AECT Code of Ethics on Commitment to Society, would this be a code violation or simply a reasonable way to address the issues within the preparation of the grant? What are some of the questions that LaShandra should ask? What approach might be the best for LaShandra at this time?

The second section of the Code of Professional Ethics addresses the practice of instructional technology from a societal perspective. IT professionals regularly have the opportunity to make choices in their professional activities. These activities can often involve working with others external to one's personal workplace. Societal ethics help to shape the way individuals and groups relate to one another. By following ethical principles the individual can help maintain societal order regarding interactions with learners and colleagues (Yeaman, Eastmond, & Naper, 2008). The six indicators in this section can be grouped into three categories: representation, personal gain, and professional service.

Representation. The code requires that representation of professional activities and experience be honest and forthright in a professional's documentation of expertise and experience. As well, the principles direct that one must attribute clearly the source of fact, finding, or personal opinion, whether it is in a written document or an interpersonal communication. Care should be taken when considering the sharing of professional information in a formal or informal setting and its impact on an organization. Discussion of a professional consultation with someone on the flight home from a site visit would not be appropriate as the consultation is an agreement between you and the client, not the public.

Personal gain.   When opportunities for personal gain are offered to you as an IT professional, be careful to delineate between personal and professional activities. Many institutions identify appropriate activities that contribute to personal remuneration; these guidelines must be adhered to at all times. Using accrued sick days to put on an offsite workshop for which you are paid would not be appropriate. Personal gain should not be at the expense of an employer or the association. Additionally, gifts or payments should not be accepted if the intent could be perceived as influencing professional judgment. Often, those who work for a public institution will find language that limits the specific dollar amount of a gift.

Professional service.   Work with an association might place you in a position that solicits contributions from outside vendors in support of activities such as a yearly conference. The commitment to society principles remind us that there is a need to hold tight to any obligations made in soliciting service to the organization. To not do so could jeopardize all future negotiations and disrupt the organizational function. As well, decisions about the application of educational technology should promote its effective use and minimize any negative impact that might be derived from the use. There is an expectation that anticipated outcomes be considered before implementation and that they be clearly articulated. For example, before submitting a grant proposal, a professional grant writer must communicate with grant partners about the intended outcomes and use of the technology that will be included among the items that will be purchased if the grant proposal is funded. Technology implementation should ensure responsible and effective benefits for all participants.

Commitment to the Profession

> *Dwight has been posting a monthly blog about the successes and challenges of being an instructional designer. As he was reading an article in one of the top instructional design-focused journals, he found an article that contained some very familiar suggestions for overcoming barriers to success. It appeared to Dwight that the author had gone back through his blog postings and used his ideas to develop the article, without citing Dwight's original work.*

What Should Dwight Do?

As the author of a blog, what recourse might Dwight have regarding the co-opting of his work? Which parts of the AECT Code of Ethics Commitment to the Profession provide guidance as to what recourse he might or might not have available? What would you tell him should be his next steps?

You are encouraged, as an IT professional, to address professional commitment by examining ways in which to become a proactive, responsible member of the profession. Professionals

should continually contribute to the overall understanding of practitioners' ethical practice. To that end, within category three: Commitment to the Profession, are ten indicators that represent the three major themes of professional interactions, research and dissemination, and responsibilities related to copyright.

Professional interactions.   The overall intent of the professional interactions aspect of the code is to consider the ways in which you can relate with other members of the profession and more specifically with those who are members of AECT. There is a direct connection within this category to those actions that are considered appropriate behavior toward others.

Fundamentally, the individual has the responsibility to make conscious decisions about the appropriateness of interactions with others, as colleagues and as AECT members. You need to consider the consequences of your actions as a part of the decision process, as well as the benefits of engaging in ethical behavior with other professionals. There may well be times when you determine it best for the profession to conduct yourself in a particular manner that might affect your association with other professionals. This decision is considered to be one of value to the profession as a whole rather than to a specific individual.

One role a professional is obligated to assume by the code of ethics is that of reporting on the inappropriate behaviors of others to the AECT Ethics Committee. This is often an uncomfortable responsibility, but needs to be considered one of value and importance to ensure quality among all those who represent the profession. While engaged in the reporting process every effort is made to maintain discretion regarding the privacy of personal information. As an IT professional you need to be comfortable with the understanding that these types of alerts to the AECT Ethics Committee are not viewed as vindictive or an attempt to disgrace another, but rather an effort to ensure that all who participate in the field embrace the professional values and practices that are accepted by all AECT members and the profession as a whole.

Research and dissemination.   The individual's commitment to the profession is measured by ways in which research can advance the knowledge and skills of members and our field's theoretical framework. While not clearly stated in the code, it is assumed that an individual will adhere to the governance of a review board, such as an institutional review board (IRB) of a university, to ensure that the conduct of the research is within the approved standards. Further, it is considered the responsibility of the individual to engage in a line of inquiry that will benefit the overall knowledge of the profession, but not when a level of risk to the participants is applied. In other words, as an IT professional you will ensure the protection of participants as part of the research plan and implementation.

A member who engages in scholarly inquiry is obliged to share the results of that aspect of the research that will provide benefit to the overall understanding of the field by all members of the association. There are multiple ways for sharing this knowledge. For example, your research results can be disseminated through presentations at conferences, publishing articles in journals, and teaching others in coursework or training venues. The mutual benefit of this professional collegiality for sharing research results can be used to advance knowledge within the profession.

Responsibilities related to copyright. Clearly articulated within the commitment to the profession is an adherence to the copyright law and the assurance of responsibility to inform others of the regulations of the law. An example of this adherence is properly citing image sources in a multimedia production or being able to identify the difference between paraphrasing and plagiarizing in a student assignment. This aspect of the commitment serves to ensure that the professional is informed about the nuances of copyright and how it applies within various types of situations. The requirement to inform others is that part of the professional code of ethics that may cause you concern since it implies an obligation to enforce legal issues. Informing others of their obligations to follow copyright is construed to be educational in nature, suggesting that when you observe a violation of copyright, it is your obligation as an IT professional to not only inform an individual of the issue at hand, but to make an effort to help that person understand the rationale for the copyright rules.

Developing Ethical Competence

A concluding element identified by Clark (1995) is in the area of achieving ethical competency. Clark defines this competency as the encouragement of ethical self-examination. Ethics, by definition, can have a very subjective focus as we put our values into practice. Many of the ethical decisions we have to make are not black and white; they are grey and fuzzy. It is often difficult to make such decisions. Clark suggests that after we do so, we should reflect upon how we came to that decision. He indicates that this reflective activity can transform the way we go about arriving at other ethical decisions. Thus, Clark encourages us to engage in this transformative reflection process in order to learn from our actions and grow as IT professionals.

The authors also add to Clark's competency list the overt modeling and mentoring of ethical practice. As students, instructors, and practicing IT professionals, we need to be aware that our practice reflects the field we represent. Our use of the AECT Code of Professional Ethics is what identifies us as a profession and continues to set us apart.

Summary of Key Principles

1. **A code of professional ethics promotes ethical practice in a profession.** By examining the code of ethics, a professional can identify how it fits into daily practice.

2. **The new AECT definition has included the term *ethical practice* for the first time.** By adding ethical practice to the definition of the field, AECT has prominently addressed the importance of ethical practice for the professional.

3. **The AECT Code of Ethics includes three sections: Commitment to the Individual, Commitment to Society, and Commitment to the Profession.** The code can serve as a guide for the professional when making difficult decisions.

4. **It is important to recognize how the code of ethics looks in practice.** Analysis of the components of a code of ethics offers the opportunity to recognize how implementation looks in practice.

5. **Providing guidelines for ethical competence is a means for helping the IT professional incorporate the code of ethics into daily practice.** Knowledge of the code of ethics is not sufficient when exploring the responsibilities of the IT professional, it must be integrated into practice.

Application Questions

1. **Free Expression in Cyberspace** (Location: private college): Dr. Leslie Brown has instituted a blog for her Introduction to Emerging Technology course. Her intent is to provide a forum for her students to express themselves regarding their views on the discussion topics within the course. Dr. Brown does not grade the student blog entries, although she does use them as guides for discussions within the course. She also provides students the option of anonymous postings, although she has a way of identifying those individuals. Recently, several student postings have been highly controversial regarding copyright issues in virtual worlds. College officials are concerned about the postings and how they reflect on the university. The officials have asked Dr. Brown to discontinue the use of the blog. Also, they have asked for the names of the students who posted anonymously.

   What should Dr. Brown do about the use of the blog for her course? Should she provide the officials with the names of students? What alternatives does she have in order to be able to have her students exchange ideas?

2. **Intellectual Property Issue** (Location: Somewhere University): Joel is a tenure-track faculty member who is concerned about his faculty evaluations. He has been teaching a course in Web page design since beginning to work at Somewhere University. Joel has noted in the past that some of his students have liberally "borrowed" code from existing Web pages. He realizes that he needs

to change this behavior, but he also wants his students to be successful since he believes that this will result in positive faculty evaluations.

How can Joel phrase his guide to students about the inappropriate use of "borrowed" code in their assignments? Should he introduce his students to copyright and intellectual property rights? What penalty should he introduce when students do "borrow" code from existing Web pages?

3. **Plagiarism** (Application: textbook): Dr. Carl Smythe collaborated with a colleague, Dr. Jane Black, on a book that served as a guidebook on new teaching strategies for practicing teachers. This guidebook was published through a professional association for teachers. While not broadly distributed, it did carry a copyright date and ISBN number. Dr. Black collaborated with another colleague (also someone who knows Dr. Smythe) to author a textbook, also about teaching strategies, which was published by a major textbook publishing company. When the textbook was released, Dr. Smythe noted that large sections of the guidebook had been slightly paraphrased within a chapter of the textbook, with some images being exactly the same. Although there was a citation to Drs. Smythe and Black for the guidebook, the textbook authors did not use quotations to note directly quoted material nor did they receive permission to use the images that they copied from the guidebook.

Since Dr. Smythe worked with Dr. Black, who shared authorship between the two publications, how should he approach this issue? What recourse does Dr. Smythe have regarding the issue of plagiarism in the textbook? What steps can be taken with future editions of the guidebook to ensure that this might not occur again?

4. **Insensitive behavior:** As project manager, Kesha Layton has enjoyed her leadership role and responsibilities for two newly hired instructional designers. Everett and Dale were showing potential as contributing team members and seemed to be working well with the clients and other team members. At lunch one day, Ms. Layton was sitting at a table out of view of the two new employees who were conversing in loud voices. "I can't believe what a pain Kesha has been. She thinks she knows everything and is demanding that we track all our hours on the time sheet by task. I never thought I would have to be working with a woman boss who is older than my mother. What a pain."

What should Ms. Layton do? As project manager, what options does Ms. Layton have as to what to do about this overheard private conversation? Would this be an example of an ethical violation or simply a management situation that needs to be addressed? What are the possible results if Ms. Layton chooses to ignore the conversation?

References

Association for Educational Communications and Technology. (2008). *Educational technology: A definition with commentary.* Edited by A. Januszewski & M. Molenda. New York: Laurence Erlbaum Associates.

Clark, C. M. (1995). *Thoughtful teaching.* London: Cassell.

Lucivero, F., Swierstra, T., & Boenink, M. (2011). Assessing expectations: towards a toolbox for an ethics of emerging technologies. *NanoEthics, 5*(2), 129–141.

Seels, B., & Richey, R. (1994). *Instructional technology: The definition and domains of the field.* Washington,

DC: Association for Educational Communications and Technology.

Tavani, H. (2013). *Ethics and technology: Controversies, questions, and strategies for ethical computing* (4th ed.). Hoboken, NJ: John Wiley and Sons.

Yeaman, A. R., Eastmond, Jr., J. N., & Naper, V. S. (2008). Professional ethics and educational technology. In A. Januszewski & M. Molenda (Eds.), *Educational technology: A definition with commentary* (pp. 283–326). New York: Lawrence Erlbaum Associates.

Chapter 37
Diversity and Accessibility

Joél Lewis
Stephen Sullivan
University of South Alabama

According to The Statistics Portal (2015), approximately 1.5 billion people in the world speak English; however, only 375 million are native English speakers. The United Nations Population Fund (2014) reports there are about 1.8 billion youth between the ages of ten and twenty-four, which is the largest youth population ever. Language and age are not the only changing demographics in the world. According to the United Nations Department of Economic and Social Affairs (2013), there are over 232 million international migrants in the world. The same department of the United Nations (2015) reported that people with diverse abilities should have the basic human right of equal access to information and equal opportunity to utilize communications technology. Facts like these make a case for the need of diversity and accessibility in instructional design.

So, what do these data indicate? The implications for advances in technology use, designing language options, emphasis of accessibility guidelines, and diversity training are opportunities for the field of instructional design. The data suggest that the human composition of businesses, institutions, schools, health care agencies, workplaces, and learning environments are constantly changing to include interactions between people with various perspectives, backgrounds, expectations, needs, work experience, culture, values, prior knowledge, etc. Differences such as these are how we define diversity for this chapter. Our view of diversity also has been shaped by learning from personal experiences at work, in school, and during social interactions where we were the minority and found it necessary to adapt to be successful. For us, Joél (an African American woman) and Stephen (a man with vision impairment), diversity is a concept we have attended to all our lives and continues to be at the heart of our efforts to contribute to learning communities by increasing global competency, creating diverse collaborations, and making learning accessible to all.

In reality, there is more to explore about how increasingly different learners are becoming and how diversity impacts the way people learn. Creating instruction with design considerations that more adequately incorporate diversity helps to address that reality. Accordingly, the two goals of this chapter are (1) to present design considerations for universal design as it relates to ability and multiculturalism, and (2) to propose a model of multimodal instruction as an integral part of a comprehensive strategy that includes as many learners as possible.

Universal Design in Instruction

Universal design has evolved to emphasize addressing these issues in the design of instruction and the benefits of inclusion (Hyter & Turnock, 2005). It focuses on minimizing barriers through implementing designs from the beginning that address the needs of diverse people rather than making accommodations through individual adaptation later (Rose, Harbour, Johnston, Daley, & Abarbanell, 2006). When considering reaching as many learners as possible, the instructional designer must be aware of the presence of different abilities and cultures, and technologies used by individuals to overcome learning barriers.

Types of Involvement

Disability can be divided into four categories: (1) visual involvement, (2) auditory involvement, (3) mobility involvement, and (4) cognitive involvement. For each of these categories there are assistive technologies specifically designed to aid people with disabilities in overcoming barriers in their environment (Rose et al., 2006). As designers, it is important to know the types of assistive technology available, the groups for which they have been designed, and the limitations they are designed to minimize. Table 37.1 outlines specific types of involvement and characteristics, types of technology they typically use, and design suggestions for each group.

Visual involvement includes any condition resulting in the loss of visual acuity, field of vision, or visual perception resulting in total blindness, legal blindness, low vision, and/or color blindness. Screen reader software is typically used by people who are totally blind. People who are considered legally blind may use screen magnification software, and/or a closed circuit television with split-screen capabilities. The touchscreen interface offers the user more flexibility through direct contact and interaction with what is on the screen for users with nonstandard eyesight (blindness or low vision).

Auditory involvement includes categories of deaf and hard of hearing. Being deaf or totally without hearing, just like total

TABLE 37.1	Categories of Involvement with Adaptations and Design Suggestions		
	Common Description	**Adaptations**	**Design Suggestions**
SH vision involvement	Totally blind Legally blind Color blindness	Cane, service animal, screen reader software, refreshable Braille display Magnification devices electronic and optical, screen magnification software, large-print materials	• Use alt tags for any and all graphic items. • Limit use of complicated tables or frames. • Properly label headings. • Provide skip navigation button. • Avoid using background images to convey important content information. • Offer an alternative text-only version. • Keep materials free of unnecessary clutter. • Avoid use of italics and serif (not smooth) fonts. • Use high contrast between background, text, graphics, and navigation tools. • Use basic black and white and gray when possible. • Avoid presentation of important instructional information that requires color recognition.
Hearing involvement	Deaf Hard of hearing	Close captioning, video phones, TDD, telephone relay Hearing aids, FM system, pocket talker, amplified phones	• Use text captioning for all audio, video, or other media. • Offer text transcript of video, recordings, or other audio normally heard by other students. • Provide visual as well as audio notification for any necessary cues. • Provide sign language interpreter for any live presentation such as lecture or guest speakers.
Mobility involvement	Paralysis, traumatic brain injury, spina bifida, authorities, muscular disorders	Word prediction software, eye gaze software, voice recognition software, mouth stick, alternative keyboards, adapted pointing devices or sip and puff devices	• Limit synchronous or real time chat. • Avoid simulations and games requiring high manual dexterity. • Avoid timed assessment. • Limit timed assignments. • Incorporate teamwork and group activities. • Offer generous space for mobility device. • Ensure compliance with standard physical accessibility features as described in the Americans with Disabilities Acts of 1990.
Cognitive involvement	Learning disabilities, autism, mental retardation, cerebral palsy, traumatic brain injury	Optical character recognition software	• Avoid using pop-up windows. • Make Web pages easy to navigate. • Present a logical flow of content material. • Always use page titles and sequential headings. • Make all text portions large enough to be easily seen and distinguished. • Avoid the use of flashing onscreen objects. • Allow as much time as needed. • Highlight important concepts. • Provide audio and visual presentations simultaneously.

blindness, is very rare. Hard of hearing includes varying degrees of hearing loss. Deafness is more than a typical disability. It is a culture that has its own language, traditions, and beliefs that bind these individuals together as a people. Deaf people must have equal access to all audio information. The text transcript does not replace real time text captioning. Just as it is beneficial for an individual to hear and see the action as it unfolds, it is equally beneficial for deaf persons to have an image of what is being presented as they are reading the audible portion.

Mobility involvement encompasses any difficulties with movement in the natural environment, including conditions like arthritis, cerebral palsy, muscular dystrophy, multiple sclerosis, spina bifida, spinal cord injury, or traumatic brain injury. Individuals with these conditions have a wide range of variability or level of disability that range from minor (the limited use of their hands) to quadriplegic (the inability to move their limbs at all). For mobility involvement, word prediction, eye gaze, and voice recognition are available. Other adaptive alternatives may include a mouth stick, alternative keyboards, adapted pointing devices, or sip and puff devices.

Cognitive involvement interferences include learning disabilities, autism, traumatic brain injury, cerebral palsy, epilepsy, neurological impairments, or mental illness. As with the previous groups, the levels of involvement are wide ranging, but the majority of cases can be considered mild to moderate. Software for this population identifies textual information and presents that information in multiple ways to address the needs of a wide range of perceptual and other cognitive factors such as deficits in attention, memory, perception, processing, and problem solving. By using this software, learners are able to freely manipulate the material and minimize learning barriers while maximizing transfer.

Multiple cases exist in these categories. For example, traumatic brain injury and cerebral palsy are listed under motor and cognitive involvement categories. Other examples are someone who is paraplegic and hard of hearing, the child who is autistic and legally blind, or the woman who is gifted and learning disabled. Table 37.1 illustrates the categories listed and provides adaptations and design suggestions for each group.

When dealing with individuals, no one solution works in all cases. In fact, no one solution ever works all the time, even in cases of disability that may appear to be exactly the same. When considering diversity, instructional designers must be aware that within each targeted population, each learner brings a unique set of circumstances that will impact how they learn.

Personal Story, Coauthor Stephen Sullivan

I was born with bilateral cataracts, a condition I inherited. A cataract is basically a clouded or defective lens in the eye that blocks the light from reaching the retina causing blindness. After surgical removal of the cataracts, I am legally blind with a best correction of 20/200 in one eye and 20/300 in the other. Throughout my K–12 education (especially in the early grades), I could read the print in the regular textbooks; I just had to look really closely. Perched over the book with my nose only a half-inch or so from the page, I could read aloud just as well

as any of the other students. However, watching me read like this made my teachers uncomfortable, even though I was able to participate and keep up.

When I was in fourth grade, my teacher decided that it would be best for me to use large-print books. These books were very bulky and I did not want to use them. For example, my history book in large print was actually five or six books. I had to turn the page ten or more times to my classmates' one-page turn. I found it extremely difficult to pay attention to content and get something from the lesson while attempting to keep up with the cumbersome page turning. When I was called on to read, I would often find myself on the wrong page. This rarely happened when I was using the regular book. The worst grades I ever made in my life were in fourth grade.

My experiences throughout my education and professional career have taught me how to adapt to different environments and how the perceptions of other people who are involved with me in the learning process affect my learning experience. I want the instructional content to be the focus, not my disability. But if the discussion starts out on me and how my needs should be accommodated, the attention is drawn away from the content. I want to be part of a learning environment without being special or singled out. It is possible for people who learn differently to experience inclusion in a standard learning environment by providing options. Give learners the option to learn in their own way, whether listening if eyesight is limited or reading with assistive technologies. Provide variation in presentation and assessment. From the beginning, design instruction so that each learner has the same opportunity to contribute to the learning process, engage in meaningful activities, apply knowledge to real-world situations, and equally benefit from the overall learning experience.

Multiculturalism

Multiculturalism is rooted in the representation of an individual's identification and exposure to a variety of cultures. It focuses on the complexity of individuals rather than their belonging to one particular group or demographic. In this chapter, we refer to multiculturalism generally as a representation of how people with different characteristics interact, learn, and exist together. We make the assumption that all learners are multicultural.

The relevance of culture to instructional design depends on perceived differences among people and how designers think these differences will impact learning (Rogers, Graham, & Mayes, 2007). Incorporating multiculturalism into instruction requires instructional designers to reflect on their own cultures, examine the impact of culture on instruction, and consider the implications for instruction.

Reflection may not be an easy task for some due to the dominance of social influence on individualism, immersion in the cultural environment, or rarely, experiencing being an outsider (Bucher, 2000). Depending on the culture, individualism is a characteristic that is celebrated or shunned. For example, instructional designers can examine sensitivity to multiculturalism by increasing awareness of the organization's vision of diversity, providing opportunity for the audience to disclose learning or content barriers, performing an exhaustive learner analysis, and soliciting feedback regarding multicultural factors of the learning environment.

Learners' multicultural perspectives have an impact on the outcomes of the design of instruction and learning environment, specifically on the type of delivery that creates opportunity for variation in presentation. For example, in facilitator-led instruction, some learners may find it more difficult than other learners to interact and freely speak. Activities must be all-inclusive while ensuring that each learner has an opportunity to contribute to the learning process. Table 37.2 describes some considerations for incorporating multiculturalism design strategies in different type of deliveries.

Language, cultural interpretations, and social norms require instructional designers to be strategic managers of culturally biased content, assistive technology, and sensitivity training. Language, in its most basic form, may be simple to one person, but ambiguous to another. Method of delivery, dialect, accent, style, and many other factors of language increase complexity in understanding content and application of knowledge. Therefore, the instructional designer must ensure that culturally biased language is not used and a level of comfort is maintained among learners.

Interpretations of cultural experience are essential when considering the design of instruction (Guild, 2001). How do we know what others are experiencing? Is it our job to know about other cultures? Movement beyond a limited view of the role of an instructional designer should include considerations of the possible limitations and cultures of current and future audiences. Stakeholders should be educated on the criticalness of being culturally responsive and adaptive to the challenges of all learners.

Social norms also present challenges to multiculturalism in instructional design. Standardized activities or practices for a particular group lay the foundation for learner attitudes and educational perspectives. When using examples and communicating with learners, it is not important to know every social norm but to avoid referring to political correctness, personal opinions, or controversial topics, unless the training warrants that type of discussion. Setting guidelines for these types of discussions, whether in person or online, is essential when instructing the learners to communicate with sensitivity and promoting cultural responsiveness (Rogers et al., 2007).

Several design components that are used to incorporate multiculturalism into instruction may also contribute to other components of the learning process. According to Rogers et al., (2007), authentic simulations, related resources, and opportunities for increased feedback can be included. Within the content area, avoid the following: traditions, reference to male/female relationships, teacher–student relationships, clothing, daily activities, and use of time. When appropriate, onsite visits and multicultural design teams are critical components that create a sense of culture (Rogers, Graham, & Mayes 2007). Utilizing a diverse group of reviewers during formative evaluation provides another avenue for checking inclusion. Being flexible is key to achieving active participation and accurate assessments.

Personal Story, Coauthor Joél Lewis

I am a seventh-generation descendent of Cudjoe Lewis, a slave of the *Clotilde,* the last African slave ship to import slaves to the United States. Growing up in a family rich in heritage, I remember as a child going to my grandparent's house every month to celebrate birthdays and learn of our ancestry. All of the children of the family listened to the elders tell stories,

TABLE 37.2	Considerations for Type of Delivery
Type of Delivery	**Considerations**
Self-instruction	Create opportunity for reflection Provide language options Make recommendations for successful completion Provide practical timelines List self-checks as a process evaluation tool
Facilitator-led	Utilize facility checklist for accommodations Create diverse groups Allow for flexibility in assignments and assessments Use experience and background in activities
Online (instructor-led)	Vary interaction with groups of students Utilize technology to create a sense of community Provide options in format of assignments Establish guidelines on discussion
Computer-based	Provide language options Include sensitivity statements or training Increase learner control Use a variety of images that will represent the audience
On-the-job training	Include shadowing Present situations that would require sensitivity in problem solving

created art by drawing shapes, and made music with wooden sticks. I am convinced that these experiences and other experiences helped me with transculturation, the process of adjusting to other cultures while maintaining cultural identity (Bucher, 2000). This was a necessity regardless of whether I identified in situations mostly as an African American or as a female, or even as a student. It was not until I was an adult that I began to understand how multicultural I was and how many of my characteristics have shaped who I am and my view of the world.

In various stages of my life, I can recall how multiculturalism has impacted my education. In elementary school, language was an evident barrier to my performance. Some test questions were confusing because I thought the words had a different meaning. For example, "bright" in my culture could be interpreted as a word to describe a person of light complexion but on an exam, "bright" may describe a person of high intelligence. Throughout my middle and high school education, my thoughts often led to racial identity. I attended schools that were approximately 60 percent Caucasian, 37 percent African American, and 3 percent Asian American. I was excited and proud to be in advanced, honors courses; however, I often wondered why I was one of a few minorities in those classes; while special education courses were overwhelmingly composed of African American students with low socioeconomic status. This reality prepared me for what would prove to be the likelihood of my educational and professional career.

I believe my experiences inspired me to be an instructional designer who is aware of the importance of multiculturalism. It is my responsibility to create a learning environment where multiculturalism is embraced and viewed as a valuable asset to the learning process. The multimodal model that follows includes design implications to create inclusive learning environments for physical, cognitive, and cultural diversity in order to provide the greatest opportunity for success for as many learners as possible.

Multimodal Diversity Model

Curriculum and instruction should include accessible alternatives that engage students with different backgrounds, learning styles, abilities, and disabilities (Simoncelli & Hinson, 2008). Specifically, universal design for learning uses innovative technologies to address diverse learning needs (Meo, 2008). Multimodal materials and methods provide a broad base for all learners (Pliner & Johnson, 2004). While many aspects of UDL are important, there are three basic principles: (1) multiple means of representation, (2) multiple means of expression, and (3) multiple means of engagement (Rose & Meyer, 2002). See Figure 37.1.

Multiple means of representation pertains to information that is presented to learners and is considered the "what" of learning (Rose & Meyer, 2002). This includes how the instructor introduces new ideas, connects prior knowledge, and highlights

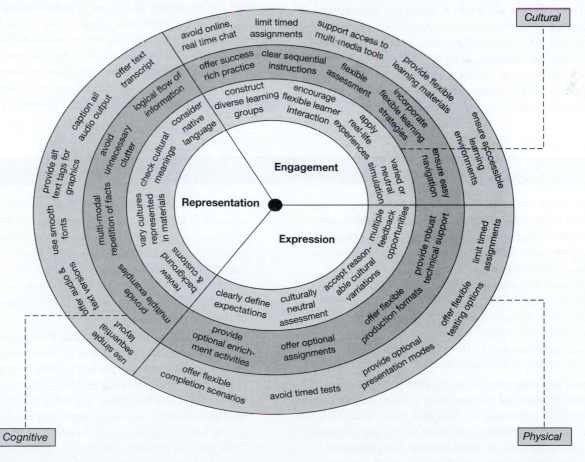

FIGURE 37.1 Multimodal Diversity Model: Strategies to use when attempting to include diverse learners in the design of instruction. This model incorporates physical, cognitive, and cultural diversity in the three principle areas of UDL: multiple means of representation, expression, and engagement.

important features, etc. (Rose et al., 2006). The introduction and presentation of instructional material to the learner, in as many formats or modes as possible, will significantly reduce the later need for accommodations. For example, making any slide or other presentation material available online for later download, providing clear and organized handouts, using smooth and generously sized fonts, and creating a high amount of contrast between background and text or images will eliminate most visual perception issues. This will also reduce acuity conflicts and the necessity for tedious note taking. Not only can this reduce the difficulties for a number of diverse learning concerns, but it also allows all learners to engage in a more active listening environment.

Multiple means of expression or performance is considered the "how" of learning (Rose & Meyer, 2002). How the learner will best express what has been learned depends on the options and flexibility of available modes. Such supports consist of testing formats, project production or presentation, group activity, term paper, etc. A second factor affecting expression is the presence of alternative supports for learning such as study groups, review sessions, and opportunities for feedback (Rose et al., 2006). By considering high flexibility and a variety of options, aspects of learner expression will result in higher learner success rates and fewer occurrences for needed accommodation.

Multiple means of engagement is considered the "why" of learning (Rose & Meyer, 2002). Just as learners differ widely in ways they learn, they also differ in what motivates or engages their learning (Rose et al., 2006). Considering the target group of learners and what they have in common is a major factor in designing of effective instruction. Some useful strategies to foster diverse learner engagement include relating the material to real-life experiences, providing clear and concise instructions, using various cultural equivalents, offering flexible instructional scenarios, and gathering plenty of learners' input.

Conclusion

A good analogy for effective instruction is a quilt. A quilt is a blanket comprised of many different pieces of material made of patterns, cut into squares, and sewn together. Each square represents the makeup of today's learners and the type of design necessary to meet their needs. Many squares of material do not look alike but must be sewn together in order to make a complete quilt. Just as each pattern of a quilt is different and colorful, this audience is diverse and unique. When one square is missing from the quilt, it is not complete. Each member of the audience is valuable and equally important to the learning process. The role of the instructional designer is to strategically bring together all the quilt squares and connect them with sound instructional design strategies. It is important to consider multiculturalism, physical involvement, and cognitive involvement while integrating diversity into instructional design. Culture, physical involvement, and cognitive involvement inclusively assist in providing greater equity in learning.

Opportunities for learners to interact and feel comfortable enough to provide feedback are important strategies in incorporating multiculturalism in instruction. In order to set a tone of sensitivity and acceptance, the design approach to engagement determines how the audience will interact in the learning environment, the perspective of the learning experience, and perceived achievement in learning outcomes. Learners need a variety of exercises and types of assessments that reflect objectives. These must also allow for interaction. Learners must exist in an environment where they can communicate their disabilities and perceived challenges to learning. As our society faces challenges in an ever-changing world, it is the role of instructional designers to reflect on personal perspectives, embrace diversity, and meet the needs of all learners.

Summary of Key Principles

1. **Implement universal design at the beginning of the design process to eliminate the need for additional accommodations after implementation has begun.** Designing instruction for diverse learners requires instructional designers to be aware of individual differences and adaptive technologies available to establish equity in learning. Considering concerns for efficiency and productivity, universal design can add to your return on investment by decreasing time to make accommodations and increasing the applicability of the instruction to a wider audience.

2. **Create learning environments that promote cultural sensitivity, flexible learner interactions, and authentic learning experiences.** As designers we have the ability to determine how learning can occur within environments. We can be creative, considerate, and comprehensive in our approaches to instruction. Be prepared to identify cultural barriers in learning, to anticipate the needs of learners and determine appropriate design implications.

3. **Make all instructional materials accessible.** Make sure any video or audio feeds are captioned and provide text transcripts for all audio portions, including visual indications of any audio cues or other necessary audio features of any kind. Creating and implementing these features takes time. Allocate enough time and resources in your project management timeline to create these design features.

4. **Organize instructional materials focusing on layout to provide logical progression of information ensuring clear and simple navigation and/or readability.** When creating text portions, consider size, readability (clear font face), and color contrast. Label with alternate text tags those items that are not text such as graphics, navigation tools, headings, and buttons. Offer full text versions when possible. Limit flashy pop-ups, complex graphics, and complicated tables and frames.

Application Questions

1. You are an adjunct instructor at a local university. A policy change has been made regarding curriculum and instruction for the upcoming semester. All courses at the university will now be developed using the three basic principles of universal design for learning of multiple means of representation, multiple means of expression, and multiple means of engagement. You are teaching a 300-level educational media course for future teachers that involves the use of the technology in the classroom. Specifically, you will be teaching these future teachers how to utilize elements and activities of the online environment such as blogging, pod and video casting, and social networking, when teaching their future K–12 students.

    a. How would you design or set up your course to meet the needs of diverse learners? How would you incorporate multimodal activities at the stages of representation, expression, and engagement?

    b. What design implications would you implement to integrate multiculturalism in this technology course for future teachers?

2. The Gulf Coast city of New Orleans, Louisiana, is often threatened by dangerous hurricanes during the time between June 1 and November 1 each year. As you may recall the city w as devastated by hurricane Katrina in August 2005. Many people lost their lives because of, among other things, a seriously flawed evacuation plan. In an effort to ensure that this never happens again, city planners and public safety officials have devised an innovative and remarkable evacuation plan in the event of another catastrophic hurricane. You have been hired to develop and implement a series of public training seminars to educate the public about the evacuation plan.

    a. What questions would you ask in a learner analysis to ensure that you collected information regarding culture and physical/cognitive impairments?

    b. What strategies would you use to meet the needs of a diverse population: culturally, economically, educationally, and otherwise?

    c. What are the challenges in implementing strategies of the multimodal diversity model?

References

Bucher, R. D. (2000). *Diversity consciousness*. Upper Saddle River, NJ: Prentice Hall.

Guild, P. B. (2001, October). Diversity, learning style, and culture. *New Horizons for Learning* Retrieved from http://www.newhorizons.org/strategies/styles/guild.htm

Hyter, M. C., & Turnock, J. L. (2005). *The Power of inclusion*. Mississauga, Ontario: Wiley.

Meo, G. (2008). Curriculum planning for all learners: Applying universal design for learning (UDL) to a high school reading comprehension program. *Preventing School Failure, 59*(2), 21–30.

Pliner. S. M., & Johnson, J. R. (2004). Historical, theoretical, and foundational principles of universal instructional design in higher education. *Equity and Excellence in Education, 37*, 105–113.

Rogers, P. C., Graham, C. R., & Mayes, T. C. (2007). Cultural competence and instructional design. *Education Tech Research Development, 55*(2), 197–217.

Rose, D. H., Harbour, W. S., Johnson, C. S., Daley, S. G., & Abarbnell, L. (2006). Universal design for learning in postsecondary education: Reflections on principles and their application. *Journal of Postsecondary Education and Disability, 19*(2), 135–151.

Rose, D. H., & Meyer, A. (2002). *Teaching every student in the digital age: Universal design for learning*. Alexandria, VA: Association for Supervision and Curriculum Development.

Simoncelli, A., & Hinson, J. M. (2008). College students with learning disabilities personal reactions to online learning. *Journal of College Reading and Learning, 38*(2), 49–62.

The Statistic Portal. (2015). The most spoken languages worldwide. Retrieved from http://www.statista.com/statistics/266808/the-most-spoken-languages-worldwide/

United Nations Department of Economic and Social Affairs. (2013). International migration. Retrieved from http://www.un.org/en/development/desa/population/theme/international-migration/

United Nations Department of Economic and Social Affairs. (2015). Inclusiveness, equal access critical to keeping persons with disabilities at heart of post-2015 efforts, special rapporteur tells commission for social development. Retrieved from http://undesadspd.org/Poverty/WhatsNew/tabid/1347/news/504/Default.aspx

United Nations Population Fund. (2014). Youth world population. Retrieved from http://www.unfpa.org/swop

Chapter 38

The Evolving Economics of Educational Materials and Open Educational Resources: Toward Closer Alignment with the Core Values of Education

David Wiley, PhD

Lumen Learning

Education Is Sharing

This chapter tells the story of the negative impact of copyright on education and the emergence of open educational resources as a response. Work in the field of open educational resources is grounded in a specific understanding of the nature of education; specifically, the notion that education is sharing. It behooves us therefore, at the outset, to be specific about what it means to share, and how it is that education is an instance of sharing.

Sharing, as it is generally understood, involves a willing offer and a willing acceptance. For example, when one child offers some M&Ms to another child, and that child happily accepts the offer, we would label this as an instance of sharing. As a counterexample, when one child offers some M&Ms to another child, and that child declines them, we would not say that sharing has occurred. Likewise, when a well-meaning parent forces one child to divide the M&Ms with another child against his or her will, we would again not say that sharing has occurred. This framework of a willing offer and a willing acceptance is the core of the commonsense meaning of sharing.

When I say that education is sharing, this is what I mean—that education involves offers willingly made and willingly accepted. When one person willingly offers to share knowledge, expertise, skills, and passion with another, and that person willingly accepts the offer, we will rightly call this education. Notice that this sharing can flow from a traditional "teacher" to a traditional "student" as well as from a "student" to a "teacher." We tend to think of education as a setting in which teachers do all the sharing, but a talented teacher is always encouraging students to share with the teacher and with other students questions, concerns, insights, etc. Homework, exams, and other assignments are nothing more than a formalized way of encouraging students to share the current state of their understanding with teachers.

Students tend to pay particular honor and tribute to those educators who offered to share something of themselves—namely, time, concern, and care beyond the requirements of the job description. Educators fondly remember those special students who offered to share something of themselves—effort, dedication, and commitment beyond what was required by the syllabus.

Truly, education is sharing.

Education as sharing takes a family of shapes and forms when we interact face to face. In this chapter, I want to focus particularly on the shapes and forms taken when the offerer and accepter are separated in time. This desire to share with others who are not immediately present leads to the creation of educational materials—textbooks, videos, podcasts, games, simulations, and other media in which instructional designers, faculty, and others attempt to reach out across the void to share what they know, think, and feel with others.

For centuries, this desire to share with others across time manifested itself primarily in writing on stone, wood, leather, pottery, papyrus, and parchment. A revolution was set off when Gutenberg combined metallic movable type, oil-based inks, and the screw press historically used to make olive oil and wine, into a practical package capable of mass producing copies of the written word. While Gutenberg's books were orders of magnitude more affordable than the handmade codices that preceded them, they were still relatively difficult to share.

As anyone who has tried to check out a popular book at the library knows, sharing books with others can be a frustrating experience. This is because books are what economists refer to as private goods, meaning they have two specific characteristics: They are rivalrous and excludable. *Rivalrous* means that one person's use of a book prevents simultaneous use of the book by others. Other examples of rivalrous goods include my car, my socks, and my chewing gum. If you are driving my car, wearing my socks, or chewing my gum, I cannot be. *Excludable* means it is possible to prevent people who haven't purchased the book from being able to enjoy the benefits of owning a copy. Examples of excludable goods also include my car, my socks, and my chewing gum. If I don't want you to drive, wear, or chew my things, I only need to keep them locked up.

Contrast the private goods nature of books with the public goods nature of the ideas, stories, and concepts expressed within a book. My knowledge of the Pythagorean theorem and its uses does not prevent you from simultaneously knowing these same things (i.e., knowledge of the theorem is nonrivalrous). Likewise, it is not practically possible for me to prevent you from learning about the Pythagorean theorem (i.e., knowledge of the theorem is nonexcludable). In a letter written to Isaac McPherson in 1813, Thomas Jefferson explained:

> If nature has made any one thing less susceptible than all others of exclusive property, it is the action of the thinking power called an idea, which an individual may exclusively possess as long as he keeps it to himself; but the moment it is divulged, it forces itself into the possession of every one, and the receiver cannot dispossess himself of it. Its peculiar character, too, is that no one possesses the less, because every other possesses the whole of it. He who receives an idea from me, receives instruction himself without lessening mine; as he who lights his taper at mine, receives light without darkening me. That ideas should freely spread from one to another over the globe, for the moral and mutual instruction of man, and improvement of his condition, seems to have been peculiarly and benevolently designed by nature, when she made them, like fire, expansible over all space, without lessening their density in any point, and like the air in which we breathe, move, and have our physical being, incapable of confinement or exclusive appropriation.

The nonrivalrous, nonexcludable nature of ideas is an absolutely key, foundational concept that typically goes completely unexamined and unappreciated in courses on instructional design, learning science, and epistemology, yet the entire enterprise of education is possible only because it is true. Ideas are public goods. To clarify this point, imagine for a moment a world in which ideas are rivalrous. To teach you everything I know about task analysis, I would have to forget everything I know about task analysis. To teach would be

immediately to forget, like handing a baton of knowledge off to the next runner in a relay race, immediately depriving the original knower of what he or she had known. In this world, Friere's (1970) description of banking education would be quite literal—teachers would not only make deposits of knowledge into students' heads, they would have to literally withdraw it from their own in order to do so.

The knowledge, skills, and attitudes that instructional designers, faculty, and others work to help students develop are public goods. In some circumstances people wish to share these ideas with people from whom they are separated by time. Since Gutenberg, this desire to share has often led people to express their ideas in books. However—and this point is critical—something crucial changes about ideas when this means of expression is employed. The pure, nonrivalrous, and nonexcludable idea is captured in a physical, rivalrous, excludable book.

Networked Digital Technologies, Sharing, and Education

The Internet has been hailed as revolutionary by many people and for many reasons. For those interested in education, perhaps the most revolutionary aspect of the Internet is its impact on our capacity to share. As indicated in Table 38.1, while expressing knowledge via a physical means, such as via printed books, captures a public good inside a private good, the Internet, which is a digital means of expression, offers a significantly different alternative. When ideas are expressed in digital form and those expressions are made available over the network, *the expressions continue to be public goods,* at least from a practical perspective (legal issues will be discussed later). While only one person can read a printed copy of *The New York Times*, and it is easy to prevent you from getting a copy of the newspaper if you won't pay, a million people can all read nytimes.com simultaneously.

The impact of the public good–preserving nature of the Internet on our capacity to share (and therefore educate) cannot be overstated. Before the Internet, if we wished to provide 100 students with a syllabus that they could read and review at a later time, we were required to print 100 copies of the syllabus. After the Internet, we need only place a single copy of the syllabus online and all students can access that one copy simultaneously. Rather than sending students to the media center where they have to wait their turn to check out a VHS cassette or DVD, we can simply post a video to YouTube. Rather than purchase dozens of copies of *Pride and Prejudice* for literature class, we can simply point students to the copy on Project Gutenberg.

TABLE 38.1	A Naïve Classification of Knowledge and Expressions of Knowledge	
Nature of Expression	**Example**	**Type of Good**
"Pure" ideas	Knowledge of details of yesterday's weather	Public goods
Physical expressions of ideas	Details of yesterday's weather published in a traditional newspaper	Private goods
Digital expressions of ideas	Details of yesterday's weather published online	Public goods

This dramatic increase in our technical capacity to share has led to a dramatic increase in people's willingness to share. It can be difficult to want to share private goods like a cherished book, a french fry, or a favorite CD, because when you take home my book or my CD, or eat my french fry, I can no longer enjoy the item. However, it is much easier to share a public good. You don't hesitate to invite your friends to watch that hysterical YouTube video you just saw, because their viewing the video does not interfere with or prevent you from doing so at the same time.

The move from physical copies of educational materials (private goods) to digital copies of educational materials (public goods) makes possible a revolution in the reach and impact of education. However, making it possible doesn't make it legal.

The Impact of Copyright Law

While the creation of the Internet continues to vastly improve our technical capability to share, and therefore educate, certain factors beyond technical capabilities must be considered. Long before the Internet was a gleam in an engineer's eye, governments began granting copyrights to authors of creative works. Copyright is a government-enforced monopoly that reserves the exclusive permission to engage in certain activities to the copyright holder, prohibiting the public from engaging in these activities without first securing the permission of the rights holder. Core among these regulated activities are the making of copies and the distributing of copies. Note that these regulated activities are also exactly those activities that are most effortlessly facilitated by the Internet.

Historically, copyright law has followed nature in recognizing an important difference between ideas (which are public goods) and the expression of ideas (which have historically been private goods). Ideas themselves are not eligible for copyright protection, while expressions of ideas are eligible for copyright protection. Early in the history of the United States, people who were interested in protecting and exercising their copyrights were required to apply for copyright protection. This was a sensible approach, as the average person had no intent to commercialize the overwhelming majority of the potentially copyrightable things created each day. This requirement to register approach recognized that commerce was the exception, not the rule, of life—commerce was a small subset of life and society.

More recently, however, as a result of agreements such as the Berne Convention and the later agreement on Trade-Related Aspects of Intellectual Property Rights (TRIPS), the full force of copyright protection is granted automatically from the moment a creative work is expressed in any medium, whether or not the creator of that work wants copyright protection. This is the case whether the means of expression is physical or digital. If your country became either a signatory to Berne or party to TRIPS, something odd has happened. The blurry picture of your carpet accidentally taken by your four-year-old now enjoys copyright protection equal to that enjoyed by *Star Wars: The Force Awakens* or the latest Beyoncé album. In the eyes of the law, commerce is now the assumed default in all aspects of life and society—commerce is the rule and sharing is the exception.

The everyday realities of life are at odds with the law's view of commerce as the default. Whether you consider people sharing billions of popular memes and photos on platforms like Facebook or Tumblr, or teachers swapping syllabi and lesson plans with each other, all of these materials are automatically and fully copyrighted by their creators and sharing them is illegal without a license granting you permission to share. As Harvard Law professor Larry Lessig has written, modern copyright law has made criminals of us all (Lessig, 2008).

"Fair use" is an exemption written directly into copyright law that allows a copyrighted work to be used without the rights holder's permission under certain circumstances. However, fair use and similar copyright exceptions theoretically provide the means for educators to make use of copyrighted materials without a copyright holder's permission in a very poorly defined set of circumstances. Large corporations that profit from selling access to copyrighted materials, however, work actively to undermine the public's practical ability to make fair uses. Copyright protections are now bolstered by legislation like the U.S. Digital Millennium Copyright Act (DMCA), which prohibits educators and others from circumventing copyright protection technology to engage in lawful uses of copyrighted material. Even when a teacher can legitimately claim that the way he or she wants to use a copyrighted work in the classroom is a fair use, the DMCA criminalizes the act of working around digital rights management in order to make a fair use.

While the Internet is constantly making it easier for us to share with each other, copyright and related laws make it increasingly difficult, and generally illegal, for us to do so. Although digital resources would otherwise be public goods that can be freely shared and used by all, the copyright restrictions automatically forced on all digital resources make them artificially excludable. In this state, they are neither public goods nor private goods, but what economists call "club goods." Club goods are resources that are nonrivalrous but excludable, like cable or satellite TV. My watching a cable television show on my television doesn't prevent you from watching the same show on your television (nonrivalrous), but the cable or satellite operator makes it impossible for either of us to do so unless we have paid to do so (excludable). In other words, you can only access club goods if you've paid to be part of the club.

A Return to Sharing: Open Educational Resources

Because digital resources are inherently public goods and consequently easy to share, they present incredible opportunities for education. There is clear and obvious alignment between the nature of education, which is sharing, and the nature of digital resources, which are nonrivalrous and nonexcludable. Only when digital resources are saddled with copyright restrictions do they lose their alignment with the educational enterprise. The fact that publishers and others go out of their way, spending millions of dollars and significant research and development effort to break this alignment by making digital resources artificially excludable, is exasperating. The unfettered sharing enabled by digital resources presents humanity's best hope for achieving education for all, yet all major education companies work proactively to undermine this capability.

A growing proportion of educators—and society more broadly—is rejecting what they feel to be the overreach of commercial concerns into their classrooms and lives. In response to this overreach, they are creating and promoting alternatives that enable broad and easy sharing within the framework of existing copyright law. The best known of these initiatives is Creative Commons, a nonprofit organization that creates and provides free, prewritten copyright licenses that creators can use to grant to the public broad permissions to use their works in a wide range of ways. According to a report written with support of major search engines like Google, Creative Commons estimates that the number of CC-licensed works available online is over 1 billion (Creative Commons, 2015).

When educational materials are licensed using an open copyright license like the Creative Commons licenses, they are called open educational resources (OER). The OER, then, are educational resources whose copyright licenses provide the public with free, irrevocable, and perpetual legal permission to engage in what Wiley (2015) calls "the 5R activities":

1. Retain: the right to make, own, and control copies of materials (e.g., download, duplicate, store, and manage your own copy)
2. Reuse: the right to use the content in a wide range of ways (e.g., in a class, in a study group, on a website, in a video)
3. Revise: the right to adapt, adjust, modify, or alter the content itself (e.g., translate the content into another language)
4. Remix: the right to combine the original or revised content with other open content to create something new (e.g., incorporate the content into a mashup)
5. Redistribute: the right to share copies of the original content, your revisions, or your remixes with others (e.g., give a copy of the content to a friend or post a copy on the Internet)

The application of an open license to a digital educational resource eliminates the artificial excludability created by copyright, and returns digital educational resources to their original state as public goods (see Table 38.2).

"Retain" is the fundamental permission of the 5Rs because it enables all the others. For example, if I can't download my own copy of a resource, I can't make changes to it. The importance of Retain becomes particularly clear in the context of the emergence of services like Spotify and Netflix at home, and library subscriptions to e-book collections, databases, and journals on campus. Each of these services rents temporary access to books, articles, songs, movies, and other materials without providing users with the possibility of buying a personal copy that they can truly own and control.

Educators, instructional designers, learners, and others must be careful not to confuse freely available resources and OER. Essentially all resources on the Internet are freely available—articles at the BBC, New York Times, and National Geographic can all be accessed and read for free online. OER, by contrast, are resources that can be accessed for free *and* provide educators, instructional designers, learners, and others with the 5R permissions to download a copy, make modifications and improvements, and share those copies freely with others.

Alignment of Educational Resources with the Core Values of Education

Education and traditional copyright are fundamentally at odds with one another. While education is sharing, the purpose of copyright has traditionally been to make sharing illegal unless permissions are secured from a rights holder. The process of securing copyright permissions is an incredibly expensive and time-consuming undertaking. This situation presents a daunting challenge for educators and instructional designers who would like to design instruction that makes use of copyrighted material. If faculty abdicate the design and creation of the educational materials used in their courses to publishers, publishers will use copyright to make those materials artificially excludable, and therefore scarce and expensive, for students.

The process of securing permissions is frequently—and increasingly—impossible. An orphan work is a copyrighted work whose copyright holder cannot be identified or contacted. For example, a photograph that does not indicate its photographer is an orphan work. If the rights holder for a work cannot be contacted, there is no way to acquire the explicit permissions necessary to share a creative work with others.

Thus, traditionally copyrighted educational materials are poorly aligned with education's core values. While education is sharing, copyright serves to complicate sharing and make it expensive. Education is already sufficiently complex without the added complications of artificial constraints placed on sharing by copyright law. Until recently, there was no widely

TABLE 38.2	A More Nuanced Classification of Knowledge and Expressions of Knowledge	
Nature of Expression	**Example**	**Type of Good**
"Pure" ideas	Knowledge of details of yesterday's weather	Public goods
Physical expressions of ideas	Details of yesterday's weather published in a traditional newspaper	Private goods
Digital expressions of ideas (traditionally copyrighted)	Details of yesterday's weather published online on CNN	Club goods
Digital expressions of ideas (openly licensed)	Details of yesterday's weather published online on Wikipedia	Public goods

available alternative to simply accepting and working within the constraints of this complication.

By contrast, open educational resources explicitly permit sharing, as explained by the 5R framework. With OER there is no need to spend time or other resources securing permissions because each is published in a manner that provides everyone—including faculty, instructional designers, and students—with free, perpetual, and irrevocable permission to adapt and share. Consequently, OER are closely aligned with education's core values and make the process of sharing as inexpensive and easy as possible.

While educators have long relied on copyright exemptions like fair use to occasionally sidestep the complexities and cost of rights clearance, fair use and related arguments made in educational settings typically require the copyrighted work to be used in a very limited context—that is, within a classroom or behind password protection. The necessity of making educational fair uses essentially in secret completely precludes the possibility of open collaboration by faculty or students across the Internet. While it is sometimes appropriate to make fair use of copyrighted works without permissions, these uses must always occur in isolation, with every faculty member or student recreating the wheel in their own local context. Traditional copyright fights against the nature of the Internet in this context in that it precludes the emergence of the network effects that are the hallmark of many innovations. In other contexts the network effect is described as the "standing on the shoulders of giants" effect, in which people are able to build on the best work done by others before them. OER permit this shoulder standing, while fair uses prohibit you from knowing whether anyone else is standing nearby.

Practical Impacts on Faculty and Students

When faculty choose to adopt OER in place of commercial educational resources, they recognize two major benefits related to the closer alignment of OER with the core values of education. First, OER adoption provides faculty with opportunities to re-professionalize, engaging in skilled activities many faculty have abandoned. Second, OER provide hitherto unknown pedagogical freedom for faculty.

Little by little, and without knowing it, faculty have slowly ceded control over the design and content of their educational materials to publishers. From this perspective, the publishing industry can be seen as responsible for the large-scale de-skilling of faculty by providing them with "easy outs" from engaging in these activities. This works particularly well for publishers over the long term, because an entire generation of faculty without these critical skills becomes wholly dependent on instructional materials created, reviewed, selected, and assembled by publishers.

Adopting OER is a completely different experience. Selecting OER does not need to be a professional and intellectual dead end for faculty. Every word, every image, every example, every definition, and every other aspect of OER is open to localization, adaptation, remixing, and improvement by faculty. Faculty might choose to ignore others' compilations of OER and build their own collection of individual OER from the ground up. On the other end of the spectrum, if a faculty member wants to simply adopt someone else's collection of OER and use it just like they used their previous commercial textbook, they have that option, too. OER provide faculty with a much greater opportunity to engage in evaluation, selection, curation, improvement, and ownership of the core tools of their trade.

Second, adopting OER instead of traditional textbooks significantly expands the academic freedom of faculty members in terms of pedagogy. There are a wide range of activities and assignments that can be made in the context of OER that simply cannot be made when a traditional textbook has been selected. For example, faculty can assign students to find OER that speak more directly and clearly to them about a course topic than current material, with the promise that the best finds will be incorporated into the official course materials. Students can write their own material, or shoot their own videos, or record their own interviews, etc., with a similar guarantee. Immediately these activities change from being disposable assignments which students invest little time in and immediately throw away after grading (like response essays), and are transformed into activities with real value that will be used and valued by their peers, winning students both personal satisfaction and a small amount of fame. Adopting OER instead of commercial materials allows faculty to invite students to become co-producers of knowledge rather than passive recipients. The permission to make that invitation simply does not exist when faculty adopt traditional textbooks.

Students are also impacted by faculty decisions to adopt OER. When every single student in a course has full, no-cost access to all the materials they are assigned to read, watch, and practice with, there is a noticeable impact on student success. The Review Project (Hilton, 2015), an ongoing, online literature review of the impacts of OER adoption, states:

> In terms of student and teacher perspective of OER, there were 2,747 students and 847 faculty members whose perceptions were surveyed across the eight studies pertaining to perceptions of OER. In no instance did a majority of students or teachers report that the OER were of inferior quality. Across multiple studies in various settings, students consistently reported that they faced financial difficulties and that OER provided a financial benefit to them. A general finding seems to be that roughly half of teachers and students find OER to be comparable to traditional resources, a sizeable minority believe they are superior, and a smaller minority find them inferior.
>
> In total, 7,779 students have utilized OER materials across the ten studies that attempted to measure results pertaining to student efficacy. While causality was not claimed by any researcher, the use of OER was sometimes correlated with higher test scores, lower failure, or withdrawal rates. None of the nine studies that measured efficacy had results in which students who utilized OER performed worse than their peers who used traditional textbooks.
>
> Even if the use of OER materials do not significantly increase student learning outcomes, this is a very important finding. Given that (1) students and teachers generally find OER to

be as good or better than traditional textbooks, and (2) students do not perform worse when utilizing OER, then (3) students, parents and taxpayers stand to save literally billions of dollars without any negative impact on learning through the adoption of OER.

Colleges and universities are relying more and more heavily on OER as evidenced by initiatives like Virginia's Zx23,

in which twenty-three Virginia colleges have committed to replace commercial textbooks with OER in all the courses necessary to complete at least one degree program on campus (Sebastian, 2015). As OER are adopted more widely it will be critically important for instructional designers, instructional technologists, educational researchers, and others to understand what they are, where they come from, and why they matter.

Summary of Key Principles

1. **Education is sharing.** Ideas, knowledge, skills, and attitudes are public goods. This means they are nonrivalrous and nonexcludable, and therefore easy to share.

2. **Expressions of ideas, knowledge, skills, and attitudes captured in physical artifacts like books are private goods, meaning they are both rivalrous and excludable, making them difficult to share.**

3. **When concrete expressions of ideas, knowledge, skills, and attitudes are converted from a physical into a digital format, this changes them from private goods back to being public goods, once again making them easier to share.**

4. **Copyright law places artificial limits on our ability to use technology to share educational materials.** This changes these public goods into club goods, once again making them difficult to share.

5. **Educational materials published under an open license are called open educational resources (OER).** When digital educational materials become OER, they are converted back into public goods. Over 1 billion openly licensed materials are published online.

6. **Open educational resources are far better aligned with the core values of education than materials published under an all rights reserved traditional copyright.** This closer alignment creates opportunities for less expensive, more flexible, more effective education.

7. **Because of their close alignment with the core values of education, adopting OER in place of traditionally copyrighted educational resources provides unique opportunities and benefits to faculty and students.** Instructional designers, faculty, and other educators and administrators should develop a basic understanding of OER.

Application Questions

1. The relationship between supply and demand is foundational to classical economics. Traditionally publishers have used copyright to make digital educational resources artificially excludable, and consequently artificially scarce, in order to maintain high prices for their products. What happens to the economics of educational publishing in a world where the supply of OER is infinite (because they are public goods)? What is the role of instructional designers in this future? What happens to the economics of education more broadly in a world where the supply of educational resources is infinite?

2. Given the existence of a large body of freely available OER that research indicates are at least equal in effectiveness to traditional educational resources, does requiring students to purchase a $150 or $250 textbook for a course raise important ethical or moral issues?

If so, what is the relationship between faculty's academic freedom to select any course materials they desire and these ethical or moral considerations? Should institutions have policies regarding these issues in the future? If so, what would an appropriate policy look like?

3. The restrictions placed on the behavior of faculty and instructional designers are as ubiquitous as the influence of gravity in our daily lives. Our intuitions about what is possible and what should not even be considered in our design practice are shaped by what we know about "how the world works" with regard to copyright. When you strip away the constraints of copyright, as open educational resources do, what new kinds of educational practice, instructional design, assessment strategies, and pedagogies become possible? How can we encourage people to escape the historical constraints of copyright to think more expansively in a world of OER?

References

Creative Commons. (2015). The state of the commons. Retrieved from https://stateof.creativecommons.org/

Freire, P. (1970). *Pedagogy of the oppressed*. New York: Herder and Herder.

Hilton, J. (2015). The review project. Retrieved from http://openedgroup.org/review/

Jefferson, T. (1813). Thomas Jefferson to Isaac McPherson. Retrieved from http://press-pubs.uchicago.edu/founders/documents/a1_8_8s12.html

Lessig, L. (2008). *Remix*. London: Bloomsbury Academic.

Sebastian, R. (2015). Zx23 project. Retrieved from http://edtech.vccs.edu/z-x-23-project/

Wiley, D. (2015). Defining the open in open content. Retrieved from http://opencontent.org/definition/

Chapter 39

Changing Conceptions of Design

Elizabeth Boling

Kennon M. Smith

Indiana University

Drawing on existing, and accelerating, philosophical and pragmatic studies of design in traditional fields like architecture, product design, and design engineering, new clarity is available within the field of educational technology regarding the true nature of what we do as instructional designers. For several decades the mainstream view in the field of educational technology has been that we are a science (Merrill, Drake, Lacy, Pratt, & the ID2 Research Group, 1996), perhaps including a bit of art, although the art is not discussed in great detail (Richey & Klein, 2010). Voices calling the scientific view of instructional design into question have sounded regularly over time, but have not significantly shifted discourse in the field. As scholars across disciplines rethink the nature of design and turn serious attention to its study and scholars within the field have paid attention to this work (Hokanson & Gibbons, 2014; Hokanson, Clinton, & Tracey, 2015), new views of design are coalescing within educational technology as well.

Existing Conception of Design in the Field of Educational Technology

Review of the literature in educational technology reveals that the term *design* is used frequently and inconsistently. Seels and Richie (1994) have identified several common uses of the word. Of these, perhaps the most widespread conception of "design" in educational technology currently is as one of the steps, or concepts, in a process-centric, ADDIE-type model that is tied to the scientific view of the field. By contrast, as we proceed to make the argument that this view is changing

and should change, we will use the term *design* in a broader sense—as encompassing the total endeavor required to improve learning and performance.

The way in which we frame our understanding of design is of no small consequence for research on and practice of design in this field. Over the last fifty years, a tremendous amount of effort has been invested in developing systems-based process models to guide instructional design work. There are now hundreds of such models (Gustafson & Branch, 2002). These models have become so pervasive and influential in framing our understanding of instructional design thinking and work, that they are sometimes seen as the embodiment of our design knowledge. Dick (1997) states, "our models have been quite useful to us in terms of summarizing the research and procedures of many contributors to our field. Our theory, as represented in our models, can be seen as a succession of 'if-then' statements" (p. 47). In other words, design (in the larger sense of "what we do") is widely considered to be equivalent to process.

Of course, educational technology is not the only design field in which process models emerged during the 1960s and 1970s (e.g., Alexander, Ishikawa, & Silverstein, 1977; Jones, 1970). Process models, or conceptual models used as tools for designing, emerged at this time in many design fields. Within a comparatively short time, however, "process . . . pursued as an end in itself resulted in abject failure" (Rowe, 1987, p. 111).

Both process models and the predominant understanding of design as a *component* within them have, in contrast, remained remarkably stable in the field of educational technology. In fact, as recently as 2010 Branch explains ADDIE (analyze, design, develop, implement, and evaluate) as "a product development paradigm" (p. 1) in which each phase "generates a deliverable . . . [which] . . . is then tested prior to becoming input for the next phase in the process" (p. 4).

Examining possible motivations for the seemingly simultaneous development of these model-based understandings of design across a number of design fields may help explain the persistence of this view in educational technology. In his analysis of the move to focus on process models in traditional design fields, Cross (2007) ascribed at least some of the activity to "aspirations to scientise design," the most positive aspects of which were efforts to establish modern design as "distinct from pre-industrial, craft-oriented design—based on scientific knowledge" (pp. 119–121). Along with the effort to make design scientific, we can see the concern that if design is *not* scientific, then it has no basis for any claims to validity. Merrill and colleagues (1996) expressed this latter view:

> Instructional design is not merely philosophy; it is not a set of procedures arrived at by collaboration; it is a set of scientific principles and technology for implementing these principles in the development of instructional experiences and environments. . . . Too much of the structure of educational technology in general and instructional design in particular is built upon the sand of relativism, rather than the rock of science. When winds of new paradigms blow and the sands of old paradigms shift, then the structure of educational technology slides toward the abyss of pseudo-science and mythology. We stand firm against the shifting sands of new paradigms and "realities." We have drawn a line in the sand. We boldly reclaim the technology of instructional design that is built upon the rock of instructional science. (p. 7)

In our view, such an argument sets up a false choice between science and not-science. We believe that instructional design is not a science and does not need to cast itself as a science in order to retain legitimacy, but that it can position itself within the design tradition and still draw upon scientific principles and processes as needed.

Questioning the View of Design in the Field of Educational Technology

Some scholars within educational technology have argued for broadening our view of design beyond that of a process-model-based science, and we review a few notable examples here. As early as 1983, Kerr made an empirical attempt to discover what designers were actually doing as they worked and concluded that our field needed to examine links with other fields of design. Almost ten years later, Murphy (1992), employing a framework from Lawson's *How Designers Think* (1980), compared the generalized characteristics of design to those of the problems we address in our field, and argued that the two were congruent. He sent out a plea to his colleagues to "look and learn from the design world" (p. 282). In 1997, Davies called for radical parallelism in the activities of design—that is, "determining goals while designing impact prototypes and simultaneously identifying appropriate subject matter content" (p. 41), and for acknowledging the chaos of the real world in our design processes. Taken together, Davies's recommendations imply a serious erosion of the central position of the process model, if not an actual

repudiation of our identity as a science. Wilson (2005a, 2005b) carried these notions further when he observed the need to consider "practitioner perspectives as a needed antidote to the surfeit of high-road theory and privileging of science over other ways of knowing and doing" in the field, and calling ID "a legitimate field of endeavor in its own right" (2005b, p. 11). His extensions to the foundations of the field imply broadening our view of design to incorporate "often neglected aspects of design . . . moral and value layers of meaning and the aesthetic side of our work" (2005a, p. 15).

Yanchar and Gabbitas (2011), in challenging the validity of eclecticism, a common (and process-centric) position in the field regarding the use of theory, introduce the notion of critical flexibility as a rigorous form of what Nelson and Stolterman (2012) might term designerly judgment, placing designers at the center of design activity. A clear implication of Parrish's (2009b) position is that methods (e.g., storytelling) might occupy a key position in designing and, therefore, a process does not itself produce design outcomes. Smith and Boling (2009) argued that our demonstrated understanding of design in the field carries with it multiple limitations, not the least of which is the failure to see designers as a key resource in designing. Rowland (2008) has explored the notion of educational technology design as "a fully developed system of inquiry for educational contexts" in which "design and research would *transform* each other . . . as independent inquiries . . . with formal intersections" (p. 7). In this view, design is cast as a legitimate form of knowledge building equal to traditionally recognized research and functioning in partnership with it; the two would work together to produce true innovations in education. None of these authors has advocated turning entirely away from the rational in design, although they do call into question the centrality of the process view and its limitations for addressing complex, mutable, human situations.

Arguments calling for a move away from the process orientation in instructional systems design (ISD) have, until recently, been hampered in part by two related assumptions. First, that process orientation is a prerequisite for serious, scientific work; and second, that art is the opposite of science. It is possible to see the view that art and science are the primary, or the only, traditions by which educational technology can identify itself played out in the 1995 exchange between Dick and Rowland in *Educational Technology*. Dick, taking his lead from some critics of ISD, squares off "creative" (or artistic) design against "systematic" (or scientific) design, with the underlying assumption that if one does not practice scientifically, one must therefore practice artistically and, presumably, with a resulting lack of rigor or credibility. Merrill and his coauthors (1996) take essentially the same position. They distinguish instructional science from "the technology of instructional design" (p. 5), stating that "instruction is a science" (p. 5), and that the technology of instructional design "is built upon the rock of instructional science" (p. 7). They do not position science in opposition to art, but in opposition to "the uncertain wilderness of philosophical relativism" (p. 7)— strongly implying the same lack of rigor.

We challenge the art versus science assumption directly, and in so doing, eliminate the need for the related, "process-model as science" assumption. Instead of viewing these traditions as oppositional, it is possible to see art and science as distinct traditions with some fundamental commonalities—particularly the search for overarching truths (Gold, 2007)—and to see *design* as a separate tradition (Nelson & Stolterman, 2012) with its own ways of knowing and of building knowledge, driven by the search for "the *ultimate particular*—the specific [instance of] design" (p. 33 italics in the original).

The view of design as a tradition, which centers on the multiple activities of designing and characterizes them all as "design," describes everything that we do in ISD (e.g., design research or analysis, prototyping evaluation, production) as part of *design* (Nelson & Stolterman, 2012). The design tradition, as it is conceived in this way, is different from—and exists on a par with—science, although it does use and rely on science, just as science uses and relies on design (Baird, 2004; Gibbons, 2013; Nelson & Stolterman, 2000; Rust, 2004). Within this view, designing is viewed as action toward concrete, although not comprehensively describable, goals within a complex conceptual space comprising possibilities and constraints in which the designer(s) and not their tools are the primary force resolving tensions into results (Boling, 2008; Cross, 2007; Goel & Pirolli, 1992; Lawson, 2005).

In the conceptual model of design as a space rather than a process, a number of "invariant features" distinguish designing from other forms of problem solving (Goel & Pirolli, 1992, (p. 395). In this design space, where a single, general process model—or a panoply of specific ones—cannot provide the direction required to transform from goal state to end state, scholars across many disciplines are establishing new value for broad design knowledge. They are studying design expertise, design knowledge, and design pedagogy (Cross, 2011; Lawson & Dorst, 2009), and recognizing the nature of design as cutting across disciplines (Durling, Rust, Chen, Ashton, & Friedman, 2009; Goel & Pirolli, 1992). Design thinking is viewed as separate from other modes of thought and valued in practice (Brown, 2008; Cross, 2007). Design knowledge and action are viewed as legitimate and important objects of study, and design is seen as a distinct form of knowledge building (Boling, 2008; Dorst, 2008; Lawson, 2005; Stolterman, McAtee, Royer, & Thadnapani, 2008).

Emerging Variance in Design Perspectives and Tools within Educational Technology

As scholars turn to the study of designing, we have come to the realization that experts do not use the tools for design that scholars develop and teach in this field (Cox & Osguthorpe, 2003; Rowland, 1992; Stolterman et al., 2008; Visscher-Voerman & Gustafson, 2004). Worse yet, while these tools are expected to support us effectively in teaching ISD (Branch, 2010; Dick, 1995), Lawson and Dorst (2009) argue that such tools may actually defeat the development of design expertise. Individuals and groups within the field of educational technology are establishing a more varied landscape of tools for design and perspectives on design than that which has prevailed in the most recent decades. Scholars in the field are adapting ideas rapidly from traditional and emerging fields of design

(e.g., architecture, product design, human-computer interaction design, software design) and working to integrate them with existing ideas.

Principles-Based Design

Several scholars have taken principles as the central concern in their studies of designing. Silber (2007) synthesized the ideas put forward by multiple design researchers, including the idea that design requires a specialized type of thinking and concluded that "ID is a set of principles and heuristics that expert IDers use to solve ill-structured problems" (p. 10). He gives six pages of "principles that IDers keep in mind as they define and solve ID problems" (p. 10) organized roughly around the concepts represented by ADDIE, which he also defines as a model. Reigeluth and Carr-Chellman (2009) take a similar, although much expanded view. They have solicited instructional theories, or "sets of goal-oriented, normative, artificial-science principles" (p. 19) from multiple authors, organizing them into types "pertaining to various aspects of instruction" (pp. 8–9)—event, analysis, planning, building, implementation, and evaluation—and presenting them in groups related to various approaches to instruction (e.g., direct instruction, problem-based instruction, simulation). Merrill (2002) has also focused on a basis in principles for designing by identifying a limited set (five) of first principles that characterize effective designs; that is, the principles are goals to be achieved in the products of design rather than guidance for the moves made during design.

Design as Problem Solving

In 2008, Jonassen countered Silber's (2007) model of designing as primarily the selection and application of principles with a different view informed by similar sources, but presented as a cyclical process. In this process, designers build a "design model that represents the proposed solution" (p. 24), both responding to constraints (technological, economic, political/organizational, environmental, learner-related, and physical) (p. 23) and creating new ones as they iterate through cycles of decision making. In this model of designing, the biases and beliefs of designers impact decision making on a par with other constraints (p. 23). His model seems to have much in common with the notion of a design space, which is constantly shaped and reshaped by designers using the faculty of judgment to execute disciplined moves that both affect the outcome of designing and are affected in their turn by subsequent moves.

Design Languages and Layers

Gibbons (2013) has explored issues surrounding the knowledge educational designers (he uses the term "technologists") use and how that knowledge is represented, drawing from diverse fields of design practice, especially engineering and architecture. He offers a view of design centered on the *product* of design rather than the *process* of design. In this view, instructional designs are a system of layers, each characterized by unique design goals, constructs, theoretical principles, design and development tools, and design processes (p. 23).

Related to this view of designing, Gibbons and Brewer (2005) explain that designers in multiple fields benefit from "the identification and use of design languages . . . [that] . . . supply the set of structures and structuring rules used to complete designs within each layer" (p. 111). They enumerate multiple benefits that would accrue from a program of design language study within the field.

Aesthetics in Design

Wilson (2005a) named aesthetics as one of two new "pillars of practice" in instructional design (p. 10), explaining that "instructional designers are designers of materials, but they are also designers of *experience*" and that their goal in this is to assist in creating "*heightened levels of immediate experience*" for learners (p. 15; italics in the original). Parrish (2009a) has elaborated this idea extensively, based in large part on a reexamination of Dewey's explanation of aesthetics. Aesthetic experiences are "those that are immersive, infused with meaning, and felt as coherent and complete" (p. 511). These qualities of experiences are seen as a critical driver for learning, not as a decorative gloss that might add appeal to a design but will ultimately distract learners from the real point of instruction. Rather than focus on design process, Parrish states that achieving such qualities requires imagination and empathy on the part of the designer (p. 254).

Agency and Design Character

Schwier, Campbell, and Kenny (2007) focus on designers themselves, describing them as "active, moral, political and influential" change agents (p. 1) operating within an emerging model that includes "interpersonal, professional, institutional and societal dimensions" (p. 2). Their model of agency stresses moral commitments, responsibilities to people and the profession, and contributions to significant social influence. Their findings are congruent with the views of scholars who place character at the center of design (Nelson & Stolterman, 2000). Osguthorpe and Osguthorpe (2007) explore issues related to the character of designers, discussing conscience and personal beliefs within an extended framework that includes historical, psychological, sociological, and philosophical foundations. Boling (2008) addresses the necessary qualities of designers. Drawing on the concept of the human instrument (Lincoln & Guba, 1985), she posits that the designer, or design team, is the only instrument complex and responsive enough to act within situations that are not comprehensively knowable. The designer's skill cannot be reduced to an algorithm, a set of principles, or a process diagram.

Performance Improvement

Many in the field now promote an expansion of the *products* of design (from instructional materials and experiences to performance interventions) while retaining an essentially scientific orientation for the *process* of designing. However, descriptions of human performance technology (HPT) make it clear that this expansion in the products of design has in turn placed pressure on the model-centric view of design as an activity. While Addison and Haig (2006) discuss "tools that can be used repeatedly and will consistently show the same outcome" (p. 38), and Pershing (1978) offers an ISD-like model for HPT, they also put forward the notion of a "design landscape" in which the performance technologist operates, and describe organizations as multidimensional contexts (spaces) for design (p. 11). In this landscape, HPT is practiced from a perspective of "holism versus reductionism" because "a given cause and its effect cannot be separated or isolated from their context" (p. 14). The terms are different than those used by other design scholars, but these ideas bear a striking resemblance to some of the conceptions of designing presented in their work. We concur with Rowland, who observed in 1995 that questions surrounding design process should not be framed as linear versus iterative, but as "'determinism' versus 'definedness'" and stated, "I believe that the field of human performance technology grew out of such concern" (p. 22). In other words, it is possible to see HPT as the outgrowth of efforts to reconceive and expand the notion of design.

Implications of Emerging Views on the Nature of Design

No single perspective is emerging to replace reliance on process models as the core of designing within the field, and we would argue that this is appropriate. While a broader, more complex view of designing seems to us to be needed in educational technology, it would be a waste to spend our collective effort seeking to capture this view in a single unifying model or theory of designing. If one entertains the view that design is a valid (and complex) tradition, not a subset or practical application of some other tradition, we see a number of implications for what we would do as a field.

Discriminate more carefully than we do now between building scientific knowledge and building design knowledge. We would not study a single design in a single context, or the process of creating a single design, and then attempt to generalize principles from that study to all other designs or even to all other designs of that general type. We would study more individual designs in context and disseminate rich descriptions of those designs as valuable contributions to the expertise of all designers in the field (Boling, 2010).

Value some types of knowledge and knowledge building differently than we do now. Precedent, the unique body of work as experienced by each designer and drawn upon for both specific and general purposes in designing, is a specific example. We have too many principles (theories) that leave designers still floundering for appropriate moves and too few examples on which to build true expertise (Boling & Smith, 2009). Craft, or skill situated in a domain (Risatti, 2013), is another example. Instructional design theory does not bridge the gap between articulated strategy and actual instruction; the knowledge to do so has been present but invisible in our field as in others (Sless, 2008), and needs to be recognized as a viable area of study. We would also privilege empirical understanding of what designers do and how they do it, using this understanding to develop tools and guidance for improving instructional design—instead of developing such tools and guidance in the absence of that understanding and conducting empirical studies to prove that designers are not using them (Stolterman et al., 2008).

Learn more about standards for discipline and judgment in design and work to establish such standards within the field. Instead of striving to identify the correct way to carry out design, or the definitive principles for producing different classes of design outcomes, we would define the parameters of disciplined judgment and action in design. Those parameters would place responsibility onto designers and design teams for recognizing and shaping the design space and employing appropriate processes and principles within it. While we place this responsibility on designers now by leaving the hard work of translating simplistic (or sometimes overly determined) models into meaningful action, that work is currently viewed at best as devising ingenious workarounds in response to constraints that prevent the ideal process from being used, and at worst as guilty deviation from a standard, or ideal, model.

Expect a broader range of capabilities from the instructional designer. Just because what we offer by virtue of our design knowledge may be better than what people had before does not mean that what we are offering is good enough, or that we are viewing ourselves in the largest sense as guarantors of design—responsible for the decisions we make about what we work on, for how we do that work, and for all the consequences of what we create (Nelson & Stolterman, 2012). Such responsibility calls for designers who are prepared far beyond their cognitive grasp of instructional theory, their ability to follow a certain process, and even their ability to conduct an empathetic, productive subject-matter expert interview. Such a responsibility calls for us to place emphasis on developing the design character of our students (Nelson & Stolterman, 2012; Korkmaz & Boling, 2014). We have to question the widespread view that starting our students off with a highly simplified representation of what we do is "a reasonable strategy for *teaching* a process to novices" (Dick, 1995). Lawson and Dorst (2009) quote Wim Groeneboom, "one of the founding fathers of the faculty of Industrial Design Engineering at TU Delft [Delft University of Technology, originally established 1842]" as saying:

> The big disadvantage [of design methods] is that through this kind of teaching we take away the insecurity of the students. It is a way of quickly and efficiently explaining design but that is deadly. Students have to learn to deal with uncertainty, and we

take that away by this kind of teaching . . . In the end, I would say that dealing with uncertainties is the core of our design profession. (p. 33)

Conclusion

Arguments can be expected to continue over what part science plays in what we do (whether science is best seen as our total definition or as a cooperative tradition), but we in educational technology have the choice at this moment to define ourselves as part of the design tradition, rather than as a branch of science or as a science-based art. If we opt not to make this choice, we run the risk that the limitations of a process-centric view, or "scientised design" (Cross, 2007, p. 119) will distort and stunt our efforts to progress as a field of practice and of study. As Dorst (2007) points out, when process models are created, other critical aspects of design (specifically the object of design, the designer, and the context of design) are "bracketed" out (p. 5). This leads to specific problems; expert designers do not use the methods or tools that scholars develop, and it becomes difficult to grapple with large changes that affect design (like digital media) (p. 7). To the extent that we lag behind in exploring and understanding the complex nature of design, other fields of practice will pick up the concerns we consider to be central to our own field and before long address them more effectively than we can do ourselves.

As active members of the design tradition, however, we become part of a diverse community that shares a broad base of fundamental characteristics in spite of any differences in focus and outcomes between us. We therefore benefit from the current surge in the study of design and designing, and can offer to others in turn the real benefit of our own disciplined outlook on the practice of design built up over recent decades. We can engage in discussions about the tools and processes we use without having to end those discussions by choosing just one of these as "the right one." We can argue productively about theories of learning and instruction because we will not be confusing these with our practice of designing. We can study the individual outcomes of design without having to distort those studies with unsupportable claims for all designs in order to make them scientific. We can use the principles we develop as what they are—tools for design— rather than as universal truths capable of generating designs all by themselves. And we can engage in legitimate scientific study of what we do, which will produce improvements in learning and performance far beyond those we are able to achieve today.

Summary of Key Principles

1. **Instructional design is not a science and does not need to cast itself as a science in order to retain legitimacy.** We can position ourselves within the design tradition and still draw upon scientific principles and processes as needed.

2. **Process models have become so pervasive and influential in framing our understanding of instructional design thinking and work that they** are sometimes seen as the embodiment of our design knowledge and all design ideas are framed within them.

3. **Experts do not use the tools for design that scholars develop and teach in this field (process models and prescriptive theories), and when used as a primary vehicle for teaching such tools may actually defeat the development of design expertise.**

4. **Scholars in the field are adapting ideas rapidly from traditional and emerging fields of design and working to integrate them with existing ideas.** No single perspective is emerging to replace reliance on process models as the core of designing within the field, and this is appropriate.

5. **Just because what we offer by virtue of our current design knowledge may be better than what people had before does not mean that what we are offering is good enough.** To the extent that we lag behind in exploring and understanding the complex nature of design, other fields of practice will pick up the concerns we consider to be central to our own field and before long address them more effectively than we can do ourselves.

Application Questions

1. Your instructor for a graduate course on New Media in Ed Tech has taken you to visit a video game design house in a nearby city. During the visit your class focused on the instructional components that are built into the games being created there, and you noted that no one you spoke to mentioned terms you might have expected to hear—task analysis, instructional strategy, and so on. When you asked about the process they use, the answers seemed vague and the designers got impatient discussing process. It almost seemed as if they made up the process as they went along for each game they designed. As a game player yourself, though, you know that the instruction in the games from this shop is really good; you have learned to play several of these games quickly compared to some others and you have admired the strategies that were used to incorporate tutorial elements into the game play. What factors might contribute to these designers being able to create effective instruction without the use of an articulated process model for doing so, and how would those factors interrelate?

2. You work in a small consulting group that develops instruction for a diverse range of clients. Recently you have been approached by a potential client who has been disappointed in what she terms "the same old modules of training." She is looking for a fresh way to approach some tricky learning situations in which new MBAs who are hired for their high levels of drive, self-confidence, and innovative thinking are being trained to use—and respect—the safeguards that large financial firms must employ to avoid major risks without squashing morale. They have substantial funding and have encouraged you to start by exploring a way to help them that will not look and feel just like the standard training so many groups produce.

   Using one or more of the new views appearing in the field (e.g., aesthetics, layers, design judgment instead of process models), how might you tackle this project? How might you structure your view of the design space this client is presenting and frame, or reframe, the problem as given to you? Which aspects of the client's request would be most difficult to address using a traditional ISD view?

References

Addison, R. M., & Haig, C. (2006). The performance architect's essential guide to the performance technology landscape. In J. A. Pershing (Ed.), *The handbook of human performance technology* (3rd ed., pp. 35–54). San Francisco: John Wiley & Sons.

Alexander, C., Ishikawa, S., & Silverstein, M. (1977). *A pattern language: Towns, buildings, construction.* New York: Oxford University Press.

Baird, D. (2004). *Thing knowledge: A philosophy of scientific instruments.* Berkeley, CA: University of California Press.

Boling, E. (2008). The designer as human instrument. *Design is not systematic: Alternative perspectives on design.* Panel presentation organized by D. Jonassen. Annual Meeting of the Association for Educational Communications and Technology, Orlando, FL.

Boling, E. (2010). The need for design cases: Disseminating design knowledge. *International Journal of Designs for Learning, 1*(1), 1–8. Retrieved from http://scholarworks.iu.edu/journals/index.php/ijdl/index

Boling, E., & Smith, K. M. (2009). Exploring standards of rigour for design cases. Undisciplined! Design Research Society Conference 2008, Sheffield Hallam University, Sheffield, UK, July 16–19.

Branch, R. M. (2010). *Instructional design: The ADDIE approach.* New York: Springer.

Brown, T. (2008, June). Design thinking. *Harvard Business Review*, 84–92.

Cox, S., & Osguthorpe, R. T. (2003). How do instructional design professionals spend their time? *TechTrends, 47*(3), 29, 45–47.

Cross, N. (2007). *Designerly ways of knowing.* London: Springer-Verlag.

Cross, N. (2011). *Design thinking: How designers think and work.* New York: Bloomsbury Academic.

Davies, I. K. (1997). Paradigms and conceptual ISD systems. In Charles R. Dills & Alexander J. Romiszowski (Eds.), *Instructional development paradigms* (pp. 31–44). Englewood Cliffs, NJ: Educational Technology Publications.

Dick, W. (1995). Instructional design and creativity: A response to the critics. *Educational Technology, 35*(4), 5–11.

Dick, W. (1997). Better instructional design theory: Process improvement or reengineering? *Educational Technology, 37*(5), 47–50.

Dorst, K. (2007). Design research: A revolution-waiting-to-happen. *Design Studies, 29*(1), 4–11.

Durling, D., Rust, C., Chen, C., Ashton, A., & Friedman, K. (2009). Undisciplined! Proceedings of the Design Research Society Conference 2008. Sheffield, UK: Sheffield-Hallam University, July 16–19.

Gibbons, A. S. (2013). *An architectural approach to instructional design.* New York: Routledge.

Gibbons, A. S., & Brewer, E. K. (2005). Elementary principles of design languages and design notation systems. In J. M. Spector, C. Ohrazda, A. Van Schaak, & D. Wiley (Eds.), *Innovations in instructional design: Essays in honor of M. David Merrill.* Mahwah, NJ: Lawrence Erlbaum.

Goel, V., & Pirolli, P. (1992). The structure of design problem spaces. *Cognitive Science, 16*(3), 395–429.

Gold, R. (2007). *The plenitude: Creativity, innovation and making stuff.* Cambridge, MA: The MIT Press.

Gustafson, K., & Branch, R. M. (2002). *Survey of instructional development models* (4th ed.). New York: ERIC Clearinghouse on Information and Technology.

Hokanson, B., Clinton, G., & Tracey, M. (Eds.). (2015). *The design of learning experience: Creating the future of educational technology.* New York: Springer.

Hokanson, B., & Gibbons, A. (Eds.). (2014). *Design in educational technology: Design thinking, design process and the design studio.* New York: Springer.

Jonassen, D. (2008). Instructional design as design problem solving: An iterative process. *Educational Technology, 48*(3), 21–26.

Jones, J. C. (1970). *Design methods: Seeds of human futures.* London: Wiley-Interscience.

Kerr, S. T. (1983). Inside the black box: Making decisions for instructional design. *British Journal of Educational Technology, 14*(1), 45–58.

Korkmaz, N., & Boling, E. (2014). In B. Hokanson & A. Gibbons (Eds.), *Design in educational technology: Design thinking, design process and the design studio* (pp 37-56). New York: Springer.

Lawson, B. (1980). *How designers think* (1st ed.). London, UK: Architectural Press.

Lawson, B. (2005). *How designers think* (3rd ed.). London, UK: Architectural Press.

Lawson, B., & Dorst, K. (2009). *Design expertise.* Oxford: Elsevier.

Lincoln, Y., & Guba, E. (1985). *Naturalistic inquiry.* Newbury Park, CA: SAGE Publications, Inc.

Merrill, M. D. (2002). First principles of instruction. *Educational Technology Research and Development, 50*(3), 43–59.

Merrill, M. D., Drake, L., Lacy, M. J., Pratt, J., & the ID2 Research Group. (1996). Reclaiming instructional design. *Educational Technology, 36*(5), 5–7.

Murphy, D. (1992). Is instructional design truly a design activity? *Educational and Training Technology International, 29*(4), 279–282.

Nelson, H., & Stolterman, E. (2000). The case for design: Creating a culture of intention. *Educational Technology, 40*(6), 29–35.

Nelson, H. G., & Stolterman, E. (2012). *The design way: Intentional change in an unpredictable world: Foundations and fundamentals of design competence* (2nd ed.). Boston, The MIT Press.

Osguthorpe, R. R., & Osguthorpe, R. D. (2007). Instructional design as a living practice: Toward a conscience of craft. *Educational Technology, 47*(4), 13–23.

Parrish, P. (2009a). Aesthetic principles for instructional design. *Educational Technology Research and Technology, 57*(4), 511–528.

Parrish, P. (2009b). Design as storytelling. *TechTrends, 50*(4), 72–82.

Pershing, J. A. (Ed.). (1978). *The handbook of human performance technology* (3rd ed., pp. 35–54). San Francisco: John Wiley & Sons.

Reigeluth, C. M., & Carr-Chellman, A. (Eds.). (2009). *Instructional-design theories and models: Building a common knowledge base* (Vol. III). New York: Routledge.

Richey, R. C., & Klein, J. D. (2010). *The instructional design knowledge base.* New York: Routledge.

Risatti, H. (2013). *A theory of craft: Function and aesthetic expression.* Chapel Hill, NC: University of North Carolina Press.

Rowe, P. (1987). *Design thinking.* Cambridge, MA: The MIT Press.

Rowland, G. (1992). What do instructional designers actually do? An initial investigation of expert practice. *Performance Improvement Quarterly, 5*(2), 65–86.

Rowland, G. (1995). Instructional design and creativity: A response to the criticized. *Educational Technology, 35*(5), 17–22.

Rowland, G. (2008). Design and research: Partners for educational innovation. *Educational Technology, 48*(6), 3–9.

Rust, C. (2004). Design enquiry: Tacit knowledge and invention in science. Art and Design Research Centre Working Paper: Sheffield-Hallam University.

Retrieved from http://www.archive.org/stream/DesignEnquiryTacitKnowledgeInventionInScience/DesignEnquiry_djvu.txt

Schwier, R., Campbell, K., & Kenny, R. (2007). Instructional designers' perceptions of their agency: Tales of change and community. In M. J. Keppell (Ed.), *Instructional Design: Case Studies in Communities of Practice*. Hershey, PA: Information Science Publishing.

Seels, B. B., & Richie, R. C. (1994). *Instructional technology: The definition and domains of the field*. Washington, DC: Association for Educational Communications and Technology.

Silber, K. (2007). A principle-based model of instructional design: A new way of thinking about and teaching ID. *Educational Technology, 47*(5), 5–19.

Sless, D. (2008). Measuring information design. *Information Design Journal, 16*(3), 250–258.

Smith, K. M., & Boling, E. (2009). What do we make of design? Design as a concept in educational technology. *Educational Technology, 49*(4), 3–17.

Stolterman, E., McAtee, J., Royer, D., & Thandapani, S. (2008). Designerly tools. Undisciplined! Proceedings of the Design Research Society Conference 2008. Sheffield, UK: Sheffield-Hallam University, July 16–19.

Visscher-Voerman, I., & Gustafson, K. L. (2004). Paradigms in the theory and practice of education and training design. *Educational Technology Research and Development, 52*(2), 69–89.

Wilson, B. G. (2005a). Broadening our foundation for instructional design: Four pillars of practice. *Educational Technology, 45*(2), 10–15.

Wilson, B. G. (2005b). Foundations for instructional design: Reclaiming the conversation. In J. M. Spector, C. Ohrazda, A. Van Schaak, & D. Wiley (Eds.), *Innovations in instructional design: Essays in honor of M. David Merrill*. Mahwah, NJ: Lawrence Erlbaum.

Yanchar, S. C. & Gabbitas, B.W. (2011). Between eclecticism and orthodoxy in instructional design. *Educational Technology Research and Development, 59*(3), 383–398.

Epilogue

Robert A. Reiser
Florida State University

John V. Dempsey
University of South Alabama

In the introduction to this book, we suggested that by the time you finished it, you might be able to provide your parents (or anyone else who is really interested) with a clear picture of the field of instructional design and technology. Now that you have completed the book, what do you think? What is your view of the field?

Don't be afraid to answer the question we just posed. As you must know by now, there are many different facets to the field, and there have been many ways in which it has been defined, so there is no "right" answer to the question. IDT professionals, including those who wrote the chapters for this book, hold a wide range of views about the nature of the field, and as far as we know, none have been designated as the "correct" one. Now that you have studied this book and, hopefully, learned a lot about the nature of our field, you should be well prepared to join the debate. Of course, your views are likely to change over time, but we think that now is a good time to reflect upon what you have learned and express your point of view to others.

So, go ahead. Call your folks and tell them what our field is all about. Perhaps they will finally understand exactly what it is that you are studying. But even if they don't understand what you are talking about, they will enjoy hearing from you!

Author Biographies

Michael W. Allen is Adjunct Associate Professor at University of Minnesota Medical School, and CEO of Allen Interactions, providers of custom-designed and produced, e-learning and blended instructional programs.

Angelia L. Bendolph is a doctoral candidate in the Instructional Design and Development program at the University of South Alabama.

Elizabeth Boling is Professor of Instruction Systems Technology and Associate Dean for Graduate Studies in the School of Education at Indiana University, and Founding Editor-in-Chief of the *International Journal of Designs for Learning*.

Curtis J. Bonk is Professor of Instructional Systems Technology at Indiana University Bloomington.

Robert Maribe Branch is Professor of Learning, Design, and Technology at the University of Georgia.

Frankie Bratton-Jeffrey is Instructional Designer for the Department of Navy Leadership Program.

Thomas Brush is the Barbara B. Jacobs Chair in Education and Technology and Chair of the Department of Instructional Systems Technology at Indiana University Bloomington.

Saul Carliner is a Professor of Educational Technology at Concordia University in Montreal and author of the award-winning book *Informal Learning Basics*.

Ruth Clark is an independent instructor and author focusing on evidence-based instruction at Clark Training & Consulting.

Markus Deimann is a MOOC Maker and Head of Research at the Lübeck University of Applied Sciences in Germany.

John V. Dempsey is the founding Director of the Innovation in Learning Center and former Professor of Instructional Design and Development at the University of South Alabama.

Vanessa P. Dennen is Professor of Instructional Systems and Learning Technologies at Florida State University, and Editor of *The Internet and Higher Education*.

Beth Dietz is Professor of Psychology at Miami University.

J. Ana Donaldson is retired from the University of Northern Iowa and past President of the Association for Educational Communications and Technology (AECT).

Marcy P. Driscoll is the Leslie J. Briggs Professor of Educational Research and Dean of the College of Education at Florida State University.

Peggy A. Ertmer is Professor Emerita of Learning Design and Technology, Purdue University, and founding Editor of the *Interdisciplinary Journal of Problem-Based Learning*.

Krista Glazewski is Associate Professor of Instructional Systems Technology at Indiana University, and co-editor of the *Interdisciplinary Journal of Problem-Based Learning*.

Begoña Gros is Professor of the Faculty of Education, University of Barcelona.

Judith A. Hale, PhD, CPT, CACP, IBSTPI Fellow, founder of Hale Associates, and CEO of The Institute for Performance Improvement is dedicated to workforce development through evidence-based certifications.

Mary C. Herring is Associate Dean and Professor in the University of Northern Iowa's College of Education, and past President of the Association for Educational Communications and Technology (AECT).

Jan Herrington is Professor of Education in the School of Education, Murdoch University, in Western Australia.

Christopher Hoadley is Associate Professor of Educational Communications & Technology at NYU and director of dolcelab, the Lab for Design of Learning, Collaboration, & Experience, at New York University.

Janet E. Hurn is Coordinator of Regional E-Learning Initiatives at Miami University, and Senior Instructor of Physics.

David W. Johnson is Professor Emeritus of Educational Psychology at the University of Minnesota and Co-Director of the Cooperative Learning Center.

R. Burke Johnson is a professor in the Department of Professional Studies at the University of South Alabama.

Roger T. Johnson is Professor of Curriculum and Instruction at the University of Minnesota and Co-Director of the Cooperative Learning Center.

Insung Jung is Professor of Education at the International Christian University, Tokyo, Japan.

John M. Keller is Emeritus Professor of the Instructional Systems and Learning Technologies Program, Department of Educational Psychology and Learning Systems, at Florida State University.

James D. Klein is the Walter Dick Distinguished Professor of Instructional Systems Design at Florida State University.

Mimi Miyoung Lee is Associate Professor in the Department of Curriculum and Instruction at the University of Houston.

Joe'l Lewis is Associate Professor of Instructional Design and Development at the University of South Alabama.

Brenda C. Litchfield is Professor of Instructional Design and Development and the Interim Director of the Innovation in Learning Center and USAonline at the University of South Alabama.

Craig Locatis is Research Project Leader in the Office of High Performance Computing and Communication, Lister Hill National Center for Biomedical Communications, National Library of Medicine, National Institutes of Health.

Richard E. Mayer is Professor of Psychology at the University of California, Santa Barbara.

Thomas A. Mays is Assistant Professor in the Department of Commerce on the Miami University regional campuses.

M. David Merrill is Professor Emeritus at Utah State University.

Gary R. Morrison is Senior Research Associate with the Center for Research and Reform in Education at Johns Hopkins University, a landscape photographer, and Professor Emeritus at Old Dominion University.

Hope Nicholas is Director of Publications for ROI Institute, the leading source of ROI competency building, implementation, ROI consulting, networking, and research.

Helmut M. Niegemann is Emeritus Professor, Learning and Interactive Media, University of Erfurt (Germany); Senior Professor Economics Education, Goethe University Frankfurt (Germany); and Visiting Research Professor, Educational Technology, Saarland University, Saarbruecken (Germany).

Anne T. Ottenbreit-Leftwich is Associate Professor of Instructional Systems Technology and the Associate Director for the MBA for Educators program at Indiana University.

Jack J. Phillips, PhD, is Chairman of ROI Institute and developer of the ROI Methodology and a world-renowned expert on accountability, measurement, and evaluation.

Patti P. Phillips, PhD, President and CEO of ROI Institute, is an internationally recognized consultant, researcher, and expert in measurement and evaluation.

Clark N. Quinn is Executive Director of Quinnovation, a global learning technology strategy consultancy, and a Principal in the Internet Time Alliance.

Thomas C. (Tom) Reeves is Professor Emeritus of Learning, Design, and Technology at the University of Georgia.

Robert A. Reiser is Associate Dean for Research, a Distinguished Teaching Professor, and the Robert M. Morgan Professor of Instructional Systems in the College of Education at Florida State University.

Thomas H. Reynolds is Professor of Teacher Education in the Sanford College of Education at National University.

Lloyd P. Rieber is Professor of Learning, Design, and Technology at the University of Georgia.

Dr. Marc Rosenberg is a leading management consultant, author, speaker, and educator in training, organizational learning, e-learning, knowledge management, and performance improvement, as well as past president and honorary life member of the International Society for Performance Improvement and an eLearning "Guild Master."

Nick Rushby is founding Director of Conation Technologies Limited, a learning technology consultancy based in the UK.

Valerie J. Shute is the Mack & Effie Tyner Campbell Endowed Professor in the College of Education at Florida State University, and co-founder of Empirical Games, LLC.

Sharon E. Smaldino is the LD & Ruth G. Morgridge Endowed Chair in Teacher Education at Northern Illinois University and past President of the Association for Educational Communications and Technology (AECT).

Kennon M. Smith is Associate Professor in the Department of Apparel Merchandising and Interior Design at Indiana University Bloomington.

Harold D. Stolovitch is Emeritus Professor, Workplace Learning and Performance, Université de Montréal, and Principal of HSA Learning & Performance Solutions LLC, a global learning and performance consulting firm.

Stephen M. Sullivan is Case Manager / Project Director with Alabama Institute for Deaf and Blind, training and advising people with nonstandard eyesight, specializing in adaptation using technology to mitigate the individual circumstances of disability.

Katsuaki Suzuki is Professor and Chair of Graduate School of Instructional Systems at Kumamoto University, Japan.

Catherine B. Tencza is the principal consultant at Tencza Designs, an international performance consulting firm.

Monica W. Tracey is Associate Professor of Learning, Design and Technology at Wayne State University, Detroit, Michigan.

Richard Van Eck is the founding Associate Dean for Teaching and Learning and the Dr. David and Lola Rognlie Monson Endowed Professor in Medical Education at the University of North Dakota School of Medicine and Health Sciences.

James Van Haneghan is Professor of Instructional Design and Development at the University of South Alabama.

Jeroen J. G. van Merrienboer is Professor of Learning and Instruction, and Research Director of the School of Health Professions Education at Maastricht University.

David Wiley is Chief Academic Officer of Lumen Learning, adjunct faculty in Brigham Young University's graduate program in Instructional Psychology and Technology, and the Education Fellow at Creative Commons.

Brent G. Wilson is Professor of Information and Learning Technologies at the University of Colorado, Denver.

David Woods is Assistant Professor in the Computer and Information Technology Department at Miami University.

Author Index

Subject Index